DICTIONARY
ASTROLOGY

By the same author

Dictionary of Occult, Hermetic and Alchemical Sigils

DICTIONARY OF
ASTROLOGY

Fred Gettings

Routledge & Kegan Paul
London, Boston and Henley

First published in 1985
by Routledge & Kegan Paul plc

14 Leicester Square, London WC2H 7PH, England

9 Park Street, Boston, Mass. 02108, USA and

Broadway House, Newtown Road,
Henley-on-Thames, Oxon RG9 1EN, England

Photographic and illustration credits
Images Colour Library, Leeds

Printed in Great Britain by
Thetford Press Limited
Thetford, Norfolk

Library of Congress Cataloging in Publication Data

Gettings, Fred.
The dictionary of astrology.
Bibliography: p.
1. Astrology — Dictionaries.   I. Title.
BF1655.G4   1985   133.5′03′21   84-18260

British Library CIP data also available

ISBN 0-7100-9672-0
ISBN 0-7102-0650-X (Pbk)

To my father Alfred Gettings —
born 19 July 1898,
died 8 December 1984

CONTENTS

INTRODUCTION

The entries and text in this dictionary have been designed to form a reference, guide and source-book for those involved in general astrological studies, as much as for those interested in specialist researches into the many realms of this art and science. Towards this end the text presents, under nearly 4,000 headings, terms derived from the major post-mediaeval tradition, as well as the most important words and concepts evolved as a result of recent fissiparous tendencies within astrology. The very nature of the history of astrology requires that the post-mediaeval sources must incorporate a few Hellenistic and Arabian terms, and even a few words derived from Babylonian and Egyptian streams: to these must be added a number of Indian (Sanskrit) concepts which have entered the mainstream of European astrology by way of Theosophy and related occult sources.

The modern revival of interest in practical and theoretical astrological studies, and the proliferation of its modern forms, are sufficient reason for the publication of this work. The truth is that all available dictionaries dealing specifically with astrological terminology are in some respects wanting: none of them serves any useful academic purpose, and most of them are frequently misleading in regard to the terms they define. It is hoped that this present work will remedy such deficiencies, and provide useful guidance for those involved in practical astrology or in the study of its various historical forms, as well as for those peripherally interested in its obvious relevance to literature and art forms prior to the 18th century.

My selection of terms from what is in effect a lexicographic labyrinth has been determined almost entirely by my own personal view of what is likely to be needed by a student who is alert to the antiquity of the art, and wishes to use astrology in a practical way, or in order to throw light on related humanistic studies. It is of paramount importance nowadays (when the fissiparous tendencies common to our entire age are eroding the traditional basis of the art) that the student be encouraged to develop an awareness of the rich antiquity of astrology. On the whole it is only specialists who are aware of just how many different forms of astrology exist, all uncomfortably lumped together under the innocent-seeming single term 'astrology'. This has always been the case: we find at the very beginnings of our records, the Dorothean Astrology was different from the Ptolemaic, and the fragmentary art known to us from the ancient mystery centres of Egypt, Babylon and Greece was different from these. There were several different forms of Arabic astrology, various forms of mediaeval astrology, and the modern syncretism has encouraged the growth of many different 'astrologies'.

The nature of the modern astrologies will of course tend to interest us more than the natures of the ancient ones. The fact is that the numerous forms of 'modern astrology' are to be distinguished from the so-called 'traditional' corpus, which tends to make use of generally accepted terminologies and concepts. In a wide generalization, I might say that the modern systems of astrology have been derived in three different ways. The first is by means of what has been called 'inspiration', by techniques resting upon various clairvoyant faculties: the "Intuitional Astrology" of Bailey is of this kind. The second is by means of the syncretic approach to the esoteric and traditional forms - a co-mingling of ideas not originally designed to be yoked together: the "Astro-Psychology" of Morrish is of this kind. The third is derived from what I can only term (with as much kindness as I can muster) 'intellectual dreaming'. Many of the modern systems, often erected behind a facade of impressive-sounding terminologies and 'research programmes', are of this kind, and are really astrological systems ungrounded in any reality. It would perhaps be unfair of me to identify such systems by name in the present context: however, one might note a peculiar intensification of this sort of astrology in recent decades by the application of computing techniques to certain branches of astrology which are - in their origin, essence and spirit - inimical to such techniques. What is often called 'traditional astrology' is being practised with

===

excellent results in Europe today as a fourth group of 'astrologies'.
Strictly speaking, however, there is no such thing as 'traditional astrology' - there exist only the various astrologies of certain periods, or of certain schools of thought. It is this simple fact which so often foxes the academic and popular historian alike. Almost every astrologer of import, from Ptolemy and Valens, through Al Biruni, Campanus, Morin and Sibly, into the grey twilight of modern systems, have developed their own 'personal' astrology. Because of this, it is essential when attempting to evaluate an astrological term or idea to establish which of the many astrologies was involved. Dante had his Alfraganus, Blake his Boehme and Varley, and (not to put too fine a point on things) Mondrian had his Blavatsky, Kandinsky his Steiner, and so on. It is by personality working into personality that the history of astrology has been made, not through the influence of this mythical astrological system which is called 'traditional'. Many individual terms may be called traditional, of course, but any reference to 'traditional astrology' is usually to the Ptolemaic which, due to a series of historical accidents, has left so strong a mark on European astrology.
One may not write on the contemporary situation in astrology without feeling the urge to lament the rapid passing of a true feeling for the ancient forms - were this passing due to a wish on behalf of the student to reject that which has been tested and found wanting, then all would be as it should be. However, the fact is that the passing of the ancient forms appears to arise from ignorance rather than from perceptivity. In a perceptive comment on the modern penchant for astrological 'research', the astrologer Davison writes of those who eagerly follow up every new method suggested, in the hope that at last they will find the solution to all their problems, 'not realizing that most of these problems spring from an imperfect acquaintance with the ordinary processes of astrology. There would be far less dissatisfaction with existing methods if students took the trouble to master them thoroughly before turning their attentions further afield.' Davison is quite right - so many astrologers follow the most arcane-seeming methods, and find themselves involved in what they happily call 'esoteric astrology', without knowing anything about the art as a whole.
The bibliography at the end of this dictionary is designed as supportive reference material, yet will also serve as an index to all the literary references made in the text. If an astrologer or historian is mentioned by name, without further commentary, then that name will refer to a relevant text in the bibliography. Within the entries themselves I have adopted the convention of using capital letters to indicate a reference to another connected entry - thus ASTROSOPHY means 'see the entry under ASTROSOPHY'. Another convention is the use of "...." to indicate an entry which is available but which need not be consulted merely for the sake of throwing more light on the term being defined - thus "Astrosophy" means 'there is a related term, namely ASTROSOPHY, which need not be consulted, unless the text indicates otherwise'. The single quotation marks '...' refer to special titles, to special names or to quotations. Mindful of the large number of specialist ABBREVIATIONS available today, I have used the following:

A	Ascendant	JU	Jupiter	PL	Pluto
AQ	Aquarius	LB	Libra	RA	Right Ascension
AR	Aries	LE	Leo	SA	Saturn
AS	Asteroids	MA	Mars	SC	Scorpio
CN	Cancer	MC	Medium Coeli	SG	Sagittarius
CP	Capricorn	ME	Mercury	SU	Sun
DH	Dragon's Head	MO	Moon	SUr	Sunrise
DS	Descendant	NE	Neptune	TA	Taurus
EA	Earth	OR	Orion	UR	Uranus
EC	Ecliptic	OS	Old Style	VE	Venus
EQ	Equator	PF	Part of Fortune	VG	Virgo
GE	Gemini	PG	Pegasus	VP	Vernal Point
IC	Imum Coeli	PI	Pisces	ZO	Zodiac (Tropical)

===

AB   See BABYLONIAN CALENDAR

ABBREVIATIONS   From relatively early times astrologers have complemented
their wide use of SIGILS with alphabetical abbreviations intended to denote
principles or data. The IC, short for the latin "Imum Coeli", is an example
derived from late mediaeval astrology: the use of H to stand for the
"Ascendant" is perhaps less evident, until one realises that the Ascendant
was originally the "Horoscopus". In modern times, no doubt under the impress
of the use of the typewriter in professional reporting - and also, no doubt,
because of a feeling that the ancient sigils are somehow 'unscientific' -
there has been a move to establish a system of alphabetical abbreviations
which might be recognised internationally among astrologers. A so-called
'internationally agreed' system of 1975 was reported by Dean and Harvey.
However, there are so many different schools of astrology, each with their
own personalized approach to the subject, that there is little hope of
'international' agreement as to which system of abbreviation should be
adopted. The list in table 1 is culled from modern astrological sources, and
sets out the main abbreviations used in post-mediaeval astrology.

---TABLE 1

A	Amplitude	MA	Mars
A	Ascendant	MC	Medium Coeli
a.d.	ante diem (see KALENDS)	ME	Mercury
AD	Admetos	MH	Midheaven
AD	Anno Domini (see FOUNDATION DATES)		
Ap	Solar Apex	MK	Dragon's Tail (Mondknoten)
AP	Apollon	MO	Moon
aq	Aquarius	N	Harmonic Number
AQ	Aquarius	NE	Neptune
ar	Aries	NN	Dragon's Head (North Node)
AR	Aries	ns	New Style (of Calendars)
AS	Ascendant	NS	New Style (of Calendars)
AS	Asteroid	OA	Oblique Ascension
AU	Astronomical Unit	OD	One Degree Method
AUC	Ab Urbe Condita (see FOUNDATION DATES)		
AV	Antivertex	OR	Orion
AX	Solar Apex	OS	Old Style (of Calendars)
b	birth (place and/or time)	p	progressed
B	Birth (place and/or time)	p	progression
ba	birthplace approximate	P	Persephone
BQ	Biquintile	P	Phase
Bi	Biquintile	P	Pluto
ca	Cancer	PA	Pallas
CA	Capricorn	PF	Part of Fortune
CE	Ceres	PG	Pegasus
CN	Cancer	pi	Pisces
cp	Capricorn	PI	Pisces
CP	Capricorn	PL	Pluto
CU	Cupido	PO	Poseidon
d	day, days	prid	Pridie (see KALENDS)
d	declination	Q	Quintessence
d	dexter	Q	Quintile
d	died	r	radical
D	Demeter	r	radix
D	Direct	R	Retrograde
D	Dragon's Head	RA	Right Ascension
DH	Dragon's Head	s	second, seconds
DR	Dragon's Head	s	sign, signs
DS	Descendant	s	sinister

DSC	Descendant	s	solar arc directions
DT	Dragon's Tail	s	stationary
EC	Ecliptic	S	Sun
EH	Equal House	sa	Sagittarius
EP	East Point	SA	Saturn
EQ	Equator	SA	Semi Arc
FS	Fixed Star	sc	Scorpio
GC	Galactic Centre	SC	Scorpio
ge	Gemini	Sd	Stationary, becoming direct
GE	Gemini	SG	Sagittarius
GMT	Greenwich Mean Time	sh	speculative horoscope
GST	Greenwich Sidereal Time	SN	Dragon's Tail (South Node)
GOH	(See KOCHIAN SYSTEM)	SO	Sun (Sol)
h	hour, hours	Sr	Stationary, becoming retr.
H	Harmonic	St	Stationary
H	Heliocentric	ST	Saturn
H	Hermes	SU	Sun
H	Horizon	SUr	Sunrise
H	Ascendant (Horoscopus)	SVP	Syncretic Vernal Point
H	Mercury (Hermes)	Sx	Sextile
HA	Hades	SyZ	Synetic Zodiac
HG	Hypergalactic Centre	SZ	Sidereal Zodiac
IAU	International Astronomical Union		
IC	Imum Coeli	t	transit
IMC	Imum Coeli	ta	Taurus
J	Jupiter	ta	time approximate
JO	Juno	TA	Taurus
JU	Jupiter	TE	Earth (Terra)
K	Saturn (Kronos)	TP	Transpluto
KdG	(See COSMOBIOLOGY)	TZ	Tropical Zodiac
KR	Kronos	U	Uranus
L	Moon (Luna)	UR	Uranus
Lb	Libra	V	Venus
LB	Libra	V	Vulcan
le	Leo	VA	Vesta
LE	Leo	VE	Venus
li	Libra	vi	Virgo
LI	Libra	VI	Virgo
LMT	Local Mean Time	VG	Virgo
LST	Local Sidereal Time	VP	Vernal Point
LY	Light Years	VU	Vulkanus
m	minute, minutes	VX	Vertex
M	Mars	y	year, years
M	Midheaven	ZE	Zeus

For abbreviations in connexion with Meridian Times, see TIME ZONES. For abbreviations for horoscopic calculation and time, see TIME. With the exceptions in Table 2 the standard modern abbreviations to denote constellations consist of the first three letters of the name - thus Andromeda is And., whilst Vulpecula is Vul.

---TABLE 2

Aps	Apus	LMi	Leo Minor
Aqr	Aquarius	Phe	Phoenix
Aql	Aquila	Psc	Pisces
Cnc	Cancer	PsA	Piscis Australis
CVn	Canes Venatici	Sge	Sagitta
CMa	Canis Major	Sgr	Sagittarius
CMi	Canis Minor	Scl	Sculptor
CrA	Corona Australis	Sct	Scutum
CrB	Corona Borealis	TrA	Triangulum Australe
Crv	Corvus	UMa	Ursa Major

===

Crt	Crater	UMi	Ursa Minor
Hya	Hydra	Vol	Piscis Volans
Hyi	Hydrus		

ABHIJIT   One of the terms used for a supposed Hindu NAKKSHATRA. The
Nakshatras are obtained by dividing the zodiacal circle into 27 arcs of 13
degrees and 20 minutes, which gives 27 such arcs. This Abhijit is
interpolated between Uttara Ashadha and Sravana, thus completing the
traditional number of 28 asterisms associated with systems of lunar mansions.
It seems that no explanation is available for this interpolation, which is
used in some systems of Horary Astrology.

ABSCISSION   Term used of an effect during a multiple ASPECT, when the
aspecting planet is forming contemporaneously one or more aspects to two or
more planets. The aspect which culminates first is said to produce an
abscission of influence ray, which mitigates the influence of the second
aspect. The term FRUSTRATION is sometimes used as synonymous with
abscission, though it is applied to the effect of the later aspect, rather
than to the activity of the prior culmination.

ABSOLUTE STELLAR MAGNITUDE   A scientific formulation denoting the apparent
magnitude of a star in relation to distance from the earth. It is based on
an estimate of how bright a star would be if it were located at a distance of
ten parsecs from the Earth.

ACCELERATION   See TIME.

ACCIDENTAL ASCENDANT   A term used in HORARY ASTROLOGY of an Ascendant
constructed for the moment at which the question is posed. A relevant natal
figure (for example, that of the querent) is adjusted to this accidental
Ascendant, and the resultant chart interpreted.

ACCIDENTAL DEBILITY   Each planet is said to have its own DEBILITY, which may
be 'essential' or 'accidental'. Wilson gives a long list of the accidentals,
along with an useful indication of 'specific values', of which the following
is merely a digest:

Besieged by SA and MA	6	In partile conjunction with SA and MA	5
In conjunction with Algol	6	If Combust	5
If retrograde	5	In the 12th house	5
Partile opposition Cauda	4	Partile opposition SA or MA	4

ACCIDENTAL DIGNITY   Each planet is said to have its own DIGNITY, which may
be either 'essential' or 'accidental'. An accidental dignity may arise due
to the planet being in a particular house, degree of the zodiac, or due to
its bearing certain special aspects. The rules for interpreting accidental
dignities are complex and even obscure, though Wilson has made some attempt
to tabulate them, along with an interesting system of 'specific values': the
following is merely a digest of the more important:

In Ascendant or Midheaven	5	Free from combustion	5
In Cazimi	5	Besieged by JU and VE	6
In partile conjunction of JU	5	In partile conjunction of VE	5
In conjunction with Cor Leonis	8	In conjunction with Spica	5
In 4th, 7th or 11th house	4	In direct motion	4

ACHERNAR   Fixed star of 1st magnitude, the alpha of Eridani. The Arabian
words from which the term is derived means 'end of the river'. Being of the
nature of Jupiter, it is said to exert a beneficial influence. Ebertin shows
that it inclines towards religion.

ACIMON   See SPICA.

===

ACQUIRIUS   Name given by Simmonite to a fixed star in the face of Aquarius -
it is probably SADALSUUD. Simmonite says that it 'denotes erudition', but
Ptolemy gives it an evil influence.

ACRAB   A modern name for the fixed star GRAFFIAS.

ACRONYCAL   Term applied to a planet in opposition to the Sun, rising after
sunset or setting before sunrise. The Acronycal Place is the degree in
direct opposition to the Sun.

ACRUX   Fixed star of 1st magnitude, the alpha of Crucis - in fact it is a
triple, the brightest star in that constellation. Of a beneficial influence,
linked with the power of Jupiter, it inclines towards occultism.

ACTINOBOLIA   Term applied to the rays of the HYLEG, when it is placed on the
diurnal arc of the figure, to the east of the Midheaven. Perhaps in origin
it was loosely related to the term ACTINOBOLISM.

ACTINOBOLISM The term appears to have been used in astrology in connexion
with the theory of ASPECTS, when it was believed that planets projected
'rays' of influence down to the earth (the etymology of the word meaning
'throwing out beams'): Ptolemy uses the word in this sense. The term has
been used to denote the idea of spirits (or even materialities) shooting
forth from some source, such as the Sun. In more recent times occultists
have adapted the word to techniques of hypnosis, and it is used at times even
to denote forms of divination involving trance, such as scrying.

ACTIVE PLANETS   Planets acting as PROMITTORS.

ACTIVE VIRTUES   In their specialist astrological sense, these are 'heat and
cold' - see VIRTUES.

ACUBENS   Fixed star (double), the alpha of constellation Cancer - the
Arabian word from which the term is derived means 'claws'. Powell uses it to
mark the termination of his sidereal Gemini (see SIDEREAL ZODIAC). It is said
to be of an evil nature, exuding an influence of Saturn conjunct Mercury.

ACULEUS   A cluster of stars (the 6M in Scorpius), often treated by
astrologers as a single "Fixed Star" influence. Set in the sting of
Scorpius, it is said to have a deleterious effect on eyesight.

ACUMEN   A cluster of stars set in the sting of Scorpius, and treated by
astrologers as of the same nature as ACULEUS.

ACVINI   The Sanscrit name for the constellation Aries - but see MESHAM.

ADAD   A Babylonian term for meteorological phenomena and astrology.

ADAR   See BABYLONIAN CALENDAR.

ADHAFERA   Fixed star (double) of 3rd magnitude, set in the mane of "Leo".
It is said to be of an evil influence, save when in the rising degree.

ADJUSTED CALCULATION DATE   Since the planetary positions in most
"Ephemerides" are given for noon, astrologers find it convenient to convert
the data of the radical horoscope to an adjusted date, so that the progressed
annual figure may be directly related to the noon date. The Adjusted
Calculation Date is therefore also called the "Noon Date", or the "Perpetual
Noon Date". The noon date may be calculated, following the normal rules of
conversion involved in the "Day for a Year" method, or may be read from a
special table.

==

ADMETOS   Name given to one of the HYPOTHETICAL PLANETS used in "Uranian
Astrology". This transplutonian is included in an ephemeris, and is claimed
to relate to 'raw material, circulation and death'.

ADNACHIEL   The ruling Angel of zodiacal Sagittarius.

ADONIS   Name given by the astrologer Sutcliffe to one of the "Hypothetical
Planets" - said to be intramercurial.

ADVANTAGE   See LINE OF ADVANTAGE.

AESTIVAL SIGNS   Sometimes the "Estival's" (from the Latin "Aestas") are the
zodiacal signs of the Summer period: Cancer, Leo and Virgo.

AESULA   See HYADES.

AETHER   Name given by early astrologers to the QUINTESSENCE, the term
probably being coined to contrast with the Latin "aer" (air), which properly
belonged to the earth, the Aether being supra-lunar. This ancient aether is
not to be confused with the ether of the modern physicists, even though this
is probably directly related to the "Etheric" of the occultists, as to the
"Astral Light" of the ancients (see Washsmuth for astrological connexions).
The aether must be distinguished from the ETHERIC SPHERE.

AETHEREUM   See MACROCOSM.

AETHERIUS   Name of a constellation, 'the Balloon', or the Globus
Aerostaticus, formed by La Lande in 1798, between the tail of the Southern
Fish and Capricornus.

AFFINITY   The term is used in traditional astrology to apply to the affinity
or attraction which is said to exist between certain pairs of planets. For
example, Mars is 'in affinity' with Venus by virtue of the sexual forces,
Venus is in 'affinity' with Mercury in an artistic sense, and so on.   The
whole realm of astrology may be defined in terms of such affinities and
repulsions, for it is deeply rooted in the theory of SYMPATHY, as Lovejoy
makes clear in his study of the "Chain of Being". In modern specialist
astrological use, the term is applied to the widely recognised fact that
astrologers appear to attract clients of a particular type - through some
sort of affinity, which is usually reflected in a "Comparison Chart".

AFFLICTION   Generally, a planet is said to be 'in affliction' with another
when it is in unfavourable aspect with it: the planet receiving the aspect
is said to be 'afflicted'. However, the term may also be used of the
conjunction of planets with certain degrees of the zodiac - as for example
when the degree is marked by a malevolent fixed star, which then 'afflicts'
the planet.   Planets may also be afflicted by PARALLEL ASPECT, or through
MUNDANE ASPECT. A planet, or a nodal point, is said to be afflicted when it
is BESIEGED by two evil planets. In a popular or even poetic sense, a native
may be 'afflicted' by an evil star, or even by his entire horoscope.

AGATHOS DAIMON   The Greek term, meaning 'good genius' (see DAIMON) applied
to the 11th locus (see LOCI), which appears to have ranked in importance
second only to the Ascendant or Midheaven. The same Greek term was applied
to the 11th locus - measured not from the Ascendant, but from the "Part of
Fortune". See also AGOTHODEMON.

AGE ALONG THE ZODIAC   Term originated by Frankland as an alternative name
for his POINT OF LIFE arc.

AGENA   Fixed star of 1st magnitude, the beta of Centaurus. Ptolemy gives it
the beneficial influence of Venus conjunct Jupiter, but others relate it to
Mercury conjunct Mars.

AGE OF AQUARIUS   See AGES, EPOCHS, PLATONIC YEAR and PRECESSION.

AGE OF JUPITER   See AGE OF SATURN.

AGE OF PISCES   See AGES, EPOCHS, PLATONIC YEAR and PRECESSION.

AGE OF SATURN   A term derived from the poetic historicism of Virgil. He
divides the historical period of mankind into two ages - those of Saturn and
Jupiter, the former corresponding to the Golden Age, familiar to us from the
description of Hesiod. The Age of Jupiter is merely a later age, one of
expansion, yet involved with a reform of those darker elements developed
towards the end of the preceding age. Both of these two ages contributed to
the development of the Ovidian FOUR AGES.

AGES   There are several different systems of Ages in astrology. Most often
the term is applied to the so-called 'Zodiacal Ages', the "Epochs", which are
said to arise due to the phenomenon of the PRECESSION of the equinoxes. The
entire period of this precession is an age of 25,920 years, which is divided
into twelve sub-periods, of 2160 years duration, allocated to each of the
twelve signs of the zodiac (see PLATONIC YEAR and THREE PROTOTYPES). There is
little agreement among astrolgers as to when the 12 epochs begin and end:
some schools insist that we are now well into the Age of Aquarius, others
that we are in the Age of Pisces, and will so remain for another century or
so, whilst yet others claim that we are in the Age of Capricorn. It is, of
course, a question of which co-ordinates and philosophical outlooks are
adopted (see, for example, AYANAMSA). Accurate dating of the epochs are a
source of much argument: confusion arises in this connexion because the
constellational system of measurement is spatial, and gives periodicities
which are of uneven length as well of indeterminate beginning and end. The
zodiacal ages are non-constellational, and there is argument as to which
fiducials determine the Zodiac proper: see both SIDEREAL CORRESPONDENCES and
SIDEREAL ZODIAC. An important astrological tradition linked with Ages is
that concerned with the periodicities during which the Archangels have rule
over the destiny of the World, and shape human history - see SECUNDADEIAN
BEINGS. In relation to personal astrology, much attention is placed on the
crisis points in the ages of the individual - see CLIMACTERICS. There is
also another system of personal Ages linked with the sequence of the planets,
which are allocated periods of rule over the growing human - see SEVEN AGES.
Yet another system is derived from the PLANETARY PERIODS.

AGES OF MAN   See CLIMACTERICS and SEVEN AGES.

AGIEL   Name given by Agrippa to the Intelligency of Saturn. He gives the
magical number of Agiel as 45, which is 3 times the linear sum (15) of the
"Magic Square" of Saturn.

AGOTHODEMON   Term derived from Ptolemy for the ELEVENTH HOUSE, properly
'agathodaemon', from the Greek toast 'Agathou Daimonos' (to the good daemon),
the Greek DAIMON being a higher spirit. See also LOT OF DAIMON.

AIDONIUS   A name given by the esotericist Thierens to a future development
of his planet Pluto (see THIERENS-PLUTO) as a realisation of the modern Mars,
in his "Etheric Spheres". It is said to represent the principle of
initiation.

AIEL   According to grimoires, this is the name given to the Governor of
zodiacal Aries: he is said to rule Sunday. See ZODIACAL SPIRITS.

AIGOKEROS   Greek name, meaning 'horned creature', used to denote the sign
and constellation Capricorn. See also KRIOS.

AIR ELEMENT   The Air Element finds expression in the zodiac through the
three signs Gemini, Libra and Aquarius. It is the element most deeply

associated with thought, and with volatility: this is recorded in the
esoteric tradition by Philalethes, who says that the air element is 'the
envelope of the life of our sensitive spirit', by which he means that the
human being swims in the world of thought, as though in a sea. Indeed,
Philalethes even calls air the 'sea of things invisible'. It is evident from
such a view that the air of the esoteric astrologer, and indeed of astrology
in general, bears little other than an analogous relationship to the air of
the physicists. This analogy is often pursued by astrologers anxious to
express in material terms the nature of the air element: it is the element
which 'carries sound', and thus permits communication between people; the
oxygen of air enlivens or feeds the flames of fire - which is to say that the
air element has an affinity with the "Fire Element". See also SANGUINE.

AIRESIS   See SECTA.

AIR SIGNS   The three zodiacal signs Gemini, Libra and Aquarius are
expressions of the "Air Element". These are sometimes called the Air
Asterisms, rather than the Air Signs. Gemini is air expressed through
"Mutability", Libra is air expressed through "Cardinality", and Aquarius is
air expressed through "Fixity". By analogy with the air of the physical
world, therefore, Gemini may be pictured as air in constant movement, an
untamed wind, blowing in many directions. Libra is air blowing in a
purposive single direction, and therefore capable of establishing specific
relationships. Aquarius is 'static air', a condition which is somewhat
contrary to nature - air under pressure, which tends under certain conditions
to explode outwards, in rapid dispersal of energies. In modern astrological
parlance, these three signs are the 'intellectual' or 'mental' signs, yet in
the ancient astrological tradition, air was associated with the thought
process - perhaps once more by analogy, for it was said that just as man
breathes in life-giving air from the world around, so he breathes in the
nutrient of thought, or 'ideas' from the world outside: by such standards,
thinking was a cosmic process. Since air was regarded as the most 'restless'
of the four elements, the three air signs were seen as being dominated by
various degrees of restlessness and vacillation. See also SANGUINE for a
portrayal of Air in human personality. The air signs are sometimes called
the "Nervous Signs", the "Sweet Signs" or the "Whole Signs". See also AIR
TRIPLICITY.

AIR TRIPLICITY   This is the generic term for the three signs linked with the
"Air Element", manifesting different aspects of the "Sanguine" temperament -
Gemini, Libra and Aquarius. Air is all-pervasive, a palpable link between
the inner world of man (lungs) and the outer environment. It is this
tendency, towards unification of the individual with the whole, which is
manifest in each of the signs of the air triplicity. Gemini seeks to unify
people, to establish useful and creative relationships. Libra is intent on
establishing unity through discovering harmonies, shared experiences and
communal responsibilities. Aquarius seeks to establish unity by bringing
together large groups of people, especially with a view to establishing
large-scale social ideals. Each of the air signs is versatile and dedicated
to human relationships, tending however to be lost in superficial and
transient matters. Since the keyword of the air triplicity is 'unification',
each of the signs is involved with establishing a relationship with the world
at large. Gemini works through Platonic relationships (predatory at worst),
Libra is concerned with unity through bonds between different sexes (notably
through marriage, or business ties), while Gemini is concerned with
friendships, especially 'distant friendships', and unions established towards
a common ideal of progress or moral good.

AKASHA   A modern Theosophical term, taken from the Sanskrit as an equivalent
for the QUINTESSENCE (fifth element), which was seen as binding together in
union or pact the other four elements. A complete definition of the term
would carry us out of the astrological domain, into the realm of occultism,
but it is sufficiently relevant to mention in this context the so-called

Akashic Chronicles (sometimes the Akashic Records) which are the historical records (that may be read only by adepts and initiates) of all thoughts and deeds which have taken place on the earth, and which are indelibly imprinted upon the Akasha.

AKRAB A variant name for the star GRAFFIAS, the beta of Scorpius, incorrectly applied by Ebertin to the delta of Scorpius, properly "Dschubba".

ALA CORVI   See ALGORAB and FIFTEEN STARS.

ALACRAB   See SCORPIUS.

ALAMAC   Fixed star (binary) set in the left foot of ANDROMEDA. The name has not been convincingly explained, and is given in several variants, such as Almach and Alamak: the entire asterism of Andromeda is sometimes called Alamac. It is said to give eminence or creative ability, and Ebertin links it with popularity and cheerfulness.

ALANGUE   See OPHIUCHUS and RASALHAGUE.

ALATUS   See PEGASUS.

ALAYODI   See CAPELLA.

ALBATEGNIAN SYSTEM   A method of HOUSE DIVISION based on the division of the Prime Vertical into diurnal and nocturnal arcs, each in turn divided (respectively) into three equal parts by two declination circles. The system, ascribed to the 10th century Arabian astrologer-prince Muhammed ben Gebir al Batani (called Albategnius in Europe), appears to have given rise to the PLACIDEAN SYSTEM, held in such apparent esteem today: however, there is much argument among scholars as to the origin of this latter system, even though it is generally agreed that it was not originated by the monk Placidus.

ALBOHAZEN SYSTEM   See HALYIAN SYSTEM.

ALCABITIAN SYSTEM   A method of HOUSE DIVISION, the principle of which is the trisection of the semi-arcs by a time division. The sidereal time is taken for the degree of the Ascendant to revolve to the cusp of the Midheaven, and this is divided into three equal parts. These divisions are then added to the sidereal time at birth, to reveal the positions of the diurnal arcs. A reverse procedure is used to determine the nocturnal arcs. It is claimed that the house grid offered by this system, unlike that of the related trisectional method of the PLACIDEAN SYSTEM, is valid for polar regions. This system is ascribed by some historians to one Alcabitius, who is supposed to have lived in the 1st century AD. However, it appears that the method is really linked with an Arabic system derived no earlier than the tenth century (see ALBATEGNIAN SYSTEM): its name probably refers not to Alcabitius, but to the Arabian astrologer Alchabitus, of the 12th century.

ALCALST   See VINDEMATRIX.

ALCHAMETH   See ARCTURUS and FIFTEEN STARS.

ALCHEMICAL MERCURY   The term Mercury is often used in esoteric and occult circles coterminous with astrology in a sense which does not refer to the purely astrological conception of MERCURY. This alchemical Mercury is really the Hermetic Mercury, which figures in alchemical treatises under a variety of spagyric names.   In the hermetic tradition, which informs exoteric astrology, Mercury is cold and moist, and therefore 'aqueous': it is therefore the 'Permanent Water', the vitalizing spirit of the body, and is linked with what the mediaeval occultists would call the "Ens Veneni", the approximate equivalent of the modern "Etheric". In this capacity, Mercury has been given many names suggestive of potent liquidity - Blessed Water,

==

Virtuous Water, Philosopher's Vinegar, Dew of Heaven, Virgin's Milk, and so
on. It is sometimes said that the whole alchemical art depends upon a true
understanding of the nature of this Mercury, which is directly linked with
the QUINTESSENCE.

ALCOHODEN Arabian astrological term for the HYLEG.

ALCOR   A fixed star, set in the constellation of URSA MAJOR. It is not a
conspicuous star (perhaps more so now than in the 8th century), and was used
by the desert Arabs as a test of good vision. Allen records that they were
used to regard CANOPUS as the highest, and Alcor as the lowest, in visual
scale. It seems that the adage 'Vidit Alcor at non lunam plenam' (He sees
Alcor, but not the full Moon) was at one time the equivalent of our proverb,
'He cannot see the wood for the trees'.

ALCYONE   Fixed star of 3rd magnitude, the brightest of the PLEIADES, set in
the shoulder of constellation Taurus. Early astronomers regarded it as a
sort of central sun to the universe, and accorded it considerable importance:
the Arabian astrologers called it 'Al Wasat' (the central one), while the
Babylonian astrologers called it 'Temennu', (foundation stone). Powell
commences his Taurus with this star in his SIDEREAL ZODIAC, locating it in
the 6th degree. It is said by modern astrologers to be of the nature
equivalent to Moon conjunct Mars.

ALDEBARAN   Fixed star of 1st magnitude, the alpha of constellation Taurus,
set in the left eye of the Bull, its name (perhaps) derived from the Arabian
'Al Dabaranu' (the forecaster). It was the 'Star of the tablet' for the
Babylonians (see MUL-APIN TABLES), and because of its almost perfect
opposition to ANTARES was used as a fiducial in the "Babylonian Zodiac": see
the figure 28, under FIFTEEN STARS. Aldebaran has many names, reflecting its
important role in astrological observation - see however STELLA DOMINATRIX.
Aldebaran was one of the four "Royal Stars" of Persian astrology. It appears
to bring good fortune and honours, when emphasized by benefic conjunction:
in Mundane Astrology, however, it is a cause of catastrophies when in aspect
with a malefic. Cornell provides a formidable list of disasters associated
with the star, and claims that when afflicting the planets it tends to cause
'extreme suffering to humanity, sickness or death', and even directions to
the angles produce periods of terrible stress.

ALEXANDRIAN CALENDAR   See EGYPTIAN CALENDAR.

ALGEBAR   See ORION.

ALGEDI   A multiple star, the alpha of Capricornus, set in the south horn of
the Goat. The name is from the Arabian 'Al Jady' (the Goat), and it is often
called Giedi. Ptolemy accords it the nature of Venus conjunct Mars, but when
conjuncted with planets in a chart its influence is towards the peculiar and
unexpected (similar to that of Uranus, as Alvidas notes).

ALGENIB   Fixed star of 3rd magnitude, the gamma of Pegasus, set in the
wing-tip of the horse, its name probably from the Arabic 'Al Janah' (the
Wing). It is said to be an unfortunate influence, projecting the nature of
Mercury conjunct Mars.

ALGENUBI   Fixed star of 3rd magnitude, the epsilon of constellation Leo,
set in the mouth of the Lion. It is said to exude a difficult influence,
being of the nature of Mars conjunct Saturn - though (by analogy?) it gives
'great power of expression'.

ALGIBBAR   See ORION and RIGEL.

ALGOL   Fixed star (binary), the beta of Perseus, set in the head of the
Gorgon Medusa. It is said to be the most evil of all stars - the 'most

==

unfortunate, violent, and dangerous star in the heavens', as Allen puts it, a
view supported by most of its traditional names. The word Algol is from the
Arabic 'Ra's al Ghul' (Demon Head), for which reason it is sometimes called
Caput Algol, almost a modern version of the Caput Medusae.   It is the 'Demon
Star', the 'Satan's Head' (Rosh ha Satan) of the Hebrews, whose astrologers
also call it Lilith after their own female demon. Ebertin gives several
interesting charts of murderers involved with dominant Algol, and, on a more
prosaic level, notes that the star appears to bring the need for false teeth
- a pale modern equivalent of the ancient tradition which has the star
afflicting the face and head to the point of decapitation or strangulation.
It is one of the FIFTEEN STARS.

ALGOMEYLA   See PROCYON.

ALGOMEYSA   See PROCYON.

ALGORAB   Fixed star (double) of 3rd magnitude, the delta of Corvus, set in
the Crow's right wing, the term being from the Arabic 'Al Ghirab' (the Crow).
It is sometimes called Ala Corvii, (crow's wing). Astrologers give it a
harmful nature, akin to Mars with Saturn. It is one of the FIFTEEN STARS.

ALHAYHOCH   Late-mediaeval name for the star ALPHECCA - see MAGICAL JEWELS.

ALHECKA   Fixed star of 3rd magnitude, set in the south horn of constellation
Taurus. Powell adopted this star as the termination of his Taurus asterism,
locating it in the 30th degree of Taurus - see SIDEREAL ZODIAC. It is said
to give a quarrelsome and difficult nature.

ALHENA   Fixed star of 2nd magnitude, the gamma of constellation Gemini, set
in the left foot of the southern twin. The term is said to be from the
Arabic 'Al Han'ah' (a burned brand-mark). Ptolemy ascribes it a nature
equivalent to Mercury conjunct Venus.

ALIEN SIGNS   A term used in Ptolemaic astrology, approximately the
equivalent of the modern DISSOCIATE SIGNS. A synonym was Disjunct Signs.

ALIOTH   One of the seven fixed stars forming the constellation URSA MAJOR,
said by Ptolemy to be of the influence equivalent to Mars.

AL JABHA   Fixed star of 3rd magnitude, set in the mane of the Lion, though
the term is from the Arabic 'Al Jeb'ha' (the Forehead). Not a beneficial
influence, it is said to carry the equivalent nature of Mercury conjunct
Saturn, and to be conducive to violence.

AL JAUZAH   See ORION.

ALLORE   See WEGA.

ALMAGEST   Sometimes called the 'Syntaxis Mathematica', this is a treatise in
13 books, dealing with astronomy and astrology, attributed to the 2nd century
astrologer Ptolemy, about whom virtually nothing is known. Much of the
astrolgical star-lore in this present text is derived from the Almagest. See
also CENTILOQUIUM and TETRABIBLOS.

ALMANAC   Name given to a booklet or set of tables, sometimes accompanied by
predictions of a public nature, or relating to weather and matters affecting
agriculture (see ASTRO-METEOROLOGY), setting out the phenomenal aspect of
future astronomical and astrological conditions. Some almanacs offer
material on a monthly basis, others on an annual. The earliest almanacs were
prophetic in nature, many of them written around simple progression
techniques, and (in connexion with weather forecasts) around ingresses into
cardinal signs. A comparison of almanac weather predictions for specific
periods in the 17th century has revealed remarkably little accuracy, and

===

no particular agreement for the same days among contemporaneous almanac
makers. See also EPHEMERIS.

ALMOCHODEN   An Arabian astrological term for the HYLEG.

ALMUCANTAR   Name of the circle of constant altitude above the horizon.

ALMUTEN   Term derived from Arabian astrology, signifying the most
influential planet in a chart, the strength being determined from essential
and accidental dignities. See DIGNITY and LORD OF THE HOROSCOPE.

ALNASL   Fixed star, the gamma of constellation Sagittarius, its Arabian name
meaning 'point', probably in reference to the head of the arrow.   Powell
chooses this star to mark the beginning of his sidereal Sagittarius (see
SIDEREAL ZODIAC), locating it in the 7th degree.

ALNILAM   Fixed star of 2nd magnitude, the epsilon of Orion, set in the belt
of the giant, the name being derived from the Arabic 'Al Nitham' (string of
pearls). It is said to be a difficult influence in a chart, and Ptolemy
gives it a nature equivalent to Jupiter conjunct Saturn.

ALPHARATZ   The name 'Schedar', with many variant spellings, is also given to
this multiple star in CASSIOPEIA: the name is said to come from the Arabic
'Al Sadr' (the Breast), where it is located. Distinguish from ALPHERATZ.

ALPHARD   Fixed star of 2nd magnitude, the alpha of Hydra, set in the neck of
the constellation, and sometimes called Cor Hydra (Hydra's Heart). It is
said to be of the nature of Venus conjunct Saturn, but of an evil influence,
even though the afflicted native may be artistic or musical.

ALPHECCA   Fixed star of 2nd magnitude, the alpha of Corona Borealis, the
term being from the Arabic 'Al Na'ir al Fakkah' (the bright one in the dish).
It is sometimes called Elpheia, and by Ebertin 'Gemma', due to a
misunderstanding. It is said to be a beneficial influence in a chart, and
Ptolemy says it is the equivalent of Mercury with Mars. See FIFTEEN STARS.

ALPHEICHIUS   See OPHIUCHUS.

ALPHERAS   See SCHEAT.

ALPHERATZ   Fixed star (double) of 2nd magnitude, the alpha of Andromeda, set
in the hair of the figure. The Arabian astrologers placed this star in
Pegasus, and called it 'Al Surrat al Faras' (the horse's navel), from which
our own term was derived.   It is sometimes called Caput Andromedae,
(Andromeda's Head). Of a beneficial nature, especially giving a good
intellect, it is linked with Venus conjunct Jupiter.

AL PHERG   Fixed star (double) of 4th magnitude, the eta of Pisces, set in
the cord joining the two fishes. Of a beneficial influence.

ALRESCHA   Fixed star (double), the alpha of constellation Pisces, marking
the knot in the cord, and hence called Nodus Piscium, Nodus Coelestis, and
the like. Powell adopted this star to mark the completion of sidereal
Pisces, locating it in the 5th degree of Aries: see SIDEREAL ZODIAC.

AL SIMAK   See ARCTURUS.

ALTAIR   Fixed star of 1st magnitude, alpha of Aquila, set in the neck of the
Eagle, the name being derived from the Arabic 'Al Tair' (the eagle). A
powerful influence, concerning which nature few authorities agree, though
Ptolemy gives it the equivalent of Mars conjunct Jupiter.

ALTARF   Fixed star, the 4th magnitude beta of constellation Cancer, the name in Arabic meaning 'the end', in reference to its position at the southern foot of the asterism. Powell adopted this star as the commencement of his sidereal Cancer, locating it the 10th degree: see SIDEREAL ZODIAC.

ALTERF   Fixed star, the lamda of constellation Leo, located by Ptolemy in the mouth of the Lion: the name derives from the corresponding "Manzil". Powell locates it as the beginning of his SIDEREAL ZODIAC Leo, in the 24th degree of Cancer.

ALTITUDE   In astrology, altitude is usually expressed in degrees, minutes and seconds, and signifies the point of elevation above or below the horizon, along the arc of the zodiac. A planet is on "Meridian Altitude" when it reaches the cusp of the Midheaven. Altitude above the horizon is usually noted positively (thus +90 for zenith) and negatively (thus -90 for nadir).

AMBIENT   Little-used term in modern astrology, originally applied to the "Tenth Sphere", the Ambient Sphere, which in the Ptolemaic cosmoconception was visualised as moving all the other "Spheres" with it. The term is now sometimes applied to the Heavens in general.

AMBRIEL   The name given in certain grimoires and methods of ceremonial magic to the governor of the zodiacal sign Gemini. The name appears in a confusing variety of contexts, however, not all of them relating to this rulership. In certain cabbalistic texts, for example, Ambriel is associated with Mars.

AMBROSIA   See HYADES.

AMPLITUDE   A term derived from the HARMONICS of the modern astrologer Addey, relating to the strength of each particular harmonic, shown as a percentage of mean distribution.

ANABIBAYON   Term given by Simmonite as a synonym for DRAGON'S HEAD. Perhaps a mistake for ANAHIBAZON.

ANAEL   The name of the Archangel associated with the Sphere of Venus.

ANAHIBAZON   Arabian astrological term for the DRAGON'S HEAD.

ANARETA   See ANARETIC and ANARETIC PLACES.

ANARETIC   Term derived from the Greek, meaning 'destroyer', and applied to the planet or degree which is for one reason or another regarded as the destroyer of life in a particular chart. The rules for determining which planet is the 'anareta', or in the anaretic place (sometimes called the 'killing place' by modern astrologers), are complex, and most astrologers warn of the difficulty of making predictions based on such rules. In some contexts the term is used of a planet which forms a difficult aspect to the HYLEG, though this does not necessarily mean that it is therefore the 'killer'. In other contexts, the term is also used of certain fixed stars which, by virtue of conjunctions in a natal chart, or by progression, pour their baneful and killing influence into that chart, and bring about the death of the native. The 'anaretic point', or 'place' is the degree occupied by such a planet or fixed star in a chart: but see also ANARETIC PLACES.

ANARETIC PLACES   The anaretic places are often said to be the degrees in a horoscope figure occupied by the radical Mars or Saturn - or by the radical Sun, Moon and Mercury, should these be badly aspected by Mars or Saturn. However, many different rules exist for determining the 'killing place', as the anaretic place is sometimes called. Cornell simplifies a complex issue by speaking of the anaretic place as that occupied by an ANARETIC planet in the 4th 6th, 8th or 12th houses. The issue remains complex, however, for besides establishing the identity of the anaretic from such places, there is the problem of determining also not only how, but when, it will bring death.

ANATOMY   See BIOLOGICAL CORRESPONDENCES and MELOTHESIC MAN.

ANCIENT MOON   Another term for OLD MOON.

ANCIENT SATURN   Another term for OLD SATURN.

ANCIENT SUN   Another term for OLD SUN.

ANDROGYNE   The term means 'having characteristics of both sexes', but in an astrological context this sense is often limited in application to the planet Mercury (see ANDROGYNOUS PLANET), which has the facility for receiving the colour and sexuality of both 'male' and 'female' planets (such as Mars and Venus, respectively), through aspect to these. In an astrological context, 'the Androgyne' is Mercury.

ANDROGYNOUS PLANET   A name for Mercury, a planet said to participate in both the feminine and masculine natures - but see for example FEMININE PLANETS. In the ancient tradition Mercury was said to be both 'dry' and 'moist', and thus linked with both the male and female natures (see SECTA). In fact, even in accord with traditional astrology, it is clear that all planets manifest a sexual duality (save for the Sun and Moon), so that when Mercury is termed 'androgynous', or is called the 'Androgyne' it is in reference to the effects observed through aspects cast to this planet. Thus, an aspect formed between the feminine Moon and a planet will tend to 'feminize' that other planet: however, an aspect received or projected by Mercury will result in a polarity which depends entirely upon the 'sexuality' or polarity of the other planet.

ANDROMEDA   Constellation, approximately from 12 degrees Aries to 15 degrees Taurus, 20 to 55 degrees north of equator (but see CONSTELLATION MAPS). In Greek mythology, Andromeda was the daughter of Cepheus, rescued from a monster by Perseus, who rode the winged horse, Pegasus. As an asterism, it is said to imbue purity of thought, honour and virtue - though Manilius tells us that when Andromeda is setting, it causes death from the bite of an animal, or by crucifixion. Among the many names for this constellation are 'Chained Woman' (Mulier Catenata), Persea (perhaps meaning 'bride of Perseus'), 'Cepheis' and 'Alamac' (after the binary of this constellation). The important stars set in the figure are ALPHERATZ, MIRACH and ALAMAC.

ANDROMEDA'S HEAD   See ALPHERATZ.

ANGELS   A name given to the "Ninth Hierarchy" of incorporeal spiritual beings above the realm of man - see SPIRITUAL HIERARCHIES. Whilst the word applies to a specific rank of the hierarchies, it is also used in a general sense of all nine levels, with resultant confusion - for example, the so-called 'Angels of the Zodiac' are actually "Archangels". According to the esoteric tradition, the Ninth Hierarchy is charged with the guidance of individuals through incarnation after incarnation. In the ecclesiastical tradition (which has deeply influenced astrological lore) St. Gregory associates the Angels with the emerald, whilst biblical exegesis associates them with the colour green: in esoteric lore, they are linked with the Sphere of the Moon. The order of the remaining eight levels of Hierarchies, from the list provided by Dionysius the Areopagite, is set out in table 3.

```
                                                        ----------TABLE 3
  RANK     SPHERE     NAME (GREEK)     OTHER NAMES
  =================================================================
  Ninth    Moon       Angeloi
  Eighth   Mercury    Archangeloi
  Seventh  Venus      Archai           Principates or Principalities
  Sixth    Sun        Exsusiai         Potestates or Powers
  Fifth    Mars       Dynamis          Virtues or Virtutes
  Fourth   Jupiter    Kyriotetes       Dominions or Dominations
  Third    Saturn     Trones           Thrones
```

==

--TABLE 3 (CONTINUED)

RANK	SPHERE	NAME (GREEK)	OTHER NAMES
Second	Fixed Stars	Seraphim	(Hebraic name)
First	Zodiac	Cherubim	(Hebraic name)

See also PLANETARY ANGELS, SECUNDADEIAN BEINGS and ZODIACAL ANGELS.

ANGELS OF THE ZODIAC   See ZODIACAL ANGELS

ANGELUS SYMBOLS   Name given to a series of short 'readings' ascribed to each
of the 360 degrees of the zodiac (in accordance with a system of DEGREE
SYMBOLS) attributed to the 16th century astrologer Johannes Angelus.

ANGLE   In relation to the horoscope figure, any of the four cardinal points
are called 'angles'. The Eastern Angle is the Ascendant of the horizon line
(AS in figure 1): in early astrology this was called Oriens, and even
Horoscopos (Greek) or Horoscopus (Latin). The Western Angle (DS in figure 1)
is the Descendant of the horizon line, in early astrology called Occidens,
'the setting of the Sun'. The South Angle (MC in figure 1) is the cusp of
the Tenth House, sometimes called the 'Medium Coeli' (Latin for 'middle of
the skies'), the Midheaven, Zenith or South Vertical, though technically
these points do not always correspond. The North Angle (IC in figure 1) is
the cusp of the Fourth House, sometimes called the 'Imum Coeli' (Latin for
'lowest part of the skies'), the Nadir, or the North Vertical. See also
ANGULARITY.

FIGURE 1 - THE ANGLES OF THE HOROSCOPE.

ANGUIS   See DRACO.

ANGULAR   See ANGULARITY.

ANGULAR HOUSES   These are the houses which fall on the ANGLE of the figure -
namely, the 1st, 4th, 7th and 10th houses, the strongest of all houses in a
horoscope. In modern astrology (see ANGULARITY) the angular houses are often
said to be those which immediately follow the angles (in clockwise
direction), the cusps regarded as marking the 'outside' limits of the houses,
rather than the most powerful part (the centres).

ANGULARITY   A planet is said to be angular when located on one of the
"Angular Houses". In many systems of interpreting houses, the cusps were
themselves regarded as the centres of houses, and thus marked the most
powerful part of the house under question. However, in modern times, the
distinction between the segment of the house and the cusp marking it has
almost been lost, with the result that in modern astrology an Angular planet
is defined in terms of angles (the two main Ascendant Axis and Midheaven
Axis), rather than in terms of houses. However, in accordance with most
astrological terms, the actual sense of the definition to be applied by the
term rather depends on the system of astrology being used. There is some

agreement among astrologers that planets 'on the angles' (however defined) are usually powerful. Ptolemy is often quoted as supporting this idea, but in fact it is difficult to be sure what Ptolemy really had in mind in regard to this matter: the few readings which have survived from Greek horoscopes, as from early Arabic figures, support the general importance of the angles. There is, also, much argument as to what arc of ORB should be applied to angularity. If it were a question of mundane position, as the original use of the term indicates, then the question of orb need hardly arise. However, if the modern interpretation is adhered to, (there is no general consensus of opinion) an orb equivalent to the 1st magnitude fixed star recognised in the MORINEAN ORBS (that is, 8 degrees) might well be regarded as applicable.

ANGULAR SIGNS   These are the CARDINAL SIGNS.

ANIADUS   A term derived from Paracelsus, which appears to be the equivalent of the stellar VIRTUE 'from which we receive celestial influences by the medium of fantasy and imagination'.

ANIDA   Term used by certain alchemists to signify the VIRTUE in things, sometimes called (as for example by Sendivogius) the 'Astral Virtue' or the 'Celestial Virtue'. Though etymologically linked with ANIADUS, it appears to be the equivalent of the ILECH.

ANIMAL SIGNS   An alternative term for FOUR-FOOTED SIGNS. It is interesting to observe that if the supposed etymology of the word 'Zodiac' (as being from the Greek 'Zoon') is correct, then all twelve signs would be animal signs. For the correct etymology, see Smith.

ANIMA MUNDI   The Latin term for 'the feminine Soul of the World', relating to the enveloping divine essence which vitalizes all beings. As Blavatsky writes, it is 'the essence of seven planes of sentience, consciousness and differentiation, moral and physical'. It is said to be of an 'igneous, ethereal nature' in the world of form, but entirely spiritual in higher realms. The higher element of the human being is said to be derived from the Anima Mundi, which is itself an emanation of a higher spiritual realm. In astrological imagery, the Anima Mundi is often given in the form of a naked woman, surrounded by the Spheres, in which are embedded the planets - one of the most famous images is that given by Fludd.

ANIMODER   A term apparently derived from Egyptian astrology by way of Ptolemy, and often misunderstood by modern astrologers. The term is used to denote a sort of rectification principle, designed to determine the exact degree of Ascendant by means of the previous syzygy to the birth. It is often wrongly confused with the TRUTINE OF HERMES.

ANNAEL   A variant for ANAEL, ruler of Venus.

ANNUAL CHART   A term used by Bradley for the SOLAR RETURN.

ANNULUS PLATONICUS   See CHAIN OF BEING. Distinguish from ANNUS PLATONICUS.

ANNUS PLATONICUS   The Latin equivalent for PLATONIC YEAR.

ANOMALISTIC PERIOD   The period of time elapsing in the movement of a planet from one Perihelion to the next. When applied to the Moon, the period marks the time elapsing beween one Perigee to the next.

ANOMALISTIC YEAR   One of the three lengths of the year, defined as the time interval between the perihelions of the orbit of the earth: it is 365.23964 days. See also TIME, TROPICAL YEAR and SIDEREAL YEAR.

ANOMALY   In relation to planetary movement, the angular distance of a planet from its perihelion or aphelion.

===

ANSER AMERICANUS   See TOUCAN.

ANTAR   See ANTARES.

ANTARES   Fixed star (binary) of 1st magnitude, the alpha of Scorpius, set in
the body of the Scorpion. This was one of the ancient ROYAL STARS, and is
sometimes called 'Cor Scorpionis' (Scorpion's Heart) and 'Shiloh'. Sometimes
called Antar, in confusion with a literary hero (see Allen), the modern name
is said to be derived from its red colour, in that it was rival even of the
planet Mars - the Greek, 'anti-Ares'. It is of an extremely powerful nature,
both martial and malefic, with the equivalent influence of Mars conjunct
Jupiter: Cornell (clearly unmindful of Algol) writes of it as 'the most
mentioned star in the textbook of Astrology, for his evils'.

ANTECANIS   See PROCYON.

ANTI-ASPECTS   A term derived from research into the relationship between
aspects and harmonics, which has suggested that there are two major
anti-aspects, and two minors. The majors are those of about 79 degrees and
101 degrees (allowing an Orb of about 3 degrees). Such angular relationships
play no part in traditional aspectal theory, though they are actually
accommodated in the Ptolemaic elemental aspectal theory (see ELEMENTAL
ASPECTS). The same is true of the so-called minor anti-aspects, which are of
about 66 degrees and 114 degrees (and allow an orb of 1 degree).

ANTICHTHON   Term of Greek origin, used to denote the 'anti-earth', the
'second earth' which was supposed to lie on the opposite side of the Sun to
our own earth, revolving invisibly to man. Historically, the idea of the
antichthon is linked with the school of Pythagoras, but it was especially
widely circulated in mediaeval astrological lore, even though it contradicted
the assumptions of the geocentric PTOLEMAIC SYSTEM, then held as a valid
model of the cosmos.

ANTI-EARTH   See ANTICHTHON.

ANTIGENETIC CHART   Term used for a chart (usually one of a related series)
cast for anniversaries of a radical natal chart, or for related periods
(months, weeks, etc.) derived from that radical in a calendrical sense.

ANTI-MIDHEAVEN   See IMUM COELI.

ANTINOUS   Constellation, approximately from 13 degrees Capricorn to 10
degrees Aquarius, 8 to 13 degrees south of the equator - but see
CONSTELLATION MAPS. Named after the favourite of Hadrian, its proximity to
the constellation Aquila has led Bayer to call it 'Ganymede', after the youth
carried off by an eagle, to become Jupiter's cupbearer: it is also
'Pocillator' (cup-bearer).

ANTIPATHY   Planets may be said to be in antipathy to each other under
certain cirumstances - most usually when they are in difficult or
inharmonious aspect. However, planets do have a natural antipathy by virtue
of their potency: for example, the Moon is by nature antipathetic to Saturn,
since the former is a dissolving influence, while the latter is a fixer
(rigidifier) of form. In "Synastry", planets (and even the same planet in
two charts) may be antipathetic when involved in difficult aspects between
the two charts. In a specialist sense, the word is sometimes applied to two
planets ruling opposing signs - thus the Mars of Aries is in antipathy with
the Venus of Libra, and the ruler of Capricorn, Saturn, is said to bear an
antipathy to the ruler of Cancer, the Moon. See also SYMPATHY.

ANTISCION   In modern astrology, the antiscion of a planet is the degree
equidistant to that planet on the opposite side of the Cancer-Capricorn axis
of a birth chart (the line falling through the first degrees of these signs).

==

This antiscion degree is a sort of mirror-image of a planetary position, or of a nodal point, and is regarded as being effective when progressed or transitted by another planet. In traditional astrology, the same term was used of two planets with the same degree of declination on the same side of the ecliptic: the same declination degree on the opposite side of the ecliptic was called a 'Contra Antiscion'. But for the modern version of this term, see CONTRASCION. The astrologer Antonio Bonattis was at pains to distinguish the modern sense of the antiscion, which he called the 'Antiscium' (plural Antiscia) from the 'declination' antiscium: interestingly, he writes of the planetary antiscion 'vibrating' to that planetary influence which mirrors it.

ANTISCIUM   See ANTISCION.

ANTISEDENT   An antisedent planet is one in retrograde motion.

ANTIVERTEX   See VERTEX.

ANURADHA   The 15th of the Hindu NAKSHATRAS.

AORION   See ORION.

APEX   See SOLAR APEX.

APEX EPHEMERIS   See GALACTIC CENTRE.

APHELION   The point in the orbit of a planet (or comet) furthest from the Sun. The plural is Aphelia.

APHETA   Term applied to a planet, or to a nodal point in a horoscope, which sustains the life of the native. See also APHETIC PLACES.   Alternative terms from different astrological traditions are HYLEG and PROROGATOR.

APHETIC PLACES   In Graeco-Roman astrology, the aphetic places were those areas in a chart which were said to maintain or enhance life. These are the central arc of 20 degrees in the 1st, 7th, 9th and 11th houses. The rules for determining which planets are aphetic or HYLEG are directly related to these aphetic places, though complex in the extreme. The Sun in an aphetic place is always given preference, followed by the Moon, and then by the planet which carries most dignity. If no planet qualifies, then the horoscope degree itself is the apheta (incidentally, this rule confirms that the relative house system places the Ascendant in the middle of the 1st house, otherwise it could not be in the aphetic place - see HOUSE SYSTEMS).

APHORISMS   A term used in astrology in relation to the collection of pithy sayings, often in the form of concentrated astrological lore, and contained in CENTILOQUIUM texts. An example from the Centiloquium of Gadbury is the aphorism, 'The Art of Astrology is certain and most indubitably true; but there are few that Practice it, who rightly understand it.'   Many aphorisms are merely simplistic generalisations of astrological traditions.

APIS   See MUSCA AUSTRALIS and MUSCA BOREALIS.

APOCALYPTIC STAR   An esoteric term used by Paracelsus for the one 'personal' star which 'exists higher than all the rest' - see ESOTERIC ASTROLOGY.

APOGEE   The point in the orbit of a planet which is farthest from the earth. The term is often used in a wide and even figurative sense, but it was originally restricted to the motion of the Moon.

APOLLO   The name of this Roman god is frequently used as a synonym for the Sun in late mediaeval texts. The fixed star CASTOR was also called Apollo by Ptolemy, a name adopted by many later astrologers. The Greek equivalent,

==

Helios, was also used in a similar dual way.

APOLLON   Name given to one of the HYPOTHETICAL PLANETS used in the "Uranian Astrology". This transneptunian planet is accorded an ephemeris, and is claimed to relate to 'expansion, science, commerce and peace'.

APORHOEA   Little used term, used of the Moon as it separates from aspect to one planet, and applies to another, when it is said to be 'in aporhoea'.

APOTELESMATIC   A term used as almost synonymous with GENETHLIACAL. It appears to have been derived from the Greek 'apotelesma' (the sum, or completion), perhaps with reference to the completing or 'casting' of a horoscope. Bosc suggests that the original application was intended to convey the idea of 'the science of influences'. In a non-specialist sense, the word is applied to the casting of horoscopes of all kinds, well beyond the limits of "Natal Astrology".

APPARENT MOTION   In astrology, the apparent motion of celestial bodies is regarded as being due to the rotary motion of the Earth, as distinct from their own "Proper Motion".

APPARENT SOLAR TIME   See TIME.

APPEARANCE   Much credence is given in popular astrology to the notion that the appearance of the native is a 'reflection' of the zodiacal or planetary dominants in his chart - that a horoscope is a significator of the physical as well as the psychic life of the native. The earliest printed textbooks set out fairly simplistic rules for determining appearances, and what has more recently been called 'facial types', in the aphorismic astrology which by-passes the more profound laws of horoscopic delineation. From such notions, a series of word-portraits, and even graphic images of facial types, claimed to correspond to the 'planets' or the 'signs', have been published - almost all of them of dubious validity. The word-portraits derive from principles set out in mediaeval astrology, the simple rule (given for example by Lilly) being that one may assess appearance from the sign ascending and from the two signs containing the Moon and the 'Lord of the Ascendant' - an axiom which is repeated even into modern textbooks. The finest of the short word-portraits (though descriptive more of 'personality' than actual appearance), linked with the Ascendant and/or Sun-sign astrology is given by Waite, the typical longer portraits are given by Pagan. However, the literature relating to types is of much the same order, and is self-proliferating. The graphic portraitures (limited to planetary types, sign and sun-signs) appears to have been derived from mediaeval physiognomy: Delaporta did not hesitate to derive facial appearances from the images of the corresponding zodiacal signs. The most sophisticated early examples may be seen in Sibly, who gave copperplate portraits set in relevant horoscopes - a considerable advance on the crude woodcuts. A 'planetary physiognomy' developed around the "Almuten", conveniently dividing mankind into seven physical types - though the astrologer-artist Varley prepared some interesting drawings to support his (unfinished) studies which seem to have been based on direct observations. The widely published planetary and zodiacal types associated with the popularisation of astrology by the Theosophists, or with such writers as Muchery, are little more than crude continuations of the mediaeval tradition: the modern practice (in popular textbooks, at least) of using photographs of famous personalities to demonstrate sun-sign or Ascendant facial types (for example, Lynch) is little more than a technical development of this ancient practice. The root of the problem is that appearance is just about as unique as the horoscope iself, and therefore does not lend itself easily to simplistic methods of classification into seven, ten or twelve types (or for that matter into the 36 'decanate types', as has been proposed). In view of the uniqueness of the chart, it is hardly surprising that Gauquelin should come to the conclusion that it was not possible 'to establish a link between the human physique and

planetary type' - thereby brushing aside a thousand-year-old tradition. There
is certainly much need for a comparative study of facial appearance in
relation to well-documented horoscopes, perhaps along the lines indicated by
Toonder, who observes the similar appearance of the Nobel prize winners
Einstein and Hahn, the tenors Gigli and Laurintz, and the writers Stephens
and Joyce. The German astrologer Wangemann has (on the account of Dean)
spent many years researching facial appearance in relation to house cusps,
which marks a departure from the traditional approach - working mainly from
the "Kochian System" which seems to lend itself to this form of research.

APPLICATION   In a strictly specialist sense, a planet is said to be applying
to another body, or to a nodal point, when it is on the point of forming an
aspect to it. Usually, it is the faster body which is said to be applying to
the slower, since it is this which is building up or forming the aspect. The
importance of the term lies in the fact that traditional astrology insists
that aspects are more powerful when in application, so that the orb of
application is more powerful than the orb of separation: but see ASYMMETRIC
ORB. The term is directly from the Latin 'applicatio', itself a translation
of Ptolemy's 'synaptein'. See DIRECT APPLICATION and RETROGRADE APPLICATION.

APPULSE   Strictly an astronomical term for a partial occultation, but
sometimes used to denote a conjunction of one orbital body with another, or
even the crossing of the meridian by such a body. In a specialist sense, it
is applied to the entry of the Moon into the Earth's shadow.

APRIL   The fourth month of the GREGORIAN CALENDAR. The etymology of the
word is probably linked with the Latin verb 'aperire' (or modern 'aperture')
and exoterically explained as the time when the 'flowers open', and so on.
In esoteric astrology, however, the month is linked with the opening of the
Earth plane to the influences of the stellar world, from which it has to some
extent been isolated in the winter time (see MARCH). It has been argued that,
in spite of the early etymologies, this term is from the Greek 'Aphrodite'
(as Aphrilis), whose festivals were celebrated in this month. Certainly, the
pagan Anglo-Saxon goddess of the Spring, Eastre, gave us the Easter-month.

APSIS   In early astrology, apsis was sometimes used as synonymous with
'orbit'. In modern astronomy, however, it is used as descriptive of one of
the two points in the elliptic orbit of such a body, at which it is at its
greatest and least distance from the 'centre' of its motion. These points
(plural 'Absides') are the APHELION and PERIHELION.

APUS   Constellation, some 75 to 80 degrees south of the equator, called
'the Bird of Paradise', and said to exude a beneficient influence.

AQUARIDS   See METEORS.

AQUARIUS   The eleventh sign of the zodiac. It corresponds as a zodiacal
sign neither in location nor extent with the constellation of the same name
(see AQUARIUS CONSTELLATION). The modern sigil for Aquarius ∿∿ is said by
some to represent the flow of water, especially that of the Nile, and this
sign (for all it is an air sign) has from the earliest days of astrology been
associated with water: on a symbolic level, however, the stream of water
which is contained in the urn of the Aquarian image (figure 2) is said to
represent spiritual knowledge, the Celestial Waters of the ancients. Some
astrologers prefer to interpret the sigil as representative of the invisible
waves of electricity (in occult terms, the 'fohat') - see however SIGILS -
ZODIAC. Aquarius is of the Air Triplicity, and of the Fixed Quality, the
influence being erratic, refined, artistic, tenacious, perverse, intuitive,
independent and original. The nature of Aquarius as it manifests in humans
is expressed in the many keywords which have been attached to it by modern
astrologers: friendly, humanitarian, progressive, persistent, inventive,
perverse, creative, tolerant, fond of science and literature, discreet and
optimistic - in a word, all the qualities which may be associated with an Air

type working with a view to establish freedom for self and others. In
excess, the Aquarian tends to be something of a crank, an opportunist, a
rebel, with both an unsympathetic and irresponsible attitude to life.
Aquarius speaks of 'freedom' more insistently than others, usually without
being able to explain fully what is meant by the word - often he or she will
attempt to destroy the status quo, rather than work at establishing something
beneficial for the future. According to the majority of modern astrologers,
Aquarius is ruled by the planet URANUS, though before this planet was
discovered in the 18th century, the sign was ruled by Saturn (see SECTA).
Mercury is exalted in Aquarius, whilst the Sun is in his detriment in this
sign. In addition to the special terms already introduced above, the various
traditional classifications present Aquarius as Diurnal, Fixed, Fortunate,
Warm, Fruitful, Human, Masculine, Mental, Moist, Nervous, Obeying, Rational,
Strong, Sweet, Vital and Whole. See also SANGUINE.

FIGURE 2 - AQUARIUS - 13TH CENTURY IMAGE FROM "SAN MINIATO ZODIAC", AND
CONSTELLATION MAP AFTER THE "MODERN ZODIAC" OF DELPORTE.

AQUARIUS CONSTELLATION   Linked in name, if not in influence, with zodiacal
Aquarius, located as indicated in figure 2, straddling the equator from 5
degrees north to 30 degrees south. The image associated with this
constellation (and hence with the sign) was even in Babylonian times that of
a man pouring water from an urn, and thus understandably in Greek astrology
was called 'Hydroxous' (water-pourer - the image in figure 2). The numerous
names given to the constellation by astrologers of different eras and places
(listed by Allen) generally allude to the idea of water, or to the image of a
'water pot'. The fixed stars within the asterism which are of importance to
astrologers are SADALMELIC and SADALSUUD, the alpha and beta of figure 2.

AQUILA   Constellation, approximately from 12 degrees Capricorn to 15 degrees
Aquarius, from 22 degrees north to 13 degrees south of the equator. This
asterism was even in early astrological texts confused with another bird, the
'Vultur Volans', and translated into English (inexactly) as the 'Flying
Grype'. The Roman astrologers knew it as 'Aquila', however, or as 'the bird
of Jupiter' (which was an eagle), while most other names from different times
and countries link the asterism with the image of a flying bird. The
important fixed star in the constellation is ALTAIR.

ARA   Name given to a constellation, the 'Altar', located to the south of
Sagittarius and, as Aratos says, 'beneath the glowing sting of that huge sign
the Scorpion'. The classical mythology is merely putting a seal on a much
more ancient idea, for it was the 'Tul-Ku' (Holy Altar) in Euphratean
astrology, but the story has it that an altar made by the Centaurs was taken
to the heavens after being used by the Gods for their oath to withstand the
Titans - hence the name 'Ara Centauri'. Mediaeval astrologers would
sometimes call it 'Puteus Sacrarius' or 'Templum', all in reference to a
sacred place, perhaps following Manilius, for whom it was 'Mundi Templum'
(Temple of the World). Ptolemy links its influence with that of Venus and

Mercury combined, and it is said to give scientific ability and concern for ecclesiastical matters.

ARABIAN DIRECTIONS   Another term for SECONDARY DIRECTIONS.

ARABIAN PARTS   See ARABIAN POINTS.

ARABIAN POINTS   A general name for a number of 'parts', some derived from early Graeco-Byzantine astrology, some from Arabic astrology, but transmitted to Europe through Arabian astrological literature. Few of these numinous points or parts are used in modern astrology, but for a complete list, see the entry under PARS.

ARABOTH   The seventh Heaven of the cabbalistic system, ruled by CASSIEL.

ARACHNE   A name applied by Vogh to what is claimed to be a 'lost' thirteenth sign of the zodiac. The new model of the zodiac which results from this addition has been called the 'Psychic Zodiac': needless to say, neither it nor the 13th sign finds a correspondence or mention in ancient astrological sources.   It is simply not possible to have a sign of less than 30 degrees. The lunar zodiac with which Vogh makes such play was a constellational lunar zodiac, but there was no Arachne in any of the lunar asterism, nor in any of the SIDEREAL ZODIAC constellations.

ARAHSAMMA   See BABYLONIAN CALENDAR.

ARATRON   First of the seven supreme angels of the cabbalistic system, one of the powers of the Arbatel corresponding to the Sphere of Saturn. He was said to be able to petrify living orgnisms, and to possess the power to change higher forms of life into lower forms - the Saturnine powers.

ARC   A segment of a curved line - in a specialist use, an arc of the zodiac, usually expressed and measured in degrees, minutes and seconds. The measurement of arc may also be translated into temporal co-ordinates, as for example in primary directions, where degree of arc is often expressed in time. See also ARC OF DIRECTION, DIURNAL ARC, NOCTURNAL ARC and SEMI-ARC.

ARCANUM   In general the term means anything hidden, but Paracelsus adopts the word for specialist astrological and alchemical use, using it to denote the secret incorporeal virtue behind or within natural forms. It is therefore a synonym in this sense for both ILECH and VIRTUE. The word is also used to denote any of the series of so-called 'Major Arcana' of the Tarot Pack - see therefore ASTROLOGICAL TAROT.

ARCHAEO-ASTRONOMY   Term used in a special sense by Krupp to designate the study of the astronomies of ancient and prehistoric times. Many of the subjects included under Krupp's editorships, such as the British stone circles and menhirs, the Mesoamerican remains, the medicine wheels of North America and the Egyptian pyramids and temples, are certainly linked with important and intriguing calendrical and astrological factors.

ARCHAI   Name given to the incorporeal beings forming the seventh Hierarchy of the spiritual realm, according to Dionysius the Areopagite (see ANGELS), the beings of the Sphere of Venus. The Archai are said to guide the motion of time itself, and in some esoteric systems they are called the Spirits of the Revolution of Time. The 'Golden Legends' of Voragine link them with the mystery of the Eucharist, which explains why they are often pictured as holding Chrismatories. Sometimes the Archai are called Principalities, an attempt to Latinize the Greek word. Saint Gregory calls them the Virtutes (sometimes translated Virtues), and associates them with the sapphire and the colour blue. In other systems, however, the Virtutes are linked with the DYNAMIS of the Martian sphere - though the connexion between the Archai and Venus is widely accepted in esoteric circles.

===

ARCHANGELS Name given to the incorporeal beings of the eighth Hierarchy, according to Dionysius the Areopagite (see ANGELS), the beings of the Sphere of Mercury. The Archangels are said to guide the spiritual destiny of groups of people, of nations, rather than individuals - this probably explains why the Archangels are often pictured as carrying formalized models of cities in their arms. St. Gregory associates the Archangels with the carbuncle stone, and biblical exegesis links them with the colour red. Since the Archangels are often called 'Angels', much confusion has arisen in astrological lore: see ARCHANGELS OF THE PLANETS, ARCHANGELS OF THE ZODIAC, CELESTIAL HIERARCHIES and TWELVE CREATIVE HIERARCHIES. For the individual Archangelic rule over elements, see GABRIEL (Water), MICHAEL (Fire), RAPHAEL (Water) and URIEL (Earth) - for Archangelic Periodicities, see SECUNDADEIAN BEINGS.

ARCHANGELS OF THE PLANETS Sometimes called by the generic term ANGELS, these spiritual beings were originally charged with the regulation of the SPHERES (rather than the planets), though this distinction is now virtually lost. The most frequently used names and planetary spheres are given in table 4. See also ARCHANGELS OF THE SEPHIROTH and PLANETARY SPIRITS.

```
-----------------------------------------------------------------TABLE 4
   Gabriel   -   Moon          Samael    -   Mars
   Raphael   -   Mercury       Zadkiel   -   Jupiter
   Anael     -   Venus         Cassiel   -   Saturn
   Michael   -   Sun
-----------------------------------------------------------------
```

ARCHANGELS OF THE SEPHIROTH The occult and cabbalistic tradition has preserved several lists of the names of the Archangels which have rule over the ten Sephirah in the Tree of Life, which is linked with various astrological correspondences. Few of the traditional lists agree in detail, but those shown in table 5, based on Grey, may be taken as representative: see QABBALISTIC ASTROLOGY. The Archangels are opposed by their Adversaries.

```
-------------------------------------------------------------TABLE 5
```

SEPHIRAH	ARCHANGEL	ADVERSARY	SPHERE
Kether (Crown)	Metatron	Thaumiel	Primum Mobile
Chockmah (Wisdom)	Raziel	Chaigidiel	Zodiac
Binah (Understanding)	Zaphkiel	Sathariel	Saturn
Chesed (Compassion)	Zadkiel	Gamchicoth	Jupiter
Geburah (Severity)	Camael	Golleb	Mars
Tiphereth (Beauty)	Michael	Togarini	Sun
Netzach (Victory)	Hamiel	Harab Serap	Venus
Hod (Splendour)	Raphael	Sammael	Mercury
Yesod (Foundation)	Gabriel	Gamaliel	Moon
Malkuth (Kingdom)	Metatron	Lilith	Man and Elements.

ARCHANGELS OF THE ZODIAC The astrological tradition has preserved many lists of ANGELS, Archangels and Spirits, which are said to be specifically in control of the twelve signs of the Zodiac. Unfortunately, few of these lists agree, but those in table 6, derived from Haywood, are representive. Those marked with an asterisk are said by some authorities not to be Archangels. The overall ruler of the zodiac is sometimes named as Maslem, but in the esoteric view, the zodiac falls under the Cherubim or Seraphim.

```
-------------------------------------------------------------TABLE 6
   AR   Malshidael, Aiei*        LB   Zuriel, Jael*, Joel*
   TA   Asmodei, Tual*           SC   Barcheil, Sozol
   GE   Ambriel                  SG   Adnacheil, Ayil
   CN   Muriel, Manuel, Cael*    CP   Hamael, Semakiel*, Casujoiah*
   LE   Vercheil, Ol*, Voel*     AQ   Cambiel, Ausiel*
   VG   Hamaeliel                PI   Barchiel, Varchiel*, Pasiel*
```

==

ARCHER Popular name for SAGITTARIUS, whose image is sometimes wrongly given as that of an archer, or a mounted archer, both forms being derived from the Babylonian image of a kind of man-beast centaur, shooting from a bow.

ARCITENENS See SAGITTARIUS CONSTELLATION.

ARC OF DIRECTION An arc measuring distance between a planet (significator) and the point where it will form an aspect with a promittor - see DIRECTIONS. The arc may be measured either in time, or in degrees of Right Ascension.

ARC OF DWARFED STATURE An arc marked from the middle of the 7th house to the middle of the 2nd house (in clockwise direction), with its most powerful influence at the cusp of the 6th house. The arc is intepreted only when the DRAGON'S HEAD is placed within its compass: such a position is supposed to stunt growth of the native.

ARC OF INCREASED STATURE An arc marked from the middle of the 1st house to the middle of the 8th house (in clockwise direction), its most powerful influence at the cusp of the 12th house. The arc is interpreted only when the DRAGON'S HEAD is placed within its compass, and such a position is supposed to increase growth of the native.

ARC SYMBOLS See DEGREE SYMBOLS.

ARCTOPHILAX See ARCTURUS.

ARC TRANSFORM CHART A figure introduced by Williamsen, as a variation of a "Harmonic Chart", derived from the theory of Harmonics, in which the determinant harmonic is the angular separation between any two planets in the radical chart. The system has been much criticized on the grounds of unwieldiness, as the simple radical gives rise to a very large number of interpretative charts.

ARCTURUS Fixed star of 1st magnitude, the alpha of Bootis, set in the left knee of the figure. The term comes from the Greek 'Arktouros' (Bear-guard), but many names have been recorded for this important star, including 'Arctophilax' (Bear-watcher), Alchameth, Azimech, Al Simak, and (in Egyptian astrology), Bau. It is a highly beneficial star, especially when rising or culminating in a chart, and Ebertin says that its Jupiter-Mars influence has a reputation for achieving 'justice through power'. See FIFTEEN STARS.

ARCTUS See both URSA MAJOR and URSA MINOR.

ARDRA The fourth of the Hindu NAKSHATRAS.

ARES One of the ancient Greek terms for Mars. Paracelsus used the same term to denote the formative power which creates differences (differentia) among species. The choice of word is probably guided by the esoteric astrological notion that Aries, ruled by "Positive Mars", is the realm of incarnation, where differentiation of spirit into form begins.

ARGION See ORION.

ARGO NAVIS Constellation, approximately from 10 degrees Cancer to 20 degrees Libra, from 15 to 65 degrees south of the ecliptic. Not surprisingly of an asterism linked with the ship of the Golden Flece, the constellation is said to give prosperity in voyages, though it is linked with drowning. Robson suggests that this explains why the first decanate of Virgo is connected with drowning, but this area of the zodiac is riddled with powerful stars which could easily bring disasters of this kind, even though they are not all set in Argo. The only Argoan fixed star which is openly associated with shipwreck is FORAMEN.

==

ARGOS   See PYXIS NAUTICA.

ARGUS   A frequent error for ARGO NAVIS.

ARIADNE'S HAIR   See COMA BERENICES.

ARIEL   Name given to one of the satellites of Uranus.

ARIES   The first sign of the zodiac. It corresponds as a sign neither in
location nor extent with the constellation of the same name - see ARIES
CONSTELLATION. The modern sigil for Aries ♈ is said by some to be a
vestigial drawing of the horns of the Ram (see figure 3) with which the sign
is associated, but some astrologers claim that it is a drawing of the human
eyebrows and nose, for Aries has rule over the human head and face in the
MELOTHESIC MAN. Some esoteric astrologers explain the sigil as a primitive
diagram of the implosion and explosion of spirit in and out of the material
body - but see SIGILS - ZODIACAL.   Aries is one of the Fire elements, of the
Cardinal Quality, and its influence is outgoing, pioneering, self-reliant,
idealistic, enthusiastic and exaggerative. There is a strong element of
selfishness, and the Arietan type tends to be insensitive to the needs of
others. This outgoing nature of Aries is expressed in many keywords attached
to the sign by modern astrologers: initiatory, freedom-loving, active,
intense, resourceful, aggressive, impulsive, inspirational, courageous,
spontaneous, audacious - in a word, all those qualities which may be
associated with a fire nature expressing itself with untrammelled confidence.
In excess, the Arietan nature may be described in terms which express its
underlying destructive nature, the keywords being: overbearing, dictatorial,
resentful, sarcastic, jealous, coarse, argumentative, violent, uncontrolled,
impatient and egotistical. Aries is ruled by the planet Mars - indeed, in
the ancient tradition by "Postive Mars" (see also SECTA), as opposed to the
"Negative Mars" which has rule over Scorpio. The sign marks the Exaltation
of the Sun, the Fall of Saturn, and the Detriment of Venus. In addition to
the special terms already introduced, the traditional classifications present
Aries as Barren, Bitter, Commanding, Diurnal, Dry, Equinoctial, Fortunate,
Four-booted, Hoarse, Hot, Hurtful, Inflammatory, Luxurious, Masculine,
Mental, Northern and Violent. See also CHOLERIC.

FIGURE 3 - THE IMAGE OF ARIES, FROM THE 13TH CENTURY "SAN MINIATO ZODIAC",
AND THE CONSTELLATION FROM THE "MODERN ZODIAC" OF DELPORTE.

ARIES CONSTELLATION   Constellation linked in name, if not in influence, with
zodiacal ARIES, located as indicated in figure 3. In popular language this
is often called the Ram, and in ancient astrological texts it was associated
with the Greek legend of the Golden Fleece, though the image appears in the
very earliest Egyptian astrology which long predates Greek culture: The
image in figure 3 is mediaeval.   The fixed stars within the asterism which
are generally considered important by astrologers are HAMAL and SHARATAN, the
alpha and beta of Aries, respectively.

ARIETAN   Pertaining to the sign or constellation of ARIES: the construction is from the Latin genitive 'Arietis'.

ARION   See ORION.

ARISTA   See SPICA and VIRGO CONSTELLATION.

ARISTARCHEIAN SYSTEM   Name given to an imperfectly recorded model of the solar system postulated by Aristarchus of Samos, in the 3rd century BC. See HELIOCENTRIC SYSTEM.

ARISTOTELIAN CYCLE   The Aristotelian Cycle, linked with the cycles set out in the Great Year of the PLATONIC CYCLE, are later glosses on Aristotle, and insist that two great catastrophes mark the direct and retrograde motions of the spheres. When the Spheres are in conjunction in Cancer, then the world is destroyed in fire. When the spheres are conjunct in Capricorn, then the world is destroyed by water or flood. Here there is a clear deviation from the original idea of sphere-cycles to planetary cycles. The Aristotelian cycle has been associated (quite needlessly) with the ordinary seasonal solar transit of the solstices, when an esoteric origin is more apposite.

ARISTOTELIAN PRINCIPLES   See PRINCIPLES.

ARISTOTELIAN SYSTEM   A model of the Universe proposed (chiefly) by Aristotle, which postulates a geocentric solar-system, with all the planets making revolutions in perfect motion, within a series of concentric spheres. The Earth itself was visualized as a sphere, bathed in three sub-lunar spheres relating to the elements - first that of Water, then of Air, and then of Fire. Set in the "Crystalline Spheres" were the Moon, Mercury, Venus, Sun, Mars, Jupiter and Saturn. These were bounded by the Sphere of Fixed Stars (the STELLATUM) which marked the end of the Universe: it was this sphere which transmitted movement to the other spheres, for which reason it was called the PRIMUM MOVENS or Primum Mobile. Everything beneath the Sphere of Moon (which of course embraced the Earth) was corruptible, but all above that sphere was bathed in incorruptible purity of the "Quintessence". This model was essentially a physical one, permeated to some extent by esoteric lore derived from Greek mystery schools: it formed the basis for the Christian and Neoplatonic cosmoconception of the CELESTIAL HIERARCHIES, the sphere of the Earth being divided into a reflective series of concentrics to accommodate the infernal regions and adversaries. The importance of the Aristotelian systems was not so much its practical value to astrologers, as its spiritual heritage.

ARKAB   Fixed star (double), the beta of Sagittarius, its name and variants (such as 'Urkab') from the Arabic 'Al Urkub', of disputed meaning.

ARMILLAX   See ASTROLABE.

ARMUS   Fixed star, the eta of Capricornus, set in the heart of the Goat. Said to be of the nature of Mercury conjunct Mars, and to give a disagreeable, contentious nature.

AROMAL PLANETS   Name given by 19th century astrologers, mainly working within the framework of Theosophy, to a large group of planets said to orbit within our Solar System, though invisible to normal sight. The astrologer Harris claims that there are more than 1,000 such aromals in our system. It is possible that certain of the HYPOTHETICAL PLANETS perceived clairvoyantly belong to this supposed class - but see also ETHEREAL PLANETS.

ARROW STAR   A name used to denote the fixed star SIRIUS, when regarded as a fiducial, derived by Fagan from the Assyrian term 'gag-i-sa'.

ARTIFICIAL GAMALEI   See GAMALEI.

ARYAN   In an astrological context, this term is usually an unfortunte
mistake for ARIETAN. The word Aryan is, of course, properly applied to a
member of a supposed race which made use of a particular form of language,
sometimes called the 'Indo-European language' - but see FIFTH ROOT RACE.

ASARU   One of the Chaldean names for the planet Jupiter.

ASCELLA   A fixed star (binary) set in the armpit of constellation
Sagittarius.   It has a beneficial influence, said to be of a nature
equivalent to Mercury conjunct Jupiter.

ASCELLI   Pair of stars, treated by astrologers as a single (though in
adjacent degrees), both set in the constellation Cancer. Robson properly
gives separate influences - the northern Ascellus tends towards defiance and
heroism, while the southern is unfavourable. Cornell, who gives both a
thoroughly evil influence, appears to have confused this pair with the
contiguous PRAESAEPE cloud.

ASCENDANT   The term is properly applied to the degree of zodiac arising on
the eastern horizon of a figure, or indeed to the degree of zodiac arising
over the eastern horizon. This degree was originally called the 'Horoscopos'
in Greek astrology, from which the modern word "Horoscope" was derived. The
term Ascendant is often used of the whole sign arising, rather than of the
degree. To avoid confusion in ordinary parlance, modern astrologers often
distinguish between the Rising Sign and the Rising Degree, both of which may
be referred to as the Ascendant. Sometimes a planet is misleadingly termed
the 'Ascendant planet', when it is in the last few degrees of the nocturnal
semi-arc. In earlier forms of astrology, it was common for all the planets
near the eastern angle to be described as 'Ascendant', but at that time the
special meaning of 'horoscope' in reference to a particular degree was not
yet obsolete, so that the distinction was clear. See also ASCENDANT SIGNS.

ASCENDANT AXIS   Term used of the horizon axis, which in the horoscope figure
usually corresponds to the axis of the Ascendant and Descendant.

ASCENDENTIA SIGNA   A curious term listed by Sendivogius, and said by him to
represent either the 'Stars of the Firmament' or the 'sydereal Spirits': but
see ASCENDANT SIGNS.

ASCENDANT SIGNS   A technical term indicating those signs which contain the
Sun when its declination is on the increase - that is, Aries, Taurus, Gemini,
Libra, Scorpio and Sagittarius. However, the term is used in a general sense
in reference to a particular Ascendant of a horoscope, in which case any of
the twelve signs may be described as being 'Ascendant Signs' - see ASCENDANT.

ASCENDING   A fairly general, if imprecise, application of this term is to any
planet or nodal point on the eastward arc of the figure. Properly speaking,
however, this pair of semi-arcs should be termed 'the ascending part of the
heavens', and a planet placed within the arcs described in such a lengthy
way. More precision is implied when reference is made to a planet within orb
of the ASCENDANT itself. See also ASCENDANT SIGNS.

ASCENDING ARC   This term, which is sometimes applied to the degree of zodiac
on the ASCENDANT, must be distinguished from the Theosophical term which is
the equivalent of the so-called 'Luminous Arc', relating to the upward
passage of life-waves from the physical realm.

ASCENSION   See RIGHT ASCENSION and OBLIQUE ASCENSION.

ASCENSIONAL DIFFERENCE   The difference between the "Right Ascension" and
"Oblique Ascension" of a body.

ASCHEMIE   See PROCYON.

ASCHERE   See PROCYON and SIRIUS.

ASCLEPIUS   See OPHIUCHUS.

ASHADHA   The Sanskrit name for Capricornus: see also MAKARAM.

ASIMEC   See SPICA.

ASLESHA   The seventh of the Hindu NAKSHATRAS, the 'embracer'.

ASMODEL   The ruling angel of zodiacal Taurus. For sigils, see SIGILS - ANGELS AND ARCHANGELS OF THE ZODIAC.

ASPECTAL PATTERN   See CONFIGURATION and MAJOR CONFIGURATION.

ASPECTARIAN   A list, usually in chronological order, of all significant aspects formed during a particular period, sometimes in relation to a particular chart. In modern times such aspectarians are often found in EPHEMERIDES. Special symbols (apart from the ABBREVIATIONS and SIGILS recorded elsewhere) include:

--TABLE 7

Declination	δ	Minute of arc	'
Eclipse of Moon	☾	New Moon	●
Eclipse of Sun	☾	North declination or latitude	+
First quarter	☽	Second of arc	"
Full Moon	O	South declination or latitude	−
Latitude	ρ	Third quarter	☾
Longitude	λ		

ASPECTS   Term applied to a large number of specific angular relationships between planets and other celestial bodies or nodal points. Most aspects are consistered ecliptically, and are generally regarded as symbolic, rather than as having any geophysical validity. In the majority of cases, aspects are also regarded as being geocentric - which is to say in terms of angular relationships relating to the Earth (the actual place of birth) as the receptive matrix. However, a number of astrologers who favour HELIOCENTRIC ASTROLOGY do make use of heliocentric aspects, and Thorburn, an astrologer who has investigated both systems, is clearly in favour of heliocentrics. The traditional forms of astrology are concerned with nine angular relationships only, these being divided into the "Major Aspects" and the "Minor Aspects", to which the mathematician-astrologer Kepler introduced a series of QUINTILE aspects (see KEPLERIAN ASPECTS), as listed in Table 8.

--TABLE 8

ASPECT NAME	ASPECT	SIGIL		GENERAL MEANING
Opposition	180 degrees	☊	☍	Tension
Trine	120 degrees	△		Expansion
Square	90 degrees	□		Difficult, but energizing
Conjunction	0 degrees	☌		Intensifies planets involved
Quincunx	150 degrees	⊼		Strain
Sesquiquadrate	135 degrees	⊡	⊡	Difficult (less than Square)
Semi-square	45 degrees	∠		Difficult
Sextile	60 degrees	⚹		Expansive (weaker than Trine)
Semi-sextile	30 degrees	⚺		Slight strain
Bi-quintile	144 degrees	±		Strengthening?
Quintile	72 degrees	Q	★	Strengthening?

The astrologer Placidus introduced an important PARALLEL aspect. There are two basic groups of traditional aspects - the "Mutual Aspects" which are those formed between two or more bodies at a specific time, and those formed between a single moving body and given points within a chart: this latter group is the DIRECTIONAL ASPECT, the PROGRESSED ASPECT and the TRANSITORY ASPECT, all used mainly in predictive astrology. For an aspect to be fully effective, it is required that it be precise (at least, as an ecliptically symbolic consideration), but it is taught by those who have researched the traditional doctrines (for example, Carter) that aspects which are "Forming" or "Separating" will still exert influences. The degree of arc wherein the aspect may be said to be operative as an influence depends upon the nature of the planets concerned, and is called an ORB. Unfortunately, there appears to be no agreement as to what orbs may be applied to the various aspects: for major aspects, some use orbs with as little as a 5 to 10 degree orb: see however ASSYMETRIC ORB and MORINEAN ORBS. The body with the faster mean motion is said to aspect the slower, which usually means that the inner planets aspect the outer planets. Forming aspects are generally regarded as being more powerful than separating aspects. Aspects are said to generate beneficial or harmful influences, depending upon the natures of the planets involved - the former are the "Benefic Aspects", the latter the "Malefic Aspects". The benefics contribute towards harmony, but may lead to a dispersion of energies. The malefics create tensions, which may be resolved and balanced, sometimes leading to a concentration of energies. The original theory of aspects, announced somewhat inconclusively by Ptolemy, appears to have been based on the interactions of the zodiacal elements, rather than being based on geometric or symbolic considerations. Thus, it was said that the harmony of the trine was a manifestation of two planets working through the same triplicity, whilst the malefic aspect of the square was a manifestation of two planets working through triplicities opposed in essential natures. In Hindu astrology there are two terms which distinguish the aspects of an elemental nature from those of a purely geometric (or symbolic) kind (see JAIMINI and TAIJAK), and a useful word has been coined from the former to denote elemental aspects - Jaiminic. Modern researchers into astrological principles have tended to ignore the symbolic nature of aspects, and the jaiminic importance of the theory of aspects, and has concentrated on the study of angular relationships as geometric propositions. The problem is that if aspects are examined in terms of three-dimensional geometry, involving the astronomical conception of an absolute plane, then the approximate conjunction (which is the basis of certain cycles) would occur only rarely. Aspects have been submitted to a certain number of statistical tests, difficult as these have proved to be. Nelson has done some useful work on the relationship between certain aspects and their influences on radio reception, whilst Dieschbourg has spent many years investigating aspects from an unconventional statistical standpoint. Almost all statistical and computerised studies have yielded disappointing results, which perhaps reflects more upon the methodology itself, than upon aspects. It is significant, for example, that most of those who have sought to establish connexions between aspects and statistical interpretation, reduce aspects to angular relationships, rather than in a jaiminic sense. In contrast, Addey's researches into a field of astrology related to aspects shows signs of revolutionizing modern astrology - see HARMONICS. In addition to the terms already mentioned, see also ABSCISSION, CAZIMI, COMBUST, DECLINATION, DEXTER, OCCULTATION, PARALLEL IN MUNDO, PARTILE ASPECT, PLATIC ASPECT and SINISTER ASPECT.

ASSOCIATION HOUSES   An alternative name for the RELATIVE HOUSES.

ASTERION   See CANES VENATICI.

ASTERISM   Literally a collection or group of stars, but usually a configuration of such stars, a 'constellation'. Since the LUNAR MANSIONS are determined by star-groups, they are sometimes called asterisms. Occasionally, the term is wrongly applied to one or other of the signs of the zodiac, which are not groups of stars.

ASTERISM IMAGE   A term coined to designate the abstract graphic image traced in imaginary lines between the stars in a particular constellation. The asterism image in figure 3 under ARIES, for example, is derived from the system of Delporte incorporated into the MODERN ZODIAC. The term is used partly to distinguish such abstract figures from the realistic IMAGE linked with the majority of the constellations, and which are in some cases associated with the signs.

ASTEROGRAM   A neologism (sometimes Asterogramme) probably originated by Sucher, and applied to horoscopes used in connexion with ASTROSOPHY. The asterogram may be geocentric or heliocentric (as in the sample chart in figure 4), but generally employs the SIDEREAL ZODIAC. The term is also extended to 'Prenatal Asterograms', as a specialist application of the EPOCHAL CHART, and to the 'Death Asterogram', cast for the moment of death.

FIGURE 4.   ASTEROGRAM FOR GOETHE'S BIRTH (AFTER SUCHER).

ASTEROID PERIODICITY   See ASTRO-ECONOMICS.

ASTEROIDS   Minor planets, the name meaning 'star-like' - the alternative (and now rare) 'Planetoid' being etymologically better. Shortly before the discovery of the so-called "New Planets", towards the end of the 18th century, it was suggested that the series of numerical progressions called Bode's Series seemed to postulate the existence of another planet between Mars and Jupiter (corresponding in the series to the progression 28). The first of these planetoids was not located by Piazzi until 1801, however: he named it CERES. In the following year another, PALLAS, was seen, and then JUNO and VESTA. Almost four decades passed before the fifth, ASTRAEA was located, but since then 2,000 have been named or (mainly) numbered, and it is estimated that there are about 50,000 in orbit. The asteroid Hildalgo (with an orbit of 13.7 years) has the longest period. Most asteroids are small by astronomical standards, though Ceres has a diameter of nearly 500 miles. The importance of the asteroids in astrology is that they were eventually vested with a supposed influence on human affairs, and in some systems of astrology have been accorded rule over certain signs: for example, Wemyss gives Pisces to the asteroids, while Dobyns links only Ceres and Vesta with this sign. Additionally, many of the HYPOTHETICAL PLANETS have been variously identified and confused with asteroids: see LUCIFER.

ASTEROID SCHEME   This term, and the variant 'Asteroid Chain', are derived from the Theosophical "Scheme of Evolution", provisionally linked with the 8th of the so-called schemes, on the grounds that the present asteroidal belt will eventually form a globe - an idea foreign to occult lore.

ASTERON The ancient Greek term for 'stars', and often used also for 'planets': Ptolemy uses the term in this general sense.

ASTRAEA   Name of one of the ASTEROIDS. The Romans used the same word
(meaning 'Starry Goddess') for the constellation and sign Virgo.

ASTRAL   The term appears to be derived from the Latin for 'star', and is
sometimes applied to the stellar world as descriptive of the fabric of the
heavens. Blavatsky suggests an origin from the Scythian 'Aist-aer' (star),
but such an etymology should not confuse the Astral with the fixed stars. In
occult and astrological terminology the Astral Plane is that contiguous in
space (if not in time) with the material realm: it is one which the
spiritual part of man enters during periods of sleep and after death. The
astral realm is one normally invisible to ordinary sight, yet it is the
proper dwelling of the higher spiritual bodies of man (the 'astral body' and
'ego' of modern occultism). It is significant that Paracelsus should coin his
term "Ens Astrale" to denote the Desire Body of man. The realm is said to be
permeated by the ASTRAL LIGHT, which is the equivalent of the ancient
"Akashya", and so the Paracelsian 'ens' does link with the stars, and
clairvoyants describe the astral body as consisting of light, like the stars
themselves, though in continuous motion. The model of man projected in
astrology is not far removed from such occultist cosmoconceptions, and
inevitably the link between the world of fixed stars and the astral has found
expression in several terms. Cornell, for example, calls the astral body the
'sidereal body', naming it the seat of the sensations, through which the
planetary influences work upon man (he appears to confuse it with the occult
Etheric Body, however, though he is on more sure grounds when he says that
the Astral Body is the realm in which Jupiter has direct relation to the
breathing and blood, and where Mars and Venus relate to the sensations and
passions.   The ASTRUM of the alchemists relates to the old conception of
hidden "Virtues", which are in turn said to proceed from the stars. In
occultism, the 'astral realm' is not linked with the stars, but with the
Sphere of the Moon, which explains why this is the 'realm of Purgatory'
(where astral deficiencies are said to be cleansed, during the postmortem
state) - see for example EIGHTH SPHERE.

ASTRAL GLOBE   See GLOBES.

ASTRAL LIGHT   See ASTRAL and AETHER.

ASTRAL SPHERE   Leadbeater, himself no astrologer, tells us that the astral
sphere of the earth extends nearly to the mean distance of the Moon's orbit.
It is not, therefore possible (as Leadbeater claims) that the astral planes
of the two worlds (Moon and Earth) touch one another when the Moon is in
perigee, but do not so touch when the Moon is in apogee. The definition
implies that the two spheres interpenetrate.

ASTRAL SPHERES   A term coined by the esoteric astrologer Thierens relating
to the future evolution of the "Spheres", and the consequent development of
new planetary bodies - see FUTURE PLANETS. These astral spheres consist of
the traditional spheres of Aquarius and Pisces, ruled by his planets NEREUS
and COELUS respectively. Together with the ETHERIC SPHERES, these make up
the LUNAR BODY of Thierens' cosmoconception. See also ASTRAL SPHERE.

ASTRAL YEAR   See SIDEREAL YEAR.

ASTRO-ALCHEMIST   A person who combines the practice of astrology with
alchemy. Many of the operations of alchemy involve the casting of charts for
propitious moments, and the careful consideration of planetary hours.

ASTRO-ALCHEMY   A term derived to denote the astrology linked with the late
mediaeval form of alchemy: this consisted mainly of a prolix terminology
that made use of astrological words and concepts in a way which recognized
the occult philosophical basis of the art. The literature of such occultists
as Boehme, Dee, Trithemius and Welling is representative of this approach to
both alchemy and astrology.

ASTRO-ARCHAEOLOGY   A term coined in modern times to designate the
quasi-archaeological theory which relates the design (and hence location and
orientation) of megalithic monuments to the celestial phenomena observed
during the long period of construction. The treatment by Michell limits the
term to megalithic circles and related structures, but it might usefully be
extended to the study of orientations which are astrologically conceived.
For example, the orientation of the SAN MINIATO ZODIAC (towards the daily
sunrise over Florence, and its demonstrable link with a FOUNDATION CHART of
1207, might be covered by the term Astro-Archaeology, or by some other
neologism, such as "Astro-Orientation".

ASTRO-BIOCHEMISTRY   A modern term used to cover the newly developing study
of astrology in relation to the TWELVE CELL-SALTS.

ASTROCARTOGRAPHY   The name given to a modern system of chart extrapolation
involving the imposition of the four angular positions of the ten planets of
the natal chart on a world map, in order to determine geographic 'power
zones' which will correspond to potentials within the native. A location,
such as a city, town or rural area, falling upon the longitudinal equivalent
of Jupiter's Midheaven position (for example) is said to evoke for the native
all the qualities associated with his or her particular natal Jupiter in
regard to his or her Midheaven propensities. The system, devised and
promulgated in America by Lewis, is also subject to the study of the
unfolding of radical potentials in terms of transits and progressions
relating to the natal chart.

ASTRO-CHRONOLOGY   Relating to the chronology of heavenly bodies - for
example, to the timing of CYCLES.

ASTRO-DIAGNOSIS   Medical diagnosis, either from a natal chart, or from a
chart set up for the time of illness. The latter method involves determining
the significator of the illness: this, along with the sign occupied by it,
may be then used to determine the part of the body afflicted. Reference was
usually made to what is called the Coley Table, devised by the astrologer of
that name. The significator of illness is said to be determined from
examination of the progressions and transits of malefics or malefic aspects.
Several methods for calculating the courses of chronic diseases have been
preserved from mediaeval astrology, of which the most influential was the
Galenic or Galen's Method, a horary method, now long out of use. The
planetary and aspectal views of astro-diagnosis may be seen contrasted in
Wemyss and Cornell. See also MEDICAL ASTROLOGY.

ASTRO-ECONOMICS   A term related to the study of supposed business cycles,
which are not all in fact astrologically derived. A science or art of
astro-economics would presumably seek to establish a connexion between
recognised cycles and astrologically recognised data: for example, sunspot
cycles, which are supposed to correlate with a 17-week cycle of stock-prices,
as well as other natural phenomena, are often dealt with in astrological
literature, yet are not really astrologically attested. A certain degree of
accuracy in establishing valid links is evident in the work of Williams,
however. Among the cycles observed by Collin are the 9-year stock market
cycle (linked with the multiple of the so-called Asteroid Periodicity), an
18-year cycle affecting house-prices (again linked with the Asteroids), and a
complex 41-month 'prices and industrial production cycle'.

ASTROGENETICS   Term, probably originated by Deusen, ostensibly to designate
a field of research involved with the study of the relationship between
genetics and astrology. The statistical findings are based on Sun Signs and
known careers of natives. As Davison rightly points out, many of Deusen's
findings duplicate the work of Krafft.

ASTRO-GEOMANCY   See GEOMANCY.

===

ASTROGNOSY Knowledge of the stars (and by extension, 'of the planets').

ASTROGONY The doctrine pertaining to the generation of the stars: most of the modern esoteric systems of astrology have their own astrogonic approach.

ASTROGRAPHY The science (once an art) of describing or mapping the heavens: see CONSTELLATION MAPS.

ASTRO-KINETICS A term adopted by Whitman in his extensive study of planetary influences and aspectal relationships. Whitman's work (thorough and informed) has resulted in his postulating that the Ptolemaic planetary rulerships over the signs should be mantained, with the "New Planets" (Uranus, Neptune and Pluto) adopted as independent planets, relegated to sub-rulerships over Aquarius, Pisces and Aries respectively. It is clear that Whitman sees the Plutonian rule over Aries as displacing 'positive Mars', whereas in fact the displacement (by Pluto) is usually of the "Negative Mars" of Scorpio - even so Whitman's general concept would respect the Ptolemaic, and insist that the three extrasaturnians should be regarded as 'subrulers' of the related signs - to which Pluto over Scorpio should be added as such a subruler.

ASTROLABE An instrument used for taking altitudes, and used by astrologers in the early mediaeval period (in fact until reliable tables were available) mainly for determining the degrees of the four cardinal points of a horoscope, and for calculating the altitudes of fixed stars and planets. A portable astrolabe was called the armillax. In popular terminology, the astrolabe is sometimes called a PLANISPHERE.

ASTROLATRY Worship of the stars as Divine Beings.

ASTROLOGER In modern times, one who practises a form or forms of ASTROLOGY. In earlier times, an observer of the stars.

ASTROLOGIC Pertaining to the realm of astrological theory or practice.

ASTROLOGICAL AGE A name wrongly given to a period usually supposed to be of 2,160 years duration - but see PRECESSION.

ASTROLOGICAL CLOCKS See ZODICAL CLOCKS.

ASTROLOGICAL FRESCOES See ZODIACAL CYCLES.

ASTROLOGICAL TAROT The many different systems of divinatory Tarot usually proclaim a relationship with astrology, especially in regard to the zodiac and constellations. There appears to be little or no agreement as to the astrological connexions which may be drawn with the 22 Major Arcana, but the schema proposed by Wirth has been widely accepted, as set out in table 9.

---TABLE 9

CARD	CARD NAME	ZODIACAL SIGN	CONSTELLATION
1	Juggler	Taurus	Orion
2	Lady Pope		Cassiopeia
3	Empress	Virgo	
4	Emperor		Hercules, Corona Borealis
5	Pope	Aries	
6	Lovers	Sagittarius	Aquila, Antinous
7	Chariot		Great Bear
8	Justice	Libra	
9	Hermit		Bootes
10	Wheel of Fortune	Capricorn	
11	Force	Leo	
12	Hanging Man		Perseus

---TABLE 9 (CONTINUED)

CARD	CARD NAME	ZODIACAL SIGN	CONSTELLATION
13	Death		Draco
14	Temperance	Aquarius	
15	The Devil		Auriga
16	House of God	Scorpio	Ophiuchus
17	The Star	Pisces	Andromeda
18	The Moon	Cancer	Canis Major and Minor
19	The Sun	Gemini	
20	Judgement		Cygnus
21	The World	Entire planisphere and Polar Star	
0	The Fool		Cepheus, Little Bear

The dubious quality of this influential 'correspondence' may be gleaned from the fact that Wirth associates the Devil arcanum with the fixed star "Capella", the alpha of Auriga, an association which is seemingly derived only from the image of "goat" - the fact is, however, that in the astrological tradition, this Capella, or Alayodi (of mediaeval astrology) was regarded as a beneficial influence, in no way demonic. It is no accident that this alpha was linked with Amalthea, after the nurse who raised Jupiter on goatsmilk, for this name-sake was the mediator between man and god. Such attempts to link the Major Arcana with the signs and constellations is based on little esoteric knowledge.

ASTROLOGICAL YEAR   See PRECESSION.

ASTROLOGICAL ZODIAC   One of Blavatsky's terms for the "Tropical Zodiac", which she distinguishes from the "Natural Zodiac": see however INTELLECTUAL ZODIAC, which is a term synonymous with the astrological zodiac.

ASTROLOGIZE   In fact, to examine by means of astrology, though in modern times the word is sometimes used scurrilously.

ASTROLOGY   The study of the relationship between the Macrocosm and the Microcosm, which (in materialistic terms) is often defined as the study of the influence of the celestial bodies on the Earth and its inhabitants. Astrology appears to be one of the most ancient of the surviving occult sciences, and a vast evidence of a highly sophisticated system in Babylonian and Egyptian cultures has survived - though the lore appears to have been well guarded by the ancient Mystery Schools. The oral traditions, as well as the development of astrological lore in ancient times, suggests an even older origin than even Babylon and Egypt, however, as recent findings in the realm of "Archaeo-Astronomy" have indicated. There are many different forms of astrology, though in popular terms the most important of these is GENETHLIACAL ASTROLOGY, which deals with the casting and interpreting of horoscopes for individual humans - this does not appear to have been practised (save for Kings, as representatives of the State) much before the 4th century BC. Two important forms (which to some extent overlap) are those called ESOTERIC ASTROLOGY and EXOTERIC ASTROLOGY, the former of which tends to deal with the individual incarnation in spiritual terms, to see the world populated by spiritual entities, and which tends to treat astrological doctrine as a sort of philosophical machine. Exoteric Astrology (the most widely practised, and usually the only one known to the average practitioner) tends to be involved with personal readings and horoscopic data, and with the predicting of events and experiences in the life of individuals. Attached to the esoteric astrological traditions in the present time are a large number of (often syncretic) teachings concerning the spiritual nature of man, as well as a corpus of traditions dealing with the hidden meanings of the signs, sigils, glyphs and symbols by which the horoscope may be understood as an esoteric diagram. Such esoteric forms are not always confined to the study of the events of a life-time, but may be directed towards the study of

==

pre-natal, pre-conceptional and post-mortem experiences, as well as to the
study of the karmic consequences operative between lifetimes.   In the
exoteric astrology, the most important forms are ASTRO-METEOROLOGY, HORARY
ASTROLOGY, MEDICAL ASTROLOGY, POLITICAL ASTROLOGY and SYNASTRY.

ASTRO-MAGICAL   Relating to divination from the stars (and planets).

ASTRO-METEOROLOGY   A term used of that branch of astrology concerned with
the predicting of weather and telluric conditions, such as earthquakes and
volcanic eruptions.   An alternative name for this study is Meteorological
Astrology.   There are few modern practitioners of this once widely-spread
art, due to the encroachment of science into a realm once considered proper
only to astrological investigation.   Astrological weather prediction appears
to have been founded upon the study of the solar ingresses into the four
cardinal signs, particularly in connexion with conjunctions and eclipses (and
in some cases, lunations).   Robson records that in some cases daily
horoscopes were cast for such predictive purposes, and points to one or two
of the rules, especially those touching upon fixed star lore.   Whilst Pearce
gives interesting material on the subject, it is significant that the last
full treatment which was not fanciful was made by Goad in the 17th century.
The interest in earthquakes and volcanic activities (and indeed in the
appearance of "Comets") still persists in popular astrological circles.
Pearce published some horoscopic data relating to earthquakes, and seems to
have predicted some of the more important ones (such as the disaster in San
Francisco, in 1906).   The modern tendency is to cast INCEPTIONAL CHARTS as a
means of studying telluric disasters and freak weather.

ASTRONOMICAL UNIT   A measure based on the Earth's mean distance from the Sun
(see SOLAR DISTANCE), which is given as 93 million miles.

ASTRONOMICAL ZODIAC   In his useful account of the early zodiacs, Powell
names that zodiac revealed in Ptolemy's star catalogue (which consists of
twelve unequal constellations) the 'Astronomical Zodiac'.   It seems to have
been the prototype of the MODERN ZODIAC, which has been mathematically
formulated: see however CONSTELLATION MAPS in connexion with the IAU ZODIAC.
Ptolemy's catalogue actually gives 48 constellations, and whilst only 12 of
these are listed as zodiacal, one or two of the other asterisms do actually
cross the determinative line of the ecliptic, as with the Modern Astronomical
Zodiac.   Ptolemy almost certainly inherited the 12 from the "Babylonian
Zodiac", or perhaps he intended to relate them to the equal-arc
(contemporaneous) "Greek Zodiac".

ASTRONOMIEN   An early term for astrologer (astronomer) - also 'Astronomian'.

ASTRONOMICON   A term usually used in reference to one of the chief early
Latin works on astrology - a poem in five books (unfinished) by the
poet-astrologer Manilius, written during the period spanning the reigns of
Augustus and Tiberius.   The text is coloured by Greek mythology, and has
indeed become a standard source for popular star lore legends: the
astrological material is said (though on dubious grounds) to be based on the
work of Asclepiades of Myrlea.   Many of the important doctrines differ from
those set out by Ptolemy in his TETRABIBLOS.   An interesting deviation is
that Manilius establishes a system of "Decans" with sign rulerships (rather
than the traditional planetary rule), with Aries for the 1st decan of Aries,
Taurus for the 2nd, and so on.   The 'house system' is an "Oktopodos" (though
perhaps based on a misunderstanding - see for example EIGHT PLACES).

ASTRO-ORIENTATION A term coined to designate the scarcely explored realm of
art-history and architecture, relating to FOUNDATION CHARTS, and the
orientation and design of buildings, as touched upon by Gettings, Nissen and
Taylor.   But see ASTROSOPHIC GEOGRAPHY.

ASTROPALMISTRY   A clumsy neologism used to designate the modern study of the

relationships between astrology and palmistry. It has been taken for granted
from very early times that the human hand is a physical model of the zodiac,
though most of the early texts on the subject tend to establish links between
the planets and parts of the hand, as in the diagram in figure 5. For a
modern survey, see PALMISTIC ZODIAC.

ME:	Little finger
SU:	Ring finger
SA:	Middle finger
JU:	Index finger
MA:	Centre of palm
VE:	Root of thumb
MO:	Lower hand mount

FIGURE 5. PLANETARY RULERSHIP OVER THE HAND (AFTER AGRIPPA).

ASTRO-PSYCHOLOGY   A term coined (seemingly) by Morrish in connexion with his
attempt to create a syncretic astrology uniting various streams of
psychology, which are essentially Jungian, Gestalt and Theosophically-derived
esoteric psychology, with a surprisingly traditional astrology. An important
element in his structure is the (ancient) idea of polarities, which he terms
'conflicts': he notes such conflicts in the "Secta" of the planets, and in
the opposites, as well as in the conventional aspects. In this syncretism,
the 'opposition' between Aries/Libra is the 'familiar theme' of War-Peace,
which he links with the Freudian 'Love-Destruction' motif. The
reconciliation of the conflict is said to come about through the germinating
force of Aries becoming 'organic structure' in Libra. Aries represents the
'Individual Potentiality' Libra represents the 'seed-process of Collective
Possibilities'. The various systems of astrologicl correspondences suggested
by Morrish often simplify beyond recognition some of the more profound
esoteric teachings concerning the relationship between the microcosm and the
macrocosm (as for example in the diagram - figure 6 - of the correspondences
between the spiritual and material planes, derived from superficial appraisal
of Theosophic teachings, and graphically presented by other esotericists in a
different way. See also ASTRO-SYBOLISM

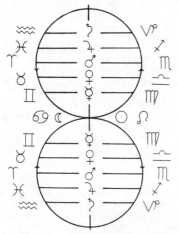

FIGURE 6.   ASTRO-PSYCHOLOGICAL CORRESPONDENCES WITH THE THEOSOPHICAL MODEL
OF MAN AND COSMOS (AFTER MORRISH).

ASTROSONICS   A name given to the branch of science (rather than astrology) concerned with the investigation of the supposed relationship between planets and frequencies. The term should not be applied to the investigation of the ratios involved in the harmonies and intervals between planets, for which there is no satisfactory term.   See CELESTIAL HARMONICS, MUSES, MUSIC OF THE SPHERES and PLANETARY TONAL INTERVALS.

ASTROSOPHIA   See ASTROSOPHY.

ASTROSOPHY A name given to a modern form of astrology, based on the indications given by Steiner, formulated and expounded by such researchers as Vreede, Thun, Sucher and Powell. Whilst essentially syncretic in form, and rooted in traditional methods, it makes frequent use of the "Sidereal Zodiac" and of "Heliocentric Charts", as well as sophisticated application of "Epoch Charts" and "Death Charts". It is rooted in a spiritual cosmoconception, and in a view of history which has given rise to such interesting generalisations as the "Three Prototypes". The connected work of Powell (in relation to the study of ancient zodiacs) has been of great importance: see for example SIDEREAL CORRESPONDENCES. The practical application of the Sidereal Zodiac to bio-dynamic farming is also associated with Astrosophy, as for example in the work of Thun: see SIDEREAL MOON RHYTHMS. For all the system of astrosophy is modern in formulation and outlook (though fortunately not beset by the modern penchant for statistics), the term has long been in use in regard to ordinary traditional astrology, and indeed figured in the title of an important (and influential) astrological text, in the Latinized 'Astrosophia', published in 1687: the 'Universa Astrosophia Naturalis' of Bonattis. The same term 'astrosophy' has been used by Volguine (circa. 1946) in a more general sense, almost as a synonym for 'astrological', as for example in his term "Astrosophic Geography".

ASTROSOPHIC GEOGRAPHY Term used by Volguine to denote the now defunct practice of siting buildings and cities in accordance with astrological principles, aimed at reflecting the heavenly patterns in the earth's geography. Such practices, relating to geographic patterns and structures, must not be confused with those relating to the FOUNDATION CHART. Volguine quotes the federation of twelve cities of the Etruscans, whose representatives gathered annually at the temple of the god Voltumna. Perhaps more apposite is the claim made by modern astrologers that the positions of churches dedicated to the Virgin Maria on the map of France are located in the same spatial relationship as that figured in the constellational Virgo: the 'earth' thereby reflecting the 'heavens'.

ASTRO-SYMBOLISM   A term coined by Morrish in connexion with his "Astro-Psychology". The symbolism described is of a highly syncretic type, mingling half-digested symbols from a variety of cultures (such as the ancient Egyptian and the Theosophically-derived Buddhist). These are not very convincingly married to traditional astrological structures, such as the zodiac, the planets, and so on, within a framework of merged Jungian, Adlerian and Theosophical psychologies of a highly personal level of interpretation. Morrish suggests, for example, that the symbol (presumably he means 'sigil') for Taurus may be taken as a coiled serpent, indicating Fohat, or Kundalini lying 'coiled' or inert and unawakened in the root of the spine. Now, whilst this interpretation is entirely personal, and bears no relation to the astrological tradition (esoteric or exoteric), it is quite erroneous to so confuse Fohat with Kundalini.

ASTRO-THEOSOPHY   A term derived from the attempt to link certain aspects of European astrology with the Oriental tenets implicit in Theosophy, towards the end of the last century. The astrologer Leo may have been the first to popularize the term (1912), but it was given earlier by Blavatsky.

ASTRO-VOCATIONAL-GUIDANCE A term coined by Morrish to denote the aspect of chart-interpretation relating to vocation and occupation.

ASTRUM   This term is usually restricted to alchemy, but is also associated with the ancient astrological doctrine of VIRTUE. The 'astrum' is a secret regenerative principle, almost the ancient equivalent of the Etheric of modern occultism (see AETHER). The astrum contains within itself all created things, and may be abstracted by alchemical processes from these things - it is the quintessence of things, the binding principle of life.

ASVINI   The 27th of the Hindu NAKSHATRAS, the 'horseman'.

ASSYMETRIC ORB   Within the astrological doctrine of ASPECTS it is maintained that the "Applying Aspect" is stronger than the "Separating Aspect", which would indicate that the orb allowed an aspect need not be distributed evenly around the precise aspect itself. The work of Wangemann appears to support the contention that such orbs should be assymmetrically disposed, to allow a wider orb for the applying aspect.

ATALIA   One of several names given to the dragon who was believed by the ancients to swallow the luminaries, and thus cause what we now call eclipses. Beck sees an image of a dragon in the Ponza zodiac (see MITHRAIC ASTROLOGY) as this Atalia, and observes that the Assyrian word for eclipse was 'Atalu'.

ATHAZER   The Moon is said to be athazer when it is in precise conjunction with the Sun, or when it bears one of a number of precise angular relationships to the Sun (some of which are actually ASPECTS). These angles, for which no orb is permitted, are 12, 45, 90, 150, 168, 180, 192, 215, 270 and 348 degrees. It is evident from these figures that the athazer is to be measured in arc along the zodiac (the last four being something of a puzzle, in that they represent 168 135 90 and 12 degrees, respectively - could there be an error in the dissident?).

ATLANTIC SISTERS   See PLEIADES.

ATLAS   See PLEIADES.

ATLAS CELESTE   The name sometimes given to the "Modern Zodiac" of Delporte - but see also CONSTELLATIONAL MAPS.

AUDACITY   Name given to one of the SEVEN LOTS of Greek astrology, the 'lot of Toma' (Daring). The degree is the same distance from the Ascendant as Mars is from the "Part of Fortune".

AUGUST   The eighth month of the GREGORIAN CALENDAR named after minor calendrical reforms by Augustus Caesar, who is said to have refused a month shorter than that named in honour of Julius (see JULY), and therefore extended this ancient Sextilis month by one day, and gave it his honorific name. The Emperor and the month have however a pertinent communal etymology, as the Latin 'augustus' originally had a religious meaning - sacred and worthy of honour, linked with the idea of augury.

AUPHANIM   One of the variant names for the OPHANIM.

AUREA CATENA HOMERI   See CHAIN OF BEING.

AURIGA   Constellation approximately 10 degrees Gemini to 3 degrees Cancer, from 30 to 60 degrees north of the equator. The image for this asterism is a charioteer without his chariot, but according to Greek legend it represents Erichtonius, who first mounted a four-horse chariot. Almost certainly it was derived from Babylonian astrology, and a large number of names have been attached to the image, linking with the idea of a 'wagoner'. Within the constellation are found an image of a goat and a kid, variously explained, but of interest to astrologers because of the emphasis placed on the relevant fixed star CAPELLA ('little goat').

AUSIEL   According to certain grimoires, the name given to the Governor of
zodiacal Aquarius. The name is not to be confused with Auriel, which is an
alternative for URIEL. See ZODIACAL SPIRITS.

AUSTRAL SIGNS   The so-called 'southern signs', which are those from Libra to
Pisces, inclusive.

AUTOZOON   A name derived from Gnostic and neo-platonic sources for the image
of the TETRAMORPH. The etymology of this Greek term is linked with that of
the zodiac - but see Smith.

AUTUMNAL EQUINOX The time of year, around 22nd September, when the Sun
reaches the 1st degree of zodiacal Libra, and thus crosses the "Colure" - see
EQUINOX and EQUINOCTIAL POINT.

AUTUMNAL QUADRANT   See QUADRANTS.

AUTUMNAL SIGNS   These are Libra, Scorpio and Sagittarius.

AVIS   See CYGNUS.

AWWA The 11th of the Araic MANZILS, from 'Al Awwa', (the barker).

AYANAMSA   A term derived from the Sanskrit (itself meaning something like
'precession') to denote the difference in degrees for any given point in time
between the fiducial of the tropical zodiac and those of the various sidereal
zodiacs. Since there is no basic agreement as to a fiducial, or even to when
the zodiacs were actually contiguous, there is no standard arc of ayanamsa.
In modern times, the ayanamsa of Markandyar gives a difference at the
beginning of our century of 22 degrees, 26 minutes and 14 seconds, while the
Fagan-Bradley ayanamsa (used by many Western siderealists) gives one degree
in excess of this. The astrologer Sucher appears to suggest an ayanamsa of 8
degrees for the middle of this century. The result of these (and many other
figures) is that the study of the ayanamsa is one of the most perplexing
realms for ·any astrologer who finds himself occupied with the problem of
converting the sidereal to the tropical for any given time. It would seem
that the vexing question of ayanamsa was no more simple in ancient times than
it is now, for at least 5 different systems have been recorded. The
Babylonian astrologers knew of two systems, one of which corresponded to a
solar longitude of Aries 10 degrees, and one of which corresponded to Aries 8
degrees: this latter system is found in astrology well into the mediaeval
period. In his study of Egyptian astrology, Fagan gives the ayanamsa of
786BC in Aries 13.8 degrees: see however PRECESSION. Dean, following the
general consensus of historical opinions, notes it significant that the zero
ayanamsa coincided with the period during which the earliest astrological
records were made, and suggests that the sidereal zodiac may be 'an artefact
of civilization rather than a genuine entity'. It would seem likely that the
two systems - tropical and sidereal - were used contemporaneously for two
separate purposes. The fact is that the "Greek Zodiac" and the "Babylonian
Zodiac", whilst relating to different co-ordinates, required only minute
adjustment even in the days of Ptolemy to bring them into correspondence: an
addition of the ayanamsa of 2 degrees and 20 minutes permits the stellar
longitude of Ptolemy's star catalogue to be almost precisely related to the
earlier Babylonian catalogue. However, the historian Neugebauer points out
that due to an error in determination of the Vernal Point, the epoch for
Ptolemy's catalogue should be 48AD, and not 138AD, as is often believed.
This would imply that in terms of a precessional rate of 1 degree in 72
years, the Babylonian stellar zodiac and the Greek tropical zodiac coincided
in 216AD.   The German Kugler, working from Babylonian tablets of lunar
computations (based on the tables of the Babylonian Kidinnu) showed that the
longitude of the vernal point was in Aries 8 degrees. The historian Weidner
located the point from later astronomical computations tables (according to
the Babylonian Naburiannu) as 10 degrees. By a systematic comparison of the

two systems, Schnabel computed the positions for the equivalent equinoctial points, and obtained for the Naburiannu tables the epoch 508BC and for Kidinnu 379BC. These figures have since been adjusted to 500BC and 373BC. See HYPSOMATIC AYANAMSA, SIDEREAL CORRESPONDENCES and SYSTEM A.

AYAR   See BABYLONIAN CALENDAR.

AYIL According to certain grimoires, this is the name given to the Governor of zodiacal Sagittarius - but see also SIZAJASEL.

AZIMECH   See ARCTURUS.

AZIMENE DEGREES A term derived from Arabian astrology, now rarely used, and applied to certain degrees or arcs in the zodiac, which are regarded as being debilitating to the native when on the Ascendant, or otherwise brought into prominence in a chart. The azimene degrees are sometimes called the 'deficient degrees', the 'weak degrees' or 'lame degrees', and may have been derived from consideration of the influence of powerful (malefic) fixed stars, now precessed. Figure 7 sets out the individual degrees and arcs accorded each sign.

FIGURE 7. THE AZIMENE DEGREES AND ARCS.

AZIMUTH A term used to denote the angle (with apex at zenith) formed by a star's vertical circle with the meridian.

AZOTH Name applied to Mercury by the alchemists, but used rarely by astrologers - for an exception, see Cornell.

AZURE DRAGON Name of the so-called 'constellation' of the Chinese heavens, which actually consists of an arc of seven "Sieu", from the asterisms 'Kio' to 'Ki', as indicated in table 48 under LUNAR MANSIONS. Properly speaking the Azure Dragon is a quadrant or arc. See also BLACK WARRIOR, RED BIRD and WHITE TIGER.

BABYLONIAN CALENDAR   The data for converting the ancient Babylonian calendar of 786-5BC (the so-called HYPSOMATIC YEAR) to the modern Gregorian system, is provided by Fagan in Table 10 below. The Babylonian equivalents are given for the first day of the ancient NEOMENIA.

-- TABLE 10

BABYLONIAN TERM		GREGORIAN DATE
Nisannu	1st Nisan	27 March
Airu	1st Ayar	26 April
Simanu	1st Sivan	25 May
Du'uzu	1st Tammuz	24 June
Abu	1st Ab	23 July
Ululu	1st Elul	22 August
Teshritu	1st Teshrit	21 September
Arakhasamma	1st Arahsamma	20 October
Kislimu	1st Kislev	19 November
Tebitu	1st Tebit	18 December
Shabatu	1st Shebat	16 January
Addaru	1st Adar	15 February

BABYLONIAN ZODIAC   The earliest formulated Babylonian Zodiac appears to be an eighteen asterism lunar zodiac, which is peripherally linked with the MUL-APIN TABLES. The first recorded use in Babylonian astrology of a system of twelve fixed-star zodiacal asterisms has been dated to the first half of the fifth century. In this system, the zodiacal belt is divided into twelve equal sectors, the signs themselves measured in terms of the fixed stars of the zodiacal belt - essentially in terms of the NORMAL STARS. The historian Powell has suggested that the transition from the system of Normal Stars to the Babylonian equal-sign zodiac was by means of the axial fiducial of the fixed stars ALDEBARAN and ANTARES, which divide the zodiac in half, and therefore provide an excellent framework for a system of arc-measurements. It would seem that the 30 degree sign was derived from analogy with the twelve month schematic year of the Babylonians (see MUL-APIN TABLES). The later GREEK ZODIAC, formally influenced by this fixed-star Babylonian Zodiac, was based on a division of the ecliptic 'line', whilst the Babylonian zodiacal belt was about 16 degrees wide - literally a pathway through the asterisms.

BACCHUS   Term applied by the astrologer Thierens in his esoteric cosmoconception to a HYPOTHETICAL PLANET, with the (inapposite) alternative name of Horus. The planet is related to the future evolution of our Cosmos, and is said to be invisibly present in the ETHERIC SPHERE.

BACKGROUND   A specialist term used of planets near to the cusps of the cadent houses, which are by virtue of this placing regarded as weak or ineffectual, and are said to be in the 'background' of the chart. See also FOREGROUND and MIDDLEGROUND.

BAILEY-PLUTO   See ESOTERIC PLUTO

BALANCE Popular name for the zodiacal sign and constellation LIBRA.

BALDAH   Al Baldah, 'the city' or 'district', the 19th of the Arabic MANZILS.

BARAQUEL   One of the Grigori (angels of Jewish legend - the term being derived from the word Egregori, meaning 'the watchers'), who instructed men in the art of astrology, according to their own higher wisdom.

===

BARREN NODE An alternative term for the DRAGON'S TAIL.

BARREN PLANETS According to Cornell, the Barren Planets are the Sun, Mars, Saturn and Uranus, which tend to 'deny or kill' children when located in the fifth or eleventh houses of parents - an idea which finds little support in traditional astrology. The Dragon's Tail is classed also as a 'barren' influence, and hence may be described as a 'barren node', being regarded as an influence equivalent to that of Saturn. Cornell's view of barren planets is highly specialized, though obviously based on a profound study of available literature.

BARREN SIGNS These are Gemini, Leo and Virgo, but it is maintained that the native may be said to be 'barren' only if one of these is upon the Ascendant, or (as some astrologers insist) on the cusp of a house of the same elemental nature. In fact, the traditional term is something of a misnomer, for these positions do not confer barrenness, so much as limit the number of children.

BARU Babylonian name for an omen-reader - see OMNIA.

BASILICA STELLA See REGULUS.

BASILISCUS See REGULUS.

BASILISK See SCORPIUS.

BATEN KAITOS Fixed star set in the body of the WHALE - the term being derived from the Arabic Al Batn al Kaitos, 'The belly of the whale'. It is regarded as an evil nature, associated with shipwrecks.

BATN AL HUT Term from the Arabic Al Batn al Hut, meaning 'the belly of the fish', the name given to the twenty-sixth of the MANZILS, now located by the beta of Andromeda.

BAU See ARCTURUS.

BEASTLY An alternative term for BESTIAL or FERAL. In his highly personal approach to Medical Astrology, Cornell comes to the conclusion that a 'beastly form' may develop if at conception (presumably he refers to a Pre-Natal Chart), the Sun and Moon are in the Sixth or Twelfth houses, in one or other of the FOUR-FOOTED SIGNS.

BEEHIVE See PRAESAEPE.

BEELZEBUB See MUSCA BOREALIS.

BEFOR One of the occult names given to the spirit of Jupiter.

BEHOLDING Those pairs of signs, which are of equal distance from the tropics, were said to 'behold' each other, and are sometimes called the Beholding Signs. These pairs are Aries-Libra, Taurus-Virgo, Gemini-Leo, Aquarius-Sagittarius and Pisces-Scorpio. Naturally, the Sun in any of these pairs gives equal ratios of day to night. Ptolemy explains the term as being connected with the fact that the pairs rise from the same part of the horizon, and set in the same parts (in a geographic sense, of course). The Beholding Signs are sometimes called 'the Signs of Equal Power', though the terminology is now largely archaic.

BELLATRIX The fixed star, gamma of Orion, set in the left shoulder of the constellation. The name, which means 'female warrior', expresses its war-like nature, for it is said by Ptolemy to be of the influence of Mars with Mercury - not altogether beneficial in a chart.

BENEFIC ASPECT A number of ASPECTS which promote a general well-being

==

between planets are termed 'benefic' - the Trine and Sextile being the most
notable examples. However, the entire nature of a particular aspect must be
taken into account if the term is to be used with any precision, since some
planets, whilst fulfilling the requirements of angular geometry (such as a
precise Trine, for example) may themselves be of an intrinsic nature which
does not promote a beneficient influence. Benefic Aspects create harmonies
which may, under certain circumstances, lead to a dispersion of energies
(towards a general laziness, for example), and this throws doubt upon the
applicability of this ancient term.

BENEFICS   The term 'benefic', whilst sometimes used of aspects (see BENEFIC
ASPECT) is also used of Planets and nodal points.   Whilst Venus and Jupiter
are the Lesser Benefic and the Greater Benefic respectively, it is often said
that the Sun, Moon and the Dragon's Head are also benefics, when well
aspected.

BENTENASH   One of the seven major fixed stars forming the constellation URSA
MAJOR (the eta of the asterism), said by Ptolemy to be of the influence
equivalent to that of Mars. Sometimes called Benetnash.

BESIEGED   When a planet is hemmed in by two malefic planets, it is said to
be besieged by them, and is regarded as being in an unfortunate position. In
the mediaeval terminology, a planet so besieged by two benefics was usually
regarded as being fortunate in influence.   In fact, the theory underlying
the tradition is merely an extension of that theory of aspects relating to
the CONJUNCTION, since the planet besieged is induced into a state of double
conjunction by forming a link between two planets which would otherwise not
necessarily be in orb, and which then mingle their influences.

BESTIAL   Originally, the Bestial Signs were those which had as zodiacal
image a whole animal. Thus Aries as Ram, Taurus as Bull, Leo as Lion and
Scorpio as Scorpion, were bestial signs. Due to linguistic change, however,
the term now carries a somewhat unfortunate connotation. There have also
been significant changes in the imagery of the signs: the original Capricorn
(once the goat-fish) has changed, so that it is now often regarded as being
entirely bestial, in its guise of Goat. Sagittarius, which was properly
half-human, half-horse, was usually termed a Bestial Sign (though see
BICORPOREAL SIGNS).   The fishes of Pisces were also regarded as 'beasts',
indicating that it is likely the classication was adopted to distinguish the
signs into the pairs of Bestial and "Human Signs".

BETELGEUZE   Fixed star, the alpha of Orion, set in the right shoulder of the
giant. The name is derived from the Arabic Ibt al Jauzah, (armpit of the
Giant). Ptolemy gives it the nature equivalent to Mars conjunct Mercury: it
is said to confer martial honour and wealth.

BHADZAPADA   The Sanskrit name for constellation Pisces - see MEENAM.

BHARANI   The 28th of the Hindu NAKSHATRAS, the 'bearer'.

BICORPOREAL   The bicorporeal signs were those with images consisting of two
separate forms - Gemini (as two humans), Sagittarius (originally a human and
horse), and Pisces (two fishes). Ptolemy included in his list of
bicorporeals the sign Virgo, an inclusion which may be explained either from
an esoteric point of view (since what was of prime importance was the corn or
child held in the hands of the celestial virgin) or from a point of view of
exoteric theory, since the biocorporeals of Ptolemy appear to have been the
equivalent of the modern "Mutable Signs". In fact, Ptolemy called these the
'Disoma', and explained the term as relating to the two kinds of weather
which the group shared: the mediaeval terminology, from which the modern
term is derived, was certainly limited to the consideration of the images.
Ptolemy says the bicorporeals make souls complex, changeable, hard to
apprehend, fond of music, and both amorous and versatile.

BIBLICAL ASTROLOGY   There have been very many attempts to relate astrology to certain passages within the Bible. Examples may be found in Beckh (in connexion specifically with the Gospel of St. Mark) and in many passing references in Butler, Heidenreich, Libra, Steiner, Wemyss, and so on. There is scarcely a 'system' of astrology which has not attempted to establish its own list of Biblical (or even theological) correspondences. The available literature may be observed in the roscicrucian literature (for example, in Boehme) or in the specialist Christological assumptions developed by Dee in connexion with his magical sigil of the "Monas". On a less exalted level, the present author has contributed somewhat to this extensive astro-biblical literature in his examination of esoteric traditions in 'The Hidden Art'. In some astrological systems, associations have been drawn between the twelve signs of the zodiac and the twelve Apostles, the twelve Tribes of Israel and the twelve stones on the Breastplate of the High Priest, while the Angels of the Seven Churches are often interpreted in planetary terms. The hierarchies of the pseudo-Dionysius are obviously astro-theological at base, as are the Seven Days (more properly, the seven epochs) of Creation, which are linked with the esoteric cosmogenesis adequately set out in such modern occult sources as Blavatsky and (specifically in astrological contexts) Heindel. See therefore, MAGICAL JEWELS, CELESTIAL HIERARCHIES, TWELVE DISCIPLES, TWELVE TRIBES OF ISRAEL and SECUNDADEIAN BEINGS. The specific symbolism and 'correspondences' established in theological and astrological literature between signs, planets and biblical references is far too complex to be examined here, but it is sufficient to note the ancient connexion between Christ and Pisces (and more especially in popular astrological literature with the Age of Pisces), due to the communality of the image of the fish, which so intrigued Augustine, and which was even a part of the pre-Christian ethos relating to the coming Messiah. In this category falls the association established between the Virgin Mary and the celestial Virgo, that gave rise to a crop of symbolism which survived (though largely misunderstood) well into the sixteenth century. The speculations regarding the STAR OF BETHLEHEM and the Magi, those Zarathustrian initiates who are so often wrongly called 'astrologers' in popular lore, have also played a prominent part in astrological literature.   There appears to be no adequate and comprehensive study of this subject of Biblical Astrology, though passing references in Blavatsky, Testa, Steiner and the remarkable Massey, for all their rejection by the academic world, are worth serious attention. In spite of the many exegetical essays relating to the astrological view of the Bible, it is sobering to note the short (though probably comprehensive) index to the biblical astronomical references given by Allen (R.H.) - 18 only are culled from the Old Testament, and 3 from the New. None of these is specifically astrological, and one or two of the 'traditional' exegetical quotations merely arise from a misunderstanding in the English translation: for example, the Genesis i.14. 'let them be for signs, and for seasons, and for days and years', is by no means a reference to the zodiacal 'signs', as is often fondly imagined by some astrologers. The link drawn in esotericism between the Secret Wisdom of the Bible and the esoteric astrological lore, is however reliable, and affords a rich field for speculative research. See also COSMIC PANTHEONS.

BIG DIPPER   One of the several names for the constellation URSA MAJOR.

BIOLOGICAL CORRESPONDENCES   In recent astrological development, the traditional image of Melothesic Man formulated in Greek astrology, has been changed to adapt to the modern (popularist) image of man. A good example of such a modern system, which incorporates not only a new series of connexions, but also the new planets, is that given by Ebertin in connexion with Cosmobiology set out in table 11.

```
-------------------------------------------------------------------TABLE 11
SU   Cell, body, heart and circulatory system.
MO   Bodily fluids, blood, lymph, the soul.
ME   The nervous system, youth.
```

==

```
-----------------------------------------------------------TABLE 11 (CONTINUED)
VE    Glands and hormonal system, growth and maturity.
MA    Muscles, middle age, prime of life.
JU    Organic system (lungs, liver, etc), the climacteric.
SA    Bones and old age.
UR    Rhythmic system (pulse, breathing, peristaltic).
NE    Weakness and slackness, paralysis and (possibly) excretory.
PL    Change, transformation and regeneration.
-------------------------------------------------------------------------
```

To the planets, Ebertin adds the following nodal influences: Dragon's Head
relates to hereditary factors, the astral body and the automonic system; the
Midheaven relates to ego-consciousness, reason as 'cerebral function', whilst
the Ascendant relates to 'environment'. In terms of glandular systems, the
esotericist Collin, working mainly within the tradition established by
Ouspensky, gives the melothesia in table 12.

```
-----------------------------------------------------------------TABLE 12
SU    Thymus glands           JU    Posterior pituitary
MO    Pancreatic system       SA    Anterior pituitary
ME    Thyroid                 UR    Sex glands
VE    Parathyroid             NE    Pineal gland
MA    Solar plexus
-------------------------------------------------------------------------
```

See also MELOTHESIC MAN.

BI-QUINTILE   An aspect of 144 degrees, arising from a division of the zodiac
into a two-fifth arc. See QUINTILE.

BIRTH   The human horoscope, around which the whole edifice of genethliacal
astrological theory has been constructed, is usually a symbolic
representation of the moment of birth. Inevitably, there is much argument as
to precisely what is meant by 'birth', as several stages and processes are
involved, each giving significantly different times. In fact, few serious
astrologers will use a chart which has not been subjected to careful
"Rectification", so that argument as to precise time of birth is often
irrelevant. Rectification aside, however, most modern astrologers would time
a birth (and cast an appropriate chart) from either the severing of the
umbilical cord, or from the first cry.

BIRTHPLACE HOUSES   English name applied to the GOH HOUSES devised by Walter
Koch: see KOCHIAN SYSTEM.

BIRTHPLACE SYSTEM   English name applied to the method of House Division
proposed by Walter Koch - see KOCHIAN SYSTEM.

BIRTH STAR   Sometimes defined as the most powerful fixed star conjunct a
planet or angle in a natal chart, or (failing such a conjunction), a star in
close orb with such a planet or angle. Sometimes also defined as the fixed
star (of astrological significance) nearest to the Ascendant: this must be
contrasted with the insistence by many astrologers that no orb should be
allowed for a fixed-star conjunction - in this connexion, see MORINEAN ORBS.
In popular journalistic astrology, the birth star is sometimes merely the
sun-sign, sometimes the planetary ruler of that sign. See also PERSONAL
STAR.

BIRTH STONES   Traditional astrological doctrines associate a number of
precious stones with each of the twelve signs of the zodiac: most of these
associations are derived from TALISMANIC MAGIC, however. The stones were
said to transmit a specific VIRTUE (in which connexion, see GAMELAI), when
used to make Seals, or even when worn unsealed as magnetic centres, to
attract the corresponding virtues of the stars. An extensive literature,

derived mainly from the Arabian-inspired mediaeval lore, presents numerous correspondencies, and interesting related documents have been published by Evans. The most reliable lists are those derived from the SCALA and CALENDRIA MAGICA of the late mediaeval tradition, but in modern times (as the representative collections in table 13 indicate) many stones are attributed to several different signs, and there appears to be little order or sense in some of the correspondences.

--TABLE 13

AR	Amethyst, diamond, garnet, bloodstone, jasper, malchite.
TA	Alabaster, emerald, coral, jade, lapis lazuli, sapphire.
GE	Aquamarine, agate, beryl, chalcedony, chrysolite, crystal, marble, topaz.
CN	Emerald, black onyx, selenite, pearl, crystal.
LE	Carbuncle, diamond, hyacinth, ruby, sardonyx.
VG	Agate, aquamarine, cornelian, hyacinth, marble, pink jasper.
LB	Alabaster, beryl, crysolite, coral, cornelian, diamond, jade, lapis lazuli, opal.
SC	Beryl, bloodstone, flint, jasper, magnet, malachite, topaz.
SG	Amethyst, carbuncle, hyacinth, moonstone, turquoise.
CP	Chrysoprase, jet, moonstone, sapphire, white onyx.
AQ	Chalcedony, hyacinth, opal, sapphire, slate.
PI	Amethyst, chrysolite, moonstone, topaz, hyacinth.

A mediaeval tradition which is a little more 'certain' is that recorded by Agrippa in his Scala Duodenarii, which gives only one jewel (lapis) to each of the signs, is in table 14.

--TABLE 14

AR	Sardonyx	TA	Sard	GE	Topaz
CN	Chalcedony	LE	Jasper	VG	Smaragdine
LB	Beryl	SC	Amethyst	SG	Hyacinth
CP	Chrysopase	AQ	Crystal	PI	Sapphire

Kircher gives the following interesting correspondences:

--TABLE 15

SIGN	GEM	CREATURE	COLOUR
AR	Amethyst	Sheep	Red
TA	Jacinth	Cattle	Dark
GE	Chrysoprase	Apes	Yellow
CN	Topaz	Water creatures	Blue
LE	Beryl	Forest creatures	Golden
VG	Chrysolite	Dogs	Green
LB	Sard	Birds	Purple
SC	Sardonyx	Birds of prey	Black
SG	Emerald	Military beasts	Flame-colour
AQ	Sapphire	Marine creatures	Deep blue
PI	Jasper	River beasts	Ash-colour

The modern esoteric astrologer Thierens provides quite a different list, which he appears to have from Pavitt:

--TABLE 16

AR	Jasper	TA	Sapphire	GE	Chalcedony
CN	Emerald	LE	Sardonyx	VG	Cornelian
LB	Chrysolite	SC	Beryl	SG	Topaz
CP	Chrysoprase	AQ	Hyacinth	PI	Amethyst

Similar lists, with many varieties of 'correspondences', could be provided, but the above is sufficient to show that there is really no traditional system of Birth Stone associations upon which one might rely. Two other lists of Magical Jewels, once pertaining to a separate tradition, have been incorporated into the general lists relating to Talismanic Magic. The first is that tradition derived from the attempt to link a magical jewel with the 'twelve stones' set in the breast-plate of the Jewish High Priest. The three lists in table 17 below represent the better type of such correspondences: the two tables derived from Wemyss are a result of an attempt to equate the Priest stones with the Foundation Stones of the New Jerusalem.

```
---------------------------------------------------------------- TABLE 17
SIGN      THIERENS       WEMYSS            WEMYSS
========================================================================
AR        Jasper         Red Jasper        Sard
TA        Sapphire       Topaz             Topaz
GE        Chalcedony     Carbuncle         Chrysolite
CN        Emerald        Emerald           Emerald
LE        Sardonyx       Lapis Lazuli      Sapphire
VG        Cornelian      Amethyst          Amethyst
LB        Crysolite      Carbuncle         Sardonyx
SC        Beryl          Agate             Jacinth
SG        Topaz          Yellow Agate      Chrysoprasos
CP        Chrysoprase    Beryl             Beryl
AQ        Hyacinth       Chalcedony        Chalcedony
PI        Amethyst       Jasper            Jasper
------------------------------------------------------------------------
```

Unfortunately, many other variant lists might be given from related sources. Another tradition, related to zodiacal associations, is that linked with FIXED STARS (a subject with which Evans has dealt in a most scholarly manner), though it must be remarked that even in mediaeval talismanic magic, these fixed stars were often associated with different jewels, a representative list given by Evans is from a fifteenth century manuscript, which provides also corresponding Sigils ('carectus' in Latin)

```
-----------------------------------------------------------------TABLE 18
Ala Corvi (Algorab)  -  Onichus (onyx)
Alayhoch (Alphecca)  -  Saphirus (sapphire)
Aldebaran  -  Carbuncle or Ruby
Pleiades  -  Cristellus (crystal)
Algol  -  Diamas (diamond)
Arcturus  -  Iaspis (Jasper)
Cauda Capricorni (Deneb Algedi)  -  Calcedonius (Chalcedony)
Cauda Urse Majoris (Polaris)  - Magnes (see below)
Cor Leonis (Regulus)  -  Gergonsa or Granatus (Garnet)
Cor Scorpionis (Antares)  -  Sardinus et Amatisto (Sardonyx/Amethyst)
Lucida Corone Scorpionis (Capella)  - Topasius (Topaz)
Spica  -  Smaragdus
Vulture Cadens (Wega)  -  Crisolitus (Chrysolite)
------------------------------------------------------------------------
```

The 'Magnes' associated with Deneb Algedi is usually translated as 'lodestone' or 'magnet stone', but the term has several different meanings in the esoteric tradition. A similar series of (varied) associations to those above, though between the planets and the range of magical stones, is too varied to be recorded here.

BI-SEPTILE   An Aspect of 102.8 degrees, arising from the multiple of the "Septile" by two, and used especially in the theory of HARMONICS.

BITTER SIGN   An archaic term, applied to each of the Fire Triplicities - Aries, Leo and Sagittarius - which were 'hot, fiery and bitter'.

BLACK WARRIOR   One of the so-called 'constellations' of the Chinese Heavens, which actually consisted of an arc of seven Sieu, from 'Tow' to 'Peih', as indicated in table 48 under LUNAR MANSIONS.   There are three other such arcs, the AZURE DRAGON, the RED BIRD and the WHITE TIGER.

BLIND TRIAL   Within an astrological context, a term used to denote a test designed to establish whether an astrologer may correctly interpret a chart cast for a person unknown to him.   In order to ensure that there is no 'unconscious bias', the blind trial is often conducted by means of a third-party (in the so-called 'Double Blind Trial'), who prepares the astrological test material on behalf of the investigator.

BLOSSOM-LIGHT TRIGON   See SIDEREAL MOON RHYTHMS.

BLUNSDON CHART   A term sometimes used for the stereographic projection of the THREE-DIMENSIONAL CHART proposed by the astrologer Blunsdon - see figure 17 under CHART SYSTEMS.

BONATIS DIRECTIONS   Name given to a system of Secondary Directions associated with the thirteenth century Italian astrologer Bonatus, and concerned with the use of a daily solar chart, cast for the return of the Sun to its own radical position, each daily chart being related to the sequence of years.   See also HIEROZ BONATIS DIRECTIONS.

BOOTES   Constellation approximately from 27 degrees Virgo to 7 degrees Scorpio, from 10 to 55 degrees north of the equator.   Several different mythical accounts of the origin of the constellation have survived.   Bootes is identified with Icarius, the Athenian who taught the use of grape to make alcohol, and with Arcas, who almost killed his mother, transformed as she was into the shape of a bear.   However, the name was used in the Odyssey, and the constellation is associated with the idea of a Herdsman.   Very many alternative names exist, including 'Bear-Watcher', 'Wagoner', 'Arctophylax', 'Atlas' and (because of its nearness to the north) 'Septentrio'.   It is said to give a fondness for rural work, as well as earthly desire.   The important stars in the astrological lists are ARCTURUS, PRINCEPS and SEGINUS.

BOREAL SIGNS   A term derived from the Greek personification (Boreus) of the North Wind, and used of the six 'Northern Signs', Aries to Virgo.

BOWL   One of the JONES PATTERNS, in which the planets are gathered into half of the chart figure (within an arc of 180 degrees):   it is said to denote a high degree of equanimity and self-containment.

BRACHIUM   Meaning 'Forearm', the Latin name given to the seventh of the LUNAR MANSIONS in some mediaeval lists.   Probably located by the fixed stars CASTOR and POLLUX.

BRHAJJATAKA   The title of a Sanscrit work on popular astrology, written in the mid-sixth century by Varahamihira.   This remains the basic textbook for the popular interpretation of horoscopes in India.   The historian Pingree says that such horoscopes are cast for perhaps 90% of the Indian population, and depend largely upon this text for interpretation.   See NADIGRANTHAMS.

BROKEN   When a planet comes to the Descendant (by transit or progression), it is said to be 'broken', and its power 'wanes' for the entire semi-arc.

BROKEN SIGNS   See IMPERFECT SIGNS

BRONZE AGE   A term derived from Hindu chronology and modern esoteric lore, and relating to an epoch, see DWAPARA YUGA and FOUR AGES.

BROTHERS AND SISTERS   The 'Point of Brothers and Sisters', not to be confused with Third House (sometimes called the 'House of Brothers and

Sisters') is one of the so-called Arabian PARS in a chart. It is determined
in a natal chart by taking the degree of Saturn to the Ascendant point, and
then adjusting the position of Jupiter to give the Point. The connexion
between Saturn and fraternity appears to have stemmed from Ptolemy, who
associated the sign on the Midheaven (linked with Capricorn, ruled by Saturn)
with Brethren.

BRUTISH   The term Brutish Signs is traditionally (though inexplicably)
applied to Leo, and to the last "Decan" (sometimes the 'last half') of
Sagittarius. Like so many similar archaic terms, the word appears to be
derived from consideration of the image of the corresponding sign: those
born under these two being said to be 'brutish, savage and inhuman'. Cornell
refines the tradition somewhat, however, by claiming that the Brutish Signs
on the Ascendant, or the luminaries in either of them, and with malefics in
the angles, 'render the native fierce, cruel and brutish'. See BESTIAL.

BUCKET   Name given to one of the JONES PATTERNS, in which a single planet is
found approximately opposite all the other planets, which are themselves
gathered within an arc of 180 degrees or less. This isolated planet (often
called the 'singleton') is regarded as a sort of 'handle', and is said to
bestow the capacity for special activity, in terms of its own nature.

BUDHAM   The Sanskrit word for Mercury, as used in Hindu astrology.

BULL   A name given to both zodiacal and constellational Taurus.

BUNDLE   One of the JONES PATTERNS, in which the planets are grouped into a
third of the horoscope circle (that is, into an arc of 120 degrees). Such a
figuration is said to denote a limited response to external stimuli, and a
greater dependence on self.

BUNGULA   A name often wrongly applied to the fixed star, alpha of Centaurus.
See RIGIL KENTAURUS.

BUTAIN   'Al Butain' (the belly), the 28th of the Arabian MANZILS.

CABBALISTIC ASTROLOGY   See QABBALISTIC ASTROLOGY.

CACADAEMON   See PERSEUS.

CACODEMON   A term once applied to the "Twelfth House", derived from a Greek
compound meaning 'evil influence'. See also DAIMON.

CADENT   The houses of the horoscope which 'fall away' from the "Angles" are
called cadent, from the Latin verb 'cadere' (to fall): these are the 3rd,
6th, 9th and 12th houses. Planets in such houses are called 'cadent
planets', and it is believed that the position marks a diminution in their
influence.

CADUCEUS   The symbolic staff or wand of the god Mercury (Hermes), and
sometimes the "Sigil" for the planet Mercury: ☿ In the ancient mysteries
this appears to have been made from a three-headed snake, but in relatively
early times it was changed to a single rod intertwined by two serpents,
linked esoterically with the human spinal column. In a specialist sense, the
word is used of an Arabian PARS, the 'part of Mercury': this point is
determined by revolving the solar degree to the Ascendant - the position of
Mercury then marks the 'Caduceus' within the houses, a point which relates to

commerce and business dealings. In his study of the "Monas", Dee formulated
a specialist theory relating a caduceus-derivation to sigillic forms.

CAEL   In certain methods of ceremonial magic, this name is given to the
governor of zodiacal Cancer.

CAELUM   Constellation, approximately from 12 degrees Taurus to 15 degrees
Gemini, and from 35 to 50 degrees north of the equator. Formed only in 1752,
the name means 'graving tool' - it is said to give artistic taste.

CAGASTER   A term (probably) originated by Paracelsus, from the Greek 'kako'
(evil) and 'astron' (star). It is applied to that spiritual force in matter
- derived from the stellar realm - which strives towards the destruction of
form. It works against the "Iliaster".

CALENDAR   A system of co-ordinating and recording Earth time with the
apparent and real cycles of cosmic bodies. See BABYLONIAN CALENDAR, CHINESE
CALENDAR, EGYPTIAN CALENDAR, EUCTEMONIAN CALENDAR, GREGORIAN CALENDAR, JULIAN
CALENDAR and ROMAN CALENDAR. See also ZODIACAL CALENDARS.

CALENDARIA MAGICA   The name used in mediaeval occultism and astrology for a
series of tables setting out the correspondences, numerological connexions
and sigillic forms between zodiacal signs, planets, elements, celestial
hierarchies and so on. The best of the surviving calendaria is that
attributed to Trithemius, which has influenced the associations passed into
astrology by the eclecticism of Agrippa. The example in table 19 is from a
15th century 'Calendarium Naturale Magicum' reproduced by Nowotny.

---TABLE 19

ONE   The One Principle of all things: God.   The 'Archetype' itself.

TWO   The polarities of Masculine (agens) - Feminine (patiens)
                                        Sun - Moon
                          Feeling (cor) - Thinking (cerebrum)

THREE The Trinity of the Godhead, and the trinity in all things.
       The three ranks of Hierarchies (suprema, media and infirma).

       HIERARCHIES   TRIUNE MAN   PRINCIPLES   ELEMENTS

       Suprema   Thinking (intellectus)   Salt   Fire
       Media   Feeling (sensitiva)   Mercury   Air
       Infirma   Body (vegetabilia)   Sulphur   Water

FOUR   ELEMENTS   Fire   Air   Water   Earth
       ANGELS   Michael   Raphael   Gabriel   Uriel
       CARDINALS   Oriens   Occidens   Septentrio   Meridies
       SOUL POWERS   Intellectus Ratio   Phantasia   Sensus
       VIRTUES   Prudence   Justice   Temperance   Fortitude
       HUMOURS   Cholera   Sanguis   Pituita*   Melancholia
       QUALITIES   Hot   Humid   Cold   Dry
       ----

       * The mediaeval term for Phlegma.

FIVE   Water   Air   Fire   Earth   'Mixtum' ("Quintessence")
       Saturn Jupiter Mars   Venus   Mercury

SIX   Seraphim   Cherubim   Thrones   Dominions   Powers   Virtutes
       Saturn   Jupiter   Mars   Venus   Mercury   Moon
       (This is an entirely fanciful set of associations - see table 3)

===

---TABLE 19 (CONTINUED)

SEVEN	Saturn	Jupiter	Mars	Sun	Venus	Mercury	Moon
	Aratron	Befor	Phalec	Och	Hagith	Ophiel	Phul
	Oriphiel	Zachariel	Samuel	Michael	Anael	Raphael	Gabriel
	Zazel*	Iophiel	Graphiel	Nachiel	Hagiel	Tiriel	Malcha
	Agiel*	Hismael	Barzabel	Soreth	Kedemel	Taphitartarat	
							Hasmodai

* These groups are planetary spirits.

EIGHT   The Stellatum (coleum stella) and the 7 planets.

NINE

SPHERES	HIERARCHIES	and RULERS	PRECIOUS STONES
Primum mobile	Seraphim	Metatron	Saphyrus
Stellatum	Cherubim	Ophaniel	Smaragdus
Saturn	Throni	Zophkiel	Carbunculus
Jupiter	Dominations	Zadkiel	Berillus
Mars	Potestates	Camael	Onijx
Sun	Virtues	Raphael*	Crysolithus
Venus	Principalities	Haniel	Iaspis
Mercury	Archangeli	Michael*	Topasius
Moon	Angeli	Gabriel	Sardius

* Michael and Raphael appear to have been confused.

TEN   Primum Mobile, the zodiac (Sphaera Zodiacus), the 7 planetary
        spheres, and the 'Earth spheres' (Sphaerae Elementaris).

ELEVEN is regarded as having no value in the system, and has no listing.

TWELVE gives the associations at their richest with the twelve signs
        of the zodiac, and their SIGILS, the names of the zodiacal angels
        (Malchidiel, Asmodel, Ambriel, Muriel, Verchiel, Hamliel, Zuriel,
        Barbiel, Adnachiel, Hanael, Gabriel and Babchiel), the twelve
        months and the Roman gods (actually called 'numina') listed under
        COSMIC PANTHEONS, the twelve "Images" of the signs, the
        corresponding "Magical Squares" and "Birth Stones".

The calendaria are usually replete with magical seals, sigils, symbols, and
the like, and constitute one of the most fascinating realms of research into
astrological and occult symbolism. See also SCALA.

CALENDRICAL ORIENTATION   A term used to denote architectural orientations in
which the axes of buildings (or some significant feature within a building)
are directed towards a calendrically determined point, such a the arc of
sunrise, or heliacal risings for a particular epoch. Such orientations are
usually derived from special astrological considerations. An example is the
SAN MINIATO ZODIAC, which has a calendrical orientation of an annual and
diurnal kind. See however ASTRO-ARCHAEOLOGY and FOUNDATION CHART.

CALLESTA   Name given to one of the satellites of Jupiter.

CAMELOPARDALIS   Constellation, approximately from 2 degrees Gemini to 15
Cancer, from 53 to 90 degrees north of the equator, the 'Giraffe'. Formed
only in 1614, it is said to confer patience and wisdom.

CAMPANEAN SYSTEM   A method of "House Division", adapted from an earlier
Arabian system by the 13th century astrologer-mathematician Giovanni Campano.
The principle underlying the method is the projection on to the ecliptic,
from the pole of the prime vertical, an equal-division of the prime vertical;

thus, the planes of the 6 intersecting great circles are always at intervals of 30 degrees. The system is one of the several 'quadrant systems' of division regarded as satisfactory by many astrologers - especially since Campanus insisted that the cusps of the houses mark the centre of the house, the strongest area of influence. One of the main objections to it is the distortion of the houses in charts cast for births near to the poles. Unfortunately, the Campanean tables are not so generally available as those drawn from the "Placidean System".

CAMPANUS HOUSES   See CAMPANEAN SYSTEM.

CANCER   The fourth sign of the zodiac. It corresponds as a zodiacal sign neither in location nor extent with the constellation of the same name - see CANCER CONSTELLATON - though the fixed stars in the asterism, along with those in part of constellation Gemini, almost entirely account for the erratic genius which is associated with natives of this sign. The modern sigil for Cancer ♋ has been variously explained. For example, Hall sees it as 'two spermatoza twisted together', intended to signify the male and female seed: however, the sigil is relatively modern, and had a different form in mediaeval astrology. The image for Cancer is nowadays a crab, as in the mediaeval form in figure 8: however, in early astrology the sign and constellation was presented more frequently in the image of a crayfish. Cancer is of the "Water Element", of the Cardinal Quality, and the influence is emotional, sensitive, imaginative, gregarious and cautious. This nature of Cancer is manifest in human beings in the many keywords attached to it by modern astrologers: romantic, sociable, shrewd, domesticated, passive, strong in feelings, and so on - in a word, all those qualities which may be associated with a sensitive water type seeking emotional unfoldment through experiencing the material realm. In excess, or when under pressure, the Cancerian nature may be described in terms which express its underlying fear of 'coming out of its crab-like shell': it is timid, self-absorbed, opinionated, acquisitive, pedestrian, driven by a fear of emotional vulnerability, moody, superficial, tending to live in the past, and so on. Like the other water signs, it may at times wish to withdraw completely from the material world. Cancer is ruled by the Moon, marks the exaltation of Jupiter, the detriment of Saturn and the fall of Mars. In addition to the special terms already mentioned, the sign Cancer is said to be Cardinal, Cold, Commanding, Crooked, Destructive, Feminine, Fruitful, Moist, Mute, Negative, Phlegmatic, Psychic, Sensitive, Unfortunate, Tropical and Weak. The powerful fixed stars associated with Cancer, which make its influence especially remarkable in the zodiacal series, are ALHENA, CANOPUS, CASTOR, DIRAH, POLLUX, PROCYON, PROPUS, SIRIUS, TEJAT and WASAT.

FIGURE 8.   THE IMAGE FOR CANCER, FROM THE "SAN MINIATO ZODIAC", AND THE CONSTELLATION FROM THE "MODERN ZODIAC" OF DELPORTE.

CANCER CONSTELLATION   Linked in name, if not in specific influence, with the zodiacal "Cancer", located as indicated in figure 8 . The image of the crab, which is pre-Grecian, is said to be that of the crab elevated to the

==

firmament by Juno for atttacking the heel of her enemy Hercules - however, see CANCER. Of particular interest to astrologers are the large number of powerful fixed stars in this constellation, and in the neighbouring Gemini, which appear to account for the erratic and eccentric genius which seems to flourish under the sign Cancer: see the Cancerian asterism stars in the list furnished for "Cancer", and FIXED STARS.

CANES VENATICI   Constellation, once linked with the neighbouring URSA MAJOR, is presented in the modern image (evolving circa 1690) of two greyhounds, Asterion and Chara (themselves asterisms), held in the rein of the constellation Bootes. Inevitably, it is linked by astrologers with a love for hunting, and it is said also to give a penetrating mind. The (double) star COR CAROLI is set in this asterism.

CANICULA   See SIRIUS.

CANIS   The 13th of the LUNAR MANSIONS in the medieval lists, 'the Dog' - probably identified by the fixed star VINDEMATRIX.

CANIS MAJOR   Constellation, approximately from 1 degree of Cancer to 1 degree of Leo, from 15 to 40 degrees south of the equator. This is the 'greater dog' distinguished from the 'lesser' of "Canis Minor". The fact that these two constellations have for centuries sandwiched the zodiacal Cancer has often been used to explain the love which the native of this sign exhibits for dogs (though in this connexion, see SIRIUS). The asterism was once simply called Canis, and was said to be the hound of Actaeon, though others gave it to Orion: there are however many names and legends attached to the asterism. Ptolemy likens the stars of the constellation (with the necessary exception of Sirius) to the nature of Venus, which makes it generally beneficial.

CANIS MINOR Constellation approximately 18 to 28 Cancer, from 1 to 10 north of the equator, the 'lesser dog', in early astrological texts called 'Procyon', along with derivatives of this Greek form meaning 'before the dog' - Prochion, Antecanis, Procanis, and so on. See however PROCYON in its modern use, for it is the influence of this fixed star which dominates the asterism.

CANOPUS Fixed star of 1st magnitude, the alpha of Argus, set originally in one of the rudders, but in later charts in one of the oars of the ship. The name is after the chief pilot of the fleet of Menelaos (at least in Greek sources), but in fact a variant name of almost similar sound (Kahi Nub) is from the Egyptian, and it is certain that some Egyptian temples were orientated towards the heliacal Canopus of the Autumnal equinox, and later (such as the Karnak temple) to its setting. To judge from the Arabian tradition, the conjunction of Canopus seems to identify the nature of any planet, and when culminating it brings glory, fame and wealth.

CAPELLA Fixed star of 1st magnitude, the alpha of constellation Auriga, set in the body of the goat, its name meaning 'little female goat'. Sometimes it is called Amalthea, after the nurse who reared Jupiter on goat's milk (see ASTROLOGICAL TAROT). In mediaeval charts and manuscripts it is called Alayodi (with variant spellings), derived from the Arabic. Ptolemy gives it the beneficial nature of Mercury conjunct Mars. See PORRIMA.

CAPILLARY DYNAMOLYSIS   A term introduced by Kolisko to denote the study of capillary action of plant saps in relation to the effects of planetary aspects. The litmus paper images made as an aid to this study are called "Morphochromatograms". See KOLISKO EFFECT.

CAPILLUS LEONIS Name meaning 'hair on the head of the Lion', given to the 11th of the LUNAR MANSIONS in mediaeval lists. Probably identified by the fixed stars Zosma and Coxa to the rear of the lion.

CAPRICORN   The tenth sign of the zodiac. It corresponds neither in location
nor extent with the constellation "Capricornus". The modern sigil for
Capricorn ♑ is said by some to be a drawing of the horns of the Goat,
with which the modern image is associated. However, Capricorn was never
properly a goat, but a goat-fish, as the Greek term "Aigokeros" itself
implied: the Babylonian prototype for the image was that of a goat with a
curled fish tail, to which the modern sigil clearly still refers - see the
mediaeval image in figure 9. Capricorn is of the Earth Element, and of the
Cardinal quality, the influence being practical, industrious, prudent,
persevering, diplomatic, cautious, methodical and ambitious. The nature of
Capricorn as it manifests in human beings is expressed in many keywords
attached to the sign by modern astrologers: dependable, concentrative,
trustworthy, efficient, just, industrious, honest, undemonstrative,
conservative, responsive, patient, systematic - in a word, all those
qualities which may be associated with an earth type working with integrity
to achieve some particular aim. In excess, or under pressure, the
Capricornian nature may be described in terms which express its underlying
need for security: secretive, fearful, miserly, unsympathetic, rigid,
suspicious, selfish, materialistic, brooding and egotistical. Like the other
earth signs, it is subject at times to deep melancholia. Capricorn is ruled
by the planet Saturn, marks the Exaltation of Mars, and the Fall of Jupiter.
In addition to the specialist terms already mentioned, Capricorn is
traditionally called Cardinal, Changeable, Cold, Crooked, Domestic, Earthy,
Egotistical, Feminine, Four-footed, Hoarse, Hurtful, Melancholic, Negative,
Nocturnal, Obeying, Southern, Tropical, Unfortunate, Violent and Wintery.

FIGURE 9.   IMAGE FOR CAPRICORN FROM THE "SAN MINIATO ZODIAC", AND THE
CONSTELLATION FROM THE "MODERN ZODIAC" OF DELPORTE.
- -

CAPRICORNUS   The constellation linked in name, if not in influence, with the
zodiacal "Capricorn", located as indicated in figure 9. In relation to its
image of Goat-fish, see CAPRICORN: the two images of Capricornus in figure
10 (on page 54) tell their own story - the first is Babylonian, the second,
12th century European - the fish in the mouth of the monster denoting Pisces
is a delightful zodiacal curiosity. The Greek myth connected with the naming
of the asterism tells that Pan, pursued by Typhon, escaped by leaping into
the Nile: his upper body turned into a goat, the lower part into a fish, and
in this guise he was taken into heaven by Jupiter - however, as the
CONSTELLATION NAMES entry indicates, the name is pre-Grecian. The most
powerful fixed stars in Capricornus to play a part in astrology are ALGIEDI,
ARMUS, BOS, CASTRA, DABIH, DORSUM and NASHIRA.

==

FIGURE 10.   IMAGES OF CAPRICORNUS FROM A 12TH CENTURY BC BABYLONIAN STELE
AND A 12TH CENTURY AD ASTROLOGICAL MANUSCRIPT (AFTER SAXL).

CAPULUS   A cluster of stars in the Perseus asterism, set in the sword hand
of the hero. It is said to cause blindness or defective eyesight.

CAPUT   A term from the Latin meaning 'head'. When so isolated, in most
astrological contexts it usually refers to 'Caput Draconis', the "Dragon's
Head". In a context of fixed stars, the isolated term may also refer to
"Algol", the Caput Algol.

CAPUT ALGOL   See ALGOL.

CAPUT ANDROMEDAE   See ALPHERATZ.

CAPUT CANIS VALIDI Name given to the 5th of the LUNAR MANSIONS in some
mediaeval lists, meaning (probably) 'the head of the mighty dog'. The
mansion was probably identified by the stars in the belt of Orion - for
example MINTAKA or HEKA.

CAPUT DRACONIS   See DRAGON'S HEAD.

CAPUT MEDUSA   See ALGOL.

CAPUT TAURI   Name given to the 3rd of the LUNAR MANSIONS in some mediaeval
lists, 'the head of Taurus' - probably located by the "Pleiades".

CARDINAL The cardinal signs are Aries, Cancer, Libra and Capricorn, and the
cardinal houses are their associates - the 1st, 4th, 7th and 10th, all so
named because they fall on the Cardinal "Angles", Aries to the East, Cancer
to the North, Libra to the West, and Capricorn to the South.

CARDINAL CROSS In traditional astrology, this is the cross formed in the
zodiac by Aries, Cancer, Libra and Capricorn (see CARDINAL). However, in
connexion with the esoteric system proposed by Bailey in her INTUITIONAL
ASTROLOGY, the cross is associated with the crisis of initiation, and with
the life of spirit and the Monad. Bailey calls it the 'Cross of
Transcendence', and traces in its sequence an evolutionary development.
Aries is the place where the initial idea to institute activity takes form:
it is the birthplace of ideas. What appears in Aries as spiritual energy
meets the soul stage of Cancer, and finds incarnation for the first time in
form. It reaches a point of equilibrium in Libra, in which soul and
personality achieve a balance of co-operation, so that in Capricorn the will
nature arrives at fulfilment, and a 'visioned goal' is reached. See also
FIXED CROSS and MUTABLE CROSS.

CARDINALITY   A term applied to one of the three "Qualities" (see FIXITY and
MUTABILITY) which acts as the mainspring of action, as the fount of energy.
The four Cardinal Signs (Aries, Cancer, Libra and Capricorn) are each in
their own way involved with initiating action, with making a movement into
the world: indeed, the alternative names for the Cardinal Quadruplicity all
suggest this idea - they are the Initiating Signs, the Leading Signs, the
Moving (or Movable) Signs. Sometimes, because they fall upon the angles of

the Macrocosmic Chart, they are called the Angular Signs.

CARDINAL QUADRUPLICITY   See CARDINALITY.

CASSIEL   The name given to the Archangel of Saturn. In certain occult
systems, Cassiel was the 'Angel of Solitude and Tears'. In the superficial
grimoire tradition he is as a demon with bat-wings, seated on a dragon.

CASSIOPEIA   Constellation, stretching from about 25 degrees Aries to the
beginning of Gemini, some 50 to 70 degrees north of the equator. The
asterism was called from very early times by this name (and variants), as
well as 'She of the Throne', sometimes 'Mulier Sedis' (the woman of the
chair), or even as 'Sedis'. Cassiopeia is supposed to have boasted that she
was more beautiful than the Nereids, and was bound in punishment to a chair,
condemned to circle the pole-star with head downwards, an eternal lesson in
humility. The astrological tradition insists that the constellation promotes
pride and boasting, and it was said by Ptolemy to exude a nature similar to
Venus with Saturn. The multiple fixed star ALPHERATZ (sometimes called
Schedar), ALMACH, MIRACH, and the nebula VERTEX (all set in the asterism) are
regarded by astrologers as powerful influences when prominent in a chart.

CASTILLO   One of the moons of Jupiter.

CASTING   The concept of 'casting a horoscope' is probably derived from the
Middle English verb 'to cast', relating to calculations made by means of
counters. Strictly speaking, the term should be limited to the procedure
preliminary to astrological interpretation, by which a horoscope figure is
drawn by means of calculations, usually derived from consultation of an
ephemeris. However, in modern use the term is employed to cover the entire
process of both drawing up a figure, and interpreting it. See COMPUTATION.

CASTOR   Fixed star (binary), the alpha of constellation Gemini, set in the
head of the mortal twin, sometimes called Eques or Apollo, along with related
variants. There is little agreement as to its intrinsic nature, though
Ptolemy likens its influence to that of Mercury, and it seems to threaten
blindness and wounds when rising.

CASTRA   Fixed star, the episilon of Capricorn, set in the belly of the goat:
an unfortunate influence.

CASUJOIAH   In certain forms of ceremonial magic, this is the name given to
the governor of zodiacal Capricorn.

CATABHISHAJ   The 28th of the Hindu, NAKSHATRS, 'Hundred Physicians'.

CATACLYSMIC PLANET   A name given to the planet URANUS.

CATAHIBAZON   See KATABABAZON.

CATHOLIC ASTROLOGY   A term derived from the Greek word used by Ptolemy
(katholike) to distinguish a form of astrology of the Genethliathic kind,
which deals with impersonal matters, such as the astrological influence which
affects all mankind, whole countries and races. See MUNDANE ASTROLOGY.

CAUDA   A term from the Latin for tail, which in most astrological contexts
refers to Cauda Draconis, the DRAGON'S TAIL. In a context of fixed stars,
the term sometimes refers to Cauda Ursae - see POLARIS.

CAUDA CAPRICORNI   See DENEB ALGEDI and FIFTEEN STARS.

CAUDA DRACONIS   See DRAGON'S TAIL.

CAUDA LEONIS   Name, 'tail of the Lion' given to the 12th of the LUNAR

==

MANSIONS in some mediaeval lists. Probably located by the fixed star
"Denebola".

CAUDA SCORPIONIS   Name, 'tail of the Scorpion', given to the 19th of the
LUNAR MANSIONS in some mediaeval lists. Probably identified by the stars
around "Shaula".

CAUDA URSAE   See FIFTEEN STARS and POLARIS.

CAZIMI   An Arabian name given to an extreme case of "Combustion", when a
planet is within 17 minutes of the Sun's longitude, and thus in conjunction
with the Sun. Authorities differ on how the cazimi is to be interpreted, but
in the tradition the placing was seen as strengthening for the planet.

CELAENO   See PLEIADES.

CELESTIAL ECLIPTIC   A term coined to distinguish the ecliptic proper, which
is the apparent path of the sun (see ECLIPTIC) from the path of the Moon's
orbit within the Ecliptic belt, which is really an orbit around the earth,
and hence called the Terrestrial Ecliptic.

CELESTIAL EQUATOR   The Great Circle of the Celestial Sphere, whose plane is
perpendicular to the axis of the Earth, is called the Celestial Equator.

CELESTIAL FIGURE   A synonym for "Chart". See also PLANISPHERE and FIGURE.

CELESTIAL HARMONICS   It has been maintained from the very earliest times
that there is a relationship between the planetary intervals, and even
between the planetary movements, and earthly music - an idea which may be
traced back to the Pythagorean concept of MUSIC OF THE SPHERES. The
developed form of the Pythagorean conception deeply influenced the esoteric
astrology of the Renaissance (mainly through the writings of Alberti and
Gafurus), especially in regard to the new awareness of the conversion of
ratios and harmonics based on planetary harmonics into spatial equivalents.
In an attempt to unify the esotericism of theology with the new materialism
of science, Kepler pointed to musical analogies in the ratios of aphelia and
periphelia, which he linked with a notion of the major scale, but his ideas
appear to have received scant understanding. In modern astrology, similar
analogies have been explored by the esotericist Collin, who claims to have
established an analogy between the tonic scale, and what he calls 'planetary
octaves', directly linked with certain multiples of planetary cycles and
groups of planetary cycles, whilst more recently Schmidt has linked musical
intervals with synodic periodicities. Some fields of modern music - for
example, certain compositions of the German Stockhausen - appear to be a
result of the search for basic cosmic harmonies linked with astrological and
esoteric notions. The earlier 'planetary music' of such composers as Holst
appear to have been more concerned with establishing soul-moods analogous to
the supposed natures of the planets, and therefore are not directly connected
with celestial harmonics, as such. Musical synthesizers are now being used
to explore the musical potential in the extrapolation and analogy-making
between mathematics and planetary motions.

CELESTIAL HIERARCHIES   The term is from the Greek compound of 'ieros'
(sacred), and 'archen' (rule), and refers as a whole to the chain of
spiritual beings which are visualised as ranged in descending order from the
realm of God to the world of man. They were given an official nomenclature
by Dionysius the Areopagite, who is said to have derived them from much
earlier sources. While this list of names and their symbolic attributes are
still used by occultists, esoteric astrologers and ecclesiastical writers,
there has been considerable elaboration on their functions since the early
days of Christianity. Each group has its distinctive function within the
spiritual realm, and since (according to the laws of sympathy) each spiritual
activity finds expression on the material realm, each group may be seen

manifest on the Earth. The schema, in accordance with the theory of
number-magic, is presented as three groups of three. In descending order of
power and responsibility, the First Hierarchy consists of the SERAPHIM, who
are directly involved with maintaining the relationship of the solar system
to the entire stellar universe, and who are often accorded rule over the
"Stellatum". Then follows the CHERUBIM, said by some authorities to be
responsible for ordering the planetary movements within the solar system, but
often accorded rule over the realm of the ZODIAC, as distinct from the fixed
stars. The Third of the First Hierarchy are the THRONES, said by some to
have rule over the realm of Time itself: esoterically, Time is regarded as
being operative only below the Sphere of Saturn, with which the Thrones are
associated - this probably explains the connexion in Greek mythology between
'Chronos' (Time) and Saturn. The Second Hierarchy consists of the DOMINIONS,
in Greek the Kyriotetes, who are said to be involved with the metamorphosis
of matter, and who are linked with the Sphere of Jupiter. Then follows the
DYNAMIS, sometimes called the Powers or Mights, who are directly charged with
rule over the Sphere of Mars. The third of the Second Hierarchy are the
POWERS, in Greek the Exsusiai, sometimes also called the the Elohim, who are
the creative beings who lend form and substance to the Earth itself, and who
have rule over the Sphere of the Sun. The Third Hierarchy consists of the
ARCHAI, sometimes called the Principalities, who have charge over the rise
and fall of the Epochs of civilisation, and the history of the world: these
beings have rule over the Sphere of Venus. Then follows the ARCHANGELS, who
have rule over individual nations of the Earth, and who are in charge of the
Sphere of Mercury. The last of the Third Hierarchy is the class of ANGELS,
who have charge over the lives of individual humans (according to the
esoteric lore, over one indiviudal from lifetime to lifetime): these are
linked with the Sphere of the Moon. At the bottom of the celestial chain is
the realm of man, which has been called the 'Tenth Hierarchy'. Below man are
the various infernal spheres of the demonic and purgatorial realms, which in
some systems are a mirror-image distortion of the celestial hierarchies:
fortunately, however, the demonic sphere plays little part in astrology. The
Celestial Hierarchies are sometimes called the 'Dionysian Hierarchies', even
in those cases where the lists do not perfectly tally with the sequence set
out by Dionysius. They are also called the 'Nine Orders'. In the present
century, following the indications of Steiner, Vreede (whilst adhering to the
traditional nomenclature and cosmic functions) has proposed a series of group
rulerships which departs from the standard, giving rule of pairs of
hierarchies over cosmic phenomena:

```
COMETS        Seraphim and Cherubim
FIXED STARS   Thrones and Spirits of Wisdom (Kyriotetes)
PLANETS       Spirits of Movement (Dynamis) and Spirits of Form (Exusiai)
MOON          Archai and Archangels
EARTH         Angels and Man
```

CELESTIAL HORIZON   The notional horizon derived from the spherical model of
our earth in relation to the CELESTIAL SPHERE, which is used in all "Tables
of Houses" as a basis for computation. The Celestial Horizon passes through
the centre of the earth. The 'Sensible Horizon' is parallel to the celestial
horizon, but passes through the eyes of the observer at any point on earth.

CELESTIAL LATITUDE   A term used in contradistinction to "Geographical
Latitude", in reference to the measurement of distance North or South of the
zodiacal circle or ecliptic. See also CELESTIAL LONGITUDE.

CELESTIAL LONGITUDE   A term used in contradistinction to "Geographical
Longitude", in reference to the measurement of distance along the zodiacal
circle, or ecliptic. By means of celestial longitude and celestial latitude,
it is possible to define the position of a stellar body in relation to the
ecliptic and hence in relation to both space and time.

CELESTIAL MERIDIAN   The Great Circle of the celestial spheres, which passes through the celestial poles and the zenith and nadir of a given place.

CELESTIAL POLES   The point where the celestial axis and the celestial sphere intersect.

CELESTIAL RIVER   See VIA LACTEA.

CELESTIAL SPHERE   An imaginary projection of the Earth, to include the visible heavens with a view to establishing a system of co-ordinates. The system of co-ordinates is designed to locate any point within this projected sphere in terms of the circumfeence of the periphery. Several such systems have been established, and are either directly or indirectly used in astrological computation: these include the ECLIPTIC SYSTEM, the EQUATORIAL SYSTEM, the HORIZONTAL SYSTEM and the VERTICAL SPHERE.

CELEUB   See PERSEUS.

CELL-SALTS   See TWELVE CELL-SALTS.

CENTAUR   Sometimes used as a popular name for zodiacal "Sagittarius", but also of CENTAURUS.

CENTAURUS   Constellation, approximately from 2 degrees Libra to 28 Scorpio, and from 28 to 68 degrees south of the equator (see also CENTAUR). The mythopoetic origin of the asterism is usually linked with the story of the centaur Chiron (after whom it is sometimes named), but it has many different designations, including Minotaur and Semi Vir (half-man). Ptolemy divides the nature of the asterism in regard to influences, and sees the human half as of the nature of Mercury conjunct Venus, and the animal part as Venus conjunct Jupiter: in general, the asterism inclines to vengeance and energy. A fixed star in the foot of the image is Rigil Kentaurus, which is sometimes shortened to 'Rigil', and hence confused with the RIGEL of Orion. For the fixed stars of importance in this asterism, see AGENA and RIGIL KENTAURUS.

CENTILOQUIUM   A series of 100 astrological aphorisms (plural 'centiloquia'), usually from the pen of one writer, but sometimes (as for example in the series attributed to Gadbury) collated from a variety of sources. The most important and influential collection, to which the term usually refers, is that wrongly attributed to Ptolemy, which in fact evinces a late mediaeval astrology quite foreign to him. The most widely known of the centiloquia in use up to the 19th century were those attributed to Hermes Trismegistus and Bethem, each of which was incorporated into the Pruckner edition of Firmicus.

CEPHEIS   See ANDROMEDA.

CEPHEUS   Constellation, approximately 17 degrees of Pisces, to the beginning of Cancer, and from 55 to 85 degrees north of equator. This asterism, named after a King of Ethiopia who figured among the Argonauts, is linked with the mythology of the adjacent constellations, Cassiopeia and Andromeda, who were his wife and daughter respectively. The asterism is regarded as exuding an influence akin to that of Jupiter with Saturn, inducing sobriety and a sense of authority, save when afflicted.

CEREBUS   A name given at one time to an asterism in HERCULES.

CERES   Name given to the first of the ASTEROIDS to be discovered by modern astronomers, in 1801. It lies in orbit between Mars and Jupiter, and has a diameter of about 490 miles. The name is derived from that of the Roman goddess of vegetation - but see also COSMIC PANTHEONS. The astrologer Dobyns associates the asteroid with the sign Virgo, along with a co-ruler "Vesta". Sometimes the constellation Virgo (and by extension, the sign Virgo) is called Ceres (more particularly 'Ceres spicifera dea' - see SPICA), as well as 'Demeter', which is the Greek equivalent goddess, whose mysteries were linked with the pre-Christian image of Virgo.

CETUS   Constellation, from about 17 degrees Pisces to 13 degrees Taurus, and 10 to 30 degrees south of the equator, the 'Whale' or 'Sea Monster' for which early pictures sometimes portray a sort of sea-dog, hence the 'Canis Tritonis', and a number of related names. In myth this asterism is the monster sent to devour Andromeda: it has an evil reputation among astrologers, and Ptolemy regards it as of an equivalent nature to Saturn. The three fixed stars within the asterism are also ill-disposed - see BATEN KAITOS, DIFDA and MENKAR.

CHAIN   In the Theosophical cosmoconception, a Chain is a series of seven "Globes". Each of the seven globes of a particular Chain may be regarded as having a definite and distinct existence in space and time, though not all globes in a particular chain are visible to ordinary sight. The Chain is properly called a "Planetary Chain", while seven successive chains are sometimes called the 'Incarnation of a Chain': see however GLOBE PERIOD.

CHAIN OF BEING   A name given to an ancient doctrine which postulates an unfaltering order of created things, ranging sequentially from the highest spiritual levels to the meanest inanimate objects on earth. The chain was visualised as a perfectly graduated hierarchy of beings, reflected in mediaeval astrology in the sophisticated theory of "Spheres", peopled by spiritual entities. This 'chain', stretching as it were from the Throne of God to the very centre of the Earth, admitted no breaks, and no chaos. Developed as a philosophical idea by Plato, added to by Aristotle, elaborated by the Neo-Platonists, this has become a stock image underlying most philosophies and cosmoconceptions, as Lovejoy has shown. Hell alone (because it had rebelled from the order of things) was disconnected from this chain, yet the vision of Dante, resting as it did upon the Redemptive thesis of theology, embraced even Hell in this chain. A symbolic model of this order, sometimes called the Annulus Platonicus, sometimes the 'Aurea Catena Homeri'('Golden Chain of Homer') was given various sigillic forms in astrological and alchemical symbolism.

CHAIN PERIOD   See GLOBE PERIOD.

CHALDEAN   From late Classical times, the word "Chaldean" has been synonymous with "astrologer", mainly because of the fame of the Mesopotamians as astronomers and astrologers: however, distinguish CHALEDEAN TERMS. Much of what is now called "Chaldean Astrology" is of the omnia kind, though it is clear from Diodorus of Sicily that the Chaldeans would cast personal horoscopes. Sachs dates the earliest known cuneiform horoscope to 410 BC, at which time a twelve-sign equal arc zodiac was in existence. It would seem that the mystery centres of the Babylonians originated the zodiac which was later amended by the Greeks to provide the names and designations with which we are now familiar - see ZODIAC and CONSTELLATION NAMES for ancient nomenclature. The names and rulerships of the planets are given in table 20.

```
----------------------------------------------------------------TABLE 20
```

PLANET	NAME	RULING SPIRIT (GOD)
MO		Sin
ME	Mustabarru	Nebu
VE	Kilbat	Ishtar
SU		Shamash
MA	Bibu	Nergal
JU	Dapinu	Marduk
SA	Kaimanu	Ninib

CHALDEAN ORDER   A name given in estoteric astrology for the septenary star, which is (wrongly) believed to have determined the days of the week. The

astrologer Libra sets out the order, ascribing a planet to each of the seven
points of the star, with the Sun at the top, as follows:

```
        SU
    VE      MA
  ME          JU      The sequence to be read:  SU MO MA ME JU VE SA
      MO  SA
```

The sequence of planets which emerges from following the inner structure of
the septenary star is, of course, different from the traditional order (which
follows the sequence of the spheres), yet it accounts for many
curious-seeming relationships established in the occult tradition - for
example, for the order of planetary rulerships given for the SECUNDADEIAN
BEINGS. The sequence does of course give rise to the order of the days of
the week, but this was not in fact determined by the Chaldean Order.

CHALDEAN TERMS   See PTOLEMAIC TERMS.

CHAMAEL A variant of "Camael", ruler of Mars.

CHAMAELEON   Constellation located close to the South Pole, formed in 1604.

CHANDRA   One of the Sanskrit names for the Moon, as used in Hindu astrology.
In this sytem, the nodes of the Moon are accorded a greater significance in
chart interpretation than in Western astrology: the ascending node is called
RAHU, the descending node KETU.

CHANGEABLE SIGNS   Six of the zodiacal signs have been traditionally
classified as 'changeable' because (it was claimed) they would change their
natures depending upon their positions in relation to the diurnal movement of
the earth. The six signs are Taurus, Gemini, Leo, Virgo, Sagittarius and
Capricorn - three sets of pairs. When eastern, Taurus was hot, Gemini and
Leo were hot and dry, Virgo was hot, Sagittarius was cold and moist, while
Capricorn was cold and dry. When western, Taurus was cold, Gemini was cold
and moist, Leo was hot and moist, Virgo cold and moist, Sagittarius hot and
dry, while Capricorn was cold and moist. The concept has little or no
application in modern astrology, and indeed the inner meanings of the pairs
of qualities has in any case been lost. See however QUALITY and PRIMORDIAL
QUALITIES. The same term 'Changeable Signs' is sometimes applied to the
signs of the Air Triplicity, which is said to promote the 'changeable'
qualities associated with the "Sanguine" temperament.

CHARA   See CANES VENATICI.

Saturn.   Signacula fiue characteres,   Demonij Saturni.
                 Intelligentiæ Saturni.

FIGURE 11. THE 'CHARACTERS' OF SATURN (AFTER AGRIPPA)

CHARACTERS A term used of certain symbols (sigils) used in astrological and
occult texts, especially so in those of late-mediaeval derivation. Many such
texts provide lists of characters which in form are usually different from
the traditional lists of sigils associated with planets and signs: in
practice, it is difficult to distinguish the two, save in so far as the
former are often vestigial drawings, while the latter are more usually quite
abstract in quality. The 3 sigils in figure 11 relate to the characters for
Saturn: the first sigil is derived from the corresponding "Magic Square" for

the planetary spirit of Saturn. Paracelsus defines the characters as being drawn from the highest stars and artificially assumed by the lower realm: such are therefore "Seals": such are often used in the manufacture of artificial Gamalai. It would appear that the characters were originally intended as receptacles of special VIRTUE or prophylactic value. In another context, Paracelsus writes of characters as being 'words', either spoken or written, which 'produce effects which Nature itself is not able to bring about, but only magical science'. Some of the planetary characters are derived from "Magical Squares" involved with occult number symbolism.

CHARIOTS   A synonym for the THRONES of the early Greek astrology.

CHART   A term synonymous for HOROSCOPE in the modern sense. It probably was once cognate with 'chart' in the sense of 'map', of Greek etymology. Certainly the late mediaeval astrologer often referred to the horoscope figure as a map, by which he meant 'map of the Heavens'. Many synonyms exist, such as FIGURE, HOROSCOPE, GENITURE, MIRROR OF HEAVEN, NATIVITY, SCHEMA, and so on. See also CHART SYSTEMS.

CHART SYSTEMS   All horoscope figures (horoscope charts), which combine the symbolic tabulation of planetary positions, ecliptic and house division into a single figure, are actually stereographic projections on to a flat surface. The choice of the matrix plane determines the kind of projection, and hence the symbolic nature of the chart - in some cases, the ecliptic is fixed, and in other cases the house system is fixed. The earliest (Greek) horoscope charts were usually circular, most often with the Ascendant ('horoscopos') to the left, with house cusps (in the equal house system) symbolically presented in such a way as to mark 'equal' divisions against the ecliptic. This system, albeit in a more sophisticated guise, is still used in connexion with the "Equal House System", as in figure 12A. By the time the Arabian-influenced Hellenistic astrological methods reached Europe (along with sophisticated methods of HOUSE DIVISIONS unknown to the Greeks) two different forms of charting were in general use - the circular method, and a form which has been called the "Quadrated Circle" - figures 12B and 12C - in one or two variants. The equal-division house system of both circular and quadrated charts presupposed that the ecliptic may be symbolically accommodated to a fixed system of houses, in the sequence set out in figure 12. The two quadrated forms have been called the 'decussata' and the 'Greek Cross Chart', for reasons which are clear from their construction.

FIGURE 12. A: STANDARD CIRCULAR CHART. B: DECUSSATA CHART. C: GREEK CROSS CHART.

In later methods, especially so in the 18th century, the compartmental symbolism was adapted to form a 'cross' from simple 'vesicae piscis', as in figure 13A, and in copperplate engravings, such as those given by Sibly, the central areas were often elaborately engraved with portraits (frequently

quite fanciful) of the native. There does not appeared to have been a
distinctive terminology to designate the different early systems - perhaps
the terms 'quadrated', 'circular' and 'vesican' might usefully be adopted.

FIGURE 13.   A: VESICAN CHART.   B: FIXED ECLIPTIC SYSTEM.

The use of the fixed ecliptic system of charting, for which the base is
represented in figure 13B, came into existence towards the end of the 19th
century, and postulated a fixed ecliptic system, into which houses might be
adapted in various degrees of arc.

FIGURE 14.   A: CONTINENTAL CHART SYSTEM.   B.   DATA FROM CONTINENTAL CHART
TRANSLATED INTO STANDARD CIRCULAR CHART FOR EASE OF READING.

This has floriated into many different systems, of which figure 14A is an
example from a 'Continental Method' used in France, in which the vernal point
is placed to the left of the circle, and the houses inserted accordingly:
the analysis in figure 14B presents the same data in a more conventional
circular chart, for ease of reading.

FIGURE 15.   A: CONTINENTAL VARIATION, HOUSE CUSPS MARKED INTO FIXED
ECLIPTIC CIRCLE.   B: CONTINENTAL METHOD TRANSLATED INTO STANDARD 'EQUAL
HOUSE' CHARTING, FOR COMPARISON.

Figure 15A is a variant of this Continental chart, the house cusps being marked to the fixed ecliptic, and thus appearing on the chart in unequal divisions, but with the Ascendant to the left. The same data is presented in figure 15B, but with equal-arc houses: one observes that the 10th house cusp (at 90 degrees to the Ascendant) does not correspond to the Medium Coeli (MC), which is inserted separately.   These are merely examples of the more frequently encountered methods of conventional charting.

FIGURE 16 - THREE DIMENSIONAL CONVERSION CHART (AFTER HIEROZ)

Many complex (and indeed unconventional) methods of charting have been developed in modern times, as the grasp on the traditional forms of astrology has been weakened. Under the impress to establish novel or 'original' methods of astrological symbolizing, such modern forms as the 'three-dimensional conversion chart' (figure 16) have been published, this one influencing the so-called "Three Dimensional Chart" of Blunsdon.

FIGURE 17. CHOISNARD CHART FOR GUSTAV ADOLPHUS, BORN STOCKHOLM 18TH DECEMBER, 1594 (O.S.).

The "Cosmogram" of Ebertin (figure 24) is a complex figure which combines certain traditional notions with a 90 degree circle designed to facilitate transfer of mid-points to the conversion of a Cosmic Picture, which is itself not a chart at all, but a diagram of a supposed planetary relationships. The "Choisnard Chart" of figure 17, which is similar in form to several variant Continental chart systems, is convention itself in comparison with the cosmopyschogram of figure 25, which for all that it accommodates in its rays astrologically based data, may scarcely be considered a chart in the ordinary sense at all. Many other systems of charting have been developed in modern astrological circles, including those relating to heliocentric astrology, of which the "Asterogram" of Sucher is an example, in figure 4. Usually, the systems are designed to present in a clear form the inter-relation of the three tabulations of ecliptic, house division, and planetary positions, so that there is generally little difficulty in converting one chart system to another. An example of a simple standard form of charting is given in figure 18, which is the astrologer Libra's "Inceptional Chart" for the ill-fated 'Titanic' - this however relates more to a type of astrology than to a method of charting.

FIGURE 18. INCEPTIONAL CHART FOR THE LAUNCHING OF THE 'TITANIC', 31ST MAY, 1911 (AFTER LIBRA).

See also EPOCHAL CHART, EQUATORIAL CHART, HARMONIC CHART, HELIOCENTRIC CHART, HORIZON CHART, JOHNDRO LOCALITY CHART, MUNDOSCOPE, POLAR CHART, PRIME VERTICAL CHART and ZENITH SYSTEM.

CHARUBEL SYMBOLS   Name given to a series of symbolic readings ascribed to the 360 degrees of the zodiac, derived by the astrologer 'Charubel' using clairvoyant means, and first published in 1898. See DEGREE SYMBOLS.

CHASING THE MOON   See HUNTING THE MOON.

CHELAE   The word is the Latin for 'claws', and in modern astrology usually reference to the "Claws" of constellation "Scorpius". In Ptolemaic astrology, the word was sometimes used of constellation Libra, which was not always distinguished from the adjacent Scorpius.

CHELUB   See PERSEUS.

CHERUB   In astrology, always a reference to the "Cherubim".

CHERUBIM   A term of uncertain Hebraic etymology (but see CHERUB) used to denote the second rank of the Celestial Hierarchies, immediately below the rank of Seraphim. The singular cherub is frequently misused in modern times, for the word should be applied in an astrological sense only to this exalted rank of spiritual beings. Cherubim are often depicted in Christian and occult iconography as having four faces, but traditions vary enormously as to their natures. The occult tradition links them with the fixed signs of the zodiac, and they are accordingly portrayed as the "Tetramorphs" or as variously combined elements of Lion, Eagle, Bull and Human. In her analysis of the esoteric background to this hierarchy, Blavatsky points out that the word 'cherub' originally meant 'serpent' and was linked with the idea of the 'serpent of eternity'. The Hebraic characters for the word are derived from an image of a 'serpent in a circle'. Such ideas are in perfect accord with the traditional association of these beings with the circle of the Zodiac. Steiner, who refers to them as 'Lords of Harmony', says that their prime function is that of controlling the relationships between the planets without our solar system. The mediaeval 'cherubin' sometimes survives in astrological contexts, but this term belongs to a period when the true nature of the Hebraic plural was misunderstood.

CHINESE CALENDAR   The Chinese system of time measurement is lunisolar, involving intercalation. The year begins with the New Moon following the entry of the Sun into Aquarius. This solar period is divided into 12 months (with an adjustment of an intercalary month every 30 months). Since the calendar began in a year equivalent to our own 2697BC, the Chinese 4682 is the equivalent of our Gregorian 1985. Little of the Chinese system has penetrated into European astrology: the ordinary and literary names for the months are complex, as are the names and affinities for the ten celestial stems, with the corresponding five "Chinese Elements". To some extent, the names of the 28 lunar mansions (called "Sieu"), and their corresponding elements and animals, along with the twelve branches and the associated symbolic animals (see CHINESE SYMBOLIC ANIMALS) have penetrated into European astrological lore in a misunderstood and superficial form. The so-called 'twelve branches' of the Chinese system, linked with the zodiac, combine with the 'ten stems' to establish a sixty-year cycle, which is the basis of the Chinese chronology.

CHINESE ELEMENTS   The Chinese distinguish five elements which, through a rich system of associations, permeate their astrological and calendrical systems. The exoteric names translate as meaning Wood, Fire, Earth, Metal and Water, but the associations and correspondences established into the microcosm and macrocosm indicate that (as indeed with the European four elements) these names denote secret principles, rather than materialities. Important to the system are the links between the elements, the planets and the binaries (Yang and Yin), as set out in table 21.

```
                                                              TABLE 21
```

ELEMENT	BINARY: YANG	- YIN	PLANET	(MEANING)
Wood	Fir	Bamboo	Jupiter	Wood Star
Fire	Burning Wood	Lamp flame	Mars	Fire Star
Earth	Hill	Plain	Saturn	Earth Star
Metal	Weapon	Kettle	Venus	Metal Star
Water	Waves	Brook	Mercury	Water Planet

CHINESE PLANETS   See Table 21 above.

CHINESE SYMBOLIC ANIMALS   The rich system of associations of the Chinese 'twelve branches' (linked with the zodiac) has penetrated popular astrological lore in Europe mainly through the names of the associated symbolic animals in their so-called 'years' which have been misunderstood by popular western astrologers, who have confused the branches with the months and with the zodiacal equivalents. Mathews gives for the Twelve Branches the equivalent poetic names, the related 'hours' and directions, as well as the correspondences of table 22.

```
                                                              TABLE 22
```

SYMBOLIC ANIMAL	ZODIACAL SIGN	SYMBOLIC ANIMAL	ZODIACAL SIGN
Rat	Aries	Horse	Libra
Ox	Taurus	Sheep	Scorpio
Tiger	Gemini	Monkey	Sagittarius
Hare (Cat)*	Cancer	Cock	Capricorn
Dragon	Leo	Dog	Aquarius
Snake	Virgo	Boar (Pig)*	Pisces

The animals in brackets with asterisk are modern European names. It is quite erroneous to confuse the 'annual readings' - which are actually designations of the 60-year cycle of the "Chinese Calendar" - with the personality readings associated with the symbolic animals. The annual designations begin with Rat (the 'year of the Rat') allocated to a particular year, combining the so-called 'ten stems' (in the cycle 1924-1984 - 'Chia') with the so-called 'twelve branches' (in the cycle 1924-1984 - 'Tzu'), to engineer a cycle of 60 years. Popular western astrology has simplified the cycle to draw attention to the 12 branches (and thus establish an accord with the zodiacal twelve) - however, there is a vast difference between the Chinese 'wooden Rat' of 1984 and the 'metal Rat' of 1992 which is missed in popular systems of interpretation, as attempted by Brau.

CHOISNARD CHART   A method of charting horoscopic data, attributed to the modern French astrologer Choisnard (though perhaps used earlier by others). Figure 17 (page 63) is an example of such a chart: the data is not inserted into a chart system which visualises the houses to be of equal extent in the symbolic projection, but adjusts the houses to fit the ecliptic, which is itself set out as a framework of 60 x 5 degree arcs (the old "Faces"), into which the planets and house cusps are inserted. The first point of Aries is always presented on the left of the figure, so that the Ascendant may be anywhere in the circle. This method of charting has gained some popularity on the Continent, but is used only rarely in England and the United States. Unfortunately, the same term (Choisnard Chart) has been applied to a system of projecting the heavens (attributed also to Choisnard) which permits a horoscope to be erected when the time of birth is not known, in which the vernal point is on the symbolic Ascendant (the actual Ascendant being unknown). It has been called the 'vernal horoscope'. See also CHART SYSTEMS.

CHOLERIC   Term applied to the "Temperament" linked with the element of Fire.

CHOLERIC QUADRANT   See QUADRANTS.

CHOLORIC   See QUADRANTS.

CHORI ANGELI   A Latin equivalent for CELESTIAL HIERARCHIES, from which the modern 'Choir of Angels' is derived.

CHOROGRAPHY   A term used by Bouche-Leclercq in connexion with the various attempts to relate geographic areas to planetary and sign influences. From the days of Ptolemy (and presumably earlier, since Ptolemy was a reporter of astrological lore) lists of planetary and zodiacal rulerships over places - first as geographic areas, later as cities and towns - were established within the astrological tradition. The 'Chorographics' of Ptolemy actually derived from the systematic application of the 'trigons' and their rulerships (in what is now an archaic concept) to the quadrants, corresponding to the longitudinal limits of the ancient "Climata". This system has all too frequently been repeated in other textbooks in a much simplified form, divorced from its original implications: many of the localities now have different names, and many of the geographic borders differ from those drawn up in Roman times, yet even so the lists of 'rulerships' are still issued in all seriousness. Other systems, derived from sources which must have been contemporaneous with Ptolemy, present quite different chorographic relationships. It is simply not possible to present a digest of all these systems, but the comparative lists in table 23 present a synoptical view of the subject (which is, in fact, exceedingly complex): such a comparative study, resting upon the material published by Bouche-Leclercq, reveals the early conflicts and contrasts which are so often ignored in modern lists (Dorotheus of Sidon, Alexandrian Paul) - the representative modern is Hall. Table 23 is designed to shown 'additions' rather than the full lists (most of the authorities correspond in several cases), while those areas which are largely meaningless to the modern mind, or which are merely historical references, have been excluded.

| | | | | | ----TABLE 23 |
SIGN	PTOLEMY	MANILIUS	DOROTHEUS	ALEX'D.	HALL
AR	Britain Gaul Germany Judaea	Egypt Hellespont Persia	Arabia Babylon	Persia	England Burgundy Japan

TABLE 23 (CONTINUED)

SIGN	PTOLEMY	MANILIUS	DOROTHEUS	ALEX'D.	HALL
TA	Asia Minor Cyclades (Cyprus, Persia)	Arabia Scythia	Egypt Media	Babylon	Greek archipelago
GE	Armenia Lower Egypt	Pontus	Cappadocia Phoenicia		Africa NE coast Wales
CN	Africa Colchis Numidia	Ethiopia India	Thrace	Armenia	Mauritius Paraguay
LE	Apulia Chaldea Gaul Italy (Phoenicia, Sicily)	Armenia Bythnia Cappadocia Macedonia		Asia	Roumania
VG	Achaia Assyria Babylon (Crete, Hellas, Mesopotamia)	Arcardy Ionia Rhodes	Cyclades Peloponnese		Brazil Crete West Indies
LB	Bactria	Italy	Cyrene	Libya	Argentina Burma North China
SC	Cappadocia Mauritania	Libya (Islands of the Mediterranean)	Sicily	Italy	Transvaal
SG	Arabia Felix Spain	Crete Sicily	Gaul	Cilicia	Australia Madagascar
CP	Illyria India (Macedonia, Thrace)	Germany Spain		Syria	Afghanistan Albania Greece
AQ	Arabia Mid Ethiopia	Lower Egypt Phoenicia		Egypt	
PI	Celicia Lydia	Chaldea Mesopotamia Red Sea		India	

The entry for Gaul under Ptolemy is perhaps 'Cisalpine Gaul', for the Gaul of Aries is certainly well ascribed. The 17th century Lucca manuscript gives Switzerland to Taurus, France to Cancer, Boehemia to Leo, Greece to Virgo, Austria to Libra, Scotland to Scorpio and Portugal to Pisces: it is more usual to ascribe Scotland to Cancer, and Ireland to Taurus. The majority of mediaeval lists of chorographies were derived from Ptolemy, but under the Arabian impulse introduced cities and towns derived from somewhat complex and unsystematic considerations - such as local dedications to gods, and "Foundation Charts". For example, the city of Florence appears to have taken its chorographic designation from the earlier rulership of the god Mars, derived ultimately from the days when the city was little more than a Roman barracks. It is likely that the designation for Rome (Leo) is related to the famous foundation chart for the city. In addition to incorporating Ptolemaic material, modern lists tend to incorporate cities and towns derived from foundation charts and ancient traditions. Most modern lists are usually indiscriminate copies of earlier ones: it is significant that as late as 1959 Hall is still ascribing 'White Russia' to Taurus, following the more reasonable ascription of the astrologer Leo, made in the 2nd decade of our century. The rulership of the United States of America, and certain of the cities, have been hotly contested for some years: at least 9 different versions for the USA are known to exist (several related to foundation charts), though the most frequently quoted is that given by Sibly, cast for the Declaration of Independence. It must be emphasised that there are many variant chorographies available, and little agreement exists among authorities either as to extant chorographies, or regarding the rules for establishing these. The general rule appears to be linked with catching what can only be called the 'feeling' of a place, which is almost certainly linked either with the zodiacal or planetary force, or even with the Archangelic ruler. In view of the actual origin of the Ptolemaic chorography, the present author has been surprised to discover much of it to be reasonably accurate: from personal experience he would confirm most of the early Ptolemaic system, with the exceptions of Gaul (hence France) which he would place under Virgo; he would place the Cyclades under Leo, and would lump together the two Egypts of the ancients under Capricorn (while admitting that the Egypt familiar to Ptolemy was no doubt very different from the modern Arabized country). Table 24 sets out a few of the city rulerships - an unpublished list from Lucca, of the 17th century, a list from the 19th century astrologer Alan Leo, and the modern Devore, who relies to some extent on Leo yet includes a useful summary of associations drawn up for American cities, recognising the while that the rulership is 'not always unanimous'.

```
---------------------------------------------------------------------TABLE 24
SIGN   LUCCA            LEO                              DEVORE
=============================================================================
AR     Faenza           Capua, Cracow, Leicester,
       Florence         Marseilles, Padua, Saragossa,
       Naples           Utretcht
TA     Bologna          Dublin, Leipzig, Mantua,         New York (SU)
       Capua            Palermo, Parma                   St. Louis (AS)
       (Pistoia, Siena, Verona)
GE     Paris            Cordova, London, Louvain,
       Trent            Mentz, Nuremburg,
       Turin            Versailles
CN     Lucca            Amsterdam, Berne, Cadiz,         New York (AS)
       Venice           Constantinople, Genoa, Lubeck    Philadelphia (SU)
       Vicenza          Milan, New York, Tunis, York
LE     Cremona          Bath, Bristol, Damascus,         Chicago (SU)
       Prague           Philadelphia, Portsmouth         Detroit
       Ravenna          Taunton                          Miami (SU)
       Rome
VG     Arezzo           Basle, Baghdad, Cheltenham,      Los Angeles (SU)
       Benvenuto        Corinth, Heidelburg, Jerusalem,  Philadelphia (AS)
       Como,            Lyons, Padua, Paris,             Washington DC.
       Ferrara          Reading
       (Navaro, Tarento, Toledo)
LB     Parma            Antwerp, Charlestown,            Chicago (AS)
       Pesaro           Frankfort, Fribourg, Lisbon,     Los Angeles (AS)
       Piacenza         Vienna                           Miami (AS)
       Siena
SC     Aquila           Fez, Frankfort (oder), Ghent,    Baltimore (AS)
       Civitavecchia    Liverpool,                       Cleveland (AS)
       Cremona          Messina                          San Francisco
       (Genoa, Padua, Rimini)                            Washington (AS)
SG     Buda             Avignon, Cologne,                Toledo (USA) (AS)
       Asti             Narbonne, Naples
CP     (Modena, Prato, Romandola)                        Boston (USA) (AS)
AQ                      Bremen, Hamburg, Ingoldstadt,    St. Louis (SU)
PI     Alessandria      Alexandria, Compostela,          Cleveland (SU)
       Ratisbon         Ratisbon, Seville, Worms
-----------------------------------------------------------------------------
```

CHRISTIAN ZODIAC   See BIBLICAL ASTROLOGY, COSMIC PANTHEONS and SAN MINIATO ZODIAC.

CHROMATIC CHART   See ZODIACAL COLOURS.

CHRONOCRATORS   In general, the term means 'rulers of time', but in specific application it is used of Jupiter and Saturn. Through the interactions of their cycles, these planets create successive conjunctions of a 20 year periodicity in signs of the same element. The "Grand Climactic" of the chronocrators marks an epoch, a complete cycle through all the triplicities of these cycles. In connexion with this important Grand Climactic, the two planets are sometimes called the Great or Grand Chronocrators. Each of the 20 year conjunctions are called 'minims' or 'specialis', the 200 year 'elemental' cycle is called 'media' or 'trigonalis', and the complete Grand Climactic of 800 years is called the 'maxima' or 'climacteria'. The same term (chronocrators) is unfortunately confusingly applied to all the traditional planets in their capacity of 'markers of time' in relation to individual human life. Systems vary (see SEVEN AGES for example), but in general tradition has it that the planets govern the life periodicities as set out in table 25.

```
-----------------------------------------------------------------TABLE 25
   MO    First 4 years of life    (in 4 year periodicity)
   ME    From 4 to 14 years       (in 10 year periodicity)
   VE    From 14 to 22 years      (in 8 year periodicity)
   SU    From 22 to 41 years      (in 19 year periodicity)
   MA    From 41 to 56 years      (in 15 year periodicity)
   JU    From 56 to 69 years      (in 12 year periodicity)
   SA    From 68 to 98 years      (in 30 year periodicity)
--------------------------------------------------------------------------
```

One of the so-called 'modern planets', Uranus, was accorded rule over the next years of life, to a cycle of 90 years. Quite unaccountable, however, is the establishing of an extrauranian cycle of 184 years, allotted to Neptune, which would bring the 'terminus vitae' to about 372 years! See CYCLES.

CHRONOS   In astrological contexts an archaic reference to Saturn.

CHRONOS AGERAOS   A name applied to the primal "Tetramorph" which united the four fixed signs of the zodiac: see ZERVAN AKARANA.

CINGULA ORIONIS   Literally, "Orion's Belt" in Latin, and usually a reference to the two powerful fixed stars in this belt - MINTAKA and ALNILAM.

CINGULUM   See MIRACH.

CIRCINUS   Constellation originated in 1752, the 'Compasses'. Astrologers say that it gives a revengeful and violent nature, but there are no powerful fixed star influences on record.

CIRCLE OF PETOSIRIS   Name applied to an ancient (certainly Hellenistic in origin) system of prognostication by simple numerology, often linked with the name of the querent - see ONOMANTIC ASTROLOGY.

CIRCLE OF POSITION   An obsolete term originally used of a system for determining the position of a fixed star by means of a circle visualized as intersecting the horizon, and passing through the star as one co-ordinate, with another circle passing through the meridian and that star as a second co-ordinate.

CIRCULAR CHART   See CHART SYSTEMS and CIRCULAR FIGURE.

CIRCULAR FIGURE   A term proposed to distinguish the various circular horoscope CHARTS (based on either equal-arc twelve-fold divisions, or on unequal-arc twelve-fold divisions, to represent the 12 houses in relation to the signs) from the "Quadrated Figure". The circular figure may also be called the Circular Chart.

CIRCUMPOLAR   Those stars which never set are called circumpolar.

CIRCUMPOLAR CONSTELLATIONS   The asterisms which, from a given point on the
Earth, do not go below the visible horizon at any time of the year. Some
constellations which are circumpolar for part of the year will 'dip' part of
their asterism below the horizon, and are not strictly circumpolar.

CITIES   For a survey of the zodiacal rule accorded cities, see CHOROGRAPHY.

CITRA   The 12th of the Hindu NAKSHATRAS, 'bright'. The same Sanskrit term
is used to designate the constellation Libra - but see also TULA.

CIVIL DAY This day-length is computed to begin at midnight, 180 degrees East
or West of Greenwich, continuing its periodicities of one hour with every 15
degrees of arc passage of the Sun. See TIME.

CLAWS   See CHELAE.

CLIMA   An obsolete term (Greek plural 'climata'), derived probably from
Hipparchus, and applied to a zone of latitude, fixed according to the ancient
principle by the maximum length of day, translated into distance. The first
of the climata does not begin at the equator, where the day is said to be
always of 12-hour duration: it begins approximately 12 and three-quarter
hours from the equator, and extends northwards to a boundary of 13 and a
quarter hours (approximating to our 13 and 21 degrees of latitude). There
were SEVEN CLIMATA, each of different mean time periods, each of different
distances. The relevance of the term is mainly historical, since the system
was based on geographic and geodesic assumptions which are now known to have
been inaccurate. They were however widely used in .ancient astrological
systems. The climata might be projected into a Celestial Sphere, as the
images of Dante make clear. However, the use of climata in connexion with
the longest daylight for a given area, as a base for astrological
computation, resulted in the climata being associated with rising times of
the ecliptic. The Roman astrologer Vettius Valens defined the climata in
terms of rising times, and the various sets of tables for the climata used by
earlier astrologers for computations linked the clima with rising times
sequential to the longest daylight. A system of "Seven Climata" was derived
from both the Babylonian SYSTEM A and SYSTEM B, though it was the latter,
with its ayanamsa of 8 degrees, which was most widely used by Hellenistic
astrologers. Ptolemy, in the Almagest, gives rising times for 11 zones,
between the longest daylights of 12 and 17 hours, and in relation to the
seven climata derived a series of astrological tabulations to which was added
an interpolation for Byzantium. Neugebauer records useful computations for
the main systems. In regard to mediaeval astrology, perhaps the most
influential tables of climata were those issued by the Arabian astrologer
Alfraganus, which formed the basis of measurement in Dante's 'Divina
Commedia': these were derived from the Hellenistic seven climata, converted
into widths in miles of the supposed inhabited area of the earth, on the
basis of 56 and two third miles being equal to one degree, which naturally
leads to a serious underestimation of dimensions in the table.

CLIMACTERIA   A term used for the 'Grand Climactic' of the 800 year cycle of
the CHRONOCRATORS. Distinguish CLIMACTERICS.

CLIMACTERIC CONJUNCTION   A term used of the conjunction of the two planets
Jupiter and Saturn, the CHRONOCRATORS.

CLIMACTERICS   From ancient times it has been believed that certain years in
the course of life are more liable to danger and/or change than others. The
most important of the climacterics are the septenary years - 7, 14, 21, 28,
etc. which are associated with lunar periodicities in the progressed chart,
and which have been linked by such esotericists as Blavatsky and Steiner with
the soul's growth. Esoterically, the full spiritual incarnation of the human
does not take place until the fourth septenary (28), and some esoteric
astrologers insist that properly speaking this is the beginning of life:

certainly, this is one of the most important of the Climacterics. The
important climacteric associated with Saturn usually falls in the 30th and
60th year, when the planet transits its natal point in a chart (just over 29
years) - but see also CHRONOCRATORS. The climacteric period associated with
the Moon's Node falls on (approximately) 18 years and 2 months, and 36 years
and 4 months: see LUNAR NODE CYCLE. Individual climacterics may only be
accurately determined from the personal chart, of course. The so-called
"historical climacterics", which have been linked with both PRECESSION and
the Archangelic Periods (see SECUNDADEIAN BEINGS) are really concerned with
the sequences of periodicities, rather than with the key-year at the
beginning of such a period. For example, in terms of the Archangelic
Periods, the years 1881 (and 1882) have been given as the Climacterics for
the beginning of the Michaelic Age in which we now live - but such a year is
not strictly speaking in itself a year of peril or of change: it merely
dates the beginning of a new era. So also with the periods of transition
which mark the progression from one Age to another, in terms of Precession.

CLIMATA   See CLIMA and SEVEN CLIMATA.

CLOCK TIME   See TIME.

CO-ASCENDANT   A term proposed as applying to the Ascendant of the so-called
"Co-latitude" of the place of birth. As Dean says, somewhat ominously, of
this and the related "Co-vertex", 'very little is known about them'.

COELI CINGULUM   See VIA LACTEA.

COELUS   A name given by the esoteric astrologer Thierens to a future
development of the planet "Uranus" in his ASTRAL SPHERES. It is said to
represent the principle of emanation.

COGNITIVE CORRESPONDENCES   While a number of variant lists of planetary
associations with the cognitive faculties of man have been preserved in the
astrological tradition, the generally agreed (if simplicitic) series are:

   ME: Sight   VE: Touch   MA: Taste   JU: Smell   SA: Hearing

Steiner introduced an entirely new list of cognitive correspondences which
are linked not with the traditional 'seven senses', but with 'twelve senses',
which are associated with the corresponding signs, set out in table 26.

```
-----------------------------------------------------------------TABLE 26
SIGN    SENSE          SIGN    SENSE                SIGN    SENSE
========================================================================
AR      Speech         LE      Life                 SG      Taste
TA      Thought        VG      Movement             CP      Sight
GE      Ego            LB      Balance              AQ      Warmth
CN      Touch          SC      Smell                PI      Hearing
------------------------------------------------------------------------
```

CO-LATITUDE   The co-latitude of a place is the complement of its latitude,
obtained by subtracting this latter from 90 degrees.

COLD   See FOUR QUALITIES and PRINCIPLES.

COLD PLANET   Saturn is sometimes called the 'cold planet': the Moon is
frequently wrongly called 'cold', whereas it is in fact made 'hot' or 'cold'
only in terms of the aspects received. See FOUR QUALITIES and PRINCIPLES.

COLEY TABLE   See ASTRO-DIAGNOSIS.

COLUMBA   Constellation, from about 5 degrees Gemini to 17 degrees Cancer,
and from 27 to 43 degrees south of equator. First noted by Bayer in 1603,

===

it was originally 'Columba Noae' (Noah's Dove), and probably because of its proximity to "Argo", sometimes called the Ark.   Astrologers grant the asterism a gentle nature, and its alpha "Phact" is also well-disposed.

COLURES   Name given to two great circles projected into the Celestial Sphere, cutting the equator at right angles, passing through the poles, one of which cuts the two equinoctial points (called the 'equinoctial colure'), the other of which cuts the solstitial points (the 'solstitial colure').

COMA BERENICES   Constellation, approximately 17 degrees Virgo to 12 degrees Libra, and 25 to 31 degrees north of the equator, with a somewhat chequered history as an asterism.   Recognized by Eratosthenes as 'Ariadne's Hair', and for centuries merged with the constellations Leo or Virgo, it was finally catalogued by Tycho in 1602 under the modern name.   The hair itself was said to have been that of the wife of Ptolemy Euergetes, a stolen sacrificial gift.   The asterism has many different names.   It is accorded a beneficial influence, which tends towards dissipation.

COMBUST   When a planet is conjunct the Sun, within an orb of 5 degrees, it is said to be 'burned' by the Sun, and is termed 'combust' or said to be 'in combustion'.   Some authorities claim that the planet in question is weakened by this combustion, but a study of Mercury (frequently combust, as one of the inner planets) would suggest otherwise.   See also CAZIMI.

COMETS   Luminous bodies, with long tails, in orbit around the Sun.   Comets are highly eccentric (at perihelion perhaps only half a million miles away from the Sun, but at aphelion hundreds of thousands of miles beyond even Pluto), and inclined to the ecliptic in almost any angle up to 90 degrees. The shortest known revolution for a comet is just over 3 years, the longest being measured in terms of centuries.   Halley's Comet returns in 75 year periods.   The term is derived from the characteristic 'tail' (from the Greek 'kome', hair, relating to the nebulous dust of the tail) the entire phenomenon of head and tail being the 'kometes', or 'hairy star'.   The tails may extend over vast distances: Halley's of 1910, for example, spanned an arc of over 150 degrees, its length being 28 million miles.   In astrological literature comets have generally acquired a bad reputation, and the earliest classifications of Ptolemy were on the level of omina texts.   In mediaeval astrology in particular the comets took on considerable importance, though generally as presage of evil and change: the appearance of the comet, its position in the zodiac (first appearance), its relation to the ecliptic belt, and other factors, were the determinants of interpretation, and few major comets have failed to make their own special reputations in literature. The comet of 1066, enshrined as detail in the Bayeux Tapestry may have meant the death of Harold, and the momentous theft of England, but seen from the point of view of the Normans it was clearly a 'good thing' - 'a comet like this is only seen when a kingdom wants a king', William is supposed to have remarked to his courtiers.   Usually, however, the presage is evil: the doom of the entire Christian world (at the hands of the Turks) was expected of the 1456 Halley.   The comet of 1528 was 'so horrible and dreadful, and engendered such terrors in the minds of men, that they died from fear alone...'   Typical of the more sane astrological literature, is that of Pearce: the great comet of 1881 was 'first seen in RA 74 45, which is the line of the 16 degrees of Gemini which had rule over Egypt - the war in Egypt (1885) and in the Sudan (1883 etc.) 'quickly followed'.   Pearce records that the astrologer Zadkiel foretold the Italian war of 1959 from the appearance of Donatti's Comet of the preceding year.   Most of the predictions are of the Mundane Astrological type, and the truth is that comets appear to play little part in Natal Astrology - however, it has been claimed that the transit of a comet over a natal point is significant.   Even modern astrological references to comets are not confined to esoteric literature: the Comet Kohoutek of the seventies produced a spawn of pseudo-astrological speculations little advanced on mediaeval sortilege.

COMMANDING A specialist term much misunderstood in modern astrology. The terms 'commanding' and 'obeying' were applied by Ptolemy and his followers to pairs of signs at equal distance from the equinoctial point. Thus Taurus has command over Pisces (which in turn 'obeys' Taurus). The pairs, with the commanders first, are Taurus-Pisces, Gemini-Aquarius, Cancer-Capricorn, Leo-Sagittarius and Virgo-Scorpio. Aries and Libra, being on the equinoctial points, are not included in the original schema. As Bouche-Leclercq points out, the original notion appears to have been that these pairs of signs 'heard' each other, the concept of one 'obeying' the other being a mere elaboration. Unfortunately, Ptolemy's ideas were misunderstood, with the result that later astrologers insisted that all the signs from Aries to Virgo were 'commanding' and those from Libra to Pisces inclusive were 'obeying': the astrologer Bonattis, in his attempt to define 'antiscia' gives the use of 'imperantes' (commanding) and 'obedientes' (obeying) as though directly from Ptolemy. As a result, the pairs were totally ignored, and a strange notion arose that the first six signs were somehow more fitted to command or lead, while the last six were fitted to obey or follow. The term is now clearly obsolete, and when used it is almost always wrongly applied.

COMMENCE   A planet coming to the Ascendant is said to 'commence', and afterwards it is said to 'increase'.

COMMON FIRE   See FIRE ELEMENT.

COMMON PLANET   Mercury is sometimes called the common planet, presumably because of its ANDROGYNE nature.

COMMON SIGNS Another term for the "Mutable Signs" - Gemini, Virgo, Sagittarius and Pisces. See MUTABILITY.

COMPARISON CHART   Term applied to the charts used to combine all the different elements from the two (or more) figures in connexion with the study of SYNASTY. It is sometimes wrongly called the "Composite Chart".

COMPOSITE CHART   A single chart detailing astrological material relating to two people, obtained by incorporating into the figure the midpoints between the two sets of planetary and nodal details within two horoscopes. This chart must be distinguished from the "Relationship Chart".

COMPUTATION   The computing or "Casting" of a horoscope usually requires the conversion of a given birth time and birth date to Greenwich Mean Time, as a prelude to calculating the Ascendant and the Houses (by whatever system) of the chart, and inserting the planetary and nodal positions. For all specialist terms used in the following account of the stages of Computation, see TIME. The first stage involves the recording of birth-date and birth-place, from which latter may be obtained the Latitude and Longitude from a Gazeteer. The second stage involves the conversion of Birth-time to Greenwich Mean Time: this requires the amendment for Zone Standard Time (see TIME ZONES), and for Summer Time, Double Summer Time and/or War Time and Daylight Saving Time. The third stage requires the consulation of an Ephemeris, to determine the Sidereal Time at Noon, according to Greenwich Mean Time, and the adjusting for the interval between this time (given for either noon or midnight, depending upon ephemeris) and the Acceleration on the Interval (explained in "Time"), at the rate of 10 secs per hour, and pro rata. The Longitudinal Equivalent is then calculated, at the rate of 4 times each degree of longitude, which number of minutes is added if the birth is to the East of Greenwich, and subtracted if to the West. This computation gives the Local Sidereal Time at Birth, a figure which may be used to determine (from a Table of Houses) the Ascendant, Midheaven, and intermediate house cusps, in terms of the Latitude of the birth. For latitudes South of the equator, the procedure is to add 12 hours to the Local Sidereal Time at Birth, and reverse the signs so that the sign opposite in the zodiac to the one given in the table of houses is used for the Ascendant. It is not

==

possible to construct accurate charts without reliable Ephemerides and Tables of Houses, and in some cases other specialist documentation (such as a Gazetteer). For modern horoscopes the series, "Die Deutsche Ephemeride" of Otto-Wilhelm-Barth-Verlag is of excellent quality. For historical charts the five-day and ten-day interval lists of Tuckerman, "Planetary, Lunar, and Solar Positions" is recommended. The problem of Time Zones and time changes is dealt with by Doane (esp. "Time Changes in the World"). Tables of Houses are published by several astrological publishers - those of Raphael "Tables of Houses for Northern Latitudes" list from the equator to 50 degrees North, with the houses for Leningrad (nearly 60 degrees North): the system is Placidean. The Chacornac "Tables de Maisons" gives a wider range of latitudes, but is also calculated according to Placidus. Wemyss gives a set of tables (for a limited range of latitudes) according to Campanus.

COMPUTERIZED CHART   More often than not, the so-called 'computerized chart' is not a chart at all in the sense of being a stereographic projection: it is usually a schematic figuration of the heavens for a particular time - most often, a birth-time. In the more sophisticated systems a stereographic projection may be implied in the calculations, but really a computerized chart is a 'reading' rather than a chart. Most of the charts available through computerized systems are little more than a complex extension of popular commercial astrology (of what specialist astrologers are wont to call 'cook-book' astrology). The print out of computerized material for the purpose of personal interpretation belongs to an altogether different category, however, and may be regarded as relieving an astrologer of much of the tedium of calculation. In regard to the complexity to which computerized charts proper may descend, Dean has a most apposite phrase, for 'computer charts whose capacity for overkill is exceeded only by their unreadability'.

CONCEPTION CHART   Usually an alternative name for the PRE-NATAL CHART cast for the (putative) moment of conception by mathematical computation from the natal chart. The same name has been applied to Collin's schema of logarithmic scales related to the 280 day period of gestation, linked with the 'creation of a body', which might be measured in terms of the Moon and Mercury cycles - though this schema was not a horoscope chart.

CONCEPTIVE SIGNS   Another term for the four FIXED SIGNS, Taurus, Leo, Scorpio and Aquarius.

CONDITIO   See SECTA.

CONFIGURATION   A term sometimes used of a pattern of ASPECTS within a chart, and sometimes of the whole chart itself. In recent years a specific application has been made of the term to cover a number of particular aspects: see MAJOR CONFIGURATION. In traditional astrology, all aspects were sometimes referred to as 'configurations'.

CONJUNCTION   An aspect maintained by two or more planets posited within the same degree of longitude. It is sometimes called the aspect of 'prominence', in that it brings the workings of the planets involved into a prominent position relative to the chart: but in this connexion, see also COMBUST. The ORB allowed a conjunction is not agreed among authorities, but some allow as much as 10 degrees for a platic aspect to be operative.

CONSTELLATION   A pattern of stars and star-groups: though the term is very frequently used wrongly to denote the SIGNS of the zodiac, which are not star-groups at all. The majority of the constellations were named and demarcated in ancient times, and all the major ones were ascribed specific influences which were regarded as being projected to the earth (in addition to the influences cast by the fixed stars of which the constellations were themselves composed - see FIXED STARS and MANSIONS). Each of the major constellations, including the important ones which bear the same names as the twelve signs of the zodiac, is treated separately under the headings:

===

CONSTELLATION (Continued)

ANDROMEDA	ANTINOUS	ANTLIA
AQUARIUS CONSTELLATION	AQUILA	ARIES CONSTELLATION
AURIGA	BOOTES	CAELUM
CANCER CONSTELLATION	CANES VENATICI	CANIS MAJOR
CANIS MINOR	CAPRICORN CONSTELLATION	CAPUT SERPENS
CENTAURUS	CETUS	COLUMBA
COMA BERENICES	CORONA AUSTRALIS	CORONA BOREALIS
CORVUS	CRATER	CYGNUS
DELPHINUS	EQUULEUS	ERIDANUS
FORNAX	GEMINI CONSTELLATION	HERCULES
HYDRA	LEO CONSTELLATION	LEO MINOR
LEPUS	LIBRA CONSTELLATION	LUPUS
LYRA	MICROSCOPIUM	MONOCEROS
OPHIUCHUS	ORION	PEGASUS
PISCES CONSTELLATION	PISCIS AUSTRINUS	PUPPIS
PYXIS	SAGITTA	SAGITTARIUS CONST.
SCORPIO CONSTELLATION	SCULPTOR	SCUTUM SOBIESKII
SERPENS	SEXTANS	TAURUS CONSTELLATION
TRIANGULUM	VELA	VIRGO CONSTELLATION
VULPECULACUM ANSERE		

The abbreviations for the above names are set out under ABBREVIATIONS. For a
list of the ancient Hebraic, Akkadian, Babylonian and Egyptian (demotic)
names for the zodiacal constellations, see CONSTELLATION NAMES. See also
CONSTELLATION MAPS.

CONSTELLATIONAL ZODIAC   A term used of a "Sidereal Zodiac" divided into
twelve unequal asterims (not signs), the boundaries or cusps of which are to
some extent arbitrary, and hence subject to some argument in specialist
astrological circles. The definitions in degrees of arc are given as:

AR 24	TA 36	GE 28	CN 21	LE 35	VG 46
LB 18	SC 31	SG 30	CP 28	AQ 25	PI 38

However, the portrayal of the ecliptical asterisms of the MODERN ZODIAC
actually involves 13 asterisms. There are several, differently defined,
constellational zodiacs in use today, the main differences arising from the
definition of arcs and extent. See CONSTELLATION NAMES.

CONSTELLATION CHART   A term sometimes used as synonymous with the
"Constellation Maps", and sometimes in reference to a horoscope chart cast
according to one of the several constellational systems, rather than
according to the more frequently used zodiacal-sign systems.

CONSTELLATION MAPS   Sometimes (confusingly) called "Constellation Charts" or
'star charts', these are maps or delineations of the heavens in terms of
individual stars or asterisms, often overlaid by schematic or pictorial
IMAGES.   There is much confusion in the early terminology: the Greeks
called the asterisms by the modern equivalent of 'signs' ('sigmata' and
'Teirea'), whilst their 'zodia', often in modern times wrongly translated as
'animals', was used of the famous ecliptical twelve (both for sign and
constellation). Their 'meteora', 'things in the heavens', was more general,
and did not always apply to our modern conception of stars, even when used in
a sense to embrace planets.   The Romans called the individual bodies 'astra'
and 'sidera', and took the Greek 'signa' for the modern signs, to be
distinguished from the constellations, which referred (as now) to all
asterisms, including the so-called 'zodiacal constellations'. That the images
should be of 'living things' is more than an etymological nuance, but seems
to have arisen from the notion that the stars themselves were living beings
(an idea mooted by Aristotle, though often wrongly attributed to Origen, some
7 centuries later). In the 3rd century BC Aratos mentions 45 constellations,

and most of these were continued into the Aratos-derived maps and texts,
though Hyginus (1st century AD?) was equally influential with his 42 figures,
from which the popular woodcuts used in a multitude of 'histories' are
derived. Most of the maps which have survived from early astonomy/astrology
are mere schemas, conveniently mythopoetic, and even esoteric, picture books,
as in the interesting example given by Aldus in figure 19 as a supposed (and
not very accurate) summary of the ancient lore. The relationship of the
twelve constellations to this planisphere is entirely fictitious, though in
some ways little different from the projections of the sophisticated
constellation map of the so-called DENDERAH ZODIAC.

FIGURE 19.   'ANTIQUE' CONSTELLATION MAP (AFTER ALDUS), WITH 'ZODIACAL
CONSTELLATIONS SEPARATELY CHARTED.

By comparison, the Arabian constellation maps are usually models of
rectitude, and reflect the important contribution made by the Arabs to the
lore of fixed star interpretation in astrological circles. However, the
accurate and 'scientific' projection of the celestial sphere is a relatively
modern thing: the mediaeval astrologer tended to rely upon tables, and even
upon direct observation, rather than upon constellational planispherical
models. In his 'Syntaxis', Ptolemy listed 48 constellations, described in
terms of 1028 stars, which has given rise to the absurd notion that the
ancients knew only that number of stars. The subsequent history of the
naming and listing of the stars in constellation lists and maps is beyond the
scope of this present work, falling as it does into the realm of the history
of astronomy, yet the following developments may be noted as being of
importance to the development of astrology. The finest sky maps which are
intended to serve other purposes than entertainment were originated after the
16th century, the earliest of the classics being the 'Uranometria' of Bayer,
published in 1603, the symbolic images of which influence almost all
subsequent atlases. The finest of the 18th century maps was probably that
produced by Flamsteed in his posthumously published 'Atlas Coelestis' of
1729, though Bode's 'Uranographia' of 1801 was probably the last of the
magnificently artistic (as opposed to strictly 'scientific') productions,
before aesthetics fell foul to scientific intent. The Bayer figures (and
indeed those of Flamsteed) relied heavily upon the woodcuts made by Durer for
the two hemispherical charts set out schematically by Heinfogel and Stabius,
though ever since called the 'Durer Map' (figure 20 - page 77). The fluidity
of boundaries (seemingly favoured even by Ptolemy, perhaps with greater
wisdom than the modern mind admits) along with the general lack of consensus
as to the nature and form of the "Images", and even the feasibility of
introducing new asterisms (usually merely severed from the older ones) made
each of the early atlases unique as works of art. There were in these
'classical' artistic productions some attempt at objective mensuration, but
in the scientific climate their fluidity and lack of consensus was anathema,
and Herschel was among the first to attempt to put an end to imprecision by

proposing to divide the skies into spherical quadrangles, thus producing
somewhat arbitrary (though clearly defined) boundaries. His idea found
little favour, however, and it was not until 1927 (after many interesting
essays) that the International Astronomical Union accepted the divisions (of
surprisingly arbitrary boundaries) proposed by the Belgian Delporte, which
are incorporated into the constellations of figure 44 in MODERN ZODIAC.
Delporte's 'Atlas Celeste' is much used by astronomers, but has been
(rightly) the subject of much learned criticism in astrological circles, not
least because its complex definition actually incorporates "Ophiuchus" as an
ecliptical constellation, and thus makes of it a zodiacal figure. A highly
significant change in form from the ancient to the modern is reflected in the
abandonment of the ancient images for the rectilinear star-groups. This is
particularly interesting, since the early maps (and even the star lists) were
linked with astrology more through mythology than any precision of definition
in regard to celestial latitude and longitude (though contemporaneous lists
did provide more-or-less accurate information relating to the conversion of
star lore to astrological practice). It is perhaps significant that the
modern constellation maps should attempt to dispense with 'living images',
and have proposed in their place a system of rectilinear abstractions, for it
is suggestive of the dehumanization process which has unfortunately
accompanied the development of the scientific outlook in astronomy.

FIGURE 20   THE SO-CALLED 'DURER MAP', CUT BY THE ARTIST DURER AFTER
HEINFOGEL AND STABIUS IN 1515 AD.

CONSTELLATION NAMES   The astrologer Fagan insists that the 'constellation
names' (among which he presumably includes the 'zodiacal names') bore the
same meanings in the 8th century BC as they do today - a point not without
dispute in academic circles, as a reading of the scholarly Sachs will
confirm. The translations offered by Fagan for the Babylonian terms, and for
the Egyptian (demotic) terms of the Graeco-Roman period, while not beyond
question, have in recent years been popularized in several histories of the
zodiac. These are set out in table 27, in which the translations under
'demotic' refer to the hieroglyphic demotic form, rather than to a direct
translation. In any case, it is clear from the translations provided by
Fagan that his basic premise is questionable even in the list he publishes.
The translation for the Babylonian Sagittarius (*), which Fagan gives as
'overseer of the Fire Ordeal' is contentious (see Akkadian in table 28).

TABLE 27

CONST.	BABYLONIAN	MEANING	DEMOTIC	MEANING
AR	Lu.hun.ga	hired labourer	Pa.Yesu	fleece
TA	Gud.an.nu	heavenly bull	Pa.ka	the bull
GE	Mash.tab.bal.gal.gal	great twins	Na-hetru	two children
CN	Al.lu	crab (?)	Pa.gerhedj	scarabaeus
LE	Ur.gu.la	great dog, lion	Pa-may-hes	fierce lion
VG	Ab.shim	spike of corn	Ta.reply	a female
LB	Zibanetum	scales	Ta-Akhet	sunrise place
SC	Gir.tab	scorpion	Ta.Djel	snake
SG	PA.BIL.SAG	overseer*	Pa.nety-ateh	arrow
CP	Sukhuyrmashu	goat-fish	Pa-her-ankh	goat face
AQ	GU.LA	giant	Pa-mu	the water
PI	Shim.mah	great swallow	Na-Thebeteyu	fish

Probably more reliable are the early constellation names derived from various (unnamed) sources by Allen, which correspond fairly closely to those recorded by Thierens for the Hebrew Cosmogony, in table 28. The list given under 'Chaldean' in this table is from Brau: it resembles the Babylonian and Akkadian list, reminding us that 'Chaldean' was once a generic name for 'astrologer'. But see also ZODIAC.

TABLE 28

CON.	AKKADIAN/PERSIAN/ASSYRIAN	MEANING	HEBREW	'CHALDEAN'
AR	I-ku-u	prince	Taleh	Kusarikkut
TA	Te te	bull of light	Shor	Te te
	Gut-an-na	heavenly bull		
GE	Do Patkar	two figures	Teomin	Tua-mu
	(Chaldean?) - Tammech	two figures		Masmasu
CN	Nan-garu (and) Puluk-ku	solar north gate(?)	Sarton	Al-lul
LE	Pap-pil-sak	great fire	Ari	A-ru
	(Babylonian) - Aru	lion		
VG	Khusak	ear of wheat	Betulah	Shi-ru
	Bealtis	wife of Bel		Ki
LB	(Euphratean) - Sugi	chariot yoke	Moznayim	Zibanitu
SC	Girtab	stinger	Akrab	Akrabu
SG	Ban	bow star (?)	Kasshat	Pabilsag
	Kakkab kastu	bow constellation		
	(Cuneiform) Utucagaba	smiting sun face		
CP	Shahu	ibex	Gedi	Sakhu
	Munaxa	goat-fish		Enzu
	Su-tul	yoke		
AQ	Ku-ur-ku	flowing-waters seat	Deli	Mulgula
	Rammanu	god of storm		Gu
PI	Nunu (and) Zib	fish*	Dagim	Nunu or Zib

* The 'Zib' of Akkadian Pisces may also mean 'boundary'.

CONTINUOUS ASTROLOGY   A term used by the historian Pingree in a brief but excellent history of astrology, as reference to that form of astrology 'designed to guarantee the astrologer constant patronage'. He is writing specifically of Hellenistic astrology, in so far as it may be gleaned from Dorotheus of Sidon, which proposed that new horoscopic diagrams (antigennesis) must be cast for every anniversary (or even at the beginning of every month, week, day or hour) for comparison with the native's birth chart. The idea is a primal conception underlying the various systems of TRANSITS and PROGRESSIONS, all of which relate to the radical chart. Continuous astrology is really the equivalent of a branch of "Predictive Astrology" which also requires a related series of progressed charts.

===

CONTRA ANTISCION   See ANTISCION.

CONTRA-DEGREE   See PROPORTIONAL ARCS.

CONTRAPARALLELS   See PARALLEL.

CONVERSE DIRECTIONS   These are "Directions" applied in an order opposite to
the natural order of the signs.   Many astrologers regard converse directions
as an invalid extension of the directing technique. See PROPORTIONAL ARCS.

COOPERTA   Name, perhaps meaning 'covered', given to the 15th of the LUNAR
MANSIONS in some mediaeval lists. Probably located by one of the less
powerful asterisms bordering the constellations Virgo and Libra.

CO-ORDINATE   In a specialist astrological sense, any of a number of
magnitudes or geometric constructions - usually projected into the "Celestial
Sphere" - which permit the astrologer to determine a position precisely.

COPERNICAN SYSTEM   The cosmo-conception which laid the basis for the most
wide-spread modern theory of the nature of the solar-system. The name is
derived from the Latinized form of the Polish name Nikolaj Kopernik, who set
out his proposed model in his 'De Revolutionibus Orbium Coelestium' (figure
22), which was not published until the end of his life, in 1543. The
original Copernican model (now much modified) proposed that the apparent
motions of the planets might be explained within a heliocentric system, with
the earth rotating diurnally on its own axis, and with each heavenly body
exerting its own gravitational force. He also placed the fixed stars at a
far greater distance from the solar system than had been visualised in the
geocentric PTOLEMAIC SYSTEM, the cosmo-conception most widely held to be true
in his day. In the same extensive text, Copernicus also proposed a new theory
to account for the "Precession" of the equinoxes

FIGURE 21. MANUSCRIPT DRAWING OF THE COPERNICAN SYSTEM FROM 'DE
REVOLUTIONIBUS ORBIUM COELESTIUM' MANUSCRIPT, PUBLISHED 1543.

COPULA   Name given to the "Spiral Nebula", now linked with CANES VENATICI.

COR CAROLI   Fixed star (double), originally included in the image of "Canes
Venatici" in the collar of the dog Chara, but set apart by Halley in 1725, as
a mark of respect for King Charles II.

COR HYDRAE   See ALPHARD.

COR LEONIS   See FIFTEEN STARS and REGULUS.

===

CORNUA ARIETIS   Name, 'the horns of Aries', given to the 1st of the LUNAR MANSIONS in some mediaeval lists. Probably located by the star "Mesarthim".

CORNUA SCORPIONIS   Name, curiously 'the horns of Scorpio', given to the 16th of the LUNAR MANSIONS in some mediaeval lists. Probably identified by the fixed stars "Zuben Elschemali" and "Zuben Elgenubi".

CORONA AUSTRALIS   Constellation, approximately 2 to 12 degrees Capricorn, and 36 to 45 degrees south of the ecliptic, the 'southern crown'. Once pictured as the crown of Sagittarius, the 'Corona Sagittarii', the circular shape of the asterism has suggested very many different names, from 'Tortoise' ('Al Kubbah' in Arabic, 'Pi' in Chinese), to garlands and 'Rota Ixionis', the wheel of Ixion. Ptolemy likens its influence to Jupiter with Saturn.

CORONA BOREALIS   Constellation, approximately 2 to 17 degrees Scorpio, and from 27 to 33 degrees north of ecliptic, the 'northern crown', said to be the garland given to Ariadne at her marriage. It is actually a 'wreath' in Greek mythology and star lore, and now with many names, sometimes indeed called after its most powerful fixed star "Alphecca", which like the asterism itself, is largely of a benevolent influence in a chart.

CORONA SUPER CAPUT SCORPIONIS   Descriptive name, 'the crown on the head of the scorpion', of the 17th of the LUNAR MANSIONS in some mediaeval lists. Identified by the fixed star "Akrab".

CORRECTION   When limited to specialist application relating to the computation of a horoscope, the adjustment of local mean time to sidereal time in order to obtain relevant birth data. See TIME.

CORRELATION   In general astrological application, this term is used to denote the comparison of charts, or selective data taken from charts, and especially to the comparative method involved in "Synastry". The term is also used more specifically in the idea of 'correlation analysis', which is a statistical method of extrapolating astrological data.

CORRESPONDENCE   In its occult sense, a term derived from the very earliest astrological lore, and used to denote the 'occult' or 'hidden' relationships between natural forms and spiritual causes, or between the microcosm and the macrocosm, which is observed acting through the "Sympathy" expressed in the "Chain of Being". Swedenborg, who used the term extensively, maintained that every natural object (that is, every sublunar object) is a result of the working of a spiritual cause, and that if the nature of the correspondence between the higher and the lower is understood, then the spiritual may be read through its physical symbol. This doctrine lies at the basis of Rosicrucian meditative endeavour.

CORRESPONDENCIES   A translation of the traditional idea of "Correspondence", intended (presumably) to point specifically to the idea of occult correspondences between things. In his brilliant study of Egyptian symbolism, Schwaller de Lubicz traces the 'attributes' or 'correspondencies' of modern astrology to the ancient Egyptian principle of related specific proportions and cubit measurements to definite 'Neters', or 'principles', which correspond (approximately) to the Platonic ideals.

COR SCORPII   See ANTARES and FIFTEEN STARS.

COR SCORPIONIS   Name given to the 18th of the LUNAR MANSIONS in some Mediaeval lists. Identified by the fixed star "Antares".

COR SERPENTIS   Fixed star, the alpha of "Serpens", set in the neck of the snake, the 'serpent's heart', and sometimes called 'Unukalhai', from the Arabic 'neck of the snake'. Ptolemy says that it has an influence like that of Saturn and Mars - it is said to bring accidents and danger from poisons.

COR TAURI   Name, 'the heart of the bull', given to the 4th of the "Lunar Mansions" in some mediaeval lists. Probably located by the star "Aldebaran".

CORVUS   Constellation, approximately 5 to 15 degrees Libra, and from 7 to 25 degrees south of the ecliptic, a 'raven' to the Greeks, 'crow' to the Romans, and earlier with a variety of bird-like names: it is part of the asterism-arc of the Chinese "Red Bird", and 'Orebh' (raven) to the Hebrews. The various legends of the dishonesty of the bird have been projected into astrological lore, for Ptolemy likens its asterism to Mars conjunct Saturn, and later astrologers link it with craftiness, ingenuity and lying. Only the delta, ALGORAB plays a part in the astrological lore: the alpha, 'Al Chiba' to the Arabs, appears to have decreased in brilliance, and to have changed colour, during the centuries.

COSIGNIFICATOR   A much over-worked term. In horary astrology, a planet in conjunction with the "Significator" of anything is its cosignificator, simply because it must be taken into consideration when the matter is being adjudged. In another sense, the Moon is regarded as 'cosignificator' with the "Lord of the Ascendant", whatever the placing of the Moon itself.   In horary charts relative to marriage (but seemingly not in charts cast for "Synastry"), the female planets, Moon and Venus, are the cosignificators if the querent is a man, while the male planets, Sun and Mars are cosignificators if the querent is a woman. Further meanings of the term are derived from the ancient tradition, in which a parallel is drawn between the basic chart (here called the "Macrocosmic Chart") and any particular manifestation of it (that is, any chart at all). Thus, Aries is said to be a 'cosignificating sign' for the Ascendant of any horoscope, simply because this sign stands on the Ascendant of the "Macrocosmic Chart". This theory of cosignification is taken to levels of theoretical refinements which, as Wilson says, 'render the science ridiculous'.

COSMECOLOGY   A neologism for a study which attempts to correlate changes and effects of a cosmic nature with observed cycles of behaviour and periodicities on the earth and human beings.

COSMICAL RISING   In a specialist sense, a term applied to the heliacal rising or setting of a planet. See ACRONYCAL.

COSMICAL SETTING   A term used of the setting of a planet or a star with the Sun in the evening.

COSMIC CROSS   When two planets in opposition are in square aspect to a third planet, they are all three said to be united in a 'cosmic cross', sometimes called a T-Square. While the formation is undeniably of a dynamic and powerful nature, its force depends upon the qualities of the three planets involved in the aspects. See also GRAND CROSS.

COSMIC CYBERNETICS   A term used by the astrologer Landscheidt for his highly personal quasi-mathematical, quasi-mystical, interpretation of certain astrological ideas, connected with the development of COSMOBIOLOGY.

COSMIC NIGHT   A modern term derived from the Theosophical use of the Sanskrit term 'Pralaya', which relates to a period of obscuration or sleep between the 'days' of creative evolution. See YUGA, where the very terms relating to 'twilight' imply a separating 'pralaya' between the ages.

COSMIC PANTHEONS   Throughout the history of astrology there has been a tendency for astrologers (and for that matter, non-astrologers) to create "correspondencies" between pantheons and the zodiac. One of the earliest attempts, which has left some mark on the development of astrology, was that of Manilius, which (for all its astrological unlikeliness) at least had the advantage of being related to only one pantheon, the Roman:

COSMIC PANTHEONS (Continued)

AR	Minerva	CN	Mercury	LB	Vulcan	CP	Vesta
TA	Venus	LE	Jupiter	SC	Mars	AQ	Juno
GE	Apollo	VG	Ceres	SG	Diana	PI	Neptune

In this connexion, see GABII ALTAR. In fact, a vast number of similar
correspondences, more or less poetic and imaginative, have been recorded, and
the important ones have been listed by Thierens and Stone, whilst a great
number are more or less taken for granted by such esotericists as Blavatsky
and Bailey.   Surprisingly, many of these "Cosmic Analogies" may be traced to
that arch-syncretist, Kircher, whose well-known zodiacal dial (figure 22)
actually hints at several important esoteric connexions, in summary of his
vast (if sometimes imaginative) erudition.   Thierens neatly summarizes the
modern syncretism along the following lines: Aries is personified by Osiris
- Taurus by Isis - Cancer by the dual Horus and Anubis - Leo is seen as one
of the 'many kings in Myths' - Virgo by the Virgin Mary, the Mother of
Krishna, and by Christ 'at the back of which the image of Isis reappears' -
Libra is the 'ideal ruler', such as we find in the legends of Rama and
Solomon - Scorpio is represented in dragon-forms, in the oriental Nagas, and
in the Chinese Lung dragons, as well as in the Phoenix (and for that matter,
in the Ansa swan) - Sagittarius is personified in Zeus (Jupiter) - Capricorn
in the Nature-god Pan, himself half 'bestial', as well as in Chronos, the
ruler of Time - Aquarius is Ouranos - whilst Pisces is inevitably Poseidon
(Neptune), and the ruler of the Cosmic Sea. This syncretic Cosmic Pantheon
has been adjusted by numerous modern accretions, many of which go back to the
early conflicts between the Romanizing-tendency of Christianity and the early
Gnosticism.   The imagery from these conflicts deeply influenced art and
literature: thus Christ has been figured as Taurus, as the descending Logos
(with Mithraic undertones) as well as Pisces, the sacrificial sufferer, the
inaugurator of the New Age. Some of this symbolism may be seen in the
twelfth century SAN MINIATO ZODIAC. The Virgin Mary is represented in Virgo,
and indeed the fixed star Spica of the constellation figured on her dress (as
the Stella Maris) well into the sixteenth century. Each of the four
EVANGELISTS are also linked with the fixed signs of the zodiac - Taurus as
St. Luke, Leo as St. Mark, Scorpio as St. John and Aquarius as St. Matthew.
But see also BIBLICAL ASTROLOGY.

FIGURE 22. THE SYNCRETIC 'KIRCHER ZODIAC' DEPICTING A NUMBER OF COSMIC
RELATIONSHIPS (AFTER KIRCHER).

COSMIC PICTURES   A 'cosmic picture' or 'planetary picture' is a term used by
Ebertin in regard to diagrammatized images of planetary relationships derived
from a "Cosmogram" by means of his "Ninety Degree Dial".   Such terms are
derived from translations from the 'Planetenbilder' proposed by the German
Witte, and used by Ebertin in his "Cosmobiology", based on the interpretation
of a series of pictures of chart groupings derived from aspects and

"Mid-points". Witte distinguishes three planetary pictures, which may be combined in a variety of ways. The mid-point between planets which is occupied by an actual body is such a 'picture'. Several 'half-sums' (mid-points) with a communal axis, though not necessarily with a planetary body posited on this communal axis, is another 'picture'. A combination of a Mid-point between the two planets which is itself aspected from another planet (or planets)to the aspectal order of 45, 90 and 135 degrees represents another such 'picture'. Such planetary pictures give rise to what Witte calls 'equations', which are really key-word equivalents. A representative 'cosmic picture' (which is also called a 'cosmic structure pattern') shown in figure 23, derived from the "Cosmogram" of figure 24, is designed to show the cosmic picture of Sun in this dial. Uranus and Mercury (conjunct Saturn) are approximately equi-distant from the Sun along the dial, and are accordingly recorded on the higher horizontal bar. Jupiter and Pluto are equi-distant from the Sun, and are recorded on the lower horizontal bar. Since the Moon is in opposition to the Sun on this dial, it is placed at the bottom of the vertical line of the cosmic picture, completing this graphic assessment of the relationship of the planets to the Sun.

FIGURE 23. COSMIC PICTURE (AFTER EBERTIN).

COSMIC STRUCTURE PATTERNS   See COSMIC PICTURES.

COSMOBIOLOGY   A term coined by the Austrian doctor Feerhow, and first used in connexion with astrology by the Swiss astrologer Krafft. It is especially used by the astrologer Ebertin in relation to his own modernized and highly personalised astrology, relating to a description of the possible correlations between cosmos and organic life, and the effects of cosmic rhythms and stellar notions on man. Ebertin, whilst profoundly aware of the traditional astrology, sought to contrast this system with his own in order to interpret destiny in terms of somatopsychic dispositions, and to 'free astrology from occultism'. He used the term "Cosmogram" for his variations of the horoscope figure, and made much use of "Planetary Pictures" involving "Mid-Points" (which play an important part in the interpretative system). The "Yearly Rhythm" tabulation, used as a basis for chart interpretation, reflects the traditional astrological view, refined by much research, and by the application of a disciplined statistical approach to the subject. The Germanic abbreviation KdG ('Kombination der Gestirneinflusse', from the title of a book published by Ebertin in 1940) is often used to denote Cosmobiology.

COSMODYNES   A term derived from the astrological research connected with the Church of Light (published largely under Doane) in regard to a system of numerical values assigned to planets, according to strength of aspect and angularities.   These numerical values for aspects and parallels range from 0 to +10, the closer the aspect, the higher the number - thus the conjunction/opposition merit the full 10, the square/trine 8, the sextile 6, the semi-square 4, and so on. Similar systems have been suggested by other astrologers (notably Carter), though not on such a firmly based research.

==

These values are weighted (see also INTENSITIES) for orb, by subtraction of 1
degree for each degree of orb. There is also a numerical value attributed to
planets in regard to proximity to the four angles (on a +8 to +14 range - the
closer, the higher). The strongest planet in a chart is that with the
highest total.

COSMOGRAM   A method of chart construction (and highly specialized
interpretation or adjustment) proposed by Ebertin, far removed from standard
"Chart Systems". The method is based on the conversion of a normal ecliptic
chart to a three-fold schema, called a "Ninety-Degree Dial", which is usually
portrayed on the cosmogram as an outer concentric dial, divided into 90 arcs
(not degrees, which suggests that the term is something of a misnomer). The
data in the inner ecliptic projection is converted to the outer dial in terms
of the following rationale, which is here related exclusively to figure 24.
The Moon, which is in 8 CA (Ebertin wrongly reports it in 7 CA) is translated
to the 8th degree of the dial. This conversion is regarded as valid, since
Cancer is one of the cardinal signs, and the first third of the dial is said
to represent the cardinal nature. On a similar basis, the MC is translated
to the dial in this first third, to 16 degrees. Mercury, being in a fixed
sign at 19 AQ is translated to the 49th degree of the dial, since the fixed
signs are related to this second-third of the sequence - thus 30 + 18 gives
48. The consequence of this progressive conversion from the ecliptic to the
dial may be studied with similar principles in mind. It is argued that from
this dial conversion it is possible to note certain emphatic areas, and
angular relationships (not aspectal relationships, of course) based on a
simple system of mid-points. The methodology of the interpretation of the
cosmogram involves the construction of several analytic diagrams from the
ninety-degree dials - see COSMIC PICTURES. See also COSMOPYSCHOGRAM: figure
25 under "Distance". The French astrologer Volguine has used the term
'cosmogram' in a general sense to apply to any representation in graphic form
of the cosmos, or of celestial relationships.

FIGURE 24. COSMOGRAM (AFTER EBERTIN).

COSMOLOGY   An alternative name for COSMOBIOLOGY.

COSMO-PSYCHIC   See THREE PROTOTYPES.

COSMOPSYCHOGRAM   A term used of a visual projection (scarcely a chart in the

conventional sense of the word) of various intensities of astrological
relationships, obtained by a structural analysis of a chart, and
incorporating the 'distance values' of the heavenly bodies. The projection
was developed by Ebertin (see COSMOBIOLOGY), based on a form used by the
German graphologist Wittlich. Each of 13 birth-chart factors are represented
by a ray on this visual projection (figure 25): the white inner portion is
said to relate to the positive value of the personality, the black portion to
its negative value. The length of the ray is determined by evaluating the
factors of mid-points and aspects. The total white section is called the
positive 'kernel'; the black section is called the negative 'mantle'. In
recent years, the internal circle, carrying the 'distance-values' has not
always been incorporated into the Cosmopsychogram: see DISTANCE.

COSMOPSYCHOLOGY   See COSMOBIOLOGY.

COUNSELLING   A term used in modern astrological circles as the equivalent
for the old 'astrological interpretation' on a one-to-one basis between
astrologer and native. The connotation of the term is coloured by the
pseudo-psychological approach to astrology which is currently fashionable,
the idea being that the astrologer (rightly or wrongly) considers himself to
be in a position to both interpret the chart and offer advice.

COUNTERPARTS   For the specifically astrological sense, see GLOBES.

CO-VERTEX   A term proposed as applying to the VERTEX of the so-called
"Co-latitude" of the place of birth. See CO-ASCENDANT.

CRAB   Popular name for both the constellation and sign "Cancer".

CRATER   Constellation contiguous with "Corvus", extending into "Libra", and
thus linked with the mythology of these constellations: the bird and cup
(crater) were transferred to heaven by Jupiter, but the asterism was linked
with the image of a cup long before Greek mythology came into existence.
While the 'kantharos' of the earliest Greek systems, it was also the
'soma-cup' of the prehistoric Indians. It is hardly surprising that one of
the fixed stars of this asterism ("Labrum") has been linked with the Grail
legends. Astrologers see the asterism as a generally beneficial influence,
and Ptolemy links it with Venus.

CREATIVE HIERARCHIES   See TWELVE CREATIVE HIERARCHIES.

CREATIVE PRINCIPLES   See SEVEN VITAL PRINCIPLES.

CREPUSCULE   Term from the Latin 'crepusculum' (twilight), and seemingly a
variation of crepuscle.

CRESCENT   In general use the term is now applied to any planet (more
particularly to the Moon) when half the disc of its body is illuminated by the
Sun. However, the derivation of the term, from the latin 'crescere' (to
grow) indicates that the word should more properly be restricted to the
partly illuminated waxing body. In graphic symbolism, the crescent 'first
quarter' is symbolised ☽ and the waning third quarter is symbolised by the
sigil ☾ See also MOON.

CRIB   See PRAESAEPE.

CRITICAL DAYS   In the specialist context of horary astrology, and in early
forms of "Medical Astrology", the critical days were those marked by the
series of directions and transits on which the Moon fell "Semi-square" to
its original position. But see also CRITICAL DEGREES.

CRITICAL DEGREES   In some forms of early "Medical Astrology", certain cusps
of the lunar MANSIONS were designated 'critical' or 'crucial' degrees. It

===

seems that some systems counted all these cuspal degrees as critical, whilst others maintained that only the cusps of the 1st, 8th, 15th and 22nd mansions were critical degrees. Since prognosis was usually concerned with the transit of the Moon through these critical degrees, the days on which such transits took place were sometimes termed 'critical degree days' or even 'critical days' (but see CRITICAL DAYS). A different system of critical degrees of the zodiac is also recorded in some astrological texts: it is said that a planet within orb (usually 2 or 3 degrees) of such degrees is found to exercise a strong influence on the life of the native, somewhat similar to the HYPSOMATA. There are one or two variations in the lists available in the popular textbooks, but the following is representative.

AR	CN	LB	CP	1, 13, 26
TA	LE	SC	AQ	9, 21
GE	VG	SG	PI	4, 17

CROCODILE   Although exoterically the Hindu astrological equivalent of the sign "Capricorn" (named Makara), the crocodile is linked by Blavatsky with esoteric astrology through the fifth group of the Hierarchies of spirits who had their abode in this constellation. The crocodile appears to be a debased symbol of the dragon, the 'dragon of wisdom', the intelligent principle in the human being, which passes from incarnation to incarnation.

CROSS   See NORTHERN CROSS and CRUX.

CROW   See CORVUS.

CRUCIAL DEGREES   See CRITICAL DEGREES.

CRUX   Constellation, approximately 2 to 12 degrees Scorpio, and from 56 to 65 degrees south of the equator, now our 'Southern Cross', though the ancients incorporated its stars into "Centaur". It was perhaps introduced as a separate asterism in the 15th century, though Al Biruni mentions a Hindu name 'Sula' (beam of crucifixion), and Allen records that it was last seen on the horizon of Jerusalem at about the time of the Crucifixion. It is more than a literary puzzle as to why Dante was familiar with its form and symbolism. Robson notes that Cabral, who disovered Brazil in 1500, called the country 'Land of the Holy Cross', and that the asterism has been reproduced on Brazilian postage stamps: Cabral might have had the asterism from his reading of earlier navigators, to whom it was a source of wonder. Astrologers link its influence with burdens and trials, and its star ACRUX plays an important role in stellar lore.

CRYSTALLINE HEAVEN   See NINTH HEAVEN.

CULMEN COELI   Little used dog-Latin for the "Tenth House".

CULMINATION   The term is used in two different senses in astrological contexts. First, it denotes the completion of a forming aspect to the "Platic".   Secondly, it denotes the arrival of a planet, fixed star, or some nodal point to the Midheaven, or the cusp of the Tenth House, by transit, direction and progression. Thus, when any celestial body crosses the meridian it is said to 'culminate'. The upper culmination is the 'maximum altitude', the lower culmination is the minimum 'altitude'. After culmination, the planet or nodal point is said to 'decrease'.

CUPIDO   Name given to one of the HYPOTHETICAL PLANETS in the "Uranian Astrology". This transneptunian is included in an ephemeris, and is claimed to relate to 'community, marriage and art'.

CURA   The Sanskrit word for "Jupiter", as used in Hindu astrology.

CUSP   In specialist astrological contexts, the term cusp has a dual reference, which is often confusingly merged into one. First, it refers to the imaginary line which separates one sign of the zodiac from another - thus the cusp between Aries and Taurus is the imaginary line which demarcates the end of the last degree of the former and the beginning of the first degree of the latter.   The existence of this term 'cusp' in reference to such a separation between signs has led to a popular notion of the "Cuspal Type", which really has no existence in serious astrology. See however CUSPAL ARC. The second meaning of the term refers to the line which demarcates the grids of the houses in a chart (see HOUSE SYSTEMS). Thus, the Ascendant line is regarded by many astrologers as the cusp of the first house: however, in some systems, such as the "Campanean System", the cusp of the house is regarded as marking the centre of that house, and forms its most influential arc of operation. In other systems, such as the "Placidean System" as it is used by many modern astrologers, the cusp of the house is regarded as marking the beginning of the name house, and the end of the preceding one: in this case, therefore, the First House is considered as beginning with the Ascendant line, and extending down to the cusp of the Second House. There is much confusion about cusps in the practice of ordinary astrology.

CUSPAL ARC   Sometimes the "Cusp" between the signs of the zodiac, or between the houses, is regarded as consisting of a small arc, rather than of a strictly precise division: such is called a 'cuspal arc'. The concept permits a degree of ambiguity as to the influence of a planet (especially so in reference to the zodiacal cusps), which is hardly necessary in view of the precision permitted by modern ephemerides.

CUSPAL DISTANCE   A term defined by the astrologer Leo as denoting the arc of Right Ascension between a planet and the house circle (cusp) of any house to which it is applying. However, the term is also used in a much more general sense in regard to distances between cusps.

CUSPAL TYPE   A term which is scarcely used in serious astrology, but which in popular versions of the art is sometimes used to describe a native born on a day near to the Sun's ingress into a sign. In most cases, the term may only be used of those natives for whom an accurate horoscope has not been cast, for such a figure would show precisely the position of the Sun, and leave no need for the term at all. In effect, the popular concept that there is such a person who may be described as a 'cuspal type' (as though this were some sort of astrological notion) belongs to the realm of superstition.

CUSTOS MESSIUM   Formerly a constellation, the 'Harvest-keeper', located near Cassiopeia and Cepheus, but no longer recognised as a separate asterism.

CYCLES In a specialist astrological sense, the term is generally used in reference to the planetary cycles, or to "Epochs", though there are actually many other cycles within the Microcosm and Macrocosm which are of interest to the astrologer - in this connexion, see also RHYTHMS. The theory of planetary cycles is based on the idea that each of the planetary bodies mark off periods which are reflected in human life and history. Synodic cycles involve two planets (interval between one conjunction and the next), sidereal cycles involve only one (a complete cycle around the Sun): within the horoscope a third cycle is determined according to "Progressions" - for example, the progression of the Moon to its natal point is equivalent to an important 28 year cycle. Other important cycles are the LUNAR NODE CYCLE of 18 years and 7 months, and the LUNAR RETURN. In many respects, the theory of cycles visualises celestial influences working to some extent outside the spheres of the individual horoscopes, even though the specific cycles within the chart have to be taken into account (and indeed form the very basis of much astrological lore). Among long-term cycles are those marked out by the CHRONOCRATORS (Jupiter and Saturn), those attributed to the Archangels (the SECUNDADEIAN PERIODS), as well as the FIRST ORDER CYCLE of the superior planets. Many of the important cycles are involved with periodicities much longer than any human life, and are quite rightly seen as influencing epochs of human history, changes in climate, social revolutions, wars, religious beliefs, political crises, and so on. The long-term cycle most frequently referred to in popular astrological lore is that subsequent to the PRECESSION of the equinoctial point. Many of the ancient cycles, which have often survived in astrological lore in a mutilated form, such as the SAROS CYCLE and the NAROS CYCLE were close approximates to the synodics (though in the latter case this is probably accidental): see MAYAN ASTROLOGY. Some useful and ingenious attempts have been made in modern times to explain or even extend the theory of cycles, among the most notable being those of Collin, who established periodicities in various human and biological phenomena related to multiples of synodic periods, and Wachsmuth, who made complex use of the Precessional periodicities: see THREE PROTOTYPES. Among the cycles observed by Collin are the 41 month cycle (prices, industrial production and sales): 4 year cycle: the 7 and a half year cycle (tree-rings, lake-deposits and barometric pressures): the 8 year cycle (cotton prices, etc.): the 9 year cycle (linked with the asteroids, affecting stock-market prices and suicides): the 9 and three-quarter year cycle, observable in a wide variety of animals: the 11 year and 2 month cycle (weather and sunspots): the important 'war peak cycle' of 15 years (involving Mars and Saturn), and an 18 year cycle (real estate and building). Collin describes also a 36 year cycle affecting European weather, an 84 year cycle relating to sexual mores, and a cycle of 165 years, involving what he terms 'regeneration', linked with the work of esoteric schools, reminding one of the 250 year cultural cycle of Pluto, noted by Rudhyar. The figures in table 29 are derived from Collins attempts to link the geocentric conjunctions of each of the planets (in terms of the first-order cycle, and the longer periodicity of the second-order cycle. He inter-relates to these the "Asteroids", projecting a 'theoretical conjunction' based on averages. The tables constructed from these cycles are designed to suggest a harmonic relationship of numbers and tones which reflect the ancient harmonies called the "Music of the Spheres".

```
-------------------------------------------------------------TABLE 29
```

PLANET	FIRST ORDER CYCLE	SECOND ORDER CYCLE
ME	117 days	8 years
VE	585 days	8 years
MA	780 days	15 years
JU	398 days	12 years
SA	378 days	30 years
UR	369 days	84 years
NE	367 days	163 years
(Asteroids	465 days	9 years)

For further information, see Bradley (solar and lunar returns), Nelson (Sunspot cycles) and Ruperti (lunar, solar and planetary cycles).

CYGNUS   Constellation, from approximately 28 degrees Capricorn to 28 degrees Pisces, and from 28 to 55 degrees north of equator, known as 'the swan' from Roman times, when it was linked with the myth of Leda and Jupiter. Before that time, however, it was simply a 'Bird' to the Greeks, and still survives in such names as Avis, Volucris and 'Al Dajaja' (hen, to the Arabian astrologers), a term used in degenerate form of its brightest star, the "Deneb Adige". Under the impress of those who sought to Christianize the zodiac, it became the 'Cross of Calvary', and to this day is sometimes called the 'Northern Cross'. Astrologers say that it gives a dreamy but cultured nature, with unsteady affections. See also ALBIREO.

CYNOSURA   See URSA MINOR.

D

DABARAN   Al Dabaran, 'the forecaster', the 2nd of the Arabian "Manzils".

DABIH   Fixed star (multiple) of 3rd magnitude, the beta of Capricornus, set in the left eye of the goat, the name linked with the Arabian "Manzil" by which the latter was identified. Ptolemy accords it the nature of Venus conjunct Saturn: when emphasized in a chart it seems to bring out suspicion and mistrust.

DAEMON   See DAIMON.

DAEMONUM STABULA   Literally 'dwelling place of the demons', a term used by Kircher for the "Lunar Mansions".

DAGON   See PISCES CONSTELLATION and PISCIS AUSTRALIS.

DAILY PROGRESSIONS   See DAILY SERIES.

DAILY SERIES   A term relating to a precise formulation of the symbolic time relationship of the 'day for a year' method (see MEASURE OF TIME). As used in "Secondary Directions", it takes the True Solar Day to be the basic unit of time involved (see TIME). The period of a day is - by symbolic projection - to be extended into a "Weekly Series" a "Monthly Series" and the "Yearly Series". The full term is 'Daily Series of Secondary Directions', sometimes reduced to the misleading term 'Daily Progressions', which might quite easily refer to other conceptions of a daily time span.

DAIMON   The term equivalent to 'daimon' or 'daemon' was used by the Greek astrologers to refer to an ancient "Pars" no longer used - see LOT OF DEMON. In late mediaeval astrology, the same term (as well as 'demon') was also used in connexion with spiritual beings (not the 'demon' of popular infernal lore), connected with planetary and zodiacal agencies: the word in this sense was almost certainly derived from the same Sanskrit root which gave 'Deva', now unfortunately wrongly linked with the elemental beings, but once the equivalent of the angels. For a list of the 'daemonia' of the planetary spheres, see INTELLIGENCY.

DARK AGE   See KALI YUGA.

DARK MOON   See LILITH.

DAY   In ordinary parlance, the day is that period of light (literally 'daylight') between sunrise and sunset, but the term is also used of the 24 hour period marked by the earth's rotation on its axis - see SOLAR DAY. For other definitions, see CIVIL DAY, JULIAN DAY, SIDEREAL DAY and TIME. The Babylonians and Hindus measured the day from sunrise to sunrise: the ancient Greeks (though not always) reckoned the day from sunset to sunset, as do the Jews. Most other nations now measure the day from midnight to midnight - but see ASTRONOMICAL DAY.

DAY FOR A YEAR   See MEASURE OF TIME.

DAY HOME   See DAY HOUSE.

DAY HOROSCOPE   A general term used of a horoscope for which the Sun is above the horizon line: it is contrasted with the "Night Horoscope".

DAY HOUSE   A confusing term arising from an early mistranslation of Greek and Latin astrological texts. In traditional astrology, a planet was considered to have rule over two signs, one being called the 'day house' of that planet, and the other sign being called the 'night house' ('diurnal' and 'nocturnal', respectively). The Sun and Moon were exceptions, for these were said to concentrate their attentions on Leo and Cancer respectively, and accordingly had only one sign each. Table 30 indicates the order of the ancient rulership.

```
-------------------------------------------------------------------TABLE 30
DAY HOUSE              PLANET                 NIGHT HOUSE
======================================================================
(Cancer         Moon)      (Sun          Leo)
Gemini          Mercury                   Virgo
Taurus          Venus                     Libra
Aries           Mars                      Scorpio
Pisces          Jupiter                   Sagittarius
Aquarius        Saturn                    Capricorn
----------------------------------------------------------------------
```

Since a sign is not a house, the term might have been translated in a way which would have avoided confusion. In modern times, 'Day Home' and 'Night Home' have been suggested as alternatives, but it is clear from such early sources as Firmicus that the original idea was linked with the equivalent of positivity and negativity - which, of course, explains the misunderstood term "Positive Mars" when used of the ruler of Aries, in contrast with the "Negative Mars" of Scorpio (prior to the introduction of Pluto as ruler of the latter sign). See PLANETARY RULERSHIP.

DAYLIGHT SAVING TIME   Called 'Summer Time' when originated in 1916, and introduced to provide an hour extra of daylight during working hours. At 2 am on the Sunday following the 3rd Saturday in April, the clock was set ahead by one hour. This was adjusted back one hour on the Sunday following the 1st Saturday in October (though in practice these days varied, resulting in the need for tables recording the history of daylight saving regulations. During the Second World War, a similar alteration by two hours was made, called 'Double Summer Time'. A related (though not synchronized) system of 'War Time' was operative in the United States of America. Some countries did not accept these regulations, and in practical terms this means that an astrologer casting horoscopes for the years after 1916 must ensure from reliable sources what sort of time was operative at the place and time of birth. Many of the tables given in standard astrological textbooks are sparse and inaccurate: 'World Daylight Saving Time' by Curran and Taylor should be consulted, but see also TIME and TIME ZONES.

DAY OF BRAHMA   See KALPA.

DAYS OF THE WEEK   As Roger Bacon intimated in the 13th century, the names of the seven days of the week appear to have been derived from the ancient astrological practice of assigning planetary rulerships to the hours of the day. The first hour of the first day was given to the rule of Saturn - hence the first day was called Saturn-day (Saturday). Each of the planets, in the ancient descending order of the "Spheres' (which is not the order of the modern astronomers, since Venus was transposed with Mercury) was then assigned to the sequence of hours, Jupiter ruling the second hour, Mars the third, and so on. By this reckoning, the 22nd hour would again be ruled by Saturn, the 23rd by Jupiter, and the 24th by Mars. The first hour of the second day would thus be ruled by the Sun - hence it was 'Sun-day' (dies Solis). The sequence of hourly rulerships gives in this way the sequence of the seven days, though the survival of the planetary names is more openly reflected in the Romance languages - for example, the French 'lunedi' is the 'Moon-day' of Monday; 'mardi' is the 'Mars-day' (our Tuesday); 'mercredi' is the 'Mercury-day' (our Wednesday); jeudi is 'Jove-day', the Jupiter-day of Thursday, and 'vendredi' is 'Venus-day' of Friday. The notion of a seven-day week developed only late in the Roman Empire, and was legalized by Constantine in the 4th century AD.

==

DAY TRIPLICITIES   Almost an archaic term, referring to the ancient tradition
that some planets are stronger when they are in certain triplicities in a
"Day Horoscope". Such are Venus, when in an earth sign; the Sun when in a
fire sign; Mars when in a water sign, and Saturn in an air sign. In fact,
this theory runs contrary to some of the traditional teachings regarding
DEBILITY and FALL.

DEATH ASTEROGRAM   A term probably originated by the modern astrologer Sucher
as synonymous with "Death Chart", though Sucher's own published death
asterograms appear to be based on one of the "Sidereal Zodiacs" with an
unconventional ayanamsa. The chart (sometimes the 'death asterogramme') is
visualized as a sort of summary of the human life to which it relates, as
well as being conceived as having some connexion with the various post-mortem
experiences of the deceased soul. As with the more conventional death chart,
it is apparent that some astrologers connect the configurations of the chart
with conditions relating to the next incarnation. The whole field is
contentious, and may not be subjected to ordinary investigatory techniques.

DEATH CHART   A name given to a horoscope figure erected for the date or time
of death, and interpreted by curious analogy with the natal chart which is
concerned with the relationships a newly incarnated soul holds to the earth
and stellar realms. Some astrologers insist that a death chart may reflect
man's post-mortem relationship with the spiritual realms (Sucher makes such a
claim in connexion with the "Death Asterogram"). Death charts may be cast
according to either the tropical or sidereal stereographic projections.
However, since the whole structure of astrological lore and symbolism is
based upon the idea of the descent of spirit and soul into incarnate form,
the application of the its rules to an 'ex-carnation' is more than
questionable practice.

DEATH POINT   The 'point of death', which is not to be confused with the
"Anaretic", is one of the so-called Arabian PARS. If the degree of the Moon
in a natal chart is revolved to the Ascendant, the cusp of the adjusted 8th
house marks the death point.

DEBILITY   Each planet is said to have its own debility, as a result of which
it is generally weakened. A planet in the opposite sign to that which it
rules is debilitated by DETRIMENT, for example, but there are many conditions
under which a planet may be regarded as being otherwise debilitated. See
DIGNITY. As with his list of dignities, Wilson gives a comprehensive list of
debilities, and ascribes them a 'specific value': the three main essential
debilities are when the planet is in its detriment (5), when it is in its
fall (4), and when it is peregrine (5). The list of accidental debilities is
much longer, and the following is merely a digest of the more important:

Besieged by Saturn and Mars	6	In partile conjunction with Saturn	5
Conjunction with Algol	6	In partile conjunction with Mars	5
Combust	5	In twelfth house	5
Retrograde	5	In partile conjunction with Cauda	4
In 6th or 8th house	4	In term of Saturn or Mars	1

DECAN   In general reference, any 10 degree arc, but more specifically a term
applied to a 10 degree arc of the zodiac, resulting in the division of the 12
signs into 36 equal arcs. In each of the signs, these divisions are called
the first, second and third decans (or 'decanates'). Great importance was
attached to the supposed influences of these zodiacal arcs in ancient
astrology - indeed, the decanate system of the Egyptians appears to have
merited as much attention as the 12 signs themselves. In modern astrology,
which rests firmly on the ancient tradition, there are two frequently used
systems for determining the supposed influences of the decan sequences. In
the first, the ruler of the first sign Aries (Mars) is given dominion over
the first decan of that sign: then the followers are each assigned to the
sequence of decan arcs throughout the zodiac, in a specific order: AR1 - MA:

AR2 - SU: AR3 - VE: TA1 - ME: TA2 - MO: TA3 - SA: GE1 - JU, etc. The
so-called 'modern planets' play no part in this sequence. The second system
does incorporate the moderns, however, since it is based on the adoption of
the ruler of the relevant sign being accorded rule over the first arc, with
the rulers of the two following signs of the same triplicity being placed
over the next two decans: AR1 - MA: AR2 - SU (SU being ruler of Leo): AR3
- JU (JU being ruler of Sagittarius): TA1 - VE, etc. In Arabian and
mediaeval European astrology the decans were highly regarded, and figured
frequently in the rich imagery of talismans.   Several early systems of
decans involved a complex nomenclature, recorded in Latin and Greek in a
modern text by Nowotny, but these are long obsolete.   Unfortunately, the
term FACE (which has quite a different application) has been used by some
astrologers as synonymous with 'decan' - this is no modern error: see for
example the Ratdolt edition of Angelus.

DECANATE   See DECAN.

DECEMBER   The twelfth month (31 days), its name being derived from the Roman
system prior to the introduction of the "Julian Calendar" reforms, when it
was the 10th month (the Latin 'decem' means 'ten'). Esoterically, the month
is still linked with the magical significance of the number 10, which
Blavatsky records as an image of the standing man (the figure 1) confronting
the entire cosmos (the zero 0), and aware of his separation from it, by means
of which he defines his own individuality (the space between the two
figures). This application to the Arabian numeration was valid within the
Roman system, for the letter X (ten) had the same symbolic meaning, though
with a different rationale. The month was specifically linked with the
festival of the Saturnalia: the esoteric significance of the X-form was
associated with the symbolism of the "Angles" of the horoscope, which were in
turn an image of the "Descent of the Soul" into matter.

DECILE   An aspect of 36 degrees, arising from a division of the zodiac into
tenths. It is sometimes called the 'semi-quintile'. See also QUINTILE.

DECLINATION   The measurement of angular distances from the "Celestial
Equator", north or south. The widest possible declination of the Sun is 23
degrees 28 minutes, when it reaches the solstital point: since the ecliptic
intersects the equator at the 1st degrees of Aries and Libra, the Sun at
these points has no declination.   The approximate maximum declination of the
Moon, Mercury, Venus and Mars is 27 degrees, whilst Jupiter, Saturn, Uranus
and Neptune have almost the same declination maximum as the Sun. In modern
notation, the positive sign (+) marks the angle north of the equator, the
negative (-) that south of the equator.

DECREASING LIGHT   A term used mainly of the Moon, after direct opposition to
the Sun, as it begins to lose light, or to "wane".   Sometimes, the term is
used of other planets. The opposite term is 'Increasing Light'.

DECREPIT QUADRANT   See QUADRANTS.

DECUMBITURE   The name given in the quasi-medical branch of "Horary
Astrology" to the chart cast for the time when the subject took to bed at the
beginning of an illness. The 'decumbiture chart' is usually concerned with
medical prognosis, and with determining the so-called 'critical days'.

DECUSSATA CHART   See CHART SYSTEMS.

DEE ZODIAC   See GLASTONBURY ZODIAC.

DEFERENT   Term used specifically in connexion with the theory of
"Epicycles" set out in the "Ptolemaic System". The complex apparent
movements of planets in the geocentric model were partly explained in terms
of their having two inter-related motions, in a conception elaborated to

==

maintain the Aristotelian doctrine that planets move in perfect circles. The
planet was visualised as striving to move in a perfect circle, its centre
moving on an imaginary circumference of an eccentrically centred circle
(centred on an imaginary line joining the earth with the Sun, but not on the
centre of the earth itself). This imaginary orbit was called the deferent,
around which the moving centre of the planet produced the effect of epicyclic
movement. The influential Arabic astrologer Alfraganus appears to have
termed the deferent the 'eccentric'.

DEFICIENT DEGREES   See AZIMENE DEGREES.

DEFLUX   A term used as an equivalent of "Separation", from the Latin
'defluxio', itself a translation of the Ptolemaic Greek 'aporroia'.

DEGREE   An arc of precisely 1/360th arc of the circumference of a circle.
The visual equivalent of a degree in practical astronomy is about twice the
apparent diameter of the Sun or Moon. See also DEGREE SYMBOLS.

DEGREE ARCS   See DEGREE AREAS.

DEGREE AREAS   A term sometimes used as the equivalent of "Degree Symbols",
which in some cases (for example, in the system of "Wemyss Degrees") relate
to 'areas' (really 'arcs'), rather than to specific degrees. Properly, the
term should be 'degree arcs'.

DEGREE DIAL   A term derived from the specialist conversion of the
"Cosmogram", and properly the 'Ninety Degree Dial' - see COSMOBIOLOGY. The
term is not to be confused with VOLVELLE.

DEGREE EXALTATIONS   See EXALTATIONS.

DEGREE RULERSHIPS   See MONOMOIRIA.

DEGREE SYMBOLS   A vast astrology literature has tabulated the specific
influences said to be exerted by individual degrees of the zodiac, regarded
as exerting effects quite independent of occupant bodies, nodes, fixed stars
and zodiacal arcs. Whilst the interpretation of individual degrees is
probably of Arabic origin, the methods by which the 'degree symbols' (that
is, the readings attached to the individual degrees) were determined has
never been adequately established. A few of the systems are undoubtedly
constructed from clairvoyant readings (as for example the modern SABIAN
SYMBOLS) but others, undoubtedly ancient, have originated in ways unknown, as
for example the VOLASFERA SYMBOLS. No satisfactory compendium or comparative
study has been made of degree symbol readings, and many astrologers doubt the
validity of all the various systems, maintaining that the individual
qualities which are associated with degrees of the zodiac may be explained by
consideration of the nature of the fixed stars, constellations and mansions,
since there is not a single degree of the zodiac free of such 'radiations' or
influences. In some systems, the 'degree symbols' are actually arcs, rather
than degrees, or even diametric axes across the zodiac. An example of an
'arc symbolism' would be the association of 25 to 29 degrees of Leo with the
art of astrology, an arc which is startlingly recurrent in the charts of
astrologers. Well over a dozen sets of 'degree symbol' systems are currently
available: Carruthers lists no fewer than 17 from post-mediaeval sources
alone, for example. In addition to those mentioned above, see also ANGELUS
SYMBOLS, CHARUBEL SYMBOLS, THEBAN CALENDAR and WEMYSS SYMBOLS. Each of the
preceding systems derived purely from the zodiacal degrees, but there is a
system derived from the constellations, which must be distinguished from
these, called STAR POINTS, and one composite system, derived from various
sources (degree symbols, fixed star influences, arcs, constellations, etc),
and linked with the constellation zodiac by Devore under the name INDIVIDUAL
DEGREES. For additional relevant material, see Carelli, Hasbrouck, Keane,
Leinbach and Matthews. See also MONOMOIRIA.

==

DEIMOS   The name of one of the two moons of Mars.

DEKAN   See DECAN.

DELATION   A term defined by Simmonite as meaning 'restoring of light', and
applied to the aspecting of an inferior planet of a superior which is either
combust or retrograde. It seems that the superior planet 'restores' to the
inferior its "Virtue".

DELINEATION   Term derived for specialist use from the old idea of 'drawing',
the word being applied to the 'drawing of a picture', but usually of the
portrait revealed in the horoscope figure.   Often, the 'delineation of a
horoscope' is the 'interpretation of a horoscope'.

DELPHINUS   Constellation, approximately 8 to 19 degrees Aquarius, from 3 to
19 degrees north of the equator, the 'Dolphin'. This was the 'Hieros
Ichthus' (sacred fish) of the ancient Greeks, who accorded it many related
names. The Dolphin was said to have been placed in the heavens by Neptune
for having persuaded Amphitrite to be his wife - hence the asterism is
sometimes called by her name. For all its reputation in mythology, the
asterism is held unfavourable by Ptolemy, who links it with the combined
natures of Mars and Saturn.

DELPORTE DIVISION   See MODERN ZODIAC.

DEMETER   Name given to one of the HYPOTHETICAL PLANETS in the system
proposed by the Dutch astrologer Ram, and accorded rule over zodiacal Cancer.
This transplutonian is included in an ephemeris, and claimed to relate to
'spiritual aptitudes, art and music'.

DEMI-DECAN   See FACE.

DEMON STAR   See ALGOL.

DENDERAH ZODIAC   Name given to an astrological bas-relief once in Denderah,
Egypt, in the Temple of Hathor. This famous circular ceiling relief was
carried by Napoleon to the Louvre, and wrongly called the Denderah Zodiac.
It is a constellation map, containing the twelve images of the zodiacal
asterisms, along with such others as Draco (see POLE STAR), symbolized as a
hippopotamus, the ancient ideogram for Sirius, and each of the planets in
their "Exaltations".   The age of this constellation map is in dispute, but
many scholars insist that whilst Ptolemaic (Fagan convincingly dates it to
April, 17 AD), it certainly contains elements from a much earlier Egyptian
astrological tradition. Breasted even suggests that the entire Temple of
Osiris, and its planet-studded constellation map (now in situ as a plaster
reproduction), stems from prototypes of about 2,900 BC. As Wachsmuth admits,
'even if this was executed at a later time, the knowledge which it embodies
had long been preserved in the Mysteries'. The fact remains that there is a
specific reference in the asterism map to 8 degrees of Aries, which relates
to a sidereal system popular in Greece and Rome, not originated until 373 BC,
which at least gives the earliest possible date for the structure. On the
other hand, it is certain that the images and symbols are themselves derived
from a very ancient tradition, which makes this 'zodiac' one of the most
fascinating astrological survivals from the past. See also ESNA ZODIACS.

DENEB   Fixed star, the zeta of Aquila, said to have derived its name from
the Arabic 'Al Dhanab' (the tail). Of the nature of Mars conjunct Jupiter.
See also DENEBOLA, for which this term is often confused.

DENEB ADIGE   Fixed star, the alpha of Cygnus, set in the tail of the Swan,
the name derived from the Arabic for 'hen's tail'. Said to be of the nature
of Mercury conjunct Venus - hence, it encourages ingenuity and mental
versatility.

DENEB ALGEDI   Fixed star, the delta of Capricornus, set in the tail of the
goat, its name from the Arabic 'tail of goat'. Powell adoped this star to
mark the termination of his sidereal Capricorn: see SIDEREAL ZODIAC. It is
said by Ptolemy to be of the nature of Jupiter conjunct Saturn.

DENEB KAITOS   Fixed star, the beta of Cetus, set in the tail of the Whale,
its name from the Arabian phrase meaning 'tail of the whale towards the
south', and sometimes called 'Difda' (the second frog) from the Arabic, which
explains the curious Latin name 'Rana Secunda' - see FOMALHAUT. It is said
to give mental disturbances when emphasised in a chart, and Ptolemy likens
its influence to that of Saturn.

DENEBOLA   Fixed star, the beta of Leo, set in the lion's tail, the name
derived from the Arabic meaning 'the tail of the lion'. Powell used the star
to terminate his sidereal Leo - see SIDEREAL ZODIAC. It is regarded as an
unfortunate influence in a chart - as Allen says, 'thus opposed to REGULUS in
character as in position'.   Ptolemy links it with the influence of Saturn
and Venus, and Simmonite to that of Uranus itself. Sometimes the star is
wrongly called "Deneb".

DEPRESSION   In a specialist sense, sometimes used as a synonym for the
planetary "Fall" - see both DIGNITY and HYPSOMATA.

DESCENDANT   As a strict technicality, the term should apply to the cusp of
the seventh house, otherwise known as the Western angle: however, it is
often used to denote the whole arc of the house.

DESCENDANT DEGREE   The degree upon the "Descendant".

DESCENDANT PLANET   Whilst one may reasonably think that this term applies to
a planet on (or at least within orb of) the "Descendant", it is in fact
applied to any planet following its "Culmination" - that is, when it is
between the 9th house and the Nadir.

DESCENDING ARC   This term, which may be applied to the degree of zodiac
descending over the cusp of the 7th house, must be distinguished from the
same Theosophical term which is the equivalent of the 'Shadowy Arc', relating
to the downward passage of life-waves into the physical realms.

DESCENT OF THE SOUL   The hermetic tradition insists that the act of rebirth
or incarnation is preceded by a descent of the soul through the planetary
spheres. It is in the descent through the spheres that the incarnating
spirit imbibes the influences proper to his being, and which are expressed in
the chart at birth. The tradition is wide-spread, under many different
terms, such as 'Spherical Descent, the 'Path of Rebirth', and so on, but the
hermetic texts most often quoted are those attributed to Macrobius and
Servius, derived from commentaries on Platonic and Virgilian texts
respectively.   The former is linked with an Orphic tradition, the latter
with an Egyptian tradition, and are accordingly dealt with under ORPHIC
DESCENT OF THE SOUL and EGYPTIAN DESCENT OF THE SOUL. Several of the more
important forms of "Esoteric Astrology" visualize a similar descent and
rebirth - especially so the astrological forms descrbied by Wachsmuth and
expressed in certain lectures by Steiner. Some esoteric astrologers insist
that the natal horoscope is itself to be interpreted as a record of the
experiences undergone by the soul during its spherical descent.

DESERTUM   Name given to the 21st of the "Lunar Mansions" in some mediaeval
lists.   Probably equated with the undistinguished stellar area along the
ecliptic between the sigma of Sagittarius (Nunki) and DABITH in Capricornus.

DETRIMENT   A specialist astrological term relating to a planet which is said
to be in its detriment, or 'in detriment', when in a sign opposite to that
which is its own sign or house. A planet in detriment is weakened.

==

DEVIL   According to the astrologer Leo, Mars has been called 'the Devil'.
If this is so, then it is likely to have been connected with the old idea of
"Negative Mars", which has rule over the 8th house, which some astrologers
link with post-mortem experiences.   Inherent in this nomenclature is the
diabolic dualism which the early Church fought to eradicate, for it seems
that Saturn went 'under the nom de guerre of Satan'. Whilst the difference
between Diabolus (Devil) and Satanus (Satan) was recognized in early occult
schools, it was largely lost in ecclesiastical literature.

DEVORE SYMBOLS   See INDIVIDUAL SYMBOLS.

DEXTER ASPECT   An ancient term, probably derived by Ptolemy (who was unaware
of the motion of the Earth) and used in reference to aspects calculated
against the order of the signs. The reverse computation is a "Sinister
Aspect". Traditionally, the dexter is more powerful, but the whole theory of
aspects requires to be considered against the natures of the planets
involved: the terms 'dexter' and 'sinister' are virtually archaic.

DHANISHTHA   The Sanskrit name for the constellation Aquarius - see KUMBHAM.

DHANUS   The Sanskrit name for zodiacal Sagittarius - but see also MULA.

DHIRA   Al Dhira, the name given to the 5th of the Arabic "Manzils", the
Arabic word meaning 'forearm', as does the mediaeval equivalent 'Brachium'.

DIAMETER   An archaic term for the aspect of "Opposition".

DIAPASON   Ratio connected with the planetary system set out in the theory of
the "Music of the Spheres", and depending upon the supposed planetary
distances. This is the Octave, a ratio of two to one, and in the planetary
diagrams it embraces the Sphere of the Moon up to the Stellatum itself,
including thereby eight spheres.

DIAPENTE   Ratio connected with the planetary system set out in the theory of
the "Music of the Spheres", and depending upon the supposed planetary
distances. This is the interval of the Fifth, or the 'sesquialtera', a ratio
of two to three. In the planetary diagram this ratio embraces the sphere of
the Moon up to and including the solar sphere.

DIAPHANOUS HEAVEN   See NINTH HEAVEN.

DIATESSARON   Ratio connected with the planetary system set out in the theory
of the "Music of the Spheres", and depending upon the supposed planetary
distances. This is the interval of the Fourth, a 'sesquitertia', a ratio of
three to four. In the planetary diagrams this ratio embraces the sphere of
Mercury up to and including the solar sphere, incorporating three spheres.

DICHOTOME   Term now almost obsolete, from the Greek meaning 'cut in half',
and used of a planet (especially of the Moon) which is half illumined - that
is to say, in "Square" aspect to the Sun.

DIDEMOI   One of the several Greek names meaning 'twins', used to denote the
sign and constellation "Gemini".

DIDO   In astrology, a name given to one of the "Hypothetical Planets" by
Wemyss, said by him to be the ruler of zodiacal Virgo - a suggestion never
widely accepted. It is possible that Wemyss had in mind the influence of
Pluto, which (though not discovered by astronomers until 1930) was recognised
by some astrologers as an extraneptunian influence some years before this.
Wemyss gave his Dido a mean motion of about 1 degree per annum.

DIDYMOI   An alternative spelling for DIDEMOI.

DIFDA   A name for the fixed star DENEB KAITOS.

DIGNITY   Each planet is said to have its own dignity, which may be
'essential', 'accidental', or both: see therefore ACCIDENTAL DIGNITY. It
seems that there was once greater precision in the use of the word than is
now the case: originally, an essential dignity was manifest only through
signs, while accidental dignities were manifest through houses, but the two
have now been confused. A planet in its own sign is certainly said to be in
its essential dignity, sometimes called a 'domal dignity'. When a planet is
in the sign of its "Exaltation", it is also said to be dignified. Less
certain, however, is a tradition that a planet posited in the same triplicity
as that of which it is ruler may be said to be dignified. Mutual reception
by exaltation was sometimes regarded as an indication of dignity. The
opposite of 'dignity' is DEBILITY. When taken to extremes, the theory of
dignities is extremely complex, especially in regard to accidental dignities.
Wilson provides a fairly comprehensive list, and ascribes a system of
'specific values', of which the following are representative:

Planet in its house	5	Planet in mutual reception by house	5
Planet in exaltation	4	Planet in mutual reception by exaltation	4
In own triplicity	3	Planet in own term	2
Planet in own Face	1		

Table 31 sets out the traditional dignities and debilities.

TABLE 31

PLANET	RULES	DETRIMENT IN	EXALTATION IN	FALL IN
SU	Leo	Aquarius	Aries	Libra
MO	Cancer	Capricorn	Taurus	Scorpio
ME	Gemini	Sagittarius	Aquarius	Leo
	Virgo	Pisces	(Virgo)	(Pisces)
VE	Taurus	Scorpio	Pisces	Virgo
	Libra	Aries		
MA	Aries	Libra	Capricorn	Cancer
	Scorpio	Taurus	(Virgo)	(Pisces)
JU	Pisces	Virgo	Cancer	Capricorn
	Sagittarius	Gemini	(Capricorn)	(Cancer)
SA	Capricorn	Cancer	Libra	Aries
	Aquarius	Leo		

The information in table 31 is based on the traditional Ptolemaic
cosmoconception, which does not take into account the modern rulerships of
the suprasaturnian planets, given in table 32.

TABLE 32

PLANET	RULES	DETRIMENT IN	EXALTATION IN	FALL IN
UR	Aquarius	Leo	Scorpio	Taurus
NE	Pisces	Virgo	Cancer	Capricorn
PL	Scorpio	Taurus	Aries	Libra

Some astrologers insist that exaltation and fall take place in specific
degrees of the zodiac, as follows:

EXALTATION: SU 19 Aries; MO 3 Taurus; ME 15 Virgo; VE 27 Pisces;
MA 28 Capricorn; JU 15 Cancer; SA 21 Libra; DH 3 Gemini.

The 'degree of fall' is that directly opposite in the zodiac to the 'degree
of exaltation'. It must be observed that many authorities offer significant
variations on these traditional dignities.

DIONE   Name given to one of the moons of Saturn - see also HYADES.

DIONYSIAN HIERARCHIES   See CELESTIAL HIERARCHIES.

DIONYSIAN PERIOD   See VICTORIAN PERIOD.

DIOSCURI   Most usually the word applies to the "Gemini Constellation", but
sometimes to the two stars in this asterism, CASTOR and POLLUX.

DIOSEMAISIS   An archaic term used to denote weather-forecasting from
astrological, stellar and meteorological phenomena.

DIRAH   Fixed star (double), the mu of Gemini, set in the left foot of the
northern twin: said to be of the nature of Mercury and Venus.

DIRECT APPLICATION   The "Application" to aspect of planets when both are in
direct motion along the ecliptic. See RETROGRADE APPLICATION.

DIRECTING   See PRIMARY DIRECTIONS.

DIRECTIONAL ASPECTS   See PRIMARY DIRECTIONS.

DIRECTIONS   The art of making 'directions', as of interpreting them, is the
most important part of "Predictive Astrology", and is involved with studying
the future configurations of planets and angles in regard to a radical chart,
with a view to learning something about the future of the native. The term
is almost certainly derived from the idea of 'directing' planets and angles
to some future position. There are actually three different forms of
'directions': two are involved with symbolic time systems (see PRIMARY
SYSTEM and SECONDARY DIRECTIONS), while a third is concerned with the
projection on to the radical chart of the actual movements of the planets in
a non-symbolic way: see TRANSITS.

DIRECT MOTION   Planets moving, or appearing to move, in the direction of the
signs are said to be in 'direct motion': see RETROGRADE.

DISAPPEAR   When a planet reaches the Nadir, it is sometimes said to
'disappear', and its influence is said to 'die'. An obsolete term.

DISCORD   The 'Point of Discord' is one of the so-called Arabian "Pars". If
the degree of Mars in a natal chart is taken as the Ascendant, the adjusted
position of Jupiter marks the point of discord.

DISJUNCT SIGNS   A term used in Ptolemaic astrology, approximately the
equivalent of DISSOCIATE SIGNS. A synonymous term was 'Alien Signs'.

DISPOSITOR   Under certain circumstances, a planet may be said to 'dispose'
of another, which really means that it superimposes its own influence upon
that other planet. Such a disposing planet is called the 'dispositor'. In
fact, while the traditional basis for disposition may have been well-founded
and simple, subsequent theories have rendered the subject very complex. In
simple terms, the theory is that the ruling planet of the sign on the cusp of
the house is the dispositor of a planet actually sited in that house. This
indicates how unsatisfactory the term is, for the influence of the disposed
planet is not removed entirely (that is, 'disposed' of, in its modern
connotation), but merely subjected in its influence to the dispositor. Thus,
if Mercury disposes Jupiter, the influence of the latter is merged with the
former, and does not disappear altogether. The example is chosen to raise a
further point - that some authorities insist that Mercury itself may not be
disposed.

DISSOCIATE ASPECTS   The original theory of "Aspects" was based on the
supposed harmony and disharmony between the four elements: see ELEMENTAL

==

ASPECTS and JAIMINI. Thus, two planets in trine aspect (120 degrees apart) were harmoniously united not so much by the magic of the number 120, or by any geometric proportion, as by the fact that they were manifesting in signs of the same triplicity. Planets in square aspect were inharmoniously linked by virtue of their being in triplicities inharmonious to each other. Since orbs are permitted in calculating the power of aspects, it sometimes happens that an aspect which fulfils the requirements of geometry or mathematics does not fulfil the requirements of the elemental relationship which lies at the base of aspectal theory. Thus, for example, two planets may be technically 'conjunct' with an orb of 4 degrees, yet if these planets are near to a cusp, it is possible that they are manifesting through different elemental powers: while geometrically 'conjunct', they are not elementally conjunct. Clearly, such an aspect may in no way carry the full force of a normal aspect - if indeed it carries any aspectal force at all. Such an aspect is called a 'dissociate aspect'. Unfortunately, the same term 'dissociate' was once used as an equivalent for the QUINCUNX, though this use is now discontinued.

DISSOCIATE SIGNS   Term applied to groups of signs which are either adjacent or five signs apart. The utility of the term appears to revolve around the important (though often overlooked) distinction between DISSOCIATE ASPECTS and normal aspects.

DISTANCE   A term derived from a modern survey of the influence which "Planetary Distances" have on horoscopic factors. However, the idea was mooted, even in the late mediaeval astrology, when the conception of distance was applied to a model of our solar system very different from the present one. Few modern astrologers ascribe to the theory that planetary distances should condition the interpretation of planetary influences: it is significant that the largely experimental COSMOPSYCHOGRAM, which once incorporated 'distance data' (figure 25), does so no longer. The astrologer Schreiweis has done much work on the subject, and has come to the conclusion that the influence of distance is measurable in terms of chart influences, expressed in terms of linear distances. As evidence of his research, he provides a general schema for the interpretation in terms of groups of planetary polarities (positive for a good aspect, negative for a malefic aspect). In each case, a planet close to the Earth tends to offer an intensification of the planetary nature. These pairs of contrasts are set out for 'close' and 'far' linear distances from the Earth, though information is not available for all the planets. See DISTANCE VALUES. The ancient astrological idea of 'distance' (as for example represented in Dante's 'Convivio') was fundamental to certain concepts, but these distances were not concerned with planetary influences or powers (which were in any case regarded as being immaterial, and therefore not conditioned by spatial considerations), as with the theory of planetary harmonics, in the ancient sense of the musical tones. It was required of the theory of the SPHERES that the maximum distance of any planet should correspond precisely with the minimum distance of the superior adjacent sphere, and it was of overriding importance that these distances should be harmonically related. The harmonics of the ancient MUSIC OF THE SPHERES was initially linked with such distances, and not with planetary motions, periodicities or 'notes', as in the later astrological theory. That such distances were entirely chimerical (by modern standards, at least) is in a sense of no real importance: the conical shadow cast by the earth into space (into which shadow we may look during the night-time) was measured according to such distances, for example. According to Alfraganus, who so fundamentally influenced Dante (and hence much modern thinking), this distance was 871,000 miles, which was in turn related to strict ratios for other planetary distances within the series of concentrics. We must not forget, however, that even the order of the planets (let alone the distances between their spheres) was disputed among the early Greek astronomers who influenced the promulgation of the "Ptolemaic System", and the best generalisation which may be made about the traditional view of distances was that it was not so much the actual spatial distance between the planets which was important, as the ratios between them.

FIGURE 25.   COSMOPSYCHOGRAPH WITH RADIATING 'DISTANCE VALUES'.
(AFTER EBERTIN).

DISTANCE VALUES   A term used by Ebertin in respect of data incorporated into
his "Cosmopsychogram", the inner circle of which originally set out in
symbolic form the 'distance values' of the planets according to a fixed
system - see figure 25. The distance from the earth was marked in terms of a
scale valued as 0 for apogee to 100 at perigee. Distance value ephemerides
for years after 1881 were made available by Ebertin, but the system appears
no longer to be widely used.

DIURNAL   Pertaining to the day, which is really 'pertaining to the
periodicity of the axial rotation of the earth', rather than to any concept
of daylight. See DAY.

DIURNAL ARC   The variable arc through which any celestial body appears to
pass from sunrise to sunset.

DIURNAL HORARY TIME   See HORARY TIME.

DIURNAL HOROSCOPE A term sometimes used of a chart in which the Sun is above
the horizon - hence cast for 'day time'. In a more specialist sense it is a
term used for a figure designed to determine future events, the data for the
figure being derived from the natal figure. The chart is erected as though
the native were reborn each day at the same sidereal time, though the planets
are inserted according to the changes recorded in the ephemeris for the
future days in question.

DIURNAL HOUSE   See DAY HOUSE and MASCULINE PLANETS.

DIURNAL PLANETS   These are the Sun and Jupiter, according to Ptolemy - but
see NOCTURNAL PLANETS. In modern astrology a planet is sometimes called
'diurnal' when it is in the day quadrants of a chart.

DIURNAL RULER   Term applied to any planet that rules by day: see DAY HOUSES.

DIURNAL SIGNS   See POSITIVE SIGNS.

DIVINE PROPORTION   See GOLDEN NUMBER.

DIVINE YEAR   One of the 'years of the gods' in the Hindu system, regarded as
being equal to 360 years of mortals. See YUGA.

DIVORCE POINT   The 'point of divorce' is a modern variant on the so-called Arabian "Pars". The degree opposite the Ascendant is rotated to the Ascendant, and the adjusted natal Venus marks the point.

DODEKATAMORION CHART   A somewhat confusing term (see DODEKATEMORION) derived from the Greek to denote a chart based on a division of the ecliptic into twelve equal parts. The majority of horoscopes are of this structure.

DODEKATEMORION   An ancient system of establishing degree points, used in Hellenistic astrology (though derived from the Babylonian), and now rarely used. The dodekatemorion of any point in the zodiac (Z) is 12 times the distance from Z of the arc between Z and the beginning of the sign in which it is located. Thus, the dodekatemorion of a planet located in 22 degrees Taurus is Aquarius 16 degrees: (12 x Z) = (12 x 22) - 264 degrees:- (264 + Z) = (264 + 22) = 286 degrees - by conversion into zodiacal arc, 286 degrees equals 9 signs and 16 degrees. Therefore, the dodekatemorion is 16 Aquarius.

DODONIDES The group name of the constellations "Hyades" and "Pleiades", which make up the 'fourteen nymphs' of Dodona, the Grecian mystery centre where, according to myth, Jupiter placed in care the infant Bacchus. They were also sometimes called the 'Atlantides', their father being Atlas.

DOG DAYS. A period originally computed from the heliacal rising of the dog-star "Sirius" (the name probably from the Greek 'serios', scorching), the alpha of "Canis Major", and extended for 40 days from that time. It was said to be the hottest time of the year, and ran through some of the weeks of July and August, from approximately 4th July. The tradition is, of course, Mediterranean in origin. In the esoteric tradition, a cycle of 40 days is involved with the descent of spirit into matter.

DOG OF ORION   See CANIS MAJOR.

DOG STARS   Usually a reference to "Sirius" and "Procyon", but sometimes to the actual asterisms of "Canis Major" and "Canis Minor".

DOLPHIN One of the names given to both the constellation and zodiacal sign "Pisces". When so used it is generally in reference to the esoteric nature of the sign, and then either to the Era of Christianity, which falls under the Age of Pisces (see PRECESSION), or to the incarnate Christ. A dolphin was sometimes used as an image of Pisces, as for example in the zodiacal scheme on the ceiling of the arch in Merton College, Oxford (figure 26), though in this case it is an heraldic evocation of the armorial bearings of Fitz James, who was Warden of the college at the end of the 15th century, when the zodiac was sculpted. See also DELPHINUS.

FIGURE 26. DOLPHIN AS SYMBOL FOR PISCES, FROM FITZJAMES ARCH, MERTON COLLEGE, OXFORD. THE ZODIACAL SCULPTURES ARE DATED FOR 1497.

===

DOMAL DIGNITY   When a planet enters its own sign (that is, the sign of which it is ruler), then it is in one of its "Essential Dignities", called the 'domal dignity'.   Sometimes such a planet is said to be 'domiciled' - for which a clumsy alternative 'domicilated' is also used.   Unfortunately, the loose use of precise astrological terms in recent years has resulted in the term domiciled being applied in a non-specific sense, so that any planet is sometimes said to be 'domiciled' in any house, or indeed in any sign.

DOMICILE   See DOMAL DIGNITY.

DOMICILIUM SOLIS   Term for both the "Leo Constellation" and "Regulus".

DOMIFICATION   Specialist term meaning 'turning into houses', and relating to the procedure of applying one or other of the "House Systems" to the chart construction.

DOMINICAL CYCLE   See VICTORIAN PERIOD.

DOMINICAL LETTER   The so-called 'Sunday letter', a term sometimes included in astrological lexicons, even though it is related only to an ancient method of computing the days of the week (and specifically the movable feasts) by means of letters of the alphabet.   The term has nothing to do with astrology.

DOMINION   A planet or a sign may properly be said to have 'dominion' over some aspect of the material realm - for example, a sign may have dominion over a particular country (see CHOROGRAPHY), or over a precious stone, animal, and so on.   See however RULE.

DOMINIONS   Or Dominations, the name given to the first of the "Celestial Hierarchies" of the second rank, sometimes called the Kyriotetes, after the nomenclature proposed by Dionysius the Areopagite.   They are associated with the sphere of Jupiter.   The Dominions are said by occultists to control the metamorphosis of matter, as the expression of spiritual events.   Steiner calls them the Spirits of Wisdom.

DOOR OF BIRTH   A term used in esoteric astrology for the sign Cancer, ruled by the Archangel Gabriel - see GATE OF BIRTH.

DOOR OF DEATH   A term used in esoteric astrology for the sign Capricorn: see GATE OF DEATH.

DORADO   Constellation, the head of which marks the south pole of the ecliptic, formed only in the early seventeeth century, the name apparently intended to refer to the coryphaena 'goldfish' of the tropical seas.

DOROTHEAN ASTROLOGY   A term used by the historian Pingree in his brief but excellent history of astrology, in reference to one of the two 'intellectually respectable traditions' of Hellenistic astrology (the other being the PTOLEMAIC SYSTEM).   The term refers to the writings of Dorotheus of Sidon (c.75 AD) whose principal later adherents were Firmicus Maternus (see MATHESEOS) and Hephaestio of Thebes, probably an Egyptian astrologer, of the 5th century.   The refinements on the Hellenistic form of astrology for which the Dorothean is noteworthy is the system of "Sortes", a specialist tradition relating to the "Prorogator", and an early form of predictive astrology which has been called "Continuous Astrology".

DORSA LEONIS   Name given by Simmonite to the fixed star "Vindemiatrix", which he wrongly located in the sign Virgo.

DORSUM   Fixed star, the theta of Capricornus, set in the back of the goat: an unfortunate influence linked with bites from venomous creatures.

===

DORYPHORY   A curious survival from ancient forms of astrology, when horosocopes were often cast through direct observation of the heavens. In short, the term is really the equivalent of 'conjunction', though in a somewhat specialist sense. The 'doryphory' of the Sun is any planet which rises shortly before it, as a sort of herald (the Greek term means something like 'spear bearer'), whilst the 'doryphory' of the Moon is any planet which rises shortly after it, carrying its train, so to speak. Save in poetic language, the term is now obsolete.

DOUBLE BLIND TRIAL   See BLIND TRIAL.

DOUBLE BODIED SIGNS   See BICORPOREAL SIGNS.

DOUBLE SUMMER TIME   See DAYLIGHT SAVING TIME.

DRACO   Constellation circling the North Pole, from 63 to 81 degrees of the equator. Known even in ancient times as 'the dragon', though under different names, such as 'Serpens', 'Python' and 'Anguis': it was 'Sir' (snake) to the Babylonians, whilst the 'Al Thuban of the Arabian astrologers was actually a translation of the Greek 'dracon'. It was held in high esteem by the Egyptians, though they called it 'Hippopotamus'. In the mythology derived from the Greek legends, this is the dragon which guarded the golden apples in the Hesperides. Astrologers maintain that it gives a brilliantly analytic mind, and much travel, but of course its very extent should make one way of interpreting its effects as a whole - the fixed stars in the asterism which have proved of interest to astrologers are THUBAN and RASTABAN.

DRACONIC ZODIAC   A curious term originated (probably) by Fagan in reference to an interpretation of Babylonian imagery and mythology. The term is applied to a schema derived from the ideal sidereal longitude of the "Dragon's Head" in the first degree of Aries on the 1st Nisan of the so-called HYPSOMATIC YEAR, the positions of the traditional planets being measured from that node.

DRACONITIC PERIOD   The name given to the period of the moon's motion from one of its nodes back to the same node (27.212 days). The name is derived from the ancient terminology which postulated a link between the dragon and the sphere of the Moon - see for example DRAGON'S HEAD.

DRAGON   See ATALIA and DRACO.

DRAGON'S EYES   See RASTABAN.

DRAGON'S HEAD   The north node of the Moon, the point where this body crosses the ecliptic to begin its northward journey. The term, originally 'Caput Draconis' in traditional astrology (though with several variants) was derived from the link made between the sphere of the Moon and the celestial dragon forces: the dragon was imagined as being curled around the earth, in symbol of the lunar sphere. It is said (with little evidence) that the eclipses were explained in terms of this celestial dragon swallowing the sun and then regurgitating it. The Dragon's Head is undoubtedly a most powerful nodal point in the horoscope, though it is one usually made efficacious only by transits and progressions. It is said to have the equivalent nature of Jupiter and Venus, though some astrologers insist that when touched by directions it releases into the life of the native benefits due from karma. Some other authorities, such as Cornell, insist that it is of the nature of the Sun. For another, unrelated, use of the term see ETTANIN.

DRAGON'S TAIL   The South Node of the Moon, the point where this body crosses the ecliptic to begin its southward journey. For the possible origin of the term, see DRAGON'S HEAD. This was the 'Cauda Draconis' of traditional astrology, a powerful nodal point said to carry the influence equivalent to that of Saturn. Some astrologers insist that when touched by directions, it releases into the life of the native karmic consequences which present difficulties. In popular astrology it is regarded as a malignant force, equivalent to that of Saturn.

DRY   See PRINCIPLES and QUALITY.

DRY SIGNS   According to the ancient Ptolemaic classification, these are Aries, Taurus, Leo, Virgo, Sagittarius and Capricorn: see PRINCIPLES.

DSCHUBBA   Fixed star, the delta of Scorpius, set in the head of the Scorpion, its Arabic name meaning 'brain of the scorpion'. Powell adopted this star to mark the commencement of his sidereal Scorpio - see SIDEREAL ZODIAC. Robson appears to confuse it with his Isidis. Ptolemy says that it is of the nature of Mars and Saturn, and it is reputed to cause immorality and malevolence.

DUAL SIGNS   See BICORPOREAL SIGNS.

DUB   One of the several variant names for the constellation "Ursa Major".

DUBHE   One of the seven stars forming the constellation "Ursa Major", said by Ptolemy to be of the influence of Mars.

DUMB SIGNS   See MUTE SIGNS.

DUODENARY MEASURE   An arc, or measure, used in "Symbolic Directions", and so named by the astrologer Carter. It is based on the division of the zodiacal sign into twelfths, giving the equivalent of two-and-a-half degrees. This is the 'dwadeshamsa' of the Hindu astrology: see DWAD.

DUO PAVONES   See GEMINI CONSTELLATION.

DWAD   A dwad is an arc of 2.5 degrees, obtained by the division of a zodiacal sign by twelve. As with the "Decans" and "Faces", the sequence of the dwads is accorded a planetary rule, which follows the traditional associations of the 12 signs, starting with the actual ruler of the relevant sign. Thus, Mars being the ruler of Aries is the ruler of the 1st dwad of Aries, followed by Venus, Mercury, Moon, and so on.

DWADESHAMSA   In Hindu astrology, a term meaning 'one-twelfth', and applied both to the division of the entire circle of the zodiac into the twelve houses, and to the divison of an individual signs into the series of "Dwad". See also DUODENARY MEASURE.

DWAPARA YUGA   The 'bronze age' of the Hindu chronology, a periodicity of 864,000 mortal years. See however YUGA. The period given includes the 'twilights' or sandhya and sandhyansa, which are 200 divine years each.

DYNAMIS   The beings of the CELESTIAL HIERARCHIES linked with the planet Mars, and the rulers of the Fifth Sphere. They are sometimes called the 'Powers' or 'Mights', though the Greek term is actually cognate with the modern 'dynamic'. In Christian symbolism, these beings are often represented as subduing devils, which is clearly associated with the powerful duality of the Aries-Scorpio rulership (see NEGATIVE MARS), which visualises the higher nature of Mars as linked with the Eagle, the lower nature with the Scorpion: for the higher to develop, the lower (demonic element) must be thrust down. Steiner calls them the 'Spirits of Motion'.

DYSIS   A Greek term for the western angle of the horoscope, the cusp of the "Seventh House".

EAGLE   An astrological term with several connotations. It is the English
translation of the Latin "Aquila" constellation. Sometimes the image of the
eagle is associated with the Evangelist St. John, and hence with the zodiacal
sign Scorpio (see TETRAMORPH). Some astrologers insist that the eagle was
used in ancient times to stand in place of Scorpio itself, but there is no
evidence of this in surviving records: the rationale seems to be that since
Scorpio is the sign in which redemption takes place, then it alone of all the
twelve signs of the zodiac may be symbolized by two images. The image of the
earth-bound scorpion represents the unredeemed nature, while the image of the
aspiring eagle symbolizes the redeemed nature. The esoteric theories
underlying such astrological doctrine appear to support this view, which is
actually expressed in the imagery of Dante. The Eagle is also the attribute
of the god Jupiter, and is used as a symbol of the planet. See PHOENIX.

EAR OF CORN   See SPICA.

EARTH CHAIN   In the Theosophical cosmoconception, the Earth is regarded as a
unit globe in a series of seven globes, each possessed of counterparts (see
GLOBES), called the 'Earth Chain'. This Chain is classified according to a
convention of alphabetical letters which refer to equivalents in similar
septenary chains (see CHAIN):

    A and G are 'lower mental' and invisible to ordinary sight.
    B and F are 'astral' and invisible to ordinary sight.
    C is the physical planet Mars (and its invisible counterparts).
    D is the physical planet Earth (and its invisible counterparts).
    E is the physical planet Mercury (and its invisible counterparts).

Inevitably, this schema has been reduced to a level of ordinary
comprehensibility, with the result that the astrologer Leo blandly writes
about the 'Earth Scheme' consisting of three physical planets - Mars, Earth
and Mercury.

EARTH ELEMENT   The Earth element finds expression in the zodiac through the
three signs Taurus, Virgo and Capricorn (see EARTH SIGNS). It is the element
most deeply associated with the physical body and environment (in which
connexion, see TRIPLICITY). Earth is esoterically an 'incarnating'
principle, which seeks to either draw or invite the immaterial into physical
form: any incarnating spirit feels the weight of such form, with the result
that the element is also associated with inertia, with physical and mental
passivity, and so on, and is inclined to find pleasure in material well-being
and physical comforts. The aridity of earth calls for the enlivening
fluidity of water - which is to say that the earth element has a beneficial
affinity with the "Water Element". See also MELANCHOLIC.

EARTH SCHEME   See EARTH CHAIN.

EARTH SHINE   Term applied to the dim light on the dark side of the Moon's
crescent surface, caused by the reflection of sunlight from the earth to the
Moon.

EARTH SIGNS   The three zodiacal signs Taurus, Virgo and Capricorn are
expressions of the "Earth Element", sometimes called the 'Earth asterisms'
rather than the 'Earth signs'. Taurus is earth expressed through fixity,
Virgo is earth expressed through mutability, and Capricorn is Earth expressed
through cardinality. Therefore, by analogy with the earth of the physical
realm, Taurus seeks to be fixed in one place, enjoying the rhythmic life of a
conservative dependence upon environment: Virgo seeks to deal practically
with the passing (ephemeral) things of the world, and often finds an orderly

or even rhythmic service to others pleasurable; Capricorn is driven by an
urge towards movement, so that 'fulfilment' is usually translated as an
upward aspiration, an orderly climbing of the social ladder, often intimately
concerned with the idea of 'service' to others. In modern astrological
parlance, these three signs are the 'physical' or 'rhythmic' signs, and in
the esoteric tradition they are associated with different manifestations of
inhibited will forces. Since the Earth element was regarded as the most
'earth-bound' and conservative of the four elements, the three earth signs
were seen as being dominated by a sort of spiritual inertia (of which an
aspect is a sense of inhibition, especially in regard to self expression)
which might be thrown off only by an effort of tremendous will. An earth
type who succeeds in galvanizing his will forces becomes a most powerful
personality, and is often deeply creative. See also EARTH TRIPLICITY.

EARTH TRIGON   See SIDEREAL MOON RHYTHMS.

EARTH TRIPLICITY The earth triplicity consists of the three signs derived
from the element of earth - Taurus, Virgo and Capricorn (see EARTH SIGNS).
Taurus is visualised as the broad and fertile region of earth, the scene of
productive agriculture: Virgo is visualised as a deep valley, pervaded by a
degree of gloom and sadness; Capricorn is visualised as a high peak,
impressive in its sense of serene age. Each of the three earth signs is
restricted in its ability to express itself, and usually
achieves self-expression as a result of a drive towards self-improvement.
Since the earth triplicity is connected literally with the 'earth around' -
that is with the environment - each of the signs reflects something of this
connexion: Taurus relates to the financial standing, Virgo to the 'control'
of environment (often through occupation), while Capricorn relates to social
standing, to 'how one is seen' as a physical being in the outer world.

EARTH ZODIAC   In his presentation of the system of "Solar Biology", Butler
postulates what he calls an 'earth zodiac' or 'lunar zodiac', as a separate
zodiacal aura, enclosing the Earth and the Moon, yet between the orbits of
Venus and Mars (see figure 27). The ordinary tropical zodiac is visualised
as enclosing the solar system in the normal way.

FIGURE 27. THE EARTH ZODIAC IN THE SPHERES (AFTER BUTLER)

EAST ANGLE   See EASTERN ANGLE.

EASTER   The movable feast of Easter remains one of the few modern festivals
in the Western world which is still determined by cosmic phenomena, connected
as it is with the 84-year lunar-solar cycle. The Council of Nicaea (325 AD)
attempted to resolve early controversy about the 'date' on which the
Resurrection of Christ should be celebrated by determining that it should
fall on a specific day, rather than date (see DAYS OF THE WEEK), on the

Sunday preceding the Vernal Equinox. Eventually a method of computing this
movable feast day was developed to adopt the Sunday following the Paschal
full Moon (that is, the full Moon subsequent to the Vernal Equinox, which was
fixed calendrically as 21st March). An exception to this rule was that
should the equinox also fall on a Sunday (or, indeed, should the day coincide
with the Jewish Passover, when Christ was supposed to have been slain), the
Easter should be put forward one week. The ecclesiastical terms Pascha or
Pascale appear to have been derived from the Jewish name for the Passover
(Pesach): the English name 'Easter' appears to have been derived from a
pagan festival in honour of the Spring goddess Eastre.

EASTERN ANGLE   An alternative name for the Ascendant, or for the cusp of the
1st house: it is associated with the sign Aries, and represents the symbolic
point of sunrise in every chart, the point where the ego (or associated Mars,
ruler of Aries) begins to assert itself. See also HOROSCOPE.

EASTERN HOUSES   The eastern house is the "First House", but the term
'eastern houses' refers (confusingly) to the houses in the eastern half of
the figure - that is to the 1st, 2nd, 3rd, 10th, 11th and 12th houses.
Strictly speaking, however, the arc ends at the cusp of the 10th house, since
once a planet has culminated it ceases to be 'eastern'.

EAST POINT   In astrology, this term is often wrongly used as synonymous for
the ASCENDANT degree, while in fact the Ascendant measures the ecliptic,
which rises due east only with the vernal or autumnal equinoxes. The term is
much used however, and may be regarded as a reference to the symbolism
inherent in the stereographic projection of the chart, as the 'symbolic'
point of sunrise in each chart.

EAST POINT SYSTEM   A system of "House Division" proposed by the astrologer
Leo at the beginning of this century, for reasons which are not very clear.
The system appears to be based on an equal division of the horizon being
projected on to the ecliptic from the East Point, but the description is
confused and incomplete: most certainly it is not a workable model, for the
declination of a planet in itself is one of the most important determinants
of its house position in the projection suggested. But see also ZENITH
SYSTEM.

EBERTIN MID-POINTS   See MID-POINTS.

ECCENTRIC   An eccentric orbit is one formed about a centre which is itself
in revolution around a second centre - see DEFERENT and PTOLEMAIC SYSTEM.
The planets were sometimes called 'eccentrics', but the term is no longer
used.

ECLIPSE   See LUNAR ECLIPSE, OCCULTATION, SAROS CYCLE, SOLAR ECLIPSES and
UMBRAL ECLIPSE.

ECLIPTIC   The apparent path traced by the movement of the Sun around the
Earth, measured against the backdrop of fixed stars. It is called the
ecliptic because it is on this path that the solar and lunar eclipses take
place. The plane projected by this ecliptic to the Celestial Sphere is
inclined to the plane of the equator by 23 degrees and 27 minutes, decreasing
by 48 seconds per century, probably to reach a minimum of 22 degrees and 54
minutes around 6,600 AD. The 12 signs of the zodiac are equal-arc divisions
of the ecliptic into 30 degrees of arc each, based on time division,
reflected in both the solar and lunar calendars. The measurement of the
fixed stars against the ecliptic is based on a spatial division. See for
example SIDEREAL ZODIAC.

ECLIPTICAL INCLINATION   Traditional astrology allowed for a maximum
inclination of the planetary orbits to the ecliptic of between 7 and 9
degrees, which in some models of the zodiacal system defined the path or band

===

of the zodiac (as opposed to the ecliptic itself). The modern figures for
the maximum distances for each of the planets is set out in table 33.

```
---------------------------------------------------------------TABLE 33
 PLANET   DEG.min.SEC.          PLANET   DEG.min.SEC.
===============================================================================
 MO       5   8   0             SA       2   29  25
 ME       7   0   14            UR           46  23
 VE       3   23  39            NE       1   46  28
 MA       1   51  0             PL       17  8   34
 JU       1   18  21
-------------------------------------------------------------------------
```

ECLIPTIC SYSTEM   The name given to the system of projecting celestial
coordinates by taking the ecliptic as the frame of reference. This is the
system most used in astrology, and contrasts with the alt-aximuth system of
navigation and the equatorial system of astronomers, for whom the celestial
equator is the frame of reference. In regard to this model, see also
GALACTIC CENTRE, PRECESSION and ZODIAC.

EFFEMINATE SIGN   For obscure reasons, Wilson terms Pisces an effeminate
sign.

EGYPTIAN CALENDAR   Sometimes called the 'Alexandrian Calendar', though the
latter is really a fixed system, whilst the Egyptian Calendar proper is a
rotating system. In popular astrology there is much misunderstanding of the
Egyptian calendrical system, which is complex in the extreme - the calendars
of (so-called) 'lucky and unlucky days' which survived in mutilated forms
into mediaeval astrology (see EGYPTIAN DAYS) is different from the ordinary
complex calendar, while both are different from the religious-ritual calendar
and the funerary calendar. It is worth noting that the cycles for which
Egyptian calendrical systems are famed in popular astrology are all of a
relatively late development - the Sothic cycle is probably no older than the
Antonines (but see SOTHIC CALENDAR), and the so-called Sadu cycle (30 year
cycle) is not actually calendrical or astrological, but anniversarial,
relating to jubilees. In simple terms, the year began on the 1st day of
Thot, (our 19th July), and consisted of 365 days, divided (quite reasonably
in terms of the Nilotic inundations) into 3 seasons of 4 months, each of 30
days, with 5 epagomenal days at the end of the 12th month, which only in much
later times bore the Coptic names, in a variety of spellings:

1.	Thot	4.	Choiak	7.	Phamenot	10.	Payni

1. Thot   4. Choiak   7. Phamenot   10. Payni
2. Paophi   5. Tybi   8. Pharmouti   11. Epiphi
3. Athyr   6. Mesheir   9. Pachon   12. Mesori

EGYPTIAN CONSTELLATIONS   See CONSTELLATION NAMES.

EGYPTIAN DAYS   A series of calendrical lists of 'fortunate' or 'unfortunate'
days said with good reason to have originated from Egyptian astrological
practices, but probably derived ultimately from Assyrian sources. The lists
of good and bad days (good and bad for certain kinds of actions, etc.) are
sometimes called 'horoscopes' in popular literature, but they are not related
to astrology in this sense at all: it is likely that their original listings
were derived from solar-lunar considerations which were eventually ossified
and divorced from calendrical or astrological concepts. It seems that the
original Egyptian days were each divided into three sections, or parts, each
subject to cosmic scrutiny. A whole day might therefore be wholly good or
bad, or a proportional admixture of good or bad: there are thus three
different types of Egyptian days (rather than the so-called 'good' and 'bad'
which have survived in popular literature) the admixtures representing a
struggle between the good and bad principles. The prohibitions involve what
appears to be primitive horary astrology, such as setting out on a journey,
work, sexual congress, and so on. It is likely that the Egyptian days were

influenced by the various festival days, and later contributed to the 'fas' and 'nefas' days of the Roman system. A bowdlerized tradition of the 'Days' survived into rudimentary 'sortes' or elementary predictive methods well into mediaeval popular astrology and geomancy. The Egyptian days are sometimes called the 'Lucky and Unlucky Days'.

EGYPTIAN DESCENT OF THE SOUL   In his commentary on a section from Virgil's 'Aeneid', Servius refers to a tradition linked with the descent of the soul through the planetary spheres, prior to rebirth, which postulates a progress inimical to the good of the soul (see however ORPHIC DESCENT OF THE SOUL). This image is (perhaps rightly) linked by some scholars with the Egyptian mystery centres. Unlike the Orphic Descent, which is descriptive of a septenary, Servius describes only five of the spheres, but in so doing he expresses the negative polarity of the planets in question, which may well link with the Ptolemaic records of the "Planetary Rulership", since the Sun and the Moon do not have 'negative' or 'positive ' rule, like the other five planets, and it is indeed the luminaries which Servius leaves out. The account of the descent pictures the 'sluggishness' of Saturn, the 'desire for domination' of Jupiter, the 'passionateness' of Mars, the 'lustfulness' of Venus, and the 'cupidity' of Mercury. It is as though the pure soul is blinded by these influences, and is afterwards unable to use its own powers. The scholastic view of this curious 'Spherical Descent' is discussed by Mead, but the interesting thing is that virtually similar key-words are still used to represent the negative aspects of these planets in modern astrology.

EGYPTIAN TERMS   See PTOLEMAIC TERMS.

EGYPTO-BABYLONIAN ZODIAC   See HYPSOMATIC ZODIAC.

EIGHTH HIERARCHY   See ARCHANGELS.

EIGHTH HOUSE   The eighth of the twelve astrological "Houses", linked with the sign Scorpio and (in modern astrology) with the planet Pluto, and whilst popularly said to be the "House of Death", it is actually the house governing regeneration, of which the post-mortem experience is merely the extreme condition. It is called the 'occult house' because it has rule over hidden things - exoterically over legacies, but esoterically over 'karma', the final legacy. It is linked through Scorpio with the sexual parts - more properly with the 'generative system'. In mundane astrology it rules the public income, especially from exports, the national debt, and interest rates, as well as important financial losses and gains.

EIGHTH SPHERE   A much-misunderstood term, the real meaning of which may be grasped only from its context. In the "Ptolemaic System" the term was used of the sphere of the fixed stars (the "Stellatum"), though this designation changed as the model was adapted. In the early cosmoconceptive models the spheres were numbered from the centre outwards, though the actual numbers were merely designations, for the theory of the "Spheres" was complex, and required a large number of interacting spheres within the designate concentrics. There were, for example, a number of elemental spheres encasing the geocentric earth: this alone meant that even if we regard the spheres as numbered 'bands of interacting spheres', the eighth sphere 'stellatum' should really be numbered as the 'twelfth'. Now, in contrast to this, we find that when Copernicus introduced his own model (see COPERNICAN SYSTEM), he retained the theory of spheres (somewhat modified in the beginning, but totally rejected eventually), but numbered them inwards, towards the heliocentric centre. In the diagrammatic representation of this system, the 'stellatum' is now often numbered as the 'first sphere'. This rather tiresome distinction must be made here in order to explain why the term 'eighth sphere' is used in astrology for both the spheres of heaven (Stellatum) and the spheres associated with Hell. In popular 'occult' literature the eighth sphere is indeed equated with the sphere of the Moon, which in the esoteric tradition is linked with the post-mortem purgatorial experiences. Allied to this, the eighth sphere has been called 'the planet of death' (the planet being the Moon, of course), and it is said to mark the sphere where lost souls find their dwelling (which, of course, makes it a very different place from purgatory). In fact, there is an extensive and highly potent literature dealing with the modern esoteric astrological conception of the eighth sphere, a literature spearheaded by Harrison, who examines with profound esoteric insight the mistaken notions that link this sphere with the Moon.

EIGHT PLACES   The 'Eight Places of Manilius' have often been confused with an eight-fold "House System", though it is likely that the places were merely derived by extrapolation from the Greek LOCI - at least, the astrologer Firmicus, who was the only other astrologer besides Manilius to mention the 'eight places', considers them to be derived in such a way. The eight places are obtained by a simple division of the four quadrants, and it would seem that the interpretation of the significance of the places (or arcs, as they should be called, even though originally they may have been points) is fundamentally influenced by the related angles. Manilius himself links the angles with the planetary gods - the horoscopos with Mercury, the Dysis with Pluto - through the term 'Janua Ditis' (door of Dis) - the Midheaven with Venus, and the 'imum coeli' with Saturn. This sequence appears to be linked with one of the many prevailing theories of the FOUR AGES. At all events, the eight places, conditioned by the angular influences, are listed as follows, in the modern order of houses:

1.	Sedes Typhonis	5.	Sedes Typhonis
2.	Phoebe-Dea	6.	Phoebus-Deus
3.	Daimon	7.	Felix Fortuna
4.	Porta Laboris	8.	Porta Laboris

In connexion with 3 above, see DAIMON. The historian Bouche-Leclercq sets out an admirable analysis of the probable meaning behind the system.

ELECTION   A term used to denote a chart cast according to the rules of "Electional Astrology".

ELECTIONAL ASTROLOGY   A form of casting and interpreting charts to determine suitable times for commencing any specific activity, such as marriage, journeys, law-suits, and so on. The idea is that the astrologer seeks among the possible times practical to the querent the most satisfactory auspicious moment fitted to that particular endeavour. A chart erected for such a chosen moment is called the 'election', or the 'inceptional figure', and this is scrutinised according to the rules of "Horary Astrology" for success or failure. Electional astrology is usually practised alongside the radical and progressed natal horoscope of the querent. The rules for interpretation are complex, but follow the general drift of traditional genethliacal astrology, though with a few additional rules concerning "Dispositors" and specialist rulerships maintained by planets and houses. See also INCEPTIONAL ASTROLOGY.

ELECTRA   See PLEIADES.

ELECTRICAL ASCENDANT   See VERTEX.

ELEMENTAL ASPECTS   The original theory upon which the doctrine of ASPECTS was based related to the supposed harmonies and lack of harmonies (the "Sympathy") between the elemental natures of the signs. Thus, planets in trine were said to be operating in a harmonic sympathy because they each fell into a sign of a particular element - for example, Mercury in Aries trine Jupiter in Leo were both working through the fire element, and were thus in unison. However, when an allowance is made for orb, this original elemental nature may be ignored: an aspect may be noted on a geometric basis which does not fulfil the requirements of the elemental basis. For example, Mercury may be in 29 degrees of Aries, while Jupiter is in 2 degrees of Virgo: in terms of the geometric theory of aspects, they are in trine (with an orb of 3 degrees), yet the aspect does not respect the ancient doctrine of elemental accord, one planet being in a fire sign, the other in an earth sign. Such non-elemental aspects are undoubtedly weaker in influence than elemental aspects, and there is even good argument for discounting their influence altogether.

ELEMENTALS   A term properly applied to the classes of nature beings, the so-called 'elementary spirits' or 'Sagani' of esoteric lore. It is important to distinguish the term from "Elements" and from 'elementaries' (a word properly applied to a class of disembodied spirits, or to the astral shells of disembodied spirits). The four groups of elementals are often mentioned in astrological literature - especially so in esoteric astrology - because they are the expression on the natural plane (in the invisible realms which support the natural plane) of the activity of the four elements, from which they take their generic name. The GNOMES are the Earth beings: the SYLPHS are the Air beings: the UNDINES are the Water beings, and the SALAMANDERS are the Fire beings. It is erroneous to call these beings 'spirits' - see SOUL BEINGS.

ELEMENTAL SOUL BEINGS   See SOUL BEINGS.

ELEMENTARIES   See ELEMENTALS.

ELEMENTARY QUALITIES   A term used by Cornell to denote the ancient "Qualities": Hot and Cold, Wet and Dry.

ELEMENTORUM   See MACROCOSM.

ELEMENTS   The esoteric elements of the astrologers are four in number: Earth, Water, Air and Fire, each manifesting through a different "Quality" three times to make up the twelve divisions of the zodiac, as in table 34.

| | | | TABLE 34 |
ELEMENT	CARDINAL	FIXED	MUTABLE
Fire	Aries	Leo	Sagittarius
Earth	Capricorn	Taurus	Virgo
Air	Libra	Aquarius	Gemini
Water	Cancer	Scorpio	Pisces

Esoterically the elements of the astrologers are five in number, for it is maintained in the tradition that the four are themselves restless, and even in enmity with each other, so that they are bound into a temporary pact (such as is required by the world of material forms) by a fifth element. This fifth element maintains the pact between sublunar things, and is often called the QUINTESSENCE, the secret "Aether" of the ancients. One must observe that the occult elements are not what they seem, even in exoteric astrology. 'Let it be remembered', says Blavatsky, 'that Fire, Water and Air, or the "Elements of primary Creation" so-called, are not the compound Elements they are on Earth but noumenal homgeneous Elements - the Spirits thereof'. It is widely recognised that the fifth element, the Quintessence, will in the future become visible to human beings. Blavatsky takes this projection further however and speaks of two other elements, which will long remain invisible, rounding off the present tetrad as a septenary. This septenary is said to be the conditional modification of the one and only Element, which is 'not the Aether', to quote Blavatsky once more, 'not even A'kasa but the Source of these'. For a full survey of the elements of astrology see AIR ELEMENT, AIR SIGNS, EARTH ELEMENT, EARTH SIGNS, FIRE ELEMENT, FIRE SIGNS, WATER ELEMENT and WATER SIGNS.

ELEVATION   The altitude of a planet, nodal point or fixed star above the horizon. Sometimes the term is limited to the description of a horoscope, in which case it refers to house-placings, the 'medium coeli' being the most highly elevated of the cusps. The planet in the eastern diurnal arc nearest to this cusp is said to be 'elevated'. However, confusion proceeds from the fact that the term is also used loosely for any planet above the horizon. It is said in the ancient tradition that if either of the luminaries is elevated above a malefic, then the influence of the latter is mitigated.

ELEVENTH HOUSE   The eleventh of the twelve astrological "Houses", linked with the sign Aquarius and (in the modern systems) the planet Uranus, and associated with the native's ideals in relation to social life and evolution, as well as with the kind of acquaintances and friendships he or she will attract. The house is said to relate directly to the aspirations of the native, and for this reason it was called once the 'house of hopes and wishes', yet it does not have the same 'heart-felt' drive of the "Fifth House" in these matters, such impulses often arising more from ideals and intellectual attractions than from direct emotional involvement. The house indicates the areas which will open up the native to higher levels of consciousness - often involving connexions with development groups or political-awareness groups - as the ruling Aquarius would suggest. Through the Aquarian connexion it rules the legs and ankles of the human body, and is esoterically connected with the entire circulatory system. In mundane astrology, it has rule over the legislature, the stock exchange, public festivals, political aspirations and friendly societies.

ELGEBAR   See RIGEL.

ELGEUZE   See ORION.

EL NATH   Fixed star (double), the beta of constellation Taurus, from the Arabian 'Al Natih' (the butting one), located on the tip of the northern horn. Astrologers maintain that it brings eminence and good fortune, but its influence seems to depend upon the nature of the conjuncting planet.

ELONGATION   A term applied to the distance in degrees of arc of either of the inferior planets to the Sun. The maximum elongation of Mercury is 28 degrees, of Venus 46 degrees. The term is also used of the furthest distance which any planet may be from the Sun - see APHELION.

ELPHEIA   See ALPHECCA and FIFTEEN STARS.

ELUL   See BABYLONIAN CALENDAR.

EMBOLISMIC LUNATION   A term often used as an equivalent for the "Embolism Month". The same term was used by the astrologer Placidus de Tito to denote a chart (really a series of charts) cast for the periodic lunar returns to the same arc relationship to the natal Sun position. See also SYNODICAL LUNATION.

EMBOLISMIC MONTH   In some ancient CALENDAR systems an intercalary month is sometimes inserted in order to preserve a relationship between the days and the seasons: this is called the 'embolismic month'.

EMPYREAN   One of the ancient names for the "Tenth Sphere", though sometimes used (in post-mediaeval sources) to denote the extra-lunar spheres, and even as a synonym for 'heavens' generally. See also MACROCOSM.

ENCELADUS   Name given to one of the moons of Saturn.

ENNEAL HOROSCOPE   A chart derived from the "Novienic Moon", and used by the ancient Greeks - see NOVIENIC CHART.

ENNEATICAL   Simmonite uses this Greek-derived term, 'ennead' (ninth part) to apply to one of the climacterics, and records that it is supposed to bring 'a

==

change of fortune'. It is also used of the 9th day of an illness, when a change of condition may be expected. On the 9th day, the Moon enters orb of a beneficial trine to its radical position.

ENS ASTRALE   See ASTRAL.

ENSIS   A nebula in the sword-sheath of the constellation ORION, said to be of the nature of Moon conjunct Mars, and to cause blindness and death when prominent in a figure.

EPACT   A term with several related meanings. First, it is used to denote the number of days by which the solar year exceeds the lunar year. Secondly, it is used (though rarely in modern times) to denote any intercalated day or days. Thirdly, it is sometimes used wrongly in astrology to denote the age of the Moon on the first day of the year.

EPANAPHORA   A term derived from Greek astrology, as applied to a sign of the zodiac following (in the sequence of the signs) the angles. Thus, if Aries is on the Midheaven, Taurus is epanaphora. The term was also used of the LOCI 2, 5 8 and 11, which means that the term used in connexion with houses was the equivalent of the later SUCCEDENT. The term has been wrongly defined by some modern astrologers, probably due to a misreading of Ptolemy: because of this, the term is sometimes used to denote arcs in which the planets are at their most influential position - the main 'epanaphoric arc' is the Midheaven, while only slightly less powerful is the Ascendant, the entire 30 degree arc immediately succedent to these cusps being regarded as the epanaphorics.

EPANAPHORIC ARC   See EPANAPHORA.

EPHEMERAL MAP   A horoscope cast for purposes of HORARY ASTROLOGY.

EPHERMERAL MOTION   Term applied to the motions of the planets to distinguish from directional or progressed motions.

EPHEMERIDES   The plural for EPHEMERIS.

EPHEMERIS   A table listing the positions of the planets and nodal points, usually in longitudes, latitudes and declinations, along with related astronomical data, usually including an "Aspectarian", and sometimes even tables of houses. Ephemerides have been in use from the beginning of personal horoscopy, but the first to be printed in the West was the 'Kalendarium Novum' (a collection relating to the years 1474 to 1506) calculated by the German mathematician-astrologer Regiomontanus. Most ephemerides used by astrologers give their positions geocentrically, though modern astronomers' ephemerides list them heliocentrically. The majority of ephemerides prior to 1925 give information relative to Noon on particular days, but the introduction of the concept of the astronomical day has resulted in many ephemerides adopting Midnight as marking the time of their data. See COMPUTATION and TIME.

EPHEMERIS TIME   See TIME.

EPICYCLE   In the cosmoconception of the "Ptolemaic System", the epicycle is a small revolving circle, the circumference of which is centred upon the moving circumference of a DEFERENT circle. The theory of epicycles was originated mainly to support the Aristotelian dictum that extra-lunar bodies moved in perfect circles - a dictum openly contradicted by the appearance of things in a geocentric model. The theory appears to have been adopted by Ptolemy from Apollonius of Perga, who probably suggested the idea of epycycles in the 3rd century BC. The complex structures and models to which the epicycle theory gave rise permitted astrologers to combine the opposite motions of epicycles and deferents within a framework of velocities and

==

radical magnitudes in such a way as to account for the (visually apparent) movement of planets in a remarkably accurate way. The theory of epicycles to some extent satisfied astrological demands, and was even adopted by Copernicus, though it eventually broke down under the weight of its own complexity.

EPOCH   Originally a term used to designate a point of reference in the calculation of dates, but more recently used to designate the PRE-NATAL EPOCH. The term is also used as a synonym for 'perodicities' or 'cycles' - see for example AGES. See also PLATONIC YEAR and PRECESSION.

EPOCHAL ASTROLOGY   See PRE-NATAL EPOCH.

EPOCHAL CHART   A horoscope figure designed to symbolically present in a chart information allegedly relating to the cosmic configuration attending the moment of conception, which is often mathematically derived from the natal chart (see PRE-NATAL ASTROLOGY). It is sometimes called the 'Conception chart', or the "Pre-Natal Chart", and is generally projected geocentrically in accordance with the standard methods of "House Division". Those who favour "Astrosophy" often use a heliocentric system, and an epochal chart which is sometimes called the 'Pre-Natal Asterogram' - see ASTEROGRAM.

EQUAL DIVISION METHOD   A system of "House Division" which is to be distinguished from the MODUS EQUALIS (sometimes called by the same name). It was devised by the Australian astrologer Zariel in the 19th century, and sometimes called the 'Zariel Division'. The cusps of the 12 houses are determined by the projection on to the ecliptic from the pole of the equator twelve equal divisions of the horizon. As the astrologer Leo points out, the principle inherent in this system is tantamount to regarding the native as being born under the meridian of the birthplace, but at the equator, no matter where the place of birth. As a system it does not appear to have a wide acceptance.

EQUAL HOUSE   See MODUS EQUALIS.

EQUAL POWER   See BEHOLDING.

EQUATION OF TIME   A term usually applied to a set of tables showing the daily variation between the mean solar day and the true solar day: strictly speaking, the term should properly be applied to the variations so tabulated. The term is sometimes wrongly applied to the difference between mean time and sidereal time, which is properly "Correction of Time".

EQUATIONS   See COSMIC PICTURES.

EQUATOR   The term equator is sometimes used to denote the imaginary circle dividing the globe of Earth into two equal parts, and sometimes to the plane of this circumference, projected into the celestial sphere, the 'equatorial plane'. See also CELESTIAL EQUATOR and TERRESTRIAL EQUATOR.

EQUATORIAL CHART   A horoscope chart, or symbolic figure, erected to symbolize a plane through the equator of the earth.

EQUATORIAL SYSTEM   The equatorial system, is a model of the "Celestial Sphere", which takes as a point of reference the diurnal rotation of the Earth. The 'vertical' co-ordinates are established by extending the north and south poles into the celestial sphere, to create the corresponding "Celestial Poles". The equator is extended into the celestial sphere (hence called the "Celestial Equator") to give the second co-ordinate. The equator is subject to a time division of hour circles, measured eastwards from the standard zero circle passing through Greenwich, and location along this circle is measured in hours and minutes of Right Ascension. The plane of the equator is regarded as a second zero, paralleled by 'parallels of declination', measured by angular distance north (termed 'plus') or south (termed 'minus') of the equator. The points where the Sun's apparent orbit intersects the equator are called the 'equinoctial points', and the arc of greatest separation between the apparent path of the Sun and the equator are called the "Solstices".

EQUINOCTIAL POINTS   See ECLIPTIC.

EQUINOCTIAL PRECESSION   See PRECESSION.

EQUINOCTIAL SIGNS   These are Aries and Libra, which mark the Spring and Autumnal equinoxes, respectively.

EQUINOX   A term meaning literally 'equal night', and used of that time when the day and night are equal in length, which occurs when the Sun enters zodiacal Aries (see VERNAL EQUINOX) and Libra (see AUTUMNAL EQUINOX).

EQUULEUS   Constellation, approximately 19 to 28 degrees Aquarius, and from 1 to 12 degrees north of the equator. The image is traditionally a figure of a horse or foal, said to represent either Celeris, the brother of Pegasus (near which the constellation is located) or another horse, Cyllarus. It is said to be a fortunate influence.

EQUULEUS PICTORIS   See PICTOR.

ERIDANUS   Constellation, winding in a full 55 degrees arc south of the equator beyond the confines of Pisces, Aries and Taurus, originally called by the Greeks 'Potamus' (river). Its very extent makes its traditional associations with travel and with dangers at sea, questionable, though the power of the lucida ACHENAR is beyond doubt. See also VIA LACTEA.

EROS   One of the SEVEN LOTS of Greek astrology, the 'lot of love'. The degree of Eros is the same distance from the Ascendant as is Venus to the DAIMON.

ERRATICS   Some of the ancient astrologers used the term 'erratics' as synonymous with planets, thus contrasting their movements with the orderly sweep of the fixed stars. The Greek word from which our term 'planets' was derived carried this sense of 'erratics', and the Babylonian for planets, bibbu, meant 'wild goats'. See also ECCENTRIC.

ESNA ZODIACS   The temple of Khum at Esnah (modern Latopolis) in Egypt is famous for its bas-reliefs of a huge calendar and two so-called 'zodiacs', one of which is in the ceiling of the portico, the other in the ceiling of the inner shrine. Like the DENDERAH ZODIAC, these are constellation maps, containing planets. They run in two registers, the images of the zodiacal constellations being remarkably similar to the modern ones, which is scarcely surprising as it was such images that the Arabian astrologers transmitted to Europe by way of Greek and Roman astrology. Long believed to be of great antiquity, these maps have been dated from internal evidence, derived from the religious calendar of the Temple, to 137 BC.

ESOTERIC ASTROLOGY   The term is derived from the idea that behind the outer form of ordinary astrology (exoteric astrology) there is an esoteric form which proceeds from an entirely spiritual realm of being. It has long been recognised by the more thoughtful astrologers and historians of astrology that much of the philosophy underlying their science properly belongs to the ancient wisdom once taught in the Mystery Centres of Egypt and Greece, which has now become not only exoteric, but even badly mutilated in the process. It is equally apparent that the stream of esoteric knowledge is still available to those who are prepared to make the considerable effort required to reach into the spiritual realms from which it proceeds. Many astrologers have indeed made this effort, through the guidelines set out in the

Neoplatonic, Rosicrucian and Qabbalistic forms of astrology, with the result
that it has been possible for them to formulate some of the ancient laws of
esoteric astrology, and introduced into the exoteric art new and important
truths. Drinkwater, who recognised seven streams of Western mystery wisdom,
quite rightly saw Astrology as derived from ancient wisdom, but felt it
prudent to add that 'astrology, though originally a great mystery religon in
ancient Chaldaea, is, in its present form, too fragmentary to be considered
an independent mystery school, and students of esoteric astrology are obliged
to supplement it from other traditions, including Theosophy itself'. It is
apparent that the stream of esoteric knowledge which sprang from the ancient
mysteries is still available to those who are prepared to make the
considerable effort to reach into the spiritual realms from which it
proceeds. The theory of spiritual historicism upon which this account is
based rests on concepts very different from those considered valid in
academic circles, yet evidence for its truth is superabundant. The
Neoplatonic astrology derived from Gnosticism was essentially born of an
esoteric stream designed to counter certain of the destructive elements
inherent in orthodox theology. Through the medium of Arabian astrology, this
esoteric antique astrology flowered in mediaeval astrological forms, many
aspects of which were encapsulated in the symbolism of cathedrals and
basilican churches. The 'new' astrology of the Renaissance, which so
completely informed the arts and literature of that period, appears to have
been born of an esotericism nourished in Florence, rooted in the new image of
man derived from Neoplatonic sources, certain oriental ideas, and a spiritual
cosmoconception which is now little understood. The esoteric stream seems to
have gone into partial occultation during the period of the intellectual
Enlightenement, and survives mainly in prolix alchemical and religious texts
linked with Rosicrucianism, but in the decades around the turn of the present
century there was a proliferation of different esoteric systems, some of
which were syncretic and orientalizing rather than truely esoteric. The main
difference between the esoteric astrology of modern times and the various
exoteric forms is in the cosmogenetic and teleological aspect of the science
- almost all esoteric astrological systems are founded on the premise that
the cosmos is a living being, that the destiny of the solar system is
intimately bound up with the destiny of humanity, and that human beings
reincarnate periodically onto the earth. There is also a major difference
between esoteric and exoteric forms in the view of the purpose behind
astrology: the esoteric astrologers tend to see their studies involved with
philosophy, with the study of cosmogenesis, and so on, and tend to make
sparing use of actual personal horoscopes. Within most forms of even
exoteric astrology there is usually a residue or accretion of esoteric lore
which postulates the idea of ESOTERIC PLANETS. In many cases the esoteric
nature of the planet is merely veiled by the exoteric planet (usually of the
same name). The most notable example is the INTUITIONAL ASTROLOGY of Bailey,
which in clairvoyant methodology was based on Blavatsky, and was deeply
influenced by the Russian, yet succeeded in developing a strain of
esotericism unique to itself. Other examples are found in the esoteric
strain of qabbalistic astrology - especially in that linked with genuine
Rosicrucianism, in the orientalizing astrology promulgated by Blavatsky, in
the later ramifications of Thierens' esotericism, and in the Christianized
esoteric astrology hinted at by Steiner and studied by many of his followers,
including Vreede and Sucher. The most powerful influences of esoteric streams
on the development of astrology have been through the writings and lectures
of Steiner (see for example ASTROSOPHY and SIDEREAL MOON RHYTHMS), and the
general renewal of interest in the stream of Paracelsian, Boehmian and
Rosicrucian literature which followed on the esoteric writings of Blavatsky
and her Theosophy. Blavatsky had no follower sufficiently able to take her
esoteric lines of thought further in the realm of astrology: the astrologer
Leo (who wrote one of the earliest books purporting to deal with esoteric
astrology) was himself no esotericist, and his writings, in so far as they
continue Theosophical lines of thought, are merely attempts to form
correspondences between the orientalizing terminology of Theosophy and
traditional astrology, with some admixture of Hindu astrology. The chief

contribution of this stream of Theosophy to modern astrology, therefore, has not been in the esoteric realm, so much as in its undoubted contribution to a reassessment of traditional astrology. The soi-disant ROSICRUCIAN ASTROLOGY of Heindel is actually derived from Blavatsky and Steiner, and must not be confused with the genuine esoteric stream of mediaeval Rosicrucianism. The esoteric elements contained in the astrological writings of Collin are derived ultimately from the esoteric system propounded by Gurdjieff and his follower Ouspenksy, both of whom appear to have had scant respect for ordinary astrology.

ESOTERIC MOON   In her system of "Intuitional Astrology", the esotericist Bailey pictures the Moon of our Earth as a sort of veil, for the influence of planets which she variously identifies as "Vulcan" and "Neptune". She gives no clear indication whether these two are to be regarded as hypotheticals, with specialist influences, or as disembodied influences of one or other of the hypotheticals described under VULCAN, and the traditional NEPTUNE. Bailey puts out many curious propositions, including, 'the Earth is a satellite of the Moon', and 'The Moon is a dead planet from which all the principles are gone'. Such statements are not in accord with the ancient esoteric tradition concerning the Moon, nor in accord with the traditions of ordinary astrology. See NON-SACRED PLANETS. The hypothetical LILITH has been called the 'Esoteric Moon'.

ESOTERIC PLANETS   The term has several applications, depending upon the form of astrology under consideration.   Within the cosmoconception of "Intuitional Astrology", the term is used sometimes as synonymous with SACRED PLANETS, and sometimes in a more exclusive sense. Within this system, which traces the arising and manifestation of the SEVEN RAYS, the sacred planets (called also the 'esoteric planets') are given the unorthodox rulerships set out in table 35. For the 'Rays' see individual entries, FIRST RAY, etc.

---TABLE 35

RAY	CONSTELLATION	ORTHODOX PLANET	ESOTERIC PLANET
1st	AR	Mars	Mercury
1st	LE	Sun	Sun
1st	CP	Saturn	Saturn
2nd	GE	Mercury	Venus
2nd	VG	Mercury	Moon (veiling a planet)
2nd	PI	Jupiter	Pluto
3rd	CN	Moon	Neptune
3rd	LI	Venus	Uranus
3rd	CP	Saturn	Saturn
4th	TA	Venus	Vulcan
4th	SC	Mars	Mars
4th	SG	Jupiter	Earth
5th	LE	Sun	Sun
5th	SG	Jupiter	Earth
5th	AQ	Uranus	Jupiter
6th	VG	Mercury	Moon
6th	SG	Jupiter	Earth
6th	PI	Jupiter	Pluto
7th	AR	Mars	Mercury
7th	CN	Moon	Neptune
7th	CP	Saturn	Saturn

However, in the face of this list, Bailey does distinguish specific esoteric planets by name: ESOTERIC MOON, ESOTERIC PLUTO and ESOTERIC VULCAN, though it is evident that each of the orthodox planets has also an esoteric side or nature. It is difficult to generalize the main different views taken by practical astrologers (see ESOTERIC ASTROLOGY) of the working of the esoteric planets, but the indications given by Bailey herself of the fundamental

==

difference between the 'sacred' and the "Non-Sacred Planets" may be extended
to that between the esoteric and the exoteric. She says that it is the
development of the individual being (the native) which marks the ability to
respond (or not to respond) to the esoteric level of a given planet, or to
its esoteric equivalent: an initiate, or highly developed human being, lives
according to cosmic laws which are different to those which embrace the
average person, for the more evolved human may respond to a higher range of
vibrations marked out by, or heralded by, the esoteric planets. A careful
reading of Blavatsky will show that each of the planets is viewed as having
an esoteric nature veiled from ordinary understanding: it is this tacit
esotericism which makes many of Blavatsky's statements appear to be so
questionable to the ordinary reader, even though they are usually statements
founded on a most profound grasp of esoteric cosmogenesis.

ESOTERIC PLUTO   In her system of "Intuitional Astrology", which leans upon
the esotericism of Blavatsky, Bailey pictures the Pluto of our solar system
as a sort of veil, working through a rulership over Pisces. It is clear
however that she adopts the standard interpretation of the
destructive/regenerative polarity of the planet. In view of this, the planet
might more readily be termed the 'Bailey-Pluto', rather than 'Esoteric
Pluto', in accordance with the present tendency to distinguish by
personalized suffix the various Plutos noted by modern astrologers.

ESOTERIC SUN   Blavatsky puts into words an idea which is implicit in several
esoteric strains of astrological thought, and which is openly mentioned in
the hermetic literature of the immediate post-Christian era - that the Sun of
our solar system 'stands for, or veils, a hidden planet'. This veiling Sun
is later called the 'Esoteric Sun' in the "Intuitional Astrology" of Bailey.
The esoteric Sun is the image of divine intelligence and wisdom, and it is
this which encourages Blavatsky to an etymology which derives the Latin 'Sol'
from 'solus', meaning 'one alone', and linking the Greek 'Helios' (Sun) with
the meaning 'most high'. The Triple Sun of esotericism is linked with the
esoteric Sun, being a veil for the Trinity - the 'spiritual Sun' is God the
Father; the 'heart of the Sun' is God the Son, and the 'physical Sun' is God
the Holy Spirit. Blavatsky traces the relegation of the Sun to the status of
'planet', and the consequent loss of its esoteric and triple symbolism to the
work of the Christian astrologers 'who had not been initiated'. However, if
the esoteric documents and art-forms of the early Christians are interpreted
correctly, it will be seen that the tradition of a spiritual sun, linked
indeed with the Trinity and with the Logos, survived for well over a thousand
years into our era. The central solar-image of the SAN MINIATO ZODIAC, made
during an exoterically geocentric period, points to this mystery, for
example.   While Blavatsky makes a distinction between the visible and
spiritual Suns, she also claims that the esoteric Sun is 'the substitute for
the invisible inter-Mercurial planet'.

ESOTERIC URANUS   Both Blavatsky and Bailey write of an esoteric Uranus: as
the former says, 'Uranus is a modern name, but one thing is certain, the
ancients had a mystery planet which they never named.' It is this esoteric
Uranus which figures in the "Intuitional Astrology" of Bailey, as one of the
three synthesizing planets (the other two being Neptune and Saturn) through
which Sirius influences our solar system. See also ESOTERIC ASTROLOGY.

ESOTERIC VULCAN   In her system of "Intuitional Astrology" the esotericist
Bailey has proposed an important role for her planet Venus, sometimes called
an esoteric planet, at other times one of the SACRED PLANETS.   This Vulcan
is said to be within the orbit of Mercury, and appears to have a
crystallizing effect - at least, this is so in connexion with its rule over
Taurus in the "Unorthodox Astrological Relationships". It is this same
Vulcan which is said to be veiled by the present Moon - see ESOTERIC MOON.

ESSENTIAL DIGNITIES   See DIGNITY.

==

ESTIVAL QUADRANT   See QUADRANTS.

ESTIVAL SIGNS   See AESTIVAL SIGNS.

ETHEREAL ORBS   See ETHEREAL PLANETS.

ETHEREAL PLANETS   A term probably originated by the astrologer Harris and
applied by him to a number of planets (invisible to all but advanced
clairvoyants) said to be in orbit between Mercury and the Sun. This chain of
planets he called the 'Sisterhood', and claimed they were AROMAL PLANETS.
It seems likely that the ethereal MELODIA was of this category - but see also
HYPOTHETICAL PLANETS. Blavatsky insists that at least four (possibly six)
of our own planets are 'ethereal orbs', by which she appears to mean that the
spiritual planet is separate in space, if not also in time, from the physical
orb: for example, she gives the name Sol to a transmercurial planet, nearer
to the Sun than Mercury, which 'became invisible at the end of the Third
Race', in Lemurian times, even before the epoch of Atlantis.

ETHERIC RACE   See FIRST ROOT RACE.

ETHERIC SPHERES   A specialist esoteric term probably coined by Thierens,
relating to the future evolution of the spheres, and the consequent
development of new planetary bodies which are (supposedly) present yet
invisible to ordinary vision. Within this new development, Aries will unfold
a planet called 'Pluto' or OSIRIS; Taurus will unfold a planet called VESTA
or 'Isis': Gemini will unfold a planet called HERMES or 'Mercurius', and
Cancer will unfold a planet called BACCHUS or 'Horus'. Thierens calls these
'spheres' because they include what must be visualized as the traditional
spheres of Aries, Taurus, Gemini and Cancer. See also ASTRAL SPHERES.

ETTANIN   Fixed star (double) the gamma of Draco, and a prominent star for
the Egyptians who called it 'Isis' or 'Taurt Isis', and for whom it marked
the head of the Hippopotamus, as figured in the DENDERAH ZODIAC. Its rising
through the central passages of the temples of Hathor at Denderah was said to
be visible about 3,500 BC. The name, with many variants (a standard being
Eltanin) is from the Arabic 'Al Ras al Tinnin' (the dragon's head) wrongly
translated by Ebertin as meaning 'right eye of the dragon', and linked by him
with the Martian influence. With a well-placed Saturn, however, it is said
to be helpful for mental concentration and for 'esoteric studies'. Lying
almost at the zenith of Greenwich, it is sometimes called the 'Zenith Star'.

EUCTEMONIAN CALENDAR   During the 5th century BC the Greek astronomer
Euctemon defined a solar calendar in terms of solar months of (approximately)
30 days duration, linked with the phenomena of equinoxes and solstices.
Euctemon gave the 12 months of his calendar the same names as the zodiacal
asterisms of the BABYLONIAN ZODIAC, or at least derived them from the
corresponding images. Prior to the JULIAN CALENDAR reforms, this sequence of
solar months began with the vernal equinox in the 'month of Aries' (APRIL).
As the historian Powell says, the Euctemonian Calendar is still in vogue
today, in popular sun-sign astrology.

EUDAIMON   A Greek-derived term - sometimes 'Eudamon' or 'Eudaemon' (meaning
approximately 'good spiritual influence') - applied to the 11th house of a
horoscope figure, which was regarded as a source of benefits, just as the
twelfth house 'Cacodemon' was regarded as a source of difficulties.

EUDORA   See HYADES.

EUROPA   One of the satellites of Jupiter.

EVANGELISTS   The Christian symbolism relating to the Four Evangelists is
derived from pre-Christian astrological lore, as indicated by Guthrie among
others. The Bull of St. Luke is from the image of Taurus; the Lion of St.

Mark is from the image of Leo; the Angel of St. Matthew (carrying a book or scroll) is from the image of Aquarius (carrying an urn). The Eagle of St. John is the 'redeemed' image of Scorpio - see EAGLE. The cosmic imagery of the Evangelists is ultimately linked with the hierarchies of the CHERUBIM and the SERPAPHIM.

EVESTRUM A Paracelsian term used to denote several aspects of the 'eternal substance' of heaven. It is the ethereal and invisible substance (or rather 'agency') of the heavens, and the 'sidereal body', the 'starry body' or 'astral body' of man, which is itself built from that substance or agency.

EXALTATIONS An exaltation is a sign (or sometimes a degree) of the zodiac in which a planet is said to exert its most powerful characteristic influence. The traditional exaltations of the planets were presented in Ptolemaic astrology in terms of signs only: a planet was said to be exalted in a particular sign, the Ptolemaic order of which corresponds to the modern as set out in table 36. Ptolemy attempted a rationalization for these exaltations, but is unconvincing in his argument. The specific degrees of exaltation have come down from very ancient sources: as the astrologer Fagan has shown, these exaltation degrees are probably derived from the HYPSOMATA.

					TABLE 36
PLANET	EXALTATION	DEGREE	PLANET	EXALTATION	DEGREE
SU	Aries	19	MO	Taurus	3
ME	Virgo	15	VE	Pisces	27
MA	Capricorn	28	JU	Cancer	15
SA	Libra	21			

Following the computations of the 'hypsomatic degrees' for what he called the HYPSOMATIC YEAR, Fagan provides the exaltation degrees of the so-called new planets and the nodes as set out in table 37. It will be noted that in Hindu astrology the north node (RAHU) is exalted in Taurus, and the south node (KETU) in Scorpio. See also DIGNITIES, but distinguish from the Hellenistic, and now archaic, NATIVITY EXALTATION.

			TABLE 37
PLANET	TROPICAL	SIDEREAL	
UR	Scorpio 25 (24.9)	Sagittarius 9 (8.7)	
NE	Aquarius 5 (4.6)	Aquarius 19 (18.4)	
PL	Cancer 4 (3.9)	Cancer 18 (17.7)	
Dragon's Head	Pisces 17 (16.7)	Aries 1 (0.5)	

EXSUSIAI   See POWERS.

EZRIAN HOUSE SYSTEM   See HORIZONTAL SYSTEM.

FACE   The term has been used in a variety of specialist astrological forms, resulting in much confusion. The only proper modern application of the term is to the division of the signs of the zodiac into 72 arcs, each of 5 degrees, so that each sign is divided into 6 equal-arc divisions. Each of these 5 degree arc 'faces' has been accorded a planetary ruler, as well as specific associations (usually connected with the signs to which they relate): they are sometimes (more properly) called 'demi-decans' - but see

==

"Decan". The incorrect use of the term has sprung from a two-fold error.
The term face has been used as the equivalent of the PROPER FACE in which
connexion it is usually misapplied due to Ptolemy's own obscure and
inconclusive definition. Unaccountably, Wilson (quoting older sources)
defines face as the equivalent of a Decan, and gives traditional decanate
readings for 10 degree arcs as applicable to the 5 degree arcs - he may have
taken the word from Angelus.

FACIAL TYPES   See APPEARANCE.

FACIES   Name given to the nebula in the 'face' of the figure of
constellation Sagittarius. It has an evil reputation among astrologers, for
when operative in a chart it causes blindness, accidents and violent death.

FAELIS   The constellation of the Cat, formed almost in joke by La Lande in
1804, but never widely adopted. Located between Antlia Pneumatica and Hydra.

FAIR STAR OF THE WATERS   See SIRIUS.

FALL   A planet is said to be in its Fall when in the sign (or degree)
opposite to that of its EXALTATION (or exaltation degree). In the ancient
astrological system, a synonym for the term was 'prison', the idea being that
a planet's influence was imprisoned in the sign opposite to its Exaltation.

FALLING STAR   See METEOR.

FAMILIARITIES   The 'familiarities' of planets were the 'aspects' between
them, the 'elemental relationships' in the original sense of aspectal theory.
See FAMILIARITY.

FAMILIARITY   A term derived from mediaeval astrology, used as a synonym for
ASPECT - the 'familiarities' were often lists of aspects in a given chart or
in a table of aspects. The term is the Latin equivalent of Ptolemy's
'oikeiosis' (kinship) which appears to embrace the idea of aspects, but was
also used in a much wider sense, of all planetary relationships.

FARGH AL MUKDIM   Arabic term, 'the fore-spout of the waterbucket' (according
to Robson), the name of the 24th of the Arabic MANZILS, located by the modern
alpha and beta of "Pegasus".

FARGH AL THANI   Arabic term, 'the lower spout of the waterbucket' (according
to Robson), the name of the 25th of the Arabic MANZILS, the mediaeval
'Haurens', located by the modern alpha of "Andromeda".

FATALITY   For 'Point of Fatality', see HOUR GLASS.

FATHER   The 'Point of Father' is not to be confused with the 'House of
Father'. The former is one of the so-called Arabian PARS - if the degree of
Saturn in a natal chart is revolved to the Ascendant, the adjusted position
of the Sun marks the Point of Father. The 'House of Father' is a name given
to the "Tenth House".

FEBRUARY   Now the second month (variable, 28 days, and 29 days as
intercalary), the name being derived from the early Roman pre-JULIAN
CALENDAR, after a festival of expiation, a catharsis, the Latin 'februatio'
applying to the ceremony of purification: the name Februata being applied to
the goddess Juno who was worshipped at the ceremonies. The festival of the
Lupercales was celebrated in the middle of this month in Roman times, and as
the imagery in the vast mosaic of the months from El Djem indicates, this was
involved with purification and catharsis (see Foucher). Esoterically the
month seems to be connected with the cleansing of the feminine element in
preparation for the beginning of Spring. In the earlier European calendars,
this was the last month of the year.

FEMININE   See SECTA.

FEMININE PLANETS   The schema of PLANETARY RULERSHIPS recorded by Ptolemy
involved the idea that planets had a dual nature (though this was not claimed
of the luminaries), variously expressed in the dual rulerships over the
zodiacal signs other than Cancer and Leo. For example, the Mercury which
ruled Gemini was positive or masculine, while the same planet ruling Virgo
was negative and feminine. Although this traditional idea has been widely
misunderstood, it is still possible to find reference to such terms as
'feminine Mercury' or even 'feminine Mars', though it is more usual to find
the expression NEGATIVE MARS, (the terms 'feminine', 'negative' and
'nocturnal' being interchangeable in this context). Quite a different
tradition, connected with the old teaching of PRINCIPLES, has also emerged
from the Ptolemaic stream of astrology: this maintains that certain planets
are by their own intrinsic nature 'feminine': these are the Moon and Venus.
Of the planets, Mercury alone partakes of both the male and female qualities,
and is accordingly termed the ANDROGYNOUS PLANET.

FEMININE SIGNS   Ptolemy, reporting an ancient astrological tradition, and
presenting a male argument, says that the even-numbered signs are 'feminine'
(hence, TA, CN, VG, SC, CP and PI), whereas the others are 'masculine'.
Having so defined the term, he then gives another quite different application
for it, claiming that the sign on the Ascendant may be regarded as being
masculine, the sequence of the zodiac in the chart marking the polarity of
the sexes throughout the figure: in such a 'nomenclature', the sex of the
signs changes according to the nature of the horoscope itself.   An
increasing misuse of the term in popular astrological circles is bent on
confusing the 'signs' with the "Images": it is supposed that the signs Virgo
and Libra are feminine, presumably because the images (derived from the
constellations) are traditionally those of women - however, in terms of the
Ptolemaic definition, Libra is a masculine sign.

FERAL   A somewhat unfortunate term, meaning 'pertaining to a wild beast',
but in a specialist sense applied to the disposition of those with Leo on the
Ascendant, or with the Ascendant degree located in the last 15 degree arc of
Sagittarius. The name is clearly derived from the "Image", and has little
practical value. The term is also used of those natives whose luminaries are
so located, but with malefic planets on the angles. Curiously, the Moon is
also said to be feral when VOID OF COURSE and to remain so whilst in her
occupant sign. But see also FERAL SIGNS.

FERAL SIGNS   These are the BESTIAL SIGNS - but see also FERAL.

FIDUCIAL   The fiducial or fiduciary is a point (in astrology very often a
fixed star) determined as a fixed position for a basis of comparative
measurement. The term is derived ultimately from the Latin 'fides' (faith)
and refers to something in which one may place trust. The fixed star
"Aldebaran" was one of the earliest of fiducials - see for example STELLA
DOMINATRIX. See also AYANAMSA.

FIFTEEN STARS   Many of the mediaeval star-lists pay special attention to 15
fixed stars, each of which was accorded a sigil, and a special place in
relation to the lore of magical gems and talismans used for amuletic and
therapeutic magic (for these sigils, see SIGILS - FIXED STARS). Contrry to
what one might expect, the 15 stars were not evenly distributed throughout
the heavens, nor were all of them of the greatest magnitude. The schema in
figure 28 shows the distribution in approximate relation to the ecliptic
(here the dotted line). It will be seen from this that three of the stars
are derived from the "Royal Stars" of the ancient Persians (the missing star
being FOMALHAUT). The following list gives the modern names, followed by the
most frequently used of the mediaeval terms in brackets, the numbers
referring to the schema in figure 28:

FIFTEEN STARS (Continued)

----

1. Aldebaran   6. Procyòn   11. Polaris (Cauda Ursae)
2. Pleiades   7. Regulus (Cor Leonis 12. Alphecca (Elpheia)
3. Algol   8. Algorab (Ala Corvi) 13. Antares (Cor Scorpii)
4. Capella (Hircus)   9. Spica   14. Wega (Vultur Cadens)
5. Sirius (Canis Major) 10. Arcturus (Alchameth) 15. Deneb Algedi

----

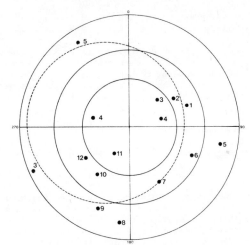

FIGURE 28.   THE FIFTEEN STARS OF MEDIAEVAL LORE (AFTER NOWOTNY).

FIFTH ELEMENT   This is the QUINTESSENCE, the secret etheric force which
unites the four elements of Earth, Air, Fire and Water.

FIFTH HEAVEN   A term used synonymously with "Fifth Sphere", which in the
cosmoconception built around the "Ptolemaic System" was the sphere of Mars,
ruled by the "Dynamis".

FIFTH HIERARCHY   See CELESTIAL HIERARCHIES.

FIFTH HOUSE   The fifth of the twelve astrological HOUSES, linked with the
nature of Leo, and with the Sun, representative of the creative power,
organisational abilities, approach to pleasures, and the general talents of
the native. It has been called the 'House of Children', and whilst this may
be taken quite literally, it must be seen as relating to a more general
conception of 'offspring', such as works of art, creative concepts, and so
on. The house has rule over the heart, loins and back of the human frame.
In Mundane Astrology it rules children, educational systems, sports,
pleasures (of a public nature), the organisational principle, and creative
arts.

FIFTH RAY   In the esoteric system of "Intuitional Astrology" described by
Bailey, the 5th of the SEVEN RAYS is called the 'Ray of Concrete Science' and
is linked with the will to act: in another context, Bailey links it with the
'cosmic seed of liberation', which is an aspect of destruction. This Fifth
Ray is said to arise in Ursa Major, and is transmitted to our solar system by
means of three zodiacal constellations (perhaps even signs?), through three
pairs of corresponding "Orthodox Planets" and "Esoteric Planets", as shown in
table 38 on page 124. The entire Fifth Ray is linked with the sacred planet
Venus - see however SACRED PLANETS. Distinguish from the FIFTH RAY TYPE.

===

FIFTH RAY (continued)

```
-----------------------------------------------------------------TABLE 38
CONSTELLATION      ORTHODOX PLANET  *      ESOTERIC PLANET
===============================================================================
   LE              Sun                    Sun
   SG              Jupiter                Earth
   AQ              Uranus                 Jupiter
-------------------------------------------------------------------------
```

FIFTH RAY TYPE   The fifth of the SEVEN RAY TYPES, associated with the planet
Jupiter: distinguish from FIFTH RAY.

FIFTH ROOT RACE   In the Theosophical cosmoconception, the Fifth Root Race is
the 5th of the seven human streams of evolution, sometimes called the Aryan
(though the modern 'Aryan Race' of non-esoteric thought is merely a
subdivision of the entire Fifth Race, and belongs to a different conception),
applied by esotericists to all the relatively advanced races of the present
surface of the Earth.

FIFTH SPHERE   The sphere of Mars - see PTOLEMAIC SYSTEM.

FIGURA COELI   A Latin term meaning 'celestial figure', used of the CHART.

FIGURE   A synonym for CHART, probably originally the 'celestial figure'.

FIGURINES   A term adopted by the German astrologer Meier in connexion with
his study of aspectal patterns. He distinguishes four groups of 'figurines',
the 'conjunction' figurine, the 'harmonious' figurine, the 'polar' figurine
and the 'polypolar'. Meier interprets these aspectal patterns in combination
with what he calls the 'Ruler of Tension', which indicates the 'type of
destiny'. The conjunction is said to exhibit little tension, the harmonious
exhibits a gifted or creative personality, whilst the polar (which includes
the polypolar) exhibits much tension in the life of the native.

FIRE ELEMENT   The fire element finds expression in the zodiac through the
three signs Aries, Leo and Sagittarius (see FIRE SIGNS). It is the element
most deeply connected with spiritual activity (in which connexion, see FIRE
TRIPLICITY). Fire is esoterically an 'expressive' principle, the important
aspect of this tradition revolving around the idea (more fully expounded in
alchemical than in astrological texts) that fire, to operate fully in accord
with its nature, needs an agency of control. Fire which is not so controlled
is called in alchemical terminology 'common fire': it generates nothing but
destruction. Therefore, when assessing the nature of a fire element in a
chart, the serious astrologer is advised to look for the 'controlling factor'
- that which gives useful direction to the creative and expressive potential
which resides in the elemental force of fire - in this connexion, see
especially FIRE SIGNS. Within all the fire conditions known to astrologers,
there is implicit (and indeed sometimes explicit) a destructive power. The
consuming nature of fire calls for a constant supply of 'oxygen', which is
expressed in the harmony the fire element bears with the AIR ELEMENT, a
harmony which may be reduced to fire being predatory at the expense of air.
See CHOLERIC.

FIRE SIGNS   The three zodiacal signs Aries, Leo and Sagittarius are
reflections on the higher plane of the FIRE ELEMENT.   The expressive and
creative power of fire works through Aries chiefly in regard to selfhood -
the native seeks outlets which permit a growth of an independent image of
self. The control of fire in this case is to be discerned in the opposite
side of the zodiac, in the less selfish nature of Libra: the all-consuming
drive towards egohood of the Arietan nature must be tempered or deflected by
a development of an awareness of others, and of a sense of harmony or balance

through relationships.   The expressive nature of fire works through Leo
mainly in regard to materiality - the native seeks to impress his own
exuberant personality and love of life on the forms of matter, which is one
reason why the Leonine nature is so often associated with artistic ability
and creativity.   The control of fire in this case is to be discerned in the
nature of the opposite sign Aquarius, which offers the possibility of
widening the scope of activity in the service of the community rather than
the isolated self.   The expressive nature of Sagittarian fire works mainly
through the mental realm, through altruistic idealism and a profound (often
practical) grasp of how the world of man may be extended into the mental
plane - through travel or education.   The destructive element enters into the
basic duality of the sign, for uncontrolled fire feeds the passions of the
lower duality of the sign, and this may consume the individual to a point
where he is deflected from his real inner being or purpose.   The clue to
control in this case lies in the opposite polarity of Gemini, which offers a
certain detachment from the passionate realm.   The three zodiacal types
inheriting the power and destructive nature of fire are often 'driven' to
creativity as though by inner tensions - they are impulsive and iconoclastic
in attitude, yet at the same time frequently full of originality and warmth.

FIRE TRIPLICITY   These are the three signs derived from the element of fire,
manifesting different aspects of the CHOLERIC temperament: Aries, Leo and
Sagittarius. Fire may be visualized as a source of great heat, smouldering,
ready to leap into high flame. Leo is a creative fire, sometimes radiating
warmth as from a hearth, usually an illumination for others. Sagittarius may
be seen as a fire-brand moving through the air, ever in movement, dangerous
when come to rest. Each of the fire signs is impulsive and dynamic,
sometimes over-confident or even brash and exhibitionist. Since the fire
triplicity is connected with the creative element of soul-life, each of the
three reflect something of this world. Aries attempts to explore and leave
his creative mark through romantic involvement with people and places -
especially so through grandiose schemes. Leo is creative by imposing his own
warmth on things of the earth - through the arts of painting and sculpture,
for example. Sagittarius seeks to leave behind his fire-spark through the
development of ideas.

FIRMAMENT   This name was originally applied to the sphere of the fixed stars
- the 'Stellatum' in the PTOLEMAIC SYSTEM. However, in general modern use,
the term is used in a general sense, to the so-called 'vault of heavens'.

FIRMAMENTO CHIERICATI   See VICENZA CYCLE.

FIRST HEAVEN   Sometimes this term used as being synonymous with 'First
Sphere', which in the Ptolemaic cosmoconception was the sphere of the Moon,
esoterically the realm of Purgatory.   In modern esotericism, however, the
term is used of the lowest realm of the heavens (the so-called 'Devachan' in
Sanskrit) into which the spirit passes after the purgatorial experience.

FIRST HIERARCHY   See CELESTIAL HIERARCHIES.

FIRST HOUSE   The first of the HOUSES of the chart, linked with the
"Ascendant", with the sign Aries, and with the planet Mars: it is the
representative of the selfhood of the native. Sometimes it is called the
'House of Fulfilment', the 'Point of Consciousness', and the 'House of Self',
and it is generally regarded as the lens through which all the influences of
the horoscope pour into the external world, through the guise of personality.
It rules the personal and natural disposition of the native, denotes the head
and face in the human frame, and is linked with the grandparents (the
grandmother for the male native, the grandfather for the female - though both
are actually important as spiritual progenitors). In Mundane Astrology the
house rules the country as a whole, the establishment or 'ruling majority',
the defendant, and those in power.

===

FIRST MOVER   A translation of PRIMUM MOVENS.

FIRST ORDER CYCLE   When the point of conjunction between two planets repeats
itself, the period elapsing between these two conjunctions is termed a 'first
order recurrence cycle', or 'first order cycle'. Future cycles of this same
first-order will eventually make up any small discrepancy as to the original
point of conjunction, so that eventually a series of first-order cycles will
result in a conjunction at the original starting point of the sequence. This
'cycle of first-order cycles' is called a 'second-order recurrence cycle', or
'second-order cycle'.

FIRST POINT   The 'first point', without further qualification, usually
refers to the first degree of Aries, to the commencement of the zodiacal
circle of measurement: it is the so-called ZERO DEGREE or 'zero point'.
Since this point is almost always identified as 0 degrees of Aries, it has
given rise to many misunderstandings in regard to the interpretation of a
chart - see therefore ROUNDING OFF.

FIRST RAY   In the "Intuitional Astrology" described by Bailey, the first of
the SEVEN RAYS is called the 'Ray of Will' or the 'Ray of Power', and is
linked with the will to incite and produce initiation or beginnings. This
first ray is said to arise in Ursa Major, and is transmitted into our solar
system by means of three 'constellations' (perhaps even signs) through their
related pairs of ORTHODOX PLANETS and ESOTERIC PLANETS, as set out in table
39. The entire First Ray is linked with the sacred planet ESOTERIC VULCAN -
but see also SACRED PLANETS. Distinguish from FIRST RAY TYPE.

```
------------------------------------------------------------------TABLE 39
   CONSTELLATION      ORTHODOX PLANET         ESOTERIC PLANET
   ===================================================================
   AR                 Mars                    Mercury
   LE                 Sun                     Sun
   CP                 Saturn                  Saturn
   -------------------------------------------------------------------
```

FIRST RAY TYPE   The first of the SEVEN RAY TYPES, associated with the planet
Saturn. Distinguish from FIRST RAY.

FIRST ROOT RACE   In the Theosophical cosmoconception, the First Root Race is
the term used to cover the first of the "Seven Races", or streams of human
evolution. The race, whilst human, had no dense bodies, and is sometimes
called the 'Etheric Race'.

FIRST SPHERE   The Sphere of the Moon - see however FIRST HEAVEN and "Eighth
Sphere".

FIRST STATION   The stationary point (see STATION) at which a planet becomes
retrograde.

FISHES   The popular name for the zodiacal sign and constellation Pisces.

FIXED CROSS   An alternative name for the "Fixed Quadruplicity" of Taurus,
Leo, Scorpio and Aquarius: see FIXITY. Not to be confused with the Major
configuration of the GRAND FIXED CROSS. The esotericist Bailey traces a
spiritual evolution in the sequence of the fixed cross, which is visualized
as a power of transmutation.

FIXED ECLIPTIC CHART   See CHART SYSTEMS.

FIXED QUADRUPLICITY   The fixed quadruplicity is Taurus, Leo, Scorpio and
Aquarius - see FIXITY.

FIXED SIGNS   These are Taurus, Leo, Scorpio and Aquarius - see FIXITY.

FIXED STARS   A most important element of early personal astrology was the
tradition of fixed star influences in the form recorded by Ptolemy, and
exploited and developed by the later Arabian astrologers. A literary
tradition has been established (itself based on the Ptolemaic model) of
equating the influence and power of the fixed stars with what have been
called the 'planetary equivalents' - for example, an evil star might be
equated with Saturn as a planetary equivalent, a benevolent star with Venus
or with the Sun. However, as the studies preserved from Arabian astrology
confirm, the influence of stars is involved with matters much deeper than
merely such planetary equivalents, for it is clear that each star emits an
influence personal to itself. Traditional astrologers insist that such
influences - unique or otherwise - may be transmitted into the life of the
native only when the stars are conjuncted by natal planets (or nodal points,
angles, and so on). The traditional view is that for a fixed star to be
operative in a chart, then it must be exactly conjunct a planet or nodal
point - however, some astrologers have adopted a system of orbs (see for
example the outstanding MORINEAN ORBS). This allowance for orb has resulted
in much confusion, since the fixed stars which figure in the astrological
tradition are so numerous that if a wide orb is permitted then there is
scarcely a horoscope figure which does not demonstrate a variety of complex
'fixed star' interpretations. If (quite sensibly) a precise conjunction is
permitted for the influence to be operative, it becomes clear that fixed
stars account for many things in charts which are otherwise quite
inexplicable - especially so in connexion with matters of genius and
eccentricity of life-history and personality. For a general survey of fixed
stars, in relation to astrological significance, Allen, Devore, Ebertin
(Hoffmann), Powell and Robson appear to be indispensable. Even so, after
allowing for radial motions, proper motions and precession - as well as for
disagreement about geometrical variations in the conversion of right
ascensions and longitudes - there is considerable disagreement among all
authorities as to precise positions and influences. The longitudes given for
each star in table 40 is that provided by Robson, subjected to correction for
precession and for rounding off, amended to 1985. The asterisks indicate
information not derived from this source. Ebertin provides a table (accurate
for 1900, 1920, 1937 and 1950) in terms of longitudes for 73 stars, along
with useful information and (somewhat dubious) case-histories. Powell
provides an accurate table of latitudes and sidereal longitudes for 106 stars
in connexion with the SIDEREAL ZODIAC. For the general significance of the
106 stars listed in table 40, see the entries under the individual star
names.

--TABLE 40

ACHERNAR (PI 15)	ARUX (SC 12)	ACUBENS (LE 14)
ACULEUS (SG 26)	ACUMEN (SG 29)	ADHAFERA (LE 29)
AGENA (SC 24)	ALAMAC (TA 14)*	ALBIREO (AQ 2)
ALCYONE (TA 30)	ALDEBARAN (GE 10)	ALGENIB (AR 9)
ALGENUBI (LE 21)	ALGOL (TA 27)	ALGORAB (LB 14)
ALHECKA (GE 25)	ALHENA (CN 9)	AL JABHAH (LE 28)
ALMACH (TA 14)	ALNILAM (GE 24)	ALPHARD (LE 28)
ALPHECCA (SC 12)	ALPHERATZ (AR 14)	ALPHERG (AR 27)
ALTAIR (AQ 2)	ANTARES (SG 10)	ARCTURUS (LB 25)
ARMUS (AQ 13)	ASCELLA (CP 14)	ASCELLI (LE 8-9)
BATEN KAITOS (AR 22)	BELLATRIX (GE 21)	BENTENASH (VG 27)*
BETELGEUZE (GE 29)	BOS (SC 30)	CANOPUS (CN 15)
CAPELLA (GE 22)	CAPHIR (LB 10)	CASTOR (CN 20)
CASTRA (AQ 20)	DABITH (AQ 4)	DENEB (CP 20)
DENEB ADIGE (PI 5)	DENEB ALGEDI (AQ 24)	DENEB KAITOS (AR 2)*
DENEBOLA (VG 22)	DIRAH (CN 5)	DORSUM (AQ 14)
DUBHE (LE 15)*	EL NATH (GE 23)	FOMALHAUT (PI 4)
GIEDI (AQ 4)	GRAFFIAS (SG 3)	HAMAL (TA 8)
HAN (SG 9)	ISIDIS (SG 3)	KHAMBALIA (SC 7)
LABRUM (VG 27)	LESATH (SG 24)	MANUBRIUM (CP 15)
MARKAB (PI 24)	MARKEB (VG 29)	MENKALINA (GE 30)

===

MENKAR (TA 14)	MINTAKA (GE 23)	MIRACH (AR 30)
MIRAK (VG 15)*	NASHIRA (AQ 22)	OCULUS (AQ 5)
PELAGUS (CP 13)	PHACT (GE 22)	POLARIS (GE 29)
POLIS (CP 3)	POLLUX (CN 23)	PRIMA HYADUM (GE 6)
PRINCEPS (SC 3)	PROCYON (CN 26)	PROPUS (CN 19)
RASALHAGUE (SG 23)	RASTABAN (SG 12)	REGULUS (LE 30)
RIGEL (GE 17)	RIGEL KENTAURUS (SC 30)*	
SABIK (SG 18)	SADALMELIK (PI 3)	SADALSUUD (AQ 24)
SCHEAT (PI 29)	SEGINUS (LB 18)	SHARATAN (TA 4)
SINISTRA (SG 30)	SIRIUS (CN 14)	SKAT (PI 9)
SPICA (LB 24)	TEJAT (CN 3)	TEREBELLUM (CP 26)
UNUKALHAI (SC 22)	VINDEMIATRIX (LEB 10)	WASAT (CN 19)
WEGA (CP 15)	ZANIAH (LB 5)	ZAVIJAVA (VG 27)
ZOSMA (VG 11)		

FIXITY   Fixity is the name applied to one of the three QUALITIES, which acts as a block to movement, and restricts the free flow of energies. The result is that the Fixed Signs (Taurus, Leo, Scorpio and Aquarius) are frequently resistant to change, though fortunately blessed with a resourcefulness and persistence which usually makes them attractive and reliable powers for good. The four FIXED SIGNS of the zodiac gave rise to the esoteric symbolism of the EVANGELISTS. Sometimes the fixed quadruplicity is called the 'Fixed Cross'.

FLAMES   In esoteric astrology the seven SACRED PLANETS are sometimes called 'the Flames'.

FLEXED   A term sometimes used as synonymous with MUTABLE.

FLORA   Name given to one of the "Asteroids", discovered in 1847.

FLYING GRYPE   See AQUILA.

FOMALHAUT   Fixed star, the alpha of "Piscis Australis", set in the mouth of the Fish, the Arabian 'fum al hut' meaning 'mouth of the fish'. This was one of the ROYAL STARS of the Persians (among whom it was called 'Hastorang'), when it marked the winter solstice. It has many names, mainly variants on the Arabian 'Al Difid al Awwal' (first frog). When rising or culminating in a chart it is said to give lasting honour, although the conjunction with planetary bodies tends to bring unfortunate strains, and intensification of energies, as well as 'secret affairs'.

FORAMEN   Fixed star (variable), the eta of "Argo Navis", which seems to take its modern name (Latin for 'opening') from the fact that it is set within the distinctive Keyhole Nebula. It is said to be of the nature of Jupiter with Saturn, and gives danger to the eyes. With the sun in conjunction it promises danger from shipwreck.

FOREGROUND   A specialist term used of planets near the angles of the chart, which due to this proximity are regarded as being especially powerful, and are thus in the 'foreground' of the chart. See also BACKGROUND and MIDDLEGROUND.

FOREHEAD OF SCORPIO   A term used by Ebertin to denote the fixed star "Graffias". Ebertin treats this beta of Scorpius as equivalent to the influence of the delta Scorpius, which he calls 'Akrab'.

FORMING   When an aspect between two or more planets or nodal points is being built up, that aspect is said to be 'forming'. When an aspect is forming, though still within a specific number of degrees of the precise aspect, it is said to be 'in forming orb'. The faster planet is described as applying to the given aspect: see APPLICATION.

FORNAX   The constellation 'Fornax Chemica', or 'Chymiae' (alchemical furnace), formed by La Caille in 1762, located 10 to 13 degrees of Taurus, and between 26 to 40 degrees beyond the equator. It is said to bring fondness for scientific work.

FORTIFIED   A term used of a planet which is strongly placed, especially by being well-aspected, or by "Elevation", or by being in a sign of its own "Dignity".

FORTNIGHT CHART   A term used by Bradley to denote half of the "Lunar Return" chart.

FORTUNA   A frequently used short-form for PARS FORTUNA.

FORTUNATE SIGNS   These are the signs Aries, Gemini, Leo, Libra, Sagittarius and Aquarius - see however SECTA.

FORTUNES   A collective term for Jupiter and Venus: the former is the 'Great Fortune', the latter the 'Lesser Fortune'.

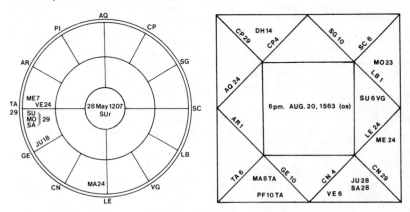

FIGURES 29 AND 30.   29: FOUNDATION CHART FOR THE "SAN MINIATO ZODIAC", CAST FOR 28TH MAY, 1207, SUNRISE (AFTER GETTINGS). 30: FOUNDATION CHART CAST FOR 6PM 20TH AUGUST, 1563 (AFTER TAYLOR)

FOUNDATION CHART   Term used for a horoscope cast in relationship to the founding time or date of a building, or an important reconstruction. In some cases - especially in mediaeval astrology, such charts were cast in advance, in order to predetermine a suitable date for commencement of the structure, or to encapsulate in the building an important astrological or symbolic lore. Of such a kind was the chart (figure 29) cast for the SAN MINIATO ZODIAC, of which only the date (1207) now remains, though a modern recasting of the relevant figure shows that the symbolism within the church was involved with the orientation of the zodiac towards a satellitium in Taurus. In some cases, foundation charts have been cast in retrospect, in order to establish certain astrological presumptions, but in general the chart is derived from "Electional Astrology". Careful examination shows that there is no clear dividing line between what has been called 'calendrical orientation' and 'foundation astrology' in connexion with ground plans (and even symbolism) for ancient temples, churches and even non-ecclesiastical buildings (see for example Taylor, Nissen and Schwaller de Lubicz). Figure 30 reproduces the horoscope cast for the laying of the foundation stone of a monastic church, recorded by Taylor: the Julian date (20th August, 1563) was the feast day of St. Bernard, but it is likely that the time was astrologically determined in the long term to include the beneficient conjunction of Jupiter with Saturn,

===

and (in the short term) to place Mercury on the Descendant, thus linking the
"Chronocrators" with the 'Nuncius' healer - the two most important
considerations in relation to a monastic church. As Plutarch records, the
foundation chart for Rome was a popular subject among astrologers, and
several variants have survived - the lack of agreement is the probable cause
of the several dating systems derived from the Roman calendar, of which some
5 different systems existed by the time of Christ (see FOUNDATION DATES).
Such things have not changed significantly in modern times - there are at
least 9 different charts for the 'foundation' of the United States of
America.

FOUNDATION DATES In ancient times, there were a variety of different systems
for determining the beginning of calendrical or other 'dating' systems. The
only ones which are relevant to European astrological charts (other than in
extremely specialist cases) are the Roman and the Christian. The Roman
system is derived from the supposed founding date of Rome, determined by the
equivalent of our 754BC. This date was designated in Latin as "Ab Urbe
Condita" - from the foundation of the City - often shortened to AUC.
According to this system, the probable birth of Jesus (in our own system,
4AD) would be given as 756 AUC. However, in respect of Roman horoscopes, see
also CALENDRICAL SYSTEMS and KALENDS. The modern European dating system did
not entirely replace the Roman until late into the mediaeval period. Shortly
after 540 AD Dionysius Exiguus suggested the foundation date from "Anno
Domini", relating to the birth of Jesus, which was gradually accepted, with
the introduction of our now familiar abbreviation AD. Unfortunately there
has been no certainty as to what this actual date was, and consequently
correlations with the Roman Foundation system have varied. The system was
not widely adopted for over a century, however, and the correlate BC is of
relatively modern adoption. Early Christian writers attemped pre-AUC and
(later) AD dating with foundation dates relating to the supposed birth of
Abraham, given as 2016 BC equivalent, and even in terms of the estimated date
of the fall of Troy (given as 1183 BC in modern equivalent). Edwards and
Schultz have made excellent attempts to marshal the material relevant to
Christology and to certain aspects of astrology. There is some evidence to
suggest that the early foundation dates were astrologically determined, as
the survival of charts for AUC indicate.

FOUR AGES   In his rag-bag of esoteric and astrological speculations, the
'Metamorphosis', Ovid mentions four 'previous ages' to the one in which
mankind presently lives (this being the 'fifth age'): he calls these ages
the Gold, Silver, Bronze and Iron, following a tradition linked with Hesiod,
these being separated from the fifth age by a great Flood. These four ages
may be linked with the esoteric theory of cosmogenesis (see for example SUN
PERIOD which corresponds to the Gold Age): there is also a correspondence
with the Hindu theory of cycles - see YUGA. In early times an important
analogy was established between the four world ages and the ages of man, the
seasons, the elements and so on:

GOLD AGE	Fire	The youth of man.
SILVER AGE	Air	Adolescence.
BRONZE AGE	Water	Maturity.
IRON AGE	Earth	Old Age.

By analogy with the four elements, which marked a descent from the refined
energy of light fire to the dark weight of earth, the Ages of Man were seen
as a descent away from the Divine Fire into the dark prison of Earth. See
also ORPHIC AGES.

FOUR ANIMALS   The astrological 'four animals' are actually three animals
united by a fourth human figure - the lion, bull and eagle linked with the
winged human. These are the four FIXED SIGNS of the zodiac. In the esoteric
astrological melothesia, the lion represents the feeling element in man (the
heart); the bull represents the will-life, or physical element; the EAGLE

represents the capacity for higher thinking, whilst the winged human
represents the union of these three capacities in the 'human' form. See
TETRAMORPHS and FOUR ZOAS.

FOUR ELEMENTS   The astrological 'four elements' are actually five in number,
the exoteric four being Earth, Air, Fire and Water, united by the fifth,
which is the "Quintessence" - see ELEMENTS. The Earth element was often
personified in the image of a bull (linked with Taurus), the Air element in
the image of an eagle (see figure 31), the Fire element with a lion (linked
with Leo - see figure 31), and the Water element was often personified in the
image of a fish or sea-horse.

FIGURE 31. PERSONIFICATION OF AIR AND FIRE (AFTER NOWOTNY).

FOUR FOOTED SIGNS   A descriptive term derived from the images associated
with certain signs, which were in turn derived from their related
constellation images.   The signs are Aries (the Ram), Taurus (the Bull), Leo
(the Lion), Sagittarius (the Centaur) and Capricorn (the Goat). They should
be called by the alternative name of 'Animal Signs', since in many zodiacal
images and constellation maps not all of these creatures are four-footed.
For example, there are many pictures of two-footed Sagittarius, while
Capricorn is scarcely anything other than a fish-tailed creature with two
legs (the goat image being relatively modern).

FOUR PRINCIPLES   See PRINCIPLES and FOUR QUALITIES.

FOUR QUALITIES   Sometimes called the 'Four Principles' to distinguish from
the 'qualities', these are the four states of being associated with the
planets and zodiacal signs in early astrology: Hot (Calidium);   Cold
(Frigidum); Humid or Wet (Humidum) and Dry (Siccum). See QUALITY.

FOUR STARS   See ROYAL STARS.

FOURTEEN STARS   The list of star-names set out under the mediaeval FIFTEEN
STARS contains one Asterism (the Pleiades), and the list is therefore
sometimes more correctly refered to as the 'Fourteen Stars'.

FOURTH HEAVEN   Sometimes this term is used as synonymous with the 'Fourth
Sphere', which in the cosmoconception built around the PTOLEMAIC SYSTEM was
the Sphere of the Sun, ruled by the "Exsusiai". In the qabbalistic system,
this heaven is sometimes called Machonon, and in common with all esoteric
systems, assigned rulership of the Archangel "Michael".

FOURTH HOUSE   The fourth of the twelve astrological HOUSES, linked with the
nature of Cancer, and with the planet Moon. It represents the domestic life
of the native, and is linked with the early environment, especially with the

mother (indeed, it was formerly called the 'House of the Mother'), though esoterically it deals with the whole experience preceding birth (see GATE OF BIRTH). This house is a useful index of the imaginative faculties and moods, and relates to 'hidden things' on account of which it has unfortunately been called the 'grave'. It is linked with the breasts and (some astrologers maintain) with the digestive organs, but it is essentially associated with the rib-cage, the protective element around the heart, and the protective attitude to kith and kin forms an important aspect of the fourth house associations. In Mundane Astrology it rules the opposition party, crops, buildings and the outcome of contests and litigation.

FOURTH RAY   In the esoteric "Intuitional Astrology" of Bailey, the fourth of the SEVEN RAYS is called the 'Ray of Harmony through Conflict', and is linked with the will to harmonize or relate, and with the illumined will. The Fourth Ray is said to arise in Ursa Major, and is transmitted to our solar system by three constellations working through pairs of corresponding "Orthodox Planets" and "Esoteric Planets", as set out in table 41. The entire Fourth Ray is linked with the sacred planet MERCURY - see however SACRED PLANETS. In connexion with the rule of esoteric Vulcan over Taurus, see also ESOTERIC VULCAN. Distinguish from FOURTH RAY TYPE.

---TABLE 41

CONSTELLATION	ORTHODOX PLANET	ESOTERIC PLANET
TA	Venus	Vulcan
SC	Mars	Mars
SG	Jupiter	Earth

FOURTH RAY TYPE   The fourth of the SEVEN RAY TYPES, associated with the planet Earth. Distinguish from FOURTH RAY.

FOURTH ROOT RACE   In the Theosophical cosmoconception, the Fourth Root Race is the name given to the fourth of the SEVEN RACES stream of evolution. This race is sometimes called the 'Atlantean', and was said to occupy mainly the lost continent of Atlantis (also called Kusha), located approximately over the present Atlantic Ocean. The main continental area was destroyed in the Miocene period, but the final submergence of Poseidonis (to which Plato refers as ancient myth) did not occur until 9,564 BC.

FOURTH SPHERE   The sphere of the Sun - see PTOLEMAIC SYSTEM.

FOUR WATCHERS   See ROYAL STARS.

FOUR ZOAS   Term originated by the poet Blake, probably under the influence of the esotericist Boehme, from the Greek plural (zoa), and derived from occult astrological lore. Blake follows the esoteric tradition in identifying the four beings with the four-fold nature of man - Tharmas is the body (probably a word derived from the Greek 'Thumos', the equivalent of the 'Etheric' - see AETHER): Urizen is Reason (thinking - probably a play on the Germanic 'Ur' and the English 'horizon'): Luvah is the emotional life (probably a play on the word 'love'), while Urthona is 'imagination' (probably again the use of the Germanic 'Ur' and the English 'Earth-owner'). These four zoas correspond to the four fixed signs of the Zodiac (with which the word 'zoa' is cognate) - Taurus, Scorpio, Leo and Aquarius, respectively - the four 'beasts' which figure in the "Tetramorph": see FOUR ANIMALS.

FRACTIONAL METHOD   A system of arc measurement used in SYMBOLIC DIRECTIONS, probably first described by the astrologer Carter, as an extension of the "One Degree Method". The method is derived from a suggestion made by Carter that the arc between any two natal planets might be divided by a conventional numerical division to give significant directions. The radical arc he called the 'primary relationship', which was susceptible to divisions which he

===

called 'secondary relationships'. Since in practice any division of the
basic primary may be used, it is a system which even Carter admits may be
'easily ridiculed', and appears to have commanded little following in circles
concerned with such projections.

FRAMING   A term derived from the interpretation of the French 'encadrement'
used by the astrologer Volguine, which has been wrongly equated with
"mid-points". An 'encadrement' is a bracketing effect of two planets on
another planet which is itself enclosed within the smaller arc of the
ecliptic which they together define. The enclosed or 'framed' planet is said
to blend its influence with both of the bracketing planets. Angles also play
a part in such framing, being regarded as the equivalent of 'planetary
influences' defining arcs. The idea (unlike the term) is by no means new,
and is indeed explicit in the theory of aspects, though the 'bracket of arc'
is limited to fairly narrow orbs.

FREDERICI HONORES   Constellation named in honour of Frederick II of Prussia,.
formed by Bode from the 34 stars in the area between Cepheus, Andromeda,
Cassiopeia and Cygnus. Now obsolete.

FRIENDLY PLANETS   Planets which have exaltations in each other's signs, or
which have communal triplicities, are said to be 'friendly' to one another.
Devore generalizes the term however by listing a number of relationships
based on the conception of 'Unfriendly Planets': Wilson (perhaps with good
reason) suggests that the whole concept is nonsensical.

FRONS LEONIS   Name given to the 10th of the LUNAR MANSIONS in some mediaeval
lists. Probably located by reference to "Regulus".

FRUITFUL SIGNS   Each of the WATER SIGNS are called 'fruitful'. The term,
now misunderstood, appears to have been used in the limited sense of being
the opposite of BARREN: the tradition now insists that such a water sign on
the cusp of the Fifth House is an indication of children.

FRUIT TRIGON   See SIDEREAL MOON RHYTHMS.

FRUSTRATION   A specialist term properly limited to HORARY ASTROLOGY. It is
applied to the action of an aspecting planet which intercedes into the effect
of another aspect (being made to the body to which it is itself applying),
and thus frustrates the promise of that other aspect. The full rule relating
to 'frustration' is a little more complex than this would suggest, however,
for it may take place only when the frustrating aspect is already within orb:
the interceding (swifter) planet which moves in to form an exact aspect
before this orb may reach fulfilment is called the 'frustrator'.

FRUSTRATOR   See FRUSTRATION.

FULL MOON   See PLANETARY PHASES.

FUNCTION   An equivalent term for KEYWORD ('Keywords of Function') applied in
a specialist sense by the astrologer Pagan. Each of the 'signs of the
Zenith' are accorded a function keyword which is included in a schema, and is
said to modify the Sun-sign of the particular chart:

AR	Warrior or Pioneer	LB	Statesman or Manager
TA	Builder or Producer	SC	Governor or Inspector
GE	Artist or Inventor	SG	Sage or Counsellor
CN	Prophet or Teacher	CP	Priest or Ambassador
LE	King or President	AQ	Truthseeker or Scientist
VG	Craftsman or Critic	PI	Poet or Interpreter

FUTURE PLANETS   A few of those planets listed by certain modern astrologers
as being among the HYPOTHETICAL PLANETS are, properly speaking, planets of

==

future development, which have been called 'future planets'. These are
putative developments of other planets which, while at the moment doubtless
in our present system (in the ordinary sense of the word) must be regarded as
'seeds' capable of growth and evolution. Among such future planets are
AIDONIUS, BACCHUS, COELUS, MERCURIUS, NEREUS and VESTA, though 'Jupiter' and
'Vulcan' are names given to future incarnations of the present Earth - see
for example JUPITER PERIOD and VULCAN PERIOD. These future planets are to be
distinguished from the esoteric SACRED PLANETS. In some cases, the
communality of names may be misleading: for example, VULCAN is a name given
to a hypothetical planet, to a future planet and to a sacred planet.
==

GABII ALTAR   A Roman altar of the Gabii family, now in the Louvre, which
bears several interesting correspondences between signs, gods/goddesses and
symbols, as follows

AR	Minerva	Owl		LB	Vulcan	Bonnet
TA	Venus	Dove		SC	Mars	Wolf
GE	Apollo	Tripod		SG	Diana	Hound
CN	Hermes	Tortoise		CP	Vesta	Lamp
LE	Jupiter	Eagle		AQ	Juno	Peacock
VG	Ceres	Basket		PI	Neptune	Dolphin

GABRIEL   The Archangel accorded rule over the Sphere of the Moon, and over
elemental Water. Gabriel is the 'Angel of the Annunciation' (see WATER
ELEMENT), which derives from the esoteric cosmology giving him rule over the
lunar sphere, the last of the planetary spheres through which the descending
spirit passes on the way to incarnation - see for example DESCENT OF THE SOUL
and GATE OF BIRTH. Gabriel is one of the SECUNDADEIAN BEINGS.

GADOS   A name ('Torch' in Greek) given by Ptolemy to the star ALDEBARAN.

GALACTIC CENTRE   A term used to denote the centre of gravity for the entire
matter of the GALAXY. The astrologer Landscheidt has provided an ephemeris
for the Galactic Centre, and the related "Solar Apex", which he calls the
'apex-ephemeris'. In 1980, the galactic centre was 26 degrees 35 minutes
Sagittarius, and the Solar Apex was 2 degrees 10 minutes Capricornus. The
progress of the former is about 1 minute per annum, the progress of the
latter being approximately 8 minutes of arc per decade. See also GALACTIC
POINT.

GALACTIC POINT   The point where the plane of the solar system cuts the plane
of the "Galaxy" (see VIA LACTEA) is located by most astrologers on the axis
of 15 degrees Sagittarius/Gemini: see however GALACTIC CENTRE. A planet on
the former degree is in direct 'conjunction' (alignment) with the galactic
centre, while a body in the latter degree will be cut off (symbolically
speaking) from a view of the galaxy by the interposed body of the earth. The
degrees are regarded as extremely critical, especially in mundane affairs:
as the astrologer Davison has remarked, Mars (conjunct with Uranus) was in
the latter degree at the exploding of the atomic bomb over Hiroshima.

GALAXY   A term derived from the Greek 'gala' (milk), in reference to the
milky appearance of the group of stars which mark out an irregular and
luminous band, which is in fact a view into the 'island universe' of stars
which contain our own solar system. This galaxy is the 'Via Lactea', and
while the term is generally applied to our own stellar system, it is also
applicable to other systems beyond our own. See also GALACTIC CENTRE.

GALEN'S METHOD   An ancient horary method of ASTRO-DIAGNOSIS.

GAMALEI   Certain natural stones or gems, which, because of some powerful astrological influence, were said by mediaeval magicians to be magically efficacious. The 'artificial gamalei' are those engraved with astrological, hermetic or magical sigils, towards talismanic ends. They are sometimes called 'Gemetrei' and 'Gamathei', but Paracelsus calls them Gamahei, and says that they are 'stones graven according to the face of heaven'. See also BIRTH STONES and SEALS.

GANYMEDE   Name given to one of the satellites of Jupiter.

GATE OF BIRTH   Name applied to the sign CANCER, not merely because of its mundane associations (see FOURTH HOUSE), but also because in the ancient "Themae Mundi" (for the beginning of the world),Cancer was often shown on the Ascendant. In esoteric astrology, it is said that the incarnating soul enters the physical realm through the 'Sphere of the Moon', which is, of course, associated with rule over Cancer, and also accounts for the term 'gate of birth'. The esoteric basis for the term is most clearly set out in Macrobius in his description of the descent of the soul through the seven zones of the planetary spheres: see STARRY CUP. In her account of esoteric astrology, Bailey says that the sign of Cancer has been recognised down the ages as the 'doorway into life of those who must know death'.

GATE OF DEATH   Name applied to the sign CAPRICORN, sometimes to the "Sphere of Saturn". In esoteric astrology it is said that the soul in its postmortem experience aspires to travel to the "Sphere of Saturn", which marks the boundaries of time, and it is almost certainly this association which gives rise to the term. Equally, since Cancer is associated with the "Gate of Birth", it is also probable that by virtue of being the extreme polarity of this sign, Capricorn was by extension associated with death, as the throne of that planet which marked the end of time. See however CROCODILE. In her account of esoteric astrology, Bailey says that the sign Capricorn has been recognized down the ages as the 'doorway into life of those who know not death'.

GAVEL POINT The 'point of Gavel', sometimes called the 'part of Pluto', and even the 'point of Organization', is one of the modern additions to the series of so-called Arabian PARS. If a chart is revolved so that the degree occupied by the Sun is transferred to the Ascendant, then the position of Pluto in this revolved arrangement is said to mark the gavel point within the houses.

GEMINATED   Virtually an obsolete synonym for 'double', apparently restricted to Horary Astrology.

GEMINI   The third sign of the zodiac, and one of the constellations. It corresponds as a zodiacal sign neither in location nor extent with the constellation of the same name - see GEMINI CONSTELLATION. The modern sigil for Gemini Ⅱ is said by some to be a drawing of the human twin holding hands with the mortal twin (see CASTOR and POLLUX). Some see the significance of the sigil as relating to the square area inside the rectilinear structure, for the rule of Gemini over the human lungs points to the permanent rhythmic relationship which the human being holds to the outer world, constantly taking in its air and oxygen, so that the inner becomes the outer, the outer the inner. The esoteric astrologers place great emphasis on the numerical relationships of 72, which may be discerned through this exchange - see Wachsmuth. Gemini is of the Air element, and of the Mutable quality, the influence being mental, intellectual and versatile: the Geminian exhibits a strong need to relate to others, and is at worst histrionic. This 'airy' nature of the sign is expressed in the many keywords attached to it by modern astrologers: versatile, idealistic, communicative, imitative, inventive, alert, inquisitive - in a word, all those qualities which may be associated with an air nature expressing itself with a view to establishing communication with the world.   In excess, the Geminian nature may be

described in terms which express the tendency to superficiality of all air
types, the keywords being: restless, impatient, unstable, superficial,
lacking in concentration, inconsistent and diffused. The type tends to
remain (at worst) childish and immature, and (at best) retains its youthful
mentality and physical appearance. Gemini is ruled by the planet Mercury and
offers no traditional DIGNITY, though some authorities (following the Arabian
astrologers) mark Gemini as the exaltation of the "Dragon's Head".

GEMINI CONSTELLATION Zodiacal constellation, the extent of which is set out
in figure 32. The Latin name Gemini (twins) merely follows a tradition
already ancient in classical times, along with the many variants (Didymoi to
the Greeks, Dioscuri to the Romans). According to ancient mythology, the
twins were sons of Leda, hence the poetic 'Ledaean Stars' of Milton - yet
their personalized names are almost legion: 'Gemini Lacones', the 'Spartan
twins', for example, though they are perhaps more famous as CASTOR and
POLLUX, less so as the pairs of Apollo and Hercules, Theseus and Piritheus.
The image for the constellation appears to have been two giants originally,
but in mediaeval times (probably under the influence of Romance literature)
the image became male and female, as in the 13th century image of the "San
Miniato Zodiac" (figure 32). Since the Arabian constellation artists present
the pair as peacocks, a mediaeval title 'Duo Pavones' sometimes occurs.
Kircher, in tortuous arguments, claims that the Egyptians regarded the twins
as Horus the Elder and Horus the Younger, though this does not appear to be
accurate, yet it links perfectly with an esoteric tradition outlined by
Steiner. The fixed star alpha is 'Castor' the mortal twin, while the beta is
'Pollux', the immortal: see also ALHENA, DIRAH, PROPUS and WASAT.

FIGURE 32. IMAGE OF GEMINI FROM THE 13TH CENTURY "SAN MINIATO ZODIAC",
AND THE CONSTELLATION FROM THE "MODERN ZODIAC" OF DELPORTE.

GEMMA One of the early names (probably late Latin) for the fixed star
ALPHECCA, which Ebertin wrongly translates as 'jewel' and relates to the
'crown' in which it is placed. The name was actually used in the sense of
'bud', in reference to the unopened blossom of the floral crown, as it was
pictured in early texts.

GEMS See BIRTH STONES.

GENERAL ASTROLOGY A term used by the historian Pingree in his division of
the forms of astrology into four distinct groups (the others being
Genethliac, Catarchic and Interrogatory). By 'general astrology' he intends
to denote that form relating the situation in the heavens at a particular

==

moment (such as eclipses, the vernal equinox, and so on) to events affecting
broad classes of people, or the entire world. The term is approximately the
equivalent of MUNDANE ASTROLOGY.

GENETHLIACAL ASTROLOGY   A term derived from the Greek and applied in general
to 'Natal Astrology', which deals with the casting and interpretation of
personal charts cast for the moment of birth.

GENETHLIACI   An archaic term for 'astrologers' - those who cast and
interpret 'genitures', or practice "Genethliacal Astrology". The term may
have been used for the first time by Isidore of Seville.

GENICULATOR   An ancient Greek name for the "Hercules Constellation".

GENITURE   Term used both to denote a personal horoscope and (incorrectly) the
interpretation of the same.

GENIUS   See AGATHOS DAIMON, which may be translated 'good genius'.

GEOARC   A subdivision of the daily orbit of a particular point on the Earth:
a measurement relating to the HOUSE SYSTEMS, and used to distinguish
measurement by HELIARC.

GEOCENTRIC   Term applied to a measurement or image of the solar system
viewed as though the Earth itself were the central point of celestial
motions. In general terms, when astrologers refer to the 'geocentric model'
they mean the PTOLEMAIC SYSTEM. Most modern systems of astrology (and
virtually all ancient astrological systems) are geocentric. However, in
modern times there has been a move to introduce a HELIOCENTRIC ASTROLOGY.

GEOCENTRIC NODES   The only geocentric nodal axis to receive much attention
in traditional astrology is that of the Moon - see DRAGON'S HEAD and DRAGON'S
TAIL - the axis of these nodes being the points where the plane of the
ecliptic is intersected by the "Terrestrial Ecliptic", which is itself
defined by the path of the Moon. The geocentric nodes of the other planets
are rarely expressed by a single axis (but see HELIOCENTRIC NODES), though in
recent years Ephemerides of geocentric planetary nodes have been made
available, and the astrologer Dobyns has related the significance of nodal
interpretation to traditional astrological concepts, including "Synastry".

GEOGRAPHICAL LATITUDE   The angular distance, north or south, of the Earth's
equator. Distinguish from LATITUDE, which in an astrological context is very
often "Celestial Latitude", save in reference to place of birth.

GEOGRAPHICAL LONGITUDE   The angular distance between the meridian of a given
place and the Prime Meridian of Greenwich, expressed in degrees east and west
of Greenwich.

GEOGRAPHIC ASTROLOGY   For a consideration of the zodiacal rulership accorded
geographic locations, see CHOROGRAPHY.

GEOMANCY Geomancy in its simplest form is really a manner of making
predictions by using stones (or indeed any inorganic materiality of the
earth, such as twigs) in order to construct a figure which is then subject to
interpretation by a series of fixed rules. These fixed rules were originally
unrelated to astrological traditions, and were limited to the consideration
of the interactions of 16 geomantic figures. The simple geomantic method was
rendered more complex by permitting an influx of astrological ideas, such as
the doctrines of elements, aspects, planetary rulerships, houses and signs,
into a divinatory system to which they did not properly belong. As a
predictive method, geomancy is therefore only peripherally connected with
astrology, and then only because the early practicioners of the art in
mediaeval Europe chose to introduce a system of recording the results of

divination within a chart which resembled the horoscope figure and which
(eventually) attached to its own system a series of associations derived from
astrological lore. Table 42 sets out the traditional associations. Of late,
due to an ignorance of historical terminologies, the word 'geomancy' has also
been misused, and applied to the study of telluric forces, the so-called
'ley-lines', which have nothing to do with the predictive art of geomancy.
By definition, geomancy looks down to the earth, while astrology looks up to
the stars, so that the recently coined term 'astro-geomancy' is something of
a misnomer.

```
-------------------------------------------------------------------TABLE 42
```

NAME OF GEOMANTIC FIGURE	ELEMENT	PLANET	SIGN
Via - Way	Water	Moon	Leo
Populus - People	Water	Moon	Capricorn
Coniunctio - Joining	Air	Mercury	Virgo
Carcer - Prison	Earth	Saturn	Pisces
Fortuna Major - Greater good	Earth	Sun	Aquarius
Fortuna Minor - Less good	Fire	Sun	Taurus
Acquisitio - Gain	Air	Jupiter	Aries
Amissio - Loss	Fire	Venus	Libra
Loetitia - Joy	Air	Jupiter	Taurus
Tristitia - Sadness	Earth	Saturn	Scorpio
Puella - Girl	Water	Venus	Libra
Puer - Boy	Fire	Mars	Aries
Albus - White	Water	Mercury	Cancer
Rubeus - Red	Fire	Mars	Gemini
Caput - Head	Earth	Caput Draconis	Virgo
Cauda - Tail	Fire	Cauda Draconis	Sagittarius

GEORGIUM SIDUS   The name given to the newly discovered URANUS by Herschel in
1781, the 'Star of George' in honour of the reigning George III. It would
appear that the name 'Uranus' was used by Bode about two years later, though
astrologers (who had for some years suspected the existence of such a planet)
had called it 'Ouranos' long before.

GEO-SOPHIC   See THREE PROTOTYPES.

GESTALT-HOROSCOPY One of the names given to the astrological system
developed by the German astrologer Dr. Walter A. Koch.

GHAFR   'Al Ghafr' (the covering), name of the 13th of the Arabian MANZILS.

GIANT   See ORION.

GIBBOR   See ORION.

GIBBOUS   A term most usually applied to the Moon in one of its "Phases", but
applicable equally to both Mercury and Venus. The Moon is said to be gibbous
when both of its sides are convex, shortly after completion of the square
aspect. See however PLANETARY PHASES.

GIEDI   See ALGEDI.

GIRTAB   See SAGITTARIUS CONSTELLATION.

GIVER OF LIFE   See HYLEG.

GLASTONBURY ZODIAC   Name given to a supposed earth-zodiac, contained within
a circle of about 9 miles diameter, with Butleigh (Somerset) at the centre,
and Glastonbury Tor to north-north west of the circle. The figures were
originally traced out by Maltwood (after whom the zodiac is sometimes named)

in the 'twenties of this century. In the sixteenth century, the scholar John Dee had mentioned the existence of a zodiac in or around Glastonbury, but his descriptions (noted in his diaries - see Deacon) are vague, and there is no evidence that this so-called 'Dee Zodiac' corresponds to the Glastonbury Zodiac. The images (which do not in every case correspond to either zodiacal or constellational images) are traced out in landscape contours, roads, earthworks, rivers, pools, and other 'natural' formations. Sometimes called the "Somerset Giants", their antiquity is (unconvincingly) claimed by Harwood Steele to have been derived from initiate knowledge brought to Britain by Sumer-Chaldean priests. The supposed zodiac, whatever it is, is certainly not Chaldean. The tracing of these figures by Maltwood was involved with her study of the Arthurian and Grail legends, the zodiac itself being the 'Round Table', and the circle of figures which her imagination projected into Ordinance Survey maps was adapted to the Grail cycle - Virgo becoming Guinevere, Aries Gawain, and so on. Many specialists, including the present writer, deny that there are any figures at all - certainly, if the projections are regarded as figures in any sense, then they do not relate to any zodiac, antique or modern, nor to any known constellational figure. A serious historian cannot but be inclined to see the zodiac as entirely a product of the human imagination: the figures are probably nothing other than autoscopic projections. From a strictly historical point of view, the figures imagined in this vast circle could not have the antiquity ascribed to them: for example, for historical reasons, Capricorn (zodiacal or constellational), could not have been imaged as a goat, no more than Cancer would have been a ship: the antiquity claimed for the zodiac would suggest that Libra and Scorpio would not have been imaged as Maltwood presents them. Modifications made by Caine to Capricorn, Scorpio and Libra are equally unconvincing, on strictly historical grounds.

GLOBE PERIOD   In the Theosophical cosmoconception, the period of time during which any given "Globe" in a CHAIN is fully active (which is to say, supportive of the main stream of life) is called a globe period. The passage of such 'life support' through all the seven globes of a particular chain is called a 'round', a septenary of rounds make up one 'chain period', and seven 'chain periods' (that is, 343 globe periods, or 49 rounds) make up what is called a single SCHEME OF EVOLUTION.

GLOBES   In the Theosophical cosmoconception, the Earth and the planets are called globes. However, each individual globe is said to possess a counterpart, often described in terms of graduations of finer substance than ordinary matter. A physical globe, such as our own Earth, for example, is regarded as the dense centre of seven interpenetrating worlds, each occupying the same space, yet all of different qualities of materiality. Such counterparts are approximately analagous to the invisible subtle sheaths which are said in occult circles to surround and interpenetrate the body of man (the so-called 'astral', 'lower mental', 'higher mental', 'buddhic' and so on - specialist Sanskrit terms not defined in the present text). Not all the globes are regarded as being physically rooted, however. For example, the globes of our EARTH CHAIN consist of 3 physical globes, along with 2 astral and 2 mental globes. The astral globe is said to possess higher corresponding bodies, something akin to the higher sheaths of the angelic realm in esoteric lore.

GLOBUS AEROSTATICUS   An obsolete constellation - see AETHERIUS.

GLUTIENS   Name given to the 23rd of the LUNAR MANSIONS in some mediaeval lists. Probably identified by the fixed star Nashira, the gamma of Capricornus.

GLYPHS   A term often wrongly used as being synonymous with SIGILS, and perhaps the most misused of all astrological specialist terms: even the careful Blavatsky misuses it. The word 'glyph' has a proper application to 'relief symbols' in sculptural and architectural forms, but not to written

===

forms. Some glyphs have undoubtedly become sigils - for example, some of the
bas-relief symbols on Egyptian tombs (properly glyphs) have become sigils, by
virtue of being translated to the written form on papyrus or paper: the
modern sigil for the Sun ⊙ was once precisely such a glyph as the Egyptian
determinate for 'god' and for 'time', it became properly the 'sigil' for the
Sun in the fifteenth century AD, when it was adopted as a symbol by Italian
astrologers. In this sense, therefore, the bas-relief images on the DENDERAH
ZODIAC may be called glyphs, but IMAGES are not ipso facto glyphs.

GNOMES   The class of ELEMENTALS linked with the Earth. They have many
different names in popular lore, but two types of gnomes mentioned in
esoteric lore are the Diemeae (the kind which live in large stones) and the
Durdales (tree spirits) - in certain of the astrological CALENDARIA MAGICA,
they are often called 'Pigmei'.

GOAT   Popular name for the zodiacal sign CAPRICORN, and used also of
Capricornus. Originally, in the Babylonian and Egyptian zodiacs and
constellation images, the sign and constellation were represented by an image
of a Goat-Fish (see figure 10).

GOH SYSTEM Abbreviated name (Geburtsorteshauser) given for the House system
introduced by the German astrologer Koch in which cusps are calculated for
the place of birth. Tables are available according to this GOH System for
all latitudes between 0 degrees and 60 degrees, for each successive degree
passing over the Midheaven. See KOCHIAN SYSTEM.

GOLDEN AGE   See FOUR AGES and KRITA YUGA.

GOLDEN FISH   See PISCIS AUSTRALIS.

GOLDEN NUMBER   In astrology the term is applied to a method for determining
the calendrical fall of the METONIC CYCLE by application to a table of such
cycles. In a non-astrological context the same term is also used of a ratio,
the 'Divine Proportion' of the ancients, which results from the division of a
line in such a way that the smaller part is in the same proportion to the
greater part as that greater part is to the whole.

GONASI   Term used by Ptolemy for the "Hercules Constellation".

GOOD DAEMON   Old name for the "Eleventh House".

GOODS POINT   The 'point of goods' is one of the so-called Arabian PARS. If
the Lord of the Second House is taken as the Ascendant of a figure, then the
new cusp of the Second house marks the point.

GORGONIFER   See PERSEUS.

GRADIAL TRANSIT   A term used first by the astrologer Sepharial in reference
to the idea that a progressed planet usually projects an ever-increasing arc
(the gradial transit arc) due to progression. This arc is presumed to remain
sensitive to major transits during the life of the native.

GRAFFIAS   Fixed star (triple), the beta of Scorpius, set in the head of the
scorpion, and hence sometimes called 'Frons Scorpii'. The probable etymology
of the term, from the Greek 'Graphaios' (crab) may explain why the scorpion
in early astrology is sometimes actually pictured as a crab, even though the
image was linked with zodiacal and constellational Cancer: Allen records
that St. Augustine believed the desert scorpion was generated from the
aquatic crab. Under the modern name 'Akrab', Powell adopted this star to
mark the termination of his sidereal Libra - see SIDEREAL ZODIAC. It has an
evil reputation among astrologers, and was said by Ptolemy to be of a nature
equivalent to Mars conjunct Saturn.

GRAND CLIMACTERIC   According to some astrologers, the 63rd year of life - but see CLIMACTERICS.

GRAND CROSS   An aspectal pattern involving at least four planets which are so placed as to form two axes of opposition which intersect at right angles. If there are no orbs involved, then each of the planets will be in a sign of a different element. The grand cross is an extension of the so-called "Cosmic Cross". It is said to bring considerable tension into the life of the native, often with creative results. See MAJOR CONFIGURATION.

GRAND FIXED CROSS   Name given to a "Major Configuration" in which two pairs of oppositions are placed in all four of the fixed quadruplicities - that is, in Taurus, Leo, Scorpio and Aquarius. Distinguish from FIXED CROSS and GRAND CROSS.

GRAND TRINE   When two planets are in trine to each other, and both separately trined by a third planet, the whole configuration is said to be a 'grand trine': it is a MAJOR CONFIGURATION. Provided there is not a disjunct trine involved in this figure, each of the planets must be in the same triplicity, and the aspect is quite rightly said to be highly beneficial.

GREAT CHAIN OF BEING   See CHAIN OF BEING.

GREAT DRAGON   A term with a variety of applications in occult, esoteric and astrological contexts. In astrology the term is sometimes used in reference to the path of the Moon (or indeed to the sphere of the Moon) which, in its intersection of the ecliptic, gives the nodes, themselves named after the image of an encircling dragon (see DRAGON'S HEAD), and often depicted as a scaled dragon. The term is also sometimes used in astrological contexts of the constellation "Draco": but see also ATALIA. In alchemy the reference is often to 'time', as the great destroyer, frequently imaged as the Ouroboros dragon, an image often found in esoteric astrological contexts. In occult thought, which touches upon modern esoteric astrology, the name is sometimes given to the dark adversary Ahriman, who is often depicted as a scaled dragon under the feet of Michael. In spiritualist circles it is a term (first used by Davis) for a mysterious portion of the heavenly Summerland, inhabited by the morally deficient beings called Diakka. While apparently relating to very different ideas within these several contexts, there is actually a unifying principle in this term, for the sphere of the Moon is traditionally linked with the diabolic post-mortem existence - but see EIGHTH SPHERE.

GREATER BENEFIC   See BENEFICS.

GREATER CLOUD   See NUBECULAE MAGELLANI.

GREATER LUMINARY   An ancient term for the Sun, in comparison with the 'lesser luminary' which is the Moon.

GREAT ILECH   The hidden "Virtue" in medicine, derived from planets or stars.

GREAT NEBULA   Name given to a nebula in the constellation "Andromeda", said by astrologers to be of an evil nature, threatening sight, and promising a violent death. It is sometimes called "Vertex", the 'Queen of the Nebulae' and 'Little Cloud'.

GREAT YEAR   In mediaeval manuscripts, 'Great Year' is a term used to denote the period of time in which all the planets will return to a given fiducial - there is little agreement as to how long this period is, however: at one extreme, William of Conches gives 49,000 years, whilst at the other extreme Petarius gives 350,635 years. This vast cycle has been confused with the PLATONIC CYCLE of 25,920 years, which is sometimes called the 'Great Year'.

==

GREEK PLANETS   The names of the Greek planets are: SU Helios - MO Selene
- ME Stilbon, Hermes - VE Phosphoros, Hesperus, Aphrodite - MA Pyroeis,
Ares - JU Phaethon, Zeus - SA Phainon, Kronos

GREEK ZODIAC The historian Powell makes a convincing case for calling the
"Tropical Zodiac" the Greek Zodiac. It is in effect a zodiac devised by
Greek astronomer-astrologers according to solar principles not inherent in
the earlier BABYLONIAN ZODIAC. The division is not of the zodiacal
asterisms, as in earlier zodiacs, but of the ecliptic itself, which is a
solar co-ordinate. The division is twelve-fold, in equal 30 degree arcs, in a
system which had been used before but which was unique in that the first arc
was conceived as being linked not with a fixed star fiducial but with solar
phenomena. This solar phenomenon was defined by the EUCTEMONIAN CALENDAR,
and the whole system of the Greek zodiac, using names derived by Euctemon
from the Babylonian zodiacal/constellational system, was probably formulated
by the Greek Hipparchus in the 2nd century BC. This appears to have been the
first zodiac technically free of the fiducials of fixed stars. Inevitably,
the very freedom of the system has given rise to the problems arising from
PRECESSION, which in turn raises the question of determining the correct
AYANAMSA. See also HELLENISTIC ZODIAC. The ancient Greek names for the
signs of the zodiac (with variant spellings) were:

AR	Krios	TA	Tauros	GE	Didymoi	CN	Karkinos
LE	Leon	VG	Parthenos	LB	Chelai (Zugos)	SC	Scorpios
SG	Toxotes	CP	Aigokeros	AQ	Hydroxous	PI	Ichthys

GREGORIAN CALENDAR   The modern European and American calendrical system,
named after the reform of the JULIAN CALENDAR initiated under Pope Gregory
XIII, and based on the work of the astrologer-physician Aloysius Lilius and a
Jesuit named Claivius. The vernal equinox had regressed by a time equivalent
of 10 days since the Council of Nicaea of 325 (see EASTER), and so by
proclamation of a Bull of 1582 the Pope annulled ten days, thereby adjusting
the calendar so that the equinox was back to the 21st March. The length of
the solar day was corrected, and the year made to commence on the 1st of
January, while the present system of leap years was established. The 97 leap
years which occur in the course of 400 years allows an error of time which is
only 26 seconds short of celestial measurement. From an astrological point
of view the changes subsequent to this Bull have led to much complication.
The Gregorian system was immediately adopted in Spain (and colonies),
Portugal and parts of Italy (then not unified). With some adjustment it was
adopted also in the Low Countries and most of France. However, it was not
adopted in England until 1752, following an Act passed in 1751, resulting in
the famous 'supression' of 11 days. Germany and Sweden had already adopted
the system in 1700. The Russians adopted it only in 1918, and the Greek
Orthodox countries (variously) between 1916 and 1923, the Turks being the
last to adopt it in 1926. Unfortunately, the correct dating (and hence
computation of horoscopes) cannot always be ascertained from the material
given here, since some localities did not adopt the changes immediately, and
in some cases the years were not always begun in Gregorian terms. In
pre-Conquest England, the year began on 25th December, but after the
Conquest, 1st January was adopted, though later changed to 25th March
following general mediaeval practice, related to the Feast of the
Annunciation. In 1752, and for all later years, it began on 1st January.

GRIFFIN   See PHOENIX.

GROUPING   A modern term used nominally as an equivalent of the technical
"Satellitium", but in general use also applied to the general configuration
of planets in a chart.

GRUS   Constellation formed and named by Bayer in 1604, though from stars
included in most earlier maps within the Southern Fish. The name means
'crane', which is highly appropriate, as Allen remarks, since the crane was

claimed to be the symbol of the astrologer in Egypt (at least, in the widely accepted mediaeval and Renaissance interpretation of Egyptian symbolism). However, in England, Bayer's term was actually translated as meaning 'bittern' or 'flamingo'.

GRYPE   This term is usually a reference to the 'Falling Grype', a mediaeval equivalent of 'Vultur Cadens', one of the important "Fifteen Stars", now called WEGA.

GUARDED   A little-used term applied in a specialist sense to one or more planets which, while elevated in the chart, are guarded on the eastern side by the Sun, and on the western side by the Moon.

GUARDIANS OF THE HEAVENS   See ROYAL STARS.

HADES   Name given to one of the "Hypothetical Planets" in the "Uranian Astrology". This transneptunian is included in an ephemeris, and is said to relate to 'lowness, dirt, antiquity and secrets'.

HAGIEL   Name given by Agrippa (quoting ancient cabbalistic sources) to the "Intelligency" of Venus. He records the magical number of Hagiel as 49, which is a typographical error, and does not follow the normal procedure of correspondences in relation to the MAGIC SQUARE of Venus.

HAGITH   One of the names for HAGIEL.

HAKAH   'Al Hak'ah' (the white spot), the 3rd of the Arabian MANZILS.

HALF MOON   See PLANETARY PHASES.

HALF-SUMS   See MID-POINTS.

HALLEY'S COMET   See COMETS.

HALYIAN SYSTEM   A method of HOUSE DIVISION closely based on he 10th century "Albategnius System", whereby the projected arc was defined by the passage of two hours of Right Ascension for each house, measured from the Ascendant. The system is ascribed to the Arabian astrologer Albohazen Haly, who lived in the 11th century, and is sometimes called the 'Albohazen System'.

HAMAL   Fixed star, the alpha of constellation Aries, set in the forehead of the Ram, the name from the Arabic 'Al Hamal (the sheep). As might be expected from its placing, the star is said to cause violence and cruelty: Ptolemy likened it to the nature of Mars conjunct Saturn. Penrose has calculated that several of the ancient Greek temples were orientated to this star, which is perhaps not surprising since the constellation of Aries was seen by the ancient Greeks as one of the symbols for Zeus.

HAMBURG SCHOOL   A name often applied to the unconventional system of "Uranian Astrology", on the grounds that Witte and Sieggruen established in Hamburg the school which developed and promulgated their ideas.

HAN   Fixed star, the zeta of "Ophiuchus", in the left knee of the figure, the name apparently from the Chinese for the feudal State of Han. It is said to be of the nature of Venus conjunct Saturn, bringing troubles and disgrace.

HANAH   'Al Han'ah' (the brand), the 4th of the Arabian MANZILS.

==

HAND OF OPHIUCHUS   Modern name for the fixed star epsilson of Ophiuchus,
apparently identified with the 'Nitach-bat' (the Man of Death) in the
Euphratean system. It is of an evil disposition.

HARMONIC CHART   Name given to the chart designed to present data according to
the system of "Harmonics" proposed by Addey. The positions of the planets
and related points are set out on a calibrated circle. The harmonic format
which arises from the insertion of 90, 72, 60 degrees (etc.) permits the
astrologer to note particular harmonics. See ARC TRANSFORM CHART.

HARMONICS   A term applied to an entirely new form of astrological research
and interpretation, based on statistical methods originally (at least)
connected with numerological theory.   The theory to which the now extensive
literature of harmonics relates is largely derived from the researches of the
astrologer Addey and his later co-workers, stemming from a seemingly
indefatigable application of statistically arranged material to
computerization. Addey found that when large numbers of birth data were
submitted to specialist statistical analysis, planetary and nodal positions
exhibited wave-like fluctuations which were not accounted for in the usual
methods of astrological interpretation. Subsequent exploration of such
analysis showed that numerical harmonic relationships seemed to apply in
various groups of charts, and Addey came to the conclusion that all integral
divisions (that is, harmonics) of the 360 degree circle were susceptible to
interpretation in terms of specialist meanings, and were therefore capable of
forming the basis for a new approach to astrological studies. Catalogues for
the harmonics which fall at and within each of the 360 degrees of the circle
are now available, designed to faciliate the use of a potential 16,000
harmonics and their equivalents in this specialized form of chart
interpretation. Although the exploration of the statistical method now
related to harmonics was pioneered by the Swiss astrologer Krafft in the
1930s, his methods were later seen to result in invalid conclusions. The
main impulse for the study came from Addey, who was of the opinion that the
significance of harmonics lay in the numerological importance underlying
them: in later times he questioned the validity of the higher harmonics -
but see for example SUBSISTENCES. Whatever the underlying reasons for the
significance of the harmonics, a system of interpretation has been built
around the intervals established by simple divisions in terms of whole
numbers. For example, the division by four is seen as relating to
'difficulty, effort and achievement' - corresponding, one notes, to the basic
four-fold division of the square aspect. The division by five, linked with
the 'mind, discrimination and the human perception', appears to rest on a
somewhat personalized view of the spiritual and material nature of man,
however, and finds no correspondence with traditional theory. The series
established by the division of the interval of nine is said to point to the
various stages of completion and fruition in the life of man - 'birth, death
and rebirth'. From a practical point of view, the difficulties with
harmonics (for those not wholly taken up with this new type of astrology) are
the very number of possible intervals available, and the actual model of man
which is supposedly portrayed or revealed in the harmonic system. It must,
however, be recognized that the use of the statistical approach to large
groups of horoscopes does appear to have established its own form of
astrology and astrological data. For example, when Seymours subjected to
such 'group analysis' the charts of 200 centegenarians, then the ordinary
standards of astrological doctrines appeared to have no really valid
application. In contrast, research by Addey into the relationship between
harmonics and longevity (involving 972 nonagenarians) established a
convincing 108th harmonic (9 x 12) relating to the number 9, itself linked
with the life-cycle. However, it is worth observing that this in no way
diminishes traditional astrology, which is itself designed to relate only to
the unique individual chart, and has never (until comparatively recent times,
in the work of Krafft, Gauquelin, and so on) been regarded as susceptible to
statistical interpolation and analysis - the very 'uniqueness' of the

individual chart seeming to prohibit such an approach. It is therefore important to recognise that what the statistically based method of harmonics establishes is the groundwork of a new approach to astrology, which does not invalidate the traditional forms. Harmonics is rooted in a statistical approach to data which is foreign to the spirit of traditional astrology: harmonics links certain data derived from astrological concepts to the field of waves, the advantage being that wave-patterns are themselves readily subjected to analysis by the computerized techniques beloved by the practitioners of harmonics. Harmonics certainly expresses more of the modern attitude to the cosmos (an attitude which is distinctly materialistic, in its striving for much-vaunted scientific objectivity) rather than to the individual chart-reading, which is the prime object of traditional astrology. Such points must be made, if only because some modern popular literature suggests that harmonics is really nothing more than a modern equivalent of the ancient aspectal theory - which is simply not the case. The aim and symbolic fruits of harmonic analysis involve a view of astrology very different from that expressed in the theory of aspects, and indeed embrace many ideas rooted in traditional astrology. There has been a move, arising mainly from the practitioners of Harmonics, to claim that the system is reflected in the much earlier divisions of Hindu astrology: however, many of the ancient methods of divisions in the Hindu system may be traced to adaptations made by Indian astrologers to the sign divisions, "Sortes" and "Loci" of Hellenistic astrology which formed the basis of Hindu exoteric astrology (see for example LORD OF THE GREEKS), which is alien to the spirit of harmonics. Much more work must be done, especially on the history of the evident adaptation of Hellenistic methods to the peculiar socio-cosmological beliefs of the Indian astrologers, before such links with the modern harmonics may be made with any real validity.

HARMONIES   See KEPLERIAN HARMONICS and PLANETARY TONAL INTERVALS.

HARMONY OF THE SPHERES   See MUSIC OF THE SPHERES.

HASALANGUE   See OPHIUCHUS.

HASMODAI   Name given to Agrippa (quoting ancient cabbalistic sources) to the 'Daemon' of the Moon, for whom he gives the magical number 369 which is the linear addition of the lunar MAGIC SQUARE. See also LUNAR INTELLIGENCY.

HASTA   Name (meaning 'the hand') given to the 11th of the Hindu NAKSHATRAS.

HASTORANG   See ROYAL STARS.

HAURIENS PRIMUS   Name given to the 26th of the LUNAR MANSIONS in some mediaeval lists. Probably identified by the fixed star Markab.

HAURIENS SECUNDUS   Name given to the 27th of the LUNAR MANSIONS in some mediaeval lists. Probably identified by the fixed star Algenib.

HAYZ   A term applied to a minor DIGNITY derived from the Arabian astrology, and limited to use in Horary Astrology. When a masculine diurnal planet is above the horizon in a diurnal chart, then it is said to be Hayz. When a feminine nocturnal planet is below the Earth in a nocturnal chart, then it is said to be Hayz. The placing was said to be mildly beneficial.

HEART   In a specialist sense, one of the Arabian PARS, the 'part of heart', sometimes called the 'part of Venus' or the 'point of Love'. If a chart is revolved so that the degree occupied by the Sun is transferred to the Ascendant, then the position of Venus in this new arrangement will mark the Heart within the houses.

HEART OF HYDRA   See ALPHARD.

HEART OF THE ROYAL LION   See REGULUS.

HEART OF THE SUN   See CAZIMI and ESOTERIC SUN.

HEART OF THE ZODIAC   A term (rarely) used in modern times to denote the zodiacal and constellational Leo.

HEAVEN   See EMPYREAN, SPHERES and TENTH SPHERE.

HEBE   Name given to one of the "Asteroids", discovered in 1847.

HE-GOAT   A term used by some modern astrologers for both the zodiacal sign Capricorn and Capricornus.

HEKA   Fixed star (double) the lamda of Orion, the name derived from the Arabic 'Al Hak'ah' (white spot): it is considered to be an unfortunate influence. See also HAKAH.

HELIACAL RISING   The first rising of a star after its period of invisibility due to conjunction with the Sun.

HELIACAL SETTING   The last setting of a star prior to its period of invisibility due to conjunction with the Sun.

HELIACAL VISIBILITY   See HELIACAL RISING, HELIACAL SETTING and MORINEAN ORBS.

HELIARC   A subdivision of the annual orbit of the earth: a measurement relating to sign divisions, and used to distinguish from measurements made in terms of GEOARC.

HELIARC FIGURE   A name for a chart cast employing the simple subdivisions of the SOLAR HOUSES.

HELIOCENTRIC ASTROLOGY   Heliocentric astrology is founded on the calculation and interpretation of charts which symbolically present data from a solar rather than from a geocentric standpoint: the heliocentric figure charts the planetary positions from a viewpoint of an observer in the centre of the sun. Special heliocentric ephemerides have been designed for astrological use, and since the heliocentric motions of planets and nodal points is more uniform than the geocentric equivalents, such tables lend themselves to ease of calculation. Since the zodiac proper is based upon a point calculated in geocentric terms, Heliocentric Astrology tends to postulate and rely upon a Constellational Zodiac, though there appears to be no precise consensus as to the limits of the twelve asterisms: but see SIDEREAL ZODIAC which is widely used by modern heliocentric astrologers, especially those concerned with Astrosophy. The heliocentric chart differs considerably from the geocentric equivalent, as the sun itself is absent (in the sense that the earth is absent from a geocentric chart), and there is no mundane system of houses, no Ascendant, and no Moon (as this is incorporated in the orb of the earth). Thus, the three fundamental influences of the geocentric chart - Sun, Moon and Ascendant - are missing. Heliocentric astrologers place great emphasis on planetary nodes, and the axes arising from these, as well as upon heliocentric aspects. The very fact that a different range of aspects is available to Venus and Mercury has perforce involved new interpretations foreign to traditional astrology (though the 16th century astrologer Morin offered such interpretations on an academic basis). It must however be realised that the projection of an aspectarian upon a heliocentric chart in no way follows the traditional rules or philosophy of astrology, since aspects were literally involved with the idea of influences (in the sense of "in-flowing" forces) of a "Jaimainic" elemental nature into the matrix of the earth, which in turn presupposed a zodiac (see ELEMENTAL ASPECTS). While heliocentric charts are championed by some modern astrologers, the non-telluric measure implies an element quite foreign to the individualizing tendency proper to traditional chart interpretation. Some interesting, if highly speculative, work has been done by Sucher (influenced by Vreede and Steiner) in connexion with heliocentric charts, relating to historical periods and epochs (see WORLD CYCLE OF MUNDANE EVENTS), though some of the historical data employed is of dubious value. Such historical interpretation is aided by the fact that heliocentric nodes advance with a fair regularity at about one degree in a century, and thus afford a most convenient time-conversion. To date, most of the studies (for example, those of Erlewine and Thorburn) of chart comparisons between geocentric and heliocentric systems, appear to have been conducted using too few cases to support valid inference. Some useful findings, especially in connexion with surveys of nodes, seen as both points and axes, and in connexion with heliocentric aspects, have been ably presented by Dean.   Heliocentric astrology is to such an extent a modern phenomenon that when the traditionalist Leo attempted to define it at the beginning of the present century, he made a large number of significant errors in his text, including the idea that it had 'sprung up in America in modern times'. The major problem is that, aside from one or two learned astrologers, the various heliocentric systems are being promulgated by students who have an insufficient knowledge of the rules and implications underlying the vast corpus of doctrines relating to traditional astrology, with all its esoteric and exoteric undertones and implications. A really satisfactory account and study of heliocentric astrology is still awaited.

HELIOCENTRIC CHART   A chart designed to stereographically project the planets against the stars from an imaginary point at the centre of the Sun, and used in "Heliocentric Astrology".   Such a projection has little relationship to the many different methods of conventional chart projection, and is in most cases a projection of the ecliptic. While there is a remarkable tendency in some astrological circles to interpret heliocentric charts from a point of view of traditions established for 'geocentric charts', much attention is paid to the planetary nodes and ingresses. Heliocentric charts are often used in "Astrosophy" (see ASTEROGRAM), and much work has been done on the heliocentric interfaces by Erlewine.

HELIOCENTRIC NODES   Since the planetary nodes advance at approximately 1 degree per century, it is possible to set down the positions of the axes in degrees valid for a long period of time. Such 'mean heliocentric nodes' as are listed in table 43 are those generally used in heliocentric astrology, expressed in whole degrees (but see ZERO DEGREE).

---TABLE 43

PLANET	NODE	PLANET	NODE	PLANET	NODE
ME	18	VE	17	MA	20
JU	10	SA	24	UR	14
NE	12	PL	20 (but see below)		

These whole degrees are valid for the mid-point of our present century, when only Jupiter's node was near to entry into the next degree (being 9.9 degrees in 1950, which will place it in the 11th degree after 1960. The information for Pluto relates to the 'true node', and may therefore be + or - 1 degree.

HELIOCENTRIC SYSTEM   A model of the solar system which places the Sun as a fixed point at the centre, and uses this as the basic co-ordinate to which all cosmic measurements are related. In astrology, this is contrasted with the GEOCENTRIC SYSTEM, which in its modern form is much adapted from the original Copernican model, and is 'heliocentric'. The idea of a heliocentric system was known to the ancient Greeks, as for example in the model proposed in outline during the 3rd century BC by Aristarchus of Samos. In setting out the form of his own PTOLEMAIC SYSTEM, Ptolemy mentions the Aristarcheian

===

model, but appears to think that it does not give a satisfactory explanation of celestial phenomena. Most modern astrology is founded upon a geocentric view of the solar system, though all information used in the calculation of nativities is now ultimately derived from the heliocentric system. See also HELIOCENTRIC ASTROLOGY.

HELIOS   The Greek astrological term for the Sun - but see APOLLO.

HELLENISTIC ZODIAC   The term is used to denote the Babylonian-based astrological computation schema of the Hellenistic period derived from tables brought from the conquered Babylon by Callisthenes (circa 331 BC): it is Hellenistic, therefore, rather than Greek (see GREEK ZODIAC). The AYANAMSA favoured was that calculated according to the tables of Naburiannu, which gave a 10 degree arc, though it sems that the Greeks incorporated it into their schema without being aware of its significance. Fagan claims that this was indeed the zodiacal schema of such well-known astrologers as Manilius, Firmicus Maternus, Vettius Valens and Manetho. He further insists that the planetary positions of the so-called DENDERAH ZODIAC are cast for the Neomenia of 17th April, 17 AD, according to the Hellenistic zodiac - a point which is much contested by other historians. See also GREEK ZODIAC.

HEMISPHERE   Half of a circle of a sphere. In relationship to the symbolic representation of the Celestial Sphere which is now called the 'horoscope figure', the visible hemisphere is usually called the DIURNAL ARC, while the obscured hemisphere is called the NOCTURNAL ARC.   The eastern hemisphere, ascending from the cusp of the imum coeli to the midheaven, is called the 'oriental arc', while the western hemisphere, descending from the midheaven to the imum coeli is called the 'occidental arc' or 'hemisphere'.

HERCULES   Name given by the astrologer Wemyss to one of the "Hypothetical Planets", said by him to be the ruler of Leo. He gives the planet a revolution of approximately 654 years. See also POLLUX.

HERCULES CONSTELLATION   Constellation, located approximately 28 degrees Libra to 2 degrees Capricorn, and from 5 to 53 degrees north of the equator. Allen quite rightly records this as one of the oldest sky figures, though it was known by quite a different name to the early Greeks, who saw it variously as a kneeling figure (hence 'Engonasi', the Kneeler). The original Engonasi was seen as a wide variety of mythical heroes, of which Hercules was merely a later type, and over 80 different names for the figure have been recorded, most of them linked with heroes. Another name has been translated as 'Phantom', though the Greek 'Eidolon' really meant something beyhond merely 'ghostly', perhaps more like 'astral form'. This latter derivation reminds us that it was considered by astrologers to give dangerous passions, such as are related to unbridled astral forces. Ptolemy likens the whole constellation to the nature of Mercury, yet curiously enough its influence is supposed to promote tenacity, fixity of aim, and general strength of character.

HERMEAN ZODIAC A term used by Massey to denote the zodiac of popular syncretic esotericism, in which the twelve signs are associated with ancient gods and mythologies - the "Hermes Zodiac", or "Hermetic Zodiac". For example, in this zodiac Pisces is figured as Ichthon ("Ichton"), and with the female goddess who brought forth the young Sun-God as a fish. One version of the hermean zodiac is that used by Kircher (figure 22 under COSMIC PANTHEONS), which contains several important hermetic associations - such as Amun for Aries, Isis for Virgo, Typhon for Scorpio, Canopus for Aquarius and Ichthon for Pisces.

HERMES   Name given to Mercury - but see GREEK PLANETS. It is also the name given to one of the "Hypothetical Planets" in the system proposed by the Dutch astrologer Ram, accorded rule over zodiacal Gemini. This transplutonian is included in an ephemeris, and claimed to relate to 'spiritual ideality and

occult ability'.   The same name was also used of a hypothetical by Thierens,
in relation to his ETHERIC SPHERE, as the future ruler of Gemini.   Thierens
gives the alternative (confusing) name 'Mercury' for this future embodiment.

HERMES ZODIAC   See HERMEAN ZODIAC.

HERMETIC MERCURY   The mercurial forces linked with planetary Mercury in
hermetic lore is something different from that associated with ordinary
Mercury - that is, with the Mercury of the non-esoteric astrological forms.
It is termed the 'Permanent Water', the 'Vitalizing Spirit', and is linked
with the quintessential forces of the world: often the magical symbol for
the SEAL OF SOLOMON is drawn with the sigil for Mercury in the central space,
to link it with the quintessence, and so placed it is no longer the ordinary
exoteric Mercury.   Many of the esoteric names for this planet suggest the
idea of 'liquid', a symbolic form for the quintessence of etheric forces -
the Blessed Water, Virtuous Water, Philosopher's Vinegar, Dew of Heaven,
Virgin's Milk, and so on.   Esoterically, the power of this hermetic Mercury
is as unifier in the human being of the polarity of thinking (imaged as Salt)
and the will-life (imaged as Sulphur).   Sometimes the thinking element in man
is symbolized by positive Mars, and the will-life by negative Mars.   Without
the control of hermetic Mercury, these polarities would ruin the life of man.

HERMETIC RULE   A term used for the so-called TRUTINE OF HERMES.

HERMETIC SORTES   Sometimes called the 'Seven Sortes' (to distinguish from
the 'Twelve Sortes' as the TWELVE PLACES of Manilius were sometimes called),
these are the ancient equivalents of the PARS, attributed to the
Trismegistian literature.   The distinction made between the hermetic sortes
and the standard 'sortes' or PARS rests in the method of computation.   The
Alexandrian Paul tells us that the hermetic 'Klipoi' (pars) are to be
calculated from the Ascendant (but see also SORTES), in the day horoscope by
direction of the signs, and in the night horoscope by inverse direction
against the signs, according to the rules set out in table 44.

```
                                                            ----TABLE 44
```

SORT NAME	PLANET	ARC BETWEEN
Nemesis	Saturn	SA and Fortuna
Victory	Jupiter	JU and Daimon
Courage	Mars	MA and Fortuna
Daimon (genius)	Sun	See DAIMON
Love	Venus	VE and Daimon
Necessity	Mercury	ME and Fortuna
Fortune	Moon	See PART OF FORTUNE

HERMETIC ZODIAC   See HERMEAN ZODIAC

HERSCHEL   See URANUS.

HESPERUS   One of the names given to the planet Venus, as the 'evening star'.
See also LUCIFER.

HEXAGON   An ancient term for the SEXTILE aspect, presumably derived from the
fact that the division of the 60 degree arc into the zodiacal circle produces
points which may be inscribed within a hexagon.

HIDDEN PLANETS   In the esoteric system developed by Bailey, it is claimed
that there are many 'hidden' planets - around 70 or so - in our solar system.
However, in her "Intuitional Astrology" only the three interlinked systems of
5 "Non-sacred Planets", 8 "Orthodox Planets" and 7 "Sacred Planets" are
generally considered.   See also AROMAL PLANETS.

==

HIDING PLACES   A term derived from Babylonian astrology, and explained by
the modern astrologer Fagan as referring to those locations (arcs) in the
heavens where the stars disappear and then re-appear in their heliacal
phenomena.

HIEMAL SIGNS   The hiemal or hyemal signs (from the Latin 'hiems', winter)
are Capricorn, Aquarius and Pisces.

HIERARCHIES   See CELESTIAL HIERARCHIES.

HIEROGLYPHIC MONAD   See MONAS HIEROGLYPHICA.

HIEROZ-BONATIS DIRECTIONS   Term used of a system of "Primary Directions"
described by the astrologer Hieroz, relating to the calculation of successive
charts from a radical, whereby the fiducial is the Sun's radical place, each
subsequent chart being derived from the Sun's return to that position.   The
system was described by Hieroz in 1941, and only ten years later did he
discover that a similar technique (see BONATIS DIRECTIONS) had been proposed
by Bonatus, as a result of which he changed the term 'Hieroz Directions' to
'Hieroz-Bonatis Directions', to accommodate the mediaeval source.

HIEROZ DIRECTIONS   See HIEROZ-BONATIS DIRECTIONS.

HINDU ZODIAC   From very ancient times the Hindu astrologers have
distinguished between the tropical and sidereal zodiacs, wisely providing
different names for the two systems.   The Sanskrit terms for the two have
been variously Anglicized, but table 45 sets out the correspondences given in
the esoteric treatments of Blavatsky, Row and Thierens, along with main
variant spellings.   It will be observed that many of the names used for the
sidereal zodiac are inevitably reduplicated in the lunar asterisms of the
Hindu NAKSHATRAS.

--TABLE 45

WESTERN NAME	HINDU TROPICAL	HINDU SIDEREAL
Aries	Mesham - Maish	Acvini
Taurus	Rishabham - Vrishab	Krttika - Krittika
Gemini	Mithunam - Mithun	Mrgacirsha - Mrigasitas
Cancer	Karkatakam - Karka	Punarvasu
Leo	Simham - Simha	Magha
Virgo	Kanya	Phalguni
Libra	Tula - Tulam	Citra
Scorpio (Scorpius)	Vrishikam - Vrishchik	Vicakha
Sagittarius	Dhanus - Dhanu	Mula
Capricorn(us)	Makaram - Makar	Ashada - Ashadha
Aquarius	Kumbham - Kumbh	Dhanishta - Cravishta
Pisces	Meenam - Meena - Minam	Bhadzapada - Bhadrapada

HIPPOS   See PEGASUS.

HIRCUS   See CAPELLA and FIFTEEN STARS.

HISMAEL   Name given by Agrippa (quoting ancient cabbalistic sources) to the
'Daemon' of Jupiter, for whom he gives the magical number 136 - see IOPHIEL.

HISTORICAL ASTROLOGY   Garacaeus distinguishes four types of astrology - the
ordinary Genethliacal, Horary, Astro-Meteorology (which he terms 'De
Mutationibus Aeris'), and a fourth, 'De Regnorum Mutationibus', which Wemyss
equates with the 'rise and fall of Kingdoms and Religions', as a sort of
'historical astrology'.   Clumsy as the term is, there appears to be no
available alternative to describe this important branch (which certainly must
not be confused with "Mundane Astrology", which is perhaps what Garacaeus had

in mind. The SECUNDADEIAN BEINGS of the occultist Trithemius were derived
from such historical astrology. See also HISTORIC ASTROLOGY.

HISTORIC ASTROLOGY   What Ptolemy called "Catholic Astrology".

HITSCHLER METHOD Name given to a method, devised by the Swiss astrologer
Hitschler, by which allocation is made of every known chemical element or
compound to a special degree of the zodiac, the list being prepared for
therapeutic purposes.

HOARSE SIGNS   One of the curious terms derived from the natures of the
images attached to the twelve signs of the zodiac, and relating to Aries,
Taurus, Leo and Capricorn. The name is said to be linked with the noises
which are made by the animals associated with the corresponding images -
though what sort of noise the goat-fish of Capricorn makes is anyone's guess.
Although Wilson follows tradition and insists that those born under these
signs will have a certain roughness or harshness of voice (those under
Capricorn apparently 'speak with a kind of whistling sound'), the fact is
that Taurus (through its ancient rule over the throat and larynx) often
produces a most beautiful and harmonious voice. See MUTE SIGNS.

HOMODROMI   A term derived from the Greek, meaning 'fellow runners', and
applied to the two planets Mercury and Venus, which by virtue of being
inferior planets may never appear to be very far from the Sun in terms of
zodiacal arc. The outer limit for Mercury is approximately 28 degrees, and
that for Venus approximately 76 degrees.

HONONYMOUS ERROR A designation used by Fagan to apply to the confusion of a
tropical sign with a sidereal sign of the same name, sigil or symbol. The
term is a useful one for purposes of discussion and reference, though Fagan's
own 'solution' to the error is questionable.   Fagan suggests that the
tropical and sidereal were coterminous in 221AD, yet the issue is not quite
so simple as he implies. The fiducial, the nature of the sidereal zodiac (in
the extent of its demarcations), and so on, make all speculation as to a
possible temporary identity of the two extremely dubious. A further
confusion in the hononymous error is the assumption that the coincidence of
two fiducials may be taken to imply an extensive coterminity of the two
sequences, and thus an identity of structure.

HORARY ASTROLOGY   The astrological art of interpreting specific questions in
terms of a chart erected for the moment when the question is formulated.
Horary astrology has its own specialist rules, though most of them are
related in a commonsense way with those of "Genethliacal Astrology".   The
astrologer Lilly, who (if his autobiography is to be believed) had a wide
practice in horary astrology, recommended that the figure be cast in respect
of propositions made and the 'doubts of the querent will be instantly
resolved'. It would seem that the horary figure represented an autoscope, a
symbolic centre for concentrating the intuitive faculties. The interesting
thing about the method is that it places the querent himself within the
framework of the conditions surrounding the question, for he or she is
represented by a planetary significator, according to clearly formulated
rules. The basic rules of the art are too complex to be set out usefully in
the present work: Wilson sacrificed a fair proportion of his book on general
astrological terms to an admittedly incomplete analysis of the horary rules
and terminology. In a sense, these rules reflect the basic tenets of
astrology, though there is a simplistic and highly symbol-conscious approach,
involving different time-scales, with planets regarded not as so many sources
of differentiated energies and spiritual qualities, as symbols of conditions
relating to the questions in hand: the planets become promittors in a horary
chart. The study of the many 'horary charts' and recorded 'interpretations'
noted in English libraries by Thomas make a fascinating background to the
investigation of social conditions in relation to astrology. The most
frequent questions are about theft, law-suits, partnerships, the safety of

==

goods and persons in sea voyages, imprisonment, lost objects and animals.
Sometimes the querent asks about death (mainly about the deaths of others),
which should properly be determined from a progressed genethliacal chart.

HORARY TIME   Horary time is measured in equal arcs marking one twelfth of
the diurnal or nocturnal arc of a star. When the days are long, then the
diurnal horary time will be longer than the nocturnal horary time, and the
corresponding 'hours' will be shorter.

HORAS   Term used in connexion with the classification of signs into two
halves of 15 degrees. The 'solar horas' are the positive halves, the 'lunar
horas' the negative halves. It is said that the horas of the positive signs
(AR, GE, LE, LB, SG, AQ) are solar in the first half, lunar in the second
half. In the negative signs (TA, CN, VG, SC, CP, PI), the first half is
lunar, the latter half solar. According to Cornell, the horas of the
negative signs are called 'magnetic' and 'magneto-electric' horas
respectively. The malefic planets in the solar horas are said to be
powerful, though weak in the lunar horas: the benefic planets are stronger
in the lunar, weaker in the solar.

HORIMEA   An obsolete term, apparently used of the HYLEG planet when it has
passed the Midheaven of a chart.

HORIZON CHART   A horoscope, or symbolic figure, erected to symbolize a
planet through the horizon - but see HORIZON SYSTEM.

HORIZON SYSTEM   A method of HOUSE DIVISION based on the projection of the
division of the horizon into twelve arcs of 30 degrees, starting from the
meridianal circle. The cusps obtained by this projection were said to be the
centre of the houses. The method is attributed to the 12th century Jewish
astrologer Ibn Ezra, and is sometimes called the 'Ezrian House System'.

HORIZONTAL SYSTEM   The horizontal system, when applied to the "Celestial
Sphere", takes as a point of reference any specific location on the Earth.
The point directly overhead is called the Zenith, the point immediately
below,the Nadir. The plane at right angles to these is called the 'Horizon',
and this (within the projection of the sphere) is regarded as having infinite
extension. This horizon plane is then regarded as being divied into the 360
degrees of equal arc. Through each of these degrees run as many vertical
circles, centred upon the mid-point between zenith and nadir, and joining
these two points. Parallels of altitude are visualized as parallel to the
plane of horizon. Measurements taken from this celestial sphere describe
precisely a location in terms of horizon plane and parallels of altitude.

HORLOGIUM OSCILLATORIUM   Constellation, 'Pendulum Clock', introduced as an
image by La Caille in 1752, and (according to Robson) inducing a 'well-stored
mind and a fondness for history'. It was for no apparent reason later
refigured and called 'Horoscope'.

HORLOGIA   See ZODIACAL CLOCKS.

HOROPLANETARY DOMIFICATION   A term constructed by the astrologer Hieroz to
denote the PLACIDEAN SYSTEM, on the grounds tht Hieroz believed that this
system was not actually proposed by Placidus (correct, as it happens) but by
Ptolemy (incorrect, as it happens). He was on safer grounds in tracing the
system to Scaliger, who mentioned it in his commentary on Manilius.

HOROSCOPE   In modern astrology the word 'horoscope' is used to denote the
symbolic figure of the heavens, the CHART, sometimes indeed the 'horoscope
figure' or the 'horoscope chart'. However, until the 18th century the word
was frequently used as synonymous not with such a chart but with the
Ascendant degree. This 18th century use was etymologically correct, for the
Greek astrology (from which much of the modern astrology derived) termed the

Ascendant the 'horoscopos' (translated into Latin as 'Horoscopus'),
apparently from two Greek terms meaning 'watching from a high vantage point'.
In spite of the objections of such people as Blundeville, the word was by the
18th century used more and more to denote the chart (see CHART SYSTEMS), so
that eventually 'horoscope' and 'chart' became synonymous. Ptolemy, who is
one of the first to even pretend to set down the rules of how the
'horoscopos' is determined, is infuriatingly vague, and seems to refer to a
method which does not correspond to anything used now. According to Ptolemy,
the degree of the zodiac ascending is to be measured according to the method
of ascensions (as the Greek 'anaphoron pragmateias' is translated), but there
is little discussion of the vexing problem of "Climata". Wilson defined the
term in its original sense, but this is now almost lost, save to a few
historians used to dealing with ancient charts and readings. See CHART
SYSTEMS, and for a meaning related to constellations HORLOGIUM OSCILLATORIUM.

HOROSCOPE CHART   See CHART SYSTEMS.

HOROSCOPOS   See HOROSCOPE.

HORUS   Name given to one of the "Hypothetical Planets" by Thierens in
relation to his esoteric view of the ETHERIC SPHERE, the future ruler of
zodiacal Cancer. The hypothetical was also called 'Bacchus'. See ORION.

HOT   See FOUR QUALITIES and PRINCIPLES.

HOUR GLASS   In a specialist sense, the 'hour glass' is one of the so-called
Arabian PARS, the 'part of Saturn', sometimes called the point or part of
Fatality, or the point of 'love of Brethren'. If a chart is revolved so that
the degree occupied by the Sun is transferred to the Ascendant, then the
position of Saturn in this new arrangement will mark the Hour Glass within
the houses.

HOURS   See PLANETARY HOURS and HORAS.

HOUSE CUSP   See CUSP.

HOUSE DIVISION   In computing an astrological chart, as a necessary
preliminary to interpretation, the astrologer usually incorporates three
quite different systems of co-ordinates into the symbolic figure. One of
these is the system of house division, a grid which fixes diurnal motion.
This grid may be inserted by means of a variety of different geometric or
symbolic systems, all of which are aimed at dividing the heaven into (usually
twelve) mundane areas called 'houses', which are marked by cusps. In almost
all methods, each quadrant of the celestial sphere is trisected by one way or
another, to give the cusps which are themselves symbolically related to the
zodiacal signs. Three separate methods have been distinguished. The first
is by direct division of the ecliptic, one of the earliest of which is the
MODUS EQUALIS, the 'equal-house' method, familiar to Hellenistic, if not to
ancient Greek astrologers, and an entirely symbolic method of dividing the
heavens. The second is that involved with division by projecting on to the
ecliptic, one of the earliest of which was the CAMPANEAN SYSTEM, which
projected from the prime vertical. The third, which involves trisecting the
semiarcs by time-based divisions, is the oldest of the non-symbolic systems,
being devised by the Arabic astrologer Haly in the 11th century - see HALYIAN
SYSTEM. The basic principles involved in the construction of the various
house systems, as projective methods, are set out under different headings.
However, the two diagrams in figure 33 point to one of these principles, in
demonstrating simplistically the difference between the constructive method
of the 'Modus Rationalis' of Regiomontanus and that of Campanus. In the
Regiomontanean system (left) it will be noted that the polar arcs (P) cut the
equator (EFGH) at the same points as do the house circles (the vertical
arcs), but they do not cut the prime vertical (ABCD) at the same points as
these house circles. In the Campanean system (right), it will be noted that
the polar arcs (P) cut the prime vertical (ABCD) at the same point as the
house circles, but they do not cut the equator (EFGH) at the same points as
these house circles. These two diagrams illustrate clearly that such house

systems are based on a solution to a problem which does not exist for
constructions involving horoscopes cast at the equator, for then the prime
vertical (ABCD) and the equator (EFGH) are identical. It is only when we
wish to determine the house divisions for a place other than the equator that
we must decide which of these two circles are to be divided equally, by (in
effect) choosing a particular house system in tabular form.

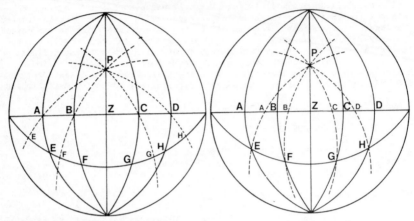

FIGURE 33. COMPARATIVE METHOD OF HOUSE DIVISION. (LEFT) THE 'MODUS
RATIONALIS' OF REGIOMONTANUS, AND (RIGHT) THE CAMPANEAN SYSTEM.

In fact, a large number of house divisions have been evolved in order to
facilitate computation of the cusps intermediate to the four angles, and the
relevant information for most systems has been made available in a variety of
TABLES OF HOUSES, which enable astrologers to insert cusps in their charts
without resorting to complex calculations, and even without understanding the
geometry or philosophy involved in what they are doing. Essentially, the
quadrant must be trisected by either time considerations or by spatial
considerations - see HOUSES. About a dozen house systems are worth mention
in modern times, though the American astrologer Munkasey has recorded 20
different systems described in extant literature, and has published tables
for 7 different methods.   In addition to those already noted, the following
list gives all the systems designed to establish a twelve-fold grid division
to symbolize diurnal motions: ALBATEGNIUS SYSTEM, ALCABITIUS SYSTEM, EAST
POINT SYSTEM, EQUAL DIVISION METHOD, HALYIAN SYSTEM, HORIZON SYSTEM, KOCHIAN
SYSTEM, MERIDIANAL SYSTEM, MORINEAN SYSTEM, NATURAL GRADUATION SYSTEM,
PLACIDEAN SYSTEM, REGIOMONTANEAN SYSTEM, PORPHYRIAN SYSTEM, TOPOCENTRIC
SYSTEM and ZENITH SYSTEM.   However, other divisions, involving a grid of 8
houses, have been recorded (see LAVAGNINI SYSTEM and OCTOPODOS). The 2nd
century AD astrologer Manilius divided the mundane belt into 8 houses of
equal arc, instead of the usual 12 - but see the TWELVE PLACES of Manilus,
which are not house divisions at all. The so-called 'Eight House System of
Firmicus' is merely the first 8 houses of the normal 12 divisions.   Dean
mentions systems of 10, 24 and 48 cusp divisions, as well as systems applied
clockwise, instead of the usual widdershins. See also the entry under
URANIAN ASTROLOGY which touches upon symbolic methods sometimes confused with
house division.   The ultimate purpose in computing the house cusps is to
locate the areas of specific mundane influence revealed by the twelve houses:
however, there is no general conformity in regard to the interpretation of
the significance of the cusps themselves, for according to some systems the
cusps mark the centre of the houses (as Campanus insisted they should) while
in others they are said to mark the boundaries.   According to the widely
accepted doctrine of "Angles" (which provide the basic grid around which the
house divisions are made), the cusps should be regarded as marking the centre
of the individual houses, on the grounds that the Ascendant is identical with
the cusp of the 1st house. The general outline of traditional interpretation
relating to the twelve houses is set out under TWELVE HOUSES.

HOUSE OF CHILDREN   See FIFTH HOUSE.

HOUSE OF DEATH   Traditional astrology uses this unfortunate term for the "Eighth House" of the horoscope figure, because of its link with the negative Mars of Scorpio. The matter dealt with in the eighth house is related more to the regeneration principle than to death (which is merely the ultimate experience of regeneration). A more recent term, the 'house of Karma', referring to the idea that karma and death are interlinked, is perhaps more suitable, provided that karma is itself seen as a redemptive process.

HOUSE OF HOPES AND WISHES   Traditional term for the "Eleventh House" of the horoscope figure. As with so many of the older terms, it contains an interesting kernel of truth, for the house is esoterically linked with the way in which the native is related to the realm of ideals, to the ancient 'world of archetypes'. This relationship is often expressed on the mundane level in terms of hopes and wishes, and perhaps explains the tradition which maintains that a malefic planet in this house may be regarded as an indication that the native will feel a sense of dissatisfaction with his or her life - in that their hopes and wishes may be continually frustrated.

HOUSE OF KARMA   See HOUSE OF DEATH.

HOUSE OF MONEY   See SECOND HOUSE.

HOUSE OF ONE'S OWN UNDOING   Traditional term for the "Twelfth House" of the horoscope figure. Like many of the ancient terms, this does encapsulate a truth when the working of the house is visualized from an external point of view. The association with zodiacal Pisces (and in modern astrology with the nebulous Neptune) means that spiritual matters generally come to a head in this house - which is one reason why it is called a 'terminal house'. The mundane division therefore represents a dissolving process, that important process of spiritual re-orientation (even of withdrawal from the material plane) which, from the outer point of view, often gives the impression of being the result of self-inflicted injury: hence it is sometimes called 'the house of sorrows'.

HOUSE OF SELF   See FIRST HOUSE.

HOUSE OF SHORT JOURNEYS   See THIRD HOUSE.

HOUSE OF SORROWS   Traditional term for the "Twelfth House" - see HOUSE OF ONE'S OWN UNDOING.

HOUSE OF FATHER   Traditional term for the "Tenth House", usually explained in terms of social conditions in the late mediaeval period (when the term was coined), for in those days the father was usually instrumental in determining the career of the native, or at least set a standard in relation to the social standing of the native. Esoterically, however, the term is linked with the idea of 'Old Father Time', the ruler (Saturn) of the associate Capricorn, which is associated with the Sphere of Saturn. In the ancient cosmoconception, this sphere marked the end of time - beyond the sphere of Saturn there was that time-less condition which was originally termed 'eternity', which is now often understood as meaning 'infinite extension of time'.

HOUSE OF THE MOTHER   See FOURTH HOUSE.

HOUSE OF THE PUBLIC   See ELEVENTH HOUSE.

HOUSE RULER   This term is misleading, for a house is not ruled by a planet. A sign is ruled by a planet. Since a sign is associated with its relevant house, however (for example Aries with the First House), the idea has arisen that the planetary ruler of the sign may also rule the related house. Properly speaking, a planet is associated with a particular house. However, when a term is so widespread in its misuse, it might be said to have acquired its meaning almost by default. The early astrologers who observed the growth of the misuse attempted to stem it by making a distinction whereby the planet was "Lord" of a house, and "Ruler" of a sign.   Unfortunately, the two terms are now regarded as being virtually interchangeable by modern astrologers.

HOUSES   The traditional horoscope figure is divided into 12 arcs, which are symbolically presented as being equal either in a spatial system or in a time system (see CHART SYSTEMS). This division is superimposed upon the projected celestial sphere, with the symbolic horizon line (usually) marking the cusps of the 1st and 7th houses (the East Point and West Point, respectively). The Tenth House cusp marks the symbolic Zenith, called the Medium Coeli, while the Fourth House cusp marks the symbolic Nadir, called the 'Imum Coeli'. The remaining eight house cusps are disposed according to one of the many different systems of HOUSE DIVISION. Each of the individual houses has many different names, derived usually from traditional astrology (for example, the Eighth House is sometimes called the "House of Death", the 'Occult House', the 'House of Karma', and so on): usually however the houses are listed by number: the sequences of houses for the various chart systems of the quadrated or circular type are given under CHART SYSTEMS. A large number of different terms and classifications have survived from ancient astrology into modern use - the most powerful houses are the "Angular" (1st, 4th, 7th and 10th); less powerful are the "Succedent" (2nd, 5th, 8th and 11th), while the weakest houses are the "Cadent" (3rd, 6th, 9th and 12th). See also EASTERN HOUSES, OCCIDENTAL HOUSES, ORIENTAL HOUSES, PSYCHIC HOUSES, RELATIVE HOUSES, TEMPORAL HOUSES and WESTERN HOUSES. See also INTERCEPTED HOUSE.

HOUSE SYSTEMS   See HOUSE DIVISION.

HUMANE   While the text of Ptolemy appears to take it for granted that the so-called "Human Signs" are humane, he distinguishes Libra (the image for which was a pair of scales) as humane because of the influence exerted by the sign.

HUMAN SIGNS   These are Gemini, Virgo and Aquarius, which are presumably so called because their images are in the form of humans - the twins, a woman holding an ear of corn or a flower, and a man pouring the water urn: but see also HUMANE. The first half of Sagittarius is traditionally included in the list, since it is imaged as half-human (usually a centaur). The whole term is used in contrast to the BESTIAL SIGNS.

HUMID   See FOUR QUALITIES.

HUMOURS   A conception of a tetrad of bodily fluids which were recognized as influencing the disposition (later the 'humour') of a person, through excess or deficiency. The humours were Phlegma, Black Bile, Yellow Bile, and Blood. These humours were dominated by a theory of Perisomata (Greek word meaning approximately 'concerning humours') which was involved with the idea that certain excesses or deficiencies produced illness - a man might be said to be 'out of humour' through lack of a bodily fluid. This perisomata theory eventually led to the development of the conception of the TEMPERAMENTS which were associated with each of the four humours and elements, their names being derived from the Greek, as in table 46.

| | | | ----TABLE 46 |
HUMOUR	GREEK EQUIVALENT	TEMPERAMENT	ELEMENT
Phlegma	Phlegma	Phlegmatic	Water
Black Bile	Melina Chole	Melancholic	Earth
Yellow Bile	Chole Nxathe	Choleric	Fire
Blood		Sanguine	Air

HUNTING THE MOON   A phrase used of a powerful and difficult aspect - Moon square Saturn. It has long been regarded as one of the most difficult of aspects, for the malignant rays of Saturn play unimpeded on the sensitive Moon, that representative of the personality and the anima (in its Jungian sense), so that male and female, age and youth, are in tension, and the form-building of Saturn is in disharmony with the diffusive form-releasing of the Moon. The aspect as a radical consideration is difficult, but for reasons connected with the cycles of the Moon and Saturn, it becomes an influence which persists in transits and progressions through the life of the individual, in that the two cycles roughly coincide: by progression, the Moon takes approximately 28 years to complete its cycle, whilst Saturn takes almost 30 years in direct motion to return to its radical position. This means that roughly every 7 years there is a major square, opposition or conjunction (of progressed and radicals) which calls into play the baleful influence of the original square aspect. These progressed aspects may be reinforced by the transits of Saturn. It has been observed that when the Moon is applying to the square, the influence becomes stronger as life proceeds. When the Moon is separating from the radical square, the influence, while strong in childhood (depending upon the orb of separation), gradually becomes weaker, and after the first 28 years is diminished. The aspect was sometimes termed 'Chasing the Moon'.

HURTFUL SIGNS   The signs Aries, Taurus, Cancer, Scorpio and Capricorn are so called, presumably because of the natures of their "Images" - the ram, bull, crab, scorpion and 'goat', respectively.

HUSBANDRY   The 'Point of Husbandry', sometimes called the point of 'Fortune in Husbandry' is one of the so-called Arabian PARS in a chart. If the degree of Venus in a natal chart is taken to the Ascendant, the adjusted position of Saturn marks the point.

HYADES   An asterism set in the forehead of the constellation Taurus, one of the most lovely groups in the night sky. In the Greek mythology they were the daughters of Atlas and Aethera, and therefore half-sisters of the "Pleiades", with whom they made up the "Dodonides". Pliny, who called them the 'Parilicium', described them as the 'violent and troublesome' stars which bring tempests, which explains one of their many appellations, 'moist daughters'. Ptolemy says that the group are of the nature of Mercury conjunct Saturn: they have an evil influence, inducing violence, poisoning and a difficult life. See also PRIMUM HYADUM.

HYDRA   A winding constellation, the 'water snake', located from about 5 degrees of Leo through to 23 degrees of Scorpio, and from 10 to 36 degrees south of the equator. As the name suggests, astrologers suppose that it threatens shipping, and gives a passionate nature. It is possible that the constellation was linked with that of Scorpius, since the early Greek sources name it 'Nepa', apparently a word of African origin, meaning 'land crab', the related word 'Nepas' meaning 'scorpion'. Allen points to its evil reputation, and records a (dubious) story that the asterism was seen as a dragon, said to symbolize the winding course of the Moon itself. He mentions also that when a comet was originated near Hydra, then it was believed that poison was being scattered through the world, but these fanciful ideas are now associated with Draco. An astrologically important star in this asterism is ALPHARD. Distinguish from HYDRUS.

HYDRA'S HEART   See ALPHARD.

HYDROXOUS   Greek term, meaning 'water power' used to designate the zodical sign and constellation Aquarius.

HYDRUS   A long and slender constellation, the 'snake' not to be confused with HYDRA, the head touching the polar stars, the tail almost reaching ACHERNAR. It was originated as a separate constellation in 1604 by Bayer, and has gained a reputation among astrologers for 'danger of poisoning'.

HYGEIA   Name given to one of the Asteroids, discovered in 1849.

HYLEG   A term derived from the Arabian astrological system, and used of a planet which (by virtue of its position in a special mundane arc) is regarded as the 'giver or sustainer of life', the "Apheta". The mundane arcs in which a planet may be hyleg are listed under HYLEGIACAL PLACES. A planet which is so hyleg is said to have influence of a beneficial kind on the length of a native's life. When such an aphetic planet progresses to an unfavourable aspect, or to a conjunction with an "Anaretic Place", then the life of the native is said to be threatened. The simplicity of the above description disguises the fact that the rules for determining hyleg are among the most complex in astrological interpretation, as the indications set out by Wilson indicate.

HYLEGIACAL PLACES   In modern astrology these are usually called the 'principal places', a specialist term used to denote mundane arcs in which the two luminaries are said to exercise the most beneficial influence within a chart, being in such arcs the promotors of life. These places, properly the 'hylegiacal arcs', are the 1st, 7th, 9th and 11th houses in popular lore, but Ptolemy located the hylegiacal arcs as being 5 degrees above the Ascendant to 25 degrees below, with a similar arc-coordination for the other houses listed above. The English astrologer Lilly called the degrees occupied by the Ascendant, Midheaven, Sun, Moon and Fortuna as the hylegiacal places, though he was certainly confusing these with the places of the MODERATORS - even so, his confusion has persisted in some astrological circles, so that the hylegiacals are sometimes misunderstood. See also APHETIC PLACES and HYLEG.

HYLEGIACAL ARC   See HYLEGIACAL PLACES.

HYPER ASTROLOGY   See HYPER-CHART.

HYPERBOREAN   See SECOND ROOT RACE.

HYPER-CHART   A term used in modern astrology (as for example by Dean) to describe a chart which would contain within its symbolic configurations all astrological data, such as angles, houses, aspects, declinations, mid-points, co-ascendants, lunations, perihelia, interfaces, asteroids, hypotheticals, and so on. The interpretation of such a chart ('hyper-astrology' as it has been called) would be beyond the grasp of an astrologer. Dean has suggested that a reasonable synthesis could be obtained within 10 years by a team of a thousand astrologers working around the clock. The fact is that by mere intellectual extrapolation and irresponsible symbolism one might establish almost any system of interpretation which ultimately will be impractical - one might, for example, quite easily propose a hyper-medicine, just as useless as hyper-astrology.

HYPERION   Name given to one of the moons of Saturn.

HYPOGEON   The Greek term meaning 'under the earth' is often interpreted in astrological circles as being the Hellenistic equivalent of the "Imum Coeli", but this is not correct. The early Greek astrologers, as well as the later Romans such as Ptolemy, defined the tenth house and the axial-correspondent fourth house by simply counting signs from their 'horoscopos' first house, which meant that they did not distinguish the medium coeli or the imum coeli in the same way as later astrologers. The term therefore originally simply meant 'fourth house'.

HYPOTHETICAL MOON   See LILITH.

HYPOTHETICAL PLANETS   Some astrologers have claimed the existence of a number of planets in our own solar system which are neither visible nor recognized by science, but which have been located (largely) by such psychic means as clairvoyance. Some astrologers have postulated the existence of over 1,000 such planets, called AROMAL PLANETS, while Blavatsky claims that there are six ETHEREAL PLANETS. At least 25 of the more widely used hypotheticals have been accorded ephemerides by various astrologers, while information regarding position, revolution and supposed influences has been furnished for some 35 such bodies. The astrologer Dean, who appears to work with statistical methods and with an analytical thoroughness which scarcely informed traditional astrological doctrine, has come to the conclusion that the hypotheticals are entirely without credibility. However, at least one hypothetical originally perceived by clairvoyant means was later recognized as a genuine non-hypothetical: see PAGAN-PLUTO. A complete list of the names of hypotheticals would actually include many 'asteroids', and the hypothetical 'moons' of certain planets, such as Jupiter: but see NON-PLANETS. The 31 names of important hypotheticals given here (in reference to specific sections in this present work) includes only such as may in theory be termed 'planets', and indeed only such as may be regarded of importance in the recent history of astrology. Unfortunately, since the work on hypotheticals has never been co-ordinated, the list includes some names that denote several hypotheticals which have been given the same name by different astrologers. See therefore the entries under the following names.

Admetos	Apollon	Cupido	Demeter	Dido
Hades	Hercules	Hermes	Horus	Isis
Jason	Kronos	La Croix	Lilith	Lion
Melodia	Midas	Minos	Moraya	Osiris
Ov	Pan	Persephone	Pluto	Polyhymnia
Poseidon	Transpluto	Vulcan	Vulkanus	Wemyss-Pluto
Zeus				

A few specialist astrologers refer to some planets as hypotheticals when they are not really hypotheticals at all. A whole group of planets frequently mentioned in esoteric literature are related to the future evolution of our present solar system, and names are used to denote the 'evolved state' of modern planets which are regarded as being just as involved in the evolution as is the human race: see FUTURE PLANETS, LUCIFER and SACRED PLANETS. The esoteric planets of Bailey's "Intuitional Astrology" also belong to a category of their own, and are scarcely hypotheticals.

HYPOTHETICALS   In astrology, usually the HYPOTHETICAL PLANETS.

HYPSOMATA   The modern teaching concerning the "Exaltations" of the planets in certain zodiacal signs, from which the theory of DIGNITIES is derived, appears to have rested on an ancient tradition of 'hypsomata' or 'degree exaltations'. The astrologer Fagan has attempted to show that these hypsomata relate to an important chart (more properly an adjusted schema) cast for the year 786-5 BC for the latitude of Babylon (figure 34), related to heliacal settings, and the use of the fixed star "Spica" (then held to be in 29 degrees of Virgo) as fiducial of the zodiac. Table 46, which is derived from Fagan's own researches, compares the hypsomata for this year (with mean difference calculations) in order to show that the luminaries and five planets were in their hypsomatic longitudes and heliacal positions during that one year, the positions of the luminaries being those of 4th April 786 BC (the 1st Nisan - see BABYLONIAN ZODIAC).

TABLE 46

PLANET	HYPSOMATA	786-5 BC	Difference
SU	AR 19	AR 18.8	+ 0.2
MO	TA 3	AR 29.4	+ 3.6
ME	VG 15	VG 16.4	- 1.4
VE	PI 27	PI 26.7	+ 0.3
MA	CP 28	AQ 0.8	- 2.8
JU	CN 15	CN 15.3	- 0.3
SA	LB 21	LB 20.6	+ 0.4
UR	SC 25		
NE	AQ 5		
PL	CN 4	(Dragon's Head in PI 17)	

The degrees given for the new planets and their nodes are extrapolated by Fagan from the 786-5 BC chart. A modern hypsomata, really an 'exaltation degree' for the node, is given as 3 degrees of Gemini by the Arabian astrologer Albiruni (11th century AD), which was repeated by the 17th century astrologer Lilly, and by this means was adopted into the western astrological tradition. The hypsomata of Fagan do correspond to the Hellenistic exaltation degrees recorded by Neugebauer, yet it is worth recording that other systems and variations have survived from ancient times. For example, the Roman encyclopaedist Pliny quotes the exaltation degrees given above, with the variations:

     SU - AR 29   MO - TA 19   SA - LB 20

Albiruni gives quite different figures, which he claims to have from Hindu astrology. The depressions (or FALL) of the planets were accorded corresponding degrees by Hellenistic astrologers, in direct opposition to the hypsomata, but this tradition does not appear to have survived in western astrology.

FIGURE 34. HOROSCOPE FOR THE 1ST NISAN OF 786 BC WHICH GAVE THE EUROPEAN HYPSOMATA (AFTER FAGAN).

HYPSOMATIC AYANAMSA   The modern astrologer Fagan has applied his theory of hypsomatic exaltations (see HYPSOMATA) to a study of the difference between the sidereal zodiac and the tropical zodiac (see AYANAMSA), to derive a mean value ayanamsa of 13.8 degrees, which would place the sidereal longitude of the vernal point for 786 BC in Aries 13.8 degrees. See however HYPSOMATIC YEAR.

HYPSOMATIC DEGREES   See EXALTATIONS.

HYPSOMATICS   A modern misuse of HYPSOMATA.

HYPSOMATIC YEAR   A term derived by Fagan from his researches into the true basis of the tradition underlying the 'exaltation degrees' and the origins of the modern zodiac. It is the year 786-5 BC - see HYPSOMATA.

HYPSOMATIC ZODIAC   A modern name (used especially by the astrologer Fagan) for the zodiac of fixed signs to distinguish this from the tropical zodiac. It is also called the 'Egypto-Babylonian Zodiac', and is based on a twelve-fold 30 degree arc, the initial point being located in the 1st degree of constellation Taurus, determined by the ancient fiducial star "Aldebaran". See HYPSOMATA.

I

IAPETUS   Name given to one of the moons of Saturn.

IATROMATHEMATICS   A term used for that division of astrology concerned with medicine - see MEDICAL ASTROLOGY.

IAU ZODIAC   Abbreviated form for the 'International Astronomical Union Zodiac' - see MODERN ZODIAC.

ICHTHUS   Greek name for the zodiacal sign and constellation Pisces.

IDES   See KALENDS.

IDLE   The astrologer Wilson classifies zodiacal Pisces as an 'idle' sign, though it is actually no less active (all things being equal in the given chart) than any of the other water signs. For another curious Wilsonian view, see EFFEMINATE SIGN.

IKLIL AL JABHAH   Name given to the 15th of the Arabian MANZILS, 'the Crown of the Forehead'.

ILECH   A term from the Paracelsian thesaurus. The 'Great Ilech' is the 'star of medicine', which is to say that it is the hidden principle VIRTUE behind the medicinal element: it is the healing power (derived from the planets and stars) which we assimilate when we take medicine. The 'Supernatural Ilech' is defined by Waite as 'the supercelestial conjunction and union of the stars of the firmament with the stars of things below'. It is, in other words, the name given to that subtle connexion which the ancients insisted link all sublunary things with the celestial realm. 'Crude Ilech' is said to be a composition of the three alchemical principles of Salt, Sulphur and Mercury which represent (in the microcosm of man) the Thinking, Willing and Feeling life, respectively. The Paracelsian term is linked with the ILIASTER.

ILIASTER   A term from mediaeval esoteric astrological lore (linked with alchemy), apparently originated by Paracelsus from the Greek word 'hyle' (matter) and 'astrum' (star). It is applied to that spiritual force in matter which strives towards perfection, and towards the building of forms. It works against the CAGASTER.

IMAGE   In connexion with astrological and esoteric symbolism one must note that the term 'image' is cognate with the word 'magic' - see SYMBOL. Specifically in connexion with astrology, the word may properly be applied to the pictorial symbols associated with the zodiacal constellations and signs. While it is taken for granted nowadays that an image of a constellation (such as the Ram of Aries - figure 35) is to be linked with the zodiacal sign of the same name, the evidence is that the images were originally associated only with the constellations (being derived ultimately from the Babylonian imagery, and continued in the planispheres so wrongly termed zodiacs - see for example DENDERAH ZODIAC). The method of symbolizing the signs is properly by means of SIGILS, while the method of symbolising constellations is properly by means of images: thus, figure 35 is an image of Aries, whilst the form ♈ is the sigil for Aries. In modern times the two systems are so interlinked for the differences to be of concern only to academic purists - but see HONONYMOUS ERROR. Many of the amulets derived from astrological symbolism were even in mediaeval times called 'imagines'. Paracelsus defines the 'science' of the image as that of representing the properties of heaven and 'impressing them' into the material realm. In the occult tradition, the man-made (or more appositely, 'magic-made') image is far more powerful than a natural SIGNATURE, for a 'like virtue is not found in any herbs' as Paracelsus says. See also GAMELEI.

FIGURE 35.   IMAGES OF THE CONSTELLATIONS - ARIES AND SAGITTARIUS.

IMAGINARY MOTION   A term used in connexion with SYMBOLIC DIRECTIONS to distinguish the symbolic arc motions imposed upon radical planets from the APPARENT MOTION of planets.

IMMERSION   A term normally applied to either the Sun or Moon when entering the eclipse, though sometimes the term is used also of an occultation.

IMMUM COELI   A technically incorrect spelling of the Latin IMUM COELI.

IMPEDED   A planet which is afflicted by an unfortunate planet, such as Mars, Saturn or Uranus, is said to be impeded or impedited. The Moon is said to be impeded when in the aspects of conjunction, square or opposition to these malefics, but also when so aligned with the Sun.

IMPEDITED   An archaic term used by Simmonite to signify bodies afflicted by evil stars. But see also IMPEDED.

IMPERFECT SIGNS   These are Leo, Virgo and Pisces, so called because (according to Wilson, at least) 'those born under them, and with bad aspects, are deformed in some way or other.'   These are also called the 'Broken Signs' and 'Mutilated Signs'. To these Hall adds Cancer and Capricorn.

IMUM COELI   A Latin term ('the lowest part of the heavens'), often wrongly applied to the cusp of the fourth house, which in many chart systems falls on the northern ANGLE of the horoscope figure: see MIDHEAVEN. The IC (as it is often abbreviated) is sometimes called the 'Anti-Midheaven'.

INCEPTIONAL ASTROLOGY   A term suggested by the astrologer Carter to distinguish two branches of astrology concerned with 'beginnings'. An inceptional chart is connected with ELECTIONAL ASTROLOGY but is not manipulative.   Most Electional Charts are cast in order to ensure favourable astrological influences for the undertaking of an enterprise - for example, in determining the appropriate moment to lay the foundation stone for a building (see FOUNDATION CHART). An inceptional chart is non-manipulative, for it is not concerned with determining a 'favourable' moment, but merely records the astrological conditions at the beginning of an enterprise (often with a view to studying the outcome of that 'beginning').   A historic inceptional chart is that cast by Flamsteed for the laying of the foundation stone of Greenwich Observatory in 1675, which has been reproduced in facsimile (figure 36) by Pearce. The aptness of this chart might suggest that it was perhaps a Foundation Chart, for Flamsteed would be quite capable of calculating a propitious moment, and 3.15 PM is certainly an odd 'accidental time' to lay a stone - it is perhaps a nominal inceptional chart, so disguised to deflect the wrath of his peers who had scant respect for

elections. An example of a simple inceptional chart is that cast for the
launching of the liner 'Titanic' (from which the disaster was noted in
advance of the event - see figure 17 under CHART SYSTEMS) or indeed several
of the charts cast for space-ship launches, the times for which are
determined by quite other considerations than astrological factors: see for
example SELENOCENTRIC CHART.

FIGURE 36. INCEPTIONAL CHART FOR THE FOUNDATION OF GREENWICH
OBSERVATORY, CAST BY FLAMSTEED FOR 3.15 PM, 10TH AUGUST, 1675
(AFTER PEARCE).

INCEPTIONAL CHART   A term used of a horoscope chart cast for purposes of
"Inceptional Astrology", to be distinguished from an "Election Chart".

INCLINATION   An astrologically specialist term used of a planetary movement
towards a position in a chart other than the natal position: it is most
frequently used in connexion with progressions (that is, within the symbolism
of the chart) but in fact all planets have inclination.   The term is also
used in regard to the plane of the orbit of a planet which subtends an angle
(the inclination) to the plane of the orbit of any other planet. Most
usually this degree of inclination is related to the ecliptic, which marks
the orbit of the earth. But see also OBLIQUITY.

INCONJUNCT   This term is frequently misused in modern astrology. It should
properly be used as an equivalent or synonym for DISJUNCT, but it has now
several meanings due to general misapplication. Devore says that a planet is
inconjunct when it forms no aspects, and is not in mutual disposition to
another planet. This definition really applies to the disjunct aspect, which
may be said to be void of influence so far as aspects are concerned.   The
term was also applied in early times to the QUINCUNX aspect of 150 degrees,
which (for all the theory underlying DISSOCIATE ASPECTS) is widely regarded
as an aspect of some power.   The term is further used not of aspects (which
are always a matter of degrees and orbs, if not of geometry) but of signs and
houses, which are loosely (and quite wrongly) said to bear aspect relations
to each other: thus, an 'inconjunct sign-aspect' is supposed to describe
some sort of relationship between signs five signs apart. By this reasoning,
every sign is inconjunct, and the term may be used only if one believes that
signs and houses may aspect one another.

INCREASE   When a planet has come to the Ascendant, it is said to 'commence',
and 'increases' for the entire semi-arc. For 'Point of Increase', see
POMEGRANATE.

INCREASE IN NUMBER   See INCREASE IN MOTION.

INCREASING LIGHT   Any planet, after conjunction with the Sun, increases in light, from a geocentric standpoint. A 'increasing' Moon is a 'waxing moon'.

INCREASING IN MOTION   Any planet accelerates as it reaches its apogee. When the Moon is thus "Swift in Motion" it is regarded as more fortunate than usual. A more ancient term was 'increase in number'.

INDICATION CYCLE   Sometimes wrongly defined as a cycle of 15 years, this is a time system (said to have been recognized by the Chaldeans) determined by segmenting the zodiacal circle by 15 degrees, allowing one degree for a year. It is not strictly speaking a cycle at all, but merely a chronological system: the name was derived from the Roman practice of using the period as suitable for the re-assessment of taxes.

INDIVIDUAL DEGREES   Devore provides a list of DEGREE SYMBOLS linked with the constellational zodiac, which he calls 'individual degrees', and which incorporates material relating to influences from fixed stars, nebulae, clusters, planetary nodes, exaltations (and falls), as well as a great deal of material relating to the aspectarian for the period between 1940 and 1946. Some of the degree interpretations are from 'ancient authorities', but since the aspectarian covers such a limited span, and certain of the nodal points are subject to precession, the overall validity of the entire list as a degree symbol system is questionable. Since the information was published by Devore, they have been called (misleadingly) the 'Devore Symbols'.

INDUS   Constellation formed by Bayer between Grus and Pavo. Robson records that it is supposed to give a penetrating mind, and an interest in orientalism, mysticism and sport.

INFANTINE QUADRANT   See QUADRANTS.

INFERIOR MID-HEAVEN   An old term for the IMUM COELI.

INFERIOR PLANETS   Originally this was a term applied to the planets 'below' (inferior to) the Sun, in the concentrics of the SPHERES of the "Ptolemaic System" - hence, the inferiors were Venus and Mercury. The change in the meaning of the word in an ordinary sense has now made it an unfortunate term, and it is usually more fitting to call them the 'lower planets', and even the 'inner planets' - both terms also derived from the Ptolemaic model.

INFLUENCE   In a general sense, the term means 'to have an effect on something', but the etymology of the word, which is from the Latin 'in-fluere' (to flow into) indicates that in origin this word was once directly linked with astrological concepts, for it was held that the Macrocosm flowed into the Microcosm.   The word is now defined in its astrological sense by the Oxford English Dictionary as 'the supposed flowing from the stars of an ethereal fluid acting upon the character and destiny of men, and affecting sublunary things generally'. Such a definition is exceedingly dated, however: the modern astrologer will see such 'supposed' influences proceding from other sources than merely the stars - for example, from the zodiac (which is not to be confused with asterisms), from the planets, from angular relationships between planets, from nodes, and a multitude of other cosmic phenomena or supposed conditions. Also, few modern astrologers would be prepared to acquiesce to the idea of 'ethereal fluid' as being a transmitter of such influences.   There is actually no more satisfactory theory of influences than that expressed in the tradition of SYMPATHIES which underlies the doctrine of the "Chain of Being" - though admittedly this is descriptive, rather than anything explanatory. A related term from Paracelsian astrology is ILECH. See also SYNCHRONICITY.

INFORTUNE MAJOR   A term used for the planet Saturn.

INFORTUNE MINOR   A term used for the planet Mars.

INFORTUNES   The two planets Mars and Saturn are traditionally the infortunes, the 'infortune minor' and the 'infortune major', respectively. To this traditional classification, some astrologers add Uranus. See MALEFICS.

INGRESS   The technical term used to denote the entry of any planet, fixed star or nodal point, into a sign or quadrant of the zodiac.

INHERITANCE   The 'point of Inheritance', sometimes called the 'point of Magistery and Possessions', is one of the so-called Arabian PARS. If the degree of Saturn in a natal chart is taken as the Ascendant, then the adjusted position of the Moon in the houses marks the point.

INITIAL CHRONOCRATORS   A term used originally in connexion with an Hellenistic astrological system of assessing age rulerships, described by Bouche-Leclercq. Only the luminaries may be the initial chronocrators: the Sun in a diurnal horoscope, the Moon in a nocturnal chart. This chronocrator stands guard over the first period of age, a period of 10 years and 9 months, or 129 months in all. This periodicity is derived from the ancient PLANETARY PERIODS, for the sum of these (MO 25, ME 20, VE 8 SU 19 MA 15, JU 12 and SA 30) gives 129, which may be read as either 'months'or 'years' according to the ancient system of numerical correspondences.

INITIATING SIGNS   These are Aries, Cancer, Libra and Capricorn.

INNER PLANET   See INFERIOR PLANETS.

INTELLECTUAL TRINITY   A term used by Butler in his "Solar Biology" in respect of the zodiacal Aries, Taurus and Gemini.

INTELLECTUAL ZODIAC   One of Blavatsky's terms for the tropical zodiac, used to distinguish this from the constellational zodiac, which she calls the "Natural Zodiac". The term 'intellectual' is being used in its ancient sense, as something related to the spiritual realm, and thus distinguished from the natural world of created forms.

INTELLIGENCY   A term used to denote a class of spirits, originally the 'intelligencies', who regulated the movement and life of the celestial "Spheres". However, the function appears to have been forgotten by about the 17th century, so that the term was (quite wrongly) equated with intelligence, and even those who recognized that term was designate of a class of spirits attached to the group an indeterminate activity and series of rulerships. Agrippa, still aware of the actual function of these beings as 'spherical regulators', gives the names shown in table 47, along with a series of sigils and magical squares for the 'intelligencies' of the planets (by which he meant 'planetary spheres', and the corresponding 'daemonia' (see DAIMONS). It is likely that the idea of the ensouled spheres entered into astrological lore by way of Aristotle himself, as indeed was the idea that these were the 'motori', or drivers of the spheres. The nomenclature is however Hebraic.

```
--------------------------------------------------------------table 47
```

PLANETARY SPHERE	INTELLIGENCIES	DAEMONIUM
Saturn	Agiel	Zazel
Jupiter	Iophiel	Hismael
Mars	Graphiel	Barbazel
Sun	Nachiel	Sorath
Venus	Hagiel	Kedemel
Mercury	Tiriel	Taphthartharach
Moon	Malcha*	Hasmodai

* In full, Malcha is 'Malcha betharsisim hed beruah Schehakim'.

INTENSITIES   A term used in connexion with the measurements for the aspects.

===

The intensities of aspects may be measured by several rule-of-thumb methods.
Carter, for example, ranks the aspects in the order of decreasing strength:
conjunction, opposition, square, trine (sextile/semi-sextile/sesquiquadrate),
and so on. This approximately corresponds to the interpretation of the two
different groups of aspects described by Ptolemy, the "Major Aspects" being
stronger, the "Minor Aspects" weaker. Morin (who in any case sought to
schematize everything in a highly personal manner) relates the opposition as
stronger than the square, the trine stronger than the sextile, on the
(dubious) grounds that each is twice the other.   Doane, in connexion with
his ASTRODYNES, offers a well-researched system of weighting, by which the
numerical values assigned to the aspects are increased by about 25% if the
luminaries are involved: this idea is far from new however, though the
weighting is special to Doane. Most disagreements among authorities as to
the ratios of intensities seem to involve the strengths of the minor aspects.

INTERCEPTED HOUSE   See INTERCEPTED SIGN.

INTERCEPTED SIGN   A term which, though frequently used, is something of a
misnomer. It is generally supposed to refer to a sign which, due to the
variations in time of right ascension, is not posited on one of the cusps in
the symbolic representation of the mundane system. In fact it is really an
'intercepted house'. Astrologers vary in their interpretation of the power
of an intercepted house - some insist that planets within such a house are
given emphasis, while others insist that there is a general weakening.
Quantitatively speaking, however, the house covers a much wider area of
influence than would a normal mundane arc, and one would therefore expect the
influence to be more considerable than normal. Certainly there is a
statistical propensity for such houses to contain more planets than other
houses.

INTERFACE   A term used in connexion with heliocentric astrology, relating to
nodes in orbital planes other than that of the ecliptic. Such nodal planes
are termed 'interfaces'.

INTERNATIONAL ASTRONOMICAL UNION ZODIAC   See MODERN ZODIAC.

INTERPOLATION   The act of inserting within a specific order of things,
especially within a series of numbers. In astrology, the term is sometimes
used of the process of determining the position of a planet between two known
positions (usually the two positions listed for a diurnal cycle in an
ephemeris). Again, the cusps of the intermediate houses, between the four
angles, are 'interpolated', according to the methods of HOUSE DIVISIONS.

INTERPRETATION   Term often used of the 'reading' of an astrological figure
according to the interacting factors seen within the chart, both from a
radical point of view, and from a point of view of transits and progressions.

INTERROGATORY ASTROLOGY   A term used by the historian Pingree in his
division of the forms of astrology into four distinct groups (the others
being Genethlialogy, General Astrology and Katarchic Astrology).
Interrogatory astrology is that concerned with answering specific questions
on the basis of the situation in the heavens at the time of making the query:
it is therefore the equivalent of "Horary Astrology".

INTERVAL   A term more appropriate than the tradition word 'aspect' to
describe the application of number symbolism involved in HARMONICS to chart
figuration. Each interval has its own significance: in the system of
Harmonics, the intervals are based on 179 harmonic numbers, yet the
significance of many of these are still to be established beyond reasonable
doubt. However, the meanings of the intervals relating to 4,5,6,7 and 8
appear to be agreed among specialists.

INTUITIONAL ASTROLOGY   In her study of "Esoteric Astrology", which in its principles and application is far removed from orthodox astrology, the esotericist Bailey suggests that it is her 'Intuitional Astrology' which must eventually supercede what is today called 'astrology'. The esoteric system proposed by Bailey, which is partly an extension of esoteric principles formulated by Blavatsky, involves the NON-SACRED PLANETS, the ORTHODOX PLANETS, the SACRED PLANETS, the SEVEN RAYS and the THREE CROSSES, among other specialist concerns and recondite terminologies. The term 'intuitional astrology' is that proposed by Bailey herself. It is well termed 'Intuitional', to distinguish it from other formulated esoteric astrological systems, as it appears to have originated largely by means of clairvoyance. By laymen the system has been variously called 'Tibetan Astrology' and 'Lucian Astrology', derived from the fact that the works of Bailey are linked with the teachings of 'a Tibetan', and are published by the Lucis Trust.

INVARIABLE PLANE   A central plane of the solar system, said to incline at approximately 1 degree and 35 minutes to the ecliptic. In astrology it has direct relevance to "Heliocentric Astrology", and to the calculative justification for many of the Great Ages which are related to the planetary perihelions involving cycles of vast duration.

INVERSION   When the extent of an aspect is subtracted from an arc of 180 degrees, the result is another aspect: each is an inversion of the other.

IO   Name given to one of the satellites of Jupiter.

IOPHIEL   Name given by Agrippa (quoting ancient cabbalistic sources) to the "Intelligency" of Jupiter. He gives the magical number of Iophiel as 136, which is 4 times the linear sum of the MAGIC SQUARE of Jupiter (34).

IRIS   Name given to one of the Asteroids, discovered in 1847.

IRON AGE   As a specialist occult term, derived from the Hindu chronology, and from modern esotericism - see KALI YUGA and FOUR AGES.

ISHTAR   One of the ancient Babylonian names for a goddess regarded as the equivalent of Venus. But see also VIRGO CONSTELLATION.

ISIDIS   Name given by Robson to a fixed star, probably the delta of Scorpius, DSCHUBBA, set in the head of the scorpion, not in the right claw.

ISIS   Name given to three different HYPOTHETICAL PLANETS. The first was that identified by the astrologer Sutcliffe, who claims it to be extraneptunian, with a periodicity of 360 years. The second Isis was that proposed by Thierens, as the future ruler of Taurus (not properly speaking a hypothetical at all - see ETHERIC SPHERES). The third is that listed by the astrologer Jayne, as a hypothetical transplutonian. Additionally, the name Isis is linked with the constellations: the Egyptian goddess of this name was the pre-Christian prototype of the Virgin Mary, and inevitably esoteric astrology has linked the Egyptian name with both the constellation and zodiacal sign Virgo, thereby echoing an ancient association, since Eratosthenes (among others) called the constellation Isis.

ITHURIEL   The name given by modern Rosicrucians to the Archangel who acts as ambassador from the planet Uranus. In earlier traditions the name is used of one of the Cherubim (as for example by Milton in 'Paradise Lost'), while in the popular demonological tradition it is used of the spirit of Mars.

IZARDS   The second series of creations of Ormuzd, the Zoroastrian being of light. They are 28 in number, and are said to watch over the virtue of the world, acting as interpreters of human prayer. The Izards are often linked with the lunar cycle of 28 days, and with the 28 "Lunar Mansions".

J

JABHA   'Al Jabhah' (forehead), name of the 8th of the Arabian MANZILS, in reference to the head of the Lion (the fiducial is the alpha of Leo).

JAEL   In some forms of ceremonial magic, the governor of zodiacal Libra.

JAIMINI   A Sanskrit term applied to one of two Hindu astrological methods of computing aspects according to elemental influences (that is, from sign to sign, rather than by geometric considerations - see ELEMENTAL ASPECTS). This method (which is like the 'Parasara' Hindu method) is similar to that described by Ptolemy in his Tetrabiblos. See also TAIJAK.

JAIMINIC   A term adapted from Hindu astrology (see JAIMINI) in application to the use of aspects viewed from a point of view of the elemental natures, to distinguish from aspects considered exclusively as geometric relationships. It was Ptolemy who introduced into astrological literature the concept equivalent to the jaiminic aspects.

JANUARY   Named as the first month of 31 days in the GREGORIAN CALENDAR, after the god Janus (who was two-faced, looking to the past and the future, and thus an excellent symbol for a cycle which has neither beginning nor end). Esoterically Janus was one of the numina which rendered sacred all entrances - the points of intersections between past and future - and he was thus associated with the ruler of time, Saturn. Long before the Julian reforms, and for some four centuries afterwrds, the esoteric significance of this month was expressed in the festival of the Compitalia, a survival in the cities of rural Lares lustral sacrifices, which may be associated with Aquarius.

JANUS   Name given to one of the HYPOTHETICAL PLANETS by Wemyss, who accorded it rule over zodiacal Sagittarius, and a revolution of 45 years, in an orbit between Saturn and Uranus. Since the planet was first announced, circa 1922, little evidence for its influence has been adduced.

JAPETUS   One of the moons of Saturn.

JEMS   See BIRTH STONES.

JEUZE   See ORION.

JOHNDRO LOCALITY CHART   A horoscope chart devised by the astrologer Johndro in which the angles are calculated according to the locality of the birth place, the so-called "Locality Angles".

JONAS THEORY   A term used specifically to denote an ovulation cycle theory, which the Czechoslovakian pyschiatrist Jonas claims to be astrologically determined. This ovulation cycle (which does not correspond to the normal ovulation cycle) is said to reach its peak each time the transits of Sun and Moon reach their monthly radical angular relationships in the female chart, allowing an orb of 15 degrees. Unfortunately, scrutiny of his statistical method, and indeed some of his astrological computations, have led to serious doubts as to the validity of the theory. Dean quite rightly comes to the conclusion that the majority of independent workers have not confirmed Jonas' findings. Jonas has also broadcast at least one other theory relating to the sexuality of the child, but it is in connexion with the former theory that his name is now widely known.

JONES PATTERNS   A term used of a system of classifying planetary groupings in personal horoscopes as an aid to rapid interpretation of underlying psychological tendencies: it is named after its originator, the American

astrologer Marc Edmund Jones. Seven different patterns have been described,
and their supposed influences outlined: see BOWL, BUCKET, BUNDLE,
LOCOMOTIVE, SEE-SAW, SPLASH and SPLAY.

JOY   This is now almost an obsolete term in its specialist astrological
sense, not because it fails to carry a useful and distinctive connotation but
because of the confusion which surrounds it in the astrological literature.
Some astrologers have substituted the term 'joy' for the planetary rulerships
over signs, as a synonym indeed for what Ptolemy called the 'thrones'. Thus,
the Sun in Leo was in its 'joy' - though Ptolemy (and others) would insist
that he was merely on its throne. Other astrologers describe the joys as
mundane affairs, as follows:

MO in Third House	ME in First House	VE in Fifth House
SU in Tenth House	MA in Sixth House	JU in Eleventh House
SA in Twelfth House		

Ptolemy had a very different view of the 'joys', however, yet as is so often
the case he is not very clear in his definition of the term. It would seem
that he intended a planet to receive joy from another planet when (though not
itself in any dignity) it was 'harmoniously linked' (whether by aspect or not
is hardly clear) with a planet which was in a dignity. In this case the
dignity appears to have become a 'joy' by means of transmission of sympathy.
Wilson attempts a general definition on much these lines, and proceeds to a
series of joys which are so prolix that they have the effect of reducing
astrology to a level which few astrologers might follow. Devore simplifies
enormously the idea of a 'joy' by suggesting that it is experienced by a
planet when another is placed in one of the former's essential dignities -
thus returning nominally to something verging on the Ptolemaic concept. The
term does actually call either for total rejection from the astrological
lexicon, or for reform.   After setting out a brief though incomplete survey
of the various 'definitions' of 'joy', Devore suggests sensibly that the joy
should be restricted to mundane considerations. It has been long held by
some astrologers that the joys should be an expression of delight felt by
planets of a similar nature when they are posited in each other's houses.
The pairs of planets are Sun and Jupiter, Saturn and Mercury, Venus and Moon.
By such standards, the Sun may be said to have his 'joy' in the Ninth House.

JUBANA   'Al Jubana' (claws), the name given to the 14th of the Arabian
"Manzils", a throwback to the Greek constellation map which placed the claws
of Scorpius where the fiducial alpha of Libra is now located.

JULIAN CALENDAR   Important calendrical system used from 45 BC to 1582 AD in
most parts of the civilized European world, and in some parts even until the
present century (see GREGORIAN CALENDAR). It forms the basis of all Roman
and mediaeval astrological computation and horoscope data. The system is
named after Julius Caesar who ordered the reforms of the ancient Roman
calendar, the work of adjustment being done mainly by Sosigines of Alexandria
and Marcus Favius.   The year contained 365 days, with an intercalary every
4th year, an adustment which permitted a close relationship with the tropical
year, and involved an error of only 11 minutes - which itself eventually
called for the reforms of Gregorius, which ousted the Julian system.   The
Julian was more than merely an adjustment of the earlier Roman system, but
the transference to a solar-based method of computation, away from the lunar
system of its predecessor. After a small necessary adjustment (required due
to a misapplication of one of Sosigines' rules) in 8 BC, the month of unequal
days, with February as the one susceptible to intercalary adjustment, were
those which we have inherited in our own Gregorian system. Indeed, the fifth
month gave us July in memory of Julius Caesar himself, while August was
derived by Augustus when he ordered the adjustment of 8 BC. The date of
primal reform was followed by the famous 'Year of Confusion' (46 BC), when in
order to adjust for precession, two months were inserted into the year.

JULIAN DAY   See JULIAN PERIOD.

JULIAN PERIOD   A period introduced by Scaliger to provide a continuous
measure of time in cycles of great extent. The period was a combination of
the solar cycle of 19 years, the lunar cycle of 28 years, and the indiction
cycle of 15 years. Scaliger artificially linked the beginning of this cycle
with the first day of the year of the Julian calendar, and began the cycle in
4713 BC. One benefit proceeding from the Julian period is that it has been
possible to establish an easily-manipulated scale of historical reference,
the Julian Day, which is merely determined in terms of daily aggregates from
the beginning of the cycle. The Julian Day is rarely used in astrology.

JULY   The seventh month (with 31 days) of the GREGORIAN CALENDAR, its name
being derived from that given to the original Roman month 'Quintilius' (the
fifth month of the JULIAN CALENDAR) in honour of Julius Caesar (born this
month), who had initiated the fundamental calendrical reforms.

JUNE   The sixth month (with 30 days) in the GREGORIAN CALENDAR. its name
probably being derived from that of the Roman goddess Juno, who was patron of
womanhood (called Pronuba) - this month being favoured for marriage (even
though the Junoesque 'Matronalia' was celebrated on the 1st March). Juno's
Grecian prototype, Hera, was certainly worshipped as the embodiment of the
fecund Earth, as many of the rituals of the Samian Hera indicate: the
imagery associated with the month is pre-Christian, and (as Foucher
indicates) is far from understood.

JUNO   Name given to one of the ASTEROIDS, discovered in 1804, and linked by
Dobyns with the sign Libra, along with a co-ruler, the asteroid "Pallas".
The same name has been given to one of the moons of Jupiter.

JUPITER   The planet in orbit between Mars and Saturn, ruler of the zodiacal
Sagittarius. Jupiter is the giant planet of our system, with an equatorial
diameter 11 times that of the earth, and with 12 satellites (four visible
with good binoculars), its rotational speed variable.   In traditional forms
of astrology, prior to the discovery of Neptune, Jupiter was said to have
rule over the zodiacal Pisces (see DAY HOUSES): modern astrologers generally
give the throne of Pisces to Neptune, however.   Jupiter is exalted in
Cancer, and has its fall in Capricorn (but see DIGNITY). The sigil for
Jupiter ♃ is said to represent the semi-circle of spiritual potential
lifting the heavy cross of materiality, which certainly symbolizes the
uplifting nature of the planet, though this sigil is actually post-mediaeval
in origin (see SIGILS - PLANETS).   Jupiter represents the profound side of
the mental life: it stands for the speculative thought of the native, and
for the spiritually expansive side of his nature. In particular Jupiter
offers an index of the moral nature of the native, and of the degree to which
he will respond enthusiastically to life and its responsibilities.   The
responsibilites themselves may come from Saturn, but how they are shouldered
depends very much upon Jupiter. When Jupiter is beneficially emphasized in
the chart (through dignity or aspect) it gives a generous, optimistic, loyal,
popular and generally successful nature. On the other hand, an unfortunately
located Jupiter tends towards uncontrolled expansion, and frequently an
inability to accept limitations - hence, self-indulgence, prodigality and
recklessness ensue. Traditionally Jupiter has rule over the thighs and liver
in the human body (see MELOTHESIC MAN), though modern astrologers place under
its rule the posterior pituitary gland, and the working of the blood: its
action seems to be involved with the regulation of blood supply and
breathing, which is the index of health in the human body. The traditional
description of the Jupiterian type is of one who has a well-formed, though
large (even plump) body, with a tendency to develop a paunch in later years.
The women are particularly beautiful: the forehead is noticeably large, the
hair dark and wavy, and in the male there is a tendency for it to recede in
later life. The eyes are usually commanding, though also kindly, and the
whole bearing a union of the dignified avuncular-paternal. The Jupiterian

usually finds expression on the physical plane through activities demanding
careful thought, speculation, growth and steady expansion - nowadays this is
especially so in the realm of law, industry and government. While the
Jupiterians are usually capable in money-matters, they do tend to be prodigal
with personal finance, yet with the special ability to handle and control the
money of others. They delight in a rich and varied life (especially one
involving travel or exploration), and are usually in great social demand.
They participate easily in public functions, and are of a philanthropic
nature, often with a fine feeling for music, and a love for philosophy which
brings them into constant contact with creative people.

JUPITER CHAIN   See JUPITER SCHEME.

JUPITER PERIOD   The name given in esoteric astrology to a future condition
(embodiment) of the earth, when humanity (having learned the lessons relating
to objective consciousness in the present cycles) will attain to
self-directed picture consciousness. Distinguish from JUPITER SCHEME.

JUPITER-SATURN CYCLES   Jupiter conjuncts with Saturn every 19.859 years, at
an advance of some 123 degrees. The first order cycle is 59.5779 years
(usually rounded off to 60 years), and a second order is 794.372 years
(usually rounded off to 795 years). See CHRONOCRATORS.

JUPITER SCHEME   The 'Jupiter Scheme' or 'Jupiterian Chain' are terms derived
specifically from the Theosophical cosmoconception linked with the SCHEME OF
EVOLUTION, and are not to be confused with the JUPITER PERIOD.   It is
claimed that while Jupiter is not yet inhabited, its moons are, and the
evolutionary development of this "Chain" will reach a very high level.

JYESTHA   The 16th of the Hindu NAKSHATRAS, 'the Oldest'.

KABBALISTIC ASTROLOGY   See QABBALISTIC ASTROLOGY.

KALB   'Al Kalb' (the heart), name given to the 16th of the Arabian MANZILS,
applying to the heart of the Scorpion, as in the medieaval lunar mansion 'Cor
Scorpionis'.

KALENDS   In the ancient Roman calendrical system there were no weeks, and
months were divided according to three points of measurement for each month
called 'Kalends', 'Nones' and 'Ides', names surviving from an ancient lunar
calendar (for example, the 'Idus' was the full moon). These were used in
astrological data and horoscopes well into late mediaeval times, surviving
even into collections of genitures of the so-called "Notable Nativities"
type. The Kalends were the 1st day of the month. The Nones were variable,
being usually the 5th day, though in March, May, July and October, it was the
7th day. The Ides were also variable, being usually the 13th day, but in the
four above months it was the 15th. Days were calculated before these points,
inclusively, so that (for example) the 29th May in our (new style) system
would be the 4th Kalends, written in horoscopic abbreviation as 'a.d.iv Kal.
Jun.' - the abbreviation 'a.d.' meaning 'ante diem', the whole phrase reading
'ante diem iv Kalendiae Junius'. The day immediately prior to a reckoning
point was indicated by the Latin 'pridie', usually shortened to 'prid': our
4th January would be written 'prid.Non.Jan.' The seven day week system
appears to have been first of all popularized by Roman astrologers (no doubt
because of the involvement with predictive techniques linked with lunar
rhythms), but not made official until the time of Constantine.

==

KALI YUGA   A Sanskrit term which has been Europeanized mainly through the
influence of Theosophy, and translated as meaning 'Iron Age', 'Black Age' or
'Dark Age'. The term often crops up in esoteric astrology because it is
widely acknowledged that we now live in this age, which the Hindus claim
began in 3,102 BC.   It is said by some occultists to be a period of 360,000
years, but others insist that the age has already terminated (circa 1880).
See YUGA, which sets out the additional periods of 'twilights' for the kali
yuga.

KALLISTOS   One of the several important variant names for "Ursa Major".

KALPA   In the Hindu chronology, a kalpa is a 'Day of Brahma', a period of
4,320 million years. The 'Night of Brahma' is of the same length. One 'Year
of Brahma' (a 'Solar Kalpa' in modern parlance) is made up of 360 such pairs,
while a century of such years makes up an entire cycle, the 'Mahakalpa' of
311,040 trillion years. Unfortunately, it is apparent that the word kalpa
is used fairly indiscriminately in reference to ages. Purucker records that
a kalpa is also a 'Mahamatava', a period equivalent to a whole lifetime of
the globes in a "Planetary Chain".

KANDRA   The Sanskrit term for the "Ascendant", as used in Hindu astrology.

KANYA   The Sanskrit name for zodiacal Virgo - but see also PHALGUNI.

KARKATAKAM   The Sanskrit name for zodiacal Cancer - but see also PUNARVASU.

KARKINOS   One of several Greek names (meaning 'crab') used to denote the
zodiacal and constellational Cancer. It is sometimes written 'Carcinos'.

KARMA   A term derived from the Sanskrit root 'kri' (to make or to do), and
meaning approximately 'action', though linked with the idea of consequence of
actions, being the 11th Nidana (chain of causation) of orthodox Buddhism. In
western occultism it is applied to the 'law of Karma', the unfolding of
destiny through repeated earth lives, in which merit and demerit are
reflected in life conditions, events and inner attitudes. In application to
astrology it is increasingly used in esoteric circles, and many astrologers
regard the natal chart as an impress of the particular karma which the
incarnating ego (that is, the native) has undertaken to resolve in this
particular lifetime. Some astrologers see the horoscope as reflecting the
whole of accumulated karma: the astrologer Robson writes, 'the horoscope is
the result of a series of past lives ... and by a study of the map of the
trend of former lives may be discovered.' Some emphasis is placed on karma
in "Astrosophy", subsequent to the work of Steiner.

KAROUBS   See OPHANIM.

KATABABAZON   Although almost archaic now, the term was once used widely as
a synonym for the "Dragon's Tail", derived from the Arabization of a Greek
term. There are many variant spellings and sounds, as for example
'Catahibazon' and 'Katahibazon'.

KATAHIBAZON   See KATABABAZON.

KATAKAM   A Sanskrit term for zodiacal Cancer, as used in Hindu astrology.

KATARCHIC ASTROLOGY   A term derived from the Greek ('Katarche', beginning)
and used to refer to that form of astrology concerned with the study of
influences arising from any given moment deemed to mark the beginning of an
enterprise or undertaking: it is in effect "Horary Astrology".

KATOTYCHE   A Greek term meaning approximately 'ill fortune', and used to
denote the "Sixth House".

KATUNE   A term used in "Mayan Astrology" to denote a period of 20 x 360 days.
Volguine links the Katune with the Jupiter/Saturn cycle, but in reality it
appears to be a system of dating.

KEMEDEL   Name given by Agrippa (quoting ancient cabbalistic sources) to the
'Daemon' of Venus, for whom he gives the magical number 157, without doubt a
misprint for 175, the value of the Venusian "Magic Square".   But see HAGIEL.

KEPHZIEL   One of the several variant names for the ruler of Saturn.

KEPLERIAN ASPECTS   A name given to a group of aspects linked with the
"Quintiles", originally proposed by the astronomer Kepler.   These are the
BI-QUINTILE, DECILE, QUINDECILE, QUINTILE, SEMI-DECILE and INCONJUNCT.
Kepler personally used the major and minor aspects of traditional astrology
in his horoscope work, but evolved the others on numerological grounds.

KEPLERIAN HARMONICS   The equation made by Kepler in his 'Harmonices Mundi'
of 1619, between the celestial motions of the solar system and musical
intervals, has never been systematically integrated into astrological theory,
mainly because the Keplerian harmonics are heliocentric, while traditional
astrology has been mainly rooted in geocentric cosmoconceptions.   In effect,
Kepler breaks away from the astrological tradition (see MUSIC OF THE SPHERES)
by rejecting the archaic notion of the spheres as a basis for harmonics, and
by rejecting even planetary distances or orbits, as these were no longer
applicable within the extension of the COPERNICAN SYSTEM proposed by Kepler
in his famous laws.   Instead, Kepler established a new harmonic series in
terms of the heliocentric diurnal angles of the planets, in their passages
through aphelion and perihelion, which he showed demonstrated a complete
system of musical intervals.   The series, set out in an excellent article by
Haase, may be digested as follows.   Saturn is connected with the Major Third,
with the Twelve Tones and the Minor Third.   Jupiter is connected with the
Octave, the Three Octaves and the Perfect Fifth.   Mars is connected with the
Minor Third (plus two octaves and plus one octave).   The Earth itself is
connected with the Diatonic Semitone, the Perfect Fifth and the Major Sixth.
Venus is connected with the Chromatic Semitone, the Minor Sixth and the
Double Octave.   Mercury is connected with the Minor Third (plus one Octave)
and the Major Sixth.   This, as Haase says, is a 'surprisingly simple
structure of the harmonies of our planetary system'.   See also PLANETARY
TONAL INTERVALS.

KERNAL   See COSMOPSYCHOGRAM.

KETU   The Sanskrit term for the "Dragon's Head", which is accorded much
importance in Hindu astrology.   For the Hindu 'Cauda', see RAHU.

KEY CYCLE   A system of calculating progressions, designed to rectify
(minute) errors implicit in the normal method.   The system is an adaptation
of "Solar Return" calculations, though adjustable to any time or space
relating to the Earth.

KEYNOTES   An equivalent term for "Keywords", applied in a special sense by
the astrologer Pagan to characteristic aims of the twelve signs:

AR	Hope	CN	Patience	LB	Beauty	CP	Reverence
TA	Peace	LE	Glory	SC	Justice	AQ	Truth
GE	Joy	VG	Purity	SG	Wisdom	PI	Love

KEYS   A term translated from the astrology of the French occultist
Christian, in reference to his 'Keys of Magism', a series of 570 fixed
readings linked with the planets, signs, houses, aspects, and so on, derived
from a syncretic interpretation of the astrological doctrines of Firmicus
Maternus, Junctinus of Florence and Pelusius.   Included in this somewhat
confused schema are the so-called 'Keys of the Annual Horoscope', which

represent 159 fixed readings (merely extended KEYWORDS) supposedly intended
to facilitate comparison of the progressed aspects to the natal chart.

KEYS OF THE ANNUAL HOROSCOPE   See KEYS.

KEYWORDS   In modern astrology a procedure has been established of portraying
the qualities of planets and signs (as well as other interpretative factors)
in terms of single words or short aphorisms, each designed to capture the
essence of the specific influences: these have been called 'keywords'. The
system was designed originally for teaching purposes, but has been used of
late (especially by Sunley) as the basis for investigating relationships
between traditional astrological forms, particularly that between the
tropical and sidereal zodiac. One of the most perceptive systematic
portrayals of planetary influences based on an extension of the keyword
system is that given by Davison, but a fine synoptical single-keyword series,
in which essentials are reduced to one word for signs, houses (Hs) and
planets, is that given by Jones:

AR	Aspiration	CN	Expansion	LB	Equivalence	CP	Discrimination
TA	Integration	LE	Assurance	SC	Creativity	AQ	Loyalty
GE	Vivification	VG	Assimilation	SG	Administration	PI	Sympathy

1st Hs	Identity	2nd Hs	Possession	3rd Hs	Convenience
4th Hs	Integration	5th Hs	Offspring	6th Hs	Obligation
7th Hs	Complementation	8th Hs	Ideality	9th Hs	Consciousness
10th Hs	Honour	11th Hs	Expectation	12th Hs	Confinement

SU	Purpose	MO	Feeling	ME	Mentality	VE	Acquisitiveness
MA	Initiative	JU	Enthusiasm	SA	Sensitiveness	UR	Independence
NE	Obligation	PL	Obsession				

See also FUNCTION, KEYNOTE and WATCHWORD.

KHAMBALIA   One of the star-names for the lamda of constellation Virgo, which
has gained a reputation in astrological textbooks not because of its size,
but (probably) because of its proximity to the ecliptic, and because it marks
one of the LUNAR MANSIONS. The name is said to be from the Coptic meaning
'crooked claw': it is said to be equivalent to Mercury conjunct Mars, and
therefore the bringer of violence: the native will have a changeable and
argumentative nature.

KIDINNU TABLES   See AYANAMSA.

KILLING PLACE   See ANARETIC PLACES.

KINSHIP   See FAMILIARITY.

KISLEV   See BABYLONIAN CALENDAR.

KNEELER   An ancient name for the "Hercules Constellation".

KNOW DATA METHODS   A term used to denote a method of checking astrological
traditions and speculations (and even formulating new astrological
hypotheses) by the empirical method of checking horoscope data (radical or
progressed) against the known case-histories of natives.

KOCHAB   Fixed star, the beta of "Ursa Minor", which Ebertin claims brings
suicide when with an afflicted Sun. Allen suggests that during the millenium
prior to our era, Kochab may have been one of the pole stars.

KOCH HOUSES   See KOCHIAN SYSTEM.

KOCHIAN SYSTEM   A method of HOUSE DIVISION devised by the German astrologer

Koch, based on the individual calculation of the cusps of intermediate houses for the place of birth. It is one of the methods which trisects the diurnal semiarc by time division. This method produces a grid which has no valid application in polar regions, and "Tables of Houses" are available only to 60 degrees of latitude, yet even so it rapidly gained support among astrologers after its introduction in 1962. 'One wonders', writes Genuit, 'why, over hundreds of years, nobody has hit upon this correct and obvious idea.' The method is sometimes called the 'GOH System' (derived from the German 'Geburtsortes Hausertabellen') and sometimes the 'Birthplace System'.

KOILON   A term derived from the ancient Greek 'koilos' (hollow), and used by esotericists to denote 'root matter'. Koilon is invisible to all but the most highly developed of clairvoyants.

KOLISKO EFFECT   A term used to denote the effect of (sidereal) planetary aspects on certain chemical reactions, recorded as litmus pictures (the so-called "Morphochromatograms"). Kolisko, following the suggestions of Steiner, established over several years' experimentation that the precipitation of mineral-salt solutions (such as argentum nitricum, ferrum sulfuricum and plumbum nitricum) left filter paper patterns which were conditioned by planetary conjunctions and oppositions, thus largely vindicating in a vividly pictorial manner Steiner's claim that 'so long as substances are in a solid state, they are subject to the forces of the Earth, but as soon as they enter the liquid state, the planetary forces come into play.' Kolisko demonstrated that the metals were affected by their corresponding 'traditional' planets (that is, silver by Moon events, iron by Martian events, lead by Saturnine events, and so on). Figure 37 gives a visual comparison of the patterns left by such precipitations, derived from a large number of photographs published by Kolisko and her followers. In connexion with this figure, which compares a non-aspectual Morphochromatogram with one demonstrating a superior conjunction of Saturn and Sun, Kolisko writes: 'under normal circumstances a picture similar to plate A was to be expected. But what did we see? Instead of heavy, massive forms an utter blank. An invisible hand had blotted out the working of the lead in the solution. And whose was the invisible hand? It was the Sun. The Sun had stood before the planet Saturn, and here below on the earth the lead could not manifest its activity. When the Stars speak, man must stand still in silent awe.' Fyfe has continued the basic research technique of Kolisko, more particularly in regard to lunar phenomena, as well as in regard to plant saps: see CAPILLARY DYNAMOLYSIS.

SU CONJ. SA
21.11.1926

FIGURE 37. PRECIPITATIONS OF LEAD SOLUTION ON LITMUS PAPER (LEFT) NORMAL CONDITIONS, COMPARED WITH (RIGHT) DURING A CONJUNCTION BETWEEN SUN AND SATURN, IN 1926 - SEE ABOVE TEXT (AFTER KOLISKO).

===

KORE   Greek term, sometimes Romanized as 'koure', of Attic origin, meaning 'maiden', and often used to denote the zodiacal and constellational Virgo. She was especially called the 'Staxeodos Koure', 'the wheat-bearing maiden'.

KORONIS   See HYADES.

KOSMOBIOLOGIE   See COSMOBIOLOGY.

KOSMOS   See MACROCOSM.

KRASIS   See MUSIC OF THE SPHERES and TEMPERAMENTS.

KRIOS   The Greek term (meaning 'ram') used to denote the zodiacal and constellational Aries.

KRITA YUGA   The Hindu 'Golden Age', a periodicity of 1,728,000 years - sometimes called the 'Satya Yuga'. This period includes the twilights 'sandhya' and 'sandhyansa' of 400 divine years each. See also YUGA.

KRITTIKA   The Sanskrit name for constellation Taurus: but see RISHABHAM. Krittika is also the name given to the 1st of the Hindu NAKSHATRAS.

KRONOS   One of the ancient terms for the planet Saturn, but not originally the Greek god-equivalent of Saturn. Kronos was in Greek mythology the youngest of the giant Titans, the son of Uranus and Gea, and was later identified with Saturnus by the Romans - presumably through his ancient association with agriculture (Gea being the Earth goddess). By the time that the astrological tradition was being set down in book form, Kronos and Saturnus were both used for the same planet: Ptolemy (writing in Greek) generally refers to the planet as Kronos. The same name (Kronos) is given to one of the several "Hypothetical Planets" used in the system of URANIAN ASTROLOGY, and is said to have a meaning linked with 'authority'.

KUJA   The Sanskrit word for the planet Mars, as used in Hindu astrology.

KUMBHAM   The Sanskrit name for zodiacal Aquarius: but see also DHANISHTHA.

KYRIOTETES   See DOMINIONS and CELESTIAL HIERARCHIES.

===

L

LABRUM   Fixed star set in constellation "Crater". It is supposed to combine the natures of Mercury and Venus, and (presumably because of its symbolic name as 'Holy Grail') it is said when rising on the Ascendant to give 'ecclesiastical preferment'.

LA CROIX   Name given by the astrologer Charubel to an extraneptunian planet, one of the HYPOTHETICAL PLANETS, which he perceived clairvoyantly some years prior to 1897, and for which he claimed a revolution period of just over 340 years. He gave it the alternative (though ambiguous) name 'Mundane Cross', and claimed for it the 'higher properties of Mars'. It has been observed that the revolution of this hypothetical is almost the same as that named "Isis". Later astrologers assigned La Croix to the day-house of Capricorn, the night-house of Aries, and exalted it in Sagittarius, though it has not been widely adopted by modern astrologers.

LADY OF HEAVEN   One of the translations of a Sumerian term for Venus.

LAGNAM   A Sanskrit term for the "Ascendant", as used in Hindu astrology.

===

LAMB   A term sometimes used of zodiacal or constellational Aries, derived
from the "Talismanic Magic" of the mediaeval period, when there was a move
(for example, in the writings of Arnaldus de Villanova) to integrate the
'pagan' elements of astrology with Christian magic.

LAMB OF GOD   A name sometimes used of zodiacal or constellational Aries -
but see also LAMB.

LAME DEGREES   See AZIMENE DEGREES and MUTILATED DEGREES.

LATITUDE   Within the limits of astrological use, the term is applied to a
system of co-ordinate measurements from the ecliptic, north or south, towards
either of the poles.

LAVAGNINI SYSTEM   A method of HOUSE DIVISION based on the attempt to apply
the equal house symbolic method (see MODUS EQUALIS) in such a way that both
Ascendant and Midheaven may be integrated for all latitudes. It is an
eight-point system, each of the points reflecting the combination of the four
angles and the pairs of zenith/nadir and east/west points. The 1st house of
the grid is determined by bisecting the angle between the Ascendant and the
east point. The 10th house is determined by the bisection of the angles
between the zenith and the MC. Over this grid the four angles are inserted,
and these cusps are regarded as marking the centre of influence of the
houses. The system is attributed to the Italian astrologer Lavagnini.

LEADING PLANET   See LOCOMOTIVE.

LEADING SIGNS   These are Aries, Cancer, Libra and Capricorn.

LEAF TRIGON   See SIDEREAL MOON RHYTHMS.

LEDAEAN STARS   See GEMINI CONSTELLATION.

LEMNISCATE   A closed figure, having a resemblance to a figure 8, the term
being derived from the Greek 'lemniscos' (ribbon). It is relevant to
astrology since certain esoteric systems (especially those of Steiner and
Vreede - but see also Schultz) insist that planets do not move in elliptical
orbits (as the developed COPERNICAN SYSTEM has taught), but in lemniscatory
patterns.

LEMURIA   A name given in esoteric circles to the long-lost culture and
continent occupied by the "Third Root Race". In its occult sense, the term
is not to be confusd with the Roman festival held in mid-May to appease
ghosts (the Latin 'lemures', meaning approximately 'shades of the departed').

LEO   The fifth sign of the zodiac, and one of the constellations. It
corresponds as a zodiacal sign neither in location nor extent with the
constellation of the same name - see LEO CONSTELLATION. The modern sigil
for Leo ♌ is said by some to be a corruption of the initial of the Greek
term for the asterism: however, the present form of the sigil appears to
derive from a late mediaeval form which is not like the lamda, and the
significance remains hidden, even though many explanations have been given by
various astrologers - see SIGILS - ZODIAC. Leo is of the Fire element, and
of the Fixed quality, the influence being creative, self-reliant,
enthusiastic, warm-hearted and positive. As with all Fire types, there is a
strong element of selfishness, but the Leonine is rarely insensitive to the
needs of others. The warm and creative outlook of Leo is expressed in many
keywords attached to the sign by modern astrologers: self-expressive,
dignified, inspirational, exuberant, magnanimous, flamboyant (sometimes
theatrical), hospitable and altruistic - in a word all those qualities which
may be associated with a Fire nature expressing itself without fear, and with
a wish to be creative. In excess the Leonine nature may be described in
terms which express its underlying selfishness, the keywords being: vain,

===

demanding, predatory, imperious, dogmatic, self-satisfied, ostentatious and
militant.   Leo is ruled by the Sun, and the sign marks the detriment of
Saturn, while some astrologers say that it marks the fall of Mercury.

LEO CONSTELLATION   Constellation linked in name, if not in influence, with
the zodiacal LEO, located as indicated in figure 38 (though it is likely that
the figure was much smaller in ancient times).   Figure 38 sets out the modern
asterism according to Delporte, derived from the MODERN ZODIAC.   Even from
early times (see BABYLONIAN ZODIAC) the asterism was named 'Lion', and its
image was that of a lion - that in figure 38 is from the mediaeval "San
Miniato Zodiac".   In classical times it was associated with the Nemean lion
of the Hercules cycle.   Ptolemy describes the influence of the constellation
in terms of the smaller asterisms of which the image is composed, but it is
said to convey the Leonine virtues of nobility and courage - for specific
influences, see the related stars ADHAFERA, DENEBOLA, REGULUS and ZOSMA.

FIGURE 38.   THE IMAGE FOR LEO, FROM THE 13TH CENTURY "SAN MINIATO ZODIAC",
AND THE CONSTELLATION FROM THE "MODERN ZODIAC" OF DELPORTE.

LEO MINOR   Constellation, 'the lesser lion', formed by Hevelius from a
number of stars between the constellations Leo and "Ursus".   It appears to be
of a nature approximate to that of the asterism Leo, bringing generosity and
nobility, combined with courage.

LEPUS   Constellation located approximately 5 degrees Gemini to 3 degrees
Cancer, and from 14 to 25 degrees south of the equator, 'the Hare' from very
early times.   In some legends this hare was placed near to the hunter
"Orion", a nearby asterism: in Egyptian astrology the asterism appears to
have been the Boat of Osiris, and thus also linked with the equivalent of
Orion.   Ptolemy gives it a nature equivalent to Mercury with Saturn, and the
tradition insists that it gives timidity, though a quick wit.

LESATH   Fixed star, the upsilon of Scorpius, set in the tail of the
scorpion, its name from the Arabic 'Al Les'ah' (the sting).   It is said to
bring danger and malevolence when emphatic in a chart, and to be of the
nature of Mercury conjunct Mars.

LESSER BENEFIC   See BENEFICS.

LESSER CLOUD   See NUBECULAE MAGELLANI.

LIBRA   The seventh sign of the zodiac, which corresponds neither in location
nor extent with the constellation of the same name (see LIBRA CONSTELLATION).
The sigil for Libra ♎ is said by some astrologers to be a vestigial
drawing of a pair of scales, with which the sign and constellation has been

associated from the very earliest times, the Babylonian name for the asterism
being 'Zibanitu' (scales).   However, one of the more frequently used of the
Egyptian hieroglyphics for the sign shows that the sigil is derived from a
picture of the Sun setting over the Earth ♎ an appropriate image for a sign
which is now associated with the Descendant, that symbolic place of sunset.
Libra is of the Air element, and of the Cardinal quality, its influence being
harmonious, elegant, orderly, comparative, peaceful, changeable and helpful.
The nature of Libra is manifest in human beings in terms of the many keywords
used by modern astrologers: gentle, artistic, sensitive, helpful, peaceful,
spiritualized, delicate, perceptive, affectionate - in a word all the
qualities which may be associated with an Air type expressing itself with a
delicate awareness of others.   In excess, the Libran nature may be described
in terms which express an impractical nature, as well as a lazy streak, the
keywords being: untidy, easily persuaded, 'lost in the clouds', unable to
cope, and so on.   The Libran says 'I want to be carried' more often than
others do, and she may do this gently or imperiously, depending upon which
side of the nature is being called into activity.   Libra is ruled by the
planet Venus, marks the exaltation of Saturn and the Fall of Pluto.

LIBRA CONSTELLATION   The constellation of Libra covers an arc of just under
21 degrees, and it would appear that at one time it was considered to be
merely an extension of the adjacent Scorpius, of which it was the 'chelae'
(claws):   figure 39 sets out the form of the asterism according to the MODERN
ZODIAC, however.   In the occult tradition, the original significance of this
constellation was intimately connected with the two signs Scorpio and Virgo,
but it is clear that the asterism was defined over three thousand years ago:
it was the Babylonian 'Zibanitu' (scales), and inevitably it was later
identified with 'Astraea', the holder of the balance which weighs the deeds
of men, though of course this goddess was linked with Virgo.   It is perhaps
no accident that the image for Libra in the mediaeval zodiac (figure 39) is
distinguished from that of Virgo merely by the attribute of the scales.
Early names which still appear in mediaeval manuscripts are 'Zichos', and the
Latin 'Jugum' (yoke or beam).   The fixed stars in the asterism which have
importance in the astrological tradition are NORTH SCALE and SOUTH SCALE,
originally the 'North Claw' and the 'South Claw', respectively.

FIGURE 39.   THE IMAGE FOR LIBRA, FROM THE 13TH CENTURY "SAN MINIATO
ZODIAC", AND THE CONSTELLATION, FROM THE "MODERN ZODIAC" OF DELPORTE.

LIFE POINT   The 'point of Life' is one of the so-called Arabian PARS.   If
the degree of the syzygy preceding the birth is used to denote a new
Ascendant in the chart, then the position of the natal moon in that new
arrangement marks the point of Life.

LIGHTENING FLASH   In a specialist sense, one of the modern additions to the
Arabian PARS, the 'part of Uranus', sometimes called the 'point of
Catastrophe'.   If a chart is so revolved that the degree occupied by the Sun

==

is transferred to the Ascendant, then the position of the radical Uranus in
this new arrangement will mark the Lightening Flash. The same term is also
used (albeit in translation) of Boehme's 'schrack', linked with the operation
of the Sun in his SEVEN PROPERTIES.

LIGHT OF TIME   This is a term used to denote the Sun in the daytime (or in
the daytime chart), the Moon in the night-time (or in the night-time chart).

LIGHT PLANETS   These are the Moon, Mercury and Venus.

LIGHTS   The Sun and Moon are the 'Lights' (also the 'Luminaries'): the Sun
is the 'Greater Light', the Moon the 'Lesser Light'. Confusingly, the Moon
and the two inferiors are also sometimes called the 'Light Planets'.

LIGHT TRIGON   See SIDEREAL MOON RHYTHMS.

LILITH   Name given to a planet generally described as one of the
"Hypothetical Planets", though it is really a 'hypothetical Moon' of the
Earth, invisible to ordinary sight save (it is said) when its body passes
between the Earth and the Sun. Lilith is called the 'Dark Moon' by
Goldstein-Jacobson, who has provided an ephemeris of positions, and gives her
a revolution of 126 years. As the choice of name would suggest, Lilith is
regarded as a sinister and malevolent planet, bringing temptations and
betrayals, and ruling such matters as abortion and stillbirth. The word
Lilith appears to have been derived from the Assyrian 'lilitu', a semi-human
succubus whose name was introduced into Rabbinic literature as the second
wife of Adam. From this ancient liason were born devils, spirits and
'lilin'. Some occultists call Lilith the 'first wife' of Adam, however.

LIMITING DATE   See ADJUSTED CALCULATION DATE.

LINE OF ADVANTAGE   Name given to an imaginary line conceived as running
between the cusps of the third decans of the 3rd and 9th houses of a chart.
When the "Dragon's Head" is to the east of this line, it is judged more
favourably than otherwise.

LINON   See PISCES CONSTELLATION.

LION   One of the modern names for zodiacal and constellational "Leo". It is
also a name given to one of the "Hypothetical Planets", listed by the
astrologer Jayne as a transplutonian.

LION'S HEART   See REGULUS.

LION'S TAIL   See DENEB.

LITTLE WORLD   See MICROCOSM.

LOADSTAR   See POLARIS.

LOCALITY ANGLES   A term derived from the work of Johndro, designed to
establish a workable chart projection called the JOHNDRO LOCALITY CHART. The
'Locality Midheaven' is the local midheaven of the birth place added to the
longitude of the Sun at birth. The 'Locality Ascendant' is derived from the
above, for the latitude of birth, in the normal way.

LOCALITY ASCENDANT   See LOCALITY ANGLES.

LOCALITY MIDHEAVEN   See LOCALITY ANGLES.

LOCAL MEAN TIME   See TIME.

LOCAL MERIDIAN   The meridian passing through the position of the observer on any part of the Earth's surface.

LOCAL SIDEREAL TIME   See TIME.

LOCI   A term derived from the Hellenistic astrological 'topoi' (places),
relating approximately to a system of 'Equal House Divisions' of 30 degree
arcs linked to the angles rather than to the ecliptic. The historian
Neugebauer records a second variant of the standard 'equal house' system,
which locates the beginning of the loci 5 degrees before the angles, though
still in the twelve-fold divisions of 30 arcs.   The order of the loci
follows the standard order of modern HOUSE DIVISION. The twelve loci which
are linked with a sequence beginning with the Ascendant are the equivalent of
the 1st house, are said to govern the following life conditions:

1. Life, spirit and 'breath' (pneuma).
2. Livelihood, property, partnerships, relations with women, business,
   profit from inheritance. It is called 'Gate of Hades'.
3. Brothers, living abroad, royalty, wealth, friends (also, 'slaves') -
   sometimes called 'Goddess'.
4. Parents, life in the temple, reputation, children, and so on.
5. Children, friendship, accomplishment and (curiously) marriage -
   sometimes called 'good fortune'.
6. Slaves, illness, enmity, infirmity - sometimes called 'bad fortune'.
7. Marriage.
8. Death, trial, penalty, loss and weakness.
9. Travel, friendship, benefit from kings, manifestations of gods,
   soothsaying - sometimes called 'God'.
10. Careers and honours, reputation, accomplishment, children, wife.
11. Friends, hopes, gifts, children and accomplishments (also, freed
    persons) - sometimes called 'good daemon'.
12. Enmity, foreign country, slaves, illness, dangers, court trials,
    infirmity, death - sometimes called 'bad daemon'.

Neugebauer records that Vettius Valens mentions the 8th locus is counted not
from the Ascendant, but from the 'Part of Fortune', though this seems to
savour of the system of "Lots", the Hellenistic equivalent of "Pars".

LOCOMOTIVE   Term applied to one of the JONES PATTERNS, in which the
distribution of the planets is such that a space of at least 120 degrees in
the figure is opposed by a more or less evenly distributed 240 degrees of
"occupied" space. The planet furthest East (read in a clockwise direction)
is said to be the "Leading Planet", and gives an especially powerful
practical drive (in terms of the planet's house). The entire Locomotive
distribution is said to give an executive ability, and at worst leads to a
ruthless selfseeking.

LONG ASCENSION   The 'Signs of Long Ascension' are those in the zodiacal arc
from Cancer to Sagittarius, inclusive.

LONGITUDE   In a strictly astrological sense, the term is used of a
co-ordinate of measurement of the zodiac, in degrees of arc, starting at the
beginning of Aries: thus, 53 degrees of longitude is 23 degrees of Taurus.

LORD   This term is used widely, and often inaccurately in modern astrology.
Properly it should apply to a planet which, by domal placing, is the most
powerful in a given chart. However, see LORD OF A HOUSE, LORD OF THE
HOROSCOPE and LORDSHIP.

LORD OF ACTION   An archaic term, originally appearing in English from the
translations of Ptolemy. As so often with Ptolemaic astrology, the rules for
determining the Lord of Action are complicated, and in fact lead in many
cases to two Lords of Action being apposite in the same chart. In its
simplest form, the Lord is that planet which makes its morning appearance

closest to the sun (and/or) nearest to the Midheaven, in the latter case when in (beneficial?) aspect to the sun. The rules need not concern us here, however, for the archaic term is of value only in so far as it points to an ancient tradition by which the "action" (that is, the profession, and professional outlook, of natives) may be determined, other than by the simplistic "Sun in Sign" or "Ascendant" or "Midheaven" interpretation. The traditional rule of planets over professions is adhered to (for example, if Mercury is the Lord, then his subjects will be writers, business men, mathematicians, teachers, bankers, soothsayers, astrologers, and 'in general those who perform their functions by means of documents'). It is interesting that among the Mercurial professions Ptolemy included 'sacrificers'.

LORD OF A HOUSE   Rather than being the 'ruler' of a house, a planet should be deemed the 'Lord' of a house (see RULE). The term was introduced by late mediaeval astrologers, intent on removing confusion in terminologies. A planet may be said to be in its "Throne" when in the sign it rules, whereas it is 'Lord' of the corresponding house. In fact, the 'Lord of the House' is the planetary ruler of the sign which occupies the cusp of that house. This term must be distinguished from "Lord of the Horoscope".

LORD OF KARMA   A term used by the esotericist Bailey of Saturn, the planet which imposes retribution, and which demands payment of all debts.

LORD OF THE GENITURE   The "Almuten" - but see also LORD OF THE HOROSCOPE.

LORD OF THE GREEKS   Name given to a scholar 'Yavanesvara', who translated into Sanskrit a 2nd century AD Grecian (probably Alexandrian) popular handbook on astrology, of which even the title is no longer known, since the original has been lost, suriving only in this translation, and in the versification made by an Indian in the 3rd century AD. This, together with another lost translation used by Satya, has formed the root of Indian astrology. Inevitably, the basic Hellenistic socio-cosmic views were adapted to Indian social conditions and philosophy, specifically to the Indian caste systems, doctrines of reincarnation, and so on. Such was also united to the Horary system of the Hindu NAKSHATRAS. The adaptation of the several Hellenistic 'sortes' and other divisions (such as the 'oktopodos') to the Hindu system has given rise to the notion that there is or was a correspondence between the Hindu system and modern HARMONICS, though the bases of division are quite different.

LORD OF THE HOROSCOPE   The European equivalent of the ALMUTEN. It is maintained that any of the planets may be so placed in the radical chart as to be deemed the most powerful influence in that chart, in which case it is called the 'Lord' or 'Ruler'. Carter suggested that such a 'Lord' stands for the native himself, while the rest of the chart stands for his external life - but this plays no part in the traditional view.   The Lord or Ruler is properly the determinant of the term often applied by astrologers to a nativity, in a simplistic manner - such as 'Martian', 'Neptunian', and so on. This mode of descriptive speech indicates that a Lord may be regarded as of about the same importance as the Ascendant, since the astrologer will speak of persons in terms of signs (that is, as an 'Arietan' or 'Leonine') in reference to the Ascendant sign. Strictly speaking, in traditional astrology at least, the term 'Lord of the Horoscope' was used of a planet emphasized by its domal position, while the 'Ruler of the Horoscope' was used of a planet emphasized by its sign-position, or by special aspectal conditions. However, in recent years, the two terms have been merged, and it is now difficult to separate domal strengths from other dignities.

LORD OF THE NATIVITY   The "Almuten": see LORD OF THE HOROSCOPE.

LORD OF THE TRIANGLE   A descriptive phrase, which might just as well be 'Lord of Triplicity', and related to an ancient system of rulerships which have disappeared from modern astrology, though it is regarded as being important by Ptolemy, and is sometimes adduced in astrological argument, as for example in connexion with the vexing question of the arc rulerships of the TERMS. The 'Lord of the Triangle' is determined as follows:

The FIRE TRIPLICITY is ruled by the Sun by day, Jupiter at night.
The EARTH TRIPLICITY is ruled by Venus by day, by Moon at night.
The AIR TRIPLICITY is ruled by Saturn by day, by Mercury at night.
The WATER TRIPLICITY is ruled by Venus by day, by Moon at night, though this last pair are regarded as 'co-workers' with the dominant ruler Mars.

LORD OF THE YEAR   A name given to a planet which has most dignity in a "Solar Revolution Chart", or in an "Ingress Figure".

LORD OF TRIPLICITY   See LORD OF THE TRIANGLE.

LORDSHIP   Properly speaking, the relationship which a planet may be said to have with its associate house is one of 'Lordship'. A planet may be said to be Lord of a particular house - even though in popular astrology a planet is often said to have 'rule' over a particular house. Thus, Mars may be said to be Lord of the 1st house, and Ruler of Aries.

LORDS OF FLAME   See SATURN PERIOD.

LORDS OF FORM   The name given to one of the TWELVE CREATIVE HIERARCHIES, associated with zodiacal Scorpio, who according to the esoteric cosmogenesis are especially concerned with the evolution of man as a spiritual being during the present "Earth Period". They are in the present stage of evolution linked with the EXSUSIAI, and therefore with the sphere of the Sun.

LORDS OF HARMONY   See CHERUBIM.

LORDS OF INDIVIDUALITY   The name given to one of the TWELVE CREATIVE HIERARCHIES, associated with zodiacal Libra, who according to the esoteric cosmogenesis prepared the 'Desire Body' of man during the MOON PERIOD.

LORDS OF LOVE   See SERAPHIM.

LORDS OF MIND   The name given to one of the TWELVE CREATIVE HIERARCHIES, associated with zodiacal Sagittarius, who according to the esoteric cosmogenesis formed the equivalent of humanity during the SATURN PERIOD. They are in the present stage of evolution linked with the ARCHAI.

LORDS OF WILL   Esoteric name for the THRONES.

LORDS OF WISDOM   The name given to one of the TWELVE CREATIVE HIERARCHIES, associated with zodiacal Virgo, who according to the esoteric cosmogenesis prepared the vital body (the Etheric Body)) of men during the SUN PERIOD.

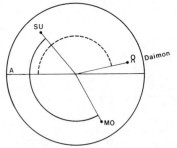

FIGURE 40.   CONSTRUCTION OF THE 'LOT OF DAIMON' (AFTER BOUCHE-LECLERCQ).

LOT OF DAIMON   One of the most important of the SEVEN LOTS of Greek
astrology, and formerly held as of equal importance to the "Part of Fortune".
The 'Daimon' of the Greeks is not the 'demon' of mediaeval lore, and the lot
is a beneficial one.   The degree of the Daimon is the same distance from the
Ascendant as the arc between the Moon and Sun (figure 40): the sigil for the
daimon used in this diagram is that used by late Greek astrologers. From the
'part of Daimon' are determined the 'lot of Love' ("Eros") and the 'lot of
Victory' - see SORTES.

LOT OF EROS   The ancient equivalent of the 'part of Venus': see HERMETIC
SORTES.

LOT OF NECESSITY   An ancient 'part of Mercury': see HERMETIC SORTES.

LOTS   See SEVEN LOTS.

LOVE   For 'part of Love', see EROS.

LOWELL-PLUTO   A name suggested for the present "Pluto" shortly after it had
been discovered by Lowell.   At that time, however, more than one astrologer
(most notably, Wemyss and Pagan) had already named two of the "Hypothetical
Planets" 'Pluto', and the new name was proposed to avoid confusion - see
however PAGAN-PLUTO and WEMYSS-PLUTO.

LOWER MIDHEAVEN   A misleading variant used for the "Imum Coeli".

LUCIAN ASTROLOGY   A misnomer, sometimes 'Lucis Astrology', for the esoteric
system proposed by Bailey as her INTUITIONAL ASTROLOGY.   The term is derived
from the name 'Lucis Trust', which publishes the works of Bailey.

LUCIDA CORONA SCORPIONIS   Late mediaeval term for the fixed star CAPELLA.

LUCIFER   In astrology the name sometimes given to the planet Venus when it
appears before the Sun (see HESPERUS) - also called the 'Morning Star'.   The
same term is also sometimes used in different senses in contexts which touch
upon astrology.   Lucifer is the celestial being wrongly equated with Satan
(probably due to a misreading of 'Isaiah' 14-12): at all events, the name
has been adopted in esoteric circles to represent the modern equivalent of
the being of the Sun (originally named 'Ormudz' in the Zoroastrian dualism)
opposed by the 'darkness', the 'Prince of Lies', who was called 'Angrimayu',
in modern occultism 'Ahriman'.   This dualism has been carried into several of
the esoteric astrological systems of modern times.   Another use of the term
is linked with the "Asteroids", for Butler has suggested that these (which he
rightly calls 'planetoids') mark the remains of a 'lost planet', which he
calls 'Lucifer' or 'Morning Star': this is clearly not the 'Morning Star' of
Venus.   In support of his suggestions, Butler quotes several clairvoyants
(such as Swedenborg and Davis), but the idea appears to be essentially
biblical in origin.   Although the name 'Lucifer' is not used in esoteric lore
in such a connexion, it is held in many occult traditions that the planetoids
are indeed a detritus of a lost planet.

LUCKY AND UNLUCKY DAYS   See EGYPTIAN DAYS.

LUMINARIES   The Sun and Moon are often called the 'luminaries' in
traditional astrology.   It is quite usual for modern astrologers to explain
this term by saying that the Moon is a 'luminary' because it 'lights up' the
night, yet the fact is that the ancients believed that all planets emitted
some degree of light in addition to that reflected by the Sun.

LUMINOSITY   The luminosity of a star (which is different from its
"Magnitude") is its 'Absolute Stellar Magnitude' - see STELLAR MAGNITUDE.

LUNA   The Latin name for the Moon.

LUNAR ASTROLOGY   The facility with which the ever-changing lunar disc might be studied against the night sky in Mediterranean lands meant that the earliest forms of astrology were based on material derived from lunar phenomena and measurements. Some of this lunar material survives in the LUNAR MANSIONS, and so on, but it is perhaps imaginative of the astrologer Fagan to claim that astrology was in ancient times 'essentially lunar' - calendrical systems may have been, yet there is little evidence from the surviving Graeco-Roman traditions (see for example BABYLONIAN ZODIAC and GREEK ZODIAC) that astrology was 'essentially lunar'. However, see LUNAR STATIONS and LUNAR ZODIAC. In modern times, particularly in the realm of "Astrosophy", there has been a renewed interest in the equivalent of lunar astrology, in connexion with bio-dynamic farming and related studies - see for example SIDEREAL MOON RHYTHMS.

LUNAR BODY   A term used in contrast with the SOLAR BODY by the esoteric astrologer Thierens intent on establishing the relationships of spheres in what he regards as the future evolution of the solar system. The 'lunar body' is made up of the "Astral Spheres" of Aquarius and Pisces, and the "Etheric Spheres" of Aries to Cancer, inclusive. The 'solar body' is made up of the spheres of the superior planets and the spheres of Venus and Mercury. See however FUTURE PLANETS.

LUNAR CYCLES   The Moon completes a cycle once every month. During this time it forms four powerful aspects with the Sun - the conjunction, opposition and two squares. Each of these four angular relationships induces a monthly rhythm in the life of individuals, the nature, intensity and timing of which will depend very much upon the positions of the natal Moon and Sun. It is for this reason that the number 4 has been associated with the Moon, which in turn explains why some writers insist that there is a four-year cycle of the Moon, which is not the case: see LUNAR NODE CYCLE and REVOLUTION PERIODS. When this quaternary is translated into years by the methods of progression, it is expressed in periodicities of 7 years, totally 28 years in a full cycle. See also AGES OF MAN, SAROS CYCLE and SIDEREAL MOON RHYTHMS.

LUNAR ECLIPSE   When the orb of the Earth interposes itself between the light of the Sun and the Moon, the phenomenon is called a 'lunar eclipse'. The Moon is usually itself visible, but with the appearance of a dark object against a dimly illumined backdrop of sky. Clearly, a lunar eclipse may take place only when the two luminaries are in the aspect of opposition. Experience has shown that eclipse leaves a sort of 'degree influence' which is only made operational later by transits or progressions. The ancient astrological rule held that the effect of a lunar eclipse would last the equivalent of one month for every hour of eclipse, timed from the beginning of the occultation. Eclipses (see also SOLAR ECLIPSE) in a chart are regarded as malignant if the degrees involved are conjunct the radical Sun, Moon, Ascendant, Midheaven, any malefic, or any of these progressed (to the time of the eclipse). Esoteric astrology insists that lunar eclipses mark the entry of evil forces into the sphere of the Earth. See also ATALIA.

LUNAR GODS   The term is usually a Theosophical equivalent for the 'Pitris', 'the ancestors of previous human races', according to occultism. In western terminology, however, the lunar gods are really the "Angels".

LUNAR HORAS   See HORAS.

LUNAR INTELLIGENCY   Following ancient cabbalistic sources, Agrippa records the Hebraic 'Schedbarschemoth Schartathan' as relating to both the 'daemon of the lunar demons' and the 'intelligency of the lunar intelligencies' (see however INTELLIGENCY), and accords them the number 3321, which is the multiple of the lunar number 9 and the linear sum of the "Magic Square" of the Moon, which is 369.

LUNAR MANSIONS   An ancient method of dividing the ecliptic belt into arcs of

12 degrees and 51 minutes, corresponding approximately to the daily mean
motion of the Moon through the ecliptic. By such divisions, 28 segments,
called 'lunar mansions' are obtained (the word 'mansions' appears to be
derived from the Arabian 'manzils'). Each of these mansions is named, and
has been subject to astrological interpretation along the lines of a "Lunar
Zodiac". Since each of the mansions is said to emit an influence, the
planets located in the individual signs transmit these influences in
accordance with their own natures, and thus determine the natural disposition
of sublunary creatures. In modern times, interpretation of the mansions
appears to be limited to a consideration of the Moon itself, however. There
are now three major extant lunar systems of 'mansions' used in astrological
circles - that derived from the Arabian system, called MANZILS; the Hindu
system of NAKSHATRAS and the Chinese SIEU, the names for which are set out in
table 48, as given by Robson: the fiducial is given for the Arabian system,
there being (slight) variations between the systems. It was the Arabian
system which most influenced the development of western astrology until the
Hindu system was popularized by Theosophy at the beginning of this century.

```
------------------------------------------------------------------TABLE 48
    CHIEF FIDUCIAL     MANZIL              NAKSHATRAS       SIEU
========================================================================
 1.  Eta Tauri         Al Thurayya         Krittika         Mao
 2.  Alpha Tauri       Al Dabaran          Rohini           Pi
 3.  Lambda Orionis    Al Hak'ah           Mrigasiras       Tsee
 4.  Gamma Geminorum   Al Han'ah           Ardra            Shen
 5.  Alpha Geminorum   Al Dhira            Punarvarsu       Tsing
 6.  44 M Cancri       Al Nathrah          Pushya           Kwei
 7.  Lambda Leonis     Al Tarf             Aslesha          Lieu
 8.  Alpha Leonis      Al Jabhah           Magha            Sing
 9.  Delta Leonis      Al Zubrah           Purva Phalguni   Chang
10.  Beta Leonis       Al Sarfah           Uttara Phalguni  Yen
11.  Beta Virginis     Al Awwa             Hasta            Tchin
12.  Alpha Virginis    Al Simak            Citra            Kio
13.  Iota Virginis     Al Ghafr            Svati            Kang
14.  Alpha Librae      Al Jubana           Visakha          Ti
15.  Beta Scorpii      Iklil al Jabhah     Anuradha         Fang
16.  Alpha Scorpii     Al Kalb             Jyestha          Sin
17.  Lambda Scorpii    Al Shaulah          Mula             Wei
18.  Zeta Sagittarii   Al Na'am            Purva Ashadha    Ki
19.  Pi Sagittarii     Al Baldah           Uttara Ashadha   Tow
20.  Alpha Capricorni  Al Sa'd al Dhabih   Abhijit          Nieu
21.  Mu Aquarii        Al Sa'd al Bula     Sravana          Mo
22.  Beta Aquarii      Al Sa'd al Su'ud    Sravishta        Heu
23.  Alpha Aquarii     Al Sa'd al Ahbiyah  Catabhishaj      Shih
24.  Alpha Pegasi      Al Fargh al Mukdim  Purva Bhadra-Pada   Shih
25.  Alpha Andromeda   Al Fargh al Thani   Uttara Bhadra-Pada  Peih
26.  Beta Andromeda    Al Batn al Hut      Revati           Goei
27.  Beta Arietis      Al Sharatain        Asvini           Leu
28.  Delta Arietis     Al Butain           Bharani          Oei
------------------------------------------------------------------------
```

LUNAR MONTH   The official 'lunar month' is 29.531 days, which marks the
cycle in which the Moon returns to its original position in relation to the
Sun. It is the 'sidereal month' (that interval between two successive
conjunctions of Sun and Moon) of 27.322 days which is used by the majority of
astrologers in regard to calculations influencing progressions: this is the
cycle reflected in the lunar periodicity of 28.

LUNAR NODE CYCLE   The movement of the nodes of the Moon (see DRAGON'S HEAD
and DRAGON'S TAIL) which move gradually around the ecliptic in contrary
direction to the movement of the planets, completes a cycle in approximately
18 years and 7 months, which is used as an important periodicity in
astrology, especially in regard to the "Climacterics" of human life.

LUNAR RETURN   A name applied to a chart cast for the time at which the moon returns to its radical position in a previous chart (most usually the natal chart of the subject). It may be measured in terms of the tropical or sidereal zodiac, though the astrologer Bradley favours the latter in his own comprehensive survey of what he calls "Solunar Returns". He insists that the 'lunar return chart', with its periodicity of approximately 27.3 days (the sidereal month) is basically a health chart. See also SENNIGHT CHART, SOLAR RETURN and SYNODICAL RETURNS.

LUNAR REVOLUTIONS   See SYNODICAL RETURNS.

LUNAR RHYTHMS   See SIDEREAL MOON RHYTHMS.

LUNAR SEMICIRCLE   Wilson defines this term as meaning 'from Aquarius to Cancer, both included'.

LUNAR STATIONS   Often used as a synonym for the LUNAR MANSIONS, even though it is clear from Arabic documents that the 'stations' were points marked by fiducials, while the mansions (or MANZILS) were constellational arcs (sometimes described as 'asterisms'). The names of the stations, as well as the related fiducials (given here in terms of the modern stars, rather than the Arabic names) are listed under "Lunar Mansions". The list is derived from the Arabic astrologer Al Biruni - but see the entries under "Manzils".

Alsharatan	(beta and gamma Arietis)
Albutain	(epsilon, delta and pi Arietis)
Althurayya	(Pleiades)
Aldabaran	(alpha Tauri)
Alhak'a	(lambda and phi, Orionis)
Alhan'a	(gamma and zeta Geminorum)
Aldhira	(alpha and beta Geminorum)
Anathra	(Praesepe, Aselli)
Altarf	(lambda Leonis, zeta Cancri)
Aljabha	(zeta, gamma, eta and alpha Leonis)
Alzubra	(delta and theta Leonis)
Alsarfa	(beta Leonis)
Al'awwa	(beta, eta, gamma, delta and epsilon Virginis)
Alsimak Al'a'zal	(alpha Virginis)
Alghafr	(iota, kappa and lambda Virginis)
Alzubana	(alpha and beta Librae)
Al'iklil	(beta, delta and pi Scorpii)
Alkalb	(alpha Scorpii)
Alshaula	(lambda and upsilon Scorpii)
Alna'a'im	(delta, epsilon and gamma Sagittarii)
Albalda	(this is the 'desert' without fiducial - see BALDAH)
Sa'd-Aldahbih	(alpha and beta Capricorni)
Sa'd-Bula	(mu, nu and epsilon Aquarii)
Sa'd Alsu'ud	(beta Aquarii)
Sa'd-Al'akhibiya	(gamma, zeta, pi, and eta Aquarii)
Alfargh Al'awwal	(alpha and beta Pegasi)
Alfargh Althani	(gamma Pegasi and alpha Andromedae)
Batn-Alhut	(beta Andromedae)

LUNAR YEAR   A lunar year is a cycle of twelve lunar months, which gives 354 days, some 11 and a quarter days shorter than the SOLAR YEAR.

LUNAR ZODIAC   It is clear from such ancient systems as the LUNAR MANSIONS that there was once a widely used system of fiducials of a constellational nature linked with the Moon. All the surviving lunar mansions have now been codified into arcs of equal extent, yet surviving traditions, and one or two interesting mediaeval terminologies, indicate that the equivalent of a lunar sidereal zodiac did exist in early times. In the schema set out in figure 49, derived from information furnished mainly by Nowotny in regard to

mediaeval star lists, it will be seen that the 28 divisions are marked by
fiducials presenting unequal divsions. Several of the names indicate
specific stars as fiducials, while one (the 'Desertum' of 21) relates to an
empty space between fiducials. Again, certain fiducials appear to have been
determined by orientation lines imagined between two stars (presumably
capable of projection), thus to allow for variations in the lunar path (take
for example the line between 'Porrima' and 'Vindemiatrix' of 13). It is
possible that the sigils derived from Agrippa for a sidereal zodiac are
probably ultimately from a tradition of a lunar zodiac, though neither sigils
nor zodiac appear to have survived into late mediaeval astrology. The
application of the lunar sidereal zodiac to astrology is not attested, save
in the codifications of the lunar mansions (much used in "Horary Astrology").
The names given in table 49 are linked with the numbers (given in the table
under 'REF' for 'reference') in the corresponding asterisms of figure 41. For
further information on these these 'mansions' or 'lunar asterisms', see the
individual entries under the mediaeval names.

FIGURE 41. 'LUNAR ZODIAC' OF UNEQUAL ARCS, CONSTRUCTED FROM A MEDIAEVAL
LIST OF "MANSIONS" (CONSTRUCTED FROM SEVERAL SOURCES - NOMENCLATURE FROM
MEDIAEVAL SOURCES QUOTED BY NOWOTNY).

TABLE 49

REF.	MEDIAEVAL NAME	FIDUCIAL
1.	Cornua arietis	Mesarthim
2.	Venter arietis	Delta or epsilon of Aries
3.	Caput tauri	Pleiades
4.	Cor tauri	Aldebaran
5.	Caput canis validi	Lambda of Orion
6.	Sidus parvum lucis magnae	Alhenna
7.	Bracchium	Between Castor and Pollux
8.	Nebulosa	Praesepe - but see NEBULOSA
9.	Oculus leonis	Alterf
10.	Frons leonis	Regulus
11.	Capillus leonis	Zosma
12.	Cauda leonis	Denebola
13.	Canis	Vindemiatrix

--TABLE 49 (CONTINUED)

REF.	MEDIAEVAL NAME	FIDUCIAL
14.	Spica	Spica
15.	Cooperta	Chi to phi of Virgo
16.	Cornua scorpionis	Zubenelgenubi to Zubenelschemali
17.	Corona super caput	Akrab
18.	Cor scorpionis	Antares
19.	Cauda scorpionis	Shaula
20.	Trabs	Between delta Scorpius & phi Sagittarius
21.	Desertum	See DESERTUM
22.	Pastor et aries	Giedi
23.	Glutiens	Between epsilon & gamma of Aquarius
24.	Sidus fortunae	Sadalsud
25.	Papilio	Mu to gamma of Aquarius
26.	Hauriens primus	Between Sheat and Markab
27.	Hauriens secundus	Between Sirrah and Algenib
29.	Piscis	Between Mirach & phi of Pisces

LUNATICUS   An ancient term used of a human being suffering from certain
forms of insanity associated with the influence of the Moon. Paracelsus
appears to have used the word alongside 'Saturninus' (i.e. 'under the
influence of Saturn') for people whose strong brain activity stifled the life
of soul, creating thereby a permanent duality, resulting in a rigidity of
outlook and unpleasant psychic characteristics. The term lunaticus is
therefore used by Paracelsus because it is the lunar part of the human being
(the soul life) which is being oppressed by the rigidity and fixity of
Saturn.

LUNATION   Term applied generally in reference to a New Moon, specifically to
the exact conjunction of the Moon with the Sun. It is also sometimes used as
an equivalent term for the SYNODIC MONTH, which is really a lunation period.

LUNATION PERIOD   See SYNODIC MONTH.

LUNE   The portion of the surface of a sphere contained within two great
semi-circles of the celestial sphere. Also, the French word for 'Moon'.

LUXURIOUS SIGN   Aries is said to be a 'luxurious sign' because of its
temperamental disposition towards luxury. The classification is misleading,
however, as all the fire signs are given to luxury, Leo far more than Aries.

MA'AT   See WEGA.

MACHON   One of the cabbalistic names for the "Fifth Heaven".

MACRO-ANTHROPOS   See THREE PROTOTYPES.

MACROCOSM   Term derived from a Greek compound meaning 'great arrangement',
and applied to the ordered systems of the celestial realms, bodies, spheres
and the related levels of consciousness. The macrocosm is sometimes called
the Kosmos (in contrast with "Cosmos") in occult circles. Any complete
entity which contains within it the working of all the laws within its
ambient macrocosm is called a 'Microcosm' or 'little world'. Man is himself
such a microcosm, and is indeed said to be the archetypal microcosm. The
study of the relationship which holds between the microcosm and macrocosm

===

forms the basis of astrology. Occultists divide the Macrocosm into three
parts. There is the 'Empyrean', which corresponds in the Microcosm to the
intellectual part of man (usually termed 'ratio', reason), located in the
head: the 'Aethereum', which corresponds to the vital faculties, located in
the heart: and the 'Elementorum', or the natural faculties, located in the
human stomach. These correspond in the astro-alchemical systems with Salt,
Mercury and Sulphur, respectively. In the astrological cosmoconception,
these correspond sequentially to the realm of the fixed stars, the planetary
spheres, and the sphere of Earth. Within the esoteric tradition, man is a
microcosm only while living in a physical body. Before birth, and after
death, he is integrated into the Macrocosm.

MACROCOSMIC CHART   A term derived in modern astrological circles to denote
the standard configuration of the schematic heavens with Aries on the
Ascendant, Taurus on the cusp of the 2nd house, and so on, without particular
reference to space or time: it is the 'ideal chart', the 'schematic chart'.
Every geocentric chart - be it natal, horary, progressed or otherwise - is
really a variation, set in space and time, of the macrocosmic chart.

MAGELLAN'S CLOUDS   See NUBECULAE MAGELLANI.

MAGHA   The 8th of the Hindu NAKSHATRAS, 'The Mighty One'. The same Sanskrit
term is used for the constellation Leo - but see also SIMHA.

MAGI   A term sometimes used as meaning 'astrologers' - but see MAGIAN.

MAGIAN   A name given to certain ancient priests connected with the worship
of a fire-god, in Assyrian, Babylonian and Persian cults. Blavatsky links
them with the Sanskrit term 'Maga', which is used of 'priests of the Sun',
mentioned in the 'Vishnu Purana'. The same Sanskrit root has given us such
words as 'magic', 'magician', 'image', 'imagination', and so on. Since the
"Wise Men' who sought out Jesus by means of the so-called "Star of Bethlehem"
have been called 'Magians' it is clear that they were more than mere
astrologers (see MAGI): they were initiates.

MAGIAN STAR   See STAR OF BETHLEHEM.

MAGICAL CALENDARS   See CALENDARIA MAGICA.

MAGICAL STONES   See BIRTH STONES.

Tabula Saturni in abaco.

Saturni.

FIGURE 42.   THE MAGIC SQUARE FOR SATURN, AND DERIVED SIGIL (AFTER AGRIPPA)

MAGIC SQUARE   Name given to an amuletic device used in the mediaeval magical
tradition, and linked with the series of numbers ascribed to the planets, or
to the spiritual rulers of the planets. Figure 42 is the traditional magical
square of Saturn: in each case, the lines add up to 15, which is the number
of Saturn. A particular relevance to astrology is that the series of sigils
associated with the planets (the so-called 'signacula' or 'characteres') the
intelligencies and the daemons of the planets, were derived from a graphic
overlay of these magic squares. In the example of Saturn (figure 42), three

==

separate lines are traced between the 9 figures in the sequence 123 46 and 987: the triple-lined figure (sigil) which results is associated with the planet Saturn. Each of the traditional planets was accorded such a magical square, with a corresponding "Intelligency" and "Daemon", each ascribed traditional numbers which were derived from the linear additions of the magic squares (and multiples thereof). These numerical values are listed under the names of the relevant spirits - see therefore: (Intelligencies) AGIEL, GRAPHIEL, HAGIEL, IOPHIEL, LUNAR INTELLIGENCY, NACHIEL and TIRIEL: (Daemons) BARZABEL, HASMODAI, HISMAEL, KEDEMEL, SORATH, TAPHTHARTHARATH and ZAZEL.

MAGNETIC ASCENDANT   See VERTEX.

MAGNETIC SIGNS   Scorpio is said to be the 'magnetic sign', though sometimes the negative signs in general are termed 'magnetic'. Cornell, however, rightly associates the term with the HORAS of the negative signs, the so-called 'magnetic' or 'magneto-electrical' horas, which are 'half-signs'.

MAGNETIC WORKBOARD   Name given to a magnetized drawing surface designed to facilitate the study of the Ebertin COSMOGRAM: the workboard includes calculation discs, plastic dials, and the so-called 'graphic 45 degree ephemeris', intended to facilitate the reading of annual configurations.

MAGNITUDE   See STELLAR MAGNITUDE.

MAGUS   A term sometimes used as meaning 'astrologer' - but see MAGIAN.

MAIA   See PLEIADES.

MAJOR ASPECTS   A term used of the group of ASPECTS given by Ptolemy - the "Conjunction", "Sextile", "Square", "Trine" and "Opposition". The MINOR ASPECTS are derived mathematically from these. A third important group, more recently derived by Kepler, are the QUINTILES.

MAJOR CONFIGURATION   A modern term used to denote a number of important aspectal patterns, which include the GRAND CROSS, the GRAND TRINE, the MYSTIC TRINE, the MYSTIC RECTANGLE, the Double BIQUINTILE, the Double QUINCUNX and the T-SQUARE. These configurations are said to focus energies in a particularly powerful way.

MAJOR PLANETS   These are Mars, Jupiter and Saturn, though some authorities include only the last two, and designate the three as "Superior Planets".

MAKARAM   The Sanskrit name for zodiacal Capricorn (though the word actually means 'crocodile': see also ASHADHA. 'Makara' is a frequent alternative in western astrological texts.

MALEFIC ASPECTS   Certain "Aspects" are said to be harmful or 'malefic' to the native. Especially so are the "Square" and "Semi-Square". These are contrasted with the 'benefics', which contribute to the harmonious working between planets. However, it is widely recognised that the malefic aspects may well create tensions (through the planets involved) yet in so doing may present a challenge to the native who, by efforts and wholesome exercise of will, may resolve the tensions, and so concentrate the energies as to render them creative forces. The ancient term is therefore quite reasonably regarded by many modern astrologers as misleading.

MALTWOOD ZODIAC   See GLASTONBURY ZODIAC

MANGER   See PRAESAEPE.

MANILIUS MEASURE   See MINOR MEASURE.

MANILIUS PLACES   See TWELVE PLACES.

MANSIONS   See LUNAR MANSIONS.

MANTLE   See COSMOPSYCHOGRAM.

MANU   See PLANETARY CHAIN LOGOS.

MANUBRIUM   A cluster of stars, often designated as the omicron of
Sagittarius, set in the face of the archer. It is said to cause blindness,
and is associated with fire and explosions.

MANZILS   The Arabian term for the LUNAR MANSIONS, from which the European
word 'mansions' appears to have been derived. The 28 asterisms of the
manzils are recorded (in the nomenclature preserved by Robson) for each of
the 12 degree 51 minute arcs, under "Lunar Mansions" - though see also LUNAR
STATIONS and LUNAR ZODIAC.

MAP   Usually, 'map of the heavens', another word for the "Horoscope" in its
modern sense. See therefore CHART.

MARCH   Named after the god Mars (the initiator) in the GREGORIAN CALENDAR,
with 31 days. Following ancient patterns, the year began in England on 25th
March (the Feast of the Annunciation) well into the 18th century - but see
"Gregorian Calendar". Esoterically, Mars and March are linked with
beginnings, and with the descent of the soul into matter. It might therefore
be said that March pierces into the opening of APRIL, that the 'Spiritus
Mundi' might delve more deeply into the 'maya' of MAY.

MARDUK   One of the Chaldean names for the planet Jupiter.

MARKAB   Fixed star, the alpha of "Pegasus", now in the wing of the flying
horse, though the Arabian name originally meant 'saddle'. Ptolemy ascribes
to it the nature of Mercury conjunct Mars, and it is said to portend danger
from cuts, stabs and fevers: it is one of those many Arabian stars which
threaten a violent death.

MARKEB   Fixed star, the kappa of "Argo", set in the buckler of the ship, and
of the same Arabian derivation as "Markab", with which it is often confused.
It is said to bring profitable journeys, and through its traditional link
with Jupiter and Saturn it brings breadth of knowledge and educational work.

MARRIAGE POINT   The 'point of Marriage' is the name given to one of the
so-called Arabian PARS. If the degree of Venus in a natal chart is taken to
the Ascendant, then the cusp of the Seventh House is said to mark the point.

MARS   The planet in orbit between the Sun and Jupiter, the planet which more
clearly resembles the Earth in regard to physical factors than any of the
other planets - though it has a diameter just over half that of the Earth.
Mars has two satellites, Phobos and Deimos. In modern astrology Mars is the
ruler of zodiacal Aries (but see also NEGATIVE MARS), with its detriment in
Libra. Some astrologers say tht it is exalted in Capricorn, with its
corresponding fall in Cancer. Mars represents the physical side of the
native's life, and is an index of his energy, endurance, and so on - of his
ability to carry projects through, and of the active side of his temperament.
Mars is directly linked with the sex drive, in which it co-operates with the
planet Venus, the former being active, the latter passive. When Mars is well
emphasized in a chart, the native is courageous, enterprising, confident,
active and proud - in particular the planet bestows great energy, with an
ability to construct or destroy, and consequent on this latter urge there is
often a general lack of refinement in the manifestation of the sign in which
it is posited. A badly placed Mars, or one badly aspected, tends towards
disruption and explosions: the native is rough, reckless, destructive and
self-centred. The sigil for Mars ♂ is said to represent the cross of
matter (the four-fold elemental life) weighing down the circle of spirit. It

is in effect the reverse of Venus in its graphic origin. Traditionally Mars has dominion over the private parts in the human being, and as it is essentially the male planet, it has particular rule over the penis - though its action is also clearly connected with the adrenals (see PLANETRY MELOTHESIA). The planet is a useful index of how quickly the physical energies may be called into play as a result of disturbances on the physical or astral plane. The Martian type usually finds expression on the physical plane through activities demanding the exertion of physical energy, and especially in connexion with activities which give rapid results. All forms of physical and manual labour fall under the rule of Mars, so that at one end of the spectrum there is building and construction work, at the other end, surgery, driving and athletics. All work involving the use of iron and steel, sharp tools and weapons of war are connected with Mars, so that military establishments, slaughterhouses, waste-disposal units, mortuaries, and so on are under its dominion. The colours of Mars are the reds, especially the more 'violent' scarlets and carmines.

MASCULINE   See SECTA.

MASCULINE DEGREES   A term applied to certain zodiacal degrees. It is said that should such a degree mark the Ascendant of a female chart, then she will have a masculine appearance. The list furnished by Cornell is:

AR	8	15	30		LE	5	15	30		SG	2	12	30
TA	11	21	30		VG	12	30			CP	11	30	
GE	16	26			LB	5	20	30		AQ	5	21	27
CN	2	10	23	30	SC	4	17	30		PI	10	23	30

MASCULINE PLANETS   With the exception of the "Luminaries", each of the planets is regarded in traditional astrology as being possessed of masculine/feminine or positive/negative polarities, which were probably derived from the PLANETARY RULERSHIP described by Ptolemy. For relevant information, see also the entry under FEMININE PLANETS. Quite a different tradition, connected with the old tradition of PRINCIPLES, has emerged from the Ptolemaic tradition - this maintains that certain planets are (by their own intrinsic nature) masculine: these are the Sun and the three superior planets Mars, Jupiter and Saturn. Ptolemy is reporting rules which were already ancient in his day when he says that these planets are masculine, that Mercury is 'common to both genders', while the Moon and Venus are feminine. He mixes (even confuses) a further strain of planetary sexuality from a different stream of astrology however, when he lists a number of rules relating to variable sexuality. Matutine planets are 'masculine', while vespertine planets are 'feminine': oriental planets are 'masculine', occidental planets 'feminine'. Cardan insists that any planet within the six-sign arc of the Sun (following the zodiacal order) are feminine, while all the rest are masculine. Wilson, after noting how complex the theory of planetary sexuality had become by his day, observes 'Modern astrologers, too, with their usual sagacity, have rendered the confusion more confused.' In modern astrology, which is fortunately something different from that known to Wilson, the sexuality of planets has retained its complexity and importance mainly in regard to "Horary Astrology" - otherwise, it is generally recognized as reasonable to treat planetary genders in terms of the gods and goddesses associated with the planets and spheres in classical terms - an exception might well be Neptune, which is really a 'feminine' influence.

MASCULINE SIGNS   In the traditional schema, the signs in alternate order, starting with Aries, and ending with Aquarius, are 'masculine'. See SECTA.

MATERNAL TRINITY   A term used by Butler in his "Solar Biology" in respect of the zodiacal signs Cancer, Leo and Virgo: the ancient 'Summer Signs'.

MATHEMATICIANS   Sometimes 'Mathematicals', a term used as synonymous with 'astrologers' in early treatises. Without doubt the word is derived from

==

the early association between mathematics and astrological practices: the "Quadripartium" of Ptolemy was in Greek the 'Mathematices Tetrabiblon', the 'Four Books of Mathematics'. By the 18th century, however, the term was often used in a pejorative sense.

MATHESEOS   The term is usually a reference to the books on astrological lore by Julius Firmicus Maternus, an astrologer who lived in the early part of the 4th century AD. The title of a good edition is given under Maternus in the bibliography, though the short title is 'Matheseos libri VIII'. The text, often described as relating to 'Roman' astrology, is actually based on a confusing series of astrological streams, partly dependent on DOROTHEAN ASTROLOGY, upon the hermetic literature associated with such sources as the so-called "Nechepso", and upon Neoplatonic sources.

MATHESIS UNIVERSALIS   A term used by the historian Haase in connexion with his study of "Keplerian Harmonics", denoting an attitude of mind expressed in the hope that 'with the help of mathematics everything could be grasped and explained'. Mathesis Universalis is concerned with a clear scientific picture or proof, and is literally materialistic in that it is quantitative, and while allowing us to 'grasp only one aspect of the world' (as Haase puts it) 'gives the erroneous impression that this picture is complete.' Haase comes to the conclusion that the great Kepler uses the methods of Mathesis Universalis to describe what the contrasting PANSOPHIA means.

MATURE QUADRANT   See QUADRANTS.

MATUTINE   Literally 'pertaining to the morning', and used sometimes of planets which are above the horizon with the rising of the Sun, at other times of planets which arise with the Sun.

MATUTINE CULMINATION   Term used by Ptolemy for one of his VISIBLE ASPECTS.

MATUTINE SETTING   Term used by Ptolemy for one of his VISIBLE ASPECTS.

MATUTINE SUBSOLAR   Term used by Ptolemy for one of his VISIBLE ASPECTS.

MAXIMA   A term for the "Grand Climactic" of 800 years: see CHRONOCRATORS.

MAXIMUM ALTITUDE   See CULMINATION.

MAY   The fifth month of the GREGORIAN CALENDAR, with a length of 31 days, named, as it is often claimed, after Maia, the daughter of Atlas and Pleione, and hence one of the sisters of the PLEIADES, which constellation rose in May. Maia was identified with her namesake 'Rhea-Cyubele', the 'Maia-Majestas', the fruitful mother, and is therefore linked with the fecundity of the Earth in this month - but, for an esoteric sequence, see MARCH. Esoterically one cannot ignore the ancient Sanskrit root 'maya', popularly translated as meaning 'illusion', though ultimately connected with the image-making faculty of humanity ('maya', 'magic','image' and 'imagination' are semantically connected). It is probably this connexion which explains the popular imagery of the Roman calendar (see for example Foucher, who deals with the Thrysdus calendrical mosaic, itself indicative of esoteric astrological nuances) which singles out the creative god Mercury, patron of the arts, to whom the 15th day of the month was sacred. For early Roman calendar, in which May was the third month, see JULIAN CALENDAR.

MAYAN ASTROLOGY   Virtually nothing is known about Mayan Astrology, though, as Volguine points out, many of the pre-Columbian buildings were 'astrological' in design - for example, the famous seven-terraced pyramid of Chicken-Itza, orientated to the cardinal points, with the step symbolism of 365, corresponds to the year. What we do know of the Mayan system suggests an extraordinary grasp of cycles, and numerical symbolism. Among the cycles was the 13-day periodicty, said to form a sign: 20 such signs gave a cycle of 260 days, called a 'Tonalamatl'. There is also a 20-day periodicity, designated in the calendar by symbols from the natural world - animals, reptiles, wind, rain, etc (see table below). Eighteen of these periods (to which were added 5 or 6 'vacant' days, 'days without a name' called 'Xma-Kaba-Kin') formed a solar year. There was a cycle of 20 solar years, or 7200 days: see also KATUNE. Volguine, apparently basing his information on Gentry, insists that the system of Secondary Directions (on a "Day for a Year" symbolism) was practised in pre-Columbian America: however, the evidence is more than dubious. There is recorded a 'Venusian Year' - the synodic period of Venus, the mean duration of her four phases - of 584 days (several names were given to this planet, including Noh-Eh, 'big star', Chac Eh, 'red star' Zaztal Eh, 'brilliant star', and so on). The Mayan manuscript in Dresden records 5 such Venus revolutions. Linked with the Venusian year is a cycle of 8 solar years (5 Venusians). Another cycle is that of 13 Venusian years. Another cycle, of 18 solar years, linked with symbols significantly close to those used for similar cycles in China. In the year-counts were several long periodicities, including 394 years, 600 years and 7,616 years. Acosta gives the following translations for the names of the zodiac:

AR Splendour of the Lamb	TA Powerful, Brilliant, Inflamed Male
GE United Stars	CN Sleeping Snake
LE Return of the Lance of the Lion	VG Divine Mother
LB Ladder	SC ?
SG ?	CP Ardent Goat or Horned One
AQ Epoch of the Waters	PI ?

The Mexican Tonalamatl, the 'Book of Days' (a sequence of 260 days), in conjunction with the the solar year, is the foundation for the calendar. The Tonalamatl is reckoned in terms of 20 distinct periods, each with symbols and hieroglyphics: The names of the days are recorded by Hastings in table 50 (for the Mayan) and Volguine, supposedly for the 'Mexican', though there is a strong Toltec element in the list.

TABLE 50

	MAYAN DAY	(HASTINGS)	(VOLGUINE)	20-DAY CYCLE	
1.	Imix	Female Breast (?)	Crocodile	Pop	Mat
2.	Ik	Wind	Jaguar	Uo	Frog
3.	Akbal	Night	Stag	Zip	Error
4.	Kan	Copious (?)	Flower	Zo'tz	Bat
5.	Chicchan	Biting Snake	Reed	Tzec	Scorpion
6.	Cimi	Death	Death	Xul	End
7.	Manik	That which hurries	Rain	Yaxkin	Renewal
8.	Lamat	?	Liana Creeper	Mol	Assemble
9.	Muluc	That heaped	Serpent	Ch'en	Alone
10.	Oc	?	Flint	Yax	Fresh
11.	Chuen	Monkey	Monkey	Zac	White
12.	Eb	Row of teeth	Lizard	Ceh	Slave
13.	Been	Worn out	Movement	Mac	Obstruct
14.	Ix	?	Dog	Mankin	Sun (?)
15.	Men	Maker	House	Muan	Bird
16.	Cib	Perfumery	Vulture	Pax	Drum
17.	Caban	That exuded (?)	Water	Kayab	Song
18.	E'tznab	Hard (?)	Wind	Cumku	Explosion
19.	Cauac	Storm	Eagle		
20.	Ahau	King, Sun	Rabbit		

MEAN MOTION   The averaged motion of a body during an orbit, based on the accepted fiction that the planet will move at a uniform rate around the Sun - the truth being rather that the motion varies in relation to the ratio of its distance from the centre. The mean daily motions, of value mainly in respect

===

to rough-and-ready progressional work, are set out in table 51.

```
--------------------------------------------------------------------TABLE 51
PLANET  DEG.Min.SEC.      PLANET  DEG.Min.SEC.      PLANET  DEG.Min.SEC.
===============================================================================
MO      13  10  35        ME       4   6   0        VE       1  36   0
MA       0  31   0        JU       0   4  59        SA       0   2   1
NE       0   0  24        UR       0   0  42        PL       0   0  14
-------------------------------------------------------------------------
```

MEAN PRECESSION   A cycle of 25,694.8 years - see however PRECESSION.

MEAN SOLAR DAY   The standard measurement of the so-called 'clock time', derived from the average of the annual series of the "True Solar Day" sequences - see TIME.

MEAN SOLAR TIME   See TIME.

MEAN TIME   A term applied to the method of converting the theoretical "Mean Motion" of the Earth into intervals of equal and regular duration - see TIME.

MEASURE OF NAIBOD   An arc used in connexion with "Symbolic Directions", based on the 'mean daily solar increment arc', which is given as 59 degrees and 8 minutes, named after the German astrologer Valentine Naibod, one of the greatest 16th century authorities on Arabic astrology.

MEASURE OF TIME   A technical term relating to the system of measuring the time of an event by conversion to arc of direction applied to particular charts. Several different systems are used: the astrologer Naibod suggests that the arc of right ascension should be converted into 1 year, 5 days and 8 hours for each degree. The Ptolemaic 'Day for a Year' system is a measure of time in which one degree is symbolically equated with a year of time: this progressional conversion is widely used in modern times.   The method recommended by Placidus de Tito involves adding the right ascension of the natal Sun to the arc of direction, thus converting to right ascension, and allowing the standard progressional technique of a "Day for a Year".

MEDIA   A term used for the 200-year cycle of the CHRONOCRATORS.

MEDICAL ASTROLOGY   The branch of astrology which deals with the study and application of particular rules of casting and interpreting in regard to questions of health. In the past it was common for astrologers and doctors to combine natal astrology and "Horary Astrology" towards this end, though there is a whole corpus of tradition attached specifically to the interpretation of purely medical considerations of a chart. The modern realm is partly represented by the Viennese Feerhov, who worked especially with astro-medical concepts linked with the alchemical allocation of human types, and the American astrologer Cornell, who, having found the astrological tradition both sparse and wanting, made a thorough record of astrological cases, which he subsequently published in encyclopaedic form. Much work has been done by Carey and Perry in relating the twelve biochemic remedies, the so-called 'Salts of Salvation' to the zodiacal signs and their physio-chemical allocations: see TWELVE CELL-SALTS. Most of the major modern astrological systems have their sub-divisions relating to medical astrology, ranging from the fixed-diagnosis system of Wemyss to the (unsystematized) link between astrology and homoeopathy of Steiner.

MEDIUM COELI   A term from the Latin meaning 'middle of the skies', the equivalent term for Midheaven, sometimes confused with the Tenth House cusp.

MEDUSA'S HEAD   See ALGOL.

MEENAM   The Sanskrit name for zodiacal Pisces - but see BHADZAPADA.

MEGREZ   One of the seven 'fixed stars' forming the constellation of "Ursa Major", said by Ptolemy to be of the influence equivalent to that of Mars.

MEIER FIGURINES   See FIGURINES.

MELANCHOLIC   One of the four TEMPERAMENTS, derived from an excess of Earth element in the psychological make-up of the personality. The melancholic temperament is conservative, withdrawn and quite stable, and is associated with the following keywords: practical, reliable, delighting in the physical and in the rhythmic, possessive, conservative, reserved, utilitarian, steadfast and hostile to novelty. Faults in the temperament (extreme melancholia) arise from a lack of fluidity, and excessive concern with materiality and self - under these conditions the type becomes commonplace, egotistical, narrow, unadventurous and miserly. See also HUMOURS.

MELANCHOLIC QUADRANT   See QUADRANTS.

MELANCHOLIC SIGNS   Term used of the "Earth Triplicity".

MELODIA   Name given to one of the "Ethereal Planets", perceived clairvoyantly by the astrologer Harris, and said to have a circumference of 50.000 miles. it is very likely that this Melodia is the same as the OV described by Charubel, which has a solar revolution of 297 years. Melodia was said to be in 18 degrees Aquarius in November 1905, which should locate it in the 1980s in the last decan of Taurus. The historic importance of Melodia from an astrological point of view is that it has been claimed to be the planet which rules the destiny of the United States of America. It has been accorded rule over Taurus (of which it is the day ruler) and Sagittarius (of which it is the night ruler), and is said to have an beneficial nature.

ARIES	Head
TAURUS	Throat
GEMINI	Arms
CANCER	Rib Cage
LEO	Heart
VIRGO	Stomach
LIBRA	Pelvis
SCORPIO	Private Parts
SAGITTARIUS	Thighs
CAPRICORN	Knee
AQUARIUS	Lower Leg
PISCES	Feet

FIGURE 43. MELOTHESIC MAN (FROM A 15TH CENTURY 'SHEPHERD'S CALENDAR'.

MELOTHESIC MAN   Term derived from the Ptolemaic astrological system for the 'zodiacal man', that image of man linked with the twelve zodiacal signs. The earliest melothesic descriptions go back to the first records of astrology, but the earliest melothesic image did not emerge in Europe until about the 12th century. Ptolemy was merely reporting an old tradition when he linked the planets and the signs to the human frame (see PLANETARY MELOTHESIA), and

it is likely that West and Toonder are not being too imaginative in showing
an ancient melothesia in early Egyptian architectural zodiacal images. The
traditional associations visualize zodiacal man as a straightened circle,
with the zodiacal sequence running from head to foot, as in figure 43. The
traditional sequence gives AR over the head (mentation): TA over the throat
(larynx and speech): GE over the 'dualities' of arms and shoulders
(externally) and the lungs (internally), and the process of breathing: CN
over the breasts and rib-cage (the 'protection' of the heart: LE over the
heart itself, seen as the centre of the emotional life: VG over the stomach
and womb (processes of elimination): LB over the small of the back and the
kidneys: SC over the sexual organs (the generative and regenerative organs,
as they are termed esoterically): SG over the hips and thighs, the liver and
the entire hepatic system: CP over the skeletal frame, and the knee in
particular, as well as the skin (which holds the frame in place, so to
speak): AQ over the shin and ankle, and (internally) over the circulatory
system: PI over the feet and the lymphatic system.   There are many modern
adaptations of these melothesic associations, and the bodily parts and
functions have been extended to include rulership over the endocrine glands
by Collin, as well as the so-called tissue salts (see TWELVE CELL-SALTS).
Steiner offers a melothesic image which links man with the esoteric view of
the tripartite union of Spirit, Soul and Body, in a series of septenaries.
The 'Spiritual' of man (the 'Thinking' of table 52), discriminating ego,
includes the head and arms: the 'Soul' life (the 'Feeling' of table 52)
reflects the emotional working of man (what Steiner elsewhere calls the
'middle man', and includes a recapitulation of the head down to the thighs:
the 'Body' life, (the 'Willing' of table 52) is expressed in a septenary
which rules the lower limbs, the moving parts of man, centred on the
power-centre of the will life, which is (esoterically) linked with the sexual
centre. The three-fold schema of septenaries is set out in table 52. This
twelve-fold system, when linked with the triadic image of man as a thinking,
feeling and willing being, is an esoteric extension of the traditional
melothesia. See also BIOLOGICAL CORRESPONDENCES and PLANETARY MELOTHESIA.

```
                                                              TABLE 52
-----------------------------------------------------------------------
  SIGN THINKING          SIGN FEELING             WILLING
=======================================================================
  AR   Upright position
  TA   Direction forwards
  GE   Symmetry              Head and feet
                        CN   Breast enclosure
                        LE   Interior - heart
                        VG   Second interior      Kidneys, solarplexus
                        LB   Balance              Balance
                        SC   Reproduction         Reproduction
  SG   Upper arm            Thigh                Thigh
  CP   Elbow                                     Knee
  AQ   Lower arm                                 Leg
  PI   hands                                     Feet
-----------------------------------------------------------------------
```

MENKALINA   Fixed star, the beta of "Auriga", set in the right shoulder of
the figure (the Arabian term 'Al Mankib' means 'the shoulder'). It is said
to bring disgrace and danger of a violent death.

MENKAR   Fixed star, the alpha of "Cetus", set in the jaws of the monster
(the Arabic 'Al Minhar' means however 'the nose'). Ptolemy says that it is
of the nature of Saturn, and it is supposed to bring disease and ruin.

MENKIB   See SCHEAT.

MENSA   Constellation formed by La Caille in 1752, originally as 'Mons
Mensae' (Table Mountain), after the African namesake - though later called
simply 'Table'. It is said to give an ambitious nature - early difficulties

in life are overcome with the passage of time.

MERCURIUS   A name given by Thierens to a future development of his own "Hermes" as Mercury-Vulcan (see however VULCAN PERIOD). It is said to be a principle of transmission. The traditional Mercury is sometimes called Mercurius in late mediaeval texts, especially in astro-alchemical contexts, in which planetary virtues and metals were rarely distinguished.

MERCURY   The planet in orbit nearest to the Sun - though in the traditional astrology founded on the pre-Copernican models (see for example PTOLEMAIC SYSTEM) it was thought to be in orbit between the Moon and Venus, and is often so depicted in diagrams of the spheres. It is the smallest of the planets, with a diameter of less than half that of the Earth. It has rule over Gemini and Virgo, with corresponding detriments in Sagittarius and Pisces. Some astrologers say that it is exalted in Aquarius, with its fall in Leo. Mercury represents the ability of the native to communicate with others: in traditional astrology, it ruled human speech. Mercury is also an index of mentality, though it is concerned with the details, with short-term reactions, with memory and with day-to-day problems, rather than with profound metaphysical thought, which is really the domain of Jupiter. When Mercury is emphasized in a chart, it is usually an indication of a quickness of mind and expression, as well as of an alert attention: the subject will be fluent in thought and talk, though probably also of a changeable disposition. A badly placed Mercury, or one badly aspected, tends towards exaggeration of speech - in lying, sarcasm or excessive volubility. The sigil for Mercury ☿ has been interpreted in many different ways, but most astrologers see in it a union of the three forms of crescent, circle and cross, as representative of the ability of Mercury to bring things together and to unify: this is the exoteric level of looking at the esoteric tradition connected with the planet in astro-alchemical circles - see ALCHEMICAL MERCURY. Traditionally, Mercury rules the hands and arms of the human body, as well as the lungs: it is linked also by some modern astrologers with the thyroid gland - but see PLANETARY MELOTHESIA. Mercury is a useful index of how the nervous energies will flow and manifest, and it is also probable that the planet has rule over perception. The Mercurial type usually finds expression on the physical plane in work requiring rapid communications, writing, or as a middle-man, salesman, and so on. He likes to exercise his wits, or even craftiness, and enjoys the manipulating of slower types, even though they often infuriate him: he often has an imitative faculty. There is usually a wish to use verbal expressions, through speech, or through literature - for this reason the type is frequently involved with journalism, publishing, travel agencies, teaching, and so on. He is at his best when dealing with other people in a manipulative or helpful way - especially in situations where financial transactions take place. Mercury is associated with mixtures of colours - with tartans, polka dots, harlequins, and so on: the true Mercurian will wear a coat of many colours, and is not especially tasteful in his choice of colours, even though he may dress fashionably. The underlying urge of Mercury is to take, rather than to give, and so the planet often assumes (chameleon-like) the influences of those planets with which he is most clearly and strongly related in a particular chart - so, incidentally, it is with the Mercurian personality, which is sensitive to environment, and will tend to pick up and imitate 'influences' from those around.

MERIDIAN   The meridian circle is that which passes through the zenith, the celestial poles, and the north and south points of the horizon.

MERIDIAN TIME   See TIME.

MERIDIANAL CULMINATION   Term used by Ptolemy for one of his VISIBLE ASPECTS.

MERIDIANAL QUADRANT   See QUADRANTS.

===

MERIDIANAL SETTING   Term used by Ptolemy for one of his VISIBLE ASPECTS.

MERIDIANAL SUBSOLAR   Term used by Ptolemy for one of his VISIBLE ASPECTS.

MERIDIAN DISTANCE   A measurement of distance between any point on the celestial equator and the nadir.

MERIDIONAL   Sometimes used as an equivalent term for 'southern'.

MEROPE   See PLEIADES.

MESARTHIM   Fixed star (double), the gamma of Aries, and sometimes called 'the first star of Aries' (and hence the 'first star' in the constellational zodiac). The origin of the name appears to have been lost. See SHARATAN.

MESHAM   The Sanskrit name for zodiacal Aries - but see also ACVINI.

METEORS   A meteor, or 'falling star', was in popular lore regarded as a sign of death, though according to Neoplatonic lore, it was a sign of conception (see however PERSONAL STAR). Eusebius of Alexandria records both beliefs. However, the fact that millions of 'shooting stars' fall to earth each day (30 million a day, so it is said, and these only such as may be seen by the human eye) means that such phenomena cannot be usefully integrated into chart interpretation. In spite of this, attempts have been made to relate the periodic meteor swarms, such as the Aquarids (end of July, in Aquarius) and the Taurids (20th November, from near Aldebaran), with genethliacal astrology. The fact that such swarms appear to radiate from a single point in the heavens is actually a sign that the earth is passing over the point at which its own orbit intersects that of the meteors (which are like the Earth itself in orbit around the Sun), yet this origin-point has been used by some astrologers as the basis for interpretation.

METEOROLOGICAL ASTROLOGY   See ASTRO-METEOROLOGY.

METIS   Name given to one of the Asteroids, discovered in 1848.

METONIC CYCLE   A cycle of 19 years, named after the Athenian astronomer Meton who first formulated its true nature. The cycle marks the return of a cycle of solar eclipses to a specific degree of the zodiac. Distinguish from the SAROS CYCLE, and see also GOLDEN NUMBER.

METONIC RETURN   Term sometimes used of a completion of the "Metonic Cycle".

MICHAEL   The "Archangel" linked with the rule of the Sphere of the Sun, and said by some to be the leader of the Archangels: Trithemius makes him the leader of the "Secundadeian Beings". The name Michael is properly pronounced 'Mikhaiel'. In the esoteric Christian tradition, Michael is the guardian of the newly dead, on whose behalf he will fight the demonic hordes. He is linked in the astrological lore with rule over the element of Fire, and is often depicted with the attributes of a golden sword and a pair of scales (derived from Egyptian symbolism, for the weighing of souls). See also FOURTH HEAVEN. For traditional symbolism, see SIGILS - PLANETARY SPIRITS.

MICRO-ASPECTS   A modern term for aspects within an extreme angle of 7.5 degrees. Within the traditional view the term has no meaning, since aspects were supposed to express elemental relationships - see ELEMENTAL ASPECTS.

MICROCOSM   Term from the Greek meaning 'little word' or 'small arrangment', and usually applied in astrological contexts to man, who is the small arrangement of the cosmos - see MACROCOSM. Technically, any complete entity which contains within it a summary of all the working of the laws within the Macrocosm is a microcosm. In terms of the occult theory of cosmo-genesis, Man is defined as the vehicle which spans the gulf between the highest and lowest manifestations of a particular world system. By such definition, each man is a model of the entire universe, and contains within him (either in developed form, or in potential) each and every manifestation to which the universe may be subject.   For example, in the triadic world of the present age, the solar force represents the creative energies of the highest order, and these find a link with the brain and heart of man.   The lunar and earthly forces, representing the lowest energies working from beneath man (sometimes indeed termed the demonic) find a centre in the sexual sphere - thus man is 'inhabited' by the (solar) angels and by the (telluric) demons, and is the unifier of these two different beings, through which he learns to exercise consciousness and love. This image is preserved in a vast number of ancient images depicting universal or microcosmic man, from the theological image of the Crucified Christ between the Sun and Moon, to the occult images popularized by Fludd: the solar image always represents the angelic nature, and the lunar image the demonic nature. A glance at the microcosmic man described by Fludd will indicate something of the triadic nature of the micro-macrocosm. Man is pictured within the ambient of the Macrocosm, as a three-fold being inhabiting a physical body. The lowest part, the 'Regio Elementaris', is quite mortal, a shade which returns after physical death to the realm of darkness - it is of the matter of Earth, of the four Elements. This is the realm charged with the faculty of perceiving colours, dimensions and materiality - the word 'matter' and the Sanskrit 'maya' (illusion) are cognate.   The highest spirit, the 'Regio Intellectus' is linked with the stars, and presents the clarity of selfhood: it governs the intellectual life of man, being objective in its view, capable of developed wisdom and justice. Connecting these two is the 'spirit of life', the 'Orbis Solis seu Cordis' (the orb of the Sun or of the Heart): the function of this third part is to remain within the true divine light within man, and to resist error: it is linked with the emotional life, detects spiritual similitudes and likenesses, and echoes the realm of the planets. No great difficulty would be required to link this triadic model with the triadic astro-alchemical model of the Paracelsian 'Crude Ilech' (which is really another name for the microcosm. The crude ilech consists of Salt (the thinking part, which is linked in the alchemical model with the lunar forces), Sulphur (the will part of man, linked in the alchemical model with the Mars forces, and with sexuality), and the mediator, Mercury (the emotional part, in the seat of the heart). This triadic relationship between the Microcosm and the ambient Macrocosm is sometimes dispensed with in occult and astrological literature, and a septenary relationship (directed to the planetary forms) is established as an alternative model of man. It is maintained in occult circles that any valid spiritual model of the microcosm (and hence of the macrocosm) must be at once a triad and a septenary. The theory of the nature of the microcosm, in its specific relationship to the Macrocosm, actually constitutes the bulk of modern occult studies, as for example developed by such esotericists as Blavatsky, Steiner and Bailey.

MICROCOSMIC MAN   See PLANETARY MELOTHESIA.

MICROSCOPIUM   Small constellation formed by La Caille in 1752, north of Capricornus. It is said to give a methodical and meticulous nature.

MIDAS   Name given to one of the "Hypothetical Planets", said to be in transplutonian orbit when listed by Jayne.

MIDDLEGROUND   A specialist term used of planets which are near the cusp of the succedent houses, and, by virtue of this placing, less effective than they would be when on the angles themselves. Such planets are said to be in the 'middleground' of the chart. See also BACKGROUND and FOREGROUND.

MIDHEAVEN   The 'Midheaven' is a term properly applied only to the culminating degree of the ecliptic. Sometimes a symbolic stereographic projection of "House Division" results in the cusp of the Tenth House not corresponding with this culminating degree (as for example in the "Modus

Equalis"), so the Tenth House cusp should not be called the Midheaven, as it so often is in popular astrology.   The method for correctly calculating by trigonometry the relationships of the Midheaven to the Ascendant (horoscopos) was known to Ptolemy, though the method was hampered by the prevalent theory of the "Climata".   The Midheaven is often called the 'Medium Coeli' (Latin for 'middle of the heavens'), frequently abbreviated to MC.

MIDHEAVEN AXIS   Term used of the vertical axis which in the horoscope figure corresponds to the axis of the Midheaven and the Imum Coeli.

MIDNIGHT MARK   A term denoting the equivalent time of midnight (Greenwich Time) in regard to the place for which the chart is calculated.

MID-POINTS   A term applied to modern astrological practice by the German astrologer Ebertin (see COSMOBIOLOGY), relating to the supposed significance of the half-sum of two other (usually planetary) factors.   The mid-point is regarded as susceptible to influences by transit or progression by planets and other nodal points - see COSMOGRAM.   Ebertin traces the use of 'half-sums' (as he also terms the mid-points) to a method of rectification used by the 13th century astrologer Bonatus, but there appears to be some misunderstanding of what Bonatus had in mind.   Mid-points were used in Europe prior to the work of such astrologers as Ebertin and Koch, even though modern astrologers often speak of the 'Ebertin mid-point system'.

MIGHTS   See DYNAMIS.

MILKY WAY   See VIA LACTEA.

MIMAS   Name given to one of the moons of Saturn.

MINAM   One of the Sanskrit terms for zodiacal Pisces, as used in Hindu astrology.   Sometimes the term is given in the form Minas.

MINIMIS   One of the terms used to denote the 20-year "Chronocrators" cycle.

MINIMUM ALTITUDE   See CULMINATION.

MINOR ASPECTS   See MAJOR ASPECTS.

MINOR MEASURE   The 'Minor Measure of Manilius' is a system of directing the horoscope figure on the basis of 72 arcs, each house representing a period of 6 years, each quadrant 18 years.   The number 72 was regarded as being of profound esoteric significance (see for example TETRACTYS), for it linked man (through the pulse beat) with the zodiac (through the precessional rate, which retrogrades the vernal point 1 degree in 72 years).   However, the fact is that the astrologer Manilius (contemporaneous with Christ) did not recognize such a rate of precession (then believed to be about 1 degree every century), so that the numerical symbolism is directly linked with the magical theory of early Gnostic speculation.   The system is really a device for projecting a time-grid (one sixth of a house being the equivalent of a year - a sort of 'face for a year' method) to measure the supposed events in terms of time, the natures of the events being revealed by progressed aspects to the radicals.   So far as the dating is concerned, the system is entirely symbolic, and deviates from standard progressional techniques.

MINOS   Name given to one of the "Hypothetical Planets", recorded by the astrologer Jayne (in 1962) as in Aquarius, and claimed to correspond to a planet sighted in 1850.

MINOTAUR   See CENTAURUS.   Sometimes the "Sagittarius Constellation" is called 'Minotaurus'.

MINTAKA   Fixed star (double), the delta of "Orion", set in he belt of the

===

giant (the name from the Arabic 'Al Mintakah' for belt) the first powerful
star visible in the rising portion of this asterism. Depending upon the
planet or nodal point which touches off its influence, the star is said to
bring good fortune, developing the better side of the planet concerned.

MINUTARY HOROSCOPE   A term applied to a horoscope symbolism linked with the
'solar radix method' of progression, based on the symbolic representation of
the sidereal measurement of the Earth's rotation.

MIRA   Fixed star (variable), the omicron of "Cetus", sometimes called the
'Stella Mira' (wonderful star), and in the 16th century the first recorded
example of a variable. It is the 'Collum Ceti' (neck of the whale) which
Ebertin wrongly translates as 'tail of the whale'. He claims that it is of
the nature of Saturn and Jupiter, yet at the same time is is far from
beneficial, for under unhelpful connexions it brings failures, fiascos,
enmity and even suicide.

MIRACH   Fixed star, the beta of "Andromeda", set in the girdle of this
figure, the name probably from the Arabian 'Mi'zar' (girdle), which has given
very many variants, such as 'Mirac', 'Mirax' and (confusingly) 'Mizar':
sometimes it is called the 'Zona Andromedae' or 'Cingulum' in reference to
the belt of Andromeda. It is said to give great physical beauty, a brilliant
mind, and good fortune in marriage: it may indeed be regarded as another
Venus in the skies when emphasized in a chart, though it is particularly
subject to disturbances from malefics.

MIRAK   One of the seven fixed stars forming "Ursa Major", which Ptolemy
equates with the influence of Mars - distinguish from the 'Mirac' of MIRACH.

MIRROR OF HEAVEN   A poetic (and indeed misleading) synonym for CHART.

MITHRAIC BULL   See TAURUS CONSTELLATION.

MITHRAIC ZODIAC   As the cult of Mithras was deeply involved with the
mysteries, little is known for sure about the unique features of the
astrology practiced by its adherents, but many astrological symbols and even
entire zodiacs associated with the cult have survived. A representative
zodiac is that from the Mithraeum on the island of Ponza, studied by
Vermaseren and Beck. It is a stucco ceiling zodiac in three concentric
zones, the outermost of which carries the twelve images presented clockwise
(set in unequal arcs, which may or may not point to a constellational map,
though Beck suggests a connexion with the distinction between 'solar and
nocturnal houses' to account for the variations). In the middle zone is a
snake, which Vermaseren sees as "Draco", but which Beck suggests may be the
'first ancient representation of the eclipsing dragon' (see ATALIA). In the
central zone are the images of Ursa Major and Ursa Minor.   Certain Mithraic
bas-reliefs depicting the slaughter of the bull contain zodiacal images - one
of the best known is the marble found in London with the tauroctonous Mithras
surrounded by a circular anti-clockwise zodiac of twelve images, with the
personifications of the winds, Sun and Moon on the outer edge. There are
also several interesting images of serpentine leontocephalous figures
(sometimes called the 'Aeon', or 'Zervan Akarana', or the 'Mithraic Kronos')
into which have been inset images of the zodiacal series.

MITHUNAM   The Sanskrit name for zodiacal Gemini - but see MRGACIRSHA.

MIXED APPLICATION This term is used to denote the APPLICATION to aspect of
one planet to another planet when one of the,two is in retrograde motion. To
be distinguished from DIRECT APPLICATION and RETROGRADE APPLICATION.

MIYAN   See REGULUS.

MIZAR   One of the seven fixed stars forming "Ursa Major", said by Ptolemy to

===

be of the influence equivalent to that of Mars. Not to be confused with the
variant 'Mizar' of "Mirach".

MODE   See QUALITIES.

MODERATORS   A defunct term applied in Ptolemaic astrology to the Sun, Moon,
Ascendant, Midheaven and Pars Fortuna, with the understanding that aspects
from these condition the influence of other planets. Since this is now quite
sensibly regarded as the basic tenet of aspectal theory (that indeed all
planets act as 'moderators' in this sense) the term is no longer valid. The
astrologer Wilson used the term in a different sense, claiming that the
moderators were so named because they each had their 'own mode of operating
on the native', which is a fairly meaningless conception within the context
of astrology. Wilson dismissed the Pars Fortuna as a moderator, for he
personally had come to the conclusion that it could have no effect in
nativities.   The astrologer Lilly so misunderstood the moderators as to call
them the 'five hylegiacal places' (see HYLEG), and as a result the term has
been misused in this sense by later astrologers.

MODERN ASTRONOMICAL ZODIAC   See MODERN ZODIAC.

MODERN PLANETS   The so-called modern planets are those which have been
discovered since the development of advanced optical instruments, and added
to the planetary schema of 'seven planets' used by the ancients. These
planets are URANUS, NEPTUNE and PLUTO, though some astrologers also include
the ASTEROIDS. See NEW PLANETS.

FIGURE 44. THE 'MODERN ASTRONOMICAL ZODIAC' BASED ON THE COMPUTATIONS OF
DELPORTE IN 1930, DEFINED BY THE INTERNATIONAL ASTRONOMICAL UNION IN 1928.

MODERN ZODIAC   The 'Modern Zodiac', sometimes called the 'Modern Astronomical Zodiac' was defined during the 1928 conference of the International Astronomical Union (hence, it is sometimes also called the 'IAU Zodiac'). Strictly speaking it is not a zodiac, but a constellational grid definition. It was published by Delporte in 1930, and within the present text his divisions are set out in the tabulations provided by Powell under SIDEREAL CORRESPONDENCES. The sequence of asterisms, with their curious grids, are given in figure 44 - but see also CONSTELLATION MAPS. The definition of the fiducial zero-point for this zodiac of unequal asterisms is uniquely defined in mathematical terms, in a complex system of arcs of constant right ascensions and declination for the equinox of 1975. However, as Powell and others have pointed out, within the system proposed, some of the constellations actually overlap, and Ophiuchus straddles the ecliptic (as may be seen in figure 44) even though this constellation is not normally taken into account in any zodiac proper. See SIDEREAL ZODIAC.

MODES   See QUALITIES.

MODUS EQUALIS   A popular system of HOUSE DIVISION, sometimes called the 'Equal House System'. It is an entirely symbolic method of dividing the ecliptic, easily constructed in the course of chart-making, and of exceedingly dubious value.   The Ascendant and the Midheaven are determined by direct division of the ecliptic, but only the Ascendant is used as fiducial for locating the cusps, which are obtained merely by adding a sequence of 30 degree arcs around the ecliptic circle from the Ascendant. In this system, the cusp of the 10th house does not always correspond to the Midheaven, and is always in mundane square to the Ascendant. It is recorded that this system was in use in the 3rd millennium BC in India, and it was certainly one of the methods used prior to Ptolemy's day by Greek and Roman astrologers. Writing in 1904, the astrologer Leo observed that the system was 'practically abandoned', but since the rise of popular (and frequently superficial) notions of astrology in this present century, and the corresponding demand for an 'easy' method of drawing up charts, the Modus Equalis has proliferated, and is now even taught in some of the more influential schools of astrology. A system proposed by the Australian astrologer Zariel hs been confused with the Modus Equalis, even though it is not a symbolic method - see EQUAL DIVISION METHOD.

MODUS RATIONALIS   See REGIOMONTANEAN SYSTEM.

MOIST   See PRINCIPLES.

MOIST DAUGHTERS   See HYADES.

MOIST SIGNS   According to the Ptolemaic astrology, these are Cancer, Scorpio and Pisces, to which some later astrologers add Gemini, Libra and Aquarius. The classification is little used today - but see SECTA.

MOISTURE   An archaic term in its ancient specialist astrological sense. It is linked with the natures of the planets, which were said to be 'dry', 'wet', 'warm' and 'cold', in accordance with the doctrine of the four qualities - see however QUALITY. The 'wet' condition (moisture) was said to increase in planets which were matutine. The Moon however increased in moisture in her 'First Quarter', when it is nocturnal and in winter time.

MONAD   In its original Greek etymology, the term 'monad' was applied to the basic indivisible unit, and it was adopted into astrological and occult terminology with a similar meaning, though with a special application to the realm of spirit, rather than matter. The 'human monad' is in modern occultism that indestructible element within each individual human, which continues through the cycles of reincarnation. See also MONAS HIEROGLYPHICA.

MONAS HIEROGLYPHICA   A name given by Dee to a sigil sometimes called the

'Monad'. The sigil itself is deceptively simple ☿ consisting basically of the standard sigil for Mercury inserted into the open sigil for Aries. The importance of the sigil lies not so much in its form as in the erudite and deeply esoteric argument used by Dee to explain its structural significance in his book (the 'Monas Hieroglyphica' of 1558). Never adequately translated from the Latin, the text is a repository of esoteric innuendos which makes it one of the more remarkable occultist products of that century, and certainly the most important attempt to construct around a single sigil a theory of graphic symbolism linked with the esoteric and astrological tradition.

MONOCEROS   Constellation on the celestial equator, parallel to the first 15 degrees of Leo, 13 to 23 degrees south of the equator. Probably formed in the early 16th century, perhaps as the image of a horse, perhaps even as the 'unicorn', as it was called by Bartschius. Robson records that it is supposed to bring an ambitious nature, with a love of travel and change.

MONOMOIRIA   A term derived from Hellenistic astrology, though probably related to earlier astrological forms, and linked with the tradition that each degree of the ecliptic is associated with a planetary influence. This theory must be differentiated from that pertaining to SYMBOLIC DEGREES, however, though it perhaps did influence this latter tradition to some extent. A number of systems for locating the particular individual degree-rulerships exist, but the one recorded by Vettius Valens is perhaps the most influential. In this system, five columns of degrees are ranged against linear arrangements of the seven planets, following the normal descending sequence from Saturn to Moon, but with each range adjusted by one sequence, so that the upper range reads in the same order as the first vertical column. In the degrees of the Monomoiria listed by Neugebauer and Bouche-Leclercq, the concept of 'zero degree' is employed, which within such a context is misleading: the tabulation in table 53 is accordingly adjusted to the standard rounding-off process required by practical astrology. The system presumes of course that the degree influence is sparked off only when that degree is tenanted by a planet.

```
------------------------------------------------------------------TABLE 53
 DEGREE                                   MONOMOIRIA
                          TENANT PLANET:  SA   JU   MA   SU   VE   ME   MO
=========================================================================
   1   8   15   22   29                   SA   JU   MA   SU   VE   ME   MO
   2   9   16   23                        JU   MA   SU   VE   ME   MO   SA
   3  10   17   24                        MA   SU   VE   ME   MO   SA   JU
   4  11   17   24                        SU   VE   ME   MO   SA   JU   MA
   5  12   19   26                        VE   ME   MO   SA   JU   MA   SU
   6  13   20   27                        ME   MO   SA   JU   MA   SU   VE
   7  14   21   28                        MO   SA   JU   MA   SU   VE   ME
-------------------------------------------------------------------------
```

MONS MAENALUS   Small constellation at the feet of the asterism "Bootes", formed by Hevelius at the end of the 17th century. It is said by astrologers to give pride and great ability, though with some destructiveness.

MONS MENSAE   See MENSA.

MONTH   The basic lunar period, reconciled into sequences of 12 by reference to the solar cycle of one year - see CALENDARS. Each of the names of the months has (or more accurately, had) some esoteric relevance to astrological lore. See therefore each of the months listed by name, JANUARY, etc.

MONTHLY DIRECTIONS   See MONTHLY SERIES.

MONTHLY SERIES   One of four measures for symbolically computing time, used in "Secondary Directions", and based on the idea that the True Solar Day should be regarded as the equivalent of a month. The full term is 'Monthly

==

Series of Secondary Directions', and (misleadingly) 'Monthly Directions'.

MOON   The satellite of the Earth, called in astrology a 'planet'. It has
rule over zodiacal Cancer and is exalted in Taurus, with its corresponding
fall in Scorpio. In a chart, the Moon represents the imaginative, reflective
side of the native, and is justifiably linked with the subconscious element
in the modern image of man. It is an index of the receptive, withdrawn,
secluded part of the person. When the Moon is emphasized in a chart, it is
usually an indication of a highly sensitive, impressionable and changeable
nature, often linked with a personality in some way associated with the past,
or with childhood. A badly placed Moon, or one badly aspected, tends to give
rise to a personality which is hypersensitive, untidy, withdrawn, morbidly
concerned with self, and strangely subject to misfortune. The sigil for the
Moon ☾ represents this body as a reflection of the Sun, the idea being
that what is important in the sigil is not so much the 'lighted crescent'
reflecting the light of the consciousness, as the part of the lunar globe
which remains in darkness - that which is not seen in nature or in sigil:
the sigil is therefore a most apt symbol of the subconscious and hidden part
of man. Traditionally, the Moon is given rule over the breasts in the human
body, though in some systems both the womb and the lymph glands are
associated with this planet - see however PLANETARY MELOTHESIA. By
association with its throne Cancer, it has rule over the human rib-cage, over
that protecting form wherein the heart rests secure. In the chart, the
position of the Moon often gives a useful index of how fluids are working
through the body. Lunar types seek positions in public life, and are very
often strangely subject to fluctuations in popularity (or to frequent changes
in jobs or locations). They generally find much happiness in the quiet
retirement of home life, and sometimes they will involve themselves with work
involving liquids, such as sailing, washing or drug-dispensing, while there
is also a tendency for them to 'protect' or 'look after' people who are
themselves dealing with liquids of some kind, or who are in need of special
nurturing. The colours associated with the Moon are white, pearl, pale
blues, silvers and iridescents: the metal of the Moon is silver, but some
astrologers now link it also with aluminium. In connexion with lunar cycles,
see EMBOLISMIC LUNATION, LUNATION, LUNAR MONTH and SAROS CYCLE.

MOON CHAIN   A term applied in the Theosophical cosmoconception to the Third
Chain of the evolution of the Earth. The planet D was the equivalent of the
Moon in the present EARTH CHAIN, and the present physical body of the Moon is
visualized as a disintegrated crust, much diminished in size, and on its way
to destruction. This Theosophical teaching is much opposed by several other
esoteric doctrines - see for example EIGHT SPHERE. The most highly developed
beings to emerge from this Chain are called the 'Sons of Twilight', the 'Sons
of the Moon', and sometimes the 'Barhishads'.

MOON-FORCES   See SUN-FORCES.

MOON PERIOD   A term which has nothing to do with the cycles of the Moon, or
the SIDEREAL MOON RHYTHMS. As a specialist term, it is derived from the
modern esoteric astrology, and relates to cosmogenesis. The Moon Period is
said to represent the third of the planetary evolutionary states, following
on the first ("Saturn Period") and the second ("Sun Period"). Initially it
was a condition of moisture, which was said to densify, though it did carry
spiritual elements from previous stages of cosmogenesis, so that while the
ancient Moon body is called 'Water', the equivalent of its atmosphere was
called 'Fire-fog'. This Moon Period, which is actually only most tenuously
linked with the present Moon of our system, is sometimes called the 'Old
Moon'. The period of the evolutionary state was said to have been overseen
by the hierarchy of Seraphim.

MOON REVOLUTION   Term derived from modern esoteric astrology, relating to
cosmogenesis. It is said that the path of the evolution of our solar system,
with its periods of activity and sleep, must recapitulate the entire sequence

===

of evolution. Since the third stage of the cosmogenesis of our present
system took place in the MOON PERIOD, the term 'Moon Revolution' pertains to
the third of these recapitulations. See also REVOLUTION PERIODS.

MOON RHYTHMS   See SIDEREAL MOON RHTYHMS.

MORAYA   Name given to one of the "Hypothetical Planets", said to be
transplutonian when listed by Jayne.

MORINEAN ORBS   These are ORBS applied to the planets and fixed stars by the
French astrologer Morin de Villefranche, determined by him as a result of
direct observations of the skies, and linked with the heliacal visibility of
the bodies. It takes about 72 minutes after sunset for the stars to become
visible on the horizon in Europe. This period was regarded by Morin as the
arc equivalent of the 'orb' of the Sun. By relating the heliacal visibility
of the known planets to the sunset arc, the orbs of the known planets were
determined. The degrees of orb given by Morin are:

    SA 7   JU 8   MA 6.5   SU 18   VE 13   ME 8   MO 12

Using exactly the same method, he determined the so-called 'orb of stars',
according to brilliance, linked with the conception of 'magnitude':

    1st mag. - 6   2nd mag. - 5   3rd mag. - 4   4th mag. - 3   and so on.

MORINEAN SYSTEM   One of the systems of HOUSE DIVISION based on projection of
equal arc divisions of the equator on to the ecliptic from the pole of the
ecliptic. It is a method proposed by the 17th century astrologer Morin de
Villefranche, and is sometimes called the 'Morinus System' (after his
Latinized name), and sometimes the 'Rational and Universal Method'.

MORINUS SYSTEM   See MORINEAN SYSTEM.

MORNING STAR   In esoteric lore, one of the names given to the PENTAGRAM, and
in exoteric lore to Venus, which draws a pentagram in the skies in her
conjunctions with the Sun (for further details, see Schultz). This form is
exoterically linked with Venus, and esoterically with what historians call
the 'orans' gesture, which is itself an imitation of the five-points of the
pentagram (echoing the two feet, the two out-stretched arms, and the head).
Strictly speaking, it is not an 'orans' (praying) gesture so much as an image
of the departed soul, symbolized in the "Astral" plane, at the beginning (in
the 'morning') of the soul's post-mortem existence - hence the link with the
'morning star' Venus.

MORPHOCHROMATOGRAM   A term introduced by Kolisko to denote the litmus
pictures (figure 37 under KOLISKO EFFECT) made in the study of fluid dynamics
related to planetary aspects.

MOTHER   The 'point of Mother' is one of the so-called Arabian PARS in a
chart. If the degree of Venus in a natal chart is revolved to the Ascendant,
the adjusted position of the Moon marks the 'point of Mother'. The Fourth
House is sometimes called the 'House of the Mother'.

MOTORI   See INTELLIGENCY.

MOVABLE SIGNS   A term applied to the Cardinal signs, which should scarcely
be described in the passive mode, in that they are really the 'Moving Signs',
the initiatory triad of the twelve.

MOVABLE ZODIAC   One of Blavatsky's several terms for the constellational
zodiac, her own 'Natural Zodiac'.

MOVING SIGNS   These are Aries, Cancer, Libra and Capricorn, the Cardinal

==

Signs - see CARDINALITY.

MRGACIRSHA   The Sanskrit name for constellation Gemini - but see MITHUNAM.

MRIGASIRAS   The 3rd of the Hindu NAKSHATRAS, 'the Head of the Stag'.

MUHURTA   See MUHURTASASTRA.

MUHURTASASTRA   A Sanskrit term used of the practice of determining the right moment for an activity - in other words, for "Electional Astrology", which in the Hindu system is dependent upon lunar factors, and makes considerable use of the "Nakshatras". Sometimes "Muhurta".

MULA   The Sanskrit name for constellation Sagittarius - but see also DHANUS. The same term is also used of the 17th of the Hindu NAKSHATRAS, 'the Root'.

MUL-APIN TABLES   The two mul-APIN tablets, dated to the 8th century BC (though incorporating material at least 500 years older) are astronomical Babylonian texts listing the rising of 18 stars and constellations in the zodiacal belt, in terms of a schematic year of 12 months. The Babylonian term means 'Plough Star', and refers to the asterism "Triangulum" and certain contiguous stars. This combination of schematic year, along with the later introduction of the axial fiducial of the fixed stars "Aldebaran" and "Antares", probably gave rise to the BABYLONIAN ZODIAC which was (according to Powell) devised as an alternative system to that of the "Normal Stars".

MULIER SEDIS   See CASSIOPEIA.

MUNDANE ASPECTS   These are ASPECTS measured without regard to the zodiac, but only in terms of subdivisions of the semi-arcs, and in terms of houses. Thus, planets separated by two houses are in 'mundane sextile', though they need not be in zodiacal sextile, and separated by 60 degrees..

MUNDANE ASTROLOGY   Astrology limited to casting and interpreting specialist charts directed towards the examination of national trends - a subdivision of what has been called "Historical Astrology". The basic charts and system of interpreting in terms of mundane astrology are different from those used in natal astrology, for special emphasis is placed on such things as solstices, lunations, eclipses and planetary conjunctions. The term is rather confusing in view of the different application of the word 'mundane' to the house systems. See WORLD CYCLE OF MUNDANE EVENTS.

MUNDANE CROSS   See LA CROIX.

MUNDANE HOUSE   Since all houses are part of the mundane figure, the term is merely prolix. A 'mundane house' is merely a 'house'.

MUNDANE PARALLEL   See PARALLEL IN MUNDO

MUNDI TEMPLUM   See ARA.

MUNDOSCOPE   A name applied to a chart calculated in such a way as to present a planet through the prime vertical for a given moment in time - this time being the ingress of the Sun or Moon into a certain sidereal sign. The chart is rarely used, but was favoured by Fagan in his researches into the sidereal zodiacs of the ancients, and adopted by the astrologer Bradley.

MUSES   In the Renaissance chart of musical correspondences given by Gafurius are a number of associations between the Spheres ("Planets"), the Muses and "Modes" (these relate to the octave species of the Greater Perfect System, but the correspondences given by Gafurius (table 54) do not appear to be the same as those established by modern musicologists.

===

MUSES (Continued).

```
=================================================================TABLE 54
SPHERE         MUSE          (MUSE ASSOCIATION)     MODE
-----------------------------------------------------------------------
Stellatum      Urania        Astronomy             Hypermixolydian
Saturn         Polyhymnia    Mimic arts            Mixolydius
Jupiter        Euterpe       Flautic art           Lydian
Mars           Erato         Lyric poetry (hymns)  Phrygian
Sun            Melpomene     Tragedy               Dorian
Venus          Terpsichore   Lyric poetry (dance)  Hypolydian
Mercury        Calliope      Heroic epic           Hypophrygian
Moon           Clio          History               Hypodorian
-----------------------------------------------------------------------
```

MUSCA AUSTRALIS   Constellation formed in the 17th century and variously
called 'Apis' (bee), 'Musca' (fly), or 'Musca Indica' (Indian fly), as well
as the 'Southern Fly' of the given term.   It is located south of the Cross,
and from 66 to 74 degrees south of the equator, east of the "Chamaeleon". It
is said to give a capricious, changeable and industrious nature.

MUSCA BOREALIS   Constellation, the 'Northern Fly', over the back of
constellation Aries, probably formed by Habrecht in the 17th century, and
sometimes (confusingly) called 'Apis' - see MUSCA AUSTRALIS. It is sometimes
called 'Vespa' (wasp), or even 'Beelzebub' after the 'Lord of the Flies'.
Robson says that it gives a practical, pleasure-loving and industrious
nature, with some sarcasm and spitefulness.

MUSCA INDICA   See MUSCA AUSTRALIS.

MUSICAL ASTROLOGY See also MUSES

MUSIC OF THE SPHERES   An idea of a 'planetary music' which has been
attributed wrongly to Pythagoras (the conception of planetary spheres itself
had not been developed before the days of Eudoxos). Pythagoras did however
lay the basis for the idea of planetary ratios (which were later used in the
'Music' or 'Harmony of the Spheres') when he showed that intervals of the
scale could be expressed in simple ratios: the intervals known to the
ancients were the 4th, 5th and octave. The discovery appears to have
resulted from a lengthy search for a way to introduce a 'blend' (the Greek
'krasis') into the pairs of opposites which were at the time believed to
underlie the basic nature of the material realm.   Pythagoras applied these
ratios to the supposed distances of the planets - an attempt which has been
likened to an anticipation of Bode's series. The 'harmonia' which was said
to reign through all things as a result of such krasis extended well beyond
the planets and music, for it coloured all created things.   In relation
specifically to music, Pythagoras maintained that since the ratios of the
scales extend into the heavens, then the whole of the sub-stellar realm
should echo to a heavenly music. Several explanations have since been given
as to why we in the sublunar sphere do not hear this music: some say that we
are deafened by its perpetual sound, while others maintain that we do hear
it, if only in our sleep, when our spirits are not so tightly bound to the
body. Modern esotericism insists that the music may be heard only by
initiates under normal circumstances, but that it becomes part of the
post-mortem experience for every other human.   Pythagoras was of the opinion
that we did not hear it because our souls were out of krasis, out of harmony
with the stellar music. When in the post-Eudoxian times the concept of the
planetary spheres was developed, the original Pythagorean idea was extended
and popularly called the 'Music of the Spheres': it was thus passed into the
Neoplatonic tradition which elaborated on the basic ideas (see for example
PLANETARY TONAL INTERVALS). The architect Alberti, and such musicologists as
Gafurus, drew a detailed picture of the planetary relationships and
corresponding tones and intervals, which so profoundly influenced humanistic

==

art and literature in respect to the notion of planetary harmonies, and which
in fact still reverberate in many of our modern conceptions of ratios and
planetary natures. Alberti adopted many of the Greek ratios, and unions of
ratios, which have subsequently been linked with the diagrams of the
planetary spheres evinced in pre-Copernican systems: see DIAPASON, DIAPENTE,
DIATESSARON and TONUS. In modern times Collin in particular has introduced a
sophisticated concept of the harmonic relationships between planets, based no
longer on distances (as is the Pythagorean model) but on revolutions and
revolution periodicities, which he links to the tonic scale. He shows that
in theory 36 octaves separate human time from what he calls 'solar time', and
the same interval separates the vibrations of human music from the vibrations
of the planetary motions. The Rosicrucian school, which has so deeply
influenced the development of esoteric astrology, maintains that humans are
not permitted to hear the music itself, but may hear copies through ordinary
mortal music, and thus not lose the longing for the celestial world beyond
the material realm. As Fludd (who believes that the music is produced from
the impinging of the moving Sun upon the paths of the planets) puts it,'music
is a faint tradition of the angelic state'. The nine MUSES of Hesiod have
been associated by occultists with the celestial music: these were the
daughters of Zeus and Mnemosyne (whose name means 'remembrance') and so we
are inclined to find in classical literature a link with the astrological
teaching which would have our souls 'recalling' the celestial world. See
also CELESTIAL HARMONICS and KEPLERIAN HARMONICS.

MUTABLE CROSS   In traditional astrology the 'mutable cross' is that which is
formed by Gemini, Virgo, Sagittarius and Pisces. This cross has been widely
developed by the esotericist Bailey in her system of astrology, and is
associated with the 'crisis of incarnation, relating to evolution, to the
kingdom of nature, to planetary initiation, body, form and personality': she
says that it is the cross of changing and absorbing experience, and
visualizes in it an evolutionary sequence in reverse movement from Pisces to
Gemini, though which the seeds of Piscean intuition flower into 'dreams of
life' in Gemini. See also CARDINAL CROSS and FIXED CROSS.

MUTABLE SIGNS   These are Gemini, Virgo, Sagittarius and Pisces.

MUTABILITY   The term applied to one of the three "Qualities" (see
CARDINALITY and FIXITY) which acts as a unifier of the impulsiveness of the
former with the rigidity of the latter, and may even be said to carry a
quality common to both. Indeed, the Mutable Signs (Gemini, Virgo,
Sagittarius and Pisces) are sometimes called the "Common Signs". The Mutable
nature is that of changeability and adaptability, but under pressure it will
give rise to instability.

MUTE SIGNS   The water triplicity are called the 'mute signs' because it has
been said that when Mercury (which rules the human voice) is afflicted in
these signs, there is a liability to dumbness or to impediment of speech.
The idea may be derived from the images for these signs - the crab of Cancer,
the scorpion of Scorpio and the fishes of Pisces emit no audible sound.

MUTILATED DEGREES   Tradition holds that some of the zodiacal degrees afflict
the native with lameness if they are emphasised in the chart in any
significant way - for example, by the Moon or the ruler of the Ascendant
occupying them. These are called the 'mutilated degrees', even though they
are properly speaking the 'mutilating degrees'. As the traditional list
below will indicate, they are in some cases 'arcs', and it is quite possible
that the original groups were linked with stellar influences, yet no
precessed ratios give a satisfactory relationship with a constellation map,
and so the tradition is hard to fathom:

    TA 6-10   CN 9-15   LE 18-25   SC 18-19
    SG 1 7-8 18-19   CP 26-29   AQ 18-19.

==

MUTUAL APPLICATION   When two planets applying to aspect move towards each
other (one being retrograde), they are said to be in 'mutual application'.

MUTUAL ASPECTS   Aspects formed between two moving bodies at a specific time
are said to be 'mutual': such aspects are formed between transitting
planets, as opposed to those formed between such a planet and a natal planet
or nodal point, or a progressed planet. The aspects listed from a natal
chart prior to the listing of progressions or transits are 'mutual aspects'.
The term is used to distinguish such angular relationships from those which
are 'Directional', 'Progressed' or 'Transitory'.

MUTUAL RECEPTION   Two planets which are posited in the essential dignities
corresponding to the other are said to be in mutual reception - see therefore
DIGNITY. Some astrologers maintain that the so-called 'domal dignities' may
also give rise to mutual reception.

MYSTICAL PLANETS   See SACRED PLANETS. The astrologer Libra discussed the
planets linked with the future development of Aries, Taurus and Gemini as
being 'still invisible on higher planes', and called these the 'invisible
mystery planets'. Libra links this future unfoldment of Aries with the
Hierarchy of the physical plane, Taurus with the Hierarchy of the astral
plane, and Gemini with the Hierarchy of the mental plane.

MYSTIC RECTANGLE   A modern term applied to a configuration of aspects in
which a pair of trines connect with a pair of sextiles in such a way that
oppositions fall across the four corners. The term, which appears to have
originated in French astrological circles, is not directly associated with
mystical tendencies within the chart - though, as Brau puts it, the mystic
rectangle 'combines the awareness of the opposition, the understanding of the
trine, and the productivity of the sextile'. One wonders, however, if the
term has arisen mainly because such a configuration is found in the chart of
Blavatsky? The mystic rectangle is a "Major Configuration".

MYSTIC TETRAD   See TETRACTYS.

==

NA'AM   'Al Na'am', the 18th of the Arabian MANZILS, 'the Ostriches'.

NABURIANNU TABLES   See AYANAMSA.

NACHIEL   Name given by Agrippa (quoting cabalistic sources) to the
"Intelligency" of the Sun, to whom he ascribes the magical number 111, the
linear sum of the "Magic Square" of the Sun.

NADI ASTROLOGY   See NADIGRANTHAMS.

NADIGRANTHAMS   General name given in Hindu astrology to collections of
palm-leaf manuscripts used in consultative astrology. The origin of these
nadigranthams is unknown, and the tendency of popularist literature is to
give them a hoary and quite improbable antiquity - some claim the authorship
of Brahma, others of Vyasa.   It is often said that the palm-leaves contain
horoscopes, but certainly such are not the main matter in those 'palmleaf
books' examined by specialists in Sanskrit. The Theosophist Row consulted an
expert in nadigranthams, and his report indicates that it was a farrago of
nonsense unrelated to astrological practice. Unaccountably, Brau makes of
the nadigranthams a sytem of astrology which he calls 'Nadi Astrology', in
which the astrologers are supposed to have delineated horoscopes cast
('sometimes centuries before') the appearance of their clients. Though

popularly believed to be true, such accounts of Indian astrology are really based on fantasy.

NADIR   The lowest point below the Earth, relative to any given position on the Earth - it is the opposite polarity of the ZENITH. Just as the zenith should not be confused with the Tenth house, so the the nadir should not be confused with the Fourth House.

NAIBODIC ARC   See TABLE OF NAIBOD.

NAIBOD'S MEASURE OF TIME   See MEASURE OF TIME.

NAKSHATRAS   The Hindu equivalent of the LUNAR MANSIONS. While there are the usual 28 mansions of nakshatras in the Hindu system, only 27 of these are used in ordinary astrology (see ABHIJIT). The arcs consist of 13 degrees and 20 minutes, and begin at "Asvini", marked by the beta of constellation Aries. Their names, and their relationships to Arabian and Chinese lunar systems, is set out under "Lunar Mansions".

NANAR   One of several Chaldean names for the Moon.

NANNAK   One of several Chaldean names for the Moon.

NARONIC MEASURE   A measure of arc used in "Symbolic Directions", based on a division of the zodiacal circle by 600 (see NAROS CYCLE), which gives arcs of three-fifths of a degree. It is claimed by Sepharial that this progression unit is a useful definition of the periods of 'depression and expansion' in life, while the astrologer Carter regards the measure as being of the utmost value in progressional work.

NAROS CYCLE   A name given to a periodicity or cycle, sometimes called the 'Naronic Cycle' or the 'Neros Cycle', claimed in esoteric circles to be one of the mystery secrets, but exoterically said to be a period of 600 years. Blavatsky claims that there were three kinds of Naros cycle - the 'greater', the 'middle' and the 'lesser', and that only the last corresponds to the cycle of 600 years.   One of the esoteric significances of the cycle of 600 is found in the numerical values and images ascribed to the Hebraic 'Tau' and 'Resh', which letters of the alphabet are associated with the cycle. The image of Resh is a circle, while the sigil for Tau is a cross: the encircled Tau (or the encircled cross) is the basis for the symbolic form of the horoscope chart - yet the numerical values of Resch (200) and Tau (400) add up to 600, thus uniting the circle and cross in the idea of the Naronic cycle.

NASHIRA   Fixed star, the gamma of Capricornus, set in the tail of the goat, the name said to be derived from the Arabic 'Al Sa'd al Nashirah' (the fortunate one). Ptolemy says it is of the nature of Saturn and Jupiter, redemptive of evil, though tending to bring danger from wild beasts.

NATAL ASTROLOGY   That branch of astrology which is concerned with the casting and interpreting of birth charts - the Latin 'natus' meaning 'birth'. It is GENETHLIACAL ASTROLOGY.

NATHRAH   'Al Nathrah' (the Crib), the 6th of the Arabian MANZILS.

NATIVE   The subject for whom a horoscope (the "Nativity") has been cast.

NATIVITY   In a specialist sense, the term used for the chart cast for a particular birth (from the Latin 'natus', birth): in modern terminology, the equivalent is "Horoscope".   In some pre-nineteenth century astrological texts the term 'nativity' was used specifically to mean 'ascendant degree', no doubt in reference to the original etymology of the word HOROSCOPE.

NATIVITY EXALTATION   The historian Neugebauer records the term 'Exaltation (of the Nativity)' in regard to a Hellenistic method of determining a 'nativity exaltation' which is to be distinguished from the planetary EXALTATIONS, even though it is now merely of historic interest. Reference is made to the astrologer Vettius Valens, who gives the exaltation sign of a given nativity in terms of the position of either the Sun or Moon in a chart. One simply counts the number of signs from the day horoscope Sun to Aries (the exaltation sign of the Sun), or from the night horoscope Moon to Taurus (the exaltation sign of the Moon), and then takes the same distance (counting in signs) from the Ascendant to mark the 'nativity exaltation'.

NATURAL ASTROLOGY A term originated (seemingly by Brau) to denote both Astronomy and "Astrometeorology", the latter the equivalent of METEOROLOGICAL ASTROLOGY. The term 'natural astrology' appears to be derived from translation of a French term which does not have an English equivalent.

NATURAL ZODIAC   One of Blavatsky's terms for the "Constellational Zodiac", which is rightly defined as 'a succession of constellations', and distinguished from her INTELLECTUAL ZODIAC.   Unfortunately, the astrologer Heindel succeeds in confusing her zodiacs, and defines the 'Natural Zodiac' as the 'twelve (sic) constellations'.

NATUS   An archaic (Latin) term for the 'Natal Chart'.

NAVAMSA   The Hindu term meaning 'ninth part', most usually the 'ninth part of a sign'. Due to a misunderstanding, the same term has been used by modern western astrologers to mean the equivalent of a nine-house system (see NOVIENIC CHART), and has also been wrongly used as applicable to HARMONICS. The astrologer Harvey has attempted to show that the navamsa chart is really a diagram of planetary positions in terms of the ninth harmonic. See also NOVENARY MEASURE.

NAVAMSA-DWADASAMSA   A term derived from Hindu astrology, meaning 'a (9 x 12) division'. It is important as an astrological division, for the 108th part of sidereal zodiacal arc (hence an arc of 16 minutes, 40 seconds) on the Ascendant is regarded as an indicator of the sex in pre-natal calculations - see EPOCHAL CHART. The problem with the method is that no fiducial is available, and no agreed "Ayanamsa", so the application of the arc is of dubious theoretical value. The epochal method of the astrologer Bailey does not use the navamsa-dwadasamsa but correlates by means of what are called "Sex Points" which are supposed to be based on the Hindu "Nakshatras", incorporating the asterism "Abhijit" to give 28 divisions of the ecliptic.

NEBO   A Chaldean god, sometimes equated with the planet Mercury.

NEBULA   A star cluster in which the individual lights of stars are merged into an indistinguishable cloud (the Greek 'nephos' means cloud, the derived mediaeval Latin 'nebulatus', cloudy). Astrologers regard the supposed influences from some nebulae as worthy of consideration in chart interpretation - see FIXED STARS.

NEBULOSA   Name given to the 8th of the lunar mansions in some of the mediaeval lists - but see table 48 in LUNAR MANSIONS. The mansion was probably located by Praesaepe, which was the only universally recognized nebula prior to the invention of the telescope. It was accordingly called 'Nubilium' (cloudy sky), 'Nebula' or 'Nebulosa in pectore Cancri' (clouds in the breast of Cancer).   See LUNAR ZODIAC.

NECESSITY   Name given to one of the SEVEN LOTS of the Greek astrologers, the lot of 'Anagke' (necessity). The degree is the same distance from the Ascendant as is Mercury from the "Part of Fortune".

NECHEPSO   See PETOSIRIS.

===

NEGATIVE MARS In the traditional system of planetary rulerships over the
signs, Mars was assigned to Scorpio: in accordance with this schema (see
PLANETARY RULERSHIPS and SECTA), the Scorpionic Mars was said to be
'feminine', 'nocturnal' and 'negative', in contrast to the 'masculine',
'diurnal' and "Positive Mars" which ruled Aries.   In post-mediaeval
astrology the basis for this use of the term was largely forgotten, and there
developed an idea of a sort of 'negative Mars' which was in some ways
different from planetary Mars. It is for this reason that one frequently
finds reference to 'negative Mars' in contexts where there is no mention of
other planets as being expressed in 'negative' or 'positive' equivalents.
The fact is that there is a 'Negative Mercury', a 'Negative Venus', and so
on. Usually the term simply means 'Mars as ruler of Scorpio', though perhaps
the word 'negative' does inadvertently point to something of the need for
redemption so characteristic a need of the sign. It must be understood,
however, that even a redeemed Scorpionic nature is ruled still by negative
Mars: but see EAGLE.

NEGATIVE PLANETS   See FEMININE PLANETS and NEGATIVE MARS.

NEGATIVE SIGNS   These are the alternate signs from Taurus to Pisces,
inclusive. But see FEMININE SIGNS, for which 'negative signs' is really an
alternative term. See also SECTA.

NEMESIS   Name given to one of the SEVEN LOTS of Greek astrology, Nemesis
being (approximately) the goddess of retribution. The degree of this lot is
at the same distance from the Ascendant as Saturn from Fortuna.

NEOMENIA   Literally the 'New Moon' from the Greek. In ancient times the new
moons of Spring and Autumn were calendrical fiducials, the first marking the
first day of the ecclesiastical year, the second marking the first day of the
civil year. As the astrologer Fagan points out, the term 'neomenia' in
antiquity had not quite the same meaning as today: in remote times the first
day of the neomenia was that day (commencing at sunset) when the thin
crescent was first visible in the western sky immediately after sunset. In
ancient times the neomenia was regarded as being inauspicious.

NEPTUNE   Planet in orbit between Uranus and Pluto, discovered in 1846 by
Galle in Berlin, following a suggestion of the Frenchman Leverrier, though it
had been observed (if mistaken for a star) by Lalande as early as 1795.
Since its discovery, Neptune has displaced Jupiter from its traditional
rulership, and has been accorded rule over the zodiacal sign Pisces.
Astrologers see it as a dissolving influence: it bestows nebulousness and
confusion, even deceptiveness when working under pressure. When working
through its beneficient side however it induces an imaginative,
inspirational, idealistic and artistic nature. The link with the 'sea' is
more than nominal (Neptune being the Roman equivalent of Poseidon, the god of
the seas), for it is generally interpreted as a symbol of the ease of contact
which the planet facilitates with the 'sea' of the unconscious: but see also
NEPTUNUS. The sigil for Neptune Ψ is popularly explained as being derived
from the trident of Neptune: but see NEW PLANETS.

NEPTUNE-PLUTO CYCLES   The synodic period for these two planets is 492.328
years, which (with a minute error of less than 3 degrees) gives the
first-order cycle. The second order cycle is a vast 72,372.25 years,
involving 147 synodics.

NEPTUNE SCHEME   The 'Neptune Scheme' or the 'Neptune Chain' are terms
derived specifically from the Theosophical cosmoconception linked with the
"Scheme of Evolution". It is claimed that the three planets in this Chain
include Neptune, and two others beyond its orbit, perhaps even Pluto, which
was unrecognized when the schema was originated. Blavatsky claimed that
Neptune is not in our own solar system, so that the formulation of this

==

scheme is derived from her followers (probably influenced by the teachings of Besant and Leadbeater).

NEPTUNI SIDUS   See PISCES CONSTELLATION.

NEPTUNUS   The name given to "Neptune" by the esoteric astrologer Thierens. He departs little from the exoteric tradition in seeing the influence of the planet (which he also designates as the Grecian 'Poseidon') as the principle of 'absorption' ruling the 'subconscious mind or dream-thinking of psycho-analysis' which will 'gather what is rejected by the wakeful or constructive mind: it may cause a morbid passivity, which leaves the mind open to become the playground for more or less 'animal' elementals or influences from the astral world, and which finally very often leads to idiocy or other phenomena of mental instability'.

NEREUS   A name given by the esoteric astrologer Thierens to a future development of his NEPTUNUS, as a transformation of the modern Jupiter in his "Astral Sphere". It is said to represent the principle of absorption.

NERGAL   A Chaldean name, probably for a personification of Mars as 'the giant king of war'. The same name is used in Hebraic astrology for Mars, though seemingly of the darker side of his nature.

NEROS   See NAROS.

NERVOUS SIGNS   Term used as a synonym for "Air Signs".

NEW MOON   See NEOMENIA.

NEW PLANETS   This is the curious term often applied to the three planets of the solar system which have been added to the traditional seven of the ancient astrological model - in order of discovery URANUS, NEPTUNE and PLUTO. Much has been written and speculated about the functions of these planets in astrological terms, and a digest is given under the respective headings. In regard to a treatment of the planets as representative of a group influence, the ideas of Walther are perhaps worthy of mention. Walther links the discovery of the new planets with the evolution of modern consciousness, to an extension of our understanding, to new technology, and so on. Yet, he does not regard the three as being divorced from the traditional seven, so much as being 'higher vibrations' of these. He compares the 84 year revolution of Uranus with the 84 day revolution of Mercury, for example, and suggests that Uranus rules those qualities which distinguish 'us' from 'others' - that which is outstanding, extraordinary or original in a native: the opposite of the peculiar and original is the trivial, the every-day. Neptune reflects Jupiter much the same way as Uranus does Mercury: Neptune urges towards self-sacrifice, and service to others: Walther says indeed that this is the planet expressive of the 'principle of the Love of Christ', and visualizes the sigil ♆ as the 'bowl of sacrifice'. The opposite of unlimited open-ness and sacrifice is egocentricity, seclusion in oneself. Pluto was visualized as a reflection of traditional Mars, as a 'higher octave of the red planet': when it is emphasized in a horoscope it may be taken as an indicator of creative faculties. The opposite of creative (or even destructive forces) of Pluto is 'paralysis of the instinct'. Walther remarks that while Neptune has a revolution approximately twice that of Uranus, Pluto has a revolution three times that of Uranus.

NEW STYLE   Term used in reference to the so-called 'new' chronology derived from the "Gregorian Calendar", to distinguish it from the earlier Julian system: in astrological charts the term is usually abbreviated to n.s. See also OLD STYLE.

NEW VENUS   See TYCHO'S STAR.

NIGHT HOME   See DAY HOUSE.

NIGHT HOUSE   Each of the traditional planets (excluding the luminaries) has an associate 'night house', a sort of mundane nocturnal lordship which is perfectly in accordance with the ancient model of planetary rulerships (see SECTA). The traditional term 'night house' is a misnomer, for it is a sign, and not a house, which is being denoted. The 'night house' of Saturn is Capricorn, of Jupiter Pisces, of Mars Scorpio, of Venus Taurus, and of Mercury Virgo. These are also the 'negative planets' (see NEGATIVE MARS). The concept is linked with the idea that each of the non-luminaries have a 'negative' and 'positive' side to their natures, finding special expression in the pairs of signs allocated to them. See also DAY HOUSE.

NIGHT OF BRAMHA   See KALPA.

NIGHT SIGN   See NIGHT HOUSE.

NINE ORDERS   One of the names for the CELESTIAL HIERARCHIES.

NINE SACRED ANIMALS   See CALENDARIA MAGICA.

NINETY DEGREE CIRCLE   A method of astrological charting, linked with the "Cosmogram" of the Ebertin COSMOLOGY.   The method was developed to combine the normal 360 degree system of chart projection with a 90 degree system in order to facilitate the study of PLANETARY PATTERNS and the study of transits and directions. It was used in connecion with a 'Ninety Degree Dial', a separate calibration designed to aid rapid assessment of the patterns.

NINIB   Name derived from Chaldean sources, and generally equated with the planet Saturn - though originally it was the name of a god.

NINTH HEAVEN   At one time the name given to the PRIMUM MOVENS, the 'Primum Mobile' of the PTOLEMAIC SYSTEM, that sphere above the eight spheres which gave the diurnal revolution to all the others: sometimes it was called the 'Crystalline Heaven', the 'diaphanous' or 'transparent' heaven (even though all the other spheres were themselves said to be both diaphanous and transparent). See however TENTH HEAVEN. The 'Ninth Heaven' was also called the 'Ninth Sphere', but unfortunately this same term was also later applied to the Earth itself, as some cosmoconceptions reckoned the concentrics in descending order from the periphery, with the 'Primum Movens' (the old Ninth Heaven) as the first.

NINTH HIERARCHY   See ANGELS.

NINTH HOUSE   The ninth of the astrological HOUSES, linked with the nature of Sagittarius, and associated with higher mentality and education. It was formerly referred to as the 'House of Religion', in the days when theology was of great popular significance, and less divorced from the life-energies of philosophy. It has rule over long journeys - originally over those which could not be made in a single day, for which some preparation was required, though it was also concerned with the idea of 'mental travel', with speculation and deeper thought. In the melothesic man it has rule over the thighs and hams. In Mundane Astrology it rules higher education, universities, transportation, immigration and long-distance communication (though not television or radio).

NINTH SPHERE   See NINTH HEAVEN.

NISAN   See BABYLONIAN CALENDAR.

NOCTUA   Name given to an obsolete constellation visualized in the tail of "Hydra", called 'Night Owl'.

==

NOCTURNAL ARC   The variable arc through which the Sun appears to pass from
sunset to sunrise.   It is, of course, the arc left when the DIURNAL ARC is
subtracted from 360 degrees, and is conditioned both by space and time: in
space by latitude, in time by the relationship between Sun and solstices.

NOCTURNAL HORARY TIME   See HORARY TIME.

NOCTURNAL HOUSE   See NIGHT HOUSE.

NOCTURNAL PLANET   A planet is said to be nocturnal when it is above the
horizon in a nocturnal nativity - when, in other words, it is in the night
sky.   The term is also used in a specialist sense recorded by Ptolemy, who
tells us that the Moon and Venus are 'nocturnal', the Sun and Jupiter
'diurnal', while Mercury is of the nature of both day and night (diurnal when
matutine, and nocturnal as an evening star).   The definition is then somewhat
clouded by the introduction of an idea which has been misunderstood by
generations of astrologers: Ptolemy assigns Saturn, a cold planet, to the
warmth of day, where its influence is mitigated - it is therefore neither a
nocturnal nor diurnal planet, but a sort of 'adopted-diurnal'.   Similarly,
Mars (which is a dry planet) is mitigated in action by the moisture of the
night: it is therefore neither nocturnal nor diurnal, but
'adopted-nocturnal'.   Later authorities, including Wilson, have misread
Ptolemy, resulting in Mars being listed as a nocturnal planet, and so on.

NOCTURNAL SIGNS   See NEGATIVE SIGNS.

NODAL   As a general term, 'nodal' applies to any sensitive degree (or arc)
on the ecliptic - for example, the Ascendant may be described as a 'nodal
point'.   More specifically, the Nodes are the points (hence the sensitive
degrees) at which the orbits of planets (or other celestial phenomena,
including even meteors) cut the plane of the ecliptic.   When in an
astrological context the term 'Node' is used, without further qualification,
the reference is usually to one of the "Nodes" of the Moon.

NODAL HOROSCOPE   A system of symbolically projecting the heavens for
astrological purposes, based on the CHOISNARD CHART, but locating the
'ascending node' of the Moon on the Ascendant.   It is a system proposed by
the astrologer Froger, whose own researches have indicated that the mean node
rather than the true node of the Moon should be adopted.

NODES   In relation to planets, the 'nodes' are the points in which the orbit
of the planet intersects the ecliptic.   The point at which the planet crosses
the ecliptic into the northern latitude is called its 'north node', while the
point where it crosses into the southern latitude is called the 'south node'.
In traditional astrology the only planetary nodes which are accorded any
importance are those of the Moon, called the "Dragon's Head" and the
"Dragon's Tail", both of which regress approximately 3 minutes of arc each
day.   In some modern forms of esoteric astrology, and in all modern forms of
heliocentric astrology, the nodes of the planets are of great importance
(indeed they are the seminal forces in a heliocentric chart).

NODUS   See PISCES CONSTELLATION.

NODUS COELESTIS   See ALRESCHA.

NODUS PISCIUM   See ALRESCHA.

NONAGEN   An aspect of 40 degrees - see NONAGON.

NONAGON   Defined by Simmonite as an aspect of 40 degrees, which divides the
heavens into nine equal arcs.   Rudhyar calls the same aspect the 'Nonagen'.

NONAGESIMAL   A name sometimes given to that point of the ecliptic which is

90 degrees from the Ascendant in the diurnal arc.   This point should not be confused with the MIDHEAVEN - in the "Modus Equalis" system of symbolic house division, the 'nonagesimal' marks the Tenth House cusp. It is sometimes misleadingly called the 'Zenith Projection'.

NON-ELEMENTAL ASPECTS   See ELEMENTAL ASPECTS.

NONES   See KALENDS.

NON-PLANETS   An unfortunate term, since strictly speaking it relates to everything in the cosmos which is not a planet, but used by Dean to include a whole range of celestial phenomena only tenuously connected. These are specifically given as COMETS, ECLIPSES, FIXED STARS, HELIOCENTRIC NODES, HYPOTHETICAL PLANETS, NODES and PARS. The classification appears to be based on the (mistaken) notion that each of these are involved with influencing degrees or arcs of degrees of the zodiac with natures analogous to those of the planets, even while they are not themselves planets. Within such a definition, many other factors should have been included, such as the FUTURE PLANETS, the SACRED PLANETS, and so on.

NON-SACRED PLANETS   The esotericist Bailey distinguishes five non-sacred planets (to be distinguished from her "Sacred Planets"), which she links with the etheric centres of the human spine. The five non-sacreds include the Earth (which is said to be on the way to becoming a 'sacred planet'), the Moon (connected with the spleen and thymus gland, and often said to 'veil' another planet - see therefore ESOTERIC MOON), Mars, which functions in connexion with the sacral centre of Man, Pluto which is connected with the solar plexus, and the Sun (which is also said to be veiled by another planet - see therefore ESOTERIC SUN), linked with the parathyroids, and acting as a mediator between the higher and lower organs. The 'non-sacreds' are not to be confused with the "Orthodox Planets" of Bailey's system.

NON-SACREDS   Another term for the NON-SACRED PLANETS.

NOON DATE   See ADJUSTED CALCULATION DATE.

NOON MARK   A term used to denote the equivalent time of noon (Greenwich Time) in regard to the place for which the chart calculations are applicable.

NOON-POINT METHOD   A term originated by the astrologer Leo, circa 1912, to describe a simple method of "Rectification", based on the fact that if the 'noon date' for a particular figure is known, then so is the exact Ascendant. The method appears to be entirely unresearched prior to publication, and is based on the chimerical application of the 'noon date' into the life of the native, at a time which is supposed to characterize 'maximum astrological intensity', which is registered either by the native or by some astrologer interested in his chart. The 'noon date' used in progressions is properly called the ADJUSTED CALCULATION DATE.

NORMA   Constellation located to the north of the asterism "Triangulum", sometimes itself called the 'Southern Triangle', sometimes 'Quadra Euclidis' (Euclid's Square). Astrologers accord it a reputation for rectitude, and an interest in geometry, etc.

NORMAL STARS   A term introduced by the historian Epping in reference to 31 stars which were sufficiently prominent in the Babylonian zodiacal belt to be used as fiducials.   The 'belt' was some 10 degrees north, and 7 and a half degrees south, of the ecliptic. In the early cuneiform texts of Babylonian astrology, planetary positions were given in reference to these normal stars. See also MUL-APIN TABLES.

NORTHERN ANGLE   The cusp of the Fourth House is called the 'northern angle', and is sometimes (wrongly) identified with the "Imum Coeli".

===

NORTHERN CLAW   See ZUBENESCHAMALI.

NORTHERN CROSS   See CYGNUS.

NORTHERN CROWN   See CORONA BOREALIS.

NORTHERN FLY   See MUSCA BOREALIS.

NORTHERN QUADRANT   See QUADRANTS.

NORTHERN SIGNS   These are the six signs from Aries to Virgo inclusive -
probably so called because in the standard chart (the MACROCOSMIC CHART) they
fall below the horizon in the nocturnal and northern arc. They are sometimes
called the Boreal Signs.

NORTH HORN   See SHARATAN.

NORTH NODE   See NODES.

NORTH POINT   The cusp of the "Northern Angle".

NORTH SCALE   See ZUBENESCHAMALI.

NOTABLE NATIVITIES   A term now used generally to denote any collection of
horoscopes, or related data, but originally derived from the title of a book
'A Thousand and One Notable Nativities', published under the name of the
astrologer Leo, comprising birth data and horoscopes derived from a large
number of astrological sources prior to the first decade of our century.
While a useful reference list (along with a second volume of related data),
especially in regard to the quoted sources, it must be used only with
caution, since some of the "Rounding Off" is not accurate, and not all the
primal sources are beyond suspicion. Many similar collections were published
in previous centuries, most notably those given by Gauricus in 1542 (figure
45), those by Junctinus in 1583, the 'Collectio Geniturarum' of Gadbury in
1662 and the many figures printed copperplate by Sibly in 1789. An
up-to-date equivalent collection (which is certainly more accurate) is in the
'Sabian Symbols' of Jones.

FIGURE 45. HOROSCOPE OF HENRY VII OF ENGLAND, CAST FOR 27TH JUNE, 1491,
AT 10.40 AM (THE CENTRAL INSCRIPTION IS INACCURATE) - (AFTER CARDAN).

NOVA   Usually defined generally as 'a new star', the nova is something of a
misnomer: as a phenomenon, it is a sudden and often very great increase in

light (and presumably in release of energies) of an extant star. Sometimes a nova is popularly described as 'an exploding star', but in fact the sudden burst of light and energy does not destroy the body, so that a nova will gradually return to being an ordinary star once again. Perhaps a nova might more usefully be defined as a temporary brilliance in a star. The observed changes do however suggest that incredible energies are involved: the nova in the Andromeda Nebula of 1885 is reported to have emitted more light in six days than our Sun will emit in a million years! The nova observed in Cassiopeia by Tycho Brahe in 1572 (it remained visible in daylight for about 18 months) is often said to have been the first to be recorded, but there are several indications of earlier ones being observed (if misunderstood). The importance of the Cassiopeia nova was the profound effect it had on men's thinking about the nature of the cosmos: few things shook the emotional security men felt in the "Ptolemaic System" more dramatically than the 1572 nova. It is likely that the 'influence' of a Nova was seen in terms similar to those of the adjacent or involved fixed stars. One wonders to what extent the dire tradition attached to Cassiopeia influenced Tycho Brahe, when he described the nova in that constellation as of an evil influence, an omen of wars, sedition, captivity, and deaths of princes, the destruction of cities, together with drought and fiery meteors in the air, bringing pestilence and venomous snakes? The causes of novae are unknown, and the attempts of astrologers to account for them within their system, to invest them with prophetic meaning, are usually quite pathetic. For example, the Nova Aquilae of 1918, which increased its brightness by 40,000 times in four days, was linked by Deluce with 'the year in which an American Expeditionary Force on foreign soil turned the tide of World War I' - a chauvinistic parochialism which is typical of this kind of astrology.

NOVEMBER   The eleventh month (30 days) of our calendar, its name being derived from the Roman system prior to the introduction of the JULIAN CALENDAR reforms, when it was the ninth month (the Latin 'novem' means nine). The esoteric significance of the month is linked with this original number, with its magical power as 3 x 3 marking the completion of two iner-related cycles, as a necessary prelude to the enactment of a new cycle which will begin in the following month.   There is a possibility that this magical connotation was linked with the change of the time of Christmas to December (originally Christmas was celebrated in January). Certainly the imagery of the important Thrysdus (El Djem) mosaic calendar (see Foucher) suggests a connexion with the Egyptian cult of Isis and Anubis, which in the later Christian imagery developed into Marian and Christophorian equivalents: in the November segment of this mosaic Anubis is dog-headed, a caduceus-bearing Mercury prototype of St. Christopher.

NOVENARY MEASURE   An arc, or measure, used in "Symbolic Directions" and derived by dividing the 30 degree sign into nine parts, to give an arc of 3 degrees and 20 minutes. This is the equivalent of the Hindu "Navamsa".

NOVIENIC CHART   The 'Novienic Equivalent Chart' is one derived in principle from the 'Enneal Horoscope' of the Greeks, which was the Sanskrit 'Navamsa Chart'.   A chart, the 'Noviens Chart' is used to determine the equivalent of the 'Novienic Moon' from the sidereal placing.   This novienic Moon is then regarded as being on the Ascendant of the chart, and the houses are disposed according to the 'Modus Equalis' symbolic division of 30 degree arcs. The rules of construction and interpretation were set out by the astrologer Fagan. See also SEXASCOPE.

NOVIENIC MOON   See NOVIENIC CHART.

NOVIENS   Sometimes used of the Novienic Moon - see NOVIENIC CHART.

NUBECULAE MAGELLANI   Constellation formed by Bayer in 1604 and named in honour of the seafarer who described them, 'Magellan's Little Clouds'. The astrological influence is said to be poetical, artistic and imaginative,

==

though involves much hard work. There are actually two separate 'clouds',
the 'Greater' (Nubecula Major) and the 'Lesser' (Nubecula Minor) - the
Greater is said to convey isolation and loneliness.

NUBECULA MAJOR   See NUBECULAE MAGELLANI.

NUBECULA MINOR   See NUBECULAE MAGELLANI.

NUBILUM   See PRAESAEPE.

NUMBER SYMBOLISM   See QABBALISTIC ASTROLOGY and TETRACTYS.

NUNCTATOR   See NUNTIUS.

NUNTIUS   One of the mediaeval esoteric names for Mercury, which pictures the
planet in its anthropomorphized role as 'messenger'. It is sometimes called
'nunctator', though in both forms it is found most often in the astrological
terminology linked with alchemy. Blavatsky writes of astrological Mercury as
'still more occult and mysterious than Venus', and likens the word Nuntis (a
term seemingly derived from the mystery wisdom) with 'Sun-Wolf' - no doubt a
reference to the Hermetic Anubis (see NOVEMBER). She is of course touching
upon the esoteric tradition which links Mercury in union with the Sun - the
Saint Christopher Mercury, who carries the Sun Child on his shoulders was
originally a dog-headed Latinized Anubis.

NUNU   See PISCES CONSTELLATION.

NUPTIAL NUMBER   In effect, the number 60, derived from the properties of the
'Pythagorean Triangle', a right-angled triangle the shorter sides of which
were ascribed the values 3 and 4 the hypotenuse yielding 5. The multiples of
these three figures (3 x 4 x 5) equals 60. This mystical number was linked
with the so-called SAROS CYCLE, as well as with the harmonics of the spheres.

==

OBERON   Name given to one of the satellites of Uranus.

OBEYING   See COMMANDING.

OBLIQUE ASCENSION   A system of measurement (usually expressed in degrees of
arc) of the circle of declination from the first degree of Aries eastwards
along the circle of the equatorial plane. If a point to be located by such a
co-ordinate is not within the plane of the equator itself, then it must form
an angle with its corresponding part of the equator when they rise together:
this angle is called the 'ascensional difference'.

OBLIQUE SPHERE   Any sphere that is not in the vertical of the Earth poles.

OBLIQUITY OF ECLIPTIC   This is expressed as the angle between the Earth's
equatorial plane and the plane of its own orbit - 23.5 degrees.

OCCIDENS   One of the Latin names for the western angle, meaning 'place of
sunset' or 'sunset', derived from an etymology linked with the idea of
killing - presumably in reference to the killing of the sunlight on the
western horizon at sunset. However occultists usually read deep significance
into the link between the west and death. For various terms, see OCCIDENTAL.

OCCIDENTAL   Literally 'westerly' or 'western' (see OCCIDENS) - but
distinguish the following derivatives, which are ambiguous: OCCIDENTAL MOON,

==

OCCIDENTAL PLANET and OCCIDENTAL SUN.

OCCIDENTAL MOON   The Moon is said to be 'occidental' (whatever its mundane placing) when decreasing in light, and hence to the west of the Sun.

OCCIDENTAL PLANET   A planet may be termed 'occidental of the Sun' when it rises or sets after the Sun - but see OCCIDENTAL.

OCCIDENTAL SUN   Specifically the term should be 'western sun' (see OCCIDENS) but in a specialist (and somewhat confusing) application the term is used of the Sun when it is in any of the two arcs of the 7th, 8th, 9th houses, and the 1st, 2nd and 3rd houses.

OCCOURSE   A term derived from translation of Ptolemy's 'eupantesis', and used in reference to the celestial changes 'experienced' by the planets, such as aspects, ingresses, occultations, and so on.   When an aspect or occultation is involved, the planet bringing about the 'occursion' was called the 'occursor'. This word is now archaic.

OCCULTATION   When a planet is hidden (the term 'occulta' means 'hidden things') by another body, it is said to be in occultation.

OCCULT HOUSE   One of the names for the EIGHTH HOUSE.

OCCURSION   See OCCOURSE.

OCH   Name of a 'daemon' listed in the grimoires as one of the seven supreme angels of the Cabbalists, and said to possess all the attributes of the Sun. He is supposed to have a complete knowledge of medicine and healing, and to be able to change base matter into gold.   He is said to be capable of prolonging human life to 600 years - which is a scarcely-veiled reference to the ancient NAROS CYCLE, itself linked with the cycles of reincarnation.

OCTANS   Constellation from approximately 20 degrees Cancer to 10 degrees Leo, and from 9 to 22 degrees south, formed by La Caille in 1752 under the original title of 'Octans Hadleianus' in honour of Hadley the inventor of the octant.   It is supposed to give a scientific mind, though may also subject the native to psychic disturbances.

OCTAVE   See CELESTIAL HARMONICS, DIAPASON and PLANETARY TONAL INTERVALS.

OCTILE   A modern name for the aspect of "Semi-Square". The term suggests that the aspect is used as a division of the zodiac according to the principles of HARMONICS, being considered as a division of the circle by 8, rather than as a pure aspect.

OCTOBER   The tenth month of the GREGORIAN CALENDAR, the 8th of the JULIAN CALENDAR (hence 'Octo', which means 'eight'), though now with 31 days. The pre-Julian calendar reckoned from March as the first month, hence the origin of the word from the Latin 'octo' (eight). Esoterically the month is still linked with the number 8 in that this begins a new septenary cycle (see SEPTEMBER), a deeper descent into matter: in the northern parts of Europe, winter was reckoned from the first full Moon of this month.

OCTOPODOS   A term derived from the Greek, referring to a system of "House Division" restricted to 8 houses (the word 'topoi' in Greek meaning 'places' or 'houses' in an astrological sense). As Fagan has shown, the system is unrelated to the conventional zodiacal signs, and is linked with the ancient three-hour 'watches' time-system. See also OKTOTOPOS.

OCULUS   Fixed star, the pi of Capricornus, set in the right eye of the goat, and said to be of the nature of Venus conjunct Saturn.

==

OCULUS LEONIS   Name given to the 9th of the LUNAR MANSIONS in some mediaeval
lists. It is probably located from the fixed star Alterf in the lion's
mouth, though termed 'eye of the lion' in reference to an earlier image of
the asterism. See table 48 under "Lunar Mansions", and LUNAR ZODIAC.

OCULUS TAURI   See ALDEBARAN.

OIKEIOSIS   See FAMILIARITY.

OKTOTOPOS   The astrologer Manilius termed his system of EIGHT PLACES the
'oktotopoi' (eight places).

OLD MOON   See MOON PERIOD.

OLD SATURN   See SATURN PERIOD.

OLD STYLE   Term used in reference to the so-called 'old' chronology of the
"Julian Calendar" which was superseded by the "Gregorian Calendar". It is
normal practice for astrologers providing astrological data which might be
taken as relating to either system to mark their data OS (or o.s.) for the
Old Style, and NS (or n.s.) for the NEW STYLE, to avoid ambiguity.

OLD SUN   See SUN PERIOD.

OMENS   See OMINA.

OMINA   The art of divination by means of 'omina' or 'celestial omens', is
not strictly speaking a part of genuine astrology, though the early forms
(widely practised in Babylonian and Egyptian societies) were incorporated
into later forms of astrology. According to the historian Pingree, the
professional omen-readers in the Mesopotamian royal courts were called the
'baru', and it was through the baru that the gods revealed the meanings of
the symbolic language of celestial phenomena. The organization of omina
material appears to have been four-fold, in terms of phenomena relating to
the Moon (Sin), the Sun (Samas), meteorological phenomena (Adad) and Venus
(Istar or Ishtar). The system of omina was widely spread in the middle east,
and even into India by the time of the Persian Empire. Pingree says that the
main impact of the texts and praxes on Indian astrology was in the field of
military astrology (yatra) and catarchic astrology (muhurta). The influence
of certain omina-based ideas may be seen in surviving astrological material
derived from 2nd century Egypt, set in the form of instructions said to have
been presented by the priest PETOSIRIS to his king NECHEPSO: several ideas
from such sources have supposedly circulated even into modern astrology, as
for example the imposing (if insubstantial) edifice of "Prenatal Astrology"
which is based on a somewhat obscure principle (see TRUTINE OF HERMES)
claimed to have been derived from Petosiris.

ONE DEGREE METHOD   A method of "Symbolic Direction" involving the taking of
one degree of zodiacal arc as equivalent to one year of life. To be
distinguished from "Day for a Year", which is used in "Secondary Directions".
A variation is the so-called RADIX METHOD.

ONOMANTIC ASTROLOGY   A form of popular astrology which should not really be
called 'astrology' at all, in so far as it is not based on an interpretation
of the heavens, but upon an exceedingly simplistic approach to numerology.
The practice is based on the conversion of letters of the alphabet (usually
the name of the querent, or the names of contestants, and so on) into
numerical equivalents, by one or other of the many rules of numerology. From
such conversions, simple diagrams (which to some extent resemble astrological
charts) are derived from which the onomantist will give response to
questions, usually on a dualistic (yes or no) basis. Certain of the
onomantic methods, such as the Hellenistic 'Circle of Petosiris', claim to
give response in matters of health, even in matters of life and death. The

idea behind this form of onomancy appears to rest on a lost hermetic
tradition that in previous times sounds and numbers were cosmically related -
several Qabbalistic systems of exegesis are based on this axiom.

OPHANIM   The Hebraic plural for the spiritual 'wheels' of the biblical
Ezekiel, which Blavatsky rightly links with the 'World Spheres': the word is
Hebraic for 'Angels of the Stellatum'. Blavatsky identifies these with the
spiritual beings now called "Cherubim" (perhaps the Assyrian 'Karoubs',
sphinxes) figured in the zodiac as the four fixed signs - see TETRAMORPHS.

OPHIEL   Name (sometimes 'Oriphiel') given to the fifth of the supreme angels
of the Cabbalists. He was said to possess the attributes of Venus, and to
have the curious ability to transmute solar forces (gold) into the Venusian
forces (copper). His seal is given in SIGILS - PLANETARY BEINGS.

OPHIUCHUS   Constellations from approximately 27 degrees Scorpio to 27
degrees Sagittarius, straddling the celestial equator in a 40 degree arc. It
is sometimes called 'Serpentarius' (serpent-holder), though the serpent
itself is usually described as a separate asterism (see DRACO). There are
very many variants of the Greek term, which in the Latinized form was very
removed from the original, as for example 'Afeichus' and 'Alpheichius'.
Equally, there were many variants of the original Latin, as for example
'Serpentiger', 'Serpentis Lator', and inevitably it was linked with the
deified initiate Asclepius, who used healing serpents in his sanctuaries.
The history of the Arabian names is the story of the degeneration of the
Arabian translation of the Greek into 'Al Hawwa', which floriated into many
terms, including 'Alangue', 'Hasalangue', and such as appear in mediaeval
texts. Ptolemy likens its influence to Saturn tempered by Venus, but in
literature the constellation has gained unpopularity as the promoter of evil
and poison (the snake in the hand?): but see the relevant star RASALAGUE.
In the MODERN ZODIAC derived from Delporte, Ophiuchus has the curious
distinction of being made 'zodiacal' - see figure 44 under "Modern Zodiac".

OPPOSITION   An "Aspect" maintained by two or more planets so placed that
they confront each other across the zodiac, being separated by 180 degrees.
It is sometimes called the 'aspect of separation', and is said to promote
tension between the planets concerned, or to intensify their actions and
influences. The amount of ORB permitted this aspect is not fully agreed
among authorities, but some permit up to 10 degrees.

ORAI   One of the Gnostic names for a ruler of Venus.

ORB   That area of influence (expressed in degrees of arc) within which
planets in ASPECT may be said to exert an influence while still forming or
separating. Sometimes an aspect is ascribed an orb, at other times the
planet is ascribed an orb. There is no fixed or agreed rule by which the orb
for each of the aspects may be determined - but some indication of the
traditional orbs is given in the relevant entries to the aspects, and table
56 sets out certain of the orbs suggested by modern astrologers, the names
relating to the bibliography. Traditionally allowances are made for orb when
any of the planets involved are retrograde. There is much argument as to the
orbs which should be allowed fixed stars - Wilson for example will permit a
1st magnitude star as much as 7.5 degrees, which essentially means that fixed
stars become operative in every natal chart. The present author allows only
0.5 degrees orb for a fixed star up to and including 3rd magnitude. The
astrologer Libra quite rightly links the specific orbs with the natures of
the planets involved. A precise orb is called 'Partile', whilst one which is
in weak orb is said to be 'Platic'. When a planet is moving towards the
partile, it is said to be 'in orb of application', and when it is separating
from the platic it is said to be 'in orb of separation'- but see also
APPLICATION and SEPARATION.   The lack of agreement about precise orbs
evinced in table 56 may probably be explained by the fact that Ptolemy's view
of aspects was coloured by the "Jaiminic" rather than by anything

geometrical: the 'traditional' Ptolemaic orbs are those given by Devore in table 56, though it is scarcely accurate to describe these planetary orbs as being 'according to Ptolemy', as Devore does. The orb attached to planets (rather than to aspects) may be seen exemplified in the closely-studied MORINEAN ORBS, for here we have an excellent practical basis for a theory, which has resulted in tables of orbs appearing in many astrological textbooks long after their calculative basis has been forgotten. However, not all authorities would accept the Morinean orbs, any more than they accept the 'traditional' orbs. Theory is very often different from practice in astrology: for example, Carter (who attempted a systematic portrayal of the aspects) is theoretically quite clear about the orbs he would allow, but the application of orbs in his practical examples of chart interpretation is even wider than those suggested by Hone.

---TABLE 56

	DEVORE	WILSON	LILLY	LEO	HONE	CORNELL	BRAU	LIBRA
MO	12	12	12			12	15	
ME	7	7	7			7		
VE	8	8	7			8		
SU	17	17	15			17	15	
MA	7	7	7			7.5		
JU	12	12	9			12		
SA	9	9	9			10		
UR	5					8	2	
NE	5					8	2	
PL							2	
Conjunction				12	8		8-10	10-12
Opposition				12	8		6-8	10-12
Trine				8	8		4-6	8
Square				8	8		5-6	8
Semi-square				4	2		2	4
Sesquiquadrate				4	2		2	4
Sextile				2	4		4-6	7
Quincunx				2	2		2	2
Parallel				1				1
Quintile					2			
Biquintile					2			

ORBIT   The path apparently followed by a planet in its revolution around the solar centre. In pre-Copernican systems the orbit was explained in terms of EPICYCLES, since it was believed that supra-lunar bodies could move only in perfect circles. In post-Copernican systems, which have developed from the COPERNICAN SYSTEM, a theory of elliptical orbit (see ORBITAL REVOLUTION) has developed, and now forms the basis for the modern model of the solar system and for computations: yet see LEMNISCATE.

ORBITAL REVOLUTION   A term often shortened in astrological texts to 'revolution': the annual motion of any celestial body around the Sun. A complete orbital revolution is a 'year' of the planet or body concerned, but this is usually translated into Earth years - that is, made into a ratio of the Earth's orbital revolution. The 'sidereal month' orbit of the Moon is 27 days, 7 hours and 43 minutes, the geocentric revolutions of the other planets are given in table 57, alongside the sidereal periods derived from Schultz.

---TABLE 57

PLANET	GEOCENTRIC - 30 DEGREE ARC	SIDEREAL
ME	14 days	87.9690 days
VE	24 and half days	224.7008 days
SU	(365 days, 6 hours, 9 minutes.)	

```
--------------------------------------------------------TABLE 57 (CONTINUED)
PLANET    GEOCENTRIC  - 30 DEGREE ARC          SIDEREAL
=============================================================================
EA                                          365.256 days
MA         2 years      6 weeks             686.9798 days
JU        12 years      1 year              4332.588 days
SA        29 years      2 and half years    10759.2 days
UR        84 years      7 years              84 years and 8 days
NE       165 years      13 and 3/4 years    164 years and 282 days
PL       248 years      20 and 3/4 years    247 years and 257 days
----------------------------------------------------------------------------
```

ORB OF APPLICATION   See ORB.

ORB OF SEPARATION   See ORB.

ORIENS   One of the Latin names (meaning 'rising', in reference to the symbolic and actual rising of the Sun) for the East Angle, the Ascendant, and the cusp of the First House. For various related terms, see ORIENTAL.

ORIENTAL   Literally 'easterly' (see ORIENS): but distinguish the following derivatives, which are sometimes confusing: ORIENTAL MOON, ORIENTAL PLANET and ORIENTAL SUN.

ORIENTAL HOUSES   See EASTERN HOUSES.

ORIENTAL MOON   The Moon is said to be 'oriental' (whatever its mundane placing) when it is increasing in light, and hence to the east of the Sun: the term is ambiguous (see ORIENTAL PLANET).

ORIENTAL PLANET   A planet may be termed 'oriental of the Sun' when it rises or sets before the Sun - see however ORIENTAL MOON.

ORIENTAL SUN   Specifically the term should mean 'the easterly Sun' (see ORIENS), or 'the Sun on the Ascendant', but (confusingly) the term is used of the Sun when it is in any of the two arcs of the 10th, 11th, 12th houses and the 4th, 5th and 6th houses.

ORION   Constellation approximately 6 degrees of Gemini to 2 degrees of Cancer, and from 13 south to 24 north of the equator, one of the most impressive of asterisms. The name is from the ancient Greek, which appears to have been derived from an earlier term which was (as Allen says) 'akin to our Warrior' in sound. The giant Orion is said to have died from the sting of Scorpius, consequent to his boast that he could slay any earthly creature. Many variants were used in the earlier texts, 'Aorion', 'Arion', 'Argion' and 'Urion', though to the Arabian astrologers he was 'Al Jabbar' (the giant), which was probably from Ptolemy's term 'Gigas', and gave rise to several curious Arabian derivatives, such as 'Algebar' (frequent in mediaeval astrological texts), 'Algibber' and so on. The interesting explanation for the early Arabian 'Al Jauzah' (wrongly translated as 'giant') is that the word was used of a black sheep with a white spot on its body, and thus made an excellent stellar reference to this brilliant asterism. The names which figure so prominently in mediaeval astrological and magical texts (Orion being used in talismanic magic to promote warrior strength) are derived from this word: 'Elgeuze', 'Jeuze', and so on. In Egypt the constellation was linked with Horus (as for example in the DENDERAH ZODIAC), though the asterism appears to have been called 'Sahu'. Related names are the Jewish 'Gibbor', and the Latin 'Venator' (huntsman) which idea probably links with its reputation in astrology for promoting 'hunting'. The asterism is said to induce a dignified, self-confident and arrogant nature when emphatic in a chart, but its several powerful stars always require special notice: see therefore BETELGEUZE, BELLALTRIX, MINTAKA, RIGEL and ANILAM.

==

ORION'S BELT   Popular name for the 'Cingula Orionis', distingished by the
stars ANILAM, Alnitak (the zeta of the constellation) and MINTAKA.

ORION'S FOOT   Popular name for the fixed star RIGEL, in the foot of "Orion".

ORIPHIEL   See OPHIEL.

ORMAZD   Sometimes called 'Ahura Mazda' (The Great Being of Light'), Ormazd
or 'Ormuzd' is the creative power of Zoroastrianism who worked against the
darkness and lies of "Ahriman" (more exactly, against the 'Angrimayu' who was
later called Ahriman in western occultism). While the latter is often
identified with the lunar forces, Ormazd is linked with the solar forces, and
Blavatsky records the esoteric teaching that he is the synthesis of the
Elohim, the creative Logoi, which are in turn associated with the realm or
sphere of the "Exsusiai".

ORPHIC   A term derived from the associations built around the legendary
magician Orpheus, who is said to have founded the Greek cult of Orphism,
which remained connected with several ancient Mystery centres. When the term
is used in (non-scholarly) astrological contexts, it is generally as a
synonym for 'esoteric', or as pertaining to the secret doctrines which
pervade astrological lore.

ORPHIC AGES   According to an account of the Orphic theogony recorded by
Servius, there are four ages of the world. The first is that of Saturn, the
second of Jupiter, the third of Neptune, and the fourth that of Pluto. The
gods must (for once) be distinguished from the 'planetary beings', since it
is clear from the context that they are intended to personify the four
elements: SA Fire, JU Air, NE Water, PL Earth. These associations have
given rise to many misunderstandings in later symbolism, but they are
probably linked with the 'stages' of the creation of the Earth outlined in
modern esotericism - see for example Waschmuth.

ORPHIC DESCENT OF THE SOUL   In his commentary on an esoteric section of
Plato's 'Republic', Macrobius quotes what he describes as Orphic initiation
knowledge relating to what the descending soul learns in its passage through
the planetary spheres, prior to rebirth. A summary of this descent reflects
much of the ancient teaching of the influences of the planets themselves.
The soul, wrapped in a luminous body, descends into the sphere of Saturn
where it develops the power of reasoning and theorizing (contemplative reason
- 'intelligentia et ratiocinatio'): in the sphere of Jupiter it develops the
power of putting into practice ('vis agendi', but more specifically in Greek,
'to praktikon'). In the sphere of Mars, it takes on the power of 'ardent
vehemence' (though the word translated is actually 'Thumikon', which in
esoteric lore is linked with magical powers). In the Sun sphere, the soul
learns 'sensing and imagining' - in a word, what Coleridge would have called
'phantasie', the power of pictorial visualization or representation. In the
sphere of Venus the soul takes on the 'power of desire', which is linked with
love. In the next sphere (Mercury), the soul is given the power of 'giving
expression', and of 'interpreting feelings' (those feelings engendered in the
previous sphere). In the final sphere, that of the Moon, the soul begins to
learn about physical bodies - actually about how to make physical bodies move
and grow, which is esoterically connected with the etheric forces - see
Waschmuth. In the lower realm, the spheres of the Earth, where it takes on
through incarnation the 'terrene' body, the soul is imprisoned in a
dark-shroud of physical. As the historian Mead remarks, the 'planetary
energies thus imbibed are in no way regarded as being either beneficient or
maleficient', and there is no question of good or bad emanation in the
spheres: see therefore the contrasting EGYPTIAN DESCENT OF THE SOUL.

ORTHODOX PLANETS   In her highly complex system of "Intuitional Astrology",
Bailey lists four different classifications of planets which include what she
calls the 'orthodox planets' - but see also ESOTERIC PLANETS, NON-SACRED

PLANETS and SACRED PLANETS.   With a single exception, the orthodox planets
correspond (at least in their rulerships) to the ancient Ptolemaic model,
with Mars ruling Aries, Venus Taurus, and so on.   The exception is that
Uranus (the only one of the so-called "Modern Planets" in this
classification) is accorded rule over Aquarius, which of course is quite in
accordance with the modern astrological view:

AR	ruled by MA	TA	ruled by VE	GE	ruled by ME
CN	ruled by MO	LE	ruled by SU	VG	ruled by ME
LB	ruled by VE	SC	ruled by MA	SG	ruled by JU
CP	ruled by SA	AQ	ruled by UR	PI	ruled by JU

It would appear that this group of orthodox planets are regarded as being
operative in the charts of ordinary people - that is, in the charts of those
who have not been initiated, or who have not otherwise undertaken to speed up
their evolutionary progress.   See also UNORTHODOX ASTROLOGICAL RELATIONSHIPS.

ORTIVE DIFFERENCE   A term derived from the Latin 'ortus solis' (rising of
the Sun) and used to denote the difference involved when directing the Sun at
its rising - though the term is also confusingly used of the same procedure
in regard to the setting of the Sun.   Precise definition of the differences
involved is not always clear: Devore suggests that the 'ortive difference'
may be an indication of some effort to accommodate the fact of horizontal
parallax, but it is equally probable that the difference is to do with the
regional variations which were so much a problem for early astrologers.   The
actual sunrise in a mountainous district is very different from that given in
tables designed for the notional horizon derived from consideration of the
Celestial Sphere.   It is certain (at least to the present writer who has had
some practical experience of the matter) that many mediaeval horoscopes were
based not on the calculated sunrise but upon the 'observational sunrise', and
that therefore a difference (which might be calculated) was involved:
perhaps this was indeed the 'ortive difference'.

OSIRIS   Name given to one of the "Hypothetical Planets" by the astrologer
Sutcliffe, as one of the four ultraneptunian bodies.   See also ISIS.   THE
remaining hypotheticals of this group were designated only by numbers.   The
Osiris of Sutcliffe is to be distinguished from its namesake discussed by
Thierens in his survey of the esoteric "Etheric Spheres", as the ruler of
Aries.

OURANOS   The ancient Greek name for the expanse of the heavens.   The god
"Uranus" was the husband of Gaia (the Earth), through whom the Titans were
fathered.   Esoterically, Ouranos and Gaia are the original parents of Man,
who belongs partly to the realm of spirit (ouranos) and partly to the realm
of elemental forces (gaia).   This is why the esoteric texts give so many
descriptive epithets for Ouranos, such as 'Waters of Space' or the 'Celestial
Ocean', for besides relating to boundless space, they relate also to Man.
The term Ouranos was sometimes used in the late 18th century as a synonym for
"Uranus", from which it must be distinguished: see also GEORGIUM SIDUS.

OUTER PLANETS   See SUPERIOR PLANETS.

OV   Designation (with the alternative name Ov.O) made by the astrologer
Charubel to an extraneptunian planet which he perceived clairvoyantly some
years prior to 1897, for which he claimed a revolution of 297 years.   He said
that it gives 'longevity and magnetic power' - in some respects this
hypothetical is similar to the then undiscovered "Pluto" (with a revolution
period of 248 years), but one wonders if it is merely accidental that
Charubel should have found this planet to be in orb of the Ascendant (12
degrees of Scorpio) of his own chart?   Ov has been identified with MELODIA.

PADUAN CYCLE Name given to one of the most ambitious of all mediaeval
astrological frescoes, in the Salone of the Palazzo della Ragione, Padua.
Three registers, totalling 333 separate compartments of largely planetary,
stellar and cosmic images, extend over 217 metres. On rather dubious
grounds, the cycle has been associated with Giotto (14th century), but later
fire damage (1426) and heavy cyclone damage (1756) demanded considerable
restoration, and at least three major restorations since. The post-1420
painters are unknown (Nicolo Mireti and Stefano de Ferrara are suggested as
masters in charge). The cycle is still the most comprehensive surviving
mediaeval attempt to relate zodiacal, constellational and seasonal imagery to
Christian theology and symbolism: unfortunately the system is far from clear
to modern minds, especially in regard to the symbolism of decans, and the
associations drawn between the apostles and the signs. The sequence is in
fact broken to the south by an old ZODIACAL CALENDAR, surrounded by a
Christian iconography which points to the ancient link between Christ and the
Sun Sphere. Some of the images are no longer understood, but some reflect
the iconography traditionally associated with Peter of Abano. A useful
synopsis by Beltrame incorporates the more scholarly (though incomplete)
treatment of Ivanoff and Barzon.

PAGAN-PLUTO Name given in comparatively recent times to the planet "Pluto".
The astrologer Pagan designated as ruler of Scorpio a 'hypothetical' planet
in 1911 (prior to the discovery of the 'new' planet Pluto) which she named
Pluto - it was a designation which influenced modern astrologers into
adopting Pluto as the ruler of this sign. The modern term 'Pluto-Pagan' is
used to distinguish the planet from various other 'Plutonic planets', such as
the LOWELL-PLUTO, the WEMYSS-PLUTO, and the THIERENS-PLUTO. Pagan herself
suggested a sigil for her Pluto ♇ which (whilst graphically more correct
than the more usual form ♇) has not been widely adopted.

PALLAS Name given to one of the ASTEROIDS, discovered in 1802, and
associated by the astrologer Dobyns with the sign Libra, along with an
asteroidal co-ruler "Juno".

PALMISTIC ZODIAC In his published research on ASTROPALMISTRY, Gettings has
proposed a schematic co-ordination between the structure of the hand
(chirognomatic and chiromantic) with the zodiac. By means of this model
(which has been called the 'palmistic zodiac') it has been possible to
demonstrate convincing relationships between personal charts and hand form.
The schema given is:

AR	Thumb (seat of Will)	LB	Mount of Venus
TA	Mount of Venus	SC	Ring Finger
GE	Line of Life	SG	Line of Head (seat of Mentation)
CN	Mount of Moon	CP	Middle Finger
LE	Line of Heart (seat of Emotions)	AQ	Line of Fate
VG	Little Finger	PI	Index Finger

PAN Name given to one of the "Hypothetical Planets" listed by the
astrologer Jayne as a transplutonian.

PANSOPHIA A term used by the historian Haase in his study of the harmonics
of Kepler as denoting an 'attitude of mind' arising from the hermetic
tradition, which (he says) strives towards presenting a unified harmonic
picture of the world, often using fantastical and seemingly obscure materials
in the picture-building. It is a holistic and hermetic attitude, which Haase
contrasts with the fissiparous attitude of the MATHESIS UNIVERSALIS. In
effect it is the late hermetic tradition as recorded in the writings of such

occultists and astrologers as Pico della Mirandola, Regiomontanus, Agrippa, Trithemius and, to some extent, Kircher and Fludd - but above all Paracelsus.

PANTHEONS   See COSMIC PANTHEONS.

PAPILIO   Name given to the 25th of the LUNAR MANSIONS in certain mediaeval lists. Probably identified by the asterisms around the urn of the "Aquarius Constellation", near to Sadachbia.   See however table 48 under "Lunar Mansions".

PARALLEL   An aspect formed between two or more planets with the same degree of declination, either north or south (together or separately) of the ecliptic. Planets so placed are said to be 'in parallel' - however, in modern astrology the term 'in parallel' is used only of those parallel on the same side of the ecliptic: those in opposite declinations are said to be 'in contraparallel'.   Traditional astrology teaches that the parallel aspect has much the same force as the CONJUNCTION, though a maximum orb of 1 degree only is permitted. The whole realm of parallel aspects is very much in dispute in modern astrology, and some astrologers regard the parallel as effective only when the planets concerned are otherwise in angular aspects. See also PARALLEL IN MUNDO.

PARALLEL IN MUNDO   Sometimes called 'Mundane Parallel', this has nothing to do with the zodiacal PARALLELS related to aspectal theory. A planet is in 'mundane parallel' with another when it is the same distance from one of the four angles. Thus, a planet on the cusp of the Second House may be in parallel (in mundo) with the planet on the cusp of the Twelfth House, since both are equidistant from the cusp of the Ascendant (First House). The theory and practice of 'in mundo' interpretation was developed by Placidus de Tito, and has not gained wide acceptance in modern astrology.

PARAN   A term derived by the astrologer Hand from the Greek PARANATELLONTA, applied to a potential relationship manifest at a moment of planetary transit, when (and only when) the natal planet is involved, and the planets of transit, cross the horizon or meridian at the same time. The term 'paranatellonta', which applied to a temporal sequence (and was sometimes used wrongly of a spatial sequence), has thus been adapted to designate a supposed influence. Whilst the term appears to rest on a confusion of the meaning of the original Greek, it is properly restricted to certain TOPOCENTRIC ASCENSIONAL TRANSITS. Brau, who gives the alternative term Paranatellon for Paran, defines it as a relationship between two planets which simultaneously cross the same angle (or different angles in the same chart). It is reasonable to link this approach to aspects with observational astrology, but it is quite wrong to claim (as Brau does) that Ptolemy wrote about Parans. This confusion might suggest that Brau is misunderstanding Ptolemy's view of the Paranatellonta.

PARANTELLON   A term sometimes used in modern astrology as an alternative for "Paran", though in a way which might suggest a basic confusion with the PARANATELLONTA: for example of mis-use, see PARAN.

PARANATELLONTA   A term derived directly from the Greek, meaning approximately "rising together", or "rising side by side", and often (wrongly) applied to the sequence of the zodiacal signs or constellations, imagined as rising over the horizon, or (less frequently) over the meridian. The term may however have been applied to other phenomena, such as the rising of star groups, with or without planets. Boll, in reference to Ptolemy's use of the word, refers to the paranatellonta in terms of star groups: the word is explained as referring to stars which rise and set at the same time as the degrees or sections of the ecliptic, but to the north or south of these (see also PARAN). In modern astrology, the term is sometimes used to refer to the mere sequence of the zodiacal signs or constellations, irrespective of their 'rising': for example, Ivanoff refers to the frescoes of the PADUAN CYCLE as a 'parantellonta'. Properly speaking, however, this is a misuse of the term.

PARANTELLONTA A modern version of PARANTELLONTA. But see also PARAN.

PARAPEGMA Originally a Greek-derived Latin term, meaning 'something fixed, or hung for display', and often applied to tables of astrological or astronomical calculations made of brass, and fixed to a wall, pillar or floor. In modern astrological use, the term might be applied to the metal or marble slabs containing astrological symbols, descriptive of the meridianal parantellonta, transits, and like phenomena, in ZODIACAL CALENDARS.

PARANSARA A name given to the Vedic sage who narrated the 'Vishnu Purana', but the name appears to have been used for various later astrologers. See however JAIMINI.

PARILICIUM See HYADES.

PARS A Latin term often translated as 'Part', derived ultimately from the Greek astrological term 'klipoi'. The term is used to cover an almost bewildering range of points derived from the adjusting planetary and nodal points to the Ascendant or other fixed points of reference, and ascribing an interpretative value to the adjusted positions of the revolved planets or nodal points. The PART OF FORTUNE, which is so important in the astrological tradition that it is sometimes merely called the 'part', is derived from the rotation of the degree held by the natal Sun until this becomes the Ascendant degree: the position of the adjusted Moon marks the point or part - but for typical construction of 'pars fortunae' see figure 46a under PART OF FORTUNE. There is a corresponding Pars for each planet (and indeed for several nodal points): in general the planetary pars are derived by revolving the Sun to the Ascendant, and then regarding the new position of the planet concerned as marking the 'pars'. Examples of the general rules for calculating others are set out under individual headings - see therefore BROTHERS AND SISTERS, COMMERCE, DISCORD, EROS, FATALITY, FATHER, GAVEL POINT, GOODS, HUSBANDRY, INCREASE, INHERITANCE, LIFE, PLAY, POINT OF BONDAGE, POINT OF FAITH, POINT OF MALE CHILDREN, POINT OF PASSIONS, POINT OF SERVANTS, POINT OF SICKNESS, POINT OF SPIRIT, POINT OF TRAVEL BY LAND, POINT OF UNDERSTANDING, MARRIAGE POINT, POMEGRANATE and PRIVATE ENEMIES. Many of the points are often (though erroneously) called 'Arabian Pars' simply because the notion entered mediaeval astrology by way of the Arabian astrologers, who had indeed developed their own idea of pars, but who were also transmitting the original conception from Greek astrology - see LOT OF DAIMON and SEVEN LOTS, for example.   The pars are really nodal points, and it is often said that they 'cast no rays' - that is, that they are not subject to influences by aspects other than the conjunction, which may also be made operative by transit or progression.

PARSEC A term derived from modern astronomy, denoting a unit expressive of vast stellar distance. One parsec equals 3.26 light years. It corresponds to the distance from which the mean distance of the Earth from the Sun would appear as a parallax of one second of arc.

PARS FORTUNAE The Latin term for the "Part of Fortune", sometimes 'pars fortuna'.

PART See PARS. When the English term 'part' is used in an astrological context, and without further qualification, it is almost invariably a reference to the PART OF FORTUNE.

PARTHENOS One of the Greek names, meaning 'virgin', used for the zodiacal sign and constellation Virgo. Sometimes the constellation was 'Parthenos Dios' (virgin goddess). See KORE.

PARTIAL ECLIPSE See UMBRAL ECLIPSE.

PARTILE ASPECT   An exact "Aspect" between two or more bodies. In general
astrological use the term is applied to aspects which are in the same degree
of longitude, but some astrologers insist that the term may be properly used
only when the aspect is exact and 'in parallel' - see PARALLEL.

PART OF DAIMON   See LOT OF DAIMON.

PART OF FORTUNE   The most important of the PARS - a nodal point in the
horoscope chart which is the same distance of zodiacal arc from the Ascendant
as the Moon is from the Sun (figure 46A). The point marks the place which
the Moon would hold at the symbolic sunrise.   Now the most important of the
Pars, in Hellenistic astrology it vied with the LOT OF DAIMON in importance.
The above account of the Pars is set out to satisfy the modern conception,
but it must be observed that this is merely one of several methods (itself
derived from Manilius) used in early astrology for determining the Pars.
Ptolemy gives a variation on this rule, as may be see in figure 46B, while
many of the ancients distinguished between a Pars originated for a day chart
from one originated from a night chart - the symbolic sunrise becoming the
symbolic moonrise. Figure 46C, derived from Firmicus, is really an extension
of the rule of Ptolemy to the night chart.

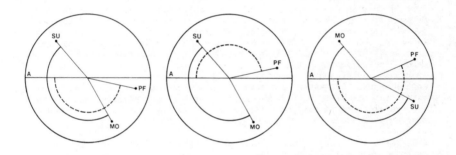

FIGURE 46. PARS FORTUNAE, CAST ACCORDING TO THE METHODS OF (A) MANILIUS,
(B) PTOLEMY AND (C) FIRMICUS.

PART OF JUPITER   The name for the so-called Arabian PARS, sometimes called
the "Pomegranate".

PART OF LOVE   See EROS.

PART OF PLUTO   See GAVEL POINT.

PASSER   The Latin for 'sparrow', an early name for the asterism later
determined by Bayer as VOLANS.

PASSIEL   Name given to two quite distinct spirits, with separate functions.
In certain methods of ceremonial magic the name is one of several attached to
the governer of zodiacal Pisces. In the Cabbalistic tradition, it is the
name given to one of the angels who has rule over Abaddon.

PASSIVE   The Sun and Moon are sometimes said to be passive, in that they
take their colouring from the signs in which they are placed: Simmonite

called the Sun and Moon the 'passive stars'. However, this is clearly a
redundant or inapplicable term with such a context, since all planets receive
such a zodiacal colouring. It is likely that the term is derived from the
Aristotelian concept of the PRINCIPLES, for the principle of Moisture is said
to be passive as indeed is the principle of Dryness. Within this
classification the dry Sun and the moist Moon might be said to be 'passive',
but the term has no application in modern astrology.

PASSIVE STARS   See PASSIVE.

PASTOR ET ARIES   Name given to the 22nd of the LUNAR MANSIONS in some
mediaeval lists. It is probably identified by the multiple star Algedi in
the horns of Capricornus - but see table 48 under "Lunar Mansions".

PATH OF REBIRTH   See DESCENT OF THE SOUL.

PATTERNS   See FIGURINES and JONES PATTERNS.

PAVO   Constellation, the 'Peacock', situated to the south of constellations
Sagittarius and the Southern Crown, and formed by Bayer in 1604. Astrologers
say that it gives vanity and love of display.

PEACOCK   See PAVO.

PEGASUS   Constellation situate to the north of the urn of Aquarius and the
eastern fish of the asterism Pisces. This is the 'Winged Horse' or 'Flying
Horse', said in Greek mythological accounts to have been born of the blood of
Medusa after her head had been cut off by Perseus: this severed head had
dropped into the sea, which may partly explain the suggested etymologies of
the word (see SCHEAT). The Greeks called the asterism 'Hippos', though
sometimes 'Hippos Ieros' (divine horse) and there are many related or derived
terms, including the Latin 'Equus', 'Equus Ales', 'Alatus' (winged),
'Sonipes' (noisy-footed), and so on. It is suggested that the Jackal-like
animal on the DENDERAH ZODIAC represents at least part of Pegasus. Ptolemy
associates its brightest stars with the influence of Mercury conjunct Mars,
and the asterism is said to bring ambition, vanity, enthusiasm and bad
judgment. Besides "Scheat", see also MARKAB.

PEG STAR   One of the names used to denote the fixed star SPICA, when
regarded as a zodiacal fiducial.

PELAGUS   Fixed star, the sigma of constellation Sagittarius, set in the
arrow of this image. It is said to be the Nunki of the ancient Euphratean
'Tablet of the Thirty Stars', associated with the sea, hence the Greek name
'Pelagus'. Ptolemy equates it with an influence similar to that of Mercury
conjunct Jupiter: it is claimed that Pelagus gives a truthful and religious
mind, and produces benefit with all planets, including even the malefics.

PENTACLE   Specifically, a geometric figure linked with the number five, such
as the five-sided pentagon or the PENTAGRAM or the PENTALPHA. However, the
term is often used in a general sense for any simple geometric figure
constructed for magical or amuletic purposes - thus the six-pointed SEAL OF
SOLOMON or the septenary CHALDEAN ORDER is sometimes called a 'Pentacle' -
see also the so-called PYTHAGOREAN PENTACLE.

PENTADES   The astrologer Fagan has argued that the so-called Egyptian
DECANS, which are supposed to relate to 'ten days star' measures, mark off
only the visible vault of the heavens, and as symbolic projections are
divorced from the material world. If this argument is sound, then the entire
circle of division would have to be taken into account, making them divisions
not of 360 degrees, but of 180 degrees, in which case they would be
'pentades'. However, there appears to be little doubt in the later
development of the Decans which influenced European astrology that they were

precisely what their name indicates - 10 degree arcs, or three-fold divisions
of the signs. Fagan's argument merely calls into question the antiquity of
the Egyptian zodiac, and permits certain of the ancient celestial diagrams to
be linked with the heliacal rising of SIRIUS.

PENTAGRAM   The 'pentagram', sometimes called the 'pentalpha', is the
five-pointed star regarded as a symbol of many esoteric qualities: it is
indeed the symbol of the microcosm, as well as of the 'etheric' (see MORNING
STAR). The pentagram has from very early times been linked esoterically with
the planet Venus. In this latter connexion, as the work of Schultz
demonstrates, when the patterns of conjunctions between Venus and Sun are
plotted over synodic periods, a pentagram is traced in the skies around the
Earth (figure 47). Sample data (additional to that in figure 47) given for a
first order cycle relating to dates of conjunctions are: 13.4.53 - 15.11.54
- 22.7.56 - 28.1.58 - 1.9.59 - 11.4.61.

FIGURES 47 AND 48. (47) PENTAGRAMMATIC FORM TRACED BY THE PERIODICITY
OF VENUS IN RELATION TO CONJUNCTIONS WITH THE SUN (AFTER SCHULTZ), AND
(48) THE HUMAN FORM CONTAINED WITHIN A PENTAGRAM (AFTER AGRIPPA).

In the 15th century Agrippa (an esotericist masquerading as a magician)
published a number of interesting figures relating the planets to the human
body and corresponding centres of rulerships. In the relevant figure for the
pentagram (figure 48) the planets accorded the points of the pentagram are a
sort of exoteric blind, for what is of real importance is the centre, marked
with the sigil for the Moon. The esotericists maintained that the pentagram
was the symbolic form of the postmortem state, and it is therefore of deep
significance that the centre of this posture (the 'etheric posture' as it is
sometimes called in esoteric circles) is placed upon the lunar sigil, for it
is through the lunar sphere which the newly departed must first travel after
death. The sexual parts, linked with the "Negative Mars" of Scorpio, marks
the unregenerate man which must be burned away in the purgatorial fires of
the lunar sphere. Agrippa makes this clear by implication when he points out
that another posture (with the arms raised) puts the centre upon the navel,
which represents the solar, life-enhancing position, yet which breaks the
pentagram-structure of the lunar-centred figure.

PENTALPHA   One of the names for the five-pointed "Pentagram", so-called
because it reproduced in its sigillic form the letter A (the Greek alpha)
five times: see figure 48.

PERILOUS YEAR The 'point of the most Perilous Year', one of the so-called Arabian PARS. If the degree of Saturn in a natal chart is rotated to the Ascendant, the position then held by the Lord of the Eighth House of that natal chart marks the point.

PERIODICAL LUNATION   See SIDEREAL LUNATION.

PERIODICITIES   See CYCLES.

PERIODIC LUNATION   Name used for a horoscope figure cast for a period of the Moon, when it returns to the exact degree of its radical place: 27 days, 7 hours and 41 minutes.

PERIODS   See INITIAL CHRONOCRATORS, PLANETARY PERIODS, PLANETARY YEARS and REVOLUTION PERIODS.

PERISOMATA   See HUMOURS.

PERPETUAL NOON DATE   See ADJUSTED CALCULATION DATE.

PERSEPHONE   Name given to one of the "Hypothetical Planets" in the system proposed by the Dutch astrologer Ram, and accorded rule over zodiacal Taurus. This transplutonian is included in an ephemeris, and claimed to relate to 'creativity and spiritual performance'. See also VIRGO CONSTELLATION.

PERSEUS   Constellation, sometimes called 'Champion', the killer of Medusa and rescuer of Andromeda. 'Perseus' is from the Greek traced back to the Babylonian 'Parasiea', though the asterism has been given many names. Some epithets are used in Latin texts, most usually in reference to his victory of Medusa (the "Algol") - 'Deferens Caput Algol', 'Victor Gorgonei Monstri', 'Gorgonifer', etc. Late mediaeval terms, 'Celeub' and 'Chelub' are almost certainly from the Arabic 'kullab', which refers to the weapon he carries. The asterism was also called 'Cacodaemon', though this probably refers to the head of Medusa (see ALGOL). The astrological association is in accord with the idea of victory - it gives intelligence, strength and an adventurous nature, though with a tendency to deception. In connexion with fixed stars, see ALGENIB.

PERSONAL DEGREE   See PERSONAL STAR.

PERSONAL STAR The popular notion that each person is linked with a particular 'personal star' may perhaps be seen as an excessively simplistic version of the idea underlying astrology: see BIRTH STAR. However, Pliny records an interesting variation of the idea, in the view that a star is born with each new birth, and then dies with the death of that person. In recent years the idea of a 'star' has been extended to the idea of 'degree of the zodiac' (which must surely contain at least one star, if not many), on the basis that the precessional rate links the Sun with one degree over a period of 72 years - see PRECESSION - which has been taken as a notional 'average period of life'. Thus, it is claimed that each person is born with a degree, and dies with that degree.

PETOSIRIS   A name or title supposedly of an Egyptian priest who wrote for his King Nechepso an astrological text which greatly influenced the antique notion of popular astrology. A number of semi-astrological hermetic doctrines, replete with magical ideas and cosmogonic formulae, have survived under the general title of 'Nechepso and Petosiris', but the style and ideas are typical of the Alexandrian School, and have been placed by Riess in the 1st century BC. See OMINA.

PHACD   One of the seven fixed stars forming the constellation of "Ursa Major", said by Ptolemy to be of the equivalent influence of Mars.

==

PHACT   Fixed star, the alpha of "Columba", sometimes called 'Phaet' or 'Phad', the name of uncertain (Arabian) origin. Lockyer maintains that at least twelve Egyptian temples were orientated towards this star. It is associated with beneficial nature of Mercury and Venus combined.

PHAINON   The Greek name (meaning 'the shiny one') for the planet Saturn. But see also PHOENON.

PHALEG   The third of the seven supreme angels of the Cabbalists, described as the 'war lord'. His seal is given in SIGILS - PLANETARY BEINGS.

PHALGUNI   The Sanskrit name for the constellation Virgo - but see KANYA.

PHASE-ANGLE   A term defined by the modern astrologer Addey, relating to the theory of HARMONICS, specifically for astrological use, though derived from general wave-theory. The 'phase-angle' is the angle between the 'peak' of a wave-form and the first degree (the 'zero point') of Aries. In consideration of this sytem of measurement, he takes the wavelength of each harmonic as being no more than 360 degrees in extent.

PHASES   See PLACES.

PHENOMENON   In ordinary use a phenomenon is something which is perceived or observed, which means that in its astrological sense the term is misused since it denotes such celestial events as ingresses, times of nodes, and so on, which may not be observed. In addition, the term covers such 'observable' events as eclipses. Ephemerides often provide lists of so-called 'phenomena' as supplementary material.

PHLEGMATIC   One of the four TEMPERAMENTS, arising from an excess of the Water element in the psychological make-up of the personality. The phlegmatic temperament is withdrawn, sensitive and unstable, and within the astrological tradition is associated with such keywords as receptive, confused, emotional, fluctuating, lacking in direction, self-protecive and slow. The type is usually very methodical, and has a great power when the forces of the temperament are rightly canalized, yet its exterior is often deceptive, unrevealing of the depths within. Faults in the temperament arise from over-sensitivity to physical phenomena, which often produces fear, or an inability to cope, under which circumstances the type is mistrustful and suspicious of radical change.

PHLEGMATIC QUADRANT   See QUADRANTS.

PHOBOS   One of the two moons of Mars.

PHOEBE   One of the poetic names given to the Moon of the Earth, but also an (unpoetic) name of one of the moons of Saturn.

PHOENICE   See POLARIS.

PHOENIX   This name was not used in an astrological context until the asterism was originated by Bayer in 1604, from stars between "Eriadanus" and "Grus". Sometimes called 'Griffin' or (confusingly) 'Eagle' (see EAGLE), this asterism was said to exert an influence conducive to good life, and to bring 'lasting fame'. The term has a rich accretion of symbolism attached to it in both alchemical and occult symbolism, however, and attempts have been made to link the 600 year cycle of the phoenix with both reincarnation theory and various planetary cycles. See NAROS CYCLE.

PHOENON   According to some authorities, one of the Greek names (meaning 'terrible' or 'cruel') for the planet Saturn. But see also PHAINON.

PHUL   The seventh of the seven supreme angels of the Cabbalists, said to

possess all the attributes of the Moon. His seal is given in SIGILS -
PLANETARY BEINGS.

PHYTO   See HYADES.

PICTOR   Constellation, formed originally by La Caille in 1752, as 'Equuleus
Pictoris' (painter's easel), but now generally known in the shortened
version. It is located south of "Columba" and is supposed to give artistic
ability, as well as a reliable nature.

PISCES   The last of the twelve signs of the zodiac, and one of the
constellations. It corresponds as a zodiacal sign neither in location nor
extent with the asterism of the same name - see PISCES CONSTELLATION.   The
modern sigil for Pisces){ is said by some to be a drawing of the two
fishes united by the so-called 'silver cord' which joins together their
mouths in the constellation image (figure 49): in this image the two fishes
usually face in opposite directions to symbolize the altercation between
spirit and soul in the human being. Pisces is of the water element and of
the mutable quality, the influence being pre-eminently emotional, intuitive
and insecure. There is a strong tendency to withdrawal and towards artistic
expression, and the Piscean type tends to be hyper-sensitive to the emotional
needs of others. The sensitive nature of Pisces is expressed in the many
keywords attached to the sign by modern astrologers: sympathetic,
imaginative, poetic, suggestible, emotionally malleable, poetic,
self-pitying, easy-going, self-indulgent, sentimental, kindly and inconstant.
    In excess, or under pressure, the Piscean nature expresses itself in terms
relating to its underlying insecurity and lack of drive, the keywords being:
dreamy, impractical, lazy, restless, unstable, chaotic, hypochondriac,
fickle, lacking in self-reliance. Pisces is ruled by the modern planet
Neptune in most modern astrological systems, though in traditional astrology
it was ruled by the beneficient and expansive Jupiter (see RULERSHIPS): the
sign marks the exaltation of Venus and the detriment of Mercury.

FIGURE 49.   IMAGE FOR PISCES FROM THE FACADE OF AMIENS CATHEDRAL, FRANCE,
AND THE CONSTELLATION OF PISCES FROM THE 'MODERN ZODIAC' OF DELPORTE.

PISCES CONSTELLATION.   Constellation of the 'Fishes', located approximately
15 degrees Pisces to 26 degrees Aries, the extent of the asterism being set
out according to the limits recognized by the MODERN ZODIAC based on Delporte
in figure 49. The image of the two fishes, joined by a connecting band (that
in figure 49 is derived from the 13th century astrological reliefs on the
facade of Amiens Cathedral), figures on the DENDERAH ZODIAC of Egypt. It was
named both 'Fish' and 'Fishes' by the Greeks, though the Romans emphasized

the duality with their 'Piscis Gemellus'. To the Babylonian astrologers 'Nunu' was also a pair of fishes, and some even more ancient remains give it as 'Nuni' (fishes) as well as 'Zib', perhaps meaning 'boundary' and pointing to its marking the 'end' of the zodiacal circle. The 'Fish' which symbolized Christ was from early Christian times linked with Pisces, yet even earlier it had been an esoteric symbol, linked with both the Greek 'fish-goddess' Atargatis, and with the Syrian 'Dagon', a fish-headed man (said to be the image of the celestial man - the seas and the spiritual realm being regarded as symbolic equivalents). This probably explains why the constellation should have been under the tutelage of Poseidon (and hence the 'Neptuni Sidus' of Manilius). Ptolemy breaks down the influence of the constellation into separate asterisms, with the result that the entire constellation is of variable influence, and may be determined only by reference to the fixed star tradition. The lucida is the so-called 'knot' (the 'Nodus') in the thread, the 'Linon' of the Greeks, the 'Nodus Piscium' of the Romans. It is the alpha of Pisces, often called 'Al Rescha' from the Arabian meaning 'the cord'. In some esoteric texts, the binding cord is sometimes called the 'Silver Cord', and is said to be linked with the subtle and invisible connexion which holds in union the spirit and soul of incarnate man.

PISCIS   Name given to the 28th of the LUNAR MANSIONS in some mediaeval lists. It is probably identified by the fixed star MIRACH. But see also table 48 under "Lunar Mansions".

PISCIS AUSTRALIS   Constellation, 'the Southern Fish', located approximately 15 degrees Aquarius to 5 degrees Pisces and 28 to 36 degrees south of the equator. It has been said that this southern fish was the parent of the "Pisces Constellation", and a curious confirmation of this is found in the legend which has the asterism formed to commemorate the change of bathing Venus into a fish. In late antiquity Venus was linked with 'Atargartis', and hence in pre-Christian mystery traditions with the fish-headed 'Dagon': in Christian mystery traditions these merged with the Virgin Mary, who gave birth to the Fish who became Christ: hence the name 'Golden Fish', though 'Greater Fish' is Grecian pre-Christian. Bayer says that the influence of the asterism is the equivalent of Saturn. FOMALHAUT, the fixed star in its mouth, was one of the four ROYAL STARS of the Persians.

PISCIS VOLANS   See VOLANS.

PITUITA   A late mediaeval term for the "Phlegmatic" humour.

PLACE   See CHOROGRAPHY.

PLACES   A translation of the Ptolemaic 'topoi', which were arcs of 2.5 degrees, obtained by dividing the zodiacal signs of 30 degrees by 12. As with the system of DECANS, each of the places was ascribed a planetary ruler. These places were also once called 'phases'. Some confusion has arisen from the fact that Ptolemy also used the same term, similarly translated, as the equivalent of 'house'.

PLACES OF THE MODERATORS   See HYLEGIACAL PLACES and MODERATORS.

PLACIDEAN MEASURE OF TIME   See MEASURE OF TIME.

PLACIDEAN SYSTEM   A widely used method of HOUSE DIVISION, sometimes called the 'Semi-Arc System', though at least three other methods employ the trisection of semi-arcs. It is a time-division, based on the addition of one third of a semi-arc to the sidereal time of ascension, in a sequence designed to determine the cusps of the 12th, 11th and 10th houses, which of course gives the degrees for the corresponding opposite cusps. The nocturnal semi-arc is treated likewise in terms of the sidereal times of descension to give the remaining cusps. The fact that the Placidean system is the most widely used in modern English astrological circles is largely due to

==

historical accident, rather than to any particular merit in the system
itself. From the 19th century most of the available 'Tables of Houses' which
were used in ephemerides (especially in the popular 'Raphael's Ephemeris'
series) were computed according to this trisection of the semi-arc, and their
availability encouraged its wide use by astrologers who did not necessarily
understand the principles involved. The system is often said to be named
after its (supposed) inventor, the astrologer Placidus di Tito, who lived in
the 17th century, but the fact is that this particular trisection method was
derived from one (correctly) ascribed to the 8th century Arabian astrologer
ben Djabir (see ALBATEGNIUS SYSTEM). See also HOROPLANETARY DOMIFICATION.

PLAKSHA   See SECOND ROOT RACE.

PLANETARY ANGELS   As with the ZODIACAL ANGELS and the ZODIACAL SPIRITS,
there is much confusion of nomenclature and role of the 'planetary angels'.
In general terms the whole schema of angelic rule is dealt with under
CELESTIAL HIERARCHIES. The true 'planetary angels' of mediaeval astrology
are the governors of the spheres, which are listed under their esoteric name
of SECUNDADEIAN BEINGS. However, the list of planetary angels most widely
used in modern astrology is:

    MO Gabriel   ME Raphael   VE Haniel   SU Michael
    MA Camael   JU Zadkiel   SA Zaphkiel

PLANETARY CHAIN   A term introduced into esoteric astrology through the
Theosophy of Blavatsky. It is claimed that each of the physical globes of
the cosmic bodies are accompanied by, and indeed nourished by, seven superior
globes which remain invisible to ordinary sight. These septenaries are
termed a CHAIN. See also GLOBES.

PLANETARY CHAIN LOGOS   In the Theosophical cosmoconception, the 'Planetary
Chain Logos' is the title given to the individual spiritual entity deputized
to take charge of a whole series of 'Seven Chains' or an entire SCHEME OF
EVOLUTION.

PLANETARY COLOURS   A number of different associations between the planets
and colours has been preserved within the astrological tradition, and it is
impossible to untangle the associations in the hope of establishing an order
in the chaos. The following are derived from lists as widely divergent as
Blavatsky, Cornell, Hall, Libra and Lilly - though it must be admitted that
each of the associations would be contested by some modern authorities.

    MO Silvers, whites, greys, 'green-silver'
    ME Yellow, azure, violet, slate colours, soft browns, 'spotted mixtures'
    VE Blues, pastel shades, greens, indigo, 'soft pale blues'
    SU Gold, orange, yellow, blue, 'yellow-brown'
    MA Red, scarlet, carmine, magenta, deep orange, 'angry shades (hues?)'
    JU Purple, violet, indigo, sky blues, 'deep tones of midnight sky'
    SA Black, grey, green, dark brown, sage green, 'dark mottled colours'

There is much argument among authorities as to the rulerships of the
extrasaturnian planets, though the following are often given:

    UR Electric colours, light blues, 'a profusion of glaring colours'
    NE Lavender, greys, whites, mauve, 'sea colours'
    PL Black, 'blood reds', 'magmatic colours'

PLANETARY HARMONICS   The modern astrologer Walter has done much research
into the theory of aspects, especially in connexion with the theory of
HARMONICS, and has come to the conclusion that there is a relationship
between harmonic numbers and the planets, as follows:

    ME 2   VE 3   SU 1   MA 5   JU 6   SA 7   UR 8   NE 9   PL 10

PLANETARY HORAS   See HORAS.

PLANETARY HOURS   In the astrological tradition every hour of the day is said to be ruled by a particular planet. It is the cycle of such planetary hours which has given rise to the names of the DAYS OF THE WEEK. Blavatsky gave an alternative system of planetary hours, dividing the day not into 24 arcs of time, but into 4, the sequence beginning in the first semi-diurnal arc of Monday with the Moon, then running through the entire week of of arcs in the traditional order of the planets. Thus Monday is said to consist of four arcs ruled in sequence by the MO, ME, VE and SU, while Tuesday is ruled by the arcs MA, JU, SA and MO. The names of the days are determined by the opening ruler. The astrologer Leo provides a similar system, allegedly based on the Egyptian time measurement systems of 3-arc days, starting Saturday with the ruler SA.

PLANETARY MAN   See PLANETARY MELOTHESIA.

PLANETARY MELOTHESIA   A term derived from Ptolemaic astrology to denote a list (really several lists) of rulerships or lordships held by the planets over various parts of the body. Ptolemy gives a list which has quite evidently influenced the later pictorial imagery of MELOTHESIC MAN:

MO   rules sense of taste, stomach, belly, womb and left-hand parts
ME   rules speech and thought, the tongue, the bile and buttocks
VE   rules sense of smell, the liver and 'flesh' (corporeality)
SU   rules sense of sight, brain, heart, sinews and right-hand parts
MA   rules left ear, kidneys, veins and genitals
JU   rules sense of touch, lungs, arteries and semen
SA   rules the right ear, spleen, bladder, phlegm and bones

Acting through their own natures, the malefics will strike those parts of the body over which they have rule. The astrologer Libra provides a list clearly derived from the zodiacal melothesia, the order of planets following the order of the signs over which they have rule:

MA   rules head and face   VE   rules throat and neck
ME   rules lungs and arms   MO   rules stomach and breasts
SU   rules heart and back   ME   rules bowels and abdomen
VE   rules reins   MA   rules generative organs, bladder.
JU   rules thighs and hips   SA   rules knees and bones
SA (UR) rules lower legs and ankles
JU (NE) rules feet and tissues

In modern times the planetary melothesia is often called (in connexion with "Melothesic Man") the 'microcosmic man' or (alone) 'planetary man'. In modern times the rulerships have been extended to the so-called 'modern planes', as well as to the prevailing image of man in terms of endoctrine glands. Collin, for example, gives a melothesic image of man as follows:

MO   rules the pancreas of the lymphatic system
ME   rules the thyroid and the pulmonary system
VE   rules the parathyroids, connected with the arterial system
SU   rules the thymus, which he associates with the function of growth
MA   rules the solar plexus and adrenal glands, the cerebro-spinal system
JU   rules the posterior pituitary, and involuntary muscular system
SA   rules the anterior pituitary, cerebral cortex and skeletal system
UR   rules the gonads and genital system, and the function of reproduction
NE   rules the pineal gland, with a function 'as yet unknown'

Perhaps the most extensive planetary melothesia, which summarizes much of the ancient tradition, is that given under the separate entries for planets by the medical astrologer Cornell.

PLANETARY MOONS   The names of the satellites (moons) of the planets are given in table 58 below.

--TABLE 58

PLANET	MOON	PLANET	MOON	PLANET	MOON
MA	Phobus	JU	Juno	SA	Mimas
MA	Daimos	JU	Europa	SA	Enceladus
		JU	Ganymede	SA	Thetys
		JU	Castillo	SA	Dione
UR	Miranda			SA	Rhea
UR	Ariel			SA	Titan
UR	Umbriel			SA	Hyperion
UR	Titania	NE	Triton	SA	Japetus
UR	Oberon	NE	Nereid	SA	Phoebe

PLANETARY ORB   In modern use the term invariably applies to the ORB ascribed to an individual planet in respect of aspects - as distinct from the orb applied to aspects themselves.   In mediaeval astrology the term was also used to denote the physical body of the planet, the 'orb' of the planet, carried within the ambient of the planetary sphere.

PLANETARY PERIODS   The theory of Planetary Periodicities really falls within the domain of CYCLES, but the term is often used in reference to a number of "periods" traditionally assigned to the planets, which are in most cases approximates only to recognised cycles, and called "Revolution Periods". There are several variant tables in the astrological traditional corpus, the variations seemingly arising from the different ideas of what the approximate periods are supposed to represent.   Table 59 sets out the traditional series.

--TABLE 59

PLANET	PTOLEMAIC PERIODS	POST-COPERNICAN PERIOD
MO	4 years	25 and 19 years
ME	10 years	10, 20, 27 and 79 years
VE	8 years	8 years
SU	19 years	
MA	15 years	79 years
JU	12 years	83 years
SA	30 years	59 years
UR		84 and 90 years
NE		164 yrs and 280 days, and 180 years
PL		247.7 years and 360 years

Some astrologers appear to use the non-Ptolemaic cycles alongside tables of mean advance (in order to determine an approximate position of a planet) when ephemerides are not available: this, of course, is bad practice, and not the reason why tables of planetary periods were constructed.   The so-called PLANETARY YEARS are also similarly misused.   In connexion with Planetary Periods, the historian Neugebauer (having referred to the 'astronomical arbitrariness' of their parameters) points out that it is significant that the lunar period is based on Egyptian years only, whilst the Venusian periods are fundamental parameters of Mesopotamian astronomy.   He also makes the point that in astrological use the periods may not be regarded only as signifying years - they are also used to represent months or days (though, not in modern astrology).   This practice corresponds, of course, to the symbolic system of progressions itself, but it is unlikely tht the Planetary Periods were designed for such a purpose.   The total of these periods is 129 years.   When counted as months, this gives 10 years and 9 months, which was one of the ancient Periodicities.   The mean values are the arithmetical mean between the extremes:

```
SU   19   (19 solar years - 235 lunar months - see METONIC CYCLE)
MO   25   (25 Egyptian years - equals 409 lunar months)
SA   30   (an approximate synodic period)
JU   12   (an approximate synodic period)
MA   15   (an approximate synodic period)
VE    8   (approximate synodic period of 99 lunar months)
ME   20   (20 Egyptian years, equivalent to 63 synodic periods)
```

Schultz, who provides so much useful material for the new esoteric approach
to astrology, gives the detailed information regarding the synodical and
sidereal planetary periods set out in table 60. His interest lies mainly in
the relatively small differences (signified under D in table 60) between
certain cyclical groups - for example, in table 60 one notes in the 7 year
cycle of Mercury, the 22 synodic periods of Mercury and the 29 sidereal
periods of Mercury, a difference of only -7.45 days. See also INITIAL
CHRONOCRATORS and REVOLUTION PERIODS.

--TABLE 60

PLANET/YEARS	DAYS	SYNODIC	(DAYS)	SIDEREAL	(DAYS)	D
ME	7	2 556.75	22	2 549.30	29	2 551.00	-7.45
ME	46	16 801.50	145	16 802.23	191	16 802.08	+0.73
ME	79	28 854.75	249	28 853.48	329	28 941.80	-1.27
VE	8	2 922.00	5	2 919.60	13	2 921.11	-2.40
MA	15	5 478.75	7	5 459.57	8	5 495.84	-19.18
MA	32	11 688.00	15	11 699.07	17	11 688.66	+11.07
MA	47	17 166.75	22	17 158.64	25	17 174.50	-8.11
MA	79	28 854.75	37	28 857.71	42	28 853.16	+2.96
JU	12	4 383.00	11	4 387.73	1	4 332.59	+4.73
JU	71	25 934.75	65	25 927.50	6	25 995.53	-7.25
JU	83	30 315.75	76	30 315.23	7	30 328.12	-0.52
SA	29	10 592.25	28	10 586.60	1	10 759.20	-5.65
SA	59	21 549.75	57	21 551.75	2	21 518.40	+1.54

PLANETARY PHASES   The 'phases' of the moons are the "Crescent" (shortly
before and after lunation) the 'half moon', in which half of the body of the
moon is lighted, the 'gibbous', when both halves of the moon are convex, and
the 'full moon', which is an opposition with the Sun. See also LUNATION.
While the term 'phases' is most usually applied to the Moon of the Earth, it
may also be applied to the inferior planets, and the "Planetary Moons".

PLANETARY PICTURES   See COSMIC PICTURES.

PLANETARY QUALITIES   The astrologer Morin published a table demonstrating
the supposed numerical values of the planets in terms of the QUALITIES
described by Ptolemy, as shown in table 61. Each of these qualities is
distributed thoughout the seven planets in equal numerical equivalents of 10.
These Morinean figures of 'weightings' were intended to be adjusted in terms
of the planetary angles, however.

--TABLE 61

PLANET	HOT	COLD	DRY	WET
MO		5		6
ME		1.5	1	
VE	0.5			4
SU	5.5		2	
MA	2.5		3	
JU	1.5		1	
SA		3.5	3	

===

PLANETARY RULERSHIP   Each planet is said to have RULE over one or more of
the signs of the zodiac.   The modern system of rulerships has been devised
mainly to accommodate the so-called 'Modern Planets', and is radically
different from the traditional schema which was introduced by Ptolemy from
antiquity.   This Ptolemaic schema was derived from a consideration of the
basic duality of each planet (rendered in modern astrology in terms derived
from the Ptolemaic system, such as 'Positive and Negative', 'Masculine and
Feminine', 'Diurnal and Nocturnal', and so on) which was itself derived from
the Egyptian cosmoconception which radically influenced Greek and Roman
astrology.   The schema set out in figure 62 reveals the application of this
duality in terms of 'signs' even though the traditional nomenclature used the
curious term 'house'.   This schema faithfully sets out the traditionalsystem
of planetary rulerships over the signs: one sees at a glance that (for
example) Jupiter has rule over Pisces and Sagittarius, the former being its
'Day Sign' (wrongly called 'Day House'), the latter being its 'Night Sign'
(wrongly called 'Night House').   The duality of the rulerships lingers on in
the modern term "Negative Mars" which of course relates to the rule of Mars
over the 'Night House' of Scorpio.

```
---------------------------------------------------------------TABLE 62
SIGN ('DAY HOUSE')        PLANET              SIGN ('NIGHT HOUSE')
=============================================================================
Cancer              MO      SU          Leo
Gemini                  ME              Virgo
Taurus                  VE              Libra
Aries                   MA              Scorpio
Pisces                  JU              Sagittarius
Aquarius                SA              Capricorn
-------------------------------------------------------------------------
```

By the time the so-called 'modern planets' had been discovered, and were
being incorporated into the system of rulerships recorded by Ptolemy, the
ancient esoteric basis for the traditional planetary rule had been largely
forgotten.   As a result, the fact that the planets (omitting the luminaries,
of course, which in any case were accorded only single rulerships) were said
to have a 'positive' (diurnal) and 'negative' (nocturnal) side to their
natures was something of a puzzle to most astrologers, and the traditional
system was readily changed to make way for the new planets, to the detriment
of astrological theory.   While there is still some disagreement about the new
rulerships (especially in connexion with the rule accorded the "Asteroids"
and certain of the "Hypothetical Planets"), the majority of modern
astrologers appear to subscribe to the system which amends the traditional
list in figure 62 with the following changes:

    SC ruled by Pluto (originally negative Mars)
    AQ ruled by Uranus (originally positive Saturn)
    PI ruled by Neptune (originally positive Jupiter)

PLANETARY SEALS Graphic symbols or sigils denoting planets, and supposed in
themselves to exert a corresponding planetary influence.   For a sample
mediaeval sequence of Planetary Seals, see Section Ten under CALENDARIA
MAGICA. Until this present century, planetary seals were accorded little
serious attention, and were regarded largely as (little understood) survivals
from late mediaeval astrology. However, in our present century, Steiner
designed a number of remarkable Seals, one from each planet, the forms
arising from deep meditative consciousness (see Kempter). These Steinerian
forms are different from the mediaeval ones, though perhaps the meditative
origin and purpose of both groups were much the same.

PLANETARY SPHERES   See SPHERES.

PLANETARY SPIRIT   The esotericist Bailey defines the term much in accord
with tradition as 'another term for the Logos of a planet'.   Such a spirit is

on what is esoterically called the 'evolutionary arc', and is more highly developed than the human - but see PLANETARY ANGELS. In spite of the accuracy of this definition, the fact is that the general term 'planetary spirit' is used widely and wildly to cover a myriad of different spiritual beings linked with the planets: see CELESTIAL HIERARCHIES, INTELLIGENCY and SECUNDADEIAN BEINGS, all of whom have at one time or another been called 'planetary spirits'.

PLANETARY TONAL INTERVALS   In an early phase of the development of the theory of the "Music of the Spheres", the 3rd century AD grammarian Censorinus recorded a number of intervals linked with the planetary DISTANCES which he insisted were derived from Pythagoras. In this system (which relates to the supposed distances not of the planets but of the spheres) the Earth to the Moon was equivalent to one tone: from Moon to Mercury half a tone: from Mercury to Venus half a tone: from Venus to the Sun one and a half tones: from Sun to Mars one tone: from Mars to Jupiter half a tone: from Jupiter to Saturn half a tone and from Saturn to the Stellatum half a tone. For a fundamental change in measurment of intervals, see KEPLERIAN HARMONICS.

PLANETARY YEAR   A large number of (variable) cycles or periods, usually called 'planetary years' have survived from ancient times, and have been radically misunderstood by many modern astrologers. Devore, for example, suggests that these were possibly guides to progression techniques (in the days when ephemerides were not readily available), and clearly does not know what the figures mean. Again, they are explained by Wemyss as relating to the 'probable length of life' of the native, in terms of the natal ruling planet, though it is clear that the figures (see 'minimum length' in table 63) are derived from the ancient PLANETARY PERIODS, which have nothing to do with the length of human life. The series of 'planetary years' in table 63 are derived from the Alexandrian Paul (though sometimes attributed to the astrologer Vettius Valens).

```
-------------------------------------------------------------TABLE 63
```

PLANET	MINIMUM LENGTH	MAXIMUM LENGTH	MEAN AGE
MO	25	108	66
ME	20	76	48
VE	8	82	45
SU	19	120	69
MA	15	66	40
JU	12	79	45
SA	30	57	43

PLANET OF DEATH   See EIGHTH SPHERE.

PLANETOIDS   See ASTEROIDS and LUCIFER.

PLANETS   In modern astronomy, the name 'Planet' is applied to all celestial bodies (with the exception of comets and meteors) which revolve around the Sun of our system, and have no light of their own. The ancients, however, believed that the planets did have a light of their own, and called the SUN and MOON planets in addition to the five 'visible' bodies MERCURY, VENUS, MARS, JUPITER and SATURN. This traditional seven of the early astrology was in relatively modern times augmented by the so-called "Modern Planets", URANUS, NEPTUNE and PLUTO, while some astrologers include the ASTEROIDS. Within the various specialist and esoteric systems of astrology, there are also the HYPOTHETICAL PLANETS, the SACRED PLANETS, and other planetary bodies, whilst in HELIOCENTRIC ASTROLOGY there is also the Earth, which figures as a planet (though in the case of heliocentric charting the Moon is generally discounted as a separate satellite). Table 64 sets out some useful data.

===

PLANET	MEAN SOLAR DISTANCE	PERIOD OF REVOLUTION	MAX. DISTANCE FROM ECLIPTIC	AXIAL ROTATION	NO. OF MOONS
MO	238,857	27d.7h.43m.11s	5deg. 8mins.	27d.7h.43m.	0
ME	35,950,000	87.97d.	7deg. 00m.14s.	59.4 days	0
VE	67,180,000	224.70d.	3deg. 23m.39s.	244 days	0
MA	141,500,000	686.98d.	1deg. 51m.	24h.37m 22.7s.	2
JU	483,300,000	11.862y.	1deg. 18m.21s.	9h.55m.(max)	12
SA	886,100,000	29.458y.	2deg. 29m.	10h.39m.(max)	10
UR	1,783,000,000	84.015y.	46m.23s.	10h.45m.	5
NE	2,793,000,000	164.788y.	1deg. 46m.28s.	15h.40m (?)	2
PL	3,666,000,000	248.4y.	17deg. 8m.34s.	6.39 days	?

———TABLE 64 (at top)

The planets with orbits outside that of the Earth are called the "Superior Planets", while those within the orbit of the Earth are called the "Inferior Planets": terms derived from the ancient theory of SPHERES. It is a basic tenet of astrology that each of the planets exercise a distinctive influence upon the Earth and its denizens, and that such influences may be studied, extrapolated and used as the basis for such things as prediction. However, the study of these influences is far from simple, since they cannot be isolated: the planets are always 'set' against some part of the zodiacal belt, and are to be studied only in relation to the influence of this (along with the influence of the fixed stars), which in turn condition the workings of the planets. Some astrologers indeed view the planets merely as the transmitters and refiners of influences within the stellar spheres: thus, the Mercury set against the zodiacal area of Aries may in itself be no different from the Mercury set against Pisces, yet the 'influence' of Mercury in these two positions is quite definitely (and demonstrably) different. Other astrologers insist that the planets are not merely 'moving lenses' in this sense, but transmit and transform according to characteristics of their own. If this latter idea is correct, then one may rightly speak of a Solar Type, or of a Mercurial Type in relation to human beings. A vast number of different classifications and nomenclatures relating to the planets have survived from traditional astrology: the names in popular use nowadays are Roman, though the antique order of the planets (each swimming within the spiritual ambient of their corresponding SPHERES) was different from the one in use to day, reflecting the order of the spiritual beings we now call the CELESTIAL HIERARCHIES. This order is set out in a woodcut of the late 15th century, used to illustrate a text by Pietro d'Abano (figure 50), for which the (almost modern sigils) give the descending order from the "Stellatum" as SA, JU, MA, SU, VE, ME and MO.

FIGURE 50. THEOLOGY AND ASTRONOMY IN DISPUTE, WITH PLANETARY SPHERES IN TRADITIONAL SEQUENCE OBSERVED IN ANTIQUITY (AFTER ABANO).

==

Among the different nomenclatures are the "Feminine Planets", the "Masculine
Planets" (see SECTA), the BENEFICS and MALEFICS, the GREATER FORTUNE and the
LESSER FORTUNE, and so on. For the sigils associated with the planets, see
SIGILS - PLANETS. The Greek names for the planets often appear in
astrological literature, though there is some disagreement as to their
meanings: Firmicus Maternus gives the classical:

MO	Selene	
ME	Stilbon	'the gleaming one'
VE	Phosphoros	'the light bearer'
SU	Helios	
MA	Piroesis	'the fiery one'
JU	Phaethon	'the bright one'
SA	Phainon	'the shiny one'

PLANISPHERE   In general terms, a plan or map formed by the projection on to
a flat surface of a sphere or part of a sphere. In particular the term is
applied to the projection of a section of the celestial sphere, as in an
Astrolabe, or even in a "Constellational Map". An astrological chart is
really a highly schematic planisphere.

PLATIC ASPECT   A weak aspect, in which the two or more aspecting bodies are
wide of ORB. The platic lacks the strength of the "Partile Aspect".

PLATONIC AGE   See PLATONIC CYCLE.

PLATONIC CYCLE   This term is sometimes wrongly identified in popular
thinking with the so-called "Platonic Year", which is a period of precession.
The Platonic Cycle is actually a 'magnus annus', the 'Great Year', in which
it is visualized that the movement of the eight spheres causes them to arrive
together in a great union at the same point (the same fiducials) from which
they began their period or cycle. In terms of the ancient cosmoconception,
once a platonic cycle was completed a retrograde motion of the spheres set
in, and a backward unfolding began, to continue for another vast periodicity
until the planetary spheres were once more aligned to their common fiducials.
The motion forward was linked in antique times with the AGE OF SATURN, under
the direction of an inner harmony. In the retrograde motion, time is
visualized as being reversed, so that men and other creatures grow young with
the progression (or rather retrogression) of time. This account may be
easily linked with the esoteric view of the disincarnate soul reaching the
last sphere of Saturn in its post-mortem experience, for with Saturn time
ends, and the soul reaches the limits of its outer movement, and begins its
descent - see ORPHIC DESCENT OF THE SOUL.

PLATONIC MONTH   A misnomer (in that it has nothing to do with a 'month' or
even with the Moon), derived from analogy with the twelve lunar months
related to the PLATONIC YEAR. It is used to denote the precession of the
Vernal Point through one sign of the zodiac, which takes 2,160 years.

PLATONIC SOLIDS   These are the so-called Platonic five regular geometric
solids: the tetrahedron, the cube, the octahedron, the dodecahedron and the
isosahedron. The importance of these solids to astrology is the repeated
attempt made by astrologers and mathematicians to show by graphic
demonstrations that these might be inscribed or circumscribed around the
planetary spheres. Kepler (in his 'Mysterium Cosmographicum') was the last
to attempt such a graphic demonstration, for his later discovery of
elliptical orbit so changed both the PTOLEMAIC SYSTEM and the COPERNICAN
SYSTEM as to render such demonstration invalid. However, it appears that the
underlying idea of geometric harmonies found expression in his later theories
of heliocentric planetary harmonies: see KEPLERIAN HARMONICS.

PLATONIC YEAR   The "Vernal Point" retrogrades through the constellations in
a period which is approximately 52,920 years (but see PRECESSION): this is

the so-called 'Platonic Year', the 'Annus Platonicus' of traditional
astrology. This period is divided into twelve equal lengths (the so-called
"Platonic Months"), corresponding to the arcs of the zodiac, and the periods
during which the Vernal Point retrogrades through the arcs are named after
the relevant signs. Unfortunately, there is no generally agreed fiducial
(see AYANAMSA), so there is no agreement among astrologers as to when such a
month begins and ends: many astrologers insist however that the Vernal Point
is retrograding through Pisces at the present time, so that mankind may be
said to be living under the impress of the 'Piscean Age'. Each of the twelve
arcs exude different influences, so that each of the so-called 'months'
(periods of 2,160 years in fact) induces fundamentally different attitudes,
mores and civilizations. These 'zodiacal ages' or 'epochs' are characterized
by more than merely the stamp of the individual sign: the four cardinal
points of the horoscope figure are visualized as working in combination to
produce what have been called in modern esoteric astrology the THREE
PROTOTYPES, which periodically repeat themselves, each in four possible
variations, thus shaping historical epochs.

PLAUSTRUM   One of the several imporant variant names for the constellation
"Ursa Major".

PLAY   The 'point of Play' is one of the so-called Arabian PARS in a chart.
If the degree of Mars in a natal chart is taken as the Ascendant, the
adjusted position of Venus is the point.

PLEIADES   One of the most famous of asterisms, set in the last few degrees
of constellation Taurus, the name usually derived from the Greek 'plein' (to
sail) on the grounds that the heliacal rising of the asterism marked the
opening of navigation for the ancient Greeks, while the setting in late
Autumn marked the close of navigation.   This etymology has however been
questioned.   Pleione was the mother of these 'Seven Sisters': they are
sometimes called the 'Atlantides' (their father being Atlas). In the Chinese
astronomy they are called the 'Seven Sisters of Industry'. However, their
names are almost legion, though emphasis is usually laid on the magical
number seven: they are the 'Seven Virgins', the 'Virgin Stars', the 'Seven
Atlantic Sisters', the 'Seven Stars', and so on.   Indeed, almost any famous
group of seven has been linked with this asterism. The names given to the
individual sisters are "Alcyone", Maia, Electra, Merope, Taygete, Celaeno and
Sterope.   Merope is sometimes called the 'Invisible Sister' because she is
the only one who married a mortal, and hid her face in shame. According to
Ptolemy, the degree of arc in which the asterism is located gives an
influence equivalent to that of Moon conjunct Mars, and its power is meant to
be evil, involving disgrace, ruin and violent death.

PLEIONE   See PLEIADES.

PLOUGH   One of the several important variant names for the constellation
"Ursa Major".

PLUTO   Planet discovered in 1930 by the Lowell Observatory, though its
existence was suspected from mathematical computations some time prior to
this date. When first announced by astronomers it was named 'Pluto-Lowell'
or "Lowell-Pluto", but it had been mentioned before this time under a variety
of different names by astrologers - these names included 'Pluto' (see
PAGAN-PLUTO). This 'modern planet' Pluto must not be confused with the
'Pluto' described by Thierens as one of the future planets of the "Etheric
Sphere", where it was to be the ruler of Aries, also named Osiris - see
THIERENS-PLUTO. Nor must it be confused with the Pluto described by Wemyss
as ruler of Cancer (the so-called WEMYSS-PLUTO). Since the modern Pluto was
discovered, it has displaced the traditional "Negative Mars" from its rule
over the zodiacal Scorpio. Astrologers see it as an eruptive and disturbing
influence, involved with the processes of elimination and regeneration. When
involutionary, it is connected with the underworld, with crime, and all that

is dark and unregenerate in our society: when evolutionary, it is connected
with esoteric movements, with all that seeks to redeem. When the planet
works through its darker nature, the individual is dominated by obsessive
psychic tendencies (which swell from the telluric unconscious realm) - yet
when the planet works through its beneficial side the same forces are used to
heal, to create and to regenerate. The sigil P is popularly explained as
being derived from a combination of the P for Pluto and the L for Lowell.
However, in 1911 the astrologer Pagan offered a much more fitting sigil in
the form of a reversed Mars $\mathcal{P}$. See also MODERN PLANETS.

POCILLATOR   See ANTINOUS.

POINT   A modern equivalent for PARS.

POINT OF BONDAGE   One of the so-called Arabian PARS in a chart. If the
figure is revolved so that the degree occupied by the dispositor of the Moon
is on the Ascendant, then the Moon position in this new arrangement marks the
point.

POINT OF FAITH   One of the so-called Arabian PARS, obtained by revolving the
figure so that the degree occupied by the Moon is on the Ascendant: the
position of Mercury relative to this new Ascendant marks the point.

POINT OF FEMALE CHILDREN   One of the so-called Arabian PARS in a chart,
obtained by revolving the figure so that the degree occupied by the Moon is
on the Ascendant: the position of Venus relative to this new Ascendant marks
the point.

POINT OF JUPITER   See PARS.

POINT OF LIFE   A term used by the astrologer Frankland in connexion with a
measure used in "Symbolic Directions": it is an arc of 4 and two sevenths of
a degree, which he considers as starting at the first degree of Aries, and
marking off in terms of such arcs yearly periods. It is a measure linked
with the septenary, for it passes through each sign in a period of seven
years, forming aspects with the radical positions. The point (or 'arc' or
'measure' as it should properly be called) is also used in a different way as
the SEPTENARY MEASURE.

POINT OF MALE CHILDREN   One of the so-called Arabian PARS obtained in the
same way as the "Point of Female Children", using Jupiter as the new
denotive.

POINT OF MARS   See PARS.

POINT OF MERCURY   See PARS.

POINT OF MOON   See PARS.

POINT OF PASSION   See SWORD.

POINT OF SATURN   See PARS.

POINT OF SERVANTS   One of the so-called Arabian PARS in a chart. If the
degree of Mercury in a natal chart is taken as the Ascendant, the adjusted
position of the Moon becomes the point of Servants.

POINT OF SICKNESS   One of the so-called Arabian PARS in a chart. If the
degree of Saturn in a natal chart is taken as the Ascendant, the adjusted
position of Mars marks the point.

POINT OF SPIRIT   One of the so-called Arabian PARS in a chart, obtained by
revolving the figure so that the degree occupied by the Moon is on the

==

Ascendant: the position of the Sun relative to this new Ascendant marks the point of Spirit.

POINT OF TRAVEL BY LAND   One of the so-called Arabian PARS. If the Lord of the Ninth is taken as the Ascendant of a figure, then the new cusp of the ninth house is said to mark the point.

POINT OF UNDERSTANDING   One of the so-called Arabian PARS in a chart. If the degree of Mercury in a natal chart is taken as the Ascendant, then the adjusted position of Mars in the new chart marks the point.

POLAR CHART   A horoscope chart cast for extreme polar regions. The main problem for horoscopes cast for polar regions is that at certain times, and in certain latitudes, the plane of the ecliptic will coincide or override the horizon plane. If a conventional system of "Chart Projection" is employed, the Ascendant may under those circumstances appear to descend - which naturally involves the astrologer in symbolic nonsense in the chart. Many attempts to resolve the problem of this 'distortion' of the traditional symbolism have led to a variety of projections being suggested, mainly by redefining the concept of the Medium Coeli.

POLARIS   Fixed star (double), the alpha of "Ursa Minor" with many different names: it was the 'Phoenice" of the early Greeks, the 'Pole Star' and even 'Stella Maris' (but see SPICA). For the Anglo-Saxons it was the 'Scip-steorra' (ship star), and for the Latins the 'Navigatoria', and even 'Loadstar' after the magnetic lodestone. It was for the Arabian astrologers 'Al Kiblah' or 'Al Rukkabah' (the Rider), and to some astrologers 'Cynosura' (dog's tail), probably because it was set in the tip of the tail of the lesser bear which was sometimes called a dog. Astrologers say that it is of the nature of Venus conjunct Saturn, and hence a difficult influence, though Robson records that the Arabian astrologers were of the opinion that the contemplation of the star would cure ophthalmia. It is one of the "Fifteen Stars" of mediaeval astrology, and thus receives a sigil: see SIGILS - FIXED STARS.

POLARITIES   The astrologer Leo defines the term 'polarities' from a point of view of solar-lunar combinations, regarding the Sun as a positive, life-giving element and the Moon as a negative, formative element. The Sun influences human character, the Moon personality, the blending of these two being the polarity. For another view of polarities, see PRINCIPLES and SECTA.

POLE OF THE ASCENDANT   The geographic latitude of the place for which an Ascendant degree has been determined - usually in preparation for a horoscope: see POLE OF THE HOROSCOPE.

POLE OF THE HOROSCOPE   An archaic term meaning the latitude of the place for which a figure has been cast.

POLE STAR   See POLARIS.

POLIS   Fixed star (triple), the mu of constellation Sagittarius, set in the upper part of his bow. The Copts gave us the name, attached however to a different image of the asterism, for 'polis' meant foal, and the word must not be confused with the same Grecian term. It is the Sagittarian impulse which has left its mark on the astrological reading of this star, for it is said to be of the nature of Mars conjunct Jupiter, and to give ambition, martial powers, ability as a horseman and keen perception.

POLLUX   Fixed star, the beta of constellation Gemini, set in the head of its namesake (the Southern Twin) who was the immortal one, sometimes linked with Hercules, (though in fact the son of Jupiter and Leda). Pollux was said to be a keen boxer, which explains one of his early names - 'Pugil'. Among the

several names used by the Arabian astrologers were derivatives of
'Rasalgeuze'. Ptolemy claims that it is of the nature of Mars, and
accordingly it is said to have a brave, spirited, audacious though cruel
influence: when rising it predicts injuries to the face, or even bad
eyesight.

POLYHYMNIA   Name given to one of the "Ethereal Planets" perceived
clairvoyantly by the astrologer Harris, said to be in orbit beyond his
MELODIA: not to be confused with the "Asteroid" of the same name.   Later
astrologers assigned Polyhymnia as the day-house planet of Cancer, the night
house planet of Libra, and said that it was exalted in Gemini, with a nature
equivalent to Moon conjunct Venus, with an admixture of Mercury.

POLYPOLAR   A term used of a horoscope chart in regard to the distribution of
aspects, derived in respect of the so-called FIGURINES of Meier, though
presumably applicable to any figure. A 'polypolar' is a figure which
includes at least two oppositions.

POMEGRANATE   In a specialist sense, one of the so-called Arabian PARS, the
'part of Jupiter', sometimes called the 'Part of Increase'. If a chart is
revolved so that the degree occupied by the Sun is transferred to the
Ascendant, then the position of Jupiter in this new arrangement will mark the
beneficial 'Pomegranate'.

PONDERABLE PLANETS   These are the planets Uranus, Jupiter and Mars according
to Simmonite, who probably forgot about Saturn, for he says that they are 'so
called because they move slower than the rest'. One might therefore add to
these the two modern planets Neptune and Pluto, both unknown to Simmonite.

PORPHYRIAN SYSTEM   A method of HOUSE DIVISIONS, the principle of which is
the trisection of the ecliptic quadrant (obtained by direct divison of the
ecliptic). The astrologer Leo rightly describes it as a 'rough and ready'
method, yet it appears to have been similar to one of the systems used by the
early Greeks, prior to its development by the Neoplatonist Porphyry (4th
century AD). However, in respect to antiquity, see also ALCABITIAN SYSTEM
and MODUS EQUALIS.

PORRIMA   Fixed star, the gamma of Virginis, set in the left arm of this
figure, and sometimes called 'Caphir'.

POSEIDON   Name given to one of the "Hypothetical Planets" used in the
Uranian System of the HAMBURG SHOOL. It is said to relate to 'mind, spirit
and ideas'. The name of this Greek sea-god was also used by Thierens in
connexion with his NEPTUNUS ('Nereus'), which he linked with the principle of
'absorption'. Since the name 'Poseidon' was in Roman times called 'Neptune',
the term is sometimes used as a synonym for the modern planet NEPTUNE.

POSITED   A term almost always used as synonymous with 'situate' or 'placed'.

POSITIVE MARS   A term which is a survival from the ancient Ptolemaic
astrological system, relating to the classification of rulerships. Each of
the planets (save for the luminaries) were accorded rule over two signs of
the zodiac (see PLANETARY RULERSHIPS), and such pairs were deemed 'positive'
or 'negative', 'solar' or 'lunar', and so on. Mars was accorded a
'negative' rule over Scorpio and a 'positive' rule over Aries. Thus the term
'positive Mars' really means 'Mars as ruler of Aries. See however NEGATIVE
MARS and SECTA.

POSITIVE PLANETS   See SECTA.

POSITIVE SIGNS   These are the signs alternating from Aries to Aquarius -
also called the 'diurnal', 'fortunate' and 'masculine' signs. See SECTA.

==

POSSESSIVE HOUSES   These are the Second, Sixth and Tenth Houses, each of
which reflects on the mundane level the influence of the 'Earth Triplicity'.

POWERS   A term used of one of the ranks of CELESTIAL HIERARCHIES, sometimes
called the Potestates or DYNAMIS. The same term is also used descriptively
of a system of astrological KEYWORDS of specific manifestations on the
physical and mental plane, of the Twelve Signs, as listed by Pagan:

```
    ------------------------------------------------------------------TABLE 65
    SIGN   PHYSICAL                      MENTAL
    ==========================================================================
    AR     Impetus                       Enterprise
    TA     Inertia                       Steadfastness
    GE     Expansion/contraction         Eagerness/Despair
    CN     Flexibility                   Adaptability
    LE     Radiation                     Faith
    VG     Crystallisation               Discrimintion
    LB     Equilibrium                   Balance
    SC     Chemical Action               Determination
    SG     Spiral Rotation*              Reason
    CP     Vibration*                    Concentration/Relaxation
    AQ     Absorption                    Curiosity
    PI     Solution                      Insight
    -------------------------------------------------------------------------
```
    * Pagan says "possibly Vibration and Spiral Rotation should be reversed".

PRAESAEPE   A star-cluster located in the head of the constellation Cancer,
known as the 'Beehive' or 'Nubilum' (cloudy), the 'Manger', the 'Crib', and
so on. It is said to be a damaging influence in a chart, bringing disgrace,
brutality and even blindness, the nature of the affliction depending upon the
planets concerned. See also ASCELLI.

PRECESSION   The 'Precession of the Equinoxes', is the term used to denote
the retrograde movement of the Vernal Point through the constellations, a
phenomenon which is perhaps connected with the nutation of the Earth upon its
poles - though the fact is that there is no really convincing explanation of
precession. In simple terms one has to visualize the two so-called zodiacs,
the tropical and the constellational, one of which 'moves', and one of which
is 'fixed' as overlapping. Because of precession, the fixed stars appear to
advance (in longitude) one arc of just over 50 seconds each year, which means
that the first point of tropical Aries seems to retrograde through the
constellations. Since the two zodiacs are of unequal segmentation (the
tropical being defined usually in terms of 30-degree arcs, the constellation
being defined usually in 12 unequal arcs - see for example MODERN ZODIAC)
there was never any point in time when the two zodiacs could have been
regarded as being coterminous throughout their extent - however, it is clear
that there would be some dates (in the past and future) when the two 'first
points' would coincide. The Vernal Point - which in terms of the seasons
marks the beginning of the year - must therefore be visualized as slipping
back (due to this precession) against the constellations. Around this cosmic
truth a wealth of astrological symbolism has been woven into a proliferation
of ideologies which tends to obscure the fact that no-one has adequately
dated the time when the two zodiacs coincided at the same fiducial, and that
there is little or no agreement as to the extent of the arcs involved in the
constellational zodiac. In fact, the Vernal Point slips back against the
backdrop of fixed stars in a motion which is theoretically steady, but which
(mainly because the ecliptic plane itself is not fixed) is minutely variable.
Schultz gives the following details for precession:

    in 1 year the rate is 50.25 seconds
    in 72 years the rate is 1 degree 0.3 minutes
    in 2,160 years the rate is 30 degrees
    in 25,920 years (72 x 30 x 12) the rate is 360 degrees

The 2,160 span is called a 'Precessional Age' or (wrongly) an 'Astrological Age': the 25,920 span is called a 'Precessional Year' or 'Great Year'. It must be observed that whilst the figures given by Schultz are accurate, very often the figures given in astrological texts are not so accurate - for example, Brau gives 25,800 for the Great Year. The real problem which arises in connexion with the application of precessional information to astrology is that the fiducials concerned are far from agreed: there is no certain showing when a particular cycle may be said to have begun - which is to say that no-one knows for sure when the sequences of the so-called "Platonic Year" began. The importance of the resultant PLATONIC YEAR is connected with a derivation from the theory of precession the important teachings concerned with the natures of the 'zodiacal ages'. Since the Vernal Point retrogrades through one 30 degree arc in 2,160 years it is maintained that the zodiacal sign through which the VP progresses leaves its own distinctive impress on history - that civilizations of particular characters, with particular natures and purposes succeed each other in epochal series of 2,160 years: see for example AGES and THREE PROTOTYPES. It is widely believed that we are at present living in the Age of Pisces (which is to say that the Vernal Point is progressing through the sign Pisces), and that this age is intimately connected with the destiny of Christianity and with Christ (symbolized as a Fish, and the centre of much Piscean imagery). In terms of the theory of precession, therefore, it is clear that the Piscean cycle will eventually come to an end, and civilization (or the world at large) will find itself under the dominion of Aquarius. Unfortunately, because of the difficulty of determining the fiducials, few astrologers agree as to when the Age of Pisces will end and (hence) when the Age of Aquarius will begin (there is even more disagreement among specialists as to precisely what Aquarius, with its ruler Uranus, will import for the world). Some astrological authorities place the beginning of the Piscean Epoch in the first centuries prior to Christ - for example, Rudhyar gives 97 BC, Thierens 125 BC, and Massey gives 255 BC. However, others insist on a much later date - the astrologer Leo loosely dates it to 'soon after the dawning of the Christian era', and other esotericists insist that we are only just beyond half way through the Epoch of Pisces, which would mean that it began about 1,000 AD. It is all a question of fiducials - unless one can actually pinpoint the beginning of a cycle reliably, one cannot say when it will end. It would seem that within very wide latitudes any astrologer is free to propose his own system. Schultz publishes the following list of stellar fiducials for the zero point of the zodiac in relation to the calendar, the dates given being BC:

16,000	Antares	14,000	Zubenelgenubi	12,700	Spica
10,500	Denebola	8,800	Regulus	7,100	Praesaepe
6,000	Castor and Pollux	4,250	Crab Nebula	3,000	Aldebaran
2,300	Pleiades	750	Hamal	0	Kaitan

The precision of such tables belies the fact that few astrologers would agree with it, and very many specialists who have laboured over the vexing question of fiducials have established their own lists. See however AYANAMSA. Since the effect of precession is that the stars appear to fall back against the Vernal Point, this means that those astrologers who seek to integrate into their charts the effects of fixed stars (translated to Right Ascension) must allow for this precessional rate. Most tables of fixed stars are accordingly dated, so that allowance may be made for precession - for example, the rounded-off degrees given under FIXED STARS are calculated for 1985, the mid-point of the 'eighties decade, and are therefore tolerably accurate for most purposes of astrology linked with this decade. By simple numerical adjustment it is possible to allow for calculations related to other times. A modern rule of thumb is derived from the rate of precession proposed by Newton, which is approximately 50 seconds of arc per year. However, the stars are far from being 'fixed', and a variety of defined motions - proper and radial motions mainly - do adjust the 'precessional rate'. Even so, in practical terms this has been shown to be sufficient for most ordinary astrological needs. It has been observed that this numerical relationship is the equivalent of 72 years to one degree of precession - approximately the mean length of human life.   Hipparchus is usually identified as the first astronomer to note (if not define) the phenomenon of precession (in the 2nd century BC) but it is evident that it was at least partly recognized by Babylonian astrologers (see for example SYSTEM A, relating to ayanamsas), and its effects were noted in the temple orientations of Egyptians and Greeks. In any case, long before the time of Hipparchus the two so-called 'zodiacs' had been clearly distinguished - but see GREEK ZODIAC. The rate of precession was not accurately determined until comparatively recent times, so that historically speaking the dates assigned to 'Zodiacal Epochs' have varied considerably. For example, Albategni gave a processional rate of 1 degree to every 60 years and 4 months. Dante was following the Arabian astrologer Alfraganus in assuming an even rate of precession of 1 degree per century, and in anticipating that the twelve 'Precessional Ages' would be of equal extent. The Arabic astrologer Albumasar suggested a theory of TREPIDATION involving an oscillation around an arc of 7 degrees, in periodicities of 900 years, rather than a direct retrogression through the constellations. Schwabe and Waschmuth have done much research into the realm of precession, and have distinguished between the zodiac and the constellations in an interesting way: they each make useful and original observations about the bearing which precession has had on historical epochs.

PRECESSIONAL AGE   A period sometimes supposed to be 2,160 years in duration: but see PRECESSION.

PRECESSIONAL YEAR   A period of 25,920 years - see PRECESSION.

PRECESSIONS   A term sometimes used as a translation of the Greek 'proegeseis' used by Ptolemy in connexion with the 'direct' movement of a planet, in contradiction to its 'retrograde' motion.

PREDICTIVE ASTROLOGY   The branch of astrology which deals with revealing the future trends implicit within a natal chart. This is the astrological realm covered in DIRECTIONS and PROGRESSIONS.

PRE-NATAL CHART   See PRE-NATAL EPOCH. Not all pre-natal charts claim to be cast for the moment of conception. Some astrologers cast such pre-natals for the so-called quickening (medically and theologically different from the conception) which is regarded generally as taking place about six weeks after conception. Other times are used also, depending upon the individual views of the astrologer as to the nature of gestation: see for example Collin.

PRE-NATAL EPOCH   Sometimes simply the 'epoch', the 'pre-natal epoch' was originally defined as a time. It was claimed to be that moment (said to occur approximately at the beginning of the gestative period) when the degree ascending on the eastern horizon and the longitude of the Moon at that moment were interchangeable with the longitude of the Ascendant degree and the longitude of the Moon (or their respective opposite points) at birth. Some astrologers would cast a chart for such a time, and regard this chart as a 'conception chart' relating to the destiny of the native as would an ordinary 'birth chart'. As formulated by Bailey, the law of the pre-natal epoch has long been supposed to recall or reflect the mythical TRUTINE OF HERMES, but an investigation into what the general law implies for particular application leads into considerable complexities which belie the simplicity of the definition. In any case, originally the term was applied not to a time but to a chart, cast for this moment of time. Eventually, by extension, the word was applied to the body of interpretative material built around the chart, so that the term 'Epochal Astrology' eventually emerged, to cover a wide field of astrology concerned fundamentally with the application of astrological doctrines to the supposed conditions of the gestation period, as well as to the relationship which is supposed to exist between the embryonic life and the subsequent natal horoscope. The idea of the epoch was largely popularized by Bailey in a system which does not bear close scrutiny, yet

there are now several different forms of pre-natal astrology derived from
other views of the periodicities of incarnation other than the precise or
postulated moment of conception - see PRE-NATAL CHART. Strictly speaking,
however, the 'pre-natal chart' described by Bailey has never pretended to be
a horoscope for conception, even though it was later frequently termed a
'conception chart' and was believed by many amateur astrologers to be just
that - it was an adjusted chart symbolically linked to the modern notion of
conception. The fact that the doctrines of the 'epoch' were popularized in
western astrology mainly by adherents of Theosophy has meant that the
majority of astrologers, not themselves of such persuasion, have failed to
grasp precisely what the epoch is indeed supposed to indicate. It is
supposed to mark the 'descent of the Monad to the Astral plane' (in the words
of Bailey) - this is by no means 'conception' in any popular sense, but from
Bailey's later observations has developed the assumption that the chart for
the epoch must therefore show the inherent character of the Ego which is
about to reincarnate: in strictly Theosophical terms, this is actually a
non-sequitur. One may therefore reasonably question the validity of the
statement of Bailey that 'the epoch has a more intimate relation with the
individual than the horoscope of birth'. Considerable research has shown
that the work of Bailey was astrologically invalid and formulated on
erroneous medical premises. The major objections are set out by Dean who
rightly comes to the conclusion that however intriguing the concept of the
pre-natal epoch in principle, 'in practice it is simply wrong'. In fact
Bailey's significance in the development of pre-natal astrology has been out
of proportion to its true worth. It is worth noting that Schwickert later
doubled the number of possible epochs (and thereby renders the complicated
more complicated) by insisting that all four angles might be used in the
lunar exchange rather than just the horizon polarity. Sepharial was probably
the first western astrologer to use pre-natal astrology or 'conception
charts' in modern times (the latter were used in Hellenistic and Roman
astrology), but he appears to have used it only as a prop for rectification,
and indeed described it as 'the only reliable method of rectification'.
However, even here it is questionable whether the method is a system of
rectification at all, since the pre-natal epoch itself is furnished in such a
way as to be derived from the fiducials of the natal chart, the former being
derived by mathematical or geometric laws from the latter.

PREVIOUS SYZYGY   See SYZYGY.

PRIMUM HYADUM   Fixed star, the gamma of constellation Taurus, literally 'the
first star of the Hyades', set in the forehead of the bull. It is said to be
of the same nature as the parent asterism, afflicting especially the eyes,
but generally being a most disturbing influence, tending towards violence and
ruin.

PRIMARY DIRECTING   Term used of the method of astrologically unfolding
potential in a radical chart, according to the PRIMARY SYSTEM - to be
distinguished from the "Secondary Directions" of the SECONDARY PROGRESSIONS.
See PRIMARY DIRECTIONS.

PRIMARY DIRECTIONS   In the method of computing known as the PRIMARY SYSTEM,
used for studying the unfolding of potential within a chart, planets are
'directed' to the precise aspect with other planets - thus, one may direct
Mars to the place of Jupiter, to calculate the future time when the
conjunction will take place in regard to the specific chart, the arc itself
being used as a basis for time conversion (on the ratio of one-nintieth of
the arc between sunrise and midheaven). Such unfolding of potential aspects
is the 'directing' of aspects, and the aspects themselves are called
"Directional". See also PROGRESSED ASPECTS.

PRIMARY SYSTEM   The general theory of astrological prediction from the
'radical chart' is based on the idea that each Earth day is the equivalent to
the advance of the Sun by approximately one degree. By analogy, this degree

is taken to be equal to the passage of one year in the life of the native: this basic analogy has given rise to a method of prediction called the "Primary System", which involves studying the unfolding of potentials between bodies and nodal points mainly in terms of aspects, the arcs of distance involved being translated into equivalence of time. In the Primary System, the distance of directed aspects is calculated as one-nintieth of the arc between the sunrise degree and the Midheaven point of the same day. Such a method is to be contrasted with the so-called SECONDARY PROGRESSIONS. The later method is more popular with modern astrologers because the time conversion factors permit greater accuracy, or at least, greater security. Primary Directions are themselves derived from the ancient concept of the "Primum Mobile", and since this means that calculations of time equivalent are made in Right Ascension along the equater (with four minutes equivalent to one year) it is very easy to make an error in conversion, or to continue error derived from wrong data (such as a mistake in the time of birth).

PRIME ESSENCES   One of the names given by Paracelsus to the traditional "Three Principles" of astrology and alchemy.

PRIME VERTICAL CHART   A horoscope chart, or symbolic figure, erected to symbolize a plane through the prime vertical. The so-called MUNDOSCOPE is such a chart system.

PRIMORDIAL QUALITIES   Term applied by de Lubicz to the two basic qualities of 'dry and hot' and 'cold and wet', represented in the Egyptian symbolism as two lions, and called Shu and Tefnu. The basic idea was adopted by the Greeks in their more exoterically sophisticated theory of QUALITY, while the Egyptian symbolism survived into Christian art.

PRIMORDIAL SEVEN   In esoteric astrology, the seven SACRED PLANETS.

PRIMUM MOVENS   In the Ptolemaic System (as in the "Aristotelian System"), the name given to the Ninth Sphere which was believed to impart movement (literally, 'the first movement') to the spheres.   See however SPHERE OF THE PRIMUM MOBILE. In later cosmoconceptions, the Primum Movens became the Tenth Sphere - but see also NINTH HEAVEN and STELLATUM.

PRINCEPS   Fixed star, the delta of constellation "Bootis", set in the club or spearshaft of the giant.   The name appears to be fairly modern - Ptolemy views all the stars of this constellation as being similar to that of Mercury with Saturn, but leaves it unnamed. In the Chinese system the star was merely one of the 'Tseih Kung' (seven princes), and the erudite Allen could find no European name for it.

PRINCEPS SIGNORUM   One of the several titles for the constellation and sign Aries, 'the leader of the signs', sometimes "Princeps Zodiaci".

PRINCEPS ZODIACI   One of the many names for the constellation and sign Aries, 'leader of the zodiac'. While it is true that Aries is noted as the 'first' of the zodiacal circle, the term is on a deeper level probably a reference to the ancient idea (recorded by Albumasar in the 9th century, that at the creation of the world all the planets were in conjunction in Aries.

PRINCIPALITIES   See ARCHAI and POWERS.

PRINCIPAL PLACES   The five houses where the two luminaries are said to be most beneficial in a horoscope figure: the 1st, 7th, 9th and 11th Houses. See also HYLEGICAL PLACES.

PRINCIPLES   The early Greek astrologers employed the four Aristotelian principles which ruled matter - terms translated as 'Hot', 'Moist', 'Dry' and 'Cold'. These were the pairs of interacting opposites said to underlie all phenomena: the hot and moist united forms and brought increase - the dry and

===

cold separated form and brought destruction. The polarities, or 'principles' (sometimes popularly called the 'Aristotelian Principles', and often confusingly called the 'qualities' - see QUALITY) played a most important part in early astrological doctrines. The planets Jupiter, Venus and Moon were said to be 'hot and moist', while Saturn was said to be 'excessively cold' and Mars 'excessively dry'. The four principles extended into a concept of Ages (for which, see SEVEN AGES), and even into the natures of the four winds, which were linked with the four seasons, the four "Angles" and the cardinal points. The East wind was 'Apeliotes' and dry. The West wind was 'Zephyrus' and moist. The South wind was 'Notus' and hot. The North wind was Boreas, and cold. See also PLANETARY QUALITIES and SEVEN PRINCIPLES.

PRINT OUT   Usually reference to a computerized print out, specifically in astrological circles to either such a data sheet giving information relating to a particular horoscope, or to a required tabulation of astrological configurations, or even to a computerized ephemeris. See also COMPUTERIZED CHART.

PRISON   A term now almost obsolete, used as the equivalent for FALL. It originated from the Greek terminology which had planets in 'phelakai', subsequently translated as 'in prison'. See also THRONES.

PRIVATE ENEMIES   The 'point of Private Enemies' is one of the so-called Arabian PARS. If the Lord of the Twelfth House is revolved to the Ascendant of a figure, then the new cusp of the Twelfth House marks the point.

PROCESSIONS   A term applied by the modern astrologer Addey to the numerical derivations of HARMONICS. A procession of nines is set out under "Subsistences".

PROCYON   Fixed star (binary), the alpha of "Canis Minor", set in the body of the dog, the name derived from the Greek 'prokuon' (before the dog) in reference to the fact that it was the star which preceeded the rising of the 'dog star' SIRIUS. The Latin equivalent name was 'Antecanis', but the mediaeval 'Aschere', 'Aschemie', 'Algomeysa' and 'Algomeyla' appear in early manuscripts, the first two said to have been derived from the Arabian phrase meaning 'bright star of Syria', so named because the star disappeared from the Arab's view at its setting over that country. A curious duality of influences is recorded: Allen, working from ancient texts not available to Robson, says that it portends wealth, fame and good fortune. Robson, who has influenced a whole generation of astrologers, records Ptolemy's view that it is of the nature of Mercury conjunct Mars, and makes of it a celestial disaster area - violence, 'elevation ending in disaster', and danger from dog-bites.

PRODITOR   See TAURUS CONSTELLATION.

PROFECTION   Sometimes given as an archaic term for 'progression': but see PROFECTIONS

PROFECTIONS   A term derived from Ptolemaic astrology relating to the rising of the signs in connexion with a simple method of progressing the chart by the rate of one sign per year. The hylegiacal degree is advanced 30 degrees for each year, irrespective of latitude: the revolved chart is considered for a given year in the life of the native in terms of this simple system as multiples of 30 degree revolutions for a year, or 2.5 degrees for each month. The astrologer Leo, however, defines profections in terms of regular progressions of the Sun and other significators, allowing to each profection the whole zodiacal circle and one sign over: thus, if the Sun in the first year is in 30 degrees of Aries, the next year it will be in 30 degrees of Taurus.

===

PROGNOSIS   A term which, whilst generally synonymous with "Prediction", is sometimes used of general chart interpretation (see PREDICTIVE ASTROLOGY).

PROGRESSED ASPECTS   See SECONDARY PROGRESSIONS.

PROGRESSED FIGURE   See SECONDARY PROGRESSIONS.

PROGRESSED HOROSCOPE   Sometimes called the 'Progressed Figure', or 'Progressed Chart', it is a horoscope figure calculated for a specific time after the Natal Chart, and schematically derived from the same. A progressed horoscope may be calculated and interpreted for any period after the birth of the native, though the progression must always be derived from the radical (the natal) chart by one or other of the several systems of PROGRESSION: for example, in the system used according to the schematic "Day for a Year", a progressed horoscope is cast for a given number of days after birth equal to the number of years elapsing from birth to the time under scrutiny, and the two charts (radical and progressed) are linked schematically by arcs denoting planetary and nodal movements. Whatever the method used, the progressed horoscope is always a record of the development inherent in the radical chart, and may be interpreted only in relation to that radical: it appears to have no other validity in itself.

PROGRESSIONS   In popular use this term is generally regarded as being an equivalent of DIRECTIONS, and it is true that in both systems of prediction, the postions of the planets and nodal points are moved forward (or backwards) according to certain rules, and both are derived from a natal chart, with a view to studying the potential and 'futurity' promised by that natal chart (often called the 'radical'). However, while progressions are involved with techniques of prediction based on the 'directing' of a radical chart, not all methods of SECONDARY DIRECTIONS are based exclusively on 'directing' forward in space and time. Some methods of secondary directions are concerned with both the idea of converse directing, and with studying the pre-radical chart. The very etymology of the word 'progressions' (from the Latin 'pro-gredior') suggests the idea of 'moving forward', and astrological purists must regard progressions as only one form of Directions.   The phrase 'progressed horoscope' is generally favoured over the phrase 'directed horoscope', however.

PROMITTOR   The 'promittor' is that which promises fulfilment, and in a specialist astrological sense refers to the potential of planets, or to the unfolding of that potential through progressions and directions. Thus, in general terms, the planets Mars and Saturn are rightly called the 'Anaretic Promittors', for they promise (among other things) the fulfilment of death - see ANARETIC. All planets promise something or other, and thus in a general sense all planets are really promittors. It is really the astrologer, in his capacity as interpreter of a chart who makes a specific planet into a promittor of a particular thing, event or condition. The term is used in a highly specialist sense of any planet to which another planet (called the 'significator') is directed to form a progressed aspect with the radical position of the promittor, by which the promise of this latter is fulfilled. The term is used widely in "Horary Astrology", but rarely in natal horoscopy.

PROPER FACE   A term derived from Ptolemy, though seemingly wrongly defined by him. A planet is said to be in its 'proper face' when it bears the same ELEMENTAL ASPECT to either of the luminaries which its own house bears to their houses. This Ptolemaic rule has been added to by later commentators, who insist that in addition to fulfilling the above requirements, the planet must be in its own house, and must also be in the ratio aspect with both the luminaries - all of which is one way of saying that a planet would rarely be in its proper face. This later concept also implies a DOMAL DIGNITY, which many experienced astrologers regard as chimerical. Some astrologers have simplified the definition of the term (though confusingly using the term 'face' as a synonym - see however FACE). Wilson, for example, who seems to be of the opinion (incorrect as it happens) that he is accurately reporting

Ptolemy's view, says that a planet is in its own face (sic) when it is at the same distance from the Sun or the Moon as its house is from their house.

PROPER MOTION   The term 'proper motion' is derived from the old sense in which 'proper' meant 'personal': in simple terms, it is the motion of a planet measurable in the plane at right angles to the line of sight. It is to be distinguished from APPARENT MOTION.

PROPHECY The foretelling of the future. In relation to astrology this is properly one of the specialist fields connected with the art of PROGRESSIONS and DIRECTIONS, by which the promise of a radical chart is unfolded and revealed in terms of cycles and dates relating to the life of the native. Unfortunately, astrology has been linked with other forms of prophecy - perhaps more accurately termed 'Astromancy' - which really play no part in the philosophical background of the science. For example, a surprising number of people use the horoscope as an 'autoscope', and make predictions according to clairvoyant principles unrelated to genuine astrology.

PROPORTIONAL ARCS   A term derived from the astrology of Sepharial, which proposes that there is a contra-degree, a nodal point, on the other side of the radical Sun, Moon, Ascendant, and Medium Coeli, equi-distant from these positions as the planets on the other side.   The proportional arc of a planet at 6 degrees Aries, in relation to (say) the Sun at 18 degrees Taurus, is 42 degrees: this arc extended to the other side of the Sun would give a nodal point (a 'sensitive degree', as Sepharial called it) in 30 degrees Gemini. The sensitive degree is said to be receptive to influences from progressions and transits. But see also CONVERSE DIRECTIONS.

PROPUS   Fixed star (binary), the eta of constellation Gemini, set in front of Castor's left foot.   It has many names attached to it, such as 'Praepes' and 'Tejat' (a modern word coined apparently from an Arabian anatomical term 'Al Tahayi').   It is said to be of the nature equivalent to Mercury conjunct Venus, and while Allen records that it 'portends lives of eminence to all born under its influence', Robson views it as an evil star, for it causes 'violence, pride, over-confidence and shamelessness'.

PROROGATOR   Pingree refers to the 'prorogator' (the Greek 'aphetis' described by Dorotheus of Sidon, circa 75 AD) as a point on the ecliptic, determined by complicated rules, which conditions the length of the native's life. This point was progressed at the rate of one degree of oblique ascension per year, towards either the Ascendant or the Descendant: as this point conjuncts a malefic, or is aspected by one, the native's life is threatened or even destroyed. In any event, he dies when the prorogator has reached the horizontal angle to which it is being directed. Pingree points out that this system is a modification of an older method (ascribed to the Babylonians) which fixed the maximum length of life as the number of degrees of oblique ascension between Ascendant and Midheaven. In later astrological texts, the prorogator was usually simply the directed "Apheta".

PROSERPINA   See VIRGO CONSTELLATION.

PSALTERIUM GEORGIANUM   An obsolete constellation, formed in 1781 in honour of George II, apparently in reference to his horoscope figure.

PSYCHIC HOUSES Sometimes also misleadingly called 'Terminal Houses', these are the Fourth House, the Eighth House and the Twelfth House - those reflecting on the mundane level the influences of the "Water Triplicity", which is concerned with issues hidden in the depths of the psyche, and is often concerned with the regenerative processes. Devore calls this group the 'Trinity of Psychism'.

PSYCHIC ZODIAC   A supposed (and entirely fictitious) zodiac of 'thirteen signs', the interloper being called ARACHNE.

==

PTOLEMAIC ASPECTS   Sometimes the "Major Aspects", which were listed by
Ptolemy, are called 'Ptolemaic Aspects', but this is misleading as they were
neither originated by him nor even well defined by him. The term appears to
have become necessary because of the introduction of the Quintile aspects,
which are (more correctly) called the "Keplerian Aspects".

PTOLEMAIC ASTROLOGY   Specifically the name applies to a corpus of
astrological traditions gathered together by Claudius Ptolemaeus in the 2nd
century of our era (see TETRABIBLOS), and in general to that corpus as it was
augmented and refined by Arabic and late mediaeval astrologers.   The
astrological conceptions, terminologies and even cosmoconceptions which go
under the name of Ptolemy were not of his making, but merely collected,
collated and partly systematized from the earlier Chaldean, Egyptian and
Greek traditions. Indeed, it is clear that the system which bears his name
is replete with ideas and terms which he himself could not always understand,
many of which he defined incompletely. It is often claimed (by those who
have not bothered to read Ptolemy, or who are unfamiliar with mediaeval
astrology) that the Ptolemaic astrology is very little different from the
late mediaeval traditions upon which modern astrology is based. This is
simply not true: the system is actually very far from the interpretational
level of traditional western forms. While many of the interpretations and
traditions (and especially many of the terminologies) he records have been
adopted (for example the tradition of the major aspects - see PTOLEMAIC
ASPECTS) just as many have become obsolete (see for example PTOLEMAIC TERMS):
just as many ascribed to him by later commentators would have been quite
foreign to his form of astrology (see for example ZIGIATUS). Only the more
important of his terms - or such as a general researcher into astrology is
likely to come across - are incorporated into this present work. See also
PTOLEMAIC SYSTEM.

PTOLEMAIC SYSTEM   The most widely adopted model of the solar system (and
indeed of the universe) used in mediaeval astrology (but see also
ARISTOTELIAN SYSTEM) until it was gradually deposed by the "Copernican
System", both as a model and as an astrological tool. The system itself is
largely set out in Ptolemy's "Almagest" and in his 'Hypotheses of the
Planets', but was much adapted and refined by later astrologers and
astronomers. It is a geocentric system, with a series of epicycles for each
of the known planets (of which there were seven, including the Sun and Moon).
The sequence of planets carried in the SPHERES was (in descending order from
the sphere of the fixed stars (usually called the "Stellatum"): SA, JU, MA,
SU, VE, ME, MO. At the centre of the concentric spheres was the Earth,
encased in a series of elemental spheres, of which Fire was the outer, Air
the next, Water the next, with the Earth at the centre. In the later models
the interior of the earth was turned into a reflection of the stellar spheres
(inverted), though given up to the various levels of the demons: these
however play little or no part in astrology. In later models, the positions
of Venus and Mercury were transposed. It is sometimes wrongly said that
there were eight spheres in the Ptolemaic system, no doubt in reference to
the stellatum of fixed stars, and the seven planets of the ancients - but
this is far from the case. The daily motion of each planet within the
spheres is a result of the whole sytem of spheres being carried by the
rotation of the stellar sphere from east to west, around a static Earth.
Ptolemy ascribed to the Aristotelian dictum that the extralunar bodies moved
in perfect circles, and in order to account for the appearances which
contradicted this theory, he imagined that each planet made an irregular
journey: though actually always moving in a perfect circle, they each
followed a complicated series of epicycles, the centres for which lay on a
"Deferent". The movement of the superior planets involved an annual
revolution of its epicycle, while the inferior planets had epicycles which
accounted for their proper periods, the deferent for their annual
irregularities. The Sun alone revolved without epicycles, in majestic sweep
around the Earth. Ptolemy was familiar with the general idea of
"Precession", which required in his system that the Stellar Sphere

(Stellatum) be carried by a further sphere (the so-called "Ninth Sphere"), which gave to the stellar sphere a diurnal motion for east to west, while this latter (carrying the planetary spheres) moved slowly in the opposite direction. The elaborate Ptolemaic system was rendered more and more complex, and required the additions of more and more spheres, until it actually became unworkable because of its own inherent complexity and was superseded by the more simple heliocentric system of Copernicus. The differences between the complicated epicycles and seemingly simple concentrics was not the only point of difficulty. The theory of precession as proposed within the Ptolemaic model actually involved ascribing the stellar sphere with two contadictory movements (see PRIMUM MOVENS). However, complex as the system was, it found favour for many centuries with astrologers because it (or rather the tables derived from it) did offer a reasonable basis for the computation of horoscopes - though these were usually backed by direct observation of the skies, which is far from the case in modern astrology. Indeed, the tables and computations offered by the system, while lacking the precision of modern tables, were reasonably accurate. The cosmoconception of Ptoemy was no more his making than was PTOLEMAIC ASTROLOGY: both were merely collected, partly systematized transmissions from earlier sources - the astrological traditions came mainly from Chaldean and Egyptian sources, the astronomical ideas from Aristotle, Plato, Eudoxus and Apollonius of Perga, to name only the major contributors.

PTOLEMAIC TERMS   A title given to a system of degree rulerships called "terms" as reproduced by Ptolemy, in contrast with the related system of termini arcs which he recorded as the CHALDEAN TERMS and the EGYPTIAN TERMS, the former resting upon the government of triplicities, the latter upon the government of houses. Terms are usually explained as being certain degrees within the signs which are supposed to have the power of influencing the nature of a planet posited within them to the nature of the planet which 'rules' the term. However, Ptolemy is far from clear as to what the terms are, or as to how they are to be interpreted: it is unlikely that they are 'sensitive degrees' at all, though this is how they are generally explained by those who quote traditional ideas without attempting to understand what Ptolemy actually said. Placidus (who did try) could not understand what Ptolemy was trying to say, and came up with his own theories instead. The present writer must admit to being more than confused by the whole matter of Ptolemaic 'terms', or 'termini', and Wilson admitted that they were for him 'wholly unintelligible'. The one thing which seems certain is that the terms are not actually sensitive degrees in the ordinary sense of the word, so that the modern commentators are quite wrong in their explanation of what Ptolemy had in mind. In the astrological literature, the notion has developed that a planet 'in its own term' (according to one of the two most widely published tables given below) was particularly powerful. However, this notion does not appear to have any support from the Ptolemaic reporting of the term. In view of this, the terms in figure 66 are given more out of antiquarian interest than with any hope to throwlight on the subject. For the sake of comparison with the 'Ptolemaic', the 'Egyptian' system is reproduced in table 66, though this was not the one most favoured by Ptolemy, who found it 'inconsistent': however, the Egyptian system was that favoured by DOROTHEAN ASTROLOGY and was thus adopted by Firmicus Maternus. Ptolemy says that the third system - our so called 'Ptolemaic' - is not his own, but one adapted from an ancient astrological document of uncertain provenance in his possession. The degrees in this system, as well as the rulerships accorded them, are set out in table 66.

--TABLE 66

SIGN	PTOLEMAIC TERMS					EGYPTIAN TERMS				
AR	JU6	VE8	ME7	MA5	SA4	JU6	VE6	ME8	MA5	SA5
TA	VE8	ME7	JU7	SA2	MA6	VE8	ME6	JU8	SA5	MA3
GE	ME7	JU6	VE7	MA6	SA4	ME6	JU6	VE5	MA7	SA6
CN	MA6	JU7	ME7	VE7	SA3	MA7	VE6	ME6	JU7	SA4

===

--TABLE 66 (CONTINUED)

SIGN	PTOLEMAIC TERMS					EGYPTIAN TERMS				
LE	JU6	ME7	SA6	VE6	MA5	JU6	VE5	SA7	ME6	MA6
VG	ME7	VE6	JU5	SA6	MA6	ME7	VE10	JU4	MA7	SA2
LB	SA6	VE5	ME5	JU8	MA6	SA6	ME8	JU7	VE7	MA2
SC	MA6	VE7	JU8	ME6	SA3	MA7	VE4	ME8	JU5	SA6
SG	JU8	VE6	ME5	SA6	MA5	JU12	VE5	ME4	SA5	MA4
CP	VE6	ME6	JU7	SA6	MA5	ME7	JU7	VE8	SA4	MA4
AQ	SA6	ME6	VE8	JU5	ME5	ME7	VE6	JU7	MA5	SA5
PI	VE8	JU6	ME6	MA5	SA5	VE12	JU4	ME3	MA9	SA2

PUGIL   See POLLUX.

PUNARVASU   The Sanskrit name for the constellation Cancer - but see
KARKATAKAM. The same name is also given to the 5th of the Hindu NAKSHATRAS,
and, according to Robson, in this latter context means 'the two good again'.

PURVA ASHADA   Name given to the 18th of the Hindu NAKSHATRAS, the meaning of
which is 'the former unconquered'.

PURVA BHADRA-PADA   Name given to the 24th of the Hindu NAKSHATRAS, meaning
'the former beautiful feet'.

PURVA PHALGUNI   Name given to the 9th of the Hindu NAKSHATRAS, meaning 'the
former bad one'.

PUSHYA   Name given to the 6th of the Hindu NAKKSHATRAS, the name meaning
'flower'.

PYROEIS   One of the Greek names for Mars, meaning 'fire' and often given
variable spellings (and various meanings) in mediaeval astrological and
alchemical texts.

PYTHAGOREAN HARMONIES   See MUSIC OF THE SPHERES.

PYTHAGOREAN PENTACLE   Name given to a six-pointed star, with an eagle
figured at the highest point, below a bull, a lion and the face of man (the
image of the four fixed signs of the zodiac - see for example TETRAMORPHS).
The imagery of the Pythagorean pentacle (which has nothing to do with
Pythagoras, even though the numbers 4 and 6 were derived in this context from
the Pythagorean SOUL-NUMBERS) was widely adopted in proto-Renaissance
ecclesiastical sculpture, and appears in mediaeval astrological, alchemical
and occult texts. The esoteric content of the pentacle was directed towards
symbolizing the human being - within the esoteric image the eagle represented
the 'thinking power' (which might soar); the lion represented the 'emotional
depth' (through the zodiacal association with Leo, which rules the heart of
man); the bull represented the physical body and will-life (Taurus being an
Earth sign), whilst the face was linked at once with the 'humanity' of
Aquarius, and with the entire human being in which the other three dwell, as
thinking, feeling and willing.

PYTHAGOREAN TRIANGLE   See NUPTIAL NUMBER.

PYTHON See DRACO.

PYXIS NAUTICA A modern constellation originated in 1752 by La Caille from
stars previously forming the ship mast of Argo Navis. Though not
particularly distinguished, the group is said to give an interest in nautical
and geographical matters.

===

QABBALISTIC ASTROLOGY The word Qabbalah relates to a complex philosophy and cosmoconception which has an oral tradition, transcribed for over a thousand years, rooted in a mystical and esoteric interpretation of scriptures. Some indeed argue Qabbalism as the roots of modern occultism. It is usual to distinguish 'Qabbalism' from 'Cabbalism', for reasons adduced by Fulcanelli - but there are many variant spellings of the name. The influence of astrology on qabbalistic thought - or, more accurately, on Christian qabbalism (in this text termed 'Cabbalism') - has been profound. Equally, the influence of Christian and Jewish cabbalism on esoteric astrology has been extensive, though they have scarcely permeated ordinary genethliacal astrology. So extensive were these fruitful influences, which may be traced through Agrippa, Boehme, Dee, Fludd, Paracelsus and Welling (to mention only those authorities whose terms are touched upon in the present work) that it is entirely beyond the scope of a short article to deal with them. Table 5 under ARCHANGELS OF THE SEPHIROTH sets out the traditional correspondences, but it is significant to observe that Fludd quite rightly (from the Christian cabbalistic point of view) gives the 'Soul of the Messiah' to rule over Malkuth, as Christ is united with the Earth: however, within the ancient hierarchies, the Archangel of the Earth is called "Uriel". Trachtenberg sets out some variations, which are perhaps only of interest to scholars: Myer, dealing mainly with Avicebron, sets out a sephirothic correspondence which ignores the Earth (Malkuth marking the Sphere of the Moon). Figure 51 is the Sephirothic Tree (with the supposed planetary rulers) given by Myer, which shows important differences from that listed under "Archangels of the Sephiroth".

FIGURE 51. SEPHIROTHIC TREE WITH ZODIACAL CORRESPONDENCES (AFTER MYER).

A correspondence between the zodiacal signs and the Hebraic letters (more accurately, their sounds and sound values) has been recorded, in some cases associated with the planetary spirits, as in table 67 (over).

===

```
------------------------------------------------------------------TABLE 67
SIGN         HEBRAIC LETTER           PLANETARY SPIRIT
=========================================================================
AR           He                       Michael
TA           Vau                      Gabriel
GE           Zain                     Raphael
CN           Heth                     Uriel
LE           Teth                     Guriel
VG           Yod (Jod)                Nuriel
LB           Lamed                    Yeschamiel
SC           Nun
SG           Samek                    Ayil
CP           Ain (Ayn)                Ubariel
AQ           Tzaddi (Tsade)
PI           Quoph (Koph)
-------------------------------------------------------------------------
```

It is often claimed in the less scholarly texts that the names of the
"Planetary Spirits" (see SECUNDADEIAN BEINGS) are qabbalistic in origin,
which is far from the truth. Trachtenberg traces the names of these
mediaeval Christian planetary rulers by way of Averroes to the Gnostics, who
were in turn influenced by the Babylonian planetary spirits, and the Persian
Amshaspands. Because of the importance attached to the sound-values of
letters and numbers in the Qabbalistic tradition, a variety of different
correspondences between numbers and zodiacal signs and planets have been
established. The sequence given by the astrologer Libra is:

```
-------------------------------------------------------------------------
AR  7      TA  6       GE  3 or 12       CN  5      LE  1      VG  1 or 10
LB  8      SC  9       SG  4             CP  3      AQ  2      PI  11

SU 1 or 4   MO 2 or 7      JU 3      ME  5      VE  6      SA  8      MA  9
-------------------------------------------------------------------------
```

QUADRA EUCLIDIS   See NORMA.

QUADRANS MURALIS   Constellation, 'Mural Quadrant', formed by La Lande in
1795 between the right foot of "Hercules" and the left foot of "Bootes". Not
recognized by modern astronomers, but said by astrologers to give rectitude,
justice and idealism.

QUADRANTINE LUNATION   A term (rarely) applied to the four major aspects of
Sun and Moon - the conjunction, opposition and two squares -- which in the
monthly cycle mark the four quarters of the celestial figure - see QUADRANTS.

QUADRANTS   The four 'quarters' of the horoscope figure. In reference to the
circle of the zodiac, the 'oriental quadrants' are from Aries to Gemini, nd
from Libra to Sagittarius, inclusive. The 'occidental quadrants' are from
Cancer to Virgo, and from Capricorn to Pisces, inclusive. Very many other
names have been used to distinuish the quadrants: the first is called
'vernal', 'sanguine' and 'infantine': the second is called 'meridianal',
'estival', 'youthful' and 'choleric' (Wilson gives 'choloric'): the third is
called 'autumnal', 'melancholic' and 'mature', while the fourth is called
'northern', 'decrepit', 'wintry' and 'phlegmatic'.

QUADRATED CHART   See CHART SYSTEMS and QUADRATED CIRCLE.

QUADRATED CIRCLE   A term probably originated by Bouche-Leclercq to apply to
the early horsocope charts symbolized in a square or otherwise quadrated
form, derived from the more usual (and older) system of symbolic projection
which was based on a circle: see CHART SYSTEMS. Two quadrated forms have
persisted into modern astrology, and each of the divsions within their
quadratures define houses in terms of the projected ecliptic. The first is

based on what might be called the 'decussata' (figure 12B under "Chart Systems"), the second on the 'Greek cross' (figure 12C).

QUADRATURES   Name given to the DICHOTOMES of the Moon.

QUADRIPARTIUM   See TETRABIBLOS.

QUADRUPEDAL   A term used to denote the five zodiacal signs represented by 'Images' which depict four-footed creatures: Aries (the ram), Taurus (the bull), Leo (the lion), Sagittarius (the horse), and Capricorn (sometimes a goat, but more properly a fish-tail - something of a foreigner in this classification). These are also called 'four-footed'.

QUADRUPLICITIES   Each of the twelve signs of the zodiac have been grouped into fours, related in such a way as to reflect the communality of QUALITY: namely, Cadinality, Fixity and Mutability. These three groups of 'quadruplicities' (sets of four) are:

    AR, CN, LB and CP   Cardinal Quadruplicity.
    TA, LE, SC and AQ   Fixed Quadruplicity.
    GE, VG, SG and PI   Mutable Quadruplicity.

QUALITIES   See QUALITY.

QUALITY   This term has (confusingly) two important technical applications in astrology. The first meaning is related to the idea of 'four qualities', linked with the innate natures of the elements: Fire is said to be of the 'hot and dry' qualities: Earth is of the 'cold and dry' qualities: Water is of the 'cold and humid' qualities: Air is of the 'hot and humid' qualities. In this sense, the 'four qualities' apparently originated by Philistion were a development of Empedocles' theory of ELEMENTS, in which Fire was hot, Air was cold, Water was moist, and Earth was dry. In relation to human beings, illness was a sign that a person was 'out of quality', or suffering from some imbalance. These qualities were eventually combined to form the limited number of dual combinations set out above, and it was in this guise that they dominated Roman and mediaeval astrology, mainly through their link with the theory of bodily humours - see TEMPERAMENTS and PRIMORDIAL QUALITIES. A second meaning is related to the idea of 'three qualities', by means of which each of the four elements finds expression in the twelve signs of the zodiac. These qualities are "Cardinality", "Fixity" and "Mutability". Thus, Aries, Cancer, Libra are of the Cardinal Quality. In this sense, the qualities are also called the "Quadruplicities" and the 'Modes'.

QUARTERLY CHARTS   A term used by Bradley to denote the four charts which may be derived from the 'quarters', or three-monthly periods in the annual SOLAR RETURN.

QUARTESSENCE   The term 'quartessence' is found mainly in the curious astrological terminology of alchemical texts. Philalethes denies the existence of the QUINTESSENCE but describes a 'quartessence', a 'fourth essence' which is the binder of the THREE PRINCIPLES, and is called by the curious designation 'moist and silent fire'.

QUARTILE   An old expression used to denote the SQUARE aspect.

QUEEN OF NEBULAE   See GREAT NEBULA.

QUERENT   A specialist term in astrology, theoretically used only to denote the one who asks the question in HORARY ASTROLOGY: sometimes however the term is used of any questioner in the various divisions of astrology. In horary astrology the significator of the querent is generally the Ascendant, or its Lord, or planets in the Ascendant sign.

QUESITED   A term usually restricted to "Horary Astrology", and related to the person or thing enquired about in respect of a horoscopic chart. The term is intended to draw a distinction between the quesited and the "Querent", the person who puts the question.

QUINCUNX   An aspect of 150 degrees, the two aspecting points being separated by five signs of the zodiac.

QUINDECILE   An aspect of 24 degrees, derived from dividing the zodiac into fifteenths.

QUINTESSENCE   The term means 'fifth element', and is a reference to the invisible power or 'essence' which binds in a unity the otherwise separate FOUR ELEMENTS. The term has had very many synonyms, of which the most frequently used are 'Aether', 'Mercury of the Philosophers' and the modern ETHERIC, the last of which has been studied in some depth by Waschmuth: however, see also QUARTESSENCE.

QUINTILE   An aspect of 72 degrees, arising from a division of the zodiac into fifths. The astrologer Morin belittled the new 'quintiles' of Kepler (see KEPLERIAN ASPECTS), and has found much support from other traditional astrologers, yet many moderns claim that this particular aspect does convey a quality of single-mindedness and power to those planets forming such an aspect.

QUINTILES   A general name sometimes given to a range of "Aspects" derived by Kepler to supplement the traditional group - see KEPLERIAN ASPECTS.

RADICAL   A term with several applications, all etymologically connected with the idea of 'root'. Generally, without a qualification or specified context, the term is the equivalent of RADICAL CHART, the name given to the primal horoscope figure. Planets disposed in such a primal figure are usually called 'radical', so that a prefix 'radical' usually indicates a planetary placing or nodal point within the radical chart: for example, 'radical Saturn' is the placing of Saturn in a given radical chart, and is normally so termed to distinguish it from the progressed Saturn. The most frequently used abbreviation for this example would be rSA and pSA.

RADICAL CHART The 'Radical' or 'Radix Chart' is the primal horoscope for a particular birth, the 'root figure' in genethliacal astrology, from which other charts (such as the Progressed Chart) may be derived, or which form the basis of later exegesis. The radical chart need not be the first chart cast for a birth (or other event) since a later rectification may reveal this to be inaccurate, and in need of adjustment: the finally adjusted recast chart is then the 'radical'.

RADICAL ELECTIONS   A term applied to certain astrologically determined times, calculated relative to a 'radical chart', and considered in relation to the unfolding tendencies and promises within that chart, expressed through transits or progressions. Usually, 'radical elections' are intended to determine fortunate or otherwise propitious astrological conditions for specific enterprises.

RADICAL POSITION   The planetary and cuspal positions in a radical chart (see "Radical") as distinguished from progressions or directions from that radical chart.

RADIX   In general this is an alternative name for the RADICAL CHART, the radix figure. Sometimes however the term may be used of the Radix System, a progressional technique (somewhat equivalent to that of the SYMBOLIC DIRECTIONS) which progresses all bodies at a rate of 59' 8" of arc equivalent to a year: see MEASURE OF NAIBOD.

RADIX COSMOGRAM   A radical horoscope figure used in COSMOBIOLOGY.

RADIX METHOD   Term used of a simple method of SYMBOLIC DIRECTIONS, involving the addition of 59' 8" of arc for each year of life: see MEASURE OF NAIBOD.

RAHU   The Sanskrit name for the "Dragon's Head" (the north Node), which is accorded great importance in Hindu astrology. See also KETU, the Sanskrit equivalent of the "Dragon's Tail".

RAM SCHOOL   Name given to a Dutch school of astrology, associated with the highly personalized system of Th. J.J. Ram, which involves (among other idiosyncratic features) the use of three hypothetical planets (Persephone, Hermes and Demeter) and an entirely new system of planetary rulerships which incorporate these transneptunians.

RANGIFER   Name of a small and faint constellation between Cassiopeia and Camelopardalis, sometimes called Tarandus, the 'Reindeer', and 'Renne', formed by Le Monnier as a momento of his stay in Lapland in 1736. Said by Robson to give a retiring nature and obscure life.

RAPHAEL   The archangel linked with the Sphere of Mercury, and one of the "Secundadeian Beings". In the cabbalistic tradition, Raphael is the healer, and is connected with the idea of knowledge gained through experience: he is linked in astrological lore with rule over the element of Air.

RAPT   In its astrological application, this term is derived from the Latin 'raptus' (carried away), in reference to the apparent diurnal movement of the heavens, by which it is carried: see however RAPT PARALLEL.

RAPT PARALLEL   This term is applied to two planets of a natal chart which, by direction, form mundane parallels (which is to say that they are equal distances from one of the four angles): see PARALLEL IN MUNDO. The origin of the word 'rapt' is explained in terms of the 'rapt motion' of the Primum Mobile, which in the Ptolemaic system of spheres was said to carry the planets in motion, and thus formed such parallels. A modern equivalent term would be 'transported parallel'.

RAS ALGETHI   Fixed star (double), the alpha of Hercules, with many variant names. Ebertin says that the influence of the star induces boldness and 'power drive'.

RASALGEUZE   See POLLUX.

RAS ALHAGAS   See RASALHAGUE.

RASALHAGUE   Fixed star, the alpha of Ophiuchus, the name from the Arabic 'Ras al Hawwa' (head of the serpent charmer), with many variants, among which 'Ras Alhagas', 'Rasalange', 'Rasalauge' and 'Alangue' are prominent. Ptolemy records it as being of the nature of Venus with Saturn, and it is said to bring misfortunes, mental depravities and perverted tastes. Alvidas claims for it a more beneficial influence, however.

RAS ELASED AUSTRALIS   A term used by Ebertin for the fixed star epsilon of constellation Leo, probably due to a misreading of the Arabian term 'Al Ras al Asad al Janubiyyah', which means 'southern star in the head of the lion'. Ebertin links the influence with higher spiritual gifts for those capable of receiving them, and with 'psychological depresssions' and even suicide for those incapable of receiving such gifts.

RASI   The Hindu term for a birthchart, usually cast for a constellational zodiac, and using equal house division, the so-called MODUS EQUALIS.

RASTABAN   Fixed star (binary), the beta of Draco, set in the head of the asterism, the name from the Arabic 'Al Ras al Thuban' (the dragon's head), but with many variants, including 'Asuia', 'Asvia' and (presumably from early star maps) 'Dragon's Eyes'. It is said to be of the nature of Mars conjunct Saturn, bringing losses, criminal inclination and (with the Moon) blindness.

RATIONAL AND UNIVERSAL METHOD   See MORINEAN SYSTEM.

RATIONAL METHOD   See REGIOMONTANEAN SYSTEM.

RAVEN   See CORVUS.

RAY   The term, now almost archaic in its original astrological sense, was once used in traditional texts as being synonymous with INFLUENCE. Significantly, the term is still cognate with 'radius', and suggests the idea of a connecting line between the circumference and the centre - an idea of importance only within a cosmoconception involving concentric spheres. The idea of 'influence rays' still persists in the term which has a planet 'falling under the rays' of another planet, when it enters orb of aspect. See in this connexion also CAST NO RAYS. The term has been widely used in the modern INTUITIONAL ASTROLOGY, though in a specialist sense - see SEVEN RAYS - not to be confused with SEVEN RAY TYPES. The term is also used of the calibrated linear scales within the centre of the COSMOPSYCHOGRAM.

RAY OF ACTIVE-INTELLIGENCE   See THIRD RAY.

RAY OF CEREMONIAL ORDER   See SEVENTH RAY.

RAY OF CONCRETE SCIENCE   See FIFTH RAY.

RAY OF DEVOTION   See SIXTH RAY.

RAY OF HARMONY THROUGH CONFLICT   See FOURTH RAY.

RAY OF IDEALISM   See SIXTH RAY.

RAY OF JUPITER   See SEVEN RAY TYPES.

RAY OF LOVE-WISDOM   See SECOND RAY.

RAY OF MARS   See SEVEN RAY TYPES.

RAY OF MERCURY   See SEVEN RAY TYPES.

RAY OF MOON   See SEVEN RAY TYPES.

RAY OF NEPTUNE   See SEVEN RAY TYPES.

RAY OF POWER   See FIRST RAY.

RAY OF SATURN   See SEVEN RAY TYPES.

RAY OF URANUS   See SEVEN RAY TYPES.

RAY OF VENUS   See SEVEN RAY TYPES.

RAY OF WILL   See FIRST RAY.

==

RAYS   See SEVEN RAYS and SEVEN RAY TYPES.

REAL ZODIAC   A term used by the astrologer Leo, but unfortunately defined (rather than described) in a most confusing manner. One the one hand he appears to consider it one of the 'sidereal zodiacs' (though of equal division), and on the other hand as the familir 'tropical zodiac'. He seems to have originated the term in order to distinguish this from the 'Supposed Zodiac' (as he terms it) of SOLAR BIOLOGY, the so-called LUNAR ZODIAC or 'Earth Zodiac', described by Butler.

RECEIVED   See RECEPTION.

RECEPTION   This term has two quite different specialist meanings. First, it is used to describe a relationship between planets: when a planet is placed in a sign over which it does not have rule, it is said to be 'in reception' or to be 'received by' the actual ruler of that sign. Secondly, when a planet is being subjected to an aspect from a faster-moving planet, it is said to be 'in reception' of that aspect, or to be 'receiving that aspect'.

RECH   See PHOENIX.

RECTIFICATION   A specialist term used to denote the process of adjusting a birth chart (itself believed to be inaccurate) by reference to known events which are dated independently of the horoscope, and hence permit correction of a progressed chart. There are several methods of rectification in modern use: for example, some astrologers use the PRE-NATAL EPOCH as the basis for rectification, whilst others employ a rule-of-thumb method (more of a preliminary to precise rectification) involving adjusting the chart to fit the known characteristics of the native to suitable angles and intermediate house-positions for planets. Some individuals use radiesthesic methods for determining the Ascendant degree, from which the related chart may be calculated, but this is a method frowned upon by serious astrologers, and, furthermore, a method which must in any case be checked against a rectification if it is to have any practical application.

RECURRENCE CYCLES   A term applied to periods of time in which conjunctions of two planets will recur in (approximately) the same degree of the zodiac. See CYCLES, FIRST ORDER CYCLE, and SECOND ORDER CYCLE.

RED BIRD   A name given to an arc of seven SIEU or Lunar Mansions in the Chinese astrological system - sometimes it is wrongly called a 'constellation'. There are three other such arcs: the AZURE DRAGON, BLACK WARRIOR and WHITE TIGER. See also CORVUS.

RE-DIRECTED   A term used of the the movement of a planet back into direct motion after being RETROGRADE.

REDUCTION   A term sometimes used to denote the conversion of sidereal material to tropical, or tropical material to sidereal.

REFRANATION   A specialist term used only in Horary Astrology. Refranation occurs when an aspect does not reach completion, due to the retrogradation of one of the aspecting planets.

REGEL   See RIGEL.

REGENERATION CYCLE   See CYCLE.

REGIA   See REGULUS.

REGIOMONTANEAN SYSTEM   A system of HOUSE DIVISION, sometimes called the 'Modus Rationalis' (Rational Method), evolved by the 15th century astrologer and mathematician Johann Muller, who worked under the pseudonym

Regiomontanus. The principle of his system is the trisection of a quadrant of the equator by great circles mutually intersecting at the north and south points of the horizon. The degrees at which these circles cut the ecliptic mark the cusps of the houses, which are regarded as being the centre of the house influence (rather than marking the outer limits of the house). Unfortunately, tables for the Regiomonantean system are not as generally available as those for the PLACIDEAN SYSTEM, though the method is certainly one of the two most rational divisions of the celestial sphere for astrological purposes. See also CAMPANEAN SYSTEM.

REGULUS   Fixed star (triple), the alpha of constellation Leo, set in the body of the lion, the name meaning 'little king', apparently so called from the belief that it ruled the affairs of the heavens. It was included in the Babylonian star-lists under the name 'Sharru' (also meaning 'king'): in India it was 'Magha', (the mighty); in Persia, 'Miyan' (the centre), and so on - a most powerful star, and one of the four ROYAL STARS of the Persians. It is sometimes called in mediaeval star lore 'Cor Leonis' (heart of the lion), and from this have come many Arabian degenerate terms, such as 'kalbelasit', 'Calb-elez-id', and so on.   Sometimes it is called the 'Heart of the Royal Lion', the 'Star Royal', and the condensed version of the entire asterism, 'Domicilium Solis':   from the Greek 'Basilikos' (king) we have 'Basilica Stella' and 'Basiliscus', and from the Latin, 'Rex' and 'Regia'. According to Ptolemy it is of the powerful nature of Mars with Jupiter, but it is regarded as being ultimately a violent and destructive star, save when culminating, when it is said to bring high honours.   The beneficial planets also bring out the best side of its influence. In contrast to Ptolemy's insistence, the European astrologers associate it with a 'kingly' influence, and (in the words of Allen) 'made it a portent of glory, riches and power to all those born under its influence.'

REINDEER   See RANGIFER.

RELATIONSHIP CHART   Term derived by Davison to denote a chart which presents in a single figure material derived from two horoscopes. The figure is cast for the mid-point in time and space between the two relevant birth datas. Sometimes confused with the "Composite Chart".

RELATIVE HOUSES   These are the THIRD HOUSE, the SEVENTH HOUSE and the ELEVENTH HOUSE - those reflecting on the mundane sphere the influence of the Air Triplicity, which calls attention to relationships, partnerships and friends. Devore calls this the 'Trinity of Association'.

REPA   See SPICA.

REPRODUCTIVE TRINITY   A term used by Butler in his SOLAR BIOLOGY in respect of the zodiacal signs Libra, Scorpio and Sagittarius.

RETICULUM RHOMBOIDALIS   Constellation, the 'Rhomboidal Net', formed by Habrecht and adopted by La Caille: it lies north of Hydrus, and is said to give tenacity, selfishness and a 'restricted life'.

RETROGRADE   Specialist astrological term derived from the Latin compound meaning 'to step backwards', and applied to the apparent motion of a planet backwards along the zodiacal belt. In traditional astrological interpretation a planet which was so retrograde carried a somewhat sinister connotation, though the tendency is for modern astrologers to either entirely dismiss the idea that retrogradation should influence the significance of planets, or to greatly amend the sinister reputation attached to the ancient interpretation. When the retrogradation ceases, and direct motion is about to begin, there is a time when the planet appears to stand still: it is then called a 'stationary' planet. The 'retrograde station' is that point of apparent stability at which the planet begins to move into retrogradation: the 'direct station' is that point of apparent stability at which the planet begins to move into direct motion along the zodiacal course.

RETROGRADE APPLICATION   The APPLICATION to aspect of a retrograde planet to
another retrograde planet.

RETROGRADE ARC   That arc of the zodiac in which any planet is retrograde,
between its 'retrograde station' and its 'direct station' (see RETROGRADE).

RETROGRADE STATION   See RETROGRADE.

REVATI   The 26th of the Hindu NAKSHATRAS.

REVOLUTION   In astrological specialist use, the return of any of the planets
to their radical places in a chart is termed a 'revolution'. The same term
is however also applied generally to any orbit - and sometimes (wrongly) to
any axial rotation of a planet. See ORBITAL REVOLUTION and REVOLUTION
PERIODS. The term is unfortunately also applied to the SOLAR RETURN, which
is sometimes wrongly called the 'Solar Revolution Method': see also SOLAR
REVOLUTION FIGURE.

REVOLUTION PERIODS   Traditional astrology has provided various scales of
'revolution periods' for the planets, some of them remarkably accurate: see
PLANETARY PERIODS. A modern series, set out in days and years, is given in
table 68.

```
--------------------------------------------------------------TABLE 68
```

PLANET	REVOLUTION IN DAYS	REVOLUTION IN YEARS
ME	87.97	0.241
VE	224.70	0.615
MA	686.98	1.881
JU	4,332.59	11.862
SA	10,759.20	29.458
UR	30,685.93	84.015
NE	60,187.64	164.788
PL	90,600.00	248.400

RHEA   Name given to one of the moons of Saturn.

RHOMBOIDAL NET   See RETICULUM RHOMBOIDALIS.

RIGEL   Fixed star, the beta of Orion, set in the left foot of the figure,
the name from the Arabic 'Rijl' (foot). It has many variant names, including
'Regel', 'Riglon', 'Rigel Algeuze', 'Algibbar', 'Algebar' and 'Elgebar'. As
with the fixed star Regulus, Ptolemy regarded it more unfavourably than
modern astrologers, according it an influence of Jupiter conjunct Saturn,
though (as Allen records of the later astrologers) it was 'said that
splendour and honours fell to the lot of those who were born under it':
certainly this is suggested by the lists of planetary influences set out by
Robson, almost all of which give good fortune and lasting honours.

RIGHT ASCENSION   A system of measurement, designed to determine the stellar
system of co-ordinates with earthly longitude. It is expressed (usually) in
degrees of declination from the first point of Aries eastwards, within the
plane of the celestial equator. In most house systems, the Midheaven is
directed by Right Ascension.

RIGIL KENTAURUS   Fixed star, the alpha of Centaurus, set in the foot of the
centaur, the name apparently from the Arabic 'Al Rijil a Kentaurus'
(centaur's foot). The star, under the name of 'Serk-t' was highly regarded
by the Egyptians, and appears to have been used for temple orientation (at
the autumnal equinox) in the 3rd and 4th millenium BC. Due to a catalogue

===

error, the star was named by Burrit 'Bungula' - from 'beta' and 'ungula' (hoof) - by which misnomer it has passed into astrological lore.

RIGLON   See RIGEL.

RIKSHA   The Sanskrit term for an ASTERISM, though also used to denote a fixed star, as well as the Hindu NAKSHATRAS.

RISHABHAM   The Sanskrit name for zodiacal Taurus - but see also KRITTIKA.

RISING SIGN   A term frequently misused in popular astrology. Properly speaking it should apply only to the sign which marks the Ascendant degree on a particular horoscope. The term is sometimes popularly used as being synonymous with ASCENDANT (especially so in the United States of America), whereas the Rising Sign is really a whole sign of thirty degrees, and the Ascendant is actually a single degree (and indeed more properly an intersection of an arc).

RISING TIMES   In ancient forms of astrology, the 'rising times' were tables derived to show how many degrees of the equator crossed the horizon of a given place, consecutively with the zodical signs: such were the basis for chart computations.   The rising times varied according to (a) the AYANAMSA used, and (b) according to the CLIMA, or location for which the information was tabulated - see for example SEVEN CLIMATA.   Determined by means of spherical trignometry, the rising times were known to Ptolemy, but previously the Babylonians had used arithmetical approximates. The equation of 1 degree of arc to four minutes of time is still used in rule-of-thumb astrology, but is far from exact in latitudes far from the equator.

RIVER OF HEAVEN   See VIA LACTEA.

ROBUR CAROLINUM   Constellation, 'Charles's Oak', formed by Halley in 1679 in commemoration of the oak in which his patron (Charles II) hid after the battle of Worcester in 1651 - in its original form, this asterism overlaid the constellation of Argo Navis.   Astrologers say that it gives an honourable, generous and steady nature.

ROHINI   The second of the Hindu NAKSHATRAS.

ROOT-EARTH TRIGON   See SIDEREAL MOON RHYTHMS.

ROOT FIGURE   See RADICAL CHART.

ROOT RACES   See SEVEN RACES.

ROSICRUCIAN ASTROLOGY   A term properly restricted to the form of astrology promulgated by the followers of Heindel, whose esoteric content was almost entirely derived from Theosophical teachings (after Blavatsky and her systematizers), and from the writings and lectures of Steiner - in both cases usually without acknowledgment.   The modern rosicrucianism must not be confused with the late-mediaeval stream of Rosicrucianism that flowered in the writings of such occultists as Dee, Fludd and Boehme, who actually influenced esoteric astrology more profoundly than they influenced the so-called 'traditional' astrology.

ROTA IXIONIS   See CORONA AUSTRALIS.

ROTATION   In correct use this term is applied to the motion of a body upon its own axis: see also REVOLUTION.

ROUND   See GLOBE PERIOD.

ROUNDING OFF   Since for most practical purposes the positions of planets in

charts are required only in terms of degrees, rather than in terms of
subdivisions of degrees, such positions are often 'rounded off'. The two
main systems of rounding off result in some cases in different figures being
obtained, so that each system employed in a particular chart, and the nature
of the conversions, must be noted.   The first system (and the most widely
used) is really a statement of the nearest whole degree: thus 12 degrees 12
minutes and 12 seconds may be given as 12 degrees, as may be 11 degrees, 43
minutes and 12 seconds.   The second system requires that the precise figure
be expressed in terms of the actual degree itself: thus, since 12 degrees,
12 minutes, 12 seconds actually marks a point in the thirteenth degree, then
this must be expressed as 13 degrees. This latter system recognizes no ZERO
DEGREE, save perhaps as an intellectual abstraction, for a planet must always
be posited in one degree or another. This latter method is of considerable
importance in regard to conversion of horoscopic material to degree symbols,
and a failure to understand the underlying conditions has frequently led to
wrongful conversions.   An example of an actual chart will therefore be
instructive: the two horoscopes in figure 52 shown an example of rounding
off the degrees in a chart erected for the birth of Goethe by the astrologer
Pearce. It is instructive to note that the corresponding data 'rounded off'
in the 'Notable Nativities' of Leo is not accurate, and may be taken as a
suitable illustration here:

    H: SC 17,   MC: VG 05,   SU: 5 VG,   MO: 12 PI,   ME: 29 LE,
        VE: 26.5 VG   MA: 3.5 CP,   JU: 26 PI,   SA: 15 SC

Whilst MO 12 is accurately rounded off, SU 05 VG should actually be SU 6 VG,
and the Ascendant should be SC 18.   The relevance of this is obvious when
one attempts to relate the figure to a degree symbol (or indeed to accurately
defined aspects) - the data given by Leo would be misleading, whilst that
given in the rounding off diagram in figure 52 would not be misleading.

FIGURE 52   HOROSCOPE FOR BIRTH OF GOETHE (28TH AUGUST, 1749 NS), NOON, AT
FRANKFORT (AFTER PEARCE), WITH 'ROUNDED-OFF' VERSION FOR COMPARISON.

ROUND TABLE   See GLASTONBURY ZODIAC.

ROYAL STARS   One of the titles given to the four stars of the ancient
Persians (beginning of the third millenium BC) which were apparently used as
markers, and sometimes called the 'Watchers of the Heavens', the 'Four
Watchers', and 'Guardians of the Heavens'. The modern names of these stars
are ALDEBARAN, ANTARES, FOMALHAUT and REGULUS, but Dupuis and Flammarion

==

named them as 'Tascheter', 'Satevis', 'Hastorgang' and 'Venant' respectively.
The right ascensions of these four are approximately six hours apart, so that
they mark the four quarters of the heavens, rather than 'cardinal points'.

RULE   This term is used of planets and signs in a wide and often
unsatisfactory manner to indicate particular relationships and
congenialities. In reference to particular relationships, a planet is often
said to have 'rule' over certain zodiacal signs, according to the ancient
system recorded by Ptolemy, which has in recent centuries been adjusted
considerably: in this connexion, see PLANETARY RULERSHIP. This particular
relationship of a planetary 'rule' over the signs has also been extended into
the misuse of the term to give 'rule' over certain houses: however, the
correct term in this context is LORDSHIP. A planet may be said to be the
Lord of a house, had to have Rule over a sign (but see also THRONE). In
reference to congenialities, the term 'rule' is used in a very wide sense to
cover relationships held by planets and signs through the ancient doctrine of
SIGNATURES. In this general sense, a planet or a sign may be said to have
rule over a particular country, a particular city, a particular animal, and
so on. A more suitable term (often used in the more scholarly textbooks) is
'dominion', though sometimes 'signature' is also used. Virtually every
tradition connected with the idea of rulership has been questioned by modern
astrologers, and there is no real consensus of opinion which may be quoted in
support of a particular theory of rulership. Dean, who appears to
misunderstand the historical basis for the ascriptions of the 'traditional'
rulerships of planets over signs, quotes many excellent testimonies both for
and against traditional rulerships, but it is interesting to note that among
those quoted against were astrologers who made use of sidereal zodiacs, which
were certainly not in the mind of the ancients who formulated the system of
rulerships which have been adopted by modern astrology. The tendency in
modern times (mainly as a result of the work being done to classify the
workings of the so-called NEW PLANETS, and in some cases because of what
might be termed 'bureaucratic aesthetics') has been to eliminate completely
the last vestiges of the dual rulerships which lay at the basis of the
Ptolemaic system: see SECTA. The Dutch astrologer Ram has suggested a schema
which incorporates a number of transplutonian HYPOTHETICAL PLANETS, and which
virtually ignores the tradtional schema: in this (though with different
hypotheticals) he was preceeded by Wemyss. The URANIAN ASTROLOGY of Witte
has also involved a new schema of hypotheticals, but it appears that many of
the modern Uranian astrologers no longer regard rulerships as having validity
at all. In the midst of so much confusion, the present author would wish to
say that a return to the (presently misunderstood) principles evinced by the
ancient Ptolemaic school will give excellent results for most purposes of
chart-interpretation. The fact is undeniable that the majority of modern
astrologers who dream up new rulerships and schemas are rarely familiar with
the spiritual truths underlying the traditions which they reject.

RULER OF TENSION   A term adopted by the German astrologer Meier in connexion
with his aspectal patterns (see FIGURINES). The rules for determining which
of the planets in a chart may be termed the 'Ruler of Tension' are complex,
seemingly involved with a simplistic numerology, but the interpretation of
the effects of the determined ruler is on the whole concomitant with the
expectations of traditional astrology: MO, for example, brings unrest and
change, whilst UR brings lack of direction or 'revolution'.

RULER OF THE HOROSCOPE   See LORD OF THE HOROSCOPE.

RULING PLANET   The 'ruling planet' of a particular horoscope is the LORD OF
THE HOROSCOPE, but the ruling planet of a sign or a house (but see RULE for
the misuse of this term) is the specific planet assigned to that sign or
house in the particular astrological system.

RUMINANT SIGNS   One of the ancient classifications which group the zodiacal
signs according to the characteristics of their IMAGE. Aries, Taurus and

===

Capricorn have been identified (through their images) with creatures which chew their cud, and may therefore be called 'ruminant'.

===

SABATHZIEL   One of several variant names for the spiritual ruler of Saturn.

SABEANS   The Sabeans, or Sabians, are in certain astrological circles regarded as being so deeply connected with early forms of astrology that the name is often used as synonymous with 'astrologers'. No doubt the term SABIAN SYMBOLS was derived from this idea.   However, there is no evidence that the ancient Sabeans (who lived in the Yemen well into the first millenium BC) practised astrology in any sense that we would now recognize. It is possible that in common with many pre-Christian tribes they were astrolators, but unlikely that they were astrologers.

SABIAN SYMBOLS   Name given to a series of DEGREE SYMBOLS ascribed to each of the 360 degrees of the zodiac, originated by psychic means in the USA by 1925. After some decades of preparatory work by many astrologers, the system was partly developed by the American Rudhyar (1936), and popularized in book form by Jones in 1953.   The particular utility of the system lies in the fact that it is attached to a supportive cross-reference of detailed and accurate horoscopes, by which the readings may be checked or exemplified.

SABIK   Fixed star, the eta of Ophiuchus, sometimes called 'Saik', set in the left knee of the asterism. Said by Ptolemy to be of the nature of Venus with Saturn, it brings perverted morals and 'success in evil deeds'.

SACRARIUS   See ARA.

SACRED ANIMALS   A term carried into English from the Hebraic 'Sepher Jesirah' by Blavatsky in reference to the ZODIAC.

SACRED PLANETS   The esotericist Bailey distinguishes seven sacred planets (as distinct from her five NON-SACRED PLANETS), which are linked with the SEVEN RAYS of her "Intuitional Astrology":

    Vulcan is linked with the FIRST RAY.
    Jupiter is linked with the SECOND RAY.
    Saturn is linked with the THIRD RAY.
    Mercury is linked with the FOURTH RAY.
    Venus is linked with the FIFTH RAY.
    Neptune is linked with the SIXTH RAY.
    Uranus is linked with the SEVENTH RAY.

The influences of these so-called 'sacreds' may not be interpreted in the ordinary astrological manner: they are intended to apply to the interpretation of charts linked only with initiates or other 'advanced' persons. Bailey says that 'the sacred planets endeavour to fuse the personality and make it the instrument of the soul and the non-sacred planets influence more specifically the form nature'. She records that the sacred planets are called the 'seven grades of psychic knowledge' or the 'seven divisions of the field of knowledge'. In another context, she gives several variant names for the informing 'lives' or beings of the seven sacred planets, such as 'Seven Planetary Logoi', 'Seven Kumaras', 'Seven Builders', 'Seven Manus', the 'Flames', the 'Primordial Seven', and so on.   The sacred planets are not to be confused with the ESOTERIC PLANETS of Bailey's system - see for example ESOTERIC MOON and ESOTERIC VULCAN.

==

SA'D AL AHBIYAH   'Al Sa'd al Ahibyah', the 23rd of the Arabian MANZILS.

SA'D AL BULA   'Al Sa'd al Bula', the 21st of the Arabian MANZILS.

SA'D AL DHABIH   'Al Sa'd al Dhabih', the 20th of the Arabian MANZILS.

SADALMELIK   Fixed star, the alpha of constellation Aquarius, set in the
right shoulder of the asterism, the name from the Arabic 'Al Sa'd al Malik'
(the lucky one of the king), and accordingly sometimes called in the Latin
approximation, 'Sidus Faustum Regis', and sometimes simply 'El Melik'. It is
equated by Ptolemy with the influence of Mercury conjunct Saturn, and is said
to bring complicated lawsuits and persecutions, as well as prominence in
occult matters.

SADALSUUD   Fixed star, the beta of constellation Aquarius, set in the left
shoulder of the asterism, the name of the Arabic 'Al Sa'd al Suud' (the
luckiest of the lucky) which accounts for the Latin approximation, 'Fortuna
Fortunarum'. It is said to bring troubles and disgrace, and Ptolemy said
that it was equivalent to the nature of Mercury conjunct Saturn, though
Simmonite likens it to that of Uranus.

SA'D AL SU'UD   'Al Sa'd al Su'ud', the 22nd of the Arabian MANZILS.

SADU CYCLE   A cycle of 30 years - see EGYPTIAN CALENDAR.

SAGITTARIUS   The ninth sign of the zodiac, which corresponds neither in
location nor meaning with the constellation of the same name - see
SAGITTARIUS CONSTELLATION. The sigil for Sagittarius ♐ is said by some to
represent the arrow of desire being shot from a vestigial bow, but many
occultists maintain that it actually consists of a four-fold cross, with an
arrow lifting this symbol of materiality into the upper spiritual realms - an
excellent symbol for the spiritualizing and expansive nature of the sign.
Sagittarius is of the Fire element and of the Mutable quality, the influence
being enterprising, open, honest, dignified, optimistic and independent. The
nature of Sagittarius as manifest in the microcosm is expressed in the many
keywords attached to it by modern astrologers: enthusiastic, philosophic,
idealistic, generous, open-minded, loyal, magnanimous, honest, frank,
restless - in a word, all the qualities which may be associated with fire
working aspirationally. In excess, the Sagittarian tends to be prodigal,
sporty, indolent, self-indulgent, conceited, dogmatic, and subject to
'pointless' wanderings. Sagittarius tends to say 'I wish to act with
dignity' more insistently than others, and he may do this creatively, and to
the benefit of others as a natural part of his being, or he may do it merely
to be seen acting in such a way, in a prodigal display of prowess or energy.
Sagittarius is ruled by the planet Jupiter.

SAGITTARIUS CONSTELLATION   Zodical constellation, the 'Archer' in many
languages, including the ancient Greek, and with many variants in the Latin,
along with Arquitenens and Arcitenens, 'the bow holder'. Figure 53, derived
from Delporte's MODERN ZODIAC, sets out the extent of the constellation.
Related terms refer to the half-human, half-animal nature of the image, which
lies at the base of the astrological lore relating to the sign: 'Semivir'
(half-man), and even 'Minotaurus' have been used, while all too frequently
the constellation is confused in literature with CENTAURUS. The Akkadian
seems to have been 'Ban', or more properly 'Mul-ban', (the star of the bow'),
and the late DENDERAH ZODIAC gives the Archer with the face of a lion. In
popular explanations of mythology, the asterism is linked with the centaur
Chiron, killed by the dropping of one of the poisoned arrows of Hercules on
his foot: however, this may go back to a misreading of Ertosthenes. The
image in figure 53 is from the mediaeval zodiac of SAN MINIATO AL MONTE, and
is that of a centaur. The fixed stars with the asterism which are regarded
as being of astrological import are ARKAB, ASCELLA, MANUBRIUM, PELAGUS, POLIS
and TEREBELLUM.

FIGURE 53.   SAGITTARIUS CONSTELLATION (AFTER DELPORTE) AND THE IMAGE FOR
SAGITTARIUS FROM THE 13TH CENTURY "SAN MINIATO ZODIAC".

SAHU   See ORION.

SAIK   See SABIK.

SALAMANDER   The class of soul beings of the Fire Element (see ELEMENTALS)
who correspond to the 'Trifertes' of esoteric lore. They are sometimes
called 'Aetnaei', and the list of correspondences in the CALENDARIA MAGICA
names them as 'Silvani'. Paracelsus appears to call them 'Rolamandri',
defined by Waite however as 'igneous men, otherwise essences of the race of
the Salamander'.

SALTS OF SALVATION   See TWELVE CELL-SALTS.

SAMAEL   A name, meaning approximately 'Venom of God', derived from the
Hebraic tradition and applied to the Archangel acting as ruler of the sphere
of Mars. Samael is one of the SECUNDADEIAN BEINGS.

SAMAS   A Babylonian name for the Sun - see OMINA. In his examination of
Mesopotamian omina material, Wiener includes under the solar omens the
phenomenon of 'doubling' - the observation of two simultaneous suns.

SANGUINE   One of the four TEMPERAMENTS, derived from an excess of the Air
element in the psychological make-up of the personality. The Sanguine
temperament strives to understand the material world through the intellect,
and is freedom-loving and idealistic. The Air temperament is associated with
the following keywords: communicative, inquisitive, original, intellectual,
quick-witted, companionable, discriminative and refined. Faults in the
temperament arise from the fact that the intellect tends to divorce the
subject from external compulsions, thus leading to daydreams, complex
ideologies, and to an inability to relate emotionally to others: under such
circumstances the type may become emotionally arid, diffused and even
dishonest in speech. See also HUMOURS.

SANGUINE QUADRANT   See QUADRANTS.

SAN MINIATO ZODIAC   The largest mediaeval (marble) floor zodiac in Europe,
set in the nave of the basilican monastic church of San Miniato al Monte, in
Florence. The historical importance of the zodiac rests in the fact that it
is linked to a highly sophisticated symbolism within the church (and indeed
on its facade) relating both to the orientation of the church and to daily

===

sunrise.   The arc of Taurus within the zodiac is directed towards the arc of
sunrise over Florence, as the schema in figure 54 indicates.   While the
zodiac is so directed, the church itself breaks all the standards of
ecclesiastical orientation, and appears to have been so directed as to permit
an extraordinary light effect (a pre-sunset phenomenon) which is also linked
with the interior symbolism of the zodiac, but which is manifest perfectly
only once each year.   The dating of the zodiac (recorded in marble in the
nave) is probably intended to point to a major satellitium of planets in
Taurus, which occured on the 28th May, 1207.   For a detailed study of the
zodiac and its related symbolism, see Gettings, in the bibliography.

FIGURE 54   THE SAN MINIATO ZODIAC, SCHEMATICALLY RELATED TO THE
ORIENTATION OF THE BASILICA AND THE ARC OF SUNRISE OVER FLORENCE.

SARFAH   'Al Sarfah', the 10th of the Arabian MANZILS.

SARIEL   A name given to one of the Grigori, who (according to Hebraic
legend) taught men the nature of the course of the Moon, and its influences,
as well as (probably) the nature of the 28 LUNAR MANSIONS.

SAROS CYCLE   A cycle of eclipses, extended over approximately 19 years, and
first described by the Chaldean astrologers.   The Moon orbits the earth in a
plane which is inclined by some 5 degrees to that of the Earth's solar orbit:
the points where these planes intersect are the nodes (see DRAGON'S HEAD and
DRAGON'S TAIL).   These two nodes regress along the Celestial Sphere, and the
rate of movement is such that it takes 223 lunar months (18 years, 11 days
and 8m hours - a figure which must be adjusted for extra or deficient leap
years) for the regressing points to return to their original positions.   This
periodicity is the Saros Cycle, during which time there are 14 partial
eclipses, 17 annular eclipses, 10 solar eclipses and 29 lunar eclipses, a
total of 70 in all.   See also METONIC CYCLE.   The same name, 'Saros Cycle',
is also applied by some astrologers to a cycle of 60 days or 60 years ('days'
and 'years' and 'ages' being interchangeable in some ancient systems - see
for example the 'days' of Biblical creation, which are actually 'ages'), or
even multiples, such as 60 x 60, or 3,600 days or years.   See NUPTIAL NUMBER.

==

SATAN   According to the astrologer Leo, Satan was one of the names of Saturn - but see also DEVIL.

SATAN'S HEAD   See ALGOL.

SATELLITE   A name given to a planet or moon (or indeed to any mechanical contrivance) which revolves in orbit around another body.

SATELLITIUM   A European astrological term used to denote a group of three or more planets in conjunction, (or, loosely speaking, grouped together in one sign, or one house, or even in an arc of less than 30 degrees). The American equivalent term is STELLIUM.

SATEVIS   See ROYAL STARS.

SATURN   Name given to the outermost of the seven traditional plants, the planetary orb within the sphere ruled by the celestial THRONES.   The influence of Saturn in the microcosm represents the restrictive side of his nature, and stands for the manner in which the human being is prepared (or is able) to pay for things received, and to demand payment from others. On a deeper level, it represents the underlying and motivating fears in the life of the native: it governs the materialistic element in life, and in particular the limitations which the native is likely to experience. When Saturn is beneficially emphasised in a chart, it is usually an indication that the subject will be practical, patient, reliable, prudent and honest, if a little austere in his attitude to life. A badly placed Saturn tends towards excessive limitation or restriction, which manifests through a deep-seated fear of life: the subject tends to be emotionally cold or despondent, narrow in outlook, and subject to melancholia. In the melothesic man, Saturn has rule over the knees, as well as over the entire skeletal frame, an expression of the cosmic fact that Saturn lends 'structure' to life's forms. In the earlier astrological tradition, the Sphere of Saturn was said to have rule over time itself - that great 'structurer' of human life. The Saturnine type usually finds expression on the physical plane through activities demanding control and organizational ability: for this reason they tend to make excellent accountants or agents, for they are particularly adapted for dealing in 'theories' of finance, though they are often personally rather parsimonious and perhaps 'over careful'. On the social plane, Saturn has rule over bureaucracy, which explains why so many Saturnine individuals are found within offices or bureaucratic organizations: this is yet another manifestation of the urge of Saturn to draw demarcations, to establish rigid structures, and to exercise control over life.

SATURNINUS   See LUNATICUS.

SATURN PERIOD   A term derived from modern esoteric astrology, relating to periods of cosmogenesis. Saturn is said to be 'the first of the planets' - though this is almost a meaningless phrase, since at that early stage of cosmogenesis Saturn was more of state of being than a planet in any sense that we might use the word now. It is described in occult literature as being something like a 'warmth globe', at a time when there was as yet no central sun or planetary system.   All potential for the future development of the solar system was contained in this Saturnine warmth globe, a state of being esoterically termed the 'Saturn Period'. This period, sometimes also called 'Old Saturn', was overseen by the hierarchy known as the 'Lords of the Flame'.

SATURN REVOLUTION   Term derived from modern esoteric astrology relating to cosmogenesis. It is said that the path or evolution in the development of the solar system, with its periods of activity and sleep (prelaya) must recapitulate, however briefly, the entire sequence of evolution up to that point. Since the cosmogenesis of our own system began in Saturn (see SATURN PERIOD), the 'Saturn Revolution' is the first of these recapitulations.

SATURN SCHEME   The 'Saturn Scheme' or 'Saturnine Chain' are terms derived specifically from the Theosophical cosmoconception linked with the SCHEME OF EVOLUTION, and are not to be confused with the SATURN PERIOD of the evolutionary sequence.

SATURN-URANUS CYCLES   Saturn conjuncts with Uranus twice in 90.726 years (first-order cycle). The period of cycles involving conjunction to opposition is 9.93 years, which has been associated with sunspot activity cycles, while the first-order cycle has been linked with fundamental political changes, and even with revolutions. There is a second-order cycle of 26 conjunctions giving a periodicity of 1179.440 years.

SCALA   A term used in late mediaeval astrology and occultism, the late Latin for 'ladder', and closely allied to the CALENDARIA MAGICA systems. The 'scalae' give lists of correspondences on a numerological basis, though (unlike the calendaria) use no symbols, signs or sigils in their constructions. The most influential scalae were those of Agrippa, which summarizes the mediaeval tradition, yet provides a little more systematization than the normal calendaria.

SCALES   A popular name for both zodiacal and constellational Libra. For 'North Scale' and 'South Scale', see ZUBENESCHAMALI and ZUBENELGENUBI, respectively.

SCERA   See SIRIUS.

SCHEAT   Fixed star, the beta of Pegasus, set in the left leg of the winged horse. Alternative names include 'Al Sa'id', 'Seat Alpheras', 'Mankib al Faras' (the Arabic for 'horses shoulder') and the derivative 'Menkib'. It has a most unfortunate reputation, for it is said to cause murder, suicide and drowning, though Ptolemy accords it the equivalent influence of Mercury conjunct Mars.   A study of the influence of planetary conjunctions with this star suggests a connexion with death through drowning, however. This may even link with an ancient Phoenician etymology - 'Pag' (or 'Pega') and 'Sus', the combination referring to the figurehead of a ship - though ancient Egyptian etymologies have also been suggested. See SKAT.

SCHEDAR   See ALPHERATZ.

SCHEMA   One of the most frequently used words in mediaeval astrology for a "Chart", the Latin term really applying to the 'scheme of the heavens', as symbolised in the chart.

SCHEME   In specialist astrological use, a modernization of the common Latin 'Schema', usually intended to mean a 'Scheme of the Heavens', and hence a synonym for CHART.

SCHEME OF EVOLUTION   According to the Theosophical cosmoconception, there are 10 separate Schemes of Evolution in our own solar system, these being the so-called 'Ten Chains' (see GLOBE PERIOD), of which only the first seven have been named (for the eighth, however, see ASTEROID SCHEME). These are:

1. The VULCAN SCHEME or Vulcanian Chain.
2. The VENUS SCHEME or Venusian Chain.
3. The EARTH SCHEME or Earth Chain.
4. The JUPITER SCHEME or Jupiterian Chain.
5. The SATURN SCHEME or Saturnine Chain.
6. The URANUS SCHEME or Uranian Chain.
7. The NEPTUNE SCHEME or Neptunian Chain.

It must be emphasised that the Vulcan of this schema (see VULCAN SCHEME) is not the same as the VULCAN hypothetical of other systems, nor is it linked with any of the VULCAN PERIOD traditions of the esoteric lore.

SCORPIO   The name given to the eighth sign of the zodiac, and sometimes to the zodiacal constellation SCORPIUS. The sigil for Scorpio ♏ is said by some to be a vestigial drawing of the male private parts, over which the sign has rule. However, esoteric astrologers claim that the sigil is really a vestigial drawing of the severed tail-half of a serpent, linking the sigil with the story of the Fall of Man. Scorpio is the only zodiacal sign to have been accorded two quite different images - that of a scorpion and that of an eagle. The former is symbol of the unregenerative scorpionic urge, while the latter symbolizes the regenerative nature - see EAGLE. Scorpio is of the water element, and of the fixed quality, the influence being magnetic, determined, secretive, shrewd, dignified, self-confident, masterful, sensitive and critical. The nature of Scorpio as it manifests in human beings is expressed in the many keywords which have been attached to it by modern astrologers: regenerative, inspirational, tenacious, forceful, magnetic, emotional, penetrating, competitive, extremist, strong in desire - in a word, all those qualities which may be associated with a water type expressing itself powerfully. In excess, the Scorpionic nature may be described in terms which express its underlying cruelty, sense of violence and instinct for crime (esoterically, the desire to have something for nothing): rebellious, degenerative, suspicious, sarcastic, cruel, selfish, violent, indulgent and domineering. The Scorpionic tends to say 'I wish to change' more insistently than the majority, and he may do this creatively, in a healing manner, or destructively, in a criminal manner, depending upon which side of his nature is being developed. In modern astrological systems, Scorpio is usually said to be ruled by the planet PLUTO, though in the traditional form it was accorded the rule of NEGATIVE MARS. It is sometimes said to mark the exaltation of Uranus, and the Fall of the Moon.

SCORPION'S HEART   See ANTARES.

FIGURE 55.   SCORPIUS, FROM THE "MODERN ZODIAC" OF DELPORTE, ALONG WITH THE IMAGE OF SCORPIO FROM THE 13TH CENTURY "SAN MINIATO ZODIAC".

SCORPIUS   Zodical constellation which in antiquity was the largest of such asterisms, incorporating in its claws (the Greek 'Chelae') what is now our separate asterism of Libra. However, the tradition is confusing, for even in antiquity the constellation was described as double, and Libra is found as a separate figure in Babylonian and Egyptian star maps. The name, properly 'Scorpius', but also sometimes 'Scorpio' (hence the two genitive Latin forms, 'Scorpii' and 'Scorpionis', the latter favoured in mediaeval astrology) was used in Roman times, the former being conveniently adopted to distinguish nominally between sign and constellation. The extent of the constellation is indicated in figure 55, derived from data furnished by Delporte's MODERN ZODIAC: the image of the scorpion in this figure is from the 13th century SAN MINIATO ZODIAC. In esoteric astrology, the association between the EAGLE and Scorpio (which figures in the important TETRAMORPH imagery) is extended from the zodiacal sign even into the constellation, for Drummond claims this name from antiquity. The asterism was also identified with the serpent - most especially with the Basilisk. The Arabic astrologers called it 'Al Akrab' (the scorpion), however, from which we have many mediaeval derivatives, such as 'Alacrab', 'Alatrap', 'Hacrab', and so on. The Akkadians called it 'Girtab' (perhaps 'the stinger', though the meaning is in dispute). In popular constellation mythology, the asterism is said to represent the scorpion which killed Orion, but it appears to have been a scorpion long before the Grecian mythology was developed. Ptolemy describes the stars in the front of Scorpius as carrying the influence of Mars, if slightly Saturnine - those in the body are said to be Mars mingled with a little Jupiter, and those in the sting are said to be Mars conjunct Mercury. However, the reputations attached to the fixed stars in the asterism are generally far from pleasant, and appear to emphasize the Martian nature: see ACULEUS, ACUMEN, ANTARES, GRAFFIAS, DSCHUBBA, SHAULA and LESATH.

SEAL   In a specialist astrological sense, a seal is one of the graphic symbols or SIGILS representing an occult prophylactic force. Just as in a non-specialist sense an official seal might be stamped on a document as a sign of ratification, so a magical seal was often used for magical purposes to imprint a magical power into some materiality, such as a sheet of paper or a strip of metal, or even a magical jem. Such a seal might be drawn, printed, incised or moulded. As a magical symbol, it was supposed to be imbued with a secret power, beneficial or maleficient, depending upon how and when it was constructed, and upon the intentions of the magician or astrologer who used it. Ancient seals, often of deep esoteric significance, have been recorded for planets, planetary spirits (and demons), decans, zodiacal angels, rulers of the spheres, and so on. It would seem that a knowledge of magical seals gave the same power over the realm of spirits as did knowledge of the demonic names: this explains why so many of the seals are so frequently incorporated into amulets and talismans such as the MAGICAL JEWELS, in which the seal was a sign that a magical VIRTUE had been imprinted into the jewel as an additional power or influence.

SEAL OF SOLOMON   Name given to the six-pointed star constructed from two interpenetrating triangles. The symbolism expressed in this figure is extremely rich: on one level it represents the triad of the macrocosm interpenetrating the triad of the microcosm (wherein it becomes a symbolic duad). On another level it is seen as the interaction of the four elements (see SIGILS - ELEMENTS) wherein it is a symbolic quaternary. Within the system of Rosicrucian symbolism, the space within the central hexagon is seen as the repository for the invisible fifth element, the QUINTESSENCE, for which the the Seal is often offered as the sigil.

SEATS   Another name for the THRONES.

SECONDARY DIRECTIONS   Term used of the method of unfolding potential in a radical chart according to the SECONDARY PROGRESSIONS, to be distinguished from the Primary Directions of the PRIMARY SYSTEM.

SECONDARY PROGRESSIONS   A term evolved to distinguish a method of unfolding potential within a radical chart from the more ancient PRIMARY SYSTEM. The basic assumption underlying the Secondary Method is that the position of planets (as well as other cosmic and mundane factors) on a certain number of days after birth will find a reflection in the life of the native that equivalent number of years after birth - that, for example, the cosmic qualities of the 7th day after birth will echo precisely in the life of the native during his seventh year. Unlike the Primary Directions of the Primary System, calculations of the unfoldment of potential are based on the

movements of the planets along the ecliptic, and thus the time equivalent is
approximately that of one day to four minutes (but see DAY FOR A YEAR):
conversion in time equivalents is therefore not so liable to error as with
the Primary System. The Secondary Progression chart is called the Progressed
Figure (or Chart), and the new aspects formed both within this figure, and
between this and its Radical Chart, are called Progressed Aspects, to be
distinguished from the differently derived Directional Aspects of the Primary
System. There is much argument about the validity of the system of Secondary
Progressions in predictive work, but much research (and practical use of the
method) in recent years has indicated that the traditional basis of the idea
(often expressed in the catch-phrase 'Day for a Year') is entirely consistent
with astrological symbolism. There is some argument among the astrological
practioners of this difficult branch of astrology about which periodicity
should be taken as representing the basic unit of the 'day'. Many modern
astrologers appear to favour the TRUE SOLAR DAY as the basis for their
computations - however, other astrologers have taken the time measurement
wrongly attributed to Ptolemy, and used in Primary Directions, which equates
the day with a transit of one degree of Right Ascension over the Midheaven,
which is then regarded as both an arc and time-span equivalent to one year of
life. Others have adopted the TABLE OF NAIBOD as a basis for symbolic
computation, whilst others use the so-called Equation of Time. A variation
is that outlined in the 17th century by Antonio de Bonattis, which involves
adding each sequential solar arc to the Midheaven, each arc then being
regarded as the equivalent of the years (in sequence). In secondary
directions, the progressed movement of the ANGLES are regarded as being of
great importance in interpretation: they are visualized as keypoints which
discharge the accumulated power of the radical and progressed planets at the
time when exact aspects are formed. So important are these that Davison, the
leading specialist in this field, suggests that it is possible to predict all
the major events of the life of the native by using only directions involving
the angles and the Sun. Davison, insists that not only should the progressed
angles and planets be taken into account, but also the CONVERSE DIRECTIONS.

SECOND HOUSE   The second of the astrological HOUSES, linked with the nature
of Taurus, and representing the possessions and feelings of the native, as
well as all those factors which lend material support to life. It was often
called the 'House of Money', though it actually relates to far more than
financial matters, even though it is indeed a useful index of how the native
will earn or otherwise come by money. Esoteric astrology suggests that this
house represents the element in life which the native will seek to redeem -
certainly it may be used as a measure of how the native will meet his
obligations. In regard to the melothesic man, the second house denotes the
throat and the larynx, and in some respects the sound of the voice. In
Mundane Astrology it rules the nation's wealth, revenues, currency and
investments (though not speculations, which belong to the Ninth House).

SECOND-ORDER CYCLE   See FIRST-ORDER CYCLE.

SECOND RAY   In the esoteric system described by Bailey, the second of the
"Seven Rays" of her INTUITIONAL ASTROLOGY is called the 'Ray of Love-Wisdom',
and is linked with the will to unify, to cause vision and is said to bring
the power to perceive. This second ray is said to arise in Ursa Major, and
is transmitted to our solar system by means of the 'constellations' (zodiacal
signs?) Gemini, Virgo and Pisces, through their pairs of corresponding
ORTHODOX PLANETS and ESOTERIC PLANETS, acccording to the schema in table 69.

CONSTELLATION (SIGN)	ORTHODOX PLANET	TABLE 69 ESOTERIC PLANET
Gemini	Mercury	Venus
Virgo	Mercury	Moon
Pisces	Jupiter	Pluto

The entire second ray is linked with the sacred planet Jupiter: but see
SACRED PLANETS.   In connexion with the 'esoteric' ruler of Virgo, above, see
also ESOTERIC MOON. Distinguish the second ray from SECOND RAY TYPE.

SECOND RAY TYPE   The second of the SEVEN RAY TYPES, associated with the
planet Venus. Distinguish from SECOND RAY.

SECOND ROOT RACE   In the Theosophical cosmoconception, the Second Root Race
is the second of the 'human races', or streams of human evolution, sometimes
called the 'Hyperborean Race', which was said to largely occupy the
long-disappeared northern continent named 'Plaksha'.

SECOND STATION   The stationary point (see STATIONS) where a planet becomes
direct of motion.

SECOND ZODIAC   See SOLAR BIOLOGY.

SECT   See SECTA.

SECTA   A Latin term derived from a late Greek specialist term 'airesis',
used by Ptolemy of the divisions of signs and planets into the feminine and
masculine (nocturnal and diurnal) groups. The Greek term was originally
involved with the idea of the 'acquisition of power', and was unfortunately
translated by the Latin 'conditio' and 'secta', and hence (even more
unfortunately) into the English 'condition' and 'sect'. See FEMININE
PLANETS, FEMININE SIGNS, MASCULINE PLANETS and MASCULINE SIGNS.

SECTIO TAURI   See TAURUS CONSTELLATION.

SECULAR HOROSCOPE   A modern term arising from the proposition that since a
chart cast for a human birth is valid as a reflection of the 'cosmic
environment', then that same chart may be cast contemporaneously to apply to
'simultaneous earthly events'. The latter chart has been called the 'secular
horoscope'. The proposition, which has attracted some notice from Dean, is
based on a misunderstanding of the nature of natal astrology, but is to some
extent in accordance with the general tenets of MUNDANE ASTROLOGY, and may
even be seen as an astrological equivalent of the Jungian SYNCHRONICITY.

SECUNDADEIAN BEINGS   The name (probably originated by the Abbot Trithemius
at the end of the 15th century from sources given by Peter of Abano) is
applied to an important group of spiritual beings assigned rule over a
sequence of repeated historical periods of 354 years' duration, sometimes
called the 'Trithemian Periods'. Each of these beings is said to be of the
rank of Archangel, though in respect to their historical charge over periods
(rather than over races of people) they are really of the rank of ARCHAI.
The names, along with many associations (including predictions relating to
certain post-15th century rules) are derived from the Hebraic-Gnostic
tradition, and are linked with the planetary spheres, rather than with the
planets themselves. Trithemius gives a survey of history in terms of the
Secundadeian Beings which has been summarized in a somewhat simplified and
personalized manner by Stein, as indicated in table 70.

SECUNDADEIAN	PLANET	STEIN SUMMARY		TABLE 70
ORPHIEL	Saturn	Light and Darkness. Christ's Time on Earth.		
ZACHARIEL	Jupiter	Order and Chaos. Monastic Life.		
SAMAEL	Mars	The Crusades.		
MICHAEL	Sun	Earth-embracing. A world economy.		
ANAEL	Venus	Persecution of Christians - faith of martyrs.		
RAPHAEL	Mercury	Ages of the Grail and Orders of Knighthood.		
GABRIEL	Moon	Feuds connected with heredity.		

Trithemius assigned the rule of solar Michael to our own epoch, which was said to have begun in 1881 (variant interpretations of his figures are recorded). The sequence of rulerships follows a special order:

SA, VE, JU, ME, MA, MO and SU

The sequence of rule was said to begin at the 'Creation of the World', which was dated by Trithemius as 5,560 BC - though at least five other dates for the Creation are given in pre-Trithemian chronologies.

SEDIS   See CASSIOPEIA.

SEED TRIGON   See SIDEREAL MOON RHYTHMS.

SEESAW   Term applied to one of the JONES PATTERNS in which the distribution of planets within the figure form a balance, separated by two 'balancing spaces' of between 60 and 90 degrees.   This distribution is said to influence the native into being able to see two sides of a problem, as well as inclining him towards mediation.

SEGINUS   Fixed star, the gamma of Bootis, set in the left shoulder of the giant, and said by Ptolemy to be of the nature of Mercury with Saturn - a far from beneficial influence.

SELENOCENTRIC CHART   A chart computed for the solar system, presuming the Moon (Greek 'Selene') to be the centre of that system.   Such a selenocentric chart was published for the landing of the first man on the Moon, in Vol.11, No.4 of the 'Astrological Journal' (1969).

SEMESTER CHART   Term used by Bradley for the last demi-solar return period expressed in a SOLAR RETURN, 'effective for the last half of the year'.

SEMI-ARC   Half of either the DIURNAL ARC or of the NOCTURNAL ARC, measuring one of the main quadrants of the horoscope figure, from the Ascendant to the Midheaven, from the Midheaven to the Descendant (both 'semi-diurnal arcs'), and from the Descendant to the Imum Coeli, and from the Imum Coeli to the Ascendant (both 'semi-nocturnal arcs').

SEMI-ARC SYSTEM   An alternative (though rarely used) alternative for the "Placidean System".

SEMI-DECILE   An aspect of 18 degrees, arising from a division of the zodiac into twentieths.   The aspect is sometimes called the 'Vigintile'.   See however QUINTILES.

SEMI-DIURNAL ARC   See SEMI-ARC.

SEMI-NOCTURNAL ARC   See SEMI-ARC.

SEMI-QUARTILE   An archaic term for the SEMI-SQUARE aspect.

SEMI-SEXTILE   An aspect of 30 degrees, the two aspecting points being separated by an arc equivalent to one sign of the zodiac.   It has been called an aspect of 'growth', and is generally regarded as beneficial.   The amount of ORB permitted this aspect is far from agreed, but some authorities allow as much as 4 degrees.

SEMI-SQUARE   An aspect of 45 degrees, the two aspecting points being separated by the equivalent arc of one and a half signs of the zodiac.   The amount of ORB permitted this aspect is far from agreed, but some authorities allow as much as 4 degrees.   Like the SQUARE, it is generally believed to be a difficult aspect.

==

SEMITA LACTEA   See VIA LACTEA.

SEPARATING   See SEPARATION.

SEPARATION   A term applied to the dissolving of an aspect: the faster moving
planet is said to 'separate' from, or to be 'in separating aspect to', the
aspected planet or nodal point. When within ORB of such separation, the
planet may be described as being in 'separating orb'. See also APPLICATION.

SEPTEMBER   The ninth month (30 days) of our GREGORIAN CALENDAR, the name
being a throw-back to the early Roman (pre-Julian) calendrical system in
which it was the seventh month (the Latin 'septem', seven), the year
beginning in March.   The esoteric magic of seven is linked with this month
still, as a fruition of a cycle in lunar terms, the fruition also of the
earth.   The Anglo-Saxons called it 'gerstmonath' (barley-month) in
recognition of the harvesting - a similar idea of 'spiritual harvesting' is
to be perceived after the age of 7 x 7 (49) in many human lives.

SEPTENARY MEASURE   A term applied to an arc of four and two-sevenths of a
degree, used in SYMBOLIC DIRECTIONS. It is derived by dividing a sign by
seven, and is also a measure used in the POINT OF LIFE system.

SEPTENTRIO   See URSA MINOR.

SEPTILE   A so-called 'aspect' of 51.4 degrees, resulting from the division
of the zodiac circle by sevenths, and used mainly in the theory of HARMONICS.
See also BI-SEPTILE and TRI-SEPTILE.

SERAPHIM A term of much-disputed etymology - though of Hebraic origin,
linked both with the idea of 'serpent (ShRPM) and 'burning' (ShRP) - and used
to denote the celestial creatures described in 'Isaiah' vi.2. as beings with
a human form and three pairs of wings. Blavatsky writes of them as 'the
Fiery Serpents of Heaven', and equates them with the four Maharajahs of the
Buddhist cosmogeny. Within the occult tradition they are linked with the
Ophanim, serpent-beings associated with the four fixed signs of the zodiac,
and thus with the four Evangelists of the Christian tradition (though see
also CHERUBIM). The Seraphim are sometimes called 'Lords of Love', and in
some occult systems are named as the rulers of the zodiac.

SERPENS   See DRACO.

SERPENS LATOR   See OPHIUCHUS.

SERPENT   See DRACO.

SERPENTARIUS   See OPHIUCHUS.

SERPENTIGER   See OPHIUCHUS.

SERTAN   A name for the fixed star ACUBENS.

SERVING TRINITY   A term used by Butler in his SOLAR BIOLOGY in respect of
the zodiacal signs Capricorn, Aquarius and Pisces.

SESQUIALTERA   See DIAPENTE.

SESQUIOCTAVE   See TONUS.

SESQUIQUADRATE   An ASPECT of 135 degrees, the two points being separated by
four and a half signs of the zodiac, the angle being compounded of a square
and a semi-square. It has been called the aspect of 'Agitation', and is
generally regarded as a difficult formation in a chart. The amount of ORB
permitted is not agreed, but some authorities allow as much as 3 degrees.

SESQUIQUINTILE   An aspect of 108 degrees - see QUINTILES.

SET   One of the several variant names for the constellation Ursa Major.

SEVEN AGES   In popular astrology, the term is usually appplied to the
various doctines relating to the division of the life of man into septenaries
- see CLIMACTERICS.   In a specialist sense, the term is sometimes applied to
the seven historic ages governed by the SECUNDADEIAN BEINGS, the so-called
'Trithemian Periods'.   In its popular sense, the division is in terms of the
seven planetary ages, following a sequence from the first sphere of the Moon,
through to the sphere of Saturn, to each sequence of which is attached a
definite number of years (see PLANETARY AGES).   Philo Judaeus notes a system
provided by Hippocrates which divides man's life unequally, but in multiples
of seven, into six ages, with the final seventh age (after 56) as that of the
'Old man'.   A list of the traditional seven is preserved under the name of
'Hermes' from a mediaeval source, giving the sequence shown in table 71.

```
------------------------------------------------------------------TABLE 71
PLANET              PERIOD          RULES AGE UP TO AN INCLUDING
==========================================================================
MO                  4 years         4
ME                  10 years        14
VE                  8 years         24
SU                  19 years        43
MA                  15 years        58
JU                  12 years        70
SA                  30 years
--------------------------------------------------------------------------
```

Saturn is traditionally accorded a period of 30 years, but in this list (and
in others) is given rule over any years after 70.   Several attempts have been
made to link these planetary ages with the list poetically set out by
Shakespeare in 'As You Like It', but it is more likely the the poet had in
mind one of the several sources from Proclus, which does not give
periodicities (perhaps taken for granted) but only the planetary rulerships:

    MO is ruler of 'nutrition and the physical life'.
    ME is ruler of 'letters, music and motley'.
    VE is ruler of the period when we 'begin to produce seed'.
    SU sees 'youth in full vigour and full perfection'.
    MA 'aspires after power and superiority over others'.
    JU gives himself 'up to prudence, and an active political life'.
    SA marks that time when we deem it 'natural to separate ourselves
        from generations, and transfer ourselves to an incorporeal life'.

The several available lists agree in spirit, if not in actual periodicities,
to the above ideals.   In more recent times attempts have been made to link
such periodicities to the extra-Saturnian planets, but much of the ancient
wisdom in the earlier lists has thereby suffered.   The most frequently quoted
of the modern lists is that given by Sepharial, but a well thought out
structure which includes the modern planets has been given in diagrammatic
form by Collin, who postulates a logarithmic sequence interacting through
three fairly distinct 'periods' of gestation (the embryonic form), childhood
and maturity.   With the modern planets incorporated, in whatever system, the
ancient concept of 'seven ages' is of necessity bypassed.

SEVEN AND A HALF DEGREE ASPECT   This aspect, for which no short name appears
to have been originated, became popular in the United States as a consequence
of the work done by Nelson on radio disturbances.   However, much more
astrologically apposite research into the aspect has been done by Wangemann,
who shows that there are 48 different multiples of this aspect, which is
naturally linked with its parent semi-square and other multipoles.   Wangemann
discovered that a small "Asymmetric Orb" of 0.7 degrees for the applying, and

==

0.1 degrees for the separating aspect, was applicable.

SEVEN BUILDERS   In esoteric astrology, the SACRED PLANETS.

SEVEN CLIMATA   The so-called 'seven climata' are tabulations of zodiacal
rising times computed for certain localities (see CLIMATA), valid for
Mediterranean areas, and derived ultimately from a method employed by
Babylonian astrologers.   Several sets of 'seven climata' exist (see SYSTEM A
and SYSTEM B, for example), but the post-Ptolemaic list, derived from 10
climata computations, to which later authorities added a necessary
interpolation for Byzantium, along with periods of longest daylight, are
shown in table 72.

```
-----------------------------------------------------------------TABLE 72
CLIMA ZONE          DAYLIGHT   NOTES
=========================================================================
```

CLIMA	ZONE	DAYLIGHT	NOTES
1	Meroe	13	
2	Syrene	13.30	
3	Lower Egypt	14	Derived directly from early figures for Alexandria, the old clima 1.
4	Rhodes	14.30	Derived by arithmetical progression from early figures for Babylon, the old clima 2.
5	Hellespont	15.00	
-	Byzantium	15.15	Interpolated from climata 5 and 6.
6	Mid. Pontus	15.30	Derived by arithmetical progression from early figures for Rome, the old clima 6.
7	Borysthenes	16	

This Hellenistic model, apparently based on a division of the habitable
quadrant of the Earth into 90 sections made by Hipparchus (who was aware of
the effect of latitude on altitude of stars) was adopted by mediaeval
astrologers from the tables converted by the Arabian Alfraganus, who
influenced the astrological thought of Dante.   The 'Seven Climata of
Alfraganus', the 'Alfraganian Climata', are the ancient climata lists
transformed into degrees of latitude and equivalent distances in miles on the
erroneous assumption that 56 and two-thirds of a mile is the equivalent of
one degree.   Thus, the influential theories of climata were concerned with
latitudes only some 700 miles north of the equator.

SEVEN FORMS   See SEVEN PROPERTIES.

SEVEN GLOBES   See GLOBES.

SEVEN KUMARAS   In esoteric astrology, the SACRED PLANETS.

SEVEN LOTS   The Alexandrian Paul records a tradition of seven 'clipoi', the
Greek term for 'lots', which were the equivalent of the modern PARS.   In
addition to the prototype of the modern PART OF FORTUNE, these were
(translated) AUDACITY, LOT OF DAIMON, LOVE, NECESSITY, NEMESIS and VICTORY.

SEVEN MANU   In esoteric astrology, the SACRED PLANETS.

SEVEN MOODS   In a series of lectures translated under the title 'Human and
Cosmic Thought', the occultist Steiner developed a schema which linked what
he called the seven philosophic moods with the seven planets:

MO	Occultism	ME	Transcendentalism	VE	Mysticism
SU	Empiricism	MA	Voluntarism	JU	Logicism
SA	Gnosis				

He distinguished the TWELVE PHILOSOPHIC TENDENCIES in terms of the twelve
signs or constellations.

SEVEN PROPERTIES   A term derived from the esoteric astrology of the German mystic Boehme, as developed by Freher, and sometimes called the 'Seven Forms', the 'Seven Working Properties', the German original term being 'wirkende Eigenschafte'. The seven forms are linked with the seven planets, though it is the principles behind the planets which interest Boehme in his esoteric account of the effects produced by their individual working, their polarities, and their balance. The 'first form' is that of Saturn, which is a harsh and hardening principle, a centripetal force, 'indrawing and compacting about its chosen centre': it is Saturn which draws and fixes. The 'second form' is Mercury (Mercurius) which strives for freedom against the restraint imposed by Saturn: it is separative and centrifugal, 'in eternal flight from fixity'. Its role is seen in the thinking mind, in 'divisive analysis'. The 'third form' is Mars, which results from the opposition of the first two, and may be likened to a turning wheel which itself represents a fusion of the centripetal and the centrifugal impulses: it is the 'turning wheel of desire'. This is the 'Ternary of Fire', which bursts forth into action into the 'fourth form' which is that of the Sun. Boehme likens this solar bursting to the crack of lightning, which is the explosion of spirit into time. The attainment of desire in this Sun form brings its own joy and harmony, which is the 'fifth form' of Venus. This form is active of harmony-producing, from the resolution of conflict to the 'mirage-paradise of misplaced hopes'. From this develops the 'sixth form', the fuller self-perception and understanding which is characteristic of Jupiter. The 'seventh form', that of the Moon, is anti-climactic, yet is involved with 'final production of concrete realization'. A relationship is established between this seventh and the first form, so that the individual actions of the planetary workings may be seen as cyclical. As Muses points out, the teleology of the pairs of antitheses (see TERNARY OF FIRE and TERNARY OF LIGHT) yield an ethically intransitive relationship: for example, the Mercury to Jupiter polarity marks a beneficient and expansive development, a natural growth, but the reverse of Jupiter to Mercury would represent the perversion of Jupiter to the ends of Mercury, so that inherent in each of the seven properties is a duality.

SEVEN RACES   In the Theosophical cosmoconception, the Seven Races are the seven streams of human evolution, four of which have run their course in the present GLOBE PERIOD, the fifth of which is still in progress (see FIFTH ROOT RACE) and two of which are to be developed in the future. See FIRST ROOT RACE, SECOND ROOT RACE, THIRD ROOT RACE and FOURTH ROOT RACE.

SEVEN RAYS   In the esoteric astrological system of INTUITIONAL ASTROLOGY described by Bailey, a series of seven rays are outlined, each originating in the constellation of Ursa Major (though besides being individually linked with the major seven stars of this asterism, they are also associated with the Pleiades and the fixed-star Sirius), and thence transmitted to our solar system by means of three 'constellations', which are the zodiacal signs, and by a conventional system of planetary rulers paralleled by an unconventional system of rulers, called respectively the 'orthodox' and the 'esoteric'. The entire sequence is set out in diagrammatic form in figure 56 - but see the following entries: FIRST RAY, SECOND RAY, THIRD RAY, FOURTH RAY, FIFTH RAY, SIXTH RAY, SEVENTH RAY. The rays set out in terms of planetary influences by Morrish are discussed under SEVEN RAY TYPES, and must not be confused with the Bailey system. The seven rays especially linked with the Theosophical Astrology are not to be confused with those of the Intuitional Astrology. The former are in fact rays emanating from the seven Planetary Spirits or 'Angels'. Strictly speaking, these rays directly influence the seven spiritual bodies of man, the first three corresponding to the three as yet undeveloped in ordinary man (Atma, Buddhi and Manas), the last four corresponding to the personality and the so-called 'bridge' which enables a reciprocate action between the higher and lower tertiaries of man's being. These septenaries are associated with eight planets (the Sun overlooking each of the seven rays) and, with an associate colour, are linked with the being of man in the schema of table 73 which is derived by Adam from the Theosophic

==

tradition which was promulgated by Leadbeater, Besant and A.E. Powell:

```
--------------------------------------------------------------TABLE 73
                                     SU
                          --------------------------------
HUMAN PRINCIPLE           UR  NE  VE  SA  ME  MA  JU  COLOUR
==============================================================================
                Atma      UR                              Violet
Ego             Buddhi        NE                          Indigo
                Manas             VE                      Sky blue
'bridge'        Antahkarana           SA                  Green
                Mental                    ME              Yellow
Personality     Astral                        MA          Orange
                Physical                          JU      Crimson-rose
--------------------------------------------------------------------------
```

Within this system, the first ray is the Ray of Uranus (linked with the Atma, itself a symbol of the redeemed physical body, and hence with the will).   The second ray is the Ray of Neptune (linked with the Buddhi, itself a symbol of the redeemed astral, and hence linked with love).   The third ray is the Ray of Venus (linked with the Manas, itself here a symbol of the redeemed mental realm of man, though in other schemas a symbol of the redeemed etheric, and hence linked with developed intuition).   The fourth ray is the Ray of Saturn, linked with the so-called 'bridge', that 'ray of light pouring from the Ego on to the personality', in other systems called the Ego itself.   The Mental realm is governed by the fifth ray, though it is connected with a higher spirituality than is usually connected with the ordinary term 'mental'. The sixth ray is the Ray of Mars, which is concerned with the emotional life, with what is esoterically called the 'astrality' of the personality.   The seventh ray is the Ray of Jupiter, concerned with the physical body (in this schema, seemingly not separated from the etheric body, which implies that it should properly be termed the 'living body').   In his treatment of this system of seven rays Adam offers some argument for amending the above classification, which he terms the 'orthodox' classification: he allots the Buddhic principle to Mercury, rather than to Neptune, and the lower mind (the Mental realm) to the Moon (which 'we are told is a substitute for Neptune').

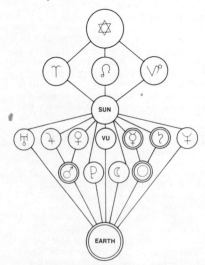

FIGURE 56.   THE SEVEN RAYS OF BAILEY'S 'INTUITIONAL ASTROLOGY'.

SEVEN RAY TYPES   In his syncretic ASTRO-PSYCHOLOGY, Morrish sets out what he calls the 'Seven Ray-Types', seemingly derived from a system of occultism which might easily be confused (in nomenclature at least) with the SEVEN RAYS of Bailey or of the Theosophical System.   Morrish sets out the First Ray as that of Saturn, 'ruler by means of set forms of obedience to established authority'.   The Second Ray is that of Venus, the 'philanthropist'.   The Third Ray is that of Mercury, the 'adaptable type - the active mental organiser'.   The Fourth Ray is that of the Earth, the 'artist' who is 'able to create material forms expressing spiritual values'. The Fifth Ray is that of Jupiter, the 'scientist or philosopher' who is to be distinguished from the Saturn-type scientist, the 'materialist' who works with set forms, with a tendency to supression. The Fifth Ray type is an idealist 'expressing itself expansively'. The Sixth Ray is that of Mars, the 'devotee-fanatic', the 'object-worshipper', the 'militant religious and partisan'. Morrish notes that while the Venusian type works for the group, the Martian type tries to force others to do so. The Seventh Ray is that of Uranus, the 'occultist', the 'research-worker and electrician' who is at the same time the 'reformer'.

SEVEN SAGES   See PLEIADES.

SEVEN SISTERS   See PLEIADES.

SEVEN SLEEPERS   One of the several important names for "Ursa Major".

SEVEN SORTES   See HERMETIC SORTES.

SEVENTH HOUSE   The seventh of the twelve astrological HOUSES, linked with the sign Libra, the Descendant House, the ancient 'Dysis'. It is associated with the influence of Venus, the ruler of Libra, and representative of the Venusian urge away from the selfhood of Mars, into relationships with others. Such relationships may be harmonious or conflicting, which explains why the house is often called the 'House of Marriage and Open Conflict'. It may be regarded as the lens through which the native sees other people in close relationships, for it has rule over partnerships and friendships - both conditioned by the ruling planet of the sign on the Descendant, and/or by planets in the house itself. At its best, the house marks the attempt to establish a free co-operation with another; at its worst, the attempt to impose ego (properly the domain of the opposite First House) on another by means of guile or coercion. It is said also to mark the native's relationship to public weal, and hence with the law, so that it is called by some the 'House of the Public': it governs also lawsuits and contracts.   In Mundane Astrology it governs the social consciousness of the people, and those who co-operate with, or oppose, the 'people' - it is also the domain of international disputes.

SEVENTH RAY   In the esoteric system described by Bailey, the seventh of the "Seven Rays" is called the 'Ray of Ceremonial Order', and is linked with the will to express, and with the 'principle of order'. The Seventh Ray is said to arise in Ursa Major, and is transmitted into our solar system by means of the zodiacal constellations (zodiacal signs?) Aries, Cancer and Capricorn, through their pairs of corresponding ORTHODOX PLANETS and ESOTERIC PLANETS, according to the schema set out in table 74.

TABLE 74

CONSTELLATION (SIGN)	ORTHODOX PLANET	ESOTERIC PLANET
Aries	Mars	Mercury
Cancer	Moon	Neptune
Capricorn	Saturn	Saturn

The entire Seventh Ray is linked with the sacred planet Uranus - see therefore SACRED PLANETS.

SEVENTH RAY TYPE   The seventh of the SEVEN RAY TYPES, associated with the
planet Uranus. Distinguish from SEVENTH RAY.

SEVEN VIRGINS   See PLEIADES.

SEVEN VITAL PRINCIPLES   A term used by Butler in his SOLAR BIOLOGY, relating
to the planetary 'powers', in which seven-fold schema he includes the Earth
(the Sun being the central source of these vital principles). The septenary
is also called the 'Seven Primate Creative Principles' and 'Creative
Principles', and finds a solar expression in the seven planets. The argument
runs that when the individual conquers or subjugates the lower part of his
being, then he attains the rewards expressed by the following principles:

UR Blessing	SA Glory	JU Honour	MA Strength
VE Riches	ME Power	TE Wisdom	

SEVEN WORKING PROPERTIES   See SEVEN PROPERTIES.

SEXASCOPE   A term used by Fagan, and applied to a system of astrological
interpretation of the NOVIENIC CHART, regarding the 'Novienic Moon' as the
significator of sexual appetite and propensities.

SEX DEGREES   A term not to be confused with SEX POINTS, but used in relation
to the various systems of DEGREE SYMBOLS as interpreted by Sepharial.

SEX POINTS   These are the so-called 'sex degrees' used by Bailey in the
calculation of the PRENATAL EPOCH, said by some to be an extension of the
'Trutine of Hermes'. The sex point is to be used (in theory at least) for
rectification of a natal chart by means of examination of the pre-natal chart
in relation to the known sexuality of a native. The sex point is actually
the place of the Moon in regard to a number of arcs determined in the
ecliptic in relation to the tropical zodiac by the Hindu NAKSHATRAS
(incorporating the asterism ABHIJIT, however) which, for the sake of
convenience are regarded as consisting of 12 degrees and 51 minutes.   The
sex point will theoretically mark an arc in the epochal chart which reveals
the actual sexuality of the native, though the laws for constructing and
interpreting the chart as a whole are somewhat complex, and perhaps even
confused.   The term 'sex point' was probably adopted to distinguish it from
the term SEX DEGREES, then used in quite a different connexion.

SEXTILE   An aspect of 60 degrees - generally regarded as a beneficial
influence, and sometimes called the aspect of opportunity.   The amount of
orb permitted this aspect is far from agreed among authorities, but some
allow as much as 4 degrees.

SHAMALI   See THIRD ROOT RACE.

SHAMAYIM   One of the names given to the first of the seven heavens of the
cabbalists, ruled by GABRIEL.

SHAMBALLA   A term with two seemingly unrelated meanings. In the
Theosophical cosmoconception (rooted in Vedic esotericism), Shamballa is said
to be a place presently located in an oasis in the Gobi Desert. It is said to
be the dwelling of high initiates, such as the 'Lords of Venus', the 'Sons of
Fire', and those who taught primitive man.   Unfortunately, the esoteric
aspect of this Shamballa has been exotericized out of all recognition in
popular occultism. The same term is used with more caution and precision by
the esotericist Bailey, who describes it as 'that major centre of our
planetary life', locating it in our solar system: she places it under the
'control' of the fixed star Polaris, as playing a part of the sequence of
projection of the SEVEN RAYS. In another context, she locates Shamballa
'where the Will of God is focused' on our planet.

SHAMSHIEL   Name given to one of the Grigori of the Hebraic tradition who taught men 'the signs of the Sun' and (probably) 'the nature of the zodiac'.

SHANI   The Sanskrit word for the planet Saturn, as used in Hindu astrology.

SHAPINGS   The term applied by Jones himself to his so-called JONES PATTERNS.

SHARATAIN   'Al Sharatain', the 27th of the Arabian MANZILS.

SHARATAN   Fixed star, the beta of constellation Aries, the name from the Arabic dual form 'Al Sharatain' which refers to the 'two signs' - this star and the gamma MESARTHIM - both of which appear to have marked the vernal equinox in the days of the astronomer Hipparchus (mid 2nd century BC), who first formulated exoterically the idea of PRECESSION.   The star is accorded an unfortunate influence (Mars conjunct Saturn), and brings physical injuries and defeats.   It is sometimes called 'Sheratan'.

SHAULA   Fixed star, the lamda of Scorpius, set in the sting of the asterism. The name has been variously corrupted to 'Shauka', 'Alascha' and 'Shomlek'. Along with the upsilon of Scorpius, it marked the "Manzil" now called SHAULAH. The star has a very unfortunate reputation.

SHAULAH   'Al Shaulah', the 17th of the Arabian MANZILS.

SHEBAT   See BABYLONIAN CALENDAR.

SHODASVARGAS   A Sanskrit term applied to the Hindu astrological chart presented in terms of 16 divisions, which may have been an elaboration of the Hellenistic 'oktotopos' division.

SHUKRA   The Sanskrit word for the planet Venus, as used in Hindu astrology.

SIDEREAL   The term 'sidereal', meaning 'pertaining to the stars', is derived from the genitive form of the Latin 'sidus' (star), 'sideris'.

SIDEREAL CORRESPONDENCES   The historian Powell, having established a "Sidereal Zodiac" defined in terms of epochal fiducials, provided a useful series of correspondences for the main sidereal zodiacal system.   In table 75 the BABYLONIAN ZODIAC is derived from the fixed star fiducial Aldebaran: the (modern) INDIAN ZODIAC is derived from the fiducial Spica, for zero degree of Libra, and the MODERN ZODIAC is defined according to the complex IAU system reported by Delporte.   The STAR CALENDAR ZODIAC is ultimately derived from the specification given by Vreede.

```
--------------------------------------------------------------TABLE 75
```

BABYLONIAN		INDIAN		MODERN		STAR CALENDAR
Deg.	Mins.	Deg.	Mins.	Deg.	Mins.	Deg.
0 AR	0	359	03	3	54	4 (5)
30 TA	0	29	03	28	38	29
60 GE	0	59	03	65	21	65
90 CN	0	89	03	93	12	93
120 LE	0	119	03	113	15	114
150 VG	0	149	03	149	04	149
180 LB	0	179	03	193	02	194 (195)
210 SC	0	209	03	216	12	213
240 SG	0	239	03	241	27	243 (244)
270 CP	0	269	03	274	52	275 (274)
300 AQ	0	299	03	302	42	302
330 PI	0	329	03	326	52	328 (327)

SIDEREAL DAY   An interval of TIME measured according to the stars - that

==

time taken for the Earth to rotate on its axis once in relation to a stellar fiducial. The sidereal day is the equivalent of 23 hours, 56 minutes and 4.09 seconds of clock time.

SIDEREAL LUNATION   A period of 27 days, 7 hours, 43 minutes and 11.5 seconds, marking two successive conjunctions of the Moon with the same degree of the zodiac - a periodic lunation.

SIDEREAL MONTH   See LUNAR MONTH.

SIDEREAL MOON RHYTHMS   A term seemingly coined in connexion with the use of the SIDEREAL ZODIAC in bio-dynamic farming, which has proceeded under the influences of the researches of Thun, supported by Kolisko and Fyfe. The planting of seeds and the preparation of the earth is regulated according to lunar positions in a recently formulated (unequal arc) constellation zodiac, which is not to be confused with either the tropical zodiac or the traditional "Constellational Zodiac". The sidereal moon rhythm is the lunar relationship to this new zodiac. The results of intensive practical research have enabled astrologers to determine that the form of the plant is linked with the influences of the fixed stars and with the movements of the planets in a most simple way - indeed, it has been shown that the triplicities of the constellations influence radically the development of all seed growth. The earth triplicity is linked with the growth of roots and root crops, and is called the 'root-earth trigon': the air triplicity is linked with the growth of blossoms and flowers, and is called the 'blossom-light trigon': the water triplicity is linked with the growth of the leaf, and is called the 'leaf-water trigon', whilst the fire triplicity is linked with the growth of fruit and seeds, and is called the 'fruit-seed warmth trigon'. The extraordinary practical value of these cosmic-agricultural researches is apparently based on considerable esoteric truth: Goethe himself announced a connexion between plant growth and the elemental SOUL BEINGS, each group of which is linked with the trigons.

SIDEREAL SIGNS   A term used by Powell in reference to the equal-arc divisions of the CONSTELLATIONAL ZODIAC, linked with the Babylonian system. It is a curious term, perhaps even a contradiction, but is intended to refer to the twelve 'box-type sectors' in the ecliptic circle, which are other than the zodiacal signs of traditional astrology. These sidereal signs appear to be analogous to this ancient constellational system as the zodiacal signs are to the zodiac. See however SIDEREAL ZODIAC.

SIDEREAL TIME   Literally, 'time by the stars', a term intended to designate a method of computing time based upon the period between specific stars over pre-determined points on the earth. See SIDEREAL DAY and TIME.

SIDEREAL YEAR   A period marking two succeedent transits of the centre of the Sun over the ecliptic meridian of a fiducial star: a period of 365.256 days. This period is sometimes called an 'astral year'.

SIDEREAL ZODIAC   As the term suggests, this is the 'zodiac of the stars', of which the CONSTELLATIONAL ZODIAC is just one example. The term is usually applied to one or other of the divisions of the stellatum into twelve areas in a band along the ecliptic, corresponding in nomenclature (though not in extent or location) to the twelve signs of the zodiac, as in figure 57. There is much disagreement among specialists as to the location and cuspal boundaries of these asterisms, however, and even lack of agreement as to how many such asterisms should be included in the 'sidereal zodiac'. Schmidt is not alone in claiming that fourteen constellations cross the ecliptic band, whilst it is evident that the number depends upon (a) the width of the band, and (b) the graphic model of the stellatum adopted. Messadie has set out calculations proposing as many as 24 asterisms along these lines. A further problem is that there is no agreement as to which stellar fiducials should be used to fix the positions of these variant zodiacal asterisms. A recent

attempt to link the sidereal zodiac to the SOLAR APEX has been made by the
sidereal astrologer Garth Allen, who has proposed a fiducial called the
'synetic vernal point' which lies 90 degrees East of the solar apex. A
brief, but well-researched, history of the early zodiacs by Powell shows that
several of the early zodiacs, including the prototype of our own modern
astronomical zodiac, were sidereal, and linked with sidereal fiducials: see
therefore ASTRONOMICAL ZODIAC, BABYLONIAN ZODIAC and GREEK ZODIAC. For a
definition of the modern astronomical zodiac, see MODERN ZODIAC. The
sidereal zodiac defined and located by Powell is of considerable importance
to the development of modern sidereal astrology, and is worth recording here.

FIGURE 57. SIDEREAL ZODIAC WITHIN AN EQUAL-ARC FRAMEWORK (AFTER POWELL).

Powell defines the sidereal fiducial in terms of a particular epoch,
restoring the ancient Babylonian fiducial of Aldebaran in 15 degrees Taurus.
The formal definition of the zero point is that exactly 45 degrees West of
Aldebaran on the 1st January, 1950. Powell provides a framework of reference
for the unequal divisions of this zodiac in terms of the 106 brightest
zodiacal stars, computed for the epoch of 1950, and additionally provides a
table of correspondences for the main 'sidereal zodiacs' in relation to his
formulated sidereal of 1950. This table may be seen schematized under
SIDEREAL CORRESPONDENCES. The sequence of unequal asterisms for the Powell
sidereal zodiac may be synopticized as follows, in terms of the diagram set
out in figure 57.

    AR   from Mesartim to tau Arietis.
    TA   from Alcyone to Alhecka.
    GE   from Propus to Pollux.
    CN   from Altarf to Acubens.
    LE   from Alterf to Denebola.
    VG   from Zavijava to mu Librae.
    LB   from Zubenelgenubi to Acrab (Graffias).
    SC   from Dschubba to Shaula.
    SG   from Alnasl to ro Sagittarii.
    CP   from sigma Capricorni to Deneb Algedi.
    AQ   from Sadalsuud to psi Aquarii.
    PI   from beta Aquarii to Alrescha.

Powell gives all magnitudes, longitudes and latitudes for all these fiducials
for the epoch of 1950.

===

SIDUS FAUSTUM REGIS   See SADALMELIK.

SIDUS FORTUNAE   'Star of Fortune', a name applied to the 24th of the LUNAR
MANSIONS in some mediaeval lists. Probably identified by the star Sadalsuud.

SIDUS PARVUM LUCIS MAGNAE   A term used to denote the 6th of the LUNAR
MANSIONS in some mediaeval lists. Probably located by the fixed star Alhena.

SIEU   The Chinese term for the equivalent of the LUNAR MANSIONS. Unlike the
Hindu "Nakshatras" or the Arabian "Manzils" and the "Lunar Stations", the
Sieu were grouped into huge constellational groups, each consisting of seven
sieu: these are the AZURE DRAGON, BLACK WARRIOR, RED BIRD and WHITE TIGER.

SIGIL   A name applied to a graphic cypher or seal or symbol, derived from
the Greek term 'sigla' (cypher) - but see also SYMBOL. It is a term now used
to denote almost any graphic symbol which incorporates a definite meaning,
but once it was restricted to magic graphic symbols. From the very earliest
times sigils have been used in astrology to denote the whole range of
planets, zodiacal signs, constellations, decans, fixed stars, the celestial
hierarchies, demons, daemons and spirits: thousands of sigils have been
recorded from such contexts. By way of example, figure 58 sets out six
sigils from a Graeco-Byzantine Decan list - the three smaller sigils
represent Mars, Sun and Venus respectively, while the three encircled sigils
represent the decans of Scorpio.

FIGURE 58. DECAN SIGILS FOR SCORPIO (AFTER NOWOTNY).

For ease of reference a series of the more important astrological sigils are
recorded in the following alphabetical entries: one may however gain some
idea of the variety involved when one considers that the five historical
variants recorded for the planet Saturn (under SIGILS - PLANETS) were
selected from over 60 recorded by the present author in a specialist context
(see bibliography). The popular notion that the sigils are derived from
vestigial drawings of the images associated with the signs and constellations
is quite erroneous, fostered seemingly by Agrippa at the end of the 15th
century. Kircher developed upon Agrippa, and established a pseudo-system of
correspondences between signs, sigils and associate gods and goddesses, some
of which are derived from esoteric sources, some of which are entirely
fanciful. On the other hand, it must be admitted that the planetary and
zodiacal sigils in use in modern astrology, whilst rarely older than the 14th
century in their present forms, were derived from esoteric schools.

SIGILLA   The Latin plural for SIGIL.

SIGILS - ASPECTS   The sigils used to denote the angular relationships
between planets appear to be as old as the aspects themselves - the post
Keplerian aspects being derived contemporaneously:

Conjunction ♂	Opposition ☍	Quincunx ⊼
Semi-sextile ⊻	Semi-square ∟	Sesquiquadrate ⌐⌐
Sextile ✶ ✻	Square ▢	Trine △

===

SIGILS - ELEMENTS   The basic range of sigils for the elements are derived from the Rosicrucian tradition, and are encapsulated in the SEAL OF SOLOMON, which unites them.   Three different systems are given in table 76.

```
-----------------------------------------------------------------TABLE 76
ELEMENT     MEDIAEVAL SIGIL    ROSICRUCIAN SIGIL    MODERN SIGIL
===========================================================================
Air
Earth
Fire
Water
Quintessence
---------------------------------------------------------------------------
```

SIGILS - FIXED STARS   Most of the mediaeval astrological sigils relating to the stars were limited to the FIFTEEN STARS, and were used mainly in talismanic magic. Agrippa, who passed the sigillic forms into the non-specialist occult stream, made a copyist error with his sigil for Capella, as a result of which the form has been erroneously accepted for this star. Although there are many variants, the ones below (called 'caracti' in many mediaeval manuscripts) are the most usual forms. In this list the second variant is that given by Agrippa, the first being from a late 14th century source:

Aldebaran   Algol   Algorab

Alphecca   Antares   Arcturus

Capella   Deneb Algedi   Pleiades

Polaris   Procyon   Regulus

Sirius   Spica   Wega

SIGILS - GENERAL   The following sigils are those most frequently used within the astrological tradition - see however the ABBREVIATIONS which are favoured in modern astrology:

Angular	Ascendant	Asteroids
Cadent	Cardinal	Ceres
Dragon's Head	Dragon's Tail	Earth
Fixed	Juno	Mutable
Pallas	Pars Fortunae	Succedent
Vesta		

SIGILS - PLANETARY SPIRITS   The sigils given in the occult and astrological tradition for the spirits - beneficial celestial beings, or the harmful demonic beings - are about as numerous as the spirits themselves. The following are only those sigilla associated with the important SECUNDADEIAN BEINGS mentioned by Trithemius:

Anael   Gabriel   Michael

Oriphiel   Raphael   Samael

Zachariel

SIGILS - PLANETS   Many of the planetary sigils used in modern astrology are derived ultimately from Graeco-Roman, Byzantine, or even Egyptian prototypes. Table 77 (over) gives only the most frequently used of the Graeco-Roman, mediaeval and modern sources.

--TABLE 77

PLANET	GRAECO-ROMAN	MEDIAEVAL	MODERN
MO	☽	☾	☽ ☾
ME			☿
VE	♀		♀
SU			☉ ♂
MA			
JU			♃
SA	♄		♄

The so-called "Modern Planets" have been accorded many variant sigils of
which the following forms are the most usual:

UR ⛢ ♅ ⚇   NE ♆ ⅏ ♆   PL ♇ ⯔ ⯕ ♇ ⯕

A number of the HYPOTHETICAL PLANETS and FUTURE PLANETS have also been
accorded sigils in modern times, as follows:

Aidonius ⚵	Apollo ⯀	Bacchus ⚘
Coelus ⚴	Dido ⊕	Hercules ⚮
Jason ⋏	Lilith ⌀	Mercurius ☿
Pagan-Pluto ⚵	Thierens-Pluto ⚵	Weymss-Pluto ♇

SIGILS - ZODIAC   The fact is that the signs of the zodiac have often been
confused with the sigils for these signs, and even with their IMAGES. Most
of the sigils used in modern times date from about the 14th century, though
they are often connected by a tortuous graphic etymology with Egyptian
(demotic), Graeco-Roman and earlier forms: there can be little doubt that
the majority of forms in use today were evolved by an esoteric school -
possibly that connected with Chartres. Table 78 lists only the most
frequently used sigils for specific periods.

--TABLE 78

SIGN	DEMOTIC	GRAECO-ROMAN	MEDIAEVAL	MODERN
AR			3°	♈
TA			oing	♉
GE			♊	♊
CN				♋
LE				♌
VG				♍
LB				♎
SC			ong	♏
SG				♐
CP				♑
AQ				♒
PI				♓

SIGN   The word 'sign' is perhaps one of the most misused of all astrological terms. Properly applied, it refers to one of the 30 degree arcs of the zodiac, of what Ptolemy called the 'zodiacos kuklos'. From early times a distinction was made by thoughtful astrologers between these signs and the constellational asterisms which had the same names as the signs. There was little confusion between the signs of the tropical zodiac and the asterisms of the constellational zodiac. The tropical was always divided into twelve equal arcs, whilst the constellations (not even visualized as a band, as a wide 'kuklos' at all) was divided into unequal asterisms, the twelve of the original 14 which touched upon the zodiacal band proper being called by the same names as those carried by the signs, even though they did not correspond in extent or location, and were only at one remote time united by a common fiducial. A 'sign' is one of the 30 degree arcs of the zodiacal circle: the term which sometimes is used in popular textbooks - 'constellational sign' - is quite meaningless. It has happened of late that popular astrologers have also written and spoken of the 'signs of the zodiac' as though these refer to the IMAGES, or (more frequently, though just as wrongly) to the SIGILS used to symbolize these. A sign is not an image, though an image may at times denote a sign. Properly speaking, the image of a sign is really derived from the ancient constellational pictures - the image of Aries is a ram, for example, that of Taurus is a bull, and so on. The signs have been classified according to ancient principles and given a bewildering variety of different group-names, many of which, whilst virtually archaic, are to be traced back to Ptolemaic astrology. A useful (if archaic) list of such group-names may be abstracted from the 17th century text of Lilly:

Airy	GE LB AQ		Barren	GE LE VG
Bestial	AR TA LE SG		Common	GE VG SG PI
Double-bodied	GE SG PI		Earthly	TA VG CP
Equinoctial	AR LB		Fiery	AR LE SG
Feminine	TA CN VG SC CP PI		Fixed	TA LE SC AQ
Fruitful	CN SC PI		Human	GE VG AQ
Masculine	AR GE LE LB SG AQ		Movable	AR CN LB CP
Northern	AR TA GE CN LE VG		Southern	LB SC SG CP AQ PI
Tropical	CN CP		Watery	CN SC PI

SIGNACULA   A term often used in mediaeval astrology as the equivalent of "Characters", sometimes of "Sigils". See also MAGIC SQUARES.

SIGNATURE   In mediaeval astrology it was taught that every material form bears an outer stamp of the planetary or zodiacal principle which underlies its nature: this is the 'signature', the 'signing' of nature. The proficient astrologer or occultist would recognize these inner principles from the outer form, and thus obtain knowledge of the real thing - of its quintessential nature - which is represented within the form. The esotericist Boehme developed the idea of 'signature' at great length, and the term has been usefully linked by Muses with the SEVEN PROPERTIES, the seven planetary natures, as a sign of the signature of all things, the outer form being regarded as 'the precise configuration of the differing representation, in relative strengths, of each of the basic properties therein'. In a general sense, the signature is the spiritual imprint of the VIRTUE. Paracelsus anticipates Goethe by visualizing the signature of things as the result of the workings of the Imagination of nature. 'There is nothing hidden which Nature has not revealed and put plainly forward,' he writes, with the signature in mind. In a later definition Paracelsus equates the 'Doctrine of Signatures' with the entire art of astrology, it being 'the science which teaches one to know the stars, what the heaven of each may be, how the heaven has produced man at his conception, and in the same way constellated him'.

SIGNIFICATOR   In a general sense, each planet is a significator of something or other - for example, the Sun is a significator of the conscious aim of the native, while the Moon is the significator of the personality, and so on. In this sense, the houses are also significators - the Second House, for example is a significator of wealth, among other things. However, the term is often used in a more specialist sense in regard to Horary Astrology, most frequently in regard to to the planets which are 'significators' of the querent: this is usually the strongest planet in the figure, which is in many cases the ruler of the Ascendant. Even within horary astrology each planet remains a significator of some event, quality or person: for example, Venus is the significator of love-affairs, the mistress, the impulse to love, and so on. See also MODERATORS and PROMITTORS.

SIGNS OF VOICE   The astrologer Wilson terms Gemini, Virgo, Libra and Aquarius (as well as the first part of Sagittarius) the 'signs of voice', because 'if either of them ascend, and Mercury be strong, the native will be a good orator'.

SIHOR   See SIRIUS.

SILVER AGE   See FOUR AGES and TRETA YUGA.

SILVER CORD   See PISCES CONSTELLATION.

SILVER RIVER   See VIA LACTEA.

SIMAK   'Al Simak', the 12th of the Arabian MANZILS.

SIMHA   One of the Sanskrit terms for zodiacal Leo, used in Hindu astrology.

SIN   A general Babylonian term for the Moon.

SINGLETON   A term sometimes used of the planetary 'handle' of the aspectal shaping called a BUCKET in the "Jones Patterns". The singleton is that planet (or conjunction of planets) which gives drive or 'purpose' to the formation, and hence to the chart as a whole.

SINISTER ASPECT   An aspect calculated in the order of the signs, to be distinguished from the reverse computation, which is the DEXTER ASPECT. The change in the meaning of the word 'sinister' (which originally meant merely 'left-handed' or 'left-hand side') has led to certain misunderstandings about this term: there is nothing unwholesome in this aspect.

SINISTRA   Name given to the relatively unimportant fixed star set in the left hand of the asterism Ophiuchus, said to give an immoral, mean and slovenly nature.

SIRIAN CYCLE   A periodicity observed by the ancients, involving the heliacal rising of the fixed star SIRIUS, in a 162 year periodicity.

SIRIUS   Fixed star (binary) the alpha of Canis Major, set in the mouth of the dog, one of the most important stars in the heavens so far as the astrological tradition is concerned. It has many names and traditions attached to it. Though now it is called the 'Dog-star', the name is often derived from the Greek 'seirios' (sparkling), even though that same term was sometimes used of all the stars (and indeed of the Sun). Some occult etymologists have linked the name with the Egyptian Osiris (which is in any case a Greek version of the Egyptian): it was for Homer the 'Star of Autumn', to the Romans 'Canicula' (little dog), and they are reported to have sacrificed a dog in their May festivals, during the so-called 'Robigalia', when the Sun reached orb of Sirius. From these names and associations came a wide variety of derivations, such as 'Latrator Anubis', 'Al Shi'ra', 'Ascher', 'Aschere', and 'Scera'. In the Egyptian astrology it was symbolized by a dog-like image as hieroglyphic, and was of considerable importance in the middle of the 4th millenium, for its heliacal rising at the summer solstice marked the beginning of both the Egyptian year and the

commencement of the Nile flooding. In the so-called zodiac at Denderah the
star is figured as a cow in a boat, but it was in earlier forms linked with
Isis, both in Denderah and at the important Isis-complex at Philae. It
appears to have been linked also with the name of Thoth, and was called
'Sihor' (Nile Star), as well as by such epithets as 'Fair Star of the
Waters', which perhaps explains the reason why Isis was called 'Stella Maris'
long before the Virgin Mary (but see STELLA MARIS). As might be imagined
from these prestigious names, astrologers link it in general with beneficial
influences: it gives honour, renown, wealth and passion. It is linked with
guardianship (in accordance with the general association with zodiacal
Cancer), and is inevitably associated with the danger of dog-bites. See also
in this last connexion PROCYON.

SIRRAH   A name for the fixed star ALPHERATZ.

SISTERHOOD   See ETHEREAL PLANETS.

SIVAN   See BABYLONIAN CALENDAR.

SIXTH HOUSE   The sixth of the astrological HOUSES, linked with the nature of
the sign Virgo, and representing the ideal of service, as well as the kind of
relationship the native will establish with those above and below (the sixth
house is sometimes said to deal with the chaos left by the leonine impulse of
the preceding fifth house, and to 'love and cherish' the associate Libra of
the following seventh house). It is sometimes called the 'House of Work',
and is frequently linked with ideals of hygiene and social care - in the
melothesic man it rules the bowels and solar plexus. In Mundane Astrology it
relates to the public health services, to such civil workers as police and
voluntary labour. It is said that strikes have their beginnings in this
house, but take their 'form' in the twelfth house.

SIXTH RAY   In the esoteric system described by Bailey, the sixth of the
"Seven Rays" is called the 'Ray of Idealism', or the 'Ray of Devotion', and
is linked with the will to create and 'bring into being'. The sixth ray is
said to arise in Ursa Major, and is transmitted into our solar system by
means of the zodiacal constellations (signs?) Virgo, Sagittarius and Pisces,
through their pairs of corresponding ORTHODOX PLANETS and ESOTERIC PLANETS,
according to the schema in table 79.

```
--------------------------------------------------------------TABLE 79
```

CONSTELLATION	ORTHODOX PLANET	ESOTERIC PLANET
Virgo	Mercury	Moon
Sagittarius	Jupiter	Earth
Pisces	Jupiter	Pluto

The entire sixth ray is linked with the sacred planet Neptune: see therefore
SACRED PLANETS. In connexion with the rule of esoteric Moon over Virgo, as
set out in the above schema, see also ESOTERIC MOON. Distinguish from SIXTH
RAY TYPE.

SIX RAY TYPE   The sixth of the SEVEN RAY TYPES, associated with the planet
Mars. Distinguish from SIXTH RAY.

SIZAJASEL   In certain systems of ceremonial magic, this is the name given to
the Governor of the zodiacal sign Sagittarius.

SKAT   Modern name for the fixed star, delta of constellation Aquarius, set
in the right leg of the asterism, once confusingly called 'Scheat' (and hence
confused with the SCHEAT of Pegasus). The term is probably derived from the
Arabic 'Al Sak' (the shin bone). Ptolemy says that it is of a nature
equivalent to Jupiter with Saturn, which is of a beneficial influence.

==

SLOW OF COURSE   Said of a planet which is moving more slowly than its mean motion: in Horary Astrology it is regarded as a debility.

SOL   The Latin name for the Sun. The same name was used by Blavatsky to denote an 'invisible trans-Mercurial planet, nearer to the Sun than Mercury' which was 'one of the most secret and highest planets'. This was probably one of the AROMAL PLANETS, but one said to have 'become invisible at the close of the Third Race' - towards the end of the Lemurian period.

SOLAR APEX   A term used to denote the objective of solar motion through space, a motion which has been identified by some astrologers with the 'target of personality' in relation to the zodiacal motion of the Sun as reflected in horoscope charts. The solar apex has been used as fiducial to overcome the anomaly of the slight proper motion of fixed stars, which makes for imprecise definition of the zodiacal fiducial. The sidereal astrologer Garth Allen proposed that the sidereal zodiac should take the solar apex as a fiducial, locating what he called the the 'synetic vernal point' 90 degrees East of the solar apex. Thus, for the first time in the history of astrology a zodiac was proposed which united the ecliptic divisions with the motion of the Sun in co-ordinates independent of the fixed stars. It was assumed by the siderelists that the solar apex was a point located in the first degree of Capricorn (but see the related figures of Landscheidt in GALACTIC CENTRE), and that this point was not subject to proper motion. However, in spite of the provision of exact degrees, and indeed of a simple ephemeris by Landscheidt, it has been shown that the apex may not be regarded as a point, but as an arc extending to almost 6 degrees, which calls into question the validity of the 'synetic vernal point' concept. See however SIDEREAL ZODIAC.

SOLAR ASTROLOGY   A term frequently misapplied as being synonymous with HELIOCENTRIC ASTROLOGY, though more properly it is used to denote that system of astrology which is involved with the casting and interpreting of charts for the moment of sunrise, or for exact local noon time, when the Sun is on the Ascendant degree or on the Medium Coeli, respectively. Usually, such astrology is used only in those cases where precise time of birth is not known, and even then only as a preparation for RECTIFICATION.

SOLAR BIOLOGY   A term seemingly originated by the astrologer Butler prior to 1887, relating to a form of astrology which, for all its strange concepts (see for example EARTH ZODIAC), and for all its being pervaded by biblical and religious references not always apposite to the case, appears to be little other than traditional genethlicacal astrology in a new guise. However, Butler says that his astrology is not involved with the prediction of coming events. The positions of the Moon are given in terms of the geocentric system in accordance with the proposition that there is a 'second zodiac' relating to the Earth, while the positions of other planets are listed according to a curious notion which requires the adjusting of the tropical positions by 180 degrees, thus segregating a 'Lunar Zodiac' (or 'Earth Zodiac') from the so-called 'Solar Zodiac', which appears to be the traditional tropical zodiac.

SOLAR BODY   See LUNAR BODY.

SOLAR CYCLE   A term most usually applied to a 'cycle' of 28 years, which is not really a solar cycle at all, but a periodicity derived from calendrical systems, in which the days of the week re-occur on the same days of the month as in the preceding period.   The genuine solar cycles are the METONIC CYCLE, the PLATONIC CYCLE and the YEAR - but see also TIME.

SOLAR DAY   The time between two consecutive transits of the Sun over a fixed point on Earth: it is in excess of the SIDEREAL DAY by approximately 1 degree of longitude (roughly 4 minutes of TIME). See also MEAN SOLAR DAY and TRUE SOLAR DAY.

==

SOLAR DISTANCE   The mean solar distance of the planets from the Sun,
expressed in thousands of miles, is as follows:

ME	35,950	VE	67,180	TE	92,870	MA	141,500
JU	483,300	SA	886,100	UR	1,783,000	NE	2,793,000
PL	3,666,000						

SOLAR ECLIPSE   When the orb of the Moon interposes itself between the earth
and the light of the Sun, the phenomenon is called a 'Solar Eclipse' - in
effect this is a platic CONJUNCTION of the luminaries.   The ancient
astrological rule held that the effect of a solar eclipse lasts as long in
years as the eclipse lasts in hours, though this 'effect' is limited to the
degree in which the eclipse took place. Eclipses (see also LUNAR ECLIPSE) in
a chart are usually regarded as malignant if the degree involved is conjunct
the Sun, Moon, Ascendant, Medium Coeli or any of the malefics, either radical
or progressed. Experience has shown that an eclipse leaves a sort of 'degree
influence' which is only made operational by later transits or progressions
which trigger off the effects. Esoteric astrology teaches that at the time
of solar eclipses evil forces are permitted to pour from the Sphere of the
Earth into the cosmos, the eclipse acting as a sort of safety-valve.

SOLAR EQUILIBRIUM   A term of recent origination, defined by Devore as having
reference to the SOLAR FIGURE cast for sunrise, and symbolically presented in
the 'Equal House' method, with houses of uniform 30 degree arcs.

SOLAR FIGURE   Term used of a particular type of horoscope erected for a
nativity for which the time of birth is not known, determining a putative
Ascendant by taking it as the Sun's degree. See SOLAR ASTROLOGY.

SOLAR FLUID   A term used in an astrological sense by Butler to denote an
'ethereal atmosphere or sea of fluidic element pervasive of, and limited by,
our solar system'. The fluid seems to correspond in quality and effect, if
not in actual distribution, with the traditional 'aether' or QUINTESSENCE,
and is almost certainly derived from the occult writings of the American
clairvoyant Davis. See however SOLAR BIOLOGY.

SOLAR HORAS   See HORAS.

SOLAR HOUSE   A system of dividing the ecliptic circle, which is not to be
confused with any of the HOUSE DIVISION methods. The 'solar houses' are
equal arc divisions of 30 degrees, supposedly subdivisions of the two-hour
periods of axial rotation of the Earth, and postulating that the Sun is on
the Ascendant at the commencement of the division.

SOLAR KALPA   See KALPA.

SOLAR RADIX METHOD   A system of progressions involving the progressing of
the horoscope as a whole by the progressive addition of an arc equivalent to
time lapsed, by the conversion of 1 hour into 15 degrees of arc. The measure
for a year (that is, the 365 and a half days of the 'mean solar year) is
equivalent to 59' 8.33", and the solar month in the system is exactly one
twelfth of that year. Since according to the theory of progressions the
diurnal is the equivalent of the annual, the same arc is measure of the day.

SOLAR RETURN   A 'solar return' is a chart cast for the time at which the Sun
returns to its radical position in a preceding chart (usually the natal
chart). It may be measured in terms of the tropical or sidereal zodiac,
though the astrologer Bradley favours the latter in his own comprehensive
survey of the 'Solunar Returns'.   He says that the 'solar return chart'
describes the events to befall the native during the following 12 months.
See also LUNAR RETURN. Subdivisions of the solar return described by Bradley
are the QUARTERLY CHARTS and the SEMESTER CHART. The solar return is
sometimes confusingly called the 'Solar Revolution' - but see REVOLUTION and

SOLAR REVOLUTION FIGURE.

SOLAR REVOLUTION   See SOLAR RETURN and SOLAR REVOLUTION FIGURE.

SOLAR REVOLUTION FIGURE   A horoscope figure cast for the moment in any year subsequent to the birth of a native when the Sun reaches the precise degree of longitude which it occupied in the radical chart. Such a figure is generally erected for purposes of prediction.

SOLAR SEMICIRCLE   Term applied to the zodiacal arc from Leo to Capricorn, inclusive.

SOLAR YEAR   Another term for the TROPICAL YEAR.

SOLAR ZODIAC   See REAL ZODIAC, SOLAR BIOLOGY and ZODIAC.

SOLID SIGNS Translations of the word 'sterea', used by Ptolemy to denote the four fixed signs of the zodiac, have given us the unfortunate term 'solid', though the Greek word really meant 'hard' or 'firm'. Ptolemy says that the 'solid signs' are persistent, firm, patient, industrious, self-controlled, hard, inflexible, and unaffected by flattery.

SOLOMON'S SEAL   See SEAL OF SOLOMON.

SOLSTICES   The points in the ecliptic at which the Sun is at its greatest distance to the North or South of the equator are called the 'solstitial points' or 'solstices' (literally, the points where the sun appears to stand still). The Summer Solstice is marked by the entry of the Sun into Cancer, the Winter Solstice by the entry of the Sun into Capricorn, round about 21st June and the 21st December, respectively.

SOLSTITIAL COLURE   See COLURE.

SOLSTITIAL POINT   See ECLIPTIC.

SOLSTITIAL POINTS   See SOLSTICES.

SOLSTITIAL SIGNS   According to Ptolemy, the solstitial signs (Cancer and Capricorn) produce souls fitted for dealing with people, fond of political activity and 'attentive to the gods', as well as fitted for the practice of astrology and divination. There is probably some confusion between the entire sign and the specific solstitial degree.

SOLUNAR RETURNS   An inclusive term for the two separate techniques involving SOLAR RETURNS and LUNAR RETURNS.

SOMERSET GIANTS See GLASTONBURY ZODIAC

SONIPES   See PEGASUS.

SORATH   Name given by Agrippa (quoting cabbalistic sources) to the Daemon of the Sun, for whom he gives the magical number 666 - but see also NACHIEL.

SORTES   The various systems of 'Sortes' (in the Greek 'klipoi' - though the term 'locus', plural 'loci', is also sometimes used - but see LOCI) derived from ancient astrology have been studied in modern times by Bouche-Leclercq, who refers to a number of Sortes no longer in use, and especially to two important 'sortes' recorded by Manilius, the equivalent of the modern "Part of Fortune" and the interesting (though now defunct) "Lot of Daimon". Manilius distinguishes between the day horoscope and the night horoscope. For the former he takes the distance between the Sun and Moon, and following the order of the signs, transfers this arc to the horoscopos (Ascendant), to locate the Pars Fortunae.   In the nocturnal chart, measurement is made

widdershins.   The modern method does not distinguish between the day and
night charts, which in effect gives precisely the same point by means of
different rules. In connexion with the Daimon (sometimes the 'klipos
daemonos', translated often as 'sortes genii', or even 'locus daemonis')
Bouche-Leclercq reports also the views of the Alexandrian Paul, who also
distinguishes between the day chart and the night chart (apparently following
some Egyptian tradition, which may not be fully understood). In the day
chart the arc from the Sun to the Moon, measured in the order of the signs,
is applied to the horoscopos against the order of the signs to mark the
Daimon. In the night chart the distance from the Sun to the Moon is measured
against the order of the signs, the arc being transferred to the horoscopos
along the order of the signs to reveal the Daimon. In these systems the
diurnal Daimon is interchangeable with the nocturnal Pars, and vice versa.
See however TWELVE SORTES. The use of 'sortes' in Hellenistic astrology was
expressed in a refined way in the 1st century AD texts of the astrologer
Dorotheus of Sidon, who placed much emphasis on the Fortunae and Daemon (as
did most early astrologers).   However, as Pingree, in his short history of
astrology, points out, the list of 'sortes' grew to such an extent that by
the 9th century the Arabian astrologer Abu Ma'shar was able to enumerate well
over a hundred.

SOSOL   In certain grimoires, the Sosol is named as Governor of Scorpio.

SOTHIC CALENDAR   A term used of one of the calendrical systems used by the
ancient Egyptians, involving four-year periods (tetracteres), which began
when the fixed star Sirius (Sothis) rose heliacally at Heliopolis. According
to Fagan, the rigorous calculations of these periodicities, involving
Newcomb's precessional constants and the 'arcus visionis' for Sirius at that
place, revealed the following series - starting 4228 BC, 2770 BC, 1314 BC and
142 AD. Fagan says that this cycle corresponds to the 'Resurrection of the
Phoenix' of Egyptian lore: it is a mean cycle of 1,456 years. Fagan further
claims that a great many of the celestial diagrams (he is careful not to call
them zodiacs or horoscopes) still preserved in ancient Egypt were computed to
mark these periodicities.

SOTHIC CYCLE   A periodicity given as a mean cycle of 1,456 years, and
sometimes as 1,460 years. See SOTHIC CALENDAR.

SOUL BEINGS   The four classes of 'elementals', often wrongly called
'elemental spirits', are generally regarded by occultists to be 'elemental
soul beings', since the very quality they lack is that of 'spirit', in that
they do not have the ego, or even the ego-potential, which is part of the
human constitution.   In the Rosicrucian tradition, which has from time to
time influenced the development of astrological thought, the four groups are
linked with the four elements (hence their generic name). The GNOMES are the
earth beings, the SALAMANDERS are the fire beings, the SYLPHS are the air
beings, and the UNDINES are the water beings.

SOUL-NUMBERS   A series of numbers linked with the Platonic theory of
harmonics and DESCENT OF THE SOUL which figured in later numerological
theories connected with astrology. The numbers are 1, 2, 3, 4, 8, 9 and 27,
but the argument as to their mystical natures is beyond the compass of the
present treatment. It is perhaps sufficient to set out the schema reproduced
by Mead relating to the circular progression and 'conversion of the soul',
for this links directly with the original Pythagorean imagery of
reincarnation, decent into multiplicity (descent into numbers) which
permeates astrological esotericism. The four stages correspond to the point,
line, plane and solid:

```
Point          1
Line       2        3
Plane      2        3    (both to the power of 2)
Solid       2    3       (both to the power of 3)
```

These are called the 'boundary numbers of the soul'. These numbers were
adopted in many esoteric schemas in regard to the cycle of descent and
re-ascent of the soul (in and out of matter): - for example, they are tacitly
assumed in the rationale given by Dee in his MONAS HIEROGLYPHICA.

SOUND VALUES   See QABBALISM.

SOUTHERN ANGLE   The cusp of the Tenth House is called the 'Southern Angle'
and is sometimes identified with the Medium Coeli: it is associated with the
sign Capricorn, and with the point of aspiration, at which the native may
achieve his 'highest' conscious aims or ambitions.

SOUTHERN CLAW   See ZUBENELGENUBI.

SOUTHERN CROSS   See CRUX.

SOUTHERN CROWN   See CORONA AUSTRALIS.

SOUTHERN FISH   See PISCIS AUSTRALIS.

SOUTHERN FLY   See MUSCA AUSTRALIS.

SOUTHERN SIGNS   These are the zodiacal signs from Libra to Pisces,
inclusive, the so-called 'Obeying Signs', south of the equatorial belt.

SOUTHERN TRIANGLE   Constellation, the 'Triangulum Australe', probably formed
by Theodor in the 16th century, south of the constellation ARA, between Pavo
and Centaur. The triangle stars, which define the asterism, are alpha, beta
and gamma. It is said to have an influence similar to that of Mercury, and
is therefore beneficial.

SOUTHERN TWIN   See POLLUX.

SOUTH NODE   The point where a planet crosses the ecliptic into the southern
latitude - see NODES.

SOUTH SCALE   See ZUBENELGENUBI.

SPECIALIS   A term used to denote the 20 year cycle of the "Chronocrators"

SPECULATION   In a strictly astrological and occult context Paracelsus
defines 'speculation' as an activity arising from the stars 'which are
concerned about man'. From the larger context of his writings, we may assume
that the term is intended to denote the relationship which exists between
what we would now call the 'archetype' (which Paracelsus variously called the
'Archaeus' or the 'Heavens') and human thinking. Hence, Paracelsus speaks of
a speculating man as one having his imagination united with heaven, and
'heaven operates so within him that more is discovered than would seem
possible by merely human methods'. The term is of specific interest in that
the mediaeval astrologers regarded astrology itself as one of the
'speculatives', in a sense very different from the modern.

SPECULUM   In astrology, a term used for a table attached to a horoscope
figure, containing information concerning astronomical data which may be
useful in interpreting the radical or progressed figure. The information
usually includes such matter as latitudes, declinations, and so on. The word
itself is from the Latin for 'mirror' - in some early texts the word is used
in a poetic sense to denote the horoscope chart, which 'mirrors' the heavens.

SPHAERA OBLIQUA   See SPHAERA RECTA.

SPHAERA RECTA   In terms of stereographic projection, the 'sphaera recta'
relates to zero geographical latitude, with reference to the phenomena of

rising and setting: the contrasting 'sphaera obliqua' is that projected for
other latitudes.

SPHAERA ZODIACUS   A Latin term used to denote (first) the STELLATUM, and
then later (archaically) the ecliptic.

SPHERE OF DEMOCRITUS   Name applied to an ancient (probably Hellenistic)
system of prognostication by means of numbers, only peripherally linked with
ONOMANTIC ASTROLOGY.

SPHERE OF HEAVEN   Sometimes called the 'Stellatum' or 'Coelum' (but see also
EIGHTH SPHERE) in the Ptolemaic System, the sphere in which dwell the beings
and orbs of the fixed stars. In the mediaeval cosmoconception the sphere was
said to be the dwelling of the CHERUBIM, ruled by the spiritual being
OPHANIEL, and linked with the image of a dove.

SPHERE OF JUPITER   In the Ptolemaic System, the sphere in which dwell the
beings and orb of the planet Jupiter. In the mediaeval cosmoconception, the
sphere was said to be the dwelling of the DOMINIONS (sometimes the
Dominations), ruled by the spiritual being ZADKIEL and the spirit Befor. The
Sphere is linked with the image of an eagle.

SPHERE OF MARS   In the Ptolemaic System, the sphere in which dwell the
beings and the orb of the planet Mars. In the mediaeval cosmoconception, the
sphere was said to be the dwelling of either the POWERS (or Potestates) or
the PRINCIPALITIES, depending upon which system of Celestial Hierarchies was
adopted - though in this connexion it is worth observing that the the Greek
term DYNAMIS for these beings appears to have been invariable, and might
reasonably be translated as 'Powers'. The sphere is ruled by the spiritual
being SAMAEL, and the spirit PHALEG, and is linked with the image of a horse.

SPHERE OF MERCURY   In the Ptolemiac System, the sphere in which dwell the
beings and orb of the planet Mercury. In the mediaeval cosmoconception, the
sphere was said to be the dwelling of the ARCHANGELS, ruled by the spiritual
being RAPHAEL and the spirit OPHIEL, and was linked with the image of a
serpent.

SPHERE OF SATURN   In the Ptolemaic System, the sphere in which dwell the
beings of Saturn, and in which the orb of this planet is carried. In the
mediaeval cosmoconception, the sphere was said to be the dwelling of the
spiritual beings called the THRONES, under the rule of ZAPHKIEL, and linked
with the spirit ARATRON. The sphere is sometimes symbolized by the image of
a dragon, and was said to mark the limits of time.

SPHERE OF THE MOON   In the Ptolemaic System, the sphere in which dwell the
beings and orb of the planet Moon - but see also EIGHT SPHERE.   In the
mediaeval cosmoconception, the sphere was said to be the dwelling of the
ANGELS, under the rule of the Archangel GABRIEL, and the spirit PHUL. The
sphere is linked with the image of an ox.

SPHERE OF THE PRIMUM MOBILE   Sometimes called the 'Primum Movens' (First
Mover) in the Ptolemaic System, this is the sphere which was supposed to give
motion to all the other spheres which it enclosed. In the mediaeval
cosmoconception, the sphere was said to be the dwelling of the SERAPHIM,
ruled by the spiritual being METATRON, and often linked with the image of a
leopard.

SPHERE OF THE SUN   In the Ptolemaic System, the sphere in which dwell the
beings and orb of the Sun. In the mediaeval cosmoconception, the sphere was
said to be the dwelling of either the VIRTUES or the POWERS (but see SPHERE
OF MARS), depending upon which system of Hierarchies was adopted. The Greek
name EXSUSIAI appears to have been invariable, however. The sphere is ruled
by the spiritual being MICHAEL, and the spirit OCH, and is linked with the

image of a lion.

SPHERE OF VENUS   In the Ptolemaic System, the sphere in which dwell the
beings and orb of the planet Venus. In the mediaeval cosmoconception, the
sphere was said to be the dwelling of either the PRINCIPALITIES or the
VIRTUES, depending upon which system of Celestial Hierarchies was adopted.
The Greek name for these beings, the ARCHAI appears to have been invariable
however, and this would therefore suggest 'principalities' as a fair
translation. The sphere is ruled by the spiritual being HANAEL and by the
spirit HAGIEL. It is linked with the image of a man.

SPHERES   The early Greek and Roman cosmoconception postulated that the seven
planets (which included the luminaries) were carried around the central Earth
in a series of spheres. The body of the planet, often called the 'planetary
orb' in later European systems, was carried along by the movement of that
sphere - a movement transmitted to it ultimately by the SPHERE OF THE PRIMUM
MOBILE, but regulated by spiritual beings. Because seven planets are
described in the Ptolemaic System (which is itself an extension of the
Aristotelian System) it is generally believed that there were only seven
planetary spheres carrying the planetary orbs - however, this is far from the
truth. The need to unite the Aristotelian dictum that 'planets move in
perfect circles' with the observable movement of these bodies required a most
sophisticated system of "Epicycles" and "Deferent" circles, and involved a
complex series of spheres within spheres. By the 16th century, shortly
before the Ptolemaic model broke down under its own weight of complexity, a
model existed which postulated the existence of as many as 79 spheres. Even
Aristotle, in his 'Metaphysics', required 55 spheres, though by the time
Dante was putting the Arabian astrology into poetic imagery a 'working model'
had been constructed with only 27 spheres. Under the impress of the
theological theory of the CELESTIAL HIERARCHIES (derived from the
pseudo-Areopagite) a system of spiritual beings, with named rulers, were
established around the theory of the spheres. One important difference
between the modern heliocentric system and the late mediaeval system
inherited by astrology was the sequence of the planets: it was believed that
Venus was nearer to the Sun, so that in most of the models of our system
prior to the 17th century, the sequence of the spheres was presented in the
order set out in figure 59. The numbers listed above the extra-lunar planets
in this figure relate to the traditional "Planetary Periods". The idea that
it was the Earth itself which revolved, rather than the vast concentrics of
spheres was suggested in Greek times, but was mooted in Europe in the 13th
century by the Franciscan monk Francois de Meyronnes.

FIGURE 59. THE ORDER OF THE SPHERES IN THE MEDIAEVAL MODEL, ALONG WITH
THE PLANETARY PERIODS.

SPHERICAL DESCENT   See DESCENT OF THE SOUL.

SPHERICAL REGULATORS   See INTELLIGENCY.

SPICA   Fixed star (binary), the alpha of constellation Virgo, set in the ear of corn held by this female figure. Its symbolic importance is just about equivalent to its astrological importance, for the Christian astrologers linked Virgo with the Virgin Mary, and the 'Spica' (ear of corn) in the arms of the asterism with Jesus, held in the arms of his Virgin mother. This imagery may be traced back to the Egyptian Isis, of course (see for example STELLA MARIS), a goddess linked with the constellation and sign Virgo. Variant names include 'Stachys', 'Arista', 'Arista Puella', and in the Arabic tradition, 'Alk Simak al A'sal', which Allen explains as meaning 'defenceless', in reference to the fact that the star appears to be unattended by others. From this Arabian notion comes certain mediaeval names - such as 'Asimec', 'Acimon', 'Almucedie' and so on. One of the names given to the star by the Egyptians was 'Repa', which means 'Lord', and Lockyer (now so often laughed to scorn by those who know less than he did) shows that the setting of Spica was a fiducial for the temple at Tel al Amarna. A few Grecian temples (including that ancient wonder at Ephesus, later the site for a cult of the Virgin Mary) were also orientated towards Spica. The astrological tradition has almost invariably associated an unfruitfulness with Virgo, and this is extended to her prime star, though it (like the asterism) also brings a noble disposition, an urge to protect the innocent, goodness and (not surprisingly) 'ecclesiastical preferment'. Ptolemy says that it is of the nature of Venus conjunct Mars - a fair, if pagan, statement of the later Christian tradition. The name Spica was also applied to the 14th of the LUNAR MANSIONS in certain mediaeval lists, which no doubt used the star as fiducial.

SPIRITS OF MOTION   See DYNAMIS.

SPIRITS OF PERSONALITY   A name given by Steiner to the ARCHAI.

SPIRITS OF REVOLUTION OF TIME   See ARCHAI.

SPIRITS OF WISDOM   See DOMINIONS.

SPIRITUAL HIERARCHIES   See CELESTIAL HIERARCHIES.

SPIRITUAL SUN   See ESOTERIC SUN.

SPLASH   Term applied to one of the JONES PATTERNS, in which the distribution of planets is generally even: this distribution is claimed to give wide interests, and lack of a one-sided nature.

SPLAY   Term applied to one of the JONES PATTERNS, in which a fairly even distribution of planets is given a focal point by the presence of a satellitium. This distribution is said to make for sturdy individuality.

SPRING SIGNS   The zodiacal signs Aries, Taurus and Gemini.

SQUARE   An aspect of 90 degrees. Since planets (or nodal points) separated by 90 degrees must be in signs which are 'opposed' in their elemental natures, it is clear that such planets must find themselves working inharmoniously: it is for this reason that the square aspect has gained such an ominous reputation in popular astrology: see ELEMENTAL ASPECTS. Serious astrologers, however, insist that the divergent natures of planets under the strain of square aspect may, when properly handled, lead to spiritual advantage, and to creativity (creativity itself being a result of the reconciliation of inner tensions, or an attempt to make such reconcilation).

SRAVANA   Name given to the 21st of the Hindu NAKSHATRAS.

==

SRAVISHTHA   Name given to the 22nd of the Hindu NAKSHATRAS.

STACHYS   See SPICA.

STAR   See FIXED STARS.

STAR CALENDAR ZODIAC   A zodiac of constellations of unequal length,
originally specified approximately in its present form by Vreede and Schultz
in 1929, and slightly corrected c. 1972, but based loosely on indications
given by Steiner in 1912 in his own Star Calendar (Sternkalender) of that
year, which reverted to an astronomical zodiac of unequal divisions. The
extent of these asterisms, expressed in sidereal longitude to the nearest
degrees, are given in the table provided by Powell under SIDEREAL
CORRESPONDENCES, and indicated graphically in figure 60.   The divisions of
the asterisms, which may appear at first glance to be rather haphazard, were
apparently derived from a careful comparison of star charts relating to the
Ptolemaic listings, yet appear to have been largely justified by the work of
Thun and others in connexion with bio-dynamic farming - see SIDEREAL MOON
RHYTHMS. Many of the charts used by the astrologer Sucher in connexion with
"Astrosophy" are based on this zodiac.

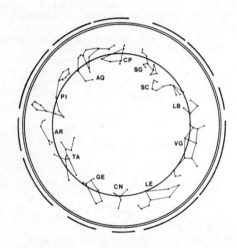

FIGURE 60. STAR CALENDAR ZODIAC (AFTER STEINER AND POWELL).

STAR CHARTS   See CONSTELLATION MAPS.

STAR OF AUTUMN   See SIRIUS.

STAR OF BETHLEHEM   Name given to the so-called 'star' followed by the Wise
Men from the East, mentioned in chapter 2 of the Gospel according to St.
Matthew. Whilst most occultists are aware that the 'star' was actually a
unique astral light, there have been many attempts by historians and
astrologers to identify the star in ordinary astronomical terms. One
explanation (for example) is that about 2 BC there was a conjunction between
the CHRONOCRATORS - yet such conjunctions are far from infrequent. Other
'explanations' include the idea that the 'star' was a NOVA - but a Nova does
not adopt 'stations', as is indicated in the Biblical description. Diodorus
of Tarsus echoes the esoteric tradition when he says quite bluntly that this
was not an ordinary star of the heavens, but a certain "virtue and

power" which had merely taken on the form of a star. In strictly Biblical terms, the Wise Men say that they had seen 'his star in the East' (ii.2), and after their visit to Herod they saw the star once again, and it 'went before them, till it came and stood over where the young child was' (ii.9). This is not the behaviour of a star. The two mentions of the 'star' in verses 2 and 9 have given rise to the idea that the Wise Men actually followed the Eastern star to Jerusalem, though this is not so claimed in the Gospel. See MAGIAN.

STAR OF MARY   See STELLA MARIS.

STAR OF THE SEA   See STELLA MARIS.

STAR POINTS   Name given to a series of readings attached to individual degrees of the constellational zodiac. They were derived psychically, by the astrologer Sepharial, towards the end of the 19th century, and are obviously linked with the influences of the fixed stars. The system is to be distinguished from the zodiacally based DEGREE SYMBOLS.

STAR ROYAL   See REGULUS.

STARRY CUP   A term derived from Macrobius, and usually claimed to relate to the constellation CRATER, though Macrobius himself says that his 'mystic secret' of the 'Starry Cup' is placed between Cancer and Leo, and refers the idea of the cup to the Bacchic intoxication 'first experienced by souls in their descent by the influx of matter into them'. This account is probably linked with the idea of the GATE OF BIRTH, located in Cancer.

STATION   Cognate with 'stationary', the term is used of those places in the orbit of a planet where it appears to be 'standing still', prior to direct or retrograde motion. When a planet is 'in its station', it appears to have no motion, and is said to be 'stationary': see however STATIONS OF THE MOON.

STATIONARY   See STATION.

STATIONS OF THE MOON   The motion of the Moon is always direct, so that properly speaking it has no STATIONS in the strict astrological meaning of the term, which implies a retrograde motion. However, the first and second DICHOTOMES of the Moon are sometimes called her first and second stations. Sometimes the points where the Moon makes entry to each of the 28 LUNAR MANSIONS are also called 'stations' or 'lunar stations': in this sense they are 'passage points' marked by fiducials.

STAXEODOS KOURE   See KORE.

STELLA DOMINATRIX   The Latin for 'master star', used of the fixed star "Aldebaran". According to Fagan this name was derived from the fact that the star was the zodiacal fiducial for the ancients, from which (he argues) 'the oldest and hence authentic zodiac began'. Certainly Aldebaran was one of the ROYAL STARS of the Persians, and was called by the Babylonians 'Ku I-kur', 'the leading star of stars'.

STELLAR MAGNITUDE   From the very earliest times stars have been classified by astrologers according to brightness (sometimes called 'apparent magnitude' in modern times). Ptolemy, for example, records such magnitudes from ancient traditions. However, magnitude tells us nothing about the actual luminosity of a star, or about its diameter. In the modern astronomical system, referred to in most astrological star lists, the stellar brightness is expressed by a formula according to which a star differs from another by one degree of magnitude when it is two and a half times brighter or fainter than the other. Thus, the star Wega is said to have a magnitude of 0.1 in comparison with Polaris, which has a magnitude of 2.2. A star of the 6th magnitude is only just visible to ordinary eyesight. See also ABSOLUTE STELLAR MAGNITUDE.

STELLA MARIS   Latin term usually translated as 'Star of the Sea', and
sometimes applied directly to the Virgin Mary, though more properly to the
star which is associated with the Virgin Mary (most often depicted on her
dress or upon her mapharion). This star may be traced back to the prototype
of early Marian symbolism, in the Egyptian Isis who was also called 'Star of
the Sea'. Astrologically, the star on the clothing of Mary is derived from
the fixed star SPICA, the lucida of Virgo, which was of course also
associated with Isis and Mary. But see also POLARIS, and in regard to the
Isidian connexion, see also SIRIUS.

STELLAR MUSIC   See MUSIC OF THE SPHERES.

STELLATUM   One of the several names given to the sphere of fixed stars in
the cosmoconception derived from the PTOLEMAIC SYSTEM. This was sometimes
called the Ninth Sphere, and the motion of the retrogression of the Vernal
Point, which was viewed as being either continuous or oscillatory (see
TREPIDATION) was said to be transmitted to it by the superior 'Primum
Mobile'. A sphere beyond the Stellatum and this Mobile was considered
Theologically necessary, as the 'eternal' realm of God and his ministering
angels, who dwelled in a sphere outside time, and in perfect motionless:
this was called the Aetherial Sphere, sometimes called the TENTH HEAVEN. It
was not until the 13th century tht the astrologer Peter of Abano suggested
that the stars themselves were not limited to a single concentric, but were
spread out in space. See also CONSTELLATIONS and FIXED STARS.

STELLIUM   See SATELLITIUM.

STEREOGRAPHIC CHART   See THREE-DIMENSIONAL CHART.

STERILE SIGNS   See BARREN SIGNS.

STRONG SIGNS   The 'strong signs' are traditionally said to be Scorpio and
Aquarius, though every sign has its own strengths and weaknesses.

SUB-DUODENARY MEASURE   An arc, or measure, used in SYMBOLIC DIRECTIONS, and
(probably) originated by Carter. It is derived by dividing the DUODENARY
MEASURE of 2 and a half degrees by twelve, to obtain an arc of 12' 30".

SUB-RULER   A term used to indicate a planet regarded as a secondary or even
tertiary 'influence' over a sign, decan or face. Whitman has made the
so-called "Modern Planets" sub-rulers in his own system of ASTRO-KINETICS.

SUBSISTENCES   A term derived from modern HARMONICS (probably) by the
astrologer Addey. The subsistences of the number 7 (for example) are the
series of harmonics which mark intervals of 9 places from the seventh degree
- that is, the 16th, 25th, 34th, etc. - all the numbers of which have digits
adding up to 7. These subsistences of 7 are derived from a procession of
nines. The subsistences of 4 are 13, 22, 31, and so on.

SUCCEDENT   Those houses which follow in succession the four angles are
called 'succedent': hence, the second, fifth, eighth and the eleventh
houses.

SUMMER SOLSTICE   See SOLSTICES.

SUN   In astrology, the solar body is termed a 'planet' simply because the
traditions and nomenclatures attached to it were established during the time
when the majority of astrological systems were geocentric. The sigil for the
Sun ⊙ is sometimes said to represent the circle of spirit containing the
central seed or nascent soul - though this sigil may not be traced back in
such an astrological context beyond the fifteenth century: see SIGILS -
PLANETARY. The Sun has rule over zodiacal Leo, is exalted in Aries, and has
its fall in Libra.   It represents the conscious element in the native, and

is usually studied as providing an index of the creative self-expression of the personality. An emphatic Sun in a chart is usually an indication of creative or artistic ability, as of a physical dignity and self-reliance, and often of a generous, affectionate and commanding nature. A badly placed Sun tends towards excess, so that the native is often showy, ostentatious, over-confident, egotistical, selfish and dictatorial. Traditionally, the Sun rules the heart of the melothesic man, and is also connected with the blood, even though it is the opposite sign Aquarius which properly rules the circulation of the blood. The Sun is a useful index of how the vital forces work through the physical body - this because spiritual (as well as physical) energies are derived ultimately from the Sun. The solar type is one who finds such energies easily, and is able to transmit them for the benefit of those around within the immediate environment: he or she is therefore often involved with activities demanding exertion and authority, even with creative enterprises on a large scale, as well as with outlets associated with the "Fifth House". Solar types seek positions where power, dignity and responsibility may be combined: they make good executives, and whilst generous are not always good accountants or even very careful with money (especially the money of other people). The metal of the Sun is gold, the ruling Archangel is MICHAEL.

SUN FORCES   A term which originated in the esoteric astrology favoured by Stein, based upon a specific cosmic interpretation of the dualism which pervades all occultism. Stein pictures the fundamental contrast underlying phenomena as the working of the dual Sun-forces and the Moon-forces: the former radiate and liberate, while the latter concentrate and wither. In fact Stein appears to use the terms as modern equivalents for the power of 'Ormudz' (the modern name for which is often given as LUCIFER) and 'Angrimayu' (the modern name for which is often given as AHRIMAN), derived from the ancient dualism of Zoroastrianism.

SUN PERIOD   A term which has nothing to do with the cycle of the Sun, or indeed with any SOLAR PERIOD. As a specialist term it is derived from modern esoteric astrology relating to cosmogenesis. The 'Sun' is said to be the second of the planetary states in the genesis of our world: it was initially a gaseous ball of warm light, from which the present solar system eventually evolved. This early period was overseen by the hierarchy of CHERUBIM. The Sun Period is sometimes called 'Old Sun'.

SUN REVOLUTION   Term derived from modern esoteric astrology, relating to cosmogenesis (see SUN PERIOD). It is said that the path of evolution of our present solar system, with its periods of activity and prelaya (sleep), as indeed the growth of every organic being, must recapitulate, however briefly, the entire sequence of evolution. Since the first stage of the cosmogenesis of our present system began in Saturn (see SATURN PERIOD) and reached its second stage in the "Sun Period", the term 'Sun Revolution' pertains to the second of these recapitulations, which is essentially one of 'warmth-light'.

SUN-SIGN ASTROLOGY   A term used to denote a popular form of so-called astrology which is based on the interpretation of character, career and psychological disposition, from the position of the Sun in regard to the tropical zodiac, to the exclusion of all other astrological factors. This system is said to be the second most popular form of 'astrology' in the world - no doubt because of its very simplicity, and for the ease with which it has been adapted for journalistic exploitation. It is interesting to observe that recent judicial interpretation in the English law courts has determined that the popular sun-sign system may not be properly described as being part of genuine astrological practice.

SUPER CHART   A term originated (probably) by Dean to denote a chart which incorporates all known astrological data in one figure. Such a chart would be entirely unreadable by ordinary means. At a very minimum, all the angles, planes, hypotheticals, nodes, parts, interactions of major and minor aspects, plus antiscions and contrascions, parallels, midpoints, and relevant progressions, would produce a chart which would be a mere plethora of sigils. The 'Hyper Chart', also mentioned by Dean, would be even more daunting, for this is conceived as including (in addition to the above) interfaces, perigrees, eclipses, lunations, satellites, fixed stars, etc, plus the imposition of derived figures such as the heliocentric equivalents, prenatals, harmonics, and so on. The concept of 'Super Chart' and 'Hyper Chart' is interesting if only because it indicates how any system of astrology must be selective if it is to be workable.

SUPERCYCLE   A somewhat misleading modern term applied to a series of (approximately) 6 sun-spot cycles in a periodicity of 132 years.

SUPERIOR MIDHEAVEN   An unnecessary term, as the MIDHEAVEN is always superior in the sense of location. It appears to have been used to distinguish this angle from the so-called 'Inferior Midheaven', which is really a confusing circumlocution for the IMUM COELI.

SUPERIOR PLANETS   Originally this was a term applied to the three planets beyond the Sun - Mars, Jupiter and Saturn: the term is therefore a relict of the Ptolemaic geocentric system, relating to positions 'higher' than the Sun sphere in regard to the Earth. See also INFERIOR PLANETS.

SUPERMIDPOINT   A term used to designate the 'ultimate midpoint', which arises after taking the midpoint of midpoints of midpoints, etc.

SUPERNATURAL ILECH   Esoteric name for the invisible influence which links the material realm with the stellar realm - but see ILECH.

SURYA   Sanskrit word for the Sun, as used in Hindu astrology.

SVATI   Name given to the 13th of the Hindu NAKSHATRAS.

SWEET SIGNS   Term used of the AIR SIGNS.

SWIFT   A planet may be said to be 'swift of motion' or 'swift in motion' when its speed over a period of 24 hours exceeds its own mean motion.

SWIFT IN MOTION   Any planet may be said to be 'swift in motion' when it is "Swift", but usually the term is reserved for the Moon, when in a motion faster than its mean rate of 13 degrees and 10 minutes. See also INCREASING IN MOTION.

SWORD   In a specialist sense, one of the so-called Arabian PARS, the 'part of Mars', sometimes called the 'Point of Passion'. If a natal chart is revolved so that the degree occupied by the Sun is on the Ascendant, then the position of Mercury in this new arrangement will mark the Sword point.

SYLPHS   The class of ELEMENTALS linked with Air. They correspond to the 'Nenuphars' of esoteric lore, while in the astrological correspondences of the CALENDARIA MAGICA they are often called 'Aerei'.

SYMBOL   The term symbol is used very loosely in astrological circles to cover such different concepts as IMAGES, SIGILS, SEALS and even SIGNS. In a strictly astrological context, a symbol is something which stands for, or represents, something else: however, a true symbol is intended to be more than merely a representative, for it should in some way act as a sort of commentary on the nature of that thing. The true nature of symbolism is perhaps most profoundly expressed in the Egyptian 'medu-neters', which the Greeks called 'hieroglyphics', for each symbol used had at least three related meanings (one strictly spiritual, linked with the equivalent of our archetypes, one linked with the potential of the thing symbolized, and a third linked with the hitherto unrealized potential of the thing in itself). In addition to these united triadic meanings, the symbol was intensified by the name ascribed to it, which (in Egyptian symbolism at least) was linked with a spritual cosmic language which would now be regarded as purely magical. Such an ancient view of symbolism - set out by de Lubicz - is to some extent still preserved in esoteric circles, but has been largely lost to modern thought, so that the union which once existed between the 'image', 'sigil', 'seal' and 'sign' (which found a single form in hieroglyphics) has been subject to fissiparous tendencies, so that whilst each word has obviously a common ideological reference, each now refers to a different system of symbolizing - the image through representation, the sigil through graphic symbolism, the seal through magical and numerologically originated symbols, and signs through a (formerly) numinous symbolism. This fragmentation of the original unity of the symbol has given rise to many misunderstandings of ancient astrological symbolisms - for example, amongmediaeval astrologers there was a tendency to infuse Christian symbolism with the old magic of seals: Arnaldus de Villanova, for example, would link the Christian image of the Lamb of God with the 'lamb' (actually the Ram) of zodiacal Aries in his magical amulets. Again, under the impulse which sought to trace Egyptian origins for the astrological glyphs and sigils, early post-mediaeval scholars suggested that the ram-horned Ammon was linked with Aries - see for example the 'etymological' suggestions of Kircher. However, a more profound knowledge of the medu-neters, and of the union between sound and symbol (which lay at the basis of Egyptian imagery) would have led not to Ammon but to the neter Khnum, who was also ram-horned, and who was specifically linked with the archetype of Aries. The error of linking Aries with Ammon gave rise to a basic misunderstanding of the nature of Aries itself. The term 'symbol', then, is often used in astrological contexts in a rather vague way, to represent almost any of the special forms of the symbol, and a definition of the term must remain a general one. Perhaps the most apposite definition is that provided by the historian Haase, who writes of the symbol as being 'essentially purposive' in that 'it points to some Higher Order for whose characteristics it is a kind of abbreviation'. See ABBREVIATIONS, IMAGE, SEAL, SIGILS, SIGN.

SYMBOLIC DEGREES   See DEGREE SYMBOLS.

SYMBOLIC DIRECTIONS   A name given to a method of astrological prediction based on 'symbolic movements' in which the measurement and timing of events is derived from a study of mathematically defined arcs, rather than planetary motions.   In Primary and Secondary Progressions, the movements of the planets are regarded as revealing the unfolding of the future from the potential contained within the radical chart, and these are therefore methods based on measurable events within the heavens. Symbolic Directions take no such measures as the basis for prediction, however, and rely entirely upon artificial arcs. The astrologer Carter distinguishes several such 'arcs of symbolic direction', five of which are set out in table 80.

NAME OF ARC	DIVISION OF	DIVISION BY	ARC	TABLE 80
Duodenary Measure	Sign	12	2.5 degrees	
Naronic Measure	Zodiac	600	0.6 degree	
Novenary Measure	Sign	9	3 deg. 20 mins.	
Septenary Measure	Sign	7	4 2/7th deg.	
Sub-Duodenary Measure	Sign	144	12.5 mins.	

Three further measures used are FRACTIONAL METHOD, MEASURE OF NAIBOD and the ONE DEGREE METHOD.   It will be observed that the Septenary Measure above is the same as the "Point of Life" used by the astrologer Frankland.

SYMBOLIC MOON   An alternative term for the Arabian PART OF FORTUNE.

===

SYMPATHY   In its specialist astrological sense, this term appears to have
two separate applications. The word is used to denote that force, subtle
influence, or spiritual empathy, which links all things in union within the
CHAIN OF BEING.   The same term is used also to describe individual
relationships between creatures and things: all sublunary things are
visualized as being either 'in sympathy' or 'in antipathy', depending upon
the elemental, planetary and zodiacal forces involved. Thus, a dog (under
the rulership of Mars) is not 'in sympathy' with a cat (under the rulerships
of Venus), and so on. This system of division extends even into the heavens,
so that planets and elements were represented as being 'in sympathy' or 'in
antipathy' (see FRIENDLY and UNFRIENDLY), and it is indeed this simple view
of nature which is the tacit rationale behind many of Ptolemy's arguments,
while the important law of CORRESPONDENCE is itself derived from the
dualistic structure. The two-fold meaning of the term has given rise to some
confusion: it is true to say that all things are 'in sympathy', in the first
sense that all things are working towards the same end within the Chain of
Being, when viewed in the light of the 'eternal plan of things'. Yet in the
second sense, it is possible to say that some things are not 'in sympathy'
when viewed in the light of transient experience, on the mundane plane. In
popular astrological literature, the two distinct uses of the term are often
merged and confused.

SYNASTRY   A term derived from the late Latin 'synastria', a neologism from
the Greek meaning approximately 'similarity of stars'. It denotes that
branch of astrology which deals with the study of agreements and
disagreements reflected in pairs of charts cast for two people (or in charts
cast for groups of people). Very often synastry is involved with comparing
two charts with a view to establishing compatability between people, or for
studying the causes and likely outcomes of crises between people. It is
widely recognized among astrologers that the charts of people who are
married, in a specific relation, in love, or otherwise karmically connected,
will have certain zodiacal degrees in common. Synastry, in that it is the
astrological study of human relationships, may be extended from ordinary
radical chart interpretation to the study of progressed charts.

SYNCHRONICITY A term originated by the psychologist C.G. Jung to designate a
psychic parallelism of events which cannot be related causally. The
parallelism, or 'connectedness' between such non-causally related events and
happenings, he termed "synchronistic". Jung quotes astrology as an excellent
example of manifest synchronicity - though many astrologers would maintain
that astrology is in fact causalistically based, when it is understood in the
light of esoteric truths. Jung himself recognised astrology as representing
"the summation of all the psychological knowledge of antiquity", and so it is
difficult to understand why he should feel the urge to coin a new term to
represent the relationship between the macrocosm and the microcosm. Could it
be that the term synchronicity is to be applied to those parallelism in
events which cannot be understood by the intellect? The interesting thing is
that the origin of the principle of Synchronicity is linked with Jung's
(somewhat limited) acquaintance with the Chinese philosophical machine, the
'I Ching' - the Chinese themselves regard the working of the oracle not in
terms of an oriental equivalent of 'synchronicity', but in terms of the
operation of spirits: i.e. animistic causality!

SYNETIC VERNAL POINT   See SOLAR APEX.

SYNODICAL LUNATION   A term applied to a 'Lunation Figure' progressed chart,
cast for the time when the progressed Moon establishes the same arc from the
progressed Sun as that held between the radical luminaries.

SYNODICAL RETURNS   A term used as an equivalent of LUNAR RETURN, applied to
a method of determining likely future events from the monthly return of the
Moon to the same elongation (arc) from the progressed Sun as the two bodies
held in the radical chart.   These 'months' are said by some astrologers to

equal a year of life, and the figures are called 'Lunar Revolutions',
presumably to distinguish them from the 'Lunar Returns', which are concerned
with monthly predictions.

SYNODIC CYCLE   A recurrence cycle between two successive conjunctions of the
same two planets. The synodic period for Jupiter-Saturn is 19.860 years, for
Saturn-Uranus 45.363 years, for Uranus-Neptune 171.403 years, for
Uranus-Pluto 127.280 years, and for Neptune-Pluto 49.328 years. See CYCLES.

SYNODIC MONTH   A lunation period of 29 days, 12 hours, 44 minutes and 2.8
seconds, the 'synodic period' between lunations.

SYNODIC PERIOD   See SYNODIC MONTH.

SYNTAXIS   See ALMAGEST.

SYSTEM A   Babylonian astrologers used two different methods for describing
the solar motion and its related phenomena, and certain of the implications
arising from these two systems continued into tabulations and methods used in
Hellenistic astrology, and even into the late mediaeval forms. They have
been called by modern historians 'System A' and 'System B'. In System A, the
AYANAMSA is 10 degrees, and in System B it is 8 degrees. These differences
are reflected in (among other things) the computations for the earliest
systems of the 'climata' (see CLIMA), each of them being linked specifically
with localities for Babylon and Alexandria, though later incorporating
computations for Rome. The traditional so-called SEVEN CLIMATA used an
ayanamsa of zero degrees, following the method of Ptolemy, who also computed
according to spherical trignometry.

SYZYGY   A term derived from the Greek meaning 'a yoking together', and used
most especially of the conjunction between the Sun and Moon. Sometimes the
term is extended (with etymological imprecision) to include oppositions
between the luminaries. It is a term entirely misused when applied to
conjunctions (or oppositions) involving planets other than the luminaries.
The term 'previous syzygy' often encountered in predictive work connected
with a radical chart refers either to the previous conjunction of the
luminaries, or to the opposition, whichever was nearer to the birth time.

TABLE OF HOUSES   A set of figures, usually arranged in columnar form,
designed to faciliate the calculation (from known sidereal times) of the
degrees arising on the Ascendant and culminating on the Midheaven, along with
intermediate house cusps, for different latitudes.

TABLE OF NAIBOD   A table setting out the MEASURE OF NAIBOD is often
published in books dealing with progressions and symbolic directions, yet
such a table is scarcely necessary in that it consists basically of the
separate additions of the annual arcs, and of the monthly arcs, according to
the requirements of the measure. The annual arc is 59' 08": the monthly arc
is 4' 56". The 06" annual increment is irrationally catered for within the
tables, but is of slight importance in predictive work by means of SYMBOLIC
DIRECTIONS.

TAIJAK   A Sanskrit term applied to the Hindu method of computing aspects
according to geometric angles, similar to the traditional method of viewing
ASPECTS in western astrology: see however ELEMENTAL ASPECTS.

TAKATA EFFECT   A name given to an effect observed and described by the

===

scientist Takata in relation to the flocculation index of blood serum which
varies by sudden increase at sunrise (with an orb of 15 minutes of time on
either side of the actual local sunrise). Similar increases have been
observed when the Earth moves into line with a group of sunspots: a
reduction effect is noted during solar eclipses, maximum reduction being at
total eclipse.

TALISMANIC MAGIC   From the very earliest times the various astrological
SIGILS, SEALS and IMAGES have been engraved or stamped on metal or pottery
talismans to make portable charms. A complex procedure was supposed to
attend the production of the genuine talisman - not only had it to be made
under the correct astrological conditions (under the appropriate planetary
hour, and so on), but it had to be manufactured in the metal or gem related
to the planetary or stellar forces being evoked in the charm. Wherever
possible many of the more potent images, sigils, symbols and names were
combined into one talismanic form. The result is that there are literally
thousands of mediaeval manuscripts dealing with the art of talismanic magic
which, in one form or another, are linked with traditional methods of
astrology. A complex art of talismanic symbolism has been attached to both
constellations and fixed stars - in connexion with the latter, see FIFTEEN
STARS - the post-mediaeval sigillic forms for these may be studied under
SIGILS - FIXED STARS. The talismanic use of seals, sigils and images
relating to the DECANS was highly complex, and at times resulted in the most
lovely symbols, a few of which have been recorded pictorially by Nowotny:
some of the talismanic lore relating to the Egyptian decans appear to have
survived even into Renaissance symbolism. The use of zodiacal and planetary
sigils and images for talismanic ends is almost in itself a chapter in the
history of astrology, but very many of the mediaeval astrological manuscripts
touch in one way or another on the magical power or significance of the basic
sigils, as the writings of Agrippa (mainly eclectic) confirm. For specific
examples of talismanic bases, see PENTAGRAM, PENTALPHA, SEAL OF SOLOMON and
TETRACTRYS.

TAMMUZ   See BABYLONIAN CALENDAR.

TAPHTHARTHARATH   Name given by Agrippa (quoting ancient cabbalistic sources)
to the daemon of Saturn, for whom he gives the magical number 2080, which is
the multiple of the number of Mercury (8) and the linear addition of the
Mercurial MAGIC SQUARE (260). See also TIRIEL.

TARANDUS   See RANGIFER.

TARF   'Al Tarf', name given to the 7th of the Arabic MANZILS.

TAROT   See ASTROLOGICAL TAROT.

TASCHETER   See ROYAL STARS.

TAURIDS   See METEORS.

TAURUS   The name of the second sign of the zodiac, also used to denote one
of the zodiacal constellations. As a sign, Taurus corresponds neither in
location nor signicance with the constellation of the same name: see TAURUS
CONSTELLATION.   The sigil for Taurus ♉ is said by some to be a drawing of
the head and horns of the bull, with which image Taurus is associated.
However, in the esoteric tradition it has been suggested that this is a
vestigial drawing of the larynx, with the Eustachian tubes, the sigil thus
linking the ideas of 'speech' and 'hearing'. This has been used as an
explanation as to why the image of the bull is sometimes linked with Christ,
for within both Taurus and Christ are contained the idea of the 'logos' or
'Word', as well as the idea of blood sacrifice. Taurus is of the Earth
element, and of the fixed quality, the influence being constructive,
strong-willed, conservative, slow, practical and sensuous. The nature of

Taurus, as it manifests in human beings, is expressed in the many keywords which have been attached to it by modern astrologers: practical, slow, heavy, possessive, conservative, intractable, relentless - in a word, all those qualities which may be associated with an Earth type expressing itself with determination. In excess the Taurean nature may be described in terms which express an underlying inertia, curiously married with a sort of magmatic violence which erupts when the subject is goaded: overbearing, deeply jealous, fixed in attitude, tyrannical, coarse, gluttonous, repetitive, selfish and unexpectedly violent or cruel. Taurus says 'this is mine' to the world more insistently than any of the other types - though he may be gentle or hard in his possessiveness, depending upon which side of his nature is being called into being. Taurus is ruled by the planet Venus, which accounts for the fact that so many Taureans are fair in form, and are so frequently associated with a beautiful or rich voice. The sign marks the exaltation of the Moon, and (according to modern schemas) the fall of Uranus. In common with the other three fixed signs of the zodiac, Taurus is linked with the TETRAMORPH, and specifically with the Evangelist Luke.

TAURUS CONSTELLATION   Constellation linked in name, if not in influence, with the zodiacal Taurus, located approximately between 17 degrees of Taurus and 23 degrees of Gemini, and straddling the equator from 2 degrees south to 34 degrees north: the representative constellation map in figure 61 is derived from data provided by Delporte in his MODERN ZODIAC.   In popular language this asterism is often called the Bull, and sometimes (misleadingly) 'Veneris Sidus' (Star of Venus), as it is the asterism associated with the rule of that planet over the sign.   In the majority of mediaeval astrological texts it is linked with the Graeco-Cretan myth of Europa, whom Jupiter carried off after he had adopted the form of a bull - however, the link with a bull was established in much earlier Egyptian and Babylonian astrology. The connexion with the myth did give rise to several variant names, such as 'Portitor', 'Proditor' (actually 'proditor Europae'), while the fact that the stellar image was often drawn as half a bull gave the term 'Sectio Tauri'. Among the many names furnished by the ancient Egyptians was 'Hapi', one of the Neters of the Nile. The Akkadian 'Te Te', given as 'Bull of Light' has been explained as a dual form in reference to the two important asterisms HYADES and PLEIADES within the constellation. The representative of the bull in figure 61 is from the 13th century SAN MINIATO ZODIAC which is orientated to a Taurean "Foundation Chart". In this latter zodiac, as in much astrological imagery, the bull of Taurus is associated with the Mithraic cult, the sign and constellation sometimes being termed the 'Mithraic Bull'. The fixed star within the constellation which is regarded as being of particular importance within the astrological tradition is ALDEBARAN.

FIGURE 61.   CONSTELLATION MAP OF TAURUS FROM THE "MODERN ZODIAC" (AFTER DELPORTE) - THE IMAGE OF TAURUS IS FROM THE 13TH CENTURY "SAN MINIATO ZODIAC" (AFTER GETTINGS).

TAURUS PONIATOVII   A constellation formed in 1777 by Poczobut of Wilna, named after the King of Poland, Poniatowski (hence sometimes it is the 'Polish Bull'). It is said to induce obstinacy, changeability, honour and renown. The constellation appears to have several earlier recognized forms - once it was part of the asterism called 'River Tigris', and once it was set out as a triangular figure.

TAYGETE   See PLEIADES.

T-CROSS   Another term used for the so-called COSMIC CROSS. See T-SQUARE.

TEBIT   See BABYLONIAN CALENDAR.

TELESCOPIUM   Constellation, the 'Telescope' or the 'Tubus Astronomicus', formed by La Caille between the constellations Ara and Sagittarius in 1752. It is said to give a keen mind and prophetic ability, along with an interest in history and the occult.

TELESCOPIUM HERSCHELLI   Constellation formed in 1781, in honour of the astronomer Herschel, but now obsolete.

TEMPERAMENT   The Grecian medical theory of HUMOURS which so radically influenced the development of early astrological theory was based on a fundamental tetrad which linked bodily fluids with certain mental dispositions, the so-called 'tempers' or temperaments. These temperaments were distinguished eventually as the CHOLERIC, MELANCHOLIC, PHLEGMATIC and SANGUINE, the etymologies for which are in each case derived from a corresponding Greek term for the humour. This tetrad of temperaments was linked to the tetrad of ELEMENTS (through the mediation of the so-called "Principles"), and was accordingly reflected in the structure of the zodiac, as indicated in the schema set out in table 81.

```
--------------------------------------------------------------TABLE 81
 TEMPERAMENT      ELEMENT         ZODIACAL SIGNS
=====================================================================
 Phlegmatic      Water           Cancer, Scorpio, Pisces
 Melancholic     Earth           Taurus, Virgo, Capricorn
 Choleric        Fire            Aries, Leo, Sagittarius
 Sanguine        Air             Gemini, Libra, Aquarius
---------------------------------------------------------------------
```

TEMPLUM   See ARA.

TEMPORAL CHART   See TOPOCENTRIC SYSTEM.

TEMPORAL HOUSES   A name applied to the 2nd, 6th and 10th houses. See also "Possessive Houses".

TEN CHAINS   See SCHEME OF EVOLUTION.

TENTH HEAVEN   Name given to the outer one of the SPHERES, which was regarded as being totally motionless. It was sometimes called the 'Empyrean', though this term (at least after the mediaeval period) was sometimes used of all the Spheres beyond the Lunar Sphere. In the early diagrammatic and literary accounts of the Spheres, there was no Tenth Sphere, no 'Tenth Heaven', the Ninth Sphere being the "Primum Mobile". Eventually however, perhaps for theological reasons, the Primum Movens was separated from the Ninth Heaven (at one time the 'Stellatum') to become a distinct sphere beyond it. The classification of the basic spheres (in the outer limits, at least) therefore depends upon context, and upon the period under review. The theological need for this outer shell, as a sort of final enclosing of the concentrics of the PTOLEMAIC SYSTEM, found its most perfect exposition in the 'Convivio' and 'Commedia' of Dante: it was regarded as the abode of God, to which all other

spheres 'aspired', their motion being a result of this aspiring love, to wish
to particpate in this 'ciel della divina pace' (heaven of divine peace).

TENTH HIERARCHY   The realm of man - the lowermost of the hierarchies (see
CELESTIAL HIERARCHIES).

TENTH HOUSE   The tenth of the astrological HOUSES, its cusp marking the
all-important Midheaven in many of the 'House Systems' (one exception being
that of the "Modus Equalis"). The tenth house is linked with Capricorn, and
has dominion over the status of the native, over the honours of his
professional life and career. It relates to the father of the native, and
was indeed referred to in early forms of astrology as the 'House of the
Father' at a time when the career was so often determined by the father as
fiat, or by the tendency to follow a family trade. In the melothesic man,
the house is connected with the knees and the skeletal system - with that
which lends structure to the human body. In Mundane Astrology it marks the
political controllers, eminent persons, the judge, president and chairmen, as
well as communal cultural ideas.

TENTH SPHERE   See TENTH HEAVEN.

TEREBELLUM   See TETRAPLEURON.

TERMINAL HOUSE   An unfortunate term used of the houses which correspond in
the basic horoscope figure to the WATER TRIPLICITY - that is to the 4th, 8th
and 12th houses. It would appear that they are so called because they each
govern the 'terminations' of certain human activities: the 4th is linked
with the end of the physical being of man; the 8th with death and
regeneration, and the 12th with the end and purpose of his personal life.

TERMINI   See TERMS.

TERMS   The planetary 'terms' consist of a series of zodiacal arcs to which
are assigned sub-ruling planets which are supposed to influence the nature of
these arcs.   These subdivisions, unlike those of the DECANS or the FACES,
are not of equal arc.   They appear now to be used only in Horary Astrology,
yet Ptolemy (who listed three different systems of such 'oria', often
translated into Latin as 'termini', and more accurately rendered into English
as 'boundaries') seems to have believed that they were valid also for Natal
Astrology. It must be observed, however, that Ptolemy was sceptical about
the terms: even so, he lists the arcs and rulerships for the EGYPTIAN TERMS
and for the CHALDEAN TERMS, and then reconstructs a further system, derived
from an old manuscript which had come into his possession, which might
conveniently be called PTOLEMAIC TERMS. Those astrologers who have at times
attempted to introduce their own tables of arc 'termini' - such as Wilson,
Sepharial and Alan Leo - show little agreement in either arcs or rulerships,
and the whole field is now extremely complex. One problem which has arisen
is the failure of astrologers to note that Ptolemy was writing about three
separate systems, and did not appear to be happy about any one.

TERNARY OF FIRE   A term derived from Boehme's esoteric astrology and linked
with his SEVEN PROPERTIES: it is the ternary of the first three principles
(Saturn, Mercury and Mars) which is a ternary harmonized by the Sun, and also
balanced against the "Ternary of Light", as set out in the schema below:

Saturn	Mercury	Mars	SUN	Venus	Jupiter	Moon
	Fire				Light	

The ternary of fire is sometimes called the 'ternary of desire', whilst the
ternary of light (VE, JU, MO) is sometimes called the 'ternary of love'.

TERNARY OF LIGHT   See TERNARY OF FIRE.

==

TERRABELLUM   See TETRAPLEURON.

TERRESTRIAL ECLIPTIC   A term coined to distinguish the orbit of the Moon, which marks the 'terrestrial ecliptic' from the 'celestial ecliptic', which is the ECLIPTIC proper.

TERRESTRIAL EQUATOR   The Great Circle of the Earth which is at every point equidistant from the two poles is called the 'Terrestrial Equator'.

TERRESTRIAL MERIDIAN   The standard modern 'Terrestrial Meridian' is the Great Circle passing through Greenwich and the poles.

TERRITORIAL SYSTEM   A method of HOUSE DIVISION based on the division of the Earth into twelve equal portions by lines passing through the poles of the Earth, linked with the ZENITH SYSTEM. Like the latter, the system was proposed by the astrologer Tucker.

TERTIARY METHOD   A term applied to a method of PROGRESSIONS involved with the projection of 'lunar returns' on to the radical chart. One system is based on adding a mean sidereal day to the birthday for every return of the Moon to its radical place, a tropical month being regarded as 27.3216 days. Another method equates the tropical year with the tropical month.

TESHRIT   See BABYLONIAN CALENDAR.

TESTIMONY   The English translation of Ptolemy's specialist use of the Greek 'marterion' (proof), a word which is cognate with our 'martyr'. Ptolemy was quite clearly using it as a synonym for ASPECT, or the act of projecting aspectal rays (see ACTINOBOLISM). However, the word has been misunderstood in modern times, and Devore defines the term as a 'partial judgment' or 'synthesis', which, within an astrological context, is quite inaccurate.

TETHYS   Name given to one of the moons of Saturn.

TETRABIBLOS   The short title given to the 'four books' of astrology ascribed to Ptolemy, consisting of a rationalized compendium of astrological lore which, even by the 2nd century of our era, was already old. The book is often called after its Latin title, the 'Quadripartium', though as Robbins says, it should more properly be called the 'Mathematical Treatise in Four Books', yet many manuscripts use the title (rarely the incipit) 'The Prognostics' address to Syrus'. It is one of the most influential of the ancient systematic treatises on astrology, and 'enjoyed almost the authority of the Bible among the astrological writers of a thousand years or more'. Many of the astrological terms and traditions still used in modern astrology have been derived from the 'Tetrabiblos', though a large number are now both misunderstood, misused and archaic. Not all the ideas and traditions ascribed to Ptolemy are found in the Tetrabiblos, or even in his other texts, mainly because the so-called 'Ptolemaic Astrology' is really an accretion of traditions established around his systematized geocentric cosmoconception. It is a regular occurrence for astrological writers to ascribe ideas to Ptolemy which he would scarcely have recognized, let alone promulgated.

TETRACTYS   A name given to a symbolic arrangement of ten points (see diagram over, page 323), which, whilst not originally of astrological import, has in one way or another been incorporated into astrological symbolism - especially so in regard to the astrological number-symbolism. Whilst the tetractys is usually traced back to the Pythagorean school, the best exoteric treatment of its symbolism is found in Philo Judaeus, who presents it as merely a matter of numerical sequence, as one of the 'numerical triangles', which have a significance mainly in regard to their corresponding 'numerical squares'. In the tables recorded by Agrippa at the end of the 15th century, 3 is the number of Saturn, 4 is the number of Jupiter, 6 is the number of the Sun, 9 is the number of Saturn and 16 the number of Jupiter. The 10 of the tetractys is not linked in a numerical way with the planets. However, this merely points to a much deeper level of numerical association, which lies at the very roots of astrological numbers. The learned Kircher shows that the tetractys is to be understood in regard to the cabbalistic numerology attached to the tetrad of the word IHVH (Jehovah), of which the corresponding numbers are given below:

.	1	H	=	10
. .	2	VH	=	15
. . .	3	HVH	=	21
. . . .	4	IHVH	=	26

The total by means of this association of numbers is 72 - the magical number of the tetractys, and one of the most pure of astrological symbolic numbers. This 'magical' 72 is linked with the pulse rate of the human blood (the microcosmic 72), and with the fact that in 72 years the Sun retrogrades in PRECESSION exactly one degree (the macrocosmic 72): Waschmuth has dealt with the number within a framework of modern occultism. As Blavatsky says, the tetractys 'has a very mystic and varied significance'. It is sometimes called the 'tetrad' or the 'mystic tetrad'.

TETRAGON   In a specialist sense, a term used as synonymous with SQUARE.

TETRAGONOUS   In a specialist (an archaic) sense, used as a synonym for 'Quartile' or 'relating to the square aspect'.

TETRAD   See both TETRACTYS and TETRAMORPH.

TETRAMORPH   A term derived from the Greek, meaning 'of a four-fold form', but in astrology applied to a composite figure which unites in a single form the images of the four fixed signs of the zodiac, themselves linked with the four elements. The so-called 'Christian' tetramorphs are not really tetramorphs at all, but four separate figures combining imagery related to the four fixed signs of the zodiac, and associated by Christian apologists with the imagery mentioned in the Bible under 'Revelations' (iv. 6-8) and 'Ezekiel' (i. 5-10), an imagery which is in any case derived from ancient pre-Christian astrological concepts, as Neuss has shown. The schema in table 82 sets out the traditional imagery of the Christian lore which has been associated with the genuine tetramorph:

---FIGURE 82

ATTRIBUTE	EVANGELIST	ELEMENT	ZODIACAL SIGN	ARCHANGEL	and SYMBOL
Human face	Matthew	Air	Aquarius	Raphael	Dragon
Lion head	Mark	Fire	Leo	Michael	Lion
Bull head	Luke	Earth	Taurus	Uriel	Bull
Eagle head, or wings	John	Water	Scorpio	Gabriel	Eagle

When this table of associations is linked with the tetramorph proper, then it is seen that the wings represent the Water element rather than the Air element (as might be imagined), since the wings are associated with the Eagle of Scorpio - the symbol of the regenerate Scorpionic nature - see EAGLE. An important change in symbolism was that linked with the adaptation of the image of the winged human water-bearer of Aquarius to symbolize Matthew, for the water urn was transformed into a book (both urn and book being bearers of spiritual energy, the latter linked with the Logos or word).

TETRAPLEURON   The name given by Ptolemy to an asterism in the form of a quadrangle in the hind quarters of the horse of constellation Sagittarius: Bayer gave the Greek in the meaningless Latin 'Terebellum'. The fixed star 'Terrabellum', the omega of the asterism, was said by Ptolemy to be of a nature similar to that of Venus with Saturn, the same as the asterism as a whole.

THEBAN CALENDAR   A name sometimes given to a system of DEGREE SYMBOLS attributed to the French occultist Christian. The system has not survived (though Sepharial claims that it was used by the occultist Levi). It is possible that the system has been confused with the readings of the DECANS (which have survived) that Christian derived mainly from the occultist Kircher: if this is the case they should properly be called 'Decan Symbols', and would have had quite a different application from degree symbols. On the other hand, the system may have been confused with his system of KEYS, which Christian derived from Firmicus, Junctinus and Pelusius.

THE GRAVE   A term sometimes used for the FOURTH HOUSE.

THEMA   In general use a synonym for CHART - really a 'theme of the Heavens'. Though no early definitions appear to be available, certain figures called 'themae' were actually schematic horoscopes or figures, as for example in the many 'themae mundi' (world charts) which were not so much horoscopes as schematic presentations of the heavens (often cosmically impossible) at the supposed beginnings of the world - in other words, the charts for 'creation'.

THIERENS-PLUTO   Name developed in comparatively recent times to distinguish the planet Pluto (also named 'Osiris') described by the esotericist Thierens from the several other Plutonic designations, such as PAGAN-PLUTO, PLUTO and WEMYSS-PLUTO. The Thierens-Pluto related to the future ETHERIC SPHERE.

THIRD HEAVEN   Usually this term is used synonymously with the Third Sphere in the concentrics of the spheres, which in the cosmoconception built around the PTOLEMAIC SYSTEM was the 'Sphere of Venus', associated in the Christian hierarchy with the ARCHAI. In the days when the sequence of the spheres was promulgated it was believed that Venus was nearer to the Sun than Mercury.

THIRD HIERARCHY   See CELESTIAL HIERARCHIES.

THIRD HOUSE   The third of the astrological HOUSES, linked with the nature of Gemini, and representing the communicative ability of the native, his mental outlook, as well as all blood ties (excluding parents).   It is the ruler of short journeys (in mediaeval astrology, journeys which might be made in less than one day) and was sometimes called the 'House of Short Journeys'.   It rules the lungs and arms in the melothesic man, and is often used as an index of the memory capability of the native. In Mundane Astrology it governs inland traffic, communications systems, public opinion and public relations. It was sometimes called the 'House of Brothers and Sisters' in connexion with the rule over 'blood ties'.

THIRD RAY   In the esoteric astrological system described by Bailey, the second of the SEVEN RAYS is called the 'Ray of Active-Intelligence', and is linked with the will to evolve, and with that which develops sensory perception into knowledge, knowledge into wisdom. This third ray is said to arise in Ursa Major, and is transmitted to our solar system by means of the zodiacal constellations (actually signs) Cancer, Libra and Capricorn, through their corresponding pairs of ORTHODOX PLANETS and ESOTERIC PLANETS according to the schema set out in table 83.

---TABLE 83

CONSTELLATION (SIGN)	ORTHODOX PLANET	ESOTERIC PLANET
Cancer	Moon	Neptune
Libra	Venus	Uranus
Capricorn	Saturn	Saturn

The entire third ray is linked with the sacred Saturn - see however SACRED
PLANETS. Distinguish from THIRD RAY TYPES.

THIRD RAY TYPES   The third of the SEVEN RAY TYPES, associated with the
planet Mercury. Distinguish from THIRD RAY.

THIRD ROOT RACE   In the Theosophical cosmoconception, the 'Third Root Race'
is the third of the seven 'human races' or streams of human evolution,
sometimes called the 'Lemurian Race', which was said to occupy the almost
completely lost continent of LEMURIA (or 'Shalmali', as it was sometimes
called), which covered approximately the present Pacific area.   During this
Root Race, the separation of humanity into the two sexes took place. Lemuria
is said to have perished before the beginning of the Eocene Age, and it was
the last sub-race of this epoch which is supposed to have left behind the
prototypes of the famous gigantic statues of Easter Island.

THIRD SPHERE   See THIRD HEAVEN.

THREE CROSSES   In her account of her INTUITIONAL ASTROLOGY, Bailey says that
the three crosses on the hill of Golgotha were biblical symbols of the three
'astrological crosses' - the CARDINAL CROSS, the FIXED CROSS and the MUTABLE
CROSS, each of which she linked with a specific Christology.

THREE DIMENSIONAL CHART   Something of a misnomer, a term applied to a method
of chart projection (figure 62) designed by Blunsdon to reveal planetary
latitudes and ecliptical longitudes in one single projection. The chart is
by no means 'three dimensional' (save in so far as all chart projections are
symbolic presentations of three-dimensionally conceived data) but
stereographic. The symbolic figure may be adapted to fit all the standard
methods of HOUSE DIVISION.

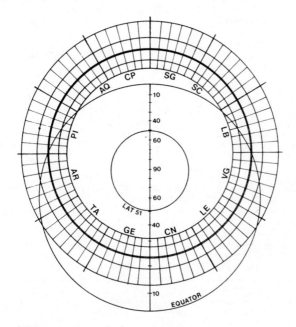

FIGURE 62. THE THREE-DIMENSIONAL CHART, OR STEREOGRAPHIC PROJECTION.
(AFTER BLUNSDON).

==

THREE PRINCIPLES   Essentially an alchemical doctrine (developed by
Paracelsus and Boehme) linked with the spiritual triad which, in the history
of occultism, is confronted with the spiritual septenary. The triad consists
of Mercury, Sulphur and Salt, and its relevance to astrology (beyond the mere
fact of the inter-relation of alchemy and astrology in many mediaeval texts)
is that the principle of Mercury relates to the occult and esoteric nature of
the planet. It is Mercury which unites these two polar opposites of Salt and
Sulphur: within the microcosm, Mercury represents the realm of emotions.
The emotional life of man reconciles the dark will-forces (Sulphur), and the
death-producing thought processes (Salt).

THREE PROTOTYPES   A term applied by Wachsmuth to denote the three typical
combinations in the world-clock, related to the zodiacal points (see PLATONIC
YEAR). Prototype 1 visualizes the (so-called) Cardinal Points in mutable
signs - for example, with Pisces marking the Vernal Point, and Gemini on the
Midheaven (figure 63A). This prototype marks 'historical epochs in which
important changes take place in man's relation to cosmic processes' along
with 'decisive turning points in the evolution of man'. In such periods, man
experiences himself as a 'cosmically orientated being', as a
'macro-anthropos'. Mankind lives at the present time within this prototype,
with Pisces on the Vernal Point, and is likely to remain in such a position
until about 2,500 AD.   Prototype 2 visualizes the Cardinal Points in fixed
signs, with (for example) Aquarius on the Vernal Point and Taurus on the
Midheaven (figure 63B). During such periods differentiation of soul and body
set it: experience is preserved in myths and images. This phase has been
described as 'cosmo-psychic'. Prototype 3 visualizes the Cardinal Points in
the Cardinal Signs, with (for example) Capricorn marking the Vernal Point,
and Aries on the Midheaven (figure 63C). In such periods, the evolution
tends towards the application of experiences to earthly activities: man
becomes to some extent independent of the cosmos. This phase has been called
the 'Geo-sophic', and within its ambient abstract thinking reaches its zenith
of activity. The system of Three Prototypes helps to present a simplified
yet cogent view of historical epochs.

FIGURE 63. THE THREE PROTOTYPES: A. THE 'MACRO-ANTHROPOS': B. THE
'COSMO-PSYCHIC': C. THE GEO-SOPHIC. (AFTER WACHSMUTH).

THRONE   A term derived from Ptolemaic astrology but widely misunderstood and
misapplied, mainly because Ptolemy was far from clear about its definition.
Fortunately, it is known that the same term was used in earlier texts than
the "Tetrabiblos" as the equivalent of EXALTATION (the corresponding Fall
being termed a 'prison', a pictorial polarity of the royal 'throne'). This

===

appears to be far from the original Ptolemaic idea, but it was used in this
sense in several mediaeval sources. A synonym appears to be 'Chariot'.
Since post-mediaeval times, some astrologers have used the term 'throne' as
being synonymous with 'rulership', so that a planet in its own throne is a
planet placed in its own sign: thus, the Sun in its throne is Sun in Leo.
This use of the term is reflected in the many late-mediaeval images of the
planetary gods presented in horse-drawn or dragon-drawn thrones, the related
signs often depicted on the wheels of the chariots.

THRONES   The third in descending order of the Celestial Hierarchy, so named
by Dionysius the Areopagite. The Thrones, sometimes called the 'Throni', the
'Troni' or the 'Seats', are the rulers over the Sphere of Saturn, and are
said by occultists to have responsibility for the flow of time itself. Their
appearance, unlike that of the celestial beings above them in rank (the
"Seraphim" and the "Cherubim"), has received scant attention: they are often
symbolized in Christian art by the attribute of a pair of scales (signs of
their role in divine justice), and whilst they have six wings (like those of
higher rank), they often are distinguished by a yellow stone - perhaps a
topaz - on their breasts. The Thrones are sometimes called the 'Lords of
Will' in modern esotericism.

THURAYYA   'Al Thurayya', the name given to the 1st of the Arabian MANZILS.

THURENE   See HYADES.

TIBETAN ASTROLOGY   In western use, a misnomer for the esoteric astrological
system proposed by Bailey, termed by her INTUITIONAL ASTROLOGY.

TIME A horoscope is usually cast from an accurate birth time, which
generally requires some conversion from the given local clock time, to relate
it to local sidereal time. That simple-sounding statement requires
considerable amplification, however, as in relation to astrological
practices, several definitions of time measurement are relevant. "Solar
Time" is time measured in relation to the Sun - the "Apparent Solar Day" is
the interval between two successive transits of the Sun - either of Midheaven
or Imum Coeli. "True Local Time" (abb. TLT) is the apparent Solar Time (i.e.,
that recorded by sundials): while not used in modern astrology, TLT is often
the basis for many pre-19th century horoscopes. "Mean Solar Time" (which is
ordinary "Clock Time") is a compensatory measurement, based on the "Mean
Solar Day". "Local Mean Time" (abb. LMT) is the mean Solar Time for any
given locality - the local variations (not measured by Clock Time) involve a
difference of four minutes for each degree of Terrestrial Longitude, which is
one hour for every 15 degrees. "Greenwich Mean Time" (abb. GMT) is the Local
Mean Time at Greenwich, England, which is on the zero line of longitude.
"Universal Time" is really 'Earth orbital time', the LMT expressed in 24 hour
notation. "Sidereal Time" is time measured according to the stars (Latin
gen. "Sideris"), the axial rotation of the earth being measured by a stellar
fiducial. A complete rotation of the earth is the "Local Sidereal Day" (abb.
LSD) - the interval of two succesive transits of a fiducial over the meridian
of a place. The LSD is said to begin when the zero point of Aries transits
the midheaven of a given locality. "Greenwich Sidereal Time" (abb. GST) is
the Local Sidereal Time at Greenwich. The difference between Sidereal Time
(ST) and Solar Time is important in chart computation. The Sidereal Day is
23 hours, 56 minutes and 4.09 seconds of Mean Solar Time. This difference is
shown in the EPHEMERIS as an increase of (approximately) 3 minutes and 56
seconds of GST for each day, and is accounted for in astrological chart
computation. "Time Acceleration" is a term used in chart calculation to
denote the difference between Sidereal Time and Mean Solar Time which has
elapsed since the GST given in the ephemeris. Such conversion is required to
convert GST to LST - the time space is fractional - in the region of 10
seconds for each hour of elapsed mean solar time. "Ephemeris Time" (abb. ET)
is Universal Time, with the addition of a (gravitational) variation so small
as to be insignificant in relation to ordinary chart computation - a list of

reductions from 1621 to 1974 is provided in the Hieratic Ephemeris, but most modern ephemerides give contemporaneous ET. Some modern Ephemerides now list the positions of planets at midnight ET. "Standard Time", (sometimes called ZONE TIME) was introduced at the end of the last century to regularize times throughout the civilised world. Towards this end, every 15 degrees of terrestrial longitude (East or West of Greenwich) was regarded as a "Standard Time Meridian", but this theoretical structure was not always adhered to, as the TIME ZONES in table 84 below indicate. "Daylight Saving Time" (abb DST), "Summer Time" and "War Time" (abb. WT) were in used during summer months in wartime and during energy crises. It is not possible to provide a simple tabulation of the complex effect this has had on determining Local Time, but in general, when DST was in operation clocks were advanced in some places half an hour, in other places and other times one hour, and (during World War II) two hours of advance gave "Double Summer Time". The rules for CHART COMPUTATION allow for such DST, provided it is known for the year in question. A good easy reference is "Whittaker's Almanac", though Brau gives a useful table of DST and WT periods in the English-speaking world, with all major variations up to 1980..

TIME DIFFERENCES See TIME ZONES

TIME ZONES For the sake of unity, in the 19th century a system of "Standard Time Meridians" or Time Zones was established, in which all clocks were set to the same local Time Zone, which in theory was centred on a Meridian which determined a Local Mean Time as standard (see TIME). To cast a horoscope for births outside the British Time Zone (centred on Greenwich) it is necessary to know the factors conditioning time in the given Time Zone, to which end a number of tables (as in table 84 below) have been provided. One of the great difficulties experienced by astrologers who regularly cast charts for foreign births is that of establishing the precise Greenwich Mean Time (and hence the Sidereal Time) from the Local Time given in accordance with localities and Time Zones. This difficulty arises because, for all the apparently simple listings given by the popular astrological textbooks, precision is not easily arrived at in view of territorial changes, which take place over comparatively short periods of time. The Preface to the useful list drawn up by Dernay in 1948 points to some of the difficulties in attempting reliable conversion. Dernay has provided an alphabetical list (now somewhat out of date) which has formed the basis for many other abridged lists in popular astrological books: such abridged lists are sometimes misleading, and may result in inaccurate charting. It is therefore perhaps unwise for an astrologer to rely too heavily on such tables (for unfamiliar locations) without checking the chart by means of a reliable method of rectification. The Time Zones most frequently given in astrological sources, with the correction factors for variation from Standard Time, are given in table 84.

---TABLE 84.

Aden Time	see below
Atlantic Standard Time	minus 4 hours
Azores Standard Time	minus 2 hours
Baghdad Time	minus 3 hours
Brazil Standard Time	minus 3 hours
Central Alaska Time	minus 10 hours
Central European Time	plus 1 hour
Central Standard Time	minus 6 hours
China Coast Time	plus 8 hours
Eastern European Time	plus 2 hours
Eastern Standard Time	minus 5 hours
Guam Standard Time	plus 10 hours
Hawaiian Standard Time	minus 10 and half hours
Indian Standard Time	plus 5 and half hours
International Date Line East	plus 12 hours
International Date Line West	minus 12 hours
Japan Standard Time	plus 9 hours

```
----------------------------------------------------------TABLE 84 (continued)
```

Java Time	plus 7 and half hours
Middle Europe Time	plus 1 hour
Mountain Standard Time	minus 7 hours
Newfoundland Standard Time	plus 3 and half hours
New Zealand Time	plus 11 and half hours
Nome Standard Time	minus 7 hours
North Sumatra Standard Time	plus 6 and half hours
Pacific Standard Time	minus 8 hours
South Australia Standard Time	plus 9 and half hours
South Sumatra Time	plus 7 hours
West Africa Time	plus 1 hour
Yukon Standard Time	minus 9 hours

During the British Protectorate, Aden Time was plus 2 hours, 29 minutes and
54 seconds. The USSR has been divided in 11 Time Zones according to
longitude, as set out in table 85.

```
-----------------------------------------------------------------TABLE 85
```

ZONE	LONGITUDINAL BAND		TIME FACTOR
1	20.30	37.30	minus 2 hours
2	37.30	52.30	minus 3 hours
3	52.30	67.30	minus 4 hours
4	67.30	82.30	minus 5 hours
5	82.30	97.30	minus 6 hours
6	97.30	112.30	minus 7 hours
7	112.30	127.30	minus 8 hours
8	127.30	142.30	minus 9 hours
9	142 30	157.30	minus 10 hours
10	157.30	172.30	minus 11 hours
11	172.30	and eastwards	minus 12 hours

The abbreviations used in connexion with the above lists have not been
standardized, but the following are frequently used:

A	Atlantic	J	Japanese	So	South
B	Baghdad	M	Mountain	Su	Sumatra
C	Central	N	North	T	Time
E	Eastern	S	Standard	W	Western
Eu	European				

Thus, C.Eu.T. is "Central European Time". Brau gives an up to date system of
Standard Time Meridians, with indications of major changes, variations and
confusions, up to 1980.

TIRIEL   Name given by Agrippa (quoting ancient cabbalistic sources) to the
"Intelligency" of Mercury. He gives the magical number of Tiriel as 260,
which is the linear sum of the MAGIC SQUARE of Mercury.

TITAN   Name given to the brightest of Saturn's moons.

TITANIA   Name given to one of the satellites of Uranus.

TONUS   Ratio connected with the planetary system set out in the theory of
the MUSIC OF THE SPHERES, and depending upon the supposed planetary
distances. It was called also the 'sesquioctave', the 'eighth'. In the
planetary diagrams this ratio is the equivalent of the distance of the Sphere
of the Moon and the Sphere of Mars (considered separately), each of which is
the ratio of an eighth of the whole series.

==

TOPOCENTRIC ASCENSIONAL TRANSITS   Mundane transits of ascension, in
connexion with (presumably) any of the charts derived from the TOPOCENTRIC
SYSTEM, correlating events with transits within an orb of one minute of time.
The literature on topocentric astrology is sometimes confusing, but it seems
that the topocentric ascensional transits involve the transits of planets,
nodal points or even house cusps, when the chart projection has been adapted
to the place of event: conjunctions, oppositions, antiscions and
contrascions are valid. A development of this particular form of predictive
astrology is the so-called PARAN. According to Dean, calculations have shown
that allowing an orb of 1 degree, at least 4 parans are present for 91% of
the time, which throws some doubt on the utility, if not the validity, of the
topocentric ascensional transit theory 'discovered' by Polich and Page.

TOPOCENTRIC ASTROLOGY   See TOPOCENTRIC SYSTEM.

TOPOCENTRIC HOUSE SYSTEM   A system of HOUSE DIVISION proposed by Polich and
Page for computing cusps for any place on earth - a system which is said to
have been derived from experience, and by the projection of known effects on
to chart schemas. In the 'topocentric' system the polar axis, which passes
through the place (the Greek 'topos') under astrological considerations is
regarded as the fixed point of reference. Rotation of the geocentric horizon
around this axis produces what is called a 'cone of rotation'. It is this
cone which is the basis upon which measurements are made in order to
determine the house cusps: hence the houses are determined by the natural
rotation of the geocentric horizon around the topocentric axis. The entire
system is actually obscure, and leaves many questions unanswered: it is
further complicated by the form in which it has been publicized. However,
standard reference Tables of Houses are available. See also TOPOCENTRIC SYSTEM.

TOPOCENTRIC SYSTEM   The term 'topocentric system' should properly be applied
to the method of chart origination and interpretation proposed by Polich and
Page, but is often used specifically (though wrongly) of the TOPOCENTRIC
HOUSE SYSTEM, upon which their methods partly depend. A good synopsis of the
entire system has been offered by Love, though the literature dealing with
topocentric astrology is curiously obscure. The topocentric astrologer is
ultimately furnished with six charts for interpretation and progression -
this points to a complexity of approach which is scacely necessary in any of
the traditional systems. Five of the charts used are derived from the
'tropical radical' chart, the 'ordinary familiar chart' of astrology, which
is however regarded as relating to the 'inner life' of the native, the
aspects acting in an interiorizing manner. From this is derived the
so-called 'topocentric mundane chart', which is held to relate to the outer
events arising from the preceding chart. Follows a 'fixed radical chart',
involving interpersonal relationships and 'destiny', to which is related the
derived 'mundane radical fixed chart' which is presumably related to events
in connexion with interpersonal relationships. These last two charts, as
their names suggest, are derived from the constellational zodiac. A (more
obscure) 'temporal chart' is concerned with suprapersonal relationships, such
as births and deaths: from this is derived the 'mundane temporal chart'.
The co-ordinate for the chart series is the Medium Coeli, which of course
presumes an accurate radical chart.

TOPOI   See LOCI.

TORCH   See ALDEBARAN.

TOTAL ECLIPSE   See UMBRAL ECLIPSE.

TOUCAN   Constellation to the south of the asterism Phoenix, almost touching
Octans, said to have been originated by Bayer in 1604, though sometimes later
called 'Anser Americanus' and even 'American Gans'. Robson says that it
gives pride with kindness.

===

TOXOTES   One of the Greek names, meaning 'archer', for the zodiacal sign and
constellation Sagittarius - it is the term used by Ptolemy.

TRABS   Name given to the 20th of the lunar MANSIONS in certain mediaeval
lists.   Probably visualized between delta (Kaus Medius) and sigma (Nunki) of
constellation Sagittarius.

TRANSITOR   The term is sometimes used in a general sense of any planet which
is transiting another planet or nodal point, though in a specialist sense it
is used of one of the major planets, the aspectal influence of which is slow.

TRANSITS   Originally this term was used in astrological circles with only
its Latin etymology in mind: the word is from the Latin 'trans-ire' (to go
across) and was applied to the crossing of any planet over any other planet,
over any nodal point, or over any place in a horoscope (or, for that matter,
in the heavens). The word may still be used in this sense. However, as the
specialist techniques of astrological prediction were developed, that branch
which was concerned with the study of the actual transits of planets over
emphatic points in a radical chart was itself called 'transits'. The word
used in this sense applies therefore to one of the subdivisions of the art of
DIRECTIONS. Unlike such predictive techniques as SECONDARY DIRECTIONS, the
study of transits is not involved with symbolic directing, using symbolic
time co-ordinates. Instead, the actual effets of planets in the stellar
spheres - in what the ancients called the ambient - during the period under
study is related to the radical chart in a non-symbolic way. Practically
this means that if an astrologer wishes to establish by means of transits the
influences playing on the life of someone born in say 1937 in the 50th life
of that person, then he will study the transits over the radical chart of
1937 which occur in the year 1987. In his excellent and influential work on
progressions and transits, the modern astrologer Davison says that those who
do combine the methods of Secondary Directions with the methods of Transits
usually regard the former as arising out of the radical chart, and the latter
as having some external force, being representative of the general conditions
of the outside world.   He maintains, however, that transits are as integral
a part of the techniques of progressions as directions of a primary and
secondary kind.

TRANSLATION   In a specialist sense, the transference of influence from a
transitting planet which occurs when it separates from aspects and casts its
rays to form another aspect with a different planet. This is sometimes
called the 'translation of light', though (unless the Sun is involved) no
light may really be said to be involved.

TRANSPLUTO   Name given to one of the HYPOTHETICAL PLANETS by the astrologer
Landscheidt. An ephemeris for the period from 1878-1987 has been made
available by the Ebertin-Verlag.

TREDECILE   Another name for the TRESILE.

TREPIDATION   A name used to denote a theory used by Arabian astrologers to
account for PRECESSION. Instead of the regression of the Vernal Point being
visualized as a steady progression, it was seen as an oscillation (or
'trepidation') around an arc of 7 degrees. This movement was incorporated
into the PTOLEMAIC SYSTEM (circa 950 AD) and was said to be communicated from
the Ninth Sphere (in some systems from the Eighth). The theory, derived from
Albumasar, gave a precessional rate of 7 degrees in 900 years.

TRESILE   An ASPECT defined by Simmonite as being derived from a 'quintile
and a half', or 3 signs and 18 degrees (108 degrees). See also QUINTILES.

TRETA YUGA   Sometimes the 'Trita Yuga', the 'Silver Age' of the Hindu
chronology, a periodicity of 1,296,000 years. See however YUGA. The period
given includes the 'twilights' or sandhya and sandhyansa.

TRIANGULUM   Constellation, 'the Triangle', located south of Andromeda, on the edge of the Milky Way, and said by Allen to be one of the most ancient of the constellations. The connexion with the Greek letter 'delta' (itself a triangle) gave the name 'Deltoton', and an inevitable association with the delta of the Nile, with the names 'Aegyptus', 'Nilus' and even 'Nili Donum' (Gift of the Nile). Other derivatives are from the Greek 'trigonon' used even by Hipparchus - 'Trigonum', 'Trigonus' and (confusingly) 'Trigon'. The Arabic 'Al Muthallath' gave rise to a plethora of mediaeval degenerate forms, including 'Almutraleh', 'Mutlat' and 'Mutlatun', etc. Ptolemy said that the stars in the asterism were of a similar influence to Mercury.

TRIANGULUM AUSTRALE   See SOUTHERN TRIANGLE.

TRIANGULUM MINOR   Constellation, the 'Lesser Triangle' formed by Helvelius alongside the major TRIANGULUM. It is now obsolete.

TRIBES OF ISRAEL   Among the several dodecanary lists of zodiacal attributes is that termed the 'Twelve Tribes' or the 'Twelve Children of Israel', which consists of an attempt (by Biblical exegesis) to relate the biblical twelve to the zodiacal twelve. There are many such lists within the astrological (and theological) traditions, but the five listed in table 86 are culled from the sources given under the headings (see bibliography). This table should at least establish that no single list is really 'definitive'.

---TABLE 86

SIGN	BUTLER	SEPHARIAL	THIERENS	LIBRA	JEREMIAS	DURANDUS
AR	Gad	Benjamin	Issachar	Gad	Naphtali	Naphtali
TA	Asher	Reuben	Zabulon	Ephraim	Joseph	Issachar
GE	Issachar	Simeon	Joseph	Benjamin	Simeon/Levi	Simeon/Levi
CN	Zebulon	Levi	Benjamin	Issachar	Issachar	Benjamin
LE	Joseph	Judah	Judah	Judah	Judah	Judah
VG	Benjamin	Zebulon	Reubon	Naphtali	Dinah	Dinah
LB	Reuben	Issachar	Gad	Asher	Dan	Asher
SC	Simeon	Dan	Ascher	Dan	Benjamin	Dan
SG	Levi	Gad	Naphtali	Manasseh	Gad	Joseph
CP	Judah	Asher	Manasseh	Zebulon	Zebulon	Gad
AQ	Dan	Naphtali	Simeon	Reuben	Reuben	Reuben
PI	Naphtali	Joseph	Levi	Simeon	Asher	Zebulon

Only the list of Sepharial follows the order of the childen given in the blessing (see Genesis xlix), with Taurus as the leader of the twelve, according to the ancient esoteric system (see for example ALDEBARAN). The church-historian Durandus, who transmits one of the earliest lists, gives the order of the twelve sons named by Jacob and then attached to these a rationale which was supposed to follow the relationship of signs.

TRIDENT   In a specialist sense, one of the modern additions to the series of Arabian PARS, the 'Part of Neptune', sometimes called the 'Point of Treachery'. If a chart is revolved so that the degree occupied by the Sun is transferred to the Ascendant, then the position of Neptune in this new arrangement will mark the Trident within the houses.   No doubt the term was originated from the supposed graphic origin of the sigil for Neptune: see SIGILS - PLANETS.

TRIGON   A term (now almost obsolete) used to denote the group of three signs linked with the same element: it is therefore the equivalent of 'triplicity'. It is sometimes used (almost archaically) to denote a TRINE aspect. For a peculiarly modern use, see also SIDEREAL MOON RHYTHM.

TRIGONOCRATORS   A term derived from the Greek, meaning 'rulers of trigons',and relating to a doctrine set out by Ptolemy which accords a planetary rule over the groups of TRIPLICITIES, as set out in table 87.

--TABLE 87

TRIPLICITY	SIGNS	PLANET BY DAY	PLANET BY NIGHT
Fire	AR LE SG	Sun	Jupiter
Earth	TA VG CP	Venus	Moon
Air	GE LB AQ	Saturn	Mercury
Water	CN SC PI	Venus*	Moon*

* The water triplicity is accorded the single rule of 'Negative Mars', but with the two co-rulers indicated above.

Unfortunately, some modern astrologers have misunderstood the idea behind the trigonocrators, and have proposed new rulerships which merely accord planetary rule over the individual zodiacal signs rather than over their elemental natures. However, the whole question of trigonocrators is involved with astrological notions which are largely archaic, and have little application to modern practice. It is clear from the "Tetrabiblos" that the concept is bound up with the 'airesis' theory to which the ancients were partial (see SECTA), but which plays no significant part in modern astrology.

TRIGONUM   See TRIANGULUM.

TRIMORIAN   A term usually applied to the 'distance of three signs', and wrongly given as a synonym for the square ASPECT.

TRINE   An ASPECT maintained by two or more planets so placed that they are separated by one third of the zodiac, which is to say by an arc of 120 degrees. This aspect is regarded as being wholly beneficial, and is sometimes called 'the aspect of good fortune'. The amount of ORB permitted is far from agreed among authorities, but some allow as much as 7 degrees.

TRINITY OF ASSOCIATION   See RELATIVE HOUSES.

TRINITY OF PSYCHISM   See PSYCHIC HOUSES.

TRINITY OF WEALTH   See POSSESSIVE HOUSES.

TRIONES   One of the several important variant names for URSA MAJOR.

TRIPLE SUN   A term derived from esoteric astrology, and intended to denote the occult maxim that the visible Sun is only the veil for two other suns, one called by Bailey 'heart of the Sun', and the other 'central spiritual Sun'. See also ESOTERIC SUN.

TRI-SEPTILE   An aspect of 154.3 degrees, arising from the multiple of the SEPTILE by 3, and used in the theory of HARMONICS.

TRITA YUGA   See TRETA YUGA.

TRITHEMIAN PERIODS   See SECUNDADEIAN BEINGS.

TRITON   Name given to the satellite of Neptune.

TRONI   See THRONES.

TROPICAL RADICAL   See TOPOCENTRIC SYSTEM.

TROPICAL SIGNS   Since Cancer and Capricorn mark the solstitial points, these are sometimes called the 'tropical signs'.

TROPICAL YEAR   A more precise term for the 'Solar Year', marking the

==

succedent transits of the centre of the Sun over the Vernal Point, a period
slightly shorter than the SIDEREAL YEAR. The tropical year is a period of
365 days, 5 hours, 48 minutes and 4.5 seconds.

TRUE SOLAR DAY   The length of time taken for the Earth to rotate on its axis
once in relation to the Sun - a periodicity different from that of the
SIDEREAL DAY. Astrologers who require day-equivalent periods for
progressions regard the True Solar Day as the most symbolically appropriate
for the 'Day for a Year' system of predictive symbolism. See TIME.

TRULLI SYMBOLS In the Puglia region of Italy, centred around the town of
Alberobello, are a number of conically-roofed houses, locally called
"trulli". Many of these have painted upon their roofs a variety of Christian
and occult symbols, several of which are astrological: the origin of this
practice is unknown, but the use of standard symbols for the modern planets,
such as Neptune and Pluto, indicates that whatever the antiquity of the
custom, new symbols are added from time to time. A recent survey has been
conducted by Goodman.

TRUTINE OF HERMES   This is a dictum attributed to the mythical Hermes
Trismegistus - 'the place of the Moon at conception was the ascendant of the
birth figure or its opposite point'. No mention of this trutine appears in
the extensive genuine trismegistic literature, and indeed the sentiment
expressed within it removes it from that type of literature: certain
Trismegistian ideas may be confused with this 'trutine', however, because of
the occult connexion between the Moon sphere and the descent into matter
(reincarnation) which is explicit in this literature. The idea does not
appear to go back beyond late mediaeval astrological speculation, though it
is perhaps Arabian in origin. Though it is often seriously quoted even in
modern astrological textbooks - especially in texts dealing with the PRENATAL
EPOCH - the trutine really belongs to the substratum of mythology of
astrology, for it enunciates a principle which is not susceptible to
verification by ordinary means. Curiously, the ANIMODER is sometimes also
linked with this concept, even though it was originally a method of
rectification unrelated to the idea of conception (which in any case, within
the framework of the Gnostic and Trismegistian literature involved a gradual
descent through the spheres, in which conception was merely a late stage).

T-SQUARE One of the aspectal patterns (see MAJOR CONFIGURATION) in which two
planets are in Opposition, with a third at their Midpoint: the resultant
pattern is in the form of a simple T. This formation is also called a
"T-Cross" - which is perhaps a more accurate designation - though this term
is also applied to two pairs of oppositions with axes in square with each
other. Since the T-Square pattern combines the restless nature of the Square
with the awareness of Opposition, it is an indication of a powerful surge of
energies: the Midpoint planet is usually the significator of the focal point
of these energies.

TUAL   In certain methods of ceremonial magic, Tual is named as the Governor
of the zodiacal sign Taurus.

TUBUS ASTRONOMICUS   See TELESCOPIUM.

TULA   The Sanskrit name for zodiacal Libra: but see also CITRA. Sometimes
the word is given in European texts as 'Tulam'.

TULAM   See TULA.

TWELFTH HOUSE   The twelfth of the astrological HOUSES, linked with the
nature of Pisces, and associated with the struggle of the individual against
the limits imposed upon him by the forms of society: it is also linked with
the powers of guilt, which always call for regeneration and rebirth. Devore
calls it the 'House of the Hangover', which corresponds approximately with

==

the traditional term 'House of One's Own Undoing'. The release from guilt
often necessitates self-sacrifice, not as a negation of self, but as a
catharsis, and such properly belongs to the realm of this house. This would
perhaps help explain the old name 'House of Bondage', which refers to
self-imposed bondage, directed from what we would now call the subconscious
levels, but which the mediaeval astrologers would link with the spiritual
impetus of Jupiter, the ancient ruler of Pisces. The twelfth is really the
house in which secret aspirations are often frustrated, or must be resolved.

TWELVE CELL-SALTS   The twelve cell-salts described and developed for medical
purposes by the homoeopathist Schuessler have been linked with the
physio-chemical and psychological allocations of the twelve signs of the
zodiac. The correspondences drawn by Carey are:

AR	Kali Phos	(Potassium Phosphate)
TA	Nat Sulph	(Sulphate of Sodium)
GE	Kali Mur	(Chloride of Potassium)
CN	Calc Fluor	(Fluoride of Lime)
LE	Mag Phos	(Phosphate of Magnesium)
VG	Kali Sulph	(Sulphate of Potassium)
LB	Nat Phos	(Sodium Phosphate)
SC	Calc Sulph	(Lime Sulphate)
SG	Silica	
CP	Calc Phos	(Lime Phosphate)
AQ	Nat Mur	(Sodium Choloride)
PI	Ferrum Phos	(Iron Phosphate)

TWELVE CREATIVE HIERARCHIES   According to esoteric astrological lore, the
twelve creative hierarchies are spiritual beings who participate, or have
participated, in the cosmogenesis of our planetary system. Each rank of
hierarchy has been linked with one of the twelve signs of the zodiac (see the
CELESTIAL HIERARCHIES, who have been linked with the planetary spheres). The
first two are not named, though linked with Aries and Taurus - the
esotericist Heindel, who has most of his learning from Steiner, says that
they 'have passed beyond the ken of anyone on Earth'. Gemini is linked with
the SERAPHIM, who oversaw the creative phase of the MOON PERIOD. Cancer is
linked with the CHERUBIM, who oversaw the creative phase of the SUN PERIOD.
Leo is linked with the group of exalted beings known in esotericism as LORDS
OF FLAME, who oversaw the creative phase of the SATURN PERIOD, which
inaugurated the cosmogenesis of our present system. The remaining seven
hierarchies are called the LORDS OF WISDOM, LORDS OF INDIVIDUALITY, LORDS OF
FORM, LORDS OF MIND, the ARCHANGELS, the ANGELS and the VIRGIN SPIRITS. With
the exception of the latter (which is the esoteric name for Mankind), these
hierarchies have also been linked with the spheres.

TWELVE HOUSES   See HOUSES and HOUSE SYSTEMS. For specific houses, see
FIRST HOUSE, which is of the same nature as the all-important "Ascendant
Degree", and which relates to selfhood: SECOND HOUSE, which deals with
finance and support: THIRD HOUSE, which deals with travel and kindred:
FOURTH HOUSE, which deals with parentage and beginnings: FIFTH HOUSE, which
deals with creativity and offspring: SIXTH HOUSE, which deals with service
to others and health: SEVENTH HOUSE, which deals with marriage and
partnerships: EIGHTH HOUSE, which deals with matters pertaining to
regeneration and death: NINTH HOUSE, which deals with distant journeys and
philosophical considerations: TENTH HOUSE, which deals with reputation and
profession: ELEVENTH HOUSE, which deals with social aspirations and
friendships, and TWELFTH HOUSE, which deals with mystical elements in the
life of the native.

TWELVE PHILOSOPHIC TENDENCIES   In a series of lectures translated under the
title 'Human and Cosmic Thought', the occultist Steiner developed a schema
which links what he called the 'twelve different shades of philosophic
outlook' with the zodiacal signs (or constellations):

AR	Idealism	TA	Rationalism	GE	Mathematicism
CN	Materialism	LE	Sensualism	VG	Phenomenalism
LB	Realism	SC	Dynamism	SG	Monadism
CP	Spiritualism	AQ	Pneumatism	PI	Psychism

Steiner distinguished the seven philosophic moods in terms of the seven planets - see therefore SEVEN MOODS.

TWELVE PLACES   The 'Twelve Places of Manilius' consists of a long-archaic system of 'significant degrees' derived from a dodecanary division of the ecliptic into 30 degree arcs, commencing at the PART OF FORTUNE. In order of zodiacal arc, these are given as:

1. Fortune and property - including slaves
2. Military affairs and voyages
3. Civil affairs and public business
4. Legal and judicial matters
5. Marriage and social life
6. Acquired wealth
7. Dangers
8. Nobility and reputation
9. Rearing of children
10. Authority
11. Health and sickness
12. Fulfilment of vows

The 'Twelve Places' are sometimes called the 'Twelve Sortes', but see also SORTES.

TWELVE PLACES OF MANILIUS   See TWELVE PLACES.

TWELVE SIGNS   See ZODIAC.

TWELVE SORTES   See TWELVE PLACES.

TWELVE SPIRITUAL BEINGS   See TWELVE CREATIVE HIERARCHIES.

TWELVE TRIBES   See TRIBES OF ISRAEL.

TWO STARS   A term sometimes used of the ancient symbol for the Dioscuri, or for the symbolic representation of Gemini, and probably originating in the astrological symbolism of certain ancient Roman coins. Two such symbolic stars are placed alongside constellation Pegasus in the VICENZA CYCLE, and these are known to have been derived from the coinage of Hadrian. In addition to connoting the standard dualistic symbolism proper to Gemini, the two stars (as Ballarin suggests) reflect the ancient duality of the 'day-life'and 'night-death', which is the main theme of the Vicenza constellational fresco.

TYCHO'S STAR   A misnomer for a NOVA popularly supposed to have been discovered by the astronomer-astrologer Tycho Brahe in 1572 (see CONSTELLATIONS). Tycho did not discover the Nova, since it was noted by many astronomers before him - probably for the first time by Schuler at Wittenburg. It was called 'New Venus' by Cornelius Gemma at least two days before Tycho actually saw it. Some astrologers regarded it as a reappearance of the "Star of Bethlehem", and inevitably predictions were soon broadcast of a Second Coming. In terms of astrology, however, it is unlikely that any other single phenomenon changed the ancient cosmoconception as profoundly as this nova, since until then it was deemed axiomatic that the supra-lunar spheres were immutable, as Aristotle had proclaimed. The nova exploded the Ptolemaic cosmoconception even more profoundly than did Copernicus.

UMBRAL ECLIPSE   The Moon is said to be in 'umbral eclipse' when it is in any way touched by the shadow of the Earth (the Latin 'umbra' means 'shadow'). The umbral eclipse becomes a 'total eclipse' when the orb of the Moon is completely swathed in the shadow of the Earth. See ECLIPSE.

UMBRIEL   Name given to one of the satellites of Uranus.

UNASPECTED PLANETS   In a specialist sense, these are planets which receive no MAJOR ASPECTS. Some astrologers maintain that an unaspected planet is an indication of 'lack of integration' of the quality represented by that planet. Other astrologers ignore the supposed influence altogether. The Australian astrologer Dean made a special study of unaspected planets, however, and suggests that such are usually inducive of a strong planetary influence, which is not always well integrated into the life of the native. If a wide orb is allowed for the major aspects, then unaspected planets are quite rare. Some astrologers maintain that planets unaspected by the major aspects are all the more susceptible to the influences of the MINOR ASPECTS.

UNDER THE SUNBEAMS   A term used to denote that a planet is within a 17 degree orb of the Sun, which is regarded by some astrologers as a debility.

UNDINES   The class of ELEMENTALS linked with Water: in the mediaeval tradition they are often called 'nympha'.

UNFORTUNATE   A term used of the signs Taurus, Cancer, Virgo, Scorpio, Capricorn and Pisces - the 'negative' signs.

UNFRIENDLY PLANETS   This is a term derived from the idea of SYMPATHY. The Sun is 'unfriendly' only to Saturn, according to some authorities, yet really the Sun is benign to all planets. The Moon is 'unfriendly' to Mars and Saturn. Venus is 'unfriendly' to Saturn. Mars is 'unfriendly' to all planets with the exception of Venus. Jupiter is 'unfriendly' to Mars. Saturn is 'unfriendly' to all save Mercury and Jupiter. See also SYMPATHY.

UNICORN   Name applied (though rarely) to Capricorn. See also MONOCEROS.

UNORTHODOX ASTROLOGICAL RELATIONSHIPS   In her highly complex system of esoteric INTUITIONAL ASTROLOGY, the esotericist Bailey presents a system of planetary rulerships over the 'constellations' (which are probably the zodiacal signs), with some planets taken from her five NON-SACRED PLANETS, and others from her series of seven SACRED PLANETS. The sequence of esoteric rulerships contrasts with that of the ORTHODOX PLANETS, as shown in table 88.

CONSTELLATION (SIGN)	ESOTERIC PLANET	ORTHODOX PLANET
Aries	Mercury	Mars
Taurus	Vulcan	Venus
Gemini	Venus	Mercury
Cancer	Neptune	Moon
Leo	Sun	Sun
Virgo	Moon	Mercury
Libra	Uranus	Venus
Scorpio	Mars	Mars
Sagittarius	Earth	Jupiter
Capricorn	Saturn	Saturn
Aquarius	Jupiter	Uranus
Pisces	Pluto	Jupiter

TABLE 88

This system of rulerships must be compared with the series set out in connexion with the esoteric SEVEN RAYS.

UNUK   An alternative name for the fixed star COR SERPENTIS.

UNUKALHAI   See COR SERPENTIS.

UPAGRAHAS   A term derived from Indian astrology, usually claimed in the west to denote 'hypothetical planets', though apparently related to the Hellenistic SORTES.

URANIA   One of the nine Muses of classical mythology, assigned in Roman times to rule over Astronomy and Astrology, her symbol being the staff pointing to the globe. The symbol is an esoteric allegory, for the staff is straight, and the globe is circular, and they both may be taken as reference to the astrological (Aristotelian) doctrine that bodies in the supra-lunar spheres move in perfect circles, while those in the sub-lunar spheres (which of course include the Earth) move in straight lines. The symbolism addresses itself to the fact that astrology is concerned with the earthly as much as with the celestial. The word 'Urania' is often applied in modern times to the whole realm of astrology, though when so used it is often in a pejorative sense.

URANIAN   The term means 'related to Urania', and it was used in this sense at least as late as 1814 by Corfield. The 'Uranian Sciences' were thus the various astrologies. In modern times the word has been used as though it meant 'relating to Uranus': see for example URANUS SCHEME. See also URANIAN ASTROLOGY.

URANIAN ASTROLOGY   Name given to a modern system of astrology derived from the theories propounded by the so-called HAMBURG SCHOOL, under the direction of Witte. The system incorporates the three basic symbolic combinations of traditional astrology, though with important differences. The theory of planetary aspects is not based on consideration of elemental natures, as in the Ptolemaic System, but arises through numerical divisions: a special DEGREE DIAL is used as an aid to recognition and interpretations - see PLANETARY PICTURES and COSMOGRAM. In addition to the standard planets recognized by more conventional astrologers, the 'Uranian Astrology' postulates eight HYPOTHETICAL PLANETS, all transneptunian (see ADMETOS, APOLLON, CUPIDO, HADES, KRONOS, POSEIDON, VULKANUS and ZEUS). The interpretation of planetary placings is not of the orthodox kind, and there is much reliance upon MIDPOINTS, ANTISCIONS and upon a limited number of aspects. The adherents of the system claim that it is empirical, but the edifice is actually so far removed from conventional astrology that it is difficult to evaluate it against normal standards.

URANIAN SCHEME   See URANUS SCHEME.

URANOGRAPHIA   A term used to denote the science of delineating or describing the sidereal heavens. See CONSTELLATION MAPS. The modern English equivalent term is 'Uranography'.

URANOMETRIA   A term used to denote any treatise on the measurement of the relative distances (and magnitudes) of heavenly bodies - though most usually of the fixed stars and the asterisms. See CONSTELLATION MAPS. The modern English equivalent term is 'Uranometry'.

URANOSCOPUS   An archaic term meaning 'star gazer', sometimes used in modern times pejoratively of an astrologer'.

URANUS   The first extrasaturnine planet to be discovered, in orbit between Saturn and the more recently discovered Neptune. It was noted by Herschel in March, 1781 - though he did not at first realize that it was a planet. When

==

a year later its true nature was determined, he called it 'Georgium Sidus' (George's Star) after the reigning George III. Continental astrologers called it 'Herschel', however, as Allen notes, 'in a much varied orthography, strangely erroneous considering the fame of its discoverer'. The same authority notes that the 'star' had been observed 22 times previously by various scientists, and it appears that the name 'Ouranos' was first used by astrologers in reference to the then hypothetical planet prior to Herschel's discovery. Certainly the eccentric astrologer and friend of William Blake, John Varley, was the first to confirm the destructive and erratic nature of the planet by direct observation of transits. In recent years the planet, under its now-standard name of Uranus, has displaced the traditional Saturn from its rule over zodiacal Aquarius, which perhaps makes sense of the old myths which visualized Ouranos as being even older than the 'Time God' Chronos, one of the ancient names for Saturn. Astrologers claim that it is the planet of change, marking social or personal revolutions and disruptions. When working through its beneficial side, it can be magnetic, original (to the point of genius or madness), reformative and unconventional. Under pressure, however, it lapses into being merely unusual, pointlessly rebellious and given to violence and/or crime. See also NEW PLANETS.

URANUS-NEPTUNE CYCLES   Uranus conjuncts with Neptune to give a first-order cycle of 171.403 years, which has been reduced to an average value of 171 years due to the renowned eccentricity of Uranus. The second-order cycle involves 21 conjunctions and a span of 3,600 years.

URANUS-PLUTO CYCLES   The synodic period for these two planets is 127.280 years, the first-order cycle being as result of two such conjunctions (254.280 years). The second-order cycles involves 27 synodics, giving a cycle of 3,432.774 years, with a small deficiency of less than 3 degrees.

URANUS SCHEME   The 'Uranus Scheme' or 'Uranian Chain' are terms derived specifically from the Theosophical cosmoconception linked with the SCHEME OF EVOLUTION, and related to a future development of one of the 'ten chains' in the present solar system.

URIEL   The Archangel accorded rule over the Earth itself.

URION   See ORION.

URKAB   See ARKAB.

URSA MAJOR   Circumpolar constellation, the 'Greater Bear' or 'Wain', with a plethora of related names, including 'Arctos', 'Kallistos' (the name of the mortal changed into a bear because of Juno's jealousy), and 'Lycaonia' after the name of Kallistos' father, and (through error) 'Arcturus', not to be confused with the star of the same name. It was the Phoenician 'Dub', and the Arabic 'Al Dubb al Akbar', and a 'bear' in the language of the North American Indians long before America was discovered by Europeans. The magical number 7 of its stars gives us many names, such as 'Seven Sleepers', 'Seven Sages', and even the unimaginative 'Seven Stars', whilst Allen records that they were called in India 'Seven Bears'. In the northern regions it was generally pictured as a cart or 'Wain', and is thus the 'Wagon', 'Arthur's Chariot', and even the Romans (touched by their spread to the north) called it 'Cursus' and 'Plaustrum' after forms of chariots: among the Goths it was 'Himmel Wagen', the 'celestial chariot'. The 'Charles's Wain' is derived from the Saxon word 'ceorl', an ordinary peasant who eventually, by linguistic adjustment, became either Charlemagne or King Charles, in the same way that Arthur the king was derived from Arcturus, the associate star. From the wagon imagery came also 'Plough', and many variants, while 'Triones' was popular with the ancients.   Allen does a scholar's justice to these names by listing some 150 important variants. In the Denderah planisphere of Egypt the asterism is symbolized as a hind-quarter of an animal and linguistically associated with Set, who had rule over all the circumpolar constellations -

hence 'Dog of Set', and 'Typhon' as names. The famous seven stars are Dubhe, Mirak, Phacd, Megrez, Alioth, Bentenash and Mizar. Ptolemy, who called the entire asterisms 'Arctos', said that each of these stars was of the equivalent nature to Mars, which would imply that the entire constellation is of the Martian quality.

URSA MINOR   Circumpolar constellation, the 'Little Bear' in comparison with the larger URSA MAJOR. It is the 'Little Dipper' against the 'Big Dipper', but sharing with this companion the name 'Septentrio', connected with the idea of 'seven' ('septem' in Latin) which eventually gave us the Latin word for the North, so prominent in these asterisms. A popular early name was 'Cynosura' (Dog's Tail') - but see also POLARIS - yet this name could be derived from that of one of the nymphs of Crete who reared Jupiter. Ptolemy tells us that the bright stars in this asterism (which he calls 'Micros Arctos') are of a similar quality to Saturn, and 'to a lesser degree, to that of Venus', a combination difficult to evaluate.

VALENS ANTHOLOGIA   Name given to the anthology of the astrologer Vettius Valens (compiled in the 2nd century AD), one of the earliest collections of horoscopic and astrological material from Hellenistic sources. The historian Sachs has dealt admirably with many of the issues raised by the horoscope figures (as for example the question of CLIMATA) which consist of some hundred literary horoscopes, apparently used by Valens as supportive examples of certain astrological doctrines. Sachs comes to the conclusion that Valens was systematically collecting and analysing a large amount of statistical material for births, histories and deaths 'in order to confirm or modify the theoretical structure of astrology'. In a modern context the term 'horoscope' may be misleading, as the material is essentially literary, and many of the individual sets of data include only the horoscopos and the positions of the luminaries. A few more complete sets do contain planetary and nodal positions, however. The basis of the computation of the horoscopos appears to belong to an astronomical theory already archaic even for Valens.

VEGA   See WEGA.

VENANT   See ROYAL STAR.

VENATOR   See ORION.

VENERIS SIDUS   See TAURUS CONSTELLATION.

VENTER ARIETIS   Name given to the 2nd lunar MANSION in some mediaeval lists. Probably located by the stars delta and epsilon of constellation Aries.

VENUS   The planet in orbit around the Sun at a mean distance of about 67 million miles, with a periodicity of about 244 days. The peculiar brilliance of Venus is due to the reflective power of the atmosphere of clouds in which the body is sheathed: a point which has not gone missed by astrologers, who point to the propensity of Venusians to deal in surfaces, and to be concerned with surface appearances. In astrology Venus represents the spiritual side of the native as manifest in his physical life, and it is an index of the ability of the subject to enjoy beauty and to co-operate with others. It is traditionally termed the planet of 'love', and is indeed a useful indicator of how the subject loves the world and all its rich manifestations: it governs also the higher emotions, and the general refinement of the individual. A Venus which is emphasised in a chart, through an essential dignity, is usually a sign of physical beauty, and of the fact that the

native will be in some way creative. Such a well-placed Venus also makes for
great popularity with the opposite sex, as well as for a harmonious emotional
life. A badly placed Venus tends to restrict in some way the urge towards
co-operation with others, and the native may be unpractical, lazy or
opportunist. The sigil for Venus ♀ is explained as representing the
circle of spirit (which contains all spiritual potential) lifted by the cross
of materiality, suggesting that the Venusian nature may be regarded as
equivalent to a 'refined or redeemed earthly quality' - it is perhaps no
accident that even a modern astronomer like Sidgwick should write of Venus as
'almost the twin sister of the earth', for as such she has been widely
regarded by many esoteric astrologers. Venus has rule over zodiacal Taurus
and Libra: in the first sign we find the love of the Earth manifesting as a
refining principle which leads to the creative manipulation of materiality,
as well as love for sensual experience such as only the physical body may
afford. In the second we find the love of the air-type, which is for
communication and harmony of expression, emphasised and intensified by the
rulership. Venus is exalted in Pisces, and has its fall in Libra.
Traditionally the planet rules the small of the back (but see MELOTHESIC MAN)
as well as the entire shape of the physical body.

VENUS PERIOD   The name given in esoteric astrology to a future condition of
our present Earth, beyond the future development of the JUPITER PERIOD, yet
prior to the final VULCAN PERIOD, when humanity will attain to objective,
self-conscious, creative being.

VENUS SCHEME   The 'Venus Scheme' or 'Venusian Chain' are terms derived from
the Theosophical SCHEME OF EVOLUTION, and claimed to relate to the most
advanced of the planetary forms.

VERNAL EQUINOX   The term means literally 'equal night of Spring'. It is
marked at the time when the Sun reaches that point at which the plane of the
ecliptic intersects the plane of the Earth's equator, which occurs twice in
each year - once when the Sun enters Aries, which is the Vernal Equinox, and
once when it enters zodiacal Libra, which is the AUTUMNAL EQUINOX. See also
VERNAL POINT.

VERNAL HOROSCOPE   An alternative term for the CHOISNARD CHART, proposed by
the astrologer Froger.

VERNAL POINT   The 'Vernal Point' is the so-called ZERO DEGREE (more properly
the Zero Point) of zodiacal Aries, which marks the "Vernal Equinox". The
gradual retrogression of this point gives rise to PRECESSION.

VERNAL QUADRANT   See QUADRANTS.

VERTEX   Name given to the GREAT NEBULA situated to the north of the head of
"Andromeda". Additionally, the 'Vertex' is a term originated by the modern
astrologer Johndro, arising from a theory (perhaps based on a suggestion made
by Collin) that the existence of a magnetic field within and around our earth
postulates that there must be two 'Ascendants' (or more properly, two
Ascendant-Descendant axes), one being magnetic, the other electrical. These
might, under certain conditions, be visualized as being at right-angles to
each other. This alternative axis is called the 'vertex-antivertex' axis:
the so-called 'magnetic ascendant' is the traditional Ascendant (that is, the
ancient 'horoscopos'), while the 'electrical ascendant' is the so-called
'vertex'. Whilst it is widely recognized that Johndro's analogy, upon which
this conception is based, is itself invalid, he claims to have shown (using
the 'Known Data Method') that the axis is linked with 'involuntary actions',
lack of choice, and 'fate'. As with so many modern astrological
speculations, there appears to be a chimerical basis for the idea of the
vertex. This curious axis cannot hold any relationship to the Ascendant or
to the Ascendant-descendant axis. The fact is that the Ascendant marks the
relationship established between a given locality on the earth and a point on

==

the zodiacal arc. The vertex-antivertex axis is the supposed expression of a
relationship contained wholly within the magnetic field of the Earth: it
could in no way (even by forced analogy) be described as an Ascendant, or
treated as an equivalent influence, precisely because it is non-zodical in
origin. See also CO-VERTEX.

VERTICAL CIRCLES   Great circles of the Celestial Sphere, passing through the
zenith and the nadir, and perpendicular to the horizon, are called the
'Vertical Circles'.

VERTICAL SPHERE   One of several CELESTIAL SPHERES, taking as its point of
reference a horizon plane as one co-ordinate, and the Midheaven of any given
point on Earth as the second. This model is the basis for many of the
systems of mundane divisions, and the numerous attempts to reconcile it with
the apparent movement of the planets have given rise to the proliferation of
different methods of HOUSE DIVISION.

VESICAN CHART   See CHART SYSTEMS.

VESPA   See MUSCA BOREALIS.

VESPER   The name (with the variant 'Vesperus') given by Roman and mediaeval
astrologers to the planet Venus when an 'evening star'. See also LUCIFER.

VESPERTINE CULMINATION   Term used by Ptolemy for one of his VISIBLE ASPECTS.

VESPERTINE SETTING   Term used by Ptolemy for one of his VISIBLE ASPECTS.

VESPERTINE SUBSOLAR   Term used by Ptolemy for one of his VISIBLE ASPECTS.

VESPERUS   See VESPER.

VESTA   A name given by the esoteric astrologer Thierens to a future
development of his Venus (also known as ISIS) and pictured as having a rule
over the Taurus of the ETHERIC SPHERES. It is said to be a principle of
conservation. The same name 'Vesta' is also used of one of the ASTEROIDS,
discovered in 1807, and linked by the astrologer Dobyns with the sign Virgo,
along with a co-ruler, the asteroid "Ceres".

VIA LACTEA   The 'Milky Way' appears something like a luminous band wrapped
around the stellar sphere - a luminosity which is caused by the light of the
myriads of closely packed stars.   In effect, when we look into this luminous
band, we are looking into the flattened structure of the galactic system,
almost along its wide major axis. Since our own solar system is embedded in
this 'flattened pancake' of luminosity, we gain the impression that the 'Via
Lactea' itself crosses the ecliptic in (approximately) the last decan of
Gemini, and over the last half of Sagittarius. When astrologers speak of
the 'influence' of this band, they usually have in mind the wide arcs which
intersect the ecliptic. Robson says that this influence is 'sympathetic,
human, artistic', and so on, but a survey of the general degree
interpretations relating to these arcs (which cannot be separated from the
influence of the fixed stars within them) shows them to be not at all
beneficial - accidents and blindness being predicted of several of the
degrees. The 'Via Lactea' or 'Galaxy' has been given many names, some of
them, as Allen remarks 'arbitary, descriptive, or fanciful titles'. The
white luminosity has linked it with milk, as set out so beautifully in the
myth of Jupiter pressing his new-born son Hercules into the breasts of his
consort Hera, and the child sucking so fiercely that the milk squirts into
the heaven, where it becomes the milky way: the milk which falls on earth
becomes the lilies. From such stories (of which there are variants) we have
'Via Lactis', 'Semita Lactea' (milky footpath) and so on. The luminosity
marks it out as a river, hence 'Eridanus', 'Stream of Ocean' and 'River of
Heaven', and the title from the Akkadian, 'River of the Divine Lady', and the

more simple Arabic 'Al Nahr' (the river). In China it was 'Tien Ho' (Celestial River), and the 'Silver River'. The idea that it was a band in the skies gave another set of names - 'Coeli Cingulum' and 'Orbis Lacteus', both relating to celestial girdles. Yet others saw it as a road, a 'via', and Allen recalls that it was for the Anglo Saxons the pathway of the giant sons of Waetla, 'Waetlinga Straet', from which some reasonably draw 'Watling Street'. Langland, in his 'Piers Plowman' makes it 'Walsyngham Way to the Virgin Mary', whilst 'Asgard Brige' was used to denote this luminous band as well as the rainbow. Yet, for every term quoted above, a dozen or more variants might be given.

VIA SOLIS   The 'Way of the Sun' - a Latin name for the ECLIPTIC.

VICAKHA   The Sanskrit name for constellation Scorpio - but see VRISHIKAM.

VICENZA CYCLE   In the Palazzo Chiericati, in Vicenza, is the so-called 'Firmamento Chiericati', a huge ceiling fresco of a well-planned constellational cycle, around an image of Apollo and Diana as personifications of Sun and Moon (this last derived from a 16th century fresco in Ferrara). The cycle was painted by Domenico Rizzo, circa 1560, but was recently restored. Over 80 identifiable constellations are incorporated into 76 frescoes, separated by bands which are themselves painted with related imagery. It has been shown that the Firmamento (in accordance with the influence of Palladio) is largely derived from zodiacal and constellational and polytheistic imagery of ancient Roman numismatics, as well as from the famous Durer print of 1515. A useful summary of such influences, and an extensive bibliographjy, has been given by Ballarin.

VICTORIAN PERIOD   A specialist astrological term, referring to a periodicity of approximately 535 years, and called after Victorius of Aquitain (and sometimes after Dionysius Exiguus, hence the alternative name 'Dionysian Period'). It was a period involved with combining the 19 year METONIC CYCLE with the so-called SOLAR CYCLE of 28 years (the Dominical cycle), to restore the new moon to the same day of the week of the same month on which the cycle began. After the Gregorian calendrical reformation its use lapsed.

VICTORY   Name given to one of the SEVEN LOTS of Greek astrology, the 'lot of Nike', the goddess of Victory. The degree of Nike is the same distance from the Ascendant as Jupiter is from the LOT OF DAEMON.

VIGINTILE   The SEMI-DECILE aspect.

VIKASHA   Name given to the 14th of the Hindu NAKSHATRAS.

VINDEMATRIX   Fixed star, the epsilon of constellation Virgo, set in the right wing of this celestial being. It has many titles, 'Vindemiator' and 'Providemiator', meaning 'grape gatherer', and in mediaeval astrology 'Alcalst' and 'Almucedie' among the related terms from the Arabian 'Al Muridin' (those who sent forth) almost certainly a mistranslation of the original Graeco-Latin term. Ptolemy says that the star is equal in influence to Mercury with Saturn, and almost all authorities claim it as an unfortunate star, bringing falsity, disgrace and folly in terms of the planetary or nodal points conjuncting it.

VIRGIN   Name given to both zodiacal Virgo and to the Virgo Constellation.

VIRGIN SPIRITS   One of the esoteric names given to present-day humanity, viewed as one of the TWELVE CREATIVE HIERARCHIES.

VIRGO   The sixth sign of the zodiac. It corresponds neither in location nor significance with the asterism of the same name: see VIRGO CONSTELLATION. The sigil for the sign ♍ is said to have been a contracted drawing of the severed serpent from which the sigils for Scorpio and Virgo were evolved, and the fact is that the Egyptian demotic scripts appear to carry such an association. The link with the head of a serpent postulated in this theory is interesting, for Virgo is indeed a sign deeply committed to the intellectual process. The sigil has also been derived from the merged letters of MV (Maria Virgo) as part of the important Marian symbolism associated with the sign and constellation: this graphic etymology is quite imaginative, however. Virgo is of the Earth element, and of the Mutable quality, the influence being discriminative, quiet, exacting, nervous, shrewd and methodical. The nature of Virgo as it manifests in human beings is expressed in the many keywords which have been attached to it by modern astrologers: dignified, clever, intelligent, nervous (though often good under pressure), graceful, mentally alert, gentle - in a word, all those qualities which may be associated with an Earth type expressing itself in the spiritual mental realm. In excess the Virgoan nature may be described in terms which express its underlying critical nature, the keywords being: carping, hyper-critical, 'bookish', shrewish and back-biting. Virgo says 'I want to clarify' more loudly than others tend to, though she may do this to be helpful, or to put others down, depending upon which side of the nature is being called into play. Virgo is traditionally ruled by Mercury, and marks the fall of Venus.

FIGURE 64.   THE CONSTELLATION VIRGO FROM THE "MODERN ZODIAC" (AFTER DELPORTE), AND THE IMAGE OF VIRGO FROM THE "SAN MINIATO ZODIAC".

VIRGO CONSTELLATION   Zodiacal constellation, located approximately in the area set out by Delporte in figure 64, straddling the ecliptic over an arc of about 30 degrees. Virtually all the ancient and modern traditions visualize the image of Virgo as a maiden, and a whole string of feminine names have been applied to her, such as 'Persephone' or 'Proserpina' - but in essence she has been regarded as the archetypal woman, the 'Kore' of the Greeks, the 'Puella' of the Romans, and in the Hindu asterisms as 'Kanya' (maiden): from very early Christian times she has been 'Virgin' or 'Virgin Mary', and in Egyptian times 'Isis'. Some of the more important variant names have revolved around the identification of the lucida in the asterism, the SPICA usually visualized as set in the Virgin's left hand or shoulder, as a child or as a sheaf of corn. The Greek name means 'ear of corn', and this was sometimes adapted by the Christians to the distaff which properly belonged to an heretical Gnostic tradition: later Christians visualized the star as an image of the Child in the arms of the Virgin Mary (but see also STELLA MARIS). The link between the star and corn was sufficient to establish the entire asterism as the corn-goddess Demeter, from which we have 'Arista' and 'Arista Puella', the 'Maiden of the Wheatfield'. But it was mainly in the image of the celestial mother that Virgo was visualized - called even 'Astraea' after the starry daughter of Themis: several of the mediaeval images of the Virgin Mary depict her dress decorated with stars (even with ears of corn) and such were doubtless derived from the pre-Christian stellar goddesses. Such images were also linked with the asterism as the Egyptian Isis and the Babylonian Ishtar. Ptolemy groups the stars of the constellation, and equates them all with beneficial influences - mainly with Mercury and Venus, yet, besides the lucida, the only star to have really caught the attention of astrologers is ZAVIJAVA.

VIRTUE   In a specialist astrological sense, the term applied to a hidden power within all sublunary things, a power which was visualized as having come from the stars. To some extent this idea is still contained in the modern use of the term in its general sense, the 'human virtue' being an inner quality proceeding from an image of the celestial or ideal man (the Latin 'vir' means 'man'). The practice of TALISMANIC MAGIC, so important a branch of mediaeval astrology, was based on the idea that it was possible to 'inject' a celestial or planetary virtue into an amulet, which would then itself contain a beneficial or protective power derived from that virtue. In esoteric lore many other terms were used to denote the celestial virtue or power - see for example ILECH and QUINTESSENCE.

VIRTUES   See VIRTUTES.

VIRTUES AND VICES   In the mediaeval tradition the seven virtues and vices were linked with the seven planets in a variety of systems, and these frequently appear in mediaeval astrological symbolism in paintings and sculpture. The correspondences in table 89 are fairly standard, of the kind used by Giotto and his school.

```
-----------------------------------------------------------------TABLE 89
```

PLANET	DAY OF WEEK	VIRTUE	VICE	PART OF MAN
SU	Sunday	Hope	Indolence	Life-force (spirit)
MO	Monday	Chastity	Envy	Psychic forces (soul)
ME	Tuesday	Wisdom	Gluttony	Intellect (mind)
VE	Wednesday	Love	Lust	Divinity in man
MA	Thursday	Courage	Wrath	Bestial lower element
JU	Friday	Faith	Pride	Higher aspirations
SA	Saturday	Prudence	Covetousness	Physical body

VIRTUTES   Name given to the incorporeal spiritual beings of the series of CELESTIAL HIERARCHIES established by Dionysius the Areopagite. Strictly speaking they should be linked with the EXSUSIAI, as rulers of the Sphere of the Sun - the 'Golden Legend' confirms this by describing the 'Virtues' (as they are sometimes called) with the divine mystery of the Eucharist, for in the esoteric lore Christ is linked with the solar sphere. However, the Virtutes have been wrongly equated with the ARCHAI (for example, by St. Gregory), which would give them rule over Venus. The rule of the ARCHAI over Venus, and of the Virtutes over the Sun is beyond dispute in astrological lore, however.

VISIBLE ASPECTS   A term used by Ptolemy in his 'Almagest' to distinguish 9 kinds of aspects which might be seen by the astrologer. These (all of which appear to involve aspects with the Sun) play no part in modern astrology, but the aspectal structure is evident from the nine terms used by Ptolemy: they are the 'matutine subsolar', 'matutine culmination', 'matutine setting', 'meridianal subsolar', 'meridianal culmination', 'meridianal setting', 'vespertine subsolar', 'vespertine culmination' and 'vespertine setting'.

VISIBLE HORIZON   See CELESTIAL HORIZON.

VITAL PRINCIPLES   See SEVEN VITAL PRINCIPLES.

VITAL SIGNS   A term applied to the three signs of the Fire Triplicity, which

===

are supposed to be profligate of their vital forces.

VOEL   In certain forms of ceremonial magic, the name is given to the
Governor of zodiacal Leo.

VOID OF COURSE   In modern astrology this old term has been misunderstood.
Originally it was derived from Horary Astrology, and applied to a planet
which passes through a zodiacal sign without encountering an aspect to or
from another planet. In Natal Astrology, a planet which formed no aspect
before leaving the sign of its radical position was also said to be 'void of
course'. Dean, studying the validity of the traditions relating to the
tropical and sidereal zodiac controversy, suggests that the 'void of course
Moon' might be used as a basis for furnishing useful checks, but makes the
mistake of defining 'void of course' in a personal way, and applying a notion
derived from Horary Astrology to realms which are unrelated to this. Dean
claims that the Moon is 'void of course' between its last major aspect in one
sign and its entry into the next.

VOLANS   Constellation, the 'Piscis Volans' (flying fish), originated by
Bayer in 1604, south of Canopus. The asterism appears to have been
recognized earlier under the name of 'Passer' (sparrow), however. Robson
tells us that it gives a quick mind, and a poetic or artistic ability.

VOLASFERA SYMBOLS   Name given to a series of readings ascribed to each of
the 360 degrees of the zodiac, according to the system of DEGREE SYMBOLS, in
a number of verbal symbols and exegeses by the Italian astrologer Borelli.
The system was popularized by the astrologer Sepharial in a translation
published at the end of the last century.

VOLUCRIS   See CYGNUS.

VOLVELLE   A name originally applied to mediaeval parchment dials (found
still in certain astrological and calendrical manuscripts) used for computing
dates of movable feasts, simple cycles (such as the phases of the Moon),
times of sunrise and sunset, tidal changes, and so on. In its simplest form
it consisted of one or more movable circles, graduated with figures, which
could be swivelled against a similar graduated background, to enable one to
make a calibrated reading of co-ordinates. In recent years a complex form of
volvelle has been developed to enable the astrologer to compute easily the
Ascendant and Midheaven degrees for given places and times. Sophisticated
plastic volvelles may be obtained nowadays, but these are rapidly being
displaced by computerized charting.

VRISHABHAM   A Sanskrit name for zodiacal Gemini, as used in Hindu astrology.

VRISHIKAM   The Sanskrit name for zodiacal Scorpio - but see also VICAKHA.

VULCAN   The term has several applications in astrology. It was a name given
by Sutcliffe to one of the intramercurial HYPOTHETICAL PLANETS. Later
astrologers assigned this Sutcliffe Vulcan to the so-called 'day-house' rule
over Scorpio, and the 'night-house' rule over Leo, and claimed that it was of
an explosive nature. This same Vulcan may be linked with one of the AROMAL
PLANETS, among which the astrologer Harris listed his own Vulcan in 1884,
though this does not appear to have been intramercurial. The Vulcan
described by Bailey in her system of "Intuitional Astrology" is actually one
of the SACRED PLANETS, and is connected especially with the FIRST RAY. The
term Vulcan is also used to veil an esoteric astrological doctrine: it is
one of the names applied to a planetary state which is supposed to represent
the future embodiment of our Earth (see FUTURE PLANETS and VULCAN PERIOD).
This latter may be connected with the Vulcan of Thierens, which he sometimes
called by the alternative name 'Mercury', or 'Mercury-Vulcan'. Thierens also
called this planet 'Vulcanus', though it is unrelated to the 'Vulkanus' of
the URANIAN ASTROLOGY. None of the hypotheticals listed above appear to

correspond with the 'Vulcan' given as an intramercurial planet by the
astrologer Weston, round about 1920. Besant mentions the intramercurial
'Vulcan' in her account of Chaldean astrology, and this appears to be
different from the Vulcan of the GLOBES, mentioned in the same text. The
astrologer Pagan also mentions a 'Vulcan', but it is far from clear which she
had in mind, though she does link it with the action of Scorpio, a sign to
which (even by 1930) she had assigned Pluto as ruler (see PAGAN-PLUTO). The
phrase chosen by Pagan to express the Vulcanian element in man is 'the stuff
of which he is made', something in man which eludes analysis, and for which
one may not give a final account. As she puts it, the 'Smith' (ie. Vulcan)
'puts everyone into the furnace, and by burning away the dross, gets down to
the essence of our (sic) being.'

VULCAN PERIOD   A term used in esoteric astrology to denote a future (and in
some respects final) condition of our present Earth, marking a future
evolution of humanity to the highest spiritual consciousness.   The term is
used only in esoteric astrology, and has nothing to do with any of the
hypotheticals listed under VULCAN.

VULCAN SCHEME   The 'Vulcan Scheme' or the 'Vulcanian Chain' are terms
derived from considerations set out under the Theosophical SCHEME OF
EVOLUTION, not to be confused with the hypotheticals listed under VULCAN. It
is claimed that this 'Vulcan Scheme' relates to a CHAIN which will produce
entities at a lower level than those of the present EARTH SCHEME.

VULCANUS   The esoteric astrologer Thierens sometimes calls his own
hypothetical VULCAN by this name.

VULKANUS   Name given to one of the HYPOTHETICAL PLANETS used in the "Uranian
Astrology", said to relate to 'power and strength', and to represent an upper
octave of Mars.

VULPECA   Constellation formed by Hevelius in 1690 as 'Vulpecula cum Ansere'
(little fox with the goose) between Sagitta and Cygnus. Inevitably
astrologers have linked the asterism with the fox-like characteristics, for
it is said to give cunning and a voracious nature.

VULTUR CADENS   See FIFTEEN STARS and WEGA.

VULTUR VOLANS   See AQUILA.

WANE   When a planet comes to the Descendant, its influence is said to be
'broken', and it is said to 'wane' for the entire semi-arc. But distinguish
the 'Waning Moon' - see DECREASING LIGHT.

WANES   See BROKEN.

WANING MOON   See DECREASING LIGHT.

WARMTH TRIGON   See SIDEREAL MOON RHYTHM.

WAR PEAK CYCLE   See CYCLE.

WASAT   Fixed star, the alpha of Gemini, the name for the Arabic 'Al Wasat'
(the middle) which some explain as reference to the proximity of the star to
the ecliptic. It is a violent star, giving (in the words of Robson)
'destructiveness as a first principle': it is especially connected with

===

chemicals and poisons - the Chinese called it 'Ta Tsun' (great wine jar).

WATCHERS OF THE HEAVENS   See ROYAL STARS.

WATCHWORD An equivalent term for KEYWORD applied in a special sense by the
astrologer Pagan. Each of the Ascendant signs are accorded a 'watchword'
which is included in an analytic schema and said to be modified (in a
particular chart) by the sign occupied by the Moon.

AR Action	TA Stability	GE Variety	CN Sympathy
LE Faith	VG Service	LB Harmony	SC Power
SG Law and Liberty	CP Excelsior	AQ Investigation	PI Unity

WATER-BEARER   One of the names for zodiacal and constellation Aquarius.

WATER ELEMENT   The water element finds expression in the zodiac through the
three signs Cancer, Scorpio and Pisces. It is the element most deeply
concerned with reflection, sensitivity and fluidity. Water is esoterically
an 'impressionable' principle, the important aspect of this tradition
revolving around the idea (more fully expressed in alchemical than in
astrological texts) that water, to operate in accordance with its true
nature, needs to be contained, and thus given form. This is why among the
Greeks (at least with Thales) water was the 'first principle' from which form
arose, the 'potentiality' of form (in the mediaeval tradition the 'first
principle' was actually the element of Fire). This partly explains the
esoteric connexion drawn between the 'dry' Moon and water, for the Moon is
that which gives growth and change to form: it perhaps also explains why the
archangelic ruler of the Moon (Gabriel) should be the announcer of a 'new
form' of spiritual existence for the Earth. The esoteric water element is
far removed from the fluidic water of the modern chemists, though suitable
analogies between the material fluid and the spiritual principle are often
found in the popular treatments of the elements.

WATERS OF SPACE   See OURANOS.

WATER SIGNS   These are Cancer, Scorpio and Pisces - see WATER TRIPLICITY.

WATER TRIPLICITY   This is the group of signs linked with the water element,
manifesting different aspects of the PHLEGMATIC temperament: Cancer, Scorpio
and Pisces.   Water may be seen in three different forms: Cancer is water as
a fluid - changeable, tending to reflect the colours of the skies and
landscapes around: Scorpio is frozen water, a shield of ice beneath which is
a depth unknown: Pisces is vaporous water, almost a dematerialized state of
being, often out of touch with ('hovering over' or 'disincarnated from') the
physical realm. Each of the water signs are extremely emotional and are
often described as 'their own worst enemies' or 'victims of circumstances'.
Since the water triplicity is concerned with the spiritual element in life,
with the dissolving of boundaries, each of the signs reflects an aspect of
this in the world. Cancer is connected with the beginnings of life, with the
fairyland world of childhood, which dissolves the world in its own
mythologies. Scorpio appears to be almost obsessed with death (in reality,
with 'resurrection' and 'redemption'), that final dissolving of physical
boundaries, with peering beyond the 'threshold' of the material. Pisces is
concerned with the idea of the poetical, with that life of spirit which is
only tenuously linked with the material realm.

WAXING MOON   See INCREASING IN LIGHT.

WEAK DEGREES   See AZIMENE DEGREES.

WEAK SIGNS   The three signs Cancer, Capricorn and Pisces are traditionally
termed 'weak signs', the basis for the classification being lost. See STRONG
SIGNS.

===

WEEKLY PROGRESSIONS   See WEEKLY SERIES.

WEEKLY SERIES   One of four measures for computing symbolic time, used in
SECONDARY DIRECTIONS, and based on the idea that the True Solar Day should be
regarded as equivalent to a week. The term is 'Weekly Series of Secondary
Directions', sometimes (confusingly) reduced to 'Weekly Directions'.

WEGA   Fixed star, the alpha of Lyra, and just as frequently called 'Vega'.
The star is of considerable importance in astrology, mainly because (under
the name 'Maat') it marked the pole and was also used for Egyptian temple
orientation. The name 'Maat' is often translated as meaning 'vulture star',
which may explain the mediaeval term 'Vultur Cadens' (falling vulture) in the
list of the FIFTEEN STARS. The Arabian 'Al Waki' itself means 'falling' and
from this we have many derivations. The Greek 'Lyra' was turned into the
late mediaeval 'Allore', 'Aloshore', and so on, whilst the Roman 'Fidus'
became 'Fidicula'. As a pole-star the Akkadians apparently called it
'Tir-anna' (Life of Heaven), and the Assyrians 'Dayan-same' (Judge of
Heaven). In spite of its link with the vulture or 'grype' (a mediaeval
variant), the influence is generally regarded as beneficial, for it brings
refinement and ideality, though a certain degree of pretentiousness and
lasciviousness. The curious thing is that Ptolemy equates the influence with
that of Venus and Mercury, yet the traditional readings for the conjunctions
with the benefics seem to give unpleasant results.

WESTERN ANGLE   The cusp of the house opposite to the Ascendant is called the
'western angle': it is associated with the sign Libra, and marks the balance
between day and night.

WESTERN HOUSES   The 'western' or 'occidental' houses are those between the
Fifth and the Ninth houses, inclusive. The Seventh House is very often
called the 'Western House'.

WEST POINT   In astrology, the term 'west point' is sometimes used as a
synonym for the Descendant, by analogy with EAST POINT.

WEMYSS DEGREES   A system of DEGREE SYMBOLS proposed by the Scottish
astrologer Wemyss, the basis of an extraordinary classification of horoscopic
material. In some cases the degree influences listed are spread over a
number of degrees, so that in many respects the method should be described as
being based on 'Arc Symbols'. Not all the degrees or arcs are accorded a
meaning, and whilst the traditional order of zodiacal signs is adhered to,
Wemyss incorporates a number of HYPOTHETICAL PLANETS as rulers in his system,
as well as changing one or two of the traditional ascriptions: Leo is given
to HERCULES, Virgo to DIDO, Libra to Neptune, Scorpio to Uranus, Sagittarius
to JASON and Pisces to the ASTEROIDS.

WEMYSS-PLUTO   The astrologer Wemyss, writing c. 1929, attempted a
revolutionary review of planetary rulerships over signs, as indicated in
WEMYSS DEGREES. One hypothetical ruler he named Pluto, as ruler of Cancer.
It was about this time that the modern planet PLUTO was discovered by Lowell,
and there was soon a consensus among astrologers (though see PAGAN-PLUTO)
that this new planet should be given rule over Scorpio. Accordingly, there
was a need to distinguish the two different 'Plutos', and the modern planet
was for a while called the 'Lowell-Pluto', and the hypothetical the
'Wemyss-Pluto'. However, Wemyss claimed a revolution of 1,366 years for his
hypothetical, which contrasts with the 248 year revolution of the modern
Pluto.

WHALE'S JAW   One of the names given in the 19th century astrological
textbooks for the fixed star MENKAR.

WHITE EAGLE   Sometimes used by modern astrologers as a term for zodiacal
Scorpio. See EAGLE.

==

WHITE TIGER   One of the so-called 'constellations' of the Chinese heavens,
which is really an arc of seven SIEU, from 'Goei' (the beta of Andromeda) to
'Shen' (the delta of Orionis).

WHOLE SIGNS   A term inexplicably applied to Taurus, Gemini, Leo, Scorpio,
Sagittarius and Aquarius - perhaps through some misunderstanding of the
classification accorded to the negative-positive polarities arising from the
SECTA.   Sometimes the three air signs Gemini, Libra and Aquarius are called
'Whole Signs', again for no apparent reason.

WINGED BULL   A name (rarely) used in modern times for zodiacal and
constellational Taurus, even though the image is not 'winged', save
indirectly through its connexion with the TETRAMORPH.

WINGED HORSE   See PEGASUS.

WINTER SOLSTICE   See SOLSTICES.

WINTRY QUADRANT   See QUADRANTS.

WORLD CYCLE OF MUNDANE EVENTS   A designation used by Tucker to refer to his
highly personal method of relating world events (Mundane events) to celestial
phenomena (in his system, aspects of the 'slow moving', extra-Jupiterian
planets, with the curious absence - in 1936 - of Pluto).   Tucker claims to
find a cycle of 128 years, relating to the return of Neptune to the same
zodiacal sign and degree at the end of every ninth period of 128 years,
around which he constructs his own World Cycle table of events.   As with all
similar attempts to establish world cycles against celestial phenomena (see
for example those of Sucher in regard to the heliocentrically considered
cycles of Astrosophy), there is an unfortunate simplicity in the approach to
historical events.   For example, the celestial phenomena (NE opposition UR,
UR conjunct SA) is associated with the 'Crusades', which for some reason
Tucker dates as 1148, when this date refers (and then only approximately) to
the Second Crusade, which was a disaster.   The Crusades were of course
conducted over an extensive period, from as early as 1096 until at least
1291.

WORLD CYCLE   See WORLD CYCLE OF MUNDANE EVENTS

WORLD SPHERES   See OPHANIM.

==

YATRA   A Sanskrit term used to denote the Hindu form of military astrology -
see OMINA.

YAVANESVARA   See LORD OF THE GREEKS.

YEAR   In general the word is applied in astrology to one of the solar
cycles, such as the 'solar year' - but see also ANOMALISTIC YEAR, SIDEREAL
YEAR and TIME.   Additionally, in esoteric astrology the term is applied to
larger periodicities which are usually multiples of the solar cycle unit:
for example, the 'Divine Year' is 311,040 million solar cycles.   Again, the
PLATONIC YEAR is a similar extension of the solar unit, linked with the
periodicities of PRECESSION.

YEAR FOR A DAY   See MEASURE OF TIME.

YEARLY CHART   A term used by Bradley for the SOLAR RETURN.

==

YEARLY PROGRESSIONS   See YEARLY SERIES.

YEARLY RHYTHM   A term used by the astrologer Ebertin to denote a system of correspondences linked with the traditional seasons, viewed from a point of view of the zodiacal cycle. In synopsis the sequence runs:

AR   The unfolding of energy relating to the time of germination, and within man, the urge to act.

TA   The creation of form, through strengthening and invigorating, in the human being constructiveness.

GE   The multiplicity and diversity of form and life, expressed in the human being through versatility.

CN   Fecundation and fertilization, in the human being receptivity and connubial love.

LE   Ripening, harvesting, linked in the human being with self-confidence.

VG   The gathering of fruit, linked with diligence and the critical faculty.

LB   Balance and adjustment in the economy of nature, linked on the human plane with the communal sense, and the sense of obligation.

SC   The death process, linked with continuation of life within the seed, as well as psychologically with the endurance principle and over-estimation of self.

SG   The season of hibernation, the cultivation of the inner life of the human and (spiritual) expansion.

CP   The season of torpidity, of 'invisible' life, which is psychologically concentrated upon the personal sense of self.

AQ   The waiting time and fasting (linked with the Lenten period), on the psychological plane connected with a 'wait and see' attitude, and readiness to help.

PI   The swelling of the seed in the watery earth, which symbolizes on a psychological level the receptivity of the human to many influences, and inner composure.

In connexion with the agricultural yearly rhythm, see SIDEREAL LUNAR ZODIAC.

YEARLY SERIES   One of the four measures for symbolically computing time, used in SECONDARY DIRECTIONS, and based on the idea that the True Solar Day should be regarded as the equivalent of a year. In other words, the term is a more precise allocation of the DAY FOR A YEAR system of progressions. The term is actually 'Yearly Series of Secondary Directions', sometimes reduced misleadingly to 'Yearly Directions'.

YEARS OF THE GODS   See DIVINE YEARS.

YED POSTERIOR   Fixed star, the epsilon of Ophiuchus, called in Euphratean astronomy 'Nitach-bat' (man of death), a star which Allen notes as one of the several 'singular survivals' in modern astrology, since it is said to be of an evil nature, like the related 'Yed Prior'.

YED PRIOR   Fixed star, the delta of Ophiuchus, the name from the Arabic 'Yad' (hand), the star being set in the hand of the asterism, and distinguished from "Yed Posterior". Like the latter, it is of an evil nature, associated with an influence of Venus with Saturn, and linked with immorality.

YLIADUS   A term used to denote an invisible spirit or agency within the human body (and indeed within the FOUR ELEMENTS): sometimes spelled 'Yliadum' or 'Yleidus', and perhaps linked with the ILIASTER.

YOUTHFUL QUADRANT   See QUADRANTS.

YUGA   In the Hindu chronology, which has had some influence on modern esoteric thought, the Yuga is a 'World Age', a thousandth part of a KALPA.

==

Each Yuga is preceded by a twilight period (sandhya) and terminated by a
twilight period (sandhyansa), and the four yugic periods (together called a
'Mahayuga' - which also incorporates the 'twilights') are named the KRITA
YUGA, the TRETA YUGA, the DWAPARA YUGA and the KALI YUGA.   The periods are
expressed in Divine Years and in the mortal years of ordinary time: in this
system the Divine Year is equal to 360 mortal years.

```
-------------------------------------------------------------------TABLE 90
   YUGIC PERIOD        DIVINE YEARS         MORTAL YEARS
================================================================================
   Krita              4,800                1,728,000
   Treta              3,600                1,296,000
   Dwapara            2,400                  864,000
   Kali               1,200                  432,000
-------------------------------------------------------------------------
```

There is much obvious confusion among western occultists regarding the 'yugic
periods'. In spite of the reliable figures listed in table 85, one still
finds certain writers maintaining that mankind entered the present age, which
is that of the 'Kali Yuga' at the death of Krishna (circa 3,102 BC) and that
this age therefore ended in 1899 (or thereabouts).

YUGIC PERIODS   See YUGA.

==

Z

ZADKIEL   One of the more important names given to the spiritual being ruling
the Sphere of Jupiter.

ZANIAH   Fixed star, the eta of constellation Virgo, set in the southern wing
of the asterism, the name being derived from an earlier Arabian minor
asterism (see ZAVIJAVA). It is said by Ptolemy to be of the nature of
Mercury conjunct Venus, and brings refinement, order and a lovable nature.

ZANRAK   A name used by Ebertin for the fixed star gamma of Eridanus,
probably in confusion with the Arabian term 'Zaurac' or 'Zaurak', which are
the standard modern names for the full 'Al Na'r al Zaurak' (the bright star
of the boat). Ebertin associates dire consequences of a prominent Zanrak,
such as 'fear of death and suicidal tendencies', though it has not received
much notice in traditional astrology. The actual 'case histories' evinced by
Ebertin suggest a tendency to isolation, rather than to anything dire.

ZARIEL DIVISION   See EQUAL DIVISION METHOD.

ZAVIJAVA   Fixed star, the beta of constellation Virgo, set below the head of
the asterism, the name from the Arabian term for the eleventh manzil (see
AWWA), which was 'the barker', the asterism itself being linked with a
kennel, of which this was (along with ZANIAH) one of the corner stars. Among
the Arab astrologers it was a beneficial star, but for obscure reasons the
Europeans have given it an influence equivalent to Mercury conjunct Mars.

ZAZEL   Name given by Agrippa (quoting ancient cabbalistic sources) to the
daemon of Saturn, for whom he gives the magical number 45 - see AGIEL.

ZENITH   The point immediately overhead from any given point on Earth is
called the zenith, which is geometrically speaking the Pole of the Horizon.
In popular speech, the Sun is sometimes said to reach its zenith, which is
merely the highest point in the ecliptic relative to a given place, though it
is rarely the zenith proper. In similar popular use, the cusp of the Tenth

===

House is sometimes called the 'zenith'.

ZENITH PROJECTION   See NONAGESIMAL.

ZENITH STAR   See ETTANIN.

ZENITH SYSTEM   A method of HOUSE DIVISION based on the projection of an
equally trisected quadrant of the ecliptic by spatial division. The method
was proposed (in somewhat obscure terms) by the astrologer Tucker, following
the suggestions of his brother (also an astrologer) and seemingly based on a
misunderstanding of Ptolemy.   Tucker claimed that the system had four main
merits: first, it divides the ecliptic by direct application; secondly, the
poles of the system coincide with the poles of the ecliptic, and thus
coincide with the poles of the horoscope being cast; thirdly, the MC of the
system will always be located 90 degrees west of the Ascendant, and fourthly,
the permanency of positions thus attained (by the 90 degree angle) will aid
purposes of accurate (statistical) research.   Unfortunately, the same term
had previously been used by the astrologer Leo some 30 years earlier, again
for a method of House Division - though this was too badly described (in what
Leo himself termed a 'somewhat hasty survey') to be of much value. Whilst
Leo's method is based on an equal division of the horizon projected on to the
ecliptic from the horizon pole, Leo for some reason linked it with the
CAMPANEAN SYSTEM, which projects the prime vertical division on to the
ecliptic from the pole of the prime vertical. The astrologer 'Chandra' quite
rightly saw Leo's system as one of the two red herrings drawn across the
trail of investigations: the other herring was Leo's unusable EAST POINT
SYSTEM.

ZERO AYANAMSA   See AYANAMSA and FIDUCIAL.

ZERO DEGREE   In a practical sense, there is no such thing as a 'zero
degree', even though the term is used widely in certain astrological circles.
Almost always, the term really means 'within the first degree', or is
a reference to the theoretical commencement of a sign. It is not uncommon for
astrologers describe planets as being in the 'zero degree' of a sign, when in
fact they mean that the planets are in the 'first degree' of that sign. The
more astute astrologers therefore speak and write of the location as being
the 'first point' of Aries, rather than of the (non-existent) zero-point, on
'zero degree', on the grounds that a circle (such as the ecliptic) may not
have a break in it. As a result of the introduction of the term, and arising
from the misunderstanding of its application, a misunderstanding has been
perpetuated in popular astrological circles which has in turn resulted in
various confusions. Frequently (because of this concept of a 'zero degree')
the degree-placing of a planet or nodal point is recorded wrongly. A planet
in (say) 10 degrees 12 minutes of Aries, or even in 10 degrees 59 minutes of
Aries, is actually in the 11th degree of that sign, though not infrequently
an astrologer will describe the first planet as being in 10 degrees, on the
principle of 'rounding off' to the nearest degree. A planet in 0 degrees, 0
minutes and 1 second of Aries is however still in the 1st degree of that
sign: it is not in a zero degree. The problems arising out of the wrong
conversion of degrees - especially in regard to correct interpretation of
platic aspects or the significance of the DEGREE SYMBOLS - are considerable.
See ROUNDING-OFF.

ZERVANA AKARANA   Name of an ancient Persian primal god, variously translated
as meaning 'without limit of time' or 'duration in a circle', though
obviously pointing to an eternal existence beyond the time-barrier of the
Sphere of Saturn. Within the realm of astrology this primal Zervan is
interesting since images used to depict him combine the symbolism of the
so-called TETRAMORPHS into one figure.

ZEUGON Greek term, sometimes Romanized as 'Zugon', meaning 'beam of a
balance', and used to denote both zodiacal and constellational Libra.

ZEUS   Name given to one of the HYPOTHETICAL PLANETS used in the "Uranian
Astrology", said to represent an upper octave of Uranus, and to be related to
'physical leadership and creativity'.

ZIB   See PISCES CONSTELLATION.

ZIGIATUS   A term now obsolete, yet worth recording if only because it
appears in so many early textbooks, yet is in fact a reflection of the nature
of the astrological tradition. According to most accounts, the term appears
to be a Latinized form of one of the Greek words meaning 'Libran', and the
upshot of its specialist use is that it denotes a person born under Libra who
is 'apt to commit suicide', who is therefore 'zigiatus'. There is not a
shred of truth in this tradition, nor does Ptolemy himself appear to use the
word or even to discussss the idea. It is to be observed that Ptolemy's
views on mental disturbances, immorality and demonic possession would find
little adherence (and indeed would probably not even be understood) in modern
astrology. In general it is his practice to write of crises and of
immoralities (which he regards as sickness of the soul) in terms of planetary
configurations, and not in terms of the signs, so that it is hardly likely
that the idea arose with Ptolemy.

ZOAS   See FOUR ZOAS.

ZODIAC   Properly speaking, the belt centred on the ecliptic, divided into
twelve arcs of 30 degrees, called the 'signs of the zodiac', with the
following order:

| Aries | Taurus | Gemini | Cancer | Leo | Virgo |
| Libra | Scorpio | Sagittarius | Capricorn | Aquarius | Pisces |

The term 'zodiac' is shamelessly misunderstood in its strictest meaning and
etymology, so that there is now much confusion in the non-specialist mind
about a thing which at one time was not confusing at all. The confusion has
arisen because of the similarity of the names used to denote the signs of the
zodiac and the twelve asterisms which are included among the 14 or so which
extend into the zodiacal belt. See however CONSTELLATIONS and SIGNS OF THE
ZODIAC, and distinguish between TROPICAL ZODIAC and the CONSTELLATIONAL
ZODIAC. The 'zodiac' is properly the 'zodiacus', a Latin term derived from
the Greek 'zodion', itself etymologically connected with the word 'zoon',
which is difficult of translation, but which (as Smith has shown) is
certainly linked with the idea of 'life' or with 'living beings'. The
popular derivations insist that the Greek zodiac was a 'circle of animals',
which is simply not true: it was a circle of 'living beings' - a concept
which of course links with the 'living beings' of Ezekiel, associated with
the CHERUBIM as the beings who dwell outside time (the limits of time being
marked in the ancient cosmoconception by the Sphere of Saturn). We see,
therefore, that when Wilson says that the zodiac 'takes its name' from the
animals associated with the signs, he is merely getting the derivation the
wrong way round. In any case, it is an elementary mistake to confuse the
SIGNS with the IMAGES. The zodiac is technically a belt, traditionally
extending 8 degrees on either side of the ecliptic (though some earlier
sources give 6 or even 9 degrees) and in modern times the belt would have to
be widened considerably to allow for the eccentricities of the so-called NEW
PLANETS. This should not however disguise the fact that the tropical zodiac
was regarded as a division of the ecliptic itself, into 12 equal-arcs of
thirty degrees. The fact that fixed stars remote in latitude from the
ecliptic were (after suitable geometric adjustment to align them to right
ascension co-ordinates) regarded as projecting their influences upon this
ecliptic, means that in effect the divisions were absolute for all latitudes.
The most influential modern attempt to define the 'sidereal zodiac', which is
distinct from the tropical zodiac, is that of Delporte - see MODERN ZODIAC.
See however SIDEREAL CORRESPONDENCESS and SIDEREAL ZODIAC. For a list of
other zodiacal systems, see ZODIACS. The names of the twelve signs and

the related constellations in early Iranian, Greek, Sanskrit (Hindu) and
Babylonian zodiacs, along with the possible translations for the last, are
given in table 91.

```
---------------------------------------------------------------TABLE 91
      IRANIAN        GREEK        SANSKRIT      BABYLONIAN
      (Sassanian)    (Classical)  (Zodiacal)    (Constellations)
========================================================================
AR    Varak          Krios        Mesham        Hunga (Hireling)
TA    Tora           Tauros       Vrisha        Gud.an.na
GE    Do-patkar      Didemoi      Mithuna       Mas.tab.ba.gal.gal
CN    Kalakang       Karkinos     Karkata       Al.lul
LE    Ser            Leon         Simha         Ur.gu.la
VG    Khusak         Parthenos    Kanya         Ab.sin (Furrow)
LB    Tarazuk        Zugos        Tula          Zibanitu (Horn?)
SC    Gazdum         Skorpios     Vrischika     Gir.tab
SG    Nemasp         Toxotes      Dhanus        Pa.bil.sag
CP    Vahik          Aigokeros    Makara        Suhur.mas (Goat-fish)
AQ    Dul            Hydroxous    Kumbha        Gu.la  (Giant?)
PI    Mahik          Ichthues     Mina          Sim.mah (Swallow?)
------------------------------------------------------------------------
```

ZODIACAL AGE   See PRECESSION.

ZODIACAL ANGELS   As with the ZODIACAL SPIRITS there is much confusion as to
the nomenclature and roles of the 'zodiacal angels', and this confusion is at
least as old as Agrippa.   However, it is the name-list preserved by Agrippa
which has been absorbed into modern astrology, to the extent that the names
are still important, even if the specific functions of the angels are now
confused.   This list, derived from his 'Duodenarii Scala' (see SCALA) is:

```
AR - Malchidiel    TA - Asmodel    GE - Ambriel    CN - Muriel
LE - Verchiel      VG - Hamaliel   LB - Zuriel     SC - Barbiel
SG - Adnachiel     CP - Hanael     AQ - Gabiel     PI - Barchiel
```

The four Archangels, whom Agrippa quite rightly describes as the 'four angels
of the cardinal divisions of the Heavens', are sometimes wrongly called
'zodiacal angels' - these are MICHAEL, RAPHAEL, GABRIEL and URIEL,
respectively of the regions of Fire, Air, Water and Earth.

ZODIACAL BAND   See ECLIPTICAL INCLINATION.

ZODIACAL CALENDARS In Italy there are several calendrical devices which
employ the sunlight to mark the progression of the days. In almost all cases
a small aperture is so arranged as to allow the sunlight to fall upon a line
which calibrates the daily zenith transits of the sun. The calibration is
generally related to the signs of the zodiac, on the standard 'sun in sign'
method. The largest Italian zodiacal calendar is that designed by Cassendi
inside San Petronio, Bologna, but a large and graphically sophisticated
external system is found beneath the arches of the Palazzo della Ragione in
Bergamo: this not only traces the zenith transits, but also the lemniscate
solar motion between the equinoxes and solstices. The small calendar on the
south wall of the Duomo in Turin is perhaps more typical, yet this appears to
mark with the solar beams only the transits through Taurus (the name Turino
is derived from the latin 'Tauro'). There are remains of zodiacal calendars
in several other places in Italy - most notably in the Salone at Padua (see
PADUAN CYCLE), and it is clear that many such calendars existed prior to the
introduction of the mechanical ZODIACAL CLOCKS.

ZODIACAL CHOROGRAPHY   See CHOROGRAPHY.

ZODIACAL CLOCKS After the introduction of the mechanical clock to Europe,
the mediaeval system of sun-driven ZODIACAL CALENDARS gradually gave rise to

===

clockwork calendars, sometimes (confusingly) called Horologia, which also
employed zodiacal imagery. Outstanding examples are still found in working
condition in Brescia, Venice and Padua, though the latter seems to have
imagery influenced by constellational rather than by zodiacal lore. It is
difficult to give precise dates for the zodiacal images on such clocks, since
frequent overhauls and restorations have usually resulted in several changes
in the original images. For example, according to Checchi the zodiacal clock
in Palazzo del Capitanio in Padua, which is said to be by Giovanni Dondi, and
dated 1344, had been restored at least six times prior to the complete
overhaul of 1838.

ZODIACAL COLOURS   A number of different associations between the signs of
the zodiac and colours have been preserved and used within the astrological
tradition, though there is more agreement here than in the associations drawn
up in connexion with the PLANETARY COLOURS. The following may be regarded as
representative, being drawn from a number of ancient and modern sources:

    AR   Red, brilliant red, orange and 'white and red'.
    TA   Red, red and citrine, white and lemon, yellow, red-orange, green,
         'cream colour' and brown.
    GE   Orange, violet, crystal blue and 'colours which clash'.
    CN   Green, soft greens, white, russet, blue-green, orange-yellow and
         'soft colours'.
    LE   Gold, orange, red, yellow, 'red and green'.
    VG   Amber, yellow-green, violet, blue, 'spotted colours', and white
         flecked with blues. Cornell surprisingly gives 'black'.
    LB   Green, yellow, crimson, white, blues, 'dark crimson', tawny and
         dark brown.
    SC   Murky red, blood red, brown, green-blue, dark red and black.
    SG   Blue, sky-blue, red, olive and blue-yellow.
    CP   Blue-violet, russet, indigo, grays and black.
    AQ   Indigo, azure, violet and strong blues, as well as light blues.
    PI   White, violet-red, blues, greens and soft pastel colours, especially
         in light blues and greens.

The 'Chromatic Chart' published by Carey is perhaps the most systematic
attempt to range the zodiacal colour associations, resting as it does on a
series of complementaries. This series, which has no satisfactory
rationalization, and which virtually ignores the traditional associations, is
given as:

    AR - Cerise or Magenta   TA - Scarlet or Cerise-Orange   GE - Orange
    CN - Orange-Yellow   LE - Yellow   VG - Yellow-Green
    LB - Green   SC - Blue-green   SG - Blue
    CP - Blue Violet   AQ - Violet   PI - Cerise-Violet

ZODIACAL CYCLES We have inherited from mediaeval astrological lore a number
of zodiacal fresco cycles which were painted to serve a variety of different
functions. The majority of these cycles are actually compendia of
astrological (and sometimes also correlated theological) lore: for example,
the largest, the PADUAN CYCLE, incorporates material from zodiacal,
planetary, constellational, seasonal and decanate imagery integrated with
both esoteric and exoteric Christian theology. In some other cases, the
cycles are essentially constellational, as for example in the VICENZA CYCLE
which was greatly influenced by Greek and Roman numismatic imagery.   In
other cases, the astrological imagery is designed to portray on a vast scale
a personal horoscope, as in the Chigi Palace in the Farnesina in Rome,
studied (with a few errors) by Gleadow. The so-called zodiacal frescoes in
the Palazzo Schiffanoia in Ferrara (now only partly complete, though recently
restored) are actually a complex series of images based upon a scholarly
reconstruction of mediaeval decanate systems probably derived ultimately from
Egyptian astrology, in turn transformed by Arabian concepts, as suggested by
Warburg and Ancona. Distinguish 'Zodiacal Cycles' from ZODIACAL SCULPTURES.

ZODIACAL DIRECTIONS   A term applied to a limited number of progressed points and planets, which may be directed in the order of the signs (hence 'direct zodiacal directions'), or against the order of the signs (hence 'converse zodiacal directions'). The term should properly be limited to the directions formed by the Ascendant, Midheaven and the luminaries.

ZODIACAL HOUSES   An ambiguous and misleading term which the astrologer Leo attempts to define in relation to signs, rather than houses - 'the signs which any planet rules, or in which it has most influence, are said to be its 'houses''. This is sheer nonsense, though it is often repeated by later writers: SIGNS are not HOUSES and never will be. The sign is a subdivision of an orbital revolution, whilst the houses are usually subdivisons of an axial rotation. A planet may be in the 'sign it rules' and in the 'house it rules' (though in this connexion, see RULERSHIP and LORD), but never in a 'zodiacal house'.

ZODIACAL LIGHT   An elongated, luminous, triangular figure with its base approximately on the horizon which, as Blavatsky claims 'is entirely unknown to science' and may 'be seen only during the morning and evening twilights'. Blavatsky says that since the nature of this 'zodiacal light' is known only to initiates, the real significance and occult meaning of the Zodiac also remains a closed book, save of course to initiates.

ZODIACAL MAN   See MELOTHESIC MAN.

ZODIACAL SCULPTURES The importance of astrological lore in relation to mediaeval theology is attested by the vast number of zodiacal sculptures which have survived on both external and internal fabrics of churches, cathedrals and public buildings. This is especially true of France and Italy. Apart from the sculptures and reliefs on the many ZODIACAL CALENDARS and ZODIACAL CYCLES, important astrological reliefs are found on the outer west-work of Amiens, Chartres and Vezelay. The 14th century zodiac at Chartres is only apparently incomplete, for the 'missing' signs (Gemini and Pisces) are located on the southern door of the west-work, in a mediaeval esoteric symbolism which has been studied in some depth by Gettings. In the narthex of Vezelay (early 14th century), interspersed with seasonal images and theological symbols, are a series of remarkable zodiacal roundels. Indeed, many French cathedrals incorporate zodiacal cycles or individual sculptures relating to cosmic lore. Italy is particularly rich in zodiacal sculptural cycles, as for example in Florence, where both the Baptistry and the church of San Miniato preserve 13th century examples (see SAN MINIATO ZODIAC). In the Baptistry at Parma, above the 12th century zodiacal sculptures by Antelami, are the remains of a system which was without doubt once complete, though now reduced to only four signs, and vestiges of frescoes. The so-called 'zodiacal portal' at La Sacra di San Michele (Val di Susa) is actually a 12th century 'constellational portal', with the 12 zodiacal images and 19 constellational images. It has been claimed by Naylor that the zodiacal sculptures (1497) in the gateway ceiling of Merton College, Oxford, are orientated in relation to a personal horoscope, but as no planets are incorporated (either as symbols or sigils), this is extremely unlikely.

ZODIACAL SPIRITS   In the esoteric tradition, the true 'zodiacal spirits' are variously the CHERUBIM and the SERAPHIM, depending upon the system of hierarchies used.   However, the term is often in modern times misused for any of the spirits associated with the individual signs of the zodiac (for example, 'Ausiel' as zodiacal spirit, or Governor, of zodiacal Aquarius). Such names go back to the time when it was believed that the planetary motions were regulated by spiritual beings. Even by the time of Agrippa, when the last fragments of the esoteric tradition relating to spirits were being put into print, there was much confusion as to spiritual beings, the ZODIACAL ANGELS, the SECUNDADEIAN BEINGS, the PLANETARY ANGELS, the rulers of the DECANS, and even the whole range of CELESTIAL HIERARCHIES being confused in name and operation.

===

ZODIACS   Many different names have been used to describe the various
zodiacal systems - for a brief outline of the main historical forms, see
ASTRONOMICAL ZODIAC, BABYLONIAN ZODIAC, CONSTELLATIONAL ZODIAC, GREEK ZODIAC,
MODERN ZODIAC, SIDEREAL ZODIAC, STAR CALENDAR ZODIAC and ZODIAC.

ZODIACUS VITAE   The Latin for 'zodiac of life', sometimes applied to the
idea that the various signs of the zodiac symbolize (in their progression
from Aries to Pisces) sequential eras or periods which may be related
analogously to the life of mankind, individual humans, mythopoetic legends,
and so on.

ZONA ANDROMEDAE   See MIRACH.

ZONES   See CHOROGRAPHY.

ZONE TIMES   See TIME ZONES.

ZOON   See ZODIAC.

ZOSMA   Fixed star (triple), the delta of constellation Leo, set in the
lion's back, the name from the Greek for 'girdle'. Another name 'Zubra' is
cognate with ZUBRAH, which means 'mane', perhaps in reference to a displaced
image. It is said to be of an influence equivalent to Saturn and Venus, and
is connected with egotism, melancholy and immorality.

ZUBENELGENUBI   Fixed star (double), the alpha of Libra, set in the 'southern
scale' of the balance. The name is from the Arabic phrase meaning 'southern
claw', from the Grecian 'Chela Notios', the reference to the claw deriving
from the image of constellation Scorpio, which at one time was pictured as
covering the Libran asterism with its own pincers, or 'claws'. There are
several derivative names and alternatives. Perhaps because of the ancient
link with the claws of Scorpio, the star is said to bring disgrace, sickness
and treachery, as well as dangers from poisoning. Ptolemy says that it is of
the nature of Mars conjunct Saturn.

ZUBENELSCHEMALI   Fixed star, the beta of constellation Libra, the name being
derived from the Arabic phrase meaning 'northern claw', itself from the
Grecian 'Chela Boreios' (see ZUBENELGENUBI). Unlike the latter star, its
'balance weight', this star is said to bring good fortune, honours and
happiness. Ptolemy likens it to the nature of Mercury conjunct Jupiter.

ZUBRAH   'Al Zubrah', the 9th of the Arabic MANZILS. See also ZOSMA.

ZUGOS   One of the Greek names for the sign and constellation Libra, used by
Ptolemy. An earlier term, 'Chelon ton Skorpion' (claws of the Scorpion)
points to a time when the constellation was regarded as being a part of the
Scorpio asterism.

===

BIBLIOGRAPHY

ABANO Pietro d'Abano   Lucidator Astronomiae. / Tractatulus... De aspectibus
planetarum versus Lunam. (trans. of supp. Hippocratus). 1608. * ACOSTA J.
Acosta   Histoire naturelle et Morale des Indes, Paris, 1600. * ADAM C.G.M.
Adam   Fresh Sidelights on Astrology. London, 1916. * ADDEY J.M. Addey
Astrology Reborn. Bournemouth, 1973 / The Discrimination of Birthtypes.
Bournemouth, 1974 / Harmonies in Astrology. 1976. * AGRIPPA H.C. Agrippa
ab Nettesheym   De Occulta Philosophia. 1533. * ALBERTI L.B. degli
Alberti   De Re Aedificatoria L.IX. 1485. * AL BIRUNI Muhammad ibn Ahmad
(Abu Al Rashan)   The Book of Instruction in the Elements of the Art of
Astrology. Written in Ghaznah, 1029 AD, trans. by R.R. Wright, London, 1934.
* ALFRAGANUS   Ahmad ibn Mohammad ibn Kathir (Al Farghani). Elementa
Astronomica. Amsterdam, 1669. * ALLEN   D.C. Allen   The Star-Crossed
Renaissance. Durham, N.Carolina, 1941. * ALLEN G. Allen   See "American
Astrology" Sep. 1957, and extensive references under DEANE below (esp.
p.47-71). * ALLEN R.H. Allen   Star Names. Their Lore and Meaning. New
York, 1963. * ALVIDAS H.C. Hodges   Science and Key of Life. 1903 etc. *
ANCONA Paolo d' Ancona   The Schifanoia Months of Ferrara (trans. L.
Krasvik). Milan, 1955. * ANGELUS J.Johannes Angelus   Astrolabium Planum
in tabulis Ascendens. Venice, 1488.   See also Johann Engel, Astrologicall
Opticks. London, 1655. See also The Faces and Degrees of the Zodiac,
reprinted by 'Raphael', c.1902 etc. * ARATUS   Arati Solensis Phaenomena,
et prognostica...etc. Paris, 1559. See also: Arati Phaenomena, Ernest
Maass. Berlin 1955. * ARISTOTLE   De Coelo, and De Generatione. In regard
to cycles, see HASTINGS below. * ARNALDUS   Arnaldi de Villanova medici
acutissimi opera nuperrime revisa... Lugduni, 1532. * ATHENAGORAS   See
W.K.C. Guthrie   Orpheus and Greek Religion. London, 1952. * BACON Roger
Bacon et. al.   The Mirror of Alchimy. London, 1597. * BAILEY   Alice A.
Bailey   Esoteric Astrology. New York & London, 1951 / The Externalization
of the Hierarchy. Tunbridge Wells, 1957. * BAILEY   E.H. Bailey   The
Prenatal Epoch. London, 1916 / Astrology and Birth Control. London, 1929.
* BALLARIN A. Ballarin, Pinacoteca di Vicenza Vicenza, 1982. * BARZON
A. Barzon I Cieli e la loro influenza   Padua, 1924. * BARRETT B.F.
Barrett   Heaven Revealed.   London, 1885. * BARRETT F.Barrett   The Magus,
or Celestial Intelligencer. London, 1801. * BARTSCHIUS Jakob Bartsch
Planisphaerium Stellatum. 1624. * BAYER   Joannes Bayer   Uranometria
omnium asterismorium. 1603. * BECK R.Beck   'Interpreting the Ponza
Zodiac'. 'Journal of Mithraic Studies', Vol. 1, No. 1, 1976. * BECKH H.
Beckh   Der Kosmische Rhythmus im Markus-Evangelium. Basel, 1928. * BESANT
A.Besant & C.W. Leadbeater Thought Forms London, 1901 / Man, Whence, How
and Whither. London, 1913. * BLAKE   See S.F.Damon   A Blake Dictionary.
Brown University, 1965, and GETTINGS below. * BLAVATSKY H.P. Blavatsky
Isis Unveiled. New York, 1877 / The Secret Doctrine. 1888 (Pasedena ed.
1970). * BLUNDEVILLE   M.B. Blundeville His Exercises. But see Gettings,
"Astrology", No.1, 1977. * BOBER H.Bober. The Zodiacal miniature of the
Tres Riches Heures of the Duke of Berry its source and meaning. "Journal of
the Warburg and Courtauld Institutes, XI, 1948. * BOEHME   Jacob Boehme
Three Principles. See also GETTINGS, LAW & MUSES below. * BOLL F.Boll,
C.Bezold & W.Gundel   Sternglaube und Sterndeutung. Stuttgart, 1966. *
BONATUS   Antonius Franciscus de Bonattis. Universa astrosophia Naturalis.
Patarii, 1687. * BONATUS G. Bonatus   De Astronomia Tractatus (ed.
Prueckner) Basle, 1550. * BORELLI   Antonio Borelli   See trans. by
'Sepharial' of La Volasfera in: 'Charubel'   Degrees of the Zodiac
Symbolized. London, 1898. * BOSC E.Bosc (J.Marcus de Vege) La Doctrine
esoterique a travers les ages. Paris, 1899. / Glossaire raisonné de la
divination.. Paris, 1910. * BOUCHE-LECLERCQ A. Bouché-Leclercq
L'Astrologie Grecque Paris, 1899 / Histoire de la divination dans
l'antiquité. Paris, 1874. * BRADLEY D.A.Bradley Profession and Birthdate.
Los Angeles, 1950 / Solar and Lunar Returns. Minnesota, 1968. * BRAHE
Tycho Brahe   Astronomiae Instauratae Progymnasmata. Francfurt 1610. * BRAU

===

J.L.Brau (et. al.) Larousse Encyclopaedia of Astrology (USA ed. 1980). *
BUTLER   Hiram E. Butler   Solar Biology. A Scientific Method. California &
London, 1920. * CARELLI   A. Carelli The 360 Degrees of the Zodiac.
Washington DC, 1951. * CAREY   G.W. Carey & I.E. Perry   The Zodiac and the
Salts of Salvation. New York, 1971. * CARRUTHERS   P.J. Carruthers   The
Degrees of the Zodiac. (Journal of Astrological Studies. No.1, 1970). *
CARTER   C.E.O. Carter The Principles of Astrology Theoretical and Applied.
London, 1925. / Symbolic Directions in Modern Astrology. London, 1929. /
Astrological Aspects. (10th ed.), London, 1969. * CHECCHI   M.Checchi (et.
al.) Guida ai monumenti e alle oggeti d'arte. Venice, 1961. * CENSORINUS
De Die Natali. Venice, 1581. * CHACORNAC   Tables de Maisons "Chacornac" -
Pour les latitudes de 0 deg. a 57 deg. Paris, 1972. * CHARUBEL
"Charubel" The Degrees of the Zodiac Symbolized. London, 1898. * CHOISNARD
P.C. Choisnard (Paul Flambart)   Langage Astral. Traité sommaire d'astrolgie
scientifique. Paris, 1930 / La Methode statistique et le bon sens en
astrologie scientifique. Paris, 1930. * CHRISTIAN   P. Christian See the
critical trans. by J. Kirkup and J.Shaw: The History and Practice of Magic.
New York, 1963. * CICERO   For the Somnium Scipionis, along with the
exposition of Macrobius, see MACROBIUS. * COLEY   H. Coley   Anima
astrologiae... London? 1676. / Clavis Astrologiae elemata... London, 1676. *
COLLIN   R. Collin The Theory of Celestial Influences   London, 1954. *
CONCHES   William of Conches   Philosophicarum et Astronomicarum. Basle,
1531. * CORFIELD   J. Corfield   "The Urania", No. 1, June, 1814. *
CORNELL   H.L. Cornell   Encyclopaedia of Medical Astrology (3rd revised
ed., with introduction by L. Lowell. Minnesota & York, 1972. * CROMBIE
A.C. Crombie Augustine to Galileo. London, 1952. * CUMONT   F.V.M. Cumont
Astrology and Religion among the Greeks and Romans. New York & London, 1912.
See also 'Les Noms de Planètes', "L'Antiquité Classique", IV-I. * DANTE
Dante Alghieri   Divina Commedia. For specialist astrological background,
see MOORE and TOYNBEE below. * DAVIS   A.J. Davis   The Principles of
Nature, her divine revelations. London, 1847. / The Penetralia. Boston, 1858
/ The Diakka, and their earthly victims, being an explanation of much that is
false and repulsive in spiritualism. New York, 1873. * DAVISON   R.C.
Davison   "Astrology". Vol.36, No.3, 1962 / The Technique of Prediction.
London, 1971. * DEAN   Geoffrey Dean (et. al.)   Recent Advances in Natal
Astrology. Subiaco, Western Australia, 1977. * DEE   John Dee   Monas
Hieroglyphica. Antwerp, 1564. None of the several available translations is
reliable. * DELAPORTA G.Battista della Porta De Humana Physiognomonia..
Hanover, 1593 / Coelestis physiognomoniae...In quibus etiam Astrologia
refellitur, et inanis et imaginaria demonstratur. Naples 1603. * DELPORTE
E. Delporte   Atlas Céleste. Cambridge, 1930 / Délimitation scientifique des
constellations. Cambridge, 1930. * DERNAY   E.Dernay Longitudes and
Latitudes Throughout the World. New York, 1948. * DEUSEN   E.L. van Deusen
Astrogenetics   London, 1976. * DEVORE   N. De Vore   Encyclopaedia of
Astrology   New York, 1947. * DIESCHBOURG   J. Dieschbourg   For personal
communications, see DEAN above, p.313ff. * DIODORUS Diodorus of Tarsus -
see "On Destiny", in Photius, cod. 233. Patr. Greque, book CIII, p.878.
(quoted in brief by FULCANELLI below). * DIONYSIUS   Dionysius the
Areopagite   Mystical Theology and the Celestial Hierarchies   (trans. by
Editors of the Shrine of Wisdom) Fintry, Brook, Nr. Godalming, 1965. *
DOANE   D.C. Doane   How to Read Cosmodynes. 1974. * DOBYNS   Z.P.Dobyns
The Node Book. Los Angeles, 1973.   For pre-1971 and post-1974 heliocentric
advance errors, see DEAN above, p.275. * DRINKWATER G.N. Drinkwater
Theosophy and the Western Mysteries. London, 1944. * DURANDUS   William
Durandus   Rationale Divinorum Officiorum, De Ecclesia et eius partibus
(sec.8). But see also NISSEN below. * EBERTIN   Reinhold Ebertin
Kombination der Gestirneinflüsse. (trans. A.G. Roosedale and L. Kratzsch:
The Combination of Stellar Influences). Aalen, 1972. See also supplement 1,
1961, trans. Ilse Hodges and C.Harvey. / Man in the Universe. An
Introduction to Cosmogiology. (trans. L. Kratzsch). Aalen, 1973 / Die
Bedeutung der Fixsterne (incorporating material by E. Ebertin and G.
Hoffmann, et. al.). Trans. Fixed Stars and their Interpretation. Aalen, 1971
/ Transits. 1972. * EDWARDS   Ormond Edwards   A New Chronology of the

Gospels. 1978. (translated Chronologie des Lebens Jesu und das Zeitgeheimnis
der Drei Jahre. Stuttgart. 1978. * ELFERNIK M.A. Elfernik   "La Descente de
l'âme d'après Macrobe." in Philosophia Antiqua Vol. 16, 1968. * EPPING   J.
Epping   Astronomisches aus Babylon oder das wissen der Chaldäer über den
gestirnten Himmel... Freiburg im Breisgau, 1889. * ERLEWINE   M. Erlewine
(et. al.) Interface - Planetary Nodes. Michigan, 1976 / M. & M. Erlewine
Astrophysical Directions   Michigan, 1977. * EUSEBIUS   Eusabius of
Alexandria   See Sermo de Astronomis. Patrum Nova Bibliotheca, 1852 and Peri
Astronommon, quam, praemissa de Magis et Stella quaestione... (ed. T.C.
Thilo)   Halae, 1834. * EVANS   Joan Evans   Magical Jewels of the Middle
Ages and the Renaissance. Oxford, 1922. * FAGAN   Cyril Fagan   Astrological
Origins.   Minnesota, 1971 / Zodiacs Old and New. London, 1951. * FEERHOV
F. Feerhov   Kursus der praktischen Astrologie. Leipzig, 1912. * FIGUIER
G.L. Figuier   Keppler, ou l'Astrologie et L'Astronomie Paris, 1889. *
FIRMICUS   Firmicus Maternus   Materni Junioris...Astronomicon libri VIII per
Nicolaum Prucknerum astrologum nuper ab innimeris mendis vindicati.   1533 /
Matheseos Liber Venice, 1499. * FLAMSTEAD   J. Flamsteed   Atlas Coelestis
(ed. M.F. & J. Hodgson) 1729. See also PEARCE below, pp 17-20. * FLUDD
Robert Fludd   Utriusque cosmi minoris et majores technica Historia...
1617-21. * FOERSTER W.J. Foerster   Johann Keppler und die Harmonie der
Sphären.   1862. * FOUCHER   L. Foucher "Découvertes Archéologiques à
Thysdrus en 1961." Institut d'Archéologie, Tunis. Notes et Documents, Vol. V
(new series). * FRANKLAND   W.Frankland   Astrological Investigations.
London, 1927 / New Meaning in Astrology. London, 1929 / Keys to Symbolic
Directing. London, 1930. * FREHER See MUSES. * FULCANELLI Fulcanelli
Le Mystere des Cathedrales: Esoteric interpretation of the Hermetic Symbols
of the Great Work. (trans. M. Sworder), London, 1971. * FYFE   Agnes Fyfe
Die Signatur des Mondes im Pflanzenreich. 1967. Moon and Plant. Capillary
Dynamic Studies. Arlesheim, 1975 / The Signature of the Planet Mercury in
Plants. / Capillary Dynamic Studies (reprinted from the British Homoeopathic
Journal. LXII No 4 (1973), LXIII No 1 (1974), LXIII No 2 (1974). * GAFURUS
F. Gafurius   Practica Musice. Mediolani, 1496. See also The Practica
Musicae of Franchinus Gafurius. (trans. I.Young) University of Wisconsin
Press. 1969. * GARDNER J.E. Gardner   Dante's Ten Heavens. A Study of the
Paradiso. London, 1898. * GAUQUELIN M. Gauquelin L'Influence des Astres.
Étude Critique et et expérimentale. Paris, 1955 / Cosmic Influences on Human
Behaviour. London, 1974. / The Cosmic Clocks: from Astrology to a Modern
Science   Chicago, 1967. * GAURICUS L. Gauricus   Tractatus Astrologicus.
1542. / Trattato d'Astrolgia Iudiciaria sopra le nativite degli huomini et
donne. 1539 / Calendarium ecclesiasticum novum... 1552. * GENTRY P.
Gentry   Cosmogonie et Astrologie de l'Extreme Occident dans le Voile d'Isis
Paris, 1922. * GENUIT   H. Genuit "In Memoriam Dr. Walter A. Koch"
"Astrology" 45, No 1, 1971. * GETTINGS   F. Gettings   The Hidden Art: A
study of occult symbolism in Art. London, 1978. / The Secrets of San Miniato
al Monte. The Christian mysteries of the nave zodiac. (Trans. French,
N.Marque; Italian, C.M. de Mariassevich, and German, H. Kahnert) Florence,
1982. / Dictionary of Occult, Hermetic and Alchemical Sigils. London, Boston,
1981. * GLEADOW R.Gleadow The Origin of the Zodiac   London, 1968. * GOAD
John Goad   Astro-Meteorologica, or Aphorisms and Discoveries of the Bodies
Caelestial... London, 1686. * GOODMAN F. Goodman "Secrets of the Stone
Towers" - "Unexplained", Vol.9, Issue, 107, 1982. * GRAY   W.G. Gray The
Ladder of Lights (or Qabalah Renovata). Toddington, 1971. * GUNDEL W.
Gundel "Dekane und Dekansternbilder" Studien der Bib. Warburg Vol. XIX 1936.
* HAASE   R. Haase   Kepler's Harmonies, between Pansophia and Mathesis
Universalis. 'Vistas in Astronomy'. Vol. 18, 1975. * HADES   A.Y.Hades
Manuel Complet d'Astrologie Scientifique et Traditionelle. Paris, 1967. *
HALL Manly P. Hall   Astrological Keywords. London, 1959. * HAND R.S.Hand
"A New Approach to Transits" - "Cosmecology Bulletin", No.4 1976. / "Science
and Symbolism in Astrology" "Geocosmic News" 5,1. Sep. 1979. * HARRIS T.L.
Harris   A Lyric of the Golden Age. New York, 1856 / Arcana of Christianity.
New York & London, 1867 / Wisdom of the Adepts. Fountain Grove, 1884. *
HARRISON   C.J.Harrison   Transcendental Univers. London, 1894. * HARWOOD
STEELE (Introduction by Harwood Steele to Itinerary of "The Somerset

===

Giants" by K.E. Maltwood - British Columbia, no date). * HASBROUCK M.M.
Hasbrouck   The Pursuit of Destiny. New York, 1976. * HASTINGS   James
Hastings (et. al.)   Encyclopaedia of Religion and Ethics. Edinburgh & New
York, 1971 ed. * HAWKINS J.R. Hawkins   Transpluto 1976. * HEIDENREICH
A. Heidenreich The Unknown in the Gospels. London, 1972. * HEINDEL   M.
Heindel   The Rosicrucian Cosmo-Conception. California & London, 1971 (26th
edition) / The Message of the Stars (with A.F. Heindel) California & London,
1919. * HEVELIUS J. Hevelius   Firmamentum Sobiescianum, sive
Uranographia... Gedani, 1690. * HIERATIC EPHEMERIS   The Complete Planetary
Ephemeris for 1950 to 2000 AD. The Hieratic Publishing Co., Massachusetts,
1975?. * HIEROZ J. Hieroz   L'Astrologie selon Morin de Villefranche...
Paris, 1962. * HITSCHLER See R.C. Davison "Atomic Medicine - the Hitschler
Method" "Astrology". Vol. 37, No. 4, 1963. * HONE M.E. Hone   The Modern
Textbook of Astrology London, 1951. * HOWE   E.Howe   Urania's Children.
The Strange World of the Astrologers. London, 1967. * HYGINUS C.J.Hyginus
Poeticon Astronomicon. Venice, 1485. See also The Myths of Hyginus (trans.
M. Grant) 1960. * ISIDORE   Incipit liber primus Ethimologiarum Isidori
Hispalensis Episcopi.. Strasbourg, 1470. / Liber ethymologiarum Isidori
Hyspalensis Episcopi. Basle, 1489. * IVANOFF N. Ivanoff Il problema
iconologico degli affreschi. In 'Il Palazzo della Ragione di Padova'. Padua,
1963. * JACOBSON R.A.Jacobson 'Using the 90-degree Dial...' in "Spica"
Vol. 9, No. 1, 1969. * JAYNE C.A. Jayne   The Unknown Planets. New York,
1974 / Horoscope Interpretation Outlined. New York, 1970 / "Astrology Now",
Vol.1, No.8, 1975. * JEREMIAS A. Jeremias   Das Alte Testament in Lichte
des alten Orients. (trans. C.L. Beaumont, The Old Testament in the Light of
the Ancient East.London, 1911), Leipsig, 1904. * JOHNDRO L.E. Johndro The
Stars. How and Why They Influence. New York, 1973 / The Earth in the
Heavens New York, 1973. * JONAS   E.Jonas (Ed.) See S.Ostrander & L.
Schroeder, Astrological Birth Control. New Jersey, 1972. * JONES   M. E.
Jones   Sabian Symbols in Astrology. New York, 1953 / The Scope of
Astrological Prediction. Washington, 1969. * JOCELYN   J. Jocelyn
Meditations on the Signs of the Zodiac London, 1970. * JUNCTINUS
F.Junctinus   Speculum Astrologiae. Lugduni, 1583 / De Divinatione, quae
fit per astra diversum. Coloniae, 1580. * JUNG   See H.I. Bach. C.G. Jung
on 'Synchronicity'. A synopsis by Bach of the article entitled
'Skynchronizitat als ein Prinzip ...' in Naturerklarung und Psyche by C.G.
Jung and W. Pauli.' 1953. * KEANE   J.L. Keane What the Degrees Mean.
Conneticut, 1976. * KEMPTER F. Kempter Rudolf Steiners Sieben Zeichen der
Planetarischen Entwicklung   Engelberg/Wuerttemberg, 1967. * KEPLER
Johannes Kepler   J. Keppleri Harmonices Mundi. Lincii, 1619 (See also
FIGUIER, FOERSTER and HAASE above and PAULI below). * KIRCHER A. Kircher
Oedipus Aegyptiacus; Hoc est, Universalis Hierglyphicae veterum...
instauratio. Rome, 1652. * KLIBANSKY (R.Klibansky, E. Panofsky and F. Saxl)
Saturn and Melancholy. London, 1964. * KOCH W.A. Koch (and W. Knappich)
Horoskop und Himmelshausen. (T1.2 Regiomontaus und das Hausersystem des
Geburtsortes) 1952 etc. / W.A.Koch & E. Schaeck   Hauser Tabellen des
Geburtsortes   1971. * KOLISKO L. Kolisko   Der Mond und das
Pflanzenwachstum. (The Moon and the Growth of Plants - trans. Pease and
Mirbt) 1936. / The Working of the Stars on Earthly Substance. Stuttgart,
1928. / Gold and the Sun. Stroud, 1947. Sternewirken in Erdenstoffen.
Saturn und Blei. Stroud, 1953. * KONIG   K. Konig   "The Zodiac" in The
Modern Mystic, Feb. 1937: Mar. 1937. * KRAFFT   K.E. Krafft Traité
d'Astro-Biologie   Brussels, 1939. * KRUPP   E.C. Krupp (Ed.) In Search of
Ancient Astronomies. London, 1979. * KUGLER F.X. Kugler   Die Babylonische
Mondrechnung... Freiburg in B. 1900 / Sternkunde und Sterndienst in Babel.
Munster, 1907. * LACAILLE L. Lacaille A catalogue of 9766 Stars in the
Southern Hemisphere... London, 1847. * LANDSCHEIDT   T. Landscheidt
Cosmic Cybernetics: the Foundations of a Modern Astrology (trans. L.
Kratzch) Aalen, 1973. * LAW   W.Law   The Works of Jacob Behmen the
Teutonic Theosopher, 1764. * LEADBEATER C.W. Leadbeater   The Astral Plane.
London, 1895. The Hidden Side of Things Adyar, 1923 (See also A.E. POWELL
below). * LEINBACH   E.V. Leinbach Degrees of the Zodiac. Virginia, 1973.
* LEO   Alan Leo See titles in Re-issue of the 'Astrology for all' Series,

of 1912, with new titles - Astrology for All: Casting the Horoscope: How to
Judge a Nativity: The Art of Synthesis: The Progressed Horoscope: The Key
to Your own Nativity, and Esoteric Astrology. See also Alan Leo's Dictionary
of Astrology, ed. by Vivian E. Robson, 1929. / Alan Leo's Astrological
Manuals, No. 11 - A Thousand and One Notable Nativities. c.1910. * LEWIS
Jim Lewis Astrocartography. San Francisco, 1976. * LEWIS C.S. Lewis The
Discarded Image   London, 1964. * LIBRA C.Aq. Libra (pseud)   Astrology. Its
Technics and Ethics (trans. G. Coba) Amersfoort, 1917. * LILLY   Wm. Lilly
Introduction to Astrology by W.L. (Zadkiel ed.) 1835 / Christian Astrology,
modestly treated... London, 1659 / Anima Astrologiae (ed. Lilly) London,
1676. * LOVE   R.G. Love   "An Outline of the Topocentric System."
"Astrology". Vol. 51, No.2, 1977. * LORENZ D.M.Lorenz   Tools of Astrology
- Houses. Eomega Grove Press, 1976. * LOVEJOY A.O. Lovejoy The Great
Chain of Being   Harvard, 1936. * LUNDY   J.P. Lundy. Monumental
Christianity, or the Art and Symbolism of the Primitive Church. London,
1882. * LYNCH   J.Lynch   The Coffee Table Book of Astrology   London,
1962. * MACROBIUS   Somnium Scipionis ex Ciceronis libro de Repubblica
excertum Venice, 1472. (see also ELFERINK). * MALTWOOD K.Maltwood   A
Guide to Glastonbury's temple of the stars. London, 1929 / See also HARWOOD
STEELE above. * MANILIUS I. Manilius   M.Manilius Astronomicon a Josepho
Scaligero. Venice, 1532. * MASSEY   G. Massey The Natural Genesis
London, 1883. * MATHEWS   Mathews' Chinese-English Dictionary   Cambridge,
Mass., 1966. * MATTHEWS E.C. Matthews. Fixed Stars and Degrees of the
Zodiac Analyzed. Bloomington, Illinois, 1968. * MAYO   J. Mayo   The
Astrologer's Astronomical Handbook   London, 1976. * MEAD G.R.S. Mead
Fragments of a Faith Forgotten   New Yorks, 1960. * MEIER H.C. Meier
Spannugsherrscher und Schiksalstypus.   Memmingen, 1939 / Spannung und
Spanniungsherrscher. "Kosmobiologisches Jahrbuch", 1977. * MESSADIE G.
Messadie Le Zodiaque a 24 Signes. Paris, 1973. * MEYER M.R. Meyer. A
Handbook for the Humanistic Astrologer. New York, 1974 / The Astrology of
Relationships   New York, 1976. * MITCHELL J. Michell   A Little History of
Astro-archaeology. London, 1977. * MOORE E. Moore   Studies in Dante
(Third Series) 1.The Astronomy of Dante. Oxford, 1968 ed. * MORRISH L.F.
Morrish Outline of Astrol-Psychology London, 1952. * MORRISON A.H.
Morrison   Astrological Review, Vol. 45. No. 1. 1973. * MUCHERY G. Muchery
The Astrological Tarot, Astromancy (trans. M. Vallior) London, 1928 / Méthode
practique d'astrologie divinatoire. Paris, 1933. / Traité complet de
chiromancie déductive et expérimentale. Paris, 1938. * MUNKASEY M.
Munkasey "The Houses: the Measurement View - Twenty Different Systems".
"Astrology Now"   Vol.1, No.8, Nov. 1975. * MUSES C.A.Muses   Illumination
on Jacob Boehme. The Works of Dionysius Andreas Freher. New York, 1951. *
MYER I. Myer. Qabbalah. The Philosophical Writings of Solomon ben Yedhuda
ibn Gebirol or Avicebron. 1972. * NAYLOR P.I.H. Naylor   Astrology. An
Historical Examination. London, 1967. * NELSON   J.H. Nelson. Cosmic
Patterns: Their Influence on Man and His Communications. Washington DC,
1974. * NEUGEBAUER   Otto Neugebauer A History of Ancient Mathematical
Astronomy, 1975. / 'Demotic Horoscopes' in The Journal of the American
Oriental Society Vol 63, 1943 / O. Neugebauer and H.B. van Hosen   Greek
horoscopes. Philadelphia, 1959 / 'Studies in Byzantine Astronomical
Terminology', "Trans. Am. Philos. Soc." 50, 2 (1960). * NISSEN   H. Nissen
Orientation, Studien zur Geschichte der Religion, 1906. * NOWOTNY   K.A.
Nowotny   De Occulta Philosophia: Agrippa ab Nettesheym. Graz, 1967. *
OUSPENSKY P.D. Ouspenksy   In Search of the Miraculous. Fragments of an
unknown teaching. London, 1949 / A New Model of the Universe   London, 1931.
* OVID Metamorphosis. * PAGAN   I.M. Pagan   From Pioneer to Poet
London. 1911. / Racial Cleavage, or The Seven Ages of Man   London, 1937. *
PANOFSKY E. Panofsky   Studies in Iconology. Oxford, 1967. * PARACELSUS
See A.E.Waite. The Hermetical and Alchemical Writings of...Paracelsus the
Great... Vol.2 - Hermetic Medicine and Hermetic Philosophy. London, 1894. *
PAULI W.P.Pauli The Influnece of Archetypal Ideas on the Scientific
Theories of Kepler. 1955. * PAVITT W.T. and K Pavitt   The Book of
Talismans   London, 1914. * PEARCE   A.J.Pearce   The Text Book of
Astrology. London, 1911. * PENROSE   F.C. Penrose   Temple Orientation

London, 1851. * PETARIUS   Dionysii Petarii   Uranologion. Basle, 1630. *
PHILALETHES See A.E. WAITE below, and Martin Rutlandus, Lexicon Alchemiae.
Frankfurt, 1583. * PINGREE See WIEDNER below. * PLINY Natural History.
II. 13. * POLICH V. Polich and A.P.N. Page. The Topocentric System of
Houses. "Spica", Vol. 3 No. 3, 1964. See also LOVE above. * POWELL   A.E.
Powell   The Solar System   London, 1930. * POWELL Robert Powell   "Mercury
Star Journal", Vol. IV, No.2, 1978. / R.Powell and P. Treadgold   The
Sidereal Zodiac. 1978.   * PTOLEMY C. Ptolemaeus Tetrabiblos. (See
ROBBINS below). * RAM   Th. J.J. Ram. Astrological Journal. Vol. 15, No.
2, 1973. * RAPHAEL   Raphael's Astronomical Ephemerides for given years. /
Raphael's Tables of Houses for Northern Latitudes   London, c.1960. *
REGIOMONTANUS   See KOCH above. * RIESS E.Reiss. Nechepsonis et
Petosiridis fragmenta magica. "Philologus", Supplementband VI, 1891-1893. *
ROBBINS   F.E. Robbins   Ptolemy, Tetrabiblos. Ed. and trans. by Robbins.
London, 1964. * ROBSON V.E. Robson   The Fixed Stars and Constellations in
Astrology. London, 1969 / (See also LEO, above) / A Student's Textbook of
Astrology   London, 1922. * ROW Subba Row Collection of Esoteric Writings.
Adya, 1902? * RUDHYAR D.Rudhyar The Astrology of Personality   New York,
1970 / The Practice of Astrology   London, 1968. * RUPERTI   A. Ruperti
Cycles of Becoming. London, 1978. * SACHS   A. Sachs   'Babylonian
Horoscopes' - Journal of Cuneiform Studies, Vol. 6, 1952. *   SCHNABEL
Kidenas, Hipparch und die Entdeckung der Praezession. 1926. * SCHULTZ
Joachim Schultz   Rhythmen der Sterne. Dornach, 1963. * SCHWABE J. Schwabe
Archetyp und Tierkreis, Grundlinien einer kosmishcen Symbolik und Mythologie
Basel, 1951. * SCHWALLER DE LUBICZ   R.A. Schwaller de Lubicz The Temple
is Man. (trans. by R. & D. Lawlor), Massachusetts, 1977. See also TOONDER
below. * SENDIVOGIUS M. Sendivogius A New Light of Alchymie. (trans.
John French) London, 1650. * SEPHARIAL "Sepharial" (pseud.) New Dictionary
of Astrology. London, (no date). / Transits and Planetary Periods. London,
1920 / The Science of Foreknowledge   London, 1918. * SIBLY E. Sibly An
Illustration of Astrology   London, 1798 / A new ... Illustration of ...
Astrology   London, 1817 / Uranoscopia   London, 1780. * SIMMONITE W.J.
Simmonite   The Complete Arcana of Practical Astrological Philosophy
London, 1890. * SMITH E.M. Smith   The Zodia   London, 1906. *
SPIEGELBERG W. Spiegelberg 'Die Ägyptischen Namen und Zeichen der
Tierkreisbilder' in "Zeitschrift fur Aegyptische Sprache und Altertumskunde"
Vol. 48 1911. * SUTCLIFFE G.E. Sutcliffe. Two Undiscovered Planets. (no
date) / The New Astronomy and Cosmic Physiology London, 1930. * STEIN
W.J. Stein Man and His Place in History. 1947. * STEINER Rudolf Steiner
The Search for the New Isis - Divine Sophia. (Trans. of four lectures given
in Dec. 1920). / Macrocosm and Microcosm. (Trans of eleven lectures given in
Vienna, March, 1910). / Man in the Light of Occultism (Trans of ten lectures
given in Christiania, June, 1912). / Occult Movements in the Nineteenth
Century. (Trans. of ten lectures given in Dornach, Oct., 1915). / An
Esoteric Cosmology. (Trans. of 18 lectures given by R.S. in Paris, 1906,
reported by Schure - English ed. 1978) / See also KEMPTER above. * STONE
J.H. van Stone   The Pathway of the Soul. London, 1912. * SUCHER   W.O.
Sucher Cosmic Christianity   1970 / Isis Sophia: An Outline of a New Star
Wisdom   1955 and 1975 / The Changing Face of Cosmology   1971. *
SWEDENBORG E. Swedenborg De Coelo et ejus miriabilibus, et de Inferno.
1758. (see also BARRETT B.F.) * SWEENEY B.M. Rhythmic Phenomena in Plants
London & New York, 1969. * TAKATA M. Takata. Zur Technik der
Glockungszahlreaktion in menschlichen serum... "Helvetica Medica Acta" Vol.
17, 1950. * TAYLOR   Rene Taylor   Architecture and Magic. In Essays in the
History of Architecture, presented to Rudolf Wittkower, 1962. * TESTA P.E.
Testa Il Simbolismo dei Giudeo-Cristiani   Bari, 1962. * THIERENS A.E.
Thierens   The Elements of Esoteric Astrology. London, 1931. * THOM
A.Thom   Megalithic Lunar Observatories   Oxford, 1973. * THOMAS K.Thomas
Religion and the Decline of Magic. London, 1971. * THORBURN   J.M.
Thorburn. Notes on the Heliocentric Co-ordinates of Planetary Positions.
"The Astrological Journal (UK)", Vol. 3, No. 3, 1961. * THUN   Maria Thun
'Nine Years Observation of Cosmic Influences on Annual Plants.' in "Star and
Furrow"   Spring, 1964. * THOMPSON C.J.S. Thompson   The Mystery and

I H
CORP
PLAN

25·11·88
29/3
17/9/90
4/6/92

REFERENCE ONLY

26·3·93
-3/10/08

13 MAY 2015

For Enquiries or Renewal at
Ardleigh Green LRC
Tel: 01708 455011 Ext: 2040

Romance of Astrology. London, 1929. * TOONDER   J.G. Toonder and J.A. West. The Case for Astrology. London, 1973. * TOYNBEE   P.J.Toynbee   Dante's Obligation to Alfraganus in the Vita Nuova and Convivio. Romania XXXII, 565ff. * TOWNLEY   J. Townley   Astrological Cycles and the Life Crisis Periods   New York, 1977. * TRITHEMIUS   J. Trithemius   De Septem Secundadeis, id est intelligentiis... Nurenberg (15)22. * TUCKER   W.J. Tucker   Astrology for Everyman. Kent, 1960. / The Principles, Theory and Practice of Scientific Prediction. London, 1936. * TUCKERMAN   B. Tuckerman Planetary, Lunar, and Solar Positions - 601 BC to AD 1 - At Five-day and Ten-day Intervals. Philadelphia, 1962. * VARLEY   J. Varley   A Treatise on Zodiacal Physiognomy. London, 1828. * VERMASEREN   M.J.Vermaseren - see 'Mithriaca' II, 1974 and BECK above. * VILLEFRANCHE   M. De Villefranche Astrologia Gallica. Paris, 1661. * VIRGIL   Georgics (for Ages, see HASTINGS above). * VOGH   J. Vogh   Arachne Rising. The Search for the Thirteenth Sign of the Zodiac.   London, 1977. * VOLGUINE   A. Volguine   Les Significations des Encadrements dans l'Horoscope. Paris, 1974. / Astrology of the Mayas and Aztecs (trans. W.J.Tucker), Sidcup, 1969. * VREEDE   E. Vreede   Anthroposophie und Astronomie. Stuttgart, 1954. * WACHSMUTH   G. Wachsmuth   The Evolution of Mankind. Dornach, 1961 (trans. from German by Norman Macbeth) / Etheric Formative Forces. Dornach, 1923. * WAERDEN   B. van der Waerden   Science Awakening II - The Birth of Astronomy Oxford, 1974. * WAITE   A.E. Waite   See PARACELSUS above. * WAITE   H.T. Waite (et. al.)   The New Waite's Compendium of Natal Astrology. London, 1971. * WALTER   H.J. Walter   Harmonische Aspectfiguren der Quintil...etc. "Kosmogiologisches Jahrbuch", 1974. * WALTHER   H.Walther   'Towards a New Astrology', "The Modern Mystic". Dec., 1939. * WANGEMANN   E. Wangemann The Astrological Aspects. "Astrology" Vol. 49, No.1, 1975. * WARBURG A.Warburg   Italienische Kunst und Internationale Astrologie im Palazzo Schifanoia im Ferrara.   "Atto del X Congresso Int. di Storia dell'Arte", 1922. * WEDEL   T.O.Wedel   The Mediaeval Attitude Towards Astrology. Folcroft, 1920. * WELLING   G. von Welling   Opus Mago-Cabbalisticum et Theosophicum...etc. Homburg vor der Hohe, 1735. * WESTON   L.H. Weston   The Planet Vulcan.   1921. * WEMYSS   M.Wemyss   The Wheel of Life, or Scientific Astrology.   London, 1930 etc. * WHITE   G. White   The Moon's Nodes   c.1950. * WIEDNER   P.P. Wiedner (ed)   See entry on ASTROLOGY by David Pingree in Dictionary of History of Ideas   New York, 1968. * WILLIAMS   D. Williams Astro Economics, 1959. * WILSON   James Wilson   A Complete Dictionary of Astrology, in which Every Technical and Abstruste Term...is ...Accurately Defined. London 1819 - but see reprint of Samuel Weiser, New York, 1974. * WIND   E.Wind   Pagan Mysteries of the Renaissance   Oxford, 1958. * WITTE A. Witte & H. Lefeldt   Rules for Planetary Pictures: The Astrology of Tomorrow. Hamburg, 1974. * WITTKOWER   R.Wittkower   Allegory and the Migration of Symbols   London, 1977 - see also TAYLOR above. * WOLFRAM E.Wolfram   The Occult Causes of Disease.   London, 1911. * ZADKIEL "Zadkiel" (R.J. Morrison)   An Introduction to Astrology. London, 1835   / The Grammar of Astrology.   London, 1849.